Building a New Global Order:

Emerging Trends in International Security

Building a New Global Order

Emerging Trends in International Security

Edited by

David Dewitt

David Haglund

John Kirton

Toronto Oxford New York
OXFORD UNIVERSITY PRESS
1993

Oxford University Press
70 Wynford Drive, Don Mills, Ontario M3C 1J9

Toronto Oxford New York
Delhi Bombay Calcutta Madras Karachi
Kuala Lumpur Singapore Hong Kong Tokyo
Nairobi Dar es Salaam Cape Town
Melbourne Auckland Madrid

and associated companies in
Berlin Ibadan

Oxford is a trademark of Oxford University Press

Canadian Cataloguing in Publication Data

Main entry under title:

Building a new global order : emerging trends in international security

Includes bibliographical references and index.
ISBN 0-19-540964-7

1. Security, International.   2. International cooperation.   I. Dewitt, David
Brian, 1948-   .   II. Haglund, David G.   III. Kirton, John J.

JX1952.B85 1993   327.1'7   C93-094581-6

Contents

List of Tables vii

List of Figures viii

Preface ix

chapter one   Introduction: The New Global Order and the
Challenges of International Security *David B. Dewitt* . . 1

part one   ***The New International Distribution of Power*** **11**

chapter two   *Quo Vadis?* The United States' Cycle of Power and its
Role in a Transforming World *Charles F. Doran* 12

chapter three   The Collapse of the USSR and World Security
S. Neil MacFarlane 40

chapter four   European Security after the Cold War:
Issues and Institutions *C.C. Pentland* 59

chapter five   The Third World in the Changing Strategic Context
Mohammed Ayoob 86

part two   ***The New Transnational Processes*** **105**

chapter six   The Dynamics of Military Technology
Andrew L. Ross 106

chapter seven   Production and Security *Robert W. Cox* 141

chapter eight   Global Communications, Culture, and Values:
Implications for Global Security *David V.J. Bell* . . . 159

chapter nine   Global Environmental Change and International
Security *Thomas F. Homer-Dixon* 185

chapter ten   Population and (In)security: National Perspectives
and Global Imperatives
Nazli Choucri and Robert C. North 229

part three   ***The New Institutions of Global Governance*** **257**

chapter eleven   Opportunities and Obstacles for Collective Security
after the Cold War
Thomas G. Weiss and Laura S. Hayes Holgate 258

chapter twelve   The United Nations' Contribution to International
                       Peace and Security
                       W. Andy Knight and Mari Yamashita 284

chapter thirteen   Bound to Leave? The Future of the NATO Stationing
                       Regime in Germany
                       David G. Haglund and Olaf Mager 313

chapter fourteen   The Seven-Power Summit as a New Security Institution
                       John Kirton 335

chapter fifteen   The Missile Technology Control Regime
                       Albert Legault 358

chapter sixteen   A New World Order? Western Public Perceptions
                       in the Post-Cold-War Era   *Don Munton* 378

chapter seventeen   Conclusion: Towards the Twenty-First Century
                       Albert Legault 401

                       Index 416

List of Tables

2.1   Some Causes of Decline and their Locus   20
9.1   Comparison of Conflict Types   214
10.1   Profile Definition   238
10.2   Growth and Development (1986)   239
10.3   Summary of Wars (1945-91)   241
10.4   Wars of 'Decolonization'   242
10.5   Civil Wars (1945-92)   244
10.6   International Wars (1945-92)   244
10.7   Refugees Crossing Borders   245
10.8   Growth, Development and Carbon Emissions   250
15.1   Weapons Proliferation   360
15.2   Nuclear Weapons Capabilities of the Threshold States   361
16.1   Perceived Likelihood of Nuclear War in 25 Years, 1988   381
16.2   Likelihood of Soviet Attack on Western Europe, 1988   383
16.3   Perceived Interests of the Soviet Union and United States, 1988   385
16.4   Confidence in the Soviet Union and United States, 1988   386
16.5   Perceptions of Greatest Threats to World Peace, 1988   391
16.6   Perceived Security Threats in the United Kingdom and Federal
        Republic of Germany, 1991   392
16.7   Perceived Theats to American National Security, 1990   393
16.8   Perceived Problems Affecting Canada's Security, 1989   393
17.1   Characteristics of the Three Major Paradigms   402

List of Figures

2.1 The Dynamics of Absolute and Relative Capability: Principles of the Power Cycle   21

2.2 War and the Power Cycle: Critical Points of Power Change and War in the German Example   28

2.3 Temporal Distribution of Critical Points by Type   29

9.1 Environmental Change and Acute Conflict   190

9.2 Some Commonly Posited Effects of Environmental Change on Agricultural Production   195

9.3 Some Posited Effects of Environmental Change on Economic Productivity in Developing Countries   198

9.4 Some Posited Types of Conflict Likely to Arise from Environmental Change in the Developing World   210

16.1 Likelihood of War   381

16.2 Threat from the Soviet Union   383

Preface

By the mid-1980s each of the editors of this volume had moved east from Vancouver, where a few years earlier we had enjoyed the stimulation and encouragement of Mark Zacher and his colleagues in the Institute of International Relations and in the Department of Political Science at UBC. As we now regularly faced growing numbers of undergraduates increasingly attracted to courses in international relations, we also began to discuss the need for a book that would make available some of the more interesting issues and ideas emerging in international politics. In particular we were concerned that while much was being written from perspectives challenging the traditional approaches to international affairs, relatively little was being done on the classic issue of international security and the related issue of international governance.

The creation of the Canadian Institute of International Peace and Security (CIIPS) by the federal government a few years earlier provided for the first time a source of financial support within Canada for innovative policy-relevant research on matters related to international peace and security. It was in response to a CIIPS Commissioned Research Programs Initiative that we submitted a proposal to explore what we then termed 'emerging trends in international security'. The project we proposed involved inviting experts spanning generations, disciplines, and nationalities first to take stock of our knowledge and understanding about a set of issues that we had identified as among those most likely to engage the security community in the near future, and, second, to speculate about the directions in which these trends might take us.

With the assistance and encouragement of Bernard Wood, then Executive Director, and Roger Hill, then Research Director, of CIIPS, we organized two international conferences that provided authors with the opportunities to present and discuss initial drafts. Just at this time, ironically, events outpaced scholarship, and whether one looked at geopolitical security issues or functional concerns, we and our colleagues realized we were engaged in a race with reality. Finally, with much good will on the part of all the authors included in this volume, we agreed to call a halt to the endless process of revising and updating. That can now wait for another volume. Rather, what we hope readers will find in the following chapters are insights and new understanding as the past is blended into today and as our previous preconceptions and analyses are proven wanting.

The book is organized around two central themes: emerging trends and international governance. The first moves from classic questions of the great powers, regional and Third World security politics, and changing political security dynamics through to an examination of some of those factors that are now increasingly understood to be of some consequence and complexity in security politics: communications, technology, population, production cycles. The second turns on the traditional question of how to promote co-operation in what many see as the anarchic world of the international community. This theme leads us into examining some of the more important post-1945 international institutional arrangements, with an eye to assessing their past, current, and future roles in dealing with the challenges of inter-state conflict as well as the broader problems of security.

We are grateful to CIIPS for its initial funding and continued support through to its unfortunate, untimely, and unnecessary demise. It remains to be seen whether serious students of international security working at Canadian universities and research institutions will ever again have a national-level institution devoted specifically to providing opportunities for Canadian and other scholars to work together on the fundamental questions of peace and war. Thanks also to the Social Sciences and Humanities Research Council of Canada for conference support; to the Department of National Defence, which through its ongoing and absolutely vital Military and Strategic Studies Program ensures that students and scholars are able to teach and study issues relevant to Canada's role in the larger international peace and security community; and to individuals in DND and in External Affairs and International Trade Canada who provided expert advice and participated in aspects of this project. In addition, we must acknowledge our home institutions—York University's Centre for International and Strategic Studies, Queen's University's Centre for International Relations, and the University of Toronto's Centre for International Studies—for providing various types of infrastructural and intellectual support. Finally, we are grateful to Brian Henderson and his colleagues at Oxford University Press for their professional advice and assistance.

David Dewitt   David Haglund   John Kirton
York University   Queen's University   University of Toronto
Toronto, Ontario   Kingston, Ontario   Toronto, Ontario

chapter one

Introduction: The New Global Order and the Challenges of International Security

David B. Dewitt

The New Global Order

Since the mid-1980s, scholars and commentators on issues of peace and war have noted the scope of political change, the rapidity with which events are known the world over, and the complexities involved in trying to understand the new security challenges. Revolutions, insurgencies, and military confrontations are now followed in detail, as they develop, in cities and countrysides in most parts of the globe. People and governments from South and North are made aware of drought, famine, and the ravages of disease not only via electronic forms of communication, but through the activities of private individuals, non-governmental organizations, and international institutions. Demographics and resource issues no longer interest only academics, market researchers, and central governments, but, because of regional and global interdependencies, are of concern both to contiguous states and to the larger international community. These classic factors of power are once more being seen as fundamental in analysing and explaining the changing security environment. The difference today is the reach of impact, the complexity of the causal process, the range of actors involved, and the acknowledgement that threat and response are no longer within the sole or even primary purview of the military.

The concepts, labels, and even norms to which those in the Western security community have grown accustomed over the past forty years or so are no longer so clearly applicable. Strategic studies now are viewed as focusing on more than the use of military force; security no longer presumes a principal concentration on challenges to a government and country from outside its borders; conflict no longer necessarily means only the violence of armed force; central governments are no longer viewed as the sole legitimate authorities for the use of coercive means; defence no longer presumes that military force is either the first or the most appropriate instrument; similarly, a threat to national security no longer necessarily evokes images of invading armies. Environmental degradation, absorptive capacity, strategic minerals, illicit drugs, unregulated movement of large amounts of capital or people, epidemic disease, and terrorism all are now seen by some, including governments and intergovernmental bodies, as potentially part of a broadened security agenda. And accompanying this proliferation of security-relevant issues and instruments are policies that begin to blur traditional dividing lines, both between jurisdictions and between concepts that were formerly discrete.

The 1991 Gulf War complicated things still further, for in the midst of the dust and fire the rhetoric of American politics turned to talk of a 'new world order'. This phrase has come to symbolize, for many, a set of expectations and hopes, few of them terribly clear or well articulated, and even fewer so far fulfilled. As the chapters that follow indicate, if there is to be a new order it will have to emerge not simply out of the ashes of the old, but rather in a dynamic tension with the powerful legacy of great-power war and resulting international institution-building during this century. The globalization of finance and production may establish interdependent networks of capital and labour, but it has yet to overcome the concomitant rise in nationalism. Indeed, the collapse of the Soviet Union, the patent failure of Marxism–Leninism, and the disillusionment of the decade of development is prompting as yet less a transformation to a new global politics than a return to traditional forms of national and micronational organization and activity. Given the extreme inequality of the global distribution of wealth, the rise of new actors who can harness the capabilities attendant on modern technology does not augur well for a more secure global environment.[1]

It may well be true that the end of the cold war provides an opportunity to raise the strategic threshold, and thereby reduce substantially the possibility of a global war. However, as the following chapters imply, one should not be too sanguine about the prospects for a 'peace dividend' in many parts of the world. The events of 1992 and 1993 in the Horn of Africa, South America, the Persian Gulf, Indochina, Central Europe, the Balkans, and Central Asia suggest that the world cannot rest easy after the last round of East–West strategic arms-control talks. As will be clear from a careful reading of this volume, the axes of conflict in the shadow of the cold war will probably be more complex, not less, and more difficult to manage, not easier. The South–

North, South–South, and North–North dynamics that are replacing the previously dominant East–West dimension will be no less strategically demanding. The spread of both conventional weapons and weapons of mass destruction, and of attendant military and industrial technologies, is but the most obvious challenge. Inevitably, global security will depend on the ability of the world's political processes to address the perceived needs, the articulated demands, and the felt insecurities of the majority of states and the majority of the globe's population, both of which lie outside the privileged group of advanced industrialized capitalist countries.

Building a New Global Order is intended to aid understanding of these very significant challenges. Although the contributors are unable to offer definitive answers, they do explore some of the more fundamental questions of the new era upon which the world has now embarked. Their purpose is to address, along with the growing community of scholars and other experts in the policy and non-governmental communities, some of the issues and problems that complicate the prospects for peace and a better quality of life among the world's communities. Examining both individual states and underlying structural factors, the book also addresses international institutions and changing global security: how the post-1945 set of organizations —the United Nations system, the European security arrangements, and the more recent process of institutionalized summits of the world's seven major powers—are coping with the changing (in)security dilemma. The aim is to bridge the gap between units that act and/or react, and the embedded conditions (contingent and otherwise) that constrain or propel security-related activities, including peace and war.

It is by now a truism to note that in many ways the world is no longer what it was during the 45 years after the collapse of fascism. Between the 1940s and the end of the 1980s, students of international affairs became captives of the cold-war politics most clearly expressed in bipolar global competition; East–West nuclear strategy; Soviet and American efforts to create friends and clients the world over, in order to contain the influence of the other; and protracted, often superpower-supported, domestic and interstate wars in much of the developing world. The politics and profits of arms proliferation, the net transfer of wealth from poor (the South) to rich (the North), the increasing numbers of peoples displaced by war, famine, and natural disasters, and the growing fears of global ecological crises have, over the past forty years or so, transformed our globe from one dominated by a few powerful states to one in which the interconnectedness of events overwhelms the capacity of any single state or even subgrouping of states to address even one of these problems adequately.[2]

Since the latter half of the 1980s, only certain aspects of this world of competition and conflict, scarcity and surplus, and peace and war have changed. Wars and revolutions continue, the distribution of skills, knowledge, and resources remains unequal, and military capacity goes unchecked. What has changed is the context—the constraints and parameters within which states act—and, in some cases, the instruments by which actors pursue their interests. The dismembering of the Soviet Union, and the concomitant rise of new or renewed states both west and east of the Urals, has tempered the East–West nuclear arms race while giving freer reign to the horizontal proliferation of conventional and unconventional weapons systems and technology. The ending (or might it be just a pause and transformation?) of the cold war has loosened the bonds of patron-client politics, thereby giving licence to the rise of micronationalisms, encouragement to narrow sectoral interests, and legitimacy to unilateral efforts to redraw subnational, national, and even international boundaries. Ironically, the demise of the Soviet state and the failure of Marxism–Leninism so long desired in the West have unleashed a maelstrom of consequences well beyond those envisioned by most political leaders.

While it may well be true that global politics has been profoundly affected by the dramatic events of the 1980s, it is no less the case that most of the challenges that the world had to face in the preceding forty years persist. Now, however, in the absence of the politics of bipolarity, there is a hiatus of uncertainty as to the shape of the new world, the preferred mechanisms to bring it into being, the priorities of the challenges that need to be addressed, the allocation of scarce resources in pursuit of those objectives, and the biggest question of all: who will decide these questions. The 'new world order' that some argued had its first major test in the 1991 Gulf War seems to be one in which, far from replacing old issues, new ones have simply been layered on top of them—and in which the constraints perversely imposed by the politics of Soviet–American relations no longer afford any semblance of an ordered agenda.

This is not to argue in favour of the past; nor is it to suggest that the interests of the advantaged minority of the globe's population—those living in relative economic prosperity, or at least within the boundaries of advanced capitalist economies—are synonymous with the interests of all. Rather, it is to point out that the collapse of the Soviet empire and of most other communist states has not made international relations, especially international security relations, any simpler or safer. While Soviet–American strategic arms control recently has counted a number of significant successes, there remain the challenges posed by others the world over seeking reassurance, if not crude military power, through the acquisition of weapons of mass destruction. Whereas Soviet–American political interests often constrained precipitous actions among former client states, their duopoly of influence is now weakened if not circumvented by the rise of new patrons quite capable of serving the needs and interests of regional, national, and communal or sectarian interests. Whereas in the past the West used the cold war and its attendant dynamics of patron–client relations and containment as excuses for ignoring human-rights abuses and systematic mass murder in far-off lands, impeding efforts by international organizations to redress these injustices, today states with the capacity to work as agents of enforcement (whether *ad hoc* or through the United Nations or regional organizations) are often frozen by indecision, uncertainty, and malaise.

The 'globalization' of international economic relations—a common phrase meant to indicate the increasingly complex intertwining of the finance, resource, labour, production, and marketing segments of economic life—is occurring at the very same time that security politics is being fragmented and regionalized. Local political forces are less in control of their economic future as a result of factors far outside their own borders. The world is beginning to witness efforts to regionalize political and security relations in order to stabilize the arena and to better harness economic capacities in the service of regional development and, at the most basic level, regime survival. The clash of global economic forces with subnational, national, and regional political interests is likely to offer one of the more profound and vital challenges to security relations in the coming decades.

The Challenges of International Security

For these reasons, among others, countries like Canada and Japan over the past few years have been articulating new concepts of interstate security. Of these, co-operative security and common security are two of the more widely used, complementing more traditional concepts such as collective security, collective defence, and mutual assurance. These latter concepts focus on the territorial state and highlight the military dimensions of (in)security and threat. The newer ones, by contrast, acknowledge a more inclusive definition of security and challenges to security encompassing but moving beyond the traditional notion of military threat and response. They recognize the continuing problems associated with military conflict, but argue that other factors increasingly threaten the survivability and coherence of the state—and not the state alone. There is an explicit identification of problems that place in dire peril not only the nation-state but also subnational units as well as transnational or regional arenas—for example, demographic factors; large or distinct population movements; illicit flow of drugs, technology, or information; air, land, and marine pollution and degradation; global ecological changes; and human-rights abuses. Further, there is a recognition that many of these new and profound problems are not amenable either to military intervention or to unilateral action. Rather, if not addressed in a co-operative and constructive undertaking, they may well lead to traditional forms of military violence, thereby threatening—in the classic sense—the state, its governing regime, and its society.

This book attempts to address many of these issues through reflection, analysis, and explanation, as well as prediction and prescription. In a single volume it assembles leading experts and asks each to explore the world of the 1990s in a historically informed, analytically rich explanatory context. Where appropriate, each author has indicated the range of options that governments or international organizations might face, or the likely impact of changes in a particular set of structural factors. Common to all the contributions is a concern for global peace and security, including the better management of competition and conflict, the prevention of major war, the enhancement of individual and community welfare, and the pursuit of more effective means to ensure that peace and security become more than the mere absence of war. Common to all, as well, is the aim to better understand some of the main challenges and issues that the world will have to face if it is to achieve these goals as it moves into the next century.

But challenges to security and the shape of a new and preferred world order were also common themes immediately following the upheavals of World War II. Out of the depths of depravity and violence emerged a newly engaged international community intent on bringing a pragmatic understanding of politics and society to efforts at rebuilding a war-exhausted world, one in which two-thirds of the globe's populations were only beginning to throw off the legacy of the age of imperialism, colonialism, and conquest. The United Nations was seen as the foundation upon which all else would be built. It was both symbolic, in striving to give voice to all sovereign states in an effort to collaborate in the establishment of a new and more peaceful world, and practical, in recognizing the unequal distribution of power and the need to create structures and procedures that would provide opportunities for universal participation and at the same time ensure that the major powers would consider it in their interests to work with and through the UN body.

Shortly thereafter the Soviet–American confrontation overwhelmed the expressed intent of the UN Charter, and for the next forty years the organization was unable to fulfil much of its original mandate. Though there were distinct successes, these were often attributed to the *ad hoc* creativity and ingenuity of diplomats and UN officials who had to work with and around the UN system in order to harness its strengths while avoiding the pitfalls of the cold war. With the Gulf War, and the sudden collapse of the Soviet Union, which was affected by and in turn affected the new political-security map of Central and Eastern Europe and the republics east of the Urals, the United Nations re-emerged as the focus of much discussion concerning a new security architecture, one in which collective security is tempered by co-operative security, and the rights of both individuals and national communities are given sufficient weight that they call into question the traditional inviolability of the nation-state.[3]

The UN Charter is clear: peace and security are collective needs and they come with shared burdens and responsibilities towards the collective both as process and as community. War is to be avoided; pacific settlement of disputes is to be pursued; and the UN system is to provide the institutional order and instruments required. In order to make this system work, it is presumed that all will carry their fair share of this burden, financially, politically, and by adhering to the shared norms of the system. In particular, this means that the Security Council and the Office of the Secretary General will be given the necessary resources — political, economic, and military — to undertake their tasks as stipulated in the Charter. A basic challenge is that the Charter is a manifesto and codification of rules, norms, and principles of the world as it should be, not the world as it is.

The post-1945 UN membership has not been 'of one world' politically, culturally, socially, economically, or normatively, nor from some perspectives has it been universal as was intended. The litany of charges against the superpowers for undermining the UN system is well known, but the problems go well beyond that. Given the very real human and regime disparities across almost every dimension, the controlled dissemination of technology by the advanced industrial world, and the introduction of weapons of mass destruction, neither collective security nor collective burden-sharing could work. In a world populated by more people and ever more states where interpersonal as well as interstate relations fall victim to the tensions inherent in systems characterized by inequalities, political relations focus on rather basic issues of competition and conflict in pursuit of survival. The generosity of spirit envisioned in the founding of the United Nations has been diffused, first by the cold war and the post-colonial struggles, and now by the quantitative and qualitative transformation of the issues. Ecological and environmental degradation is now reaching global proportions; military risk and threat are not constrained either by assuming that only five nuclear powers are worthy of recognition or by any simple ladder of escalation that presumes a universal logic and rationality; individual states no longer are able to control or even monitor all transboundary activities; and governments are no longer the sole repositories either of wealth or of instruments of coercion.

With all the stresses and strains, the glaring failures and inadequacies, and the errors of both omission and commission over the past 45 years at the United Nations, the fundamental goals of peace and security — individual, communal, and national; economic, social, and political — remain elusive for most of the world's peoples. Yet the UN is still the only forum where, in some form, and however perversely at times, the world's nation-states sit together. While other bodies — the G-7 Summit, regional organizations, the Commonwealth, *la Francophonie*, the World Bank, the CSCE, NATO, APEC, ASEAN, and so forth — purport to address particular issues or specific regional concerns, the United Nations remains the only place where all nation-states, not just the 'like-minded' or the regionally connected or those with a common heritage or language, meet within a codified normative, legal, and administrative structure.

The need for assistance in overcoming, let alone preventing, interstate as well as protracted internal violence is not in question; the following chapters make that painfully clear. Rather, given such evidence, the question is why the UN, born out of world war, is not a more central, activist, and effective participant in preventing wars, in halting wars, and in ensuring that wars do not recur. Of the 190 or so wars, both interstate and internal, that have been fought since 1945, the UN has been a responsible third party to only about one-tenth. Further, during this post-colonial period of emerging states, why has the UN system been unable to stop the ravages of internecine warfare — famine, underdevelopment, generalized human-rights abuse, refugee movements — that have so often resulted from a combination of the dynamics of post-colonialism with the power politics of the cold war? Regional organizations during this same period have exhibited much the same inability to undertake either effective preventive diplomacy or productive developmental assistance; similarly, in the absence of such diplomacy or assistance they have failed to follow through with measures that might either separate parties to the conflict, and then create opportunities for the peaceful settlement of disputes, or stimulate more positive use of local and historically embedded skills, knowledge, and resources.

Is this record likely to change in the post-cold-war era? While it is clear that the lessons of the Gulf crisis should not be over-generalized, it is also evident that more states now view the United Nations system primarily as an instrument of ratification for their own status and actions, and possibly as a means to ensure their more effective integration into the world's political and economic processes. At the same time, the continued inability of the United Nations to take decisive action in response to the violent disintegration of states, to massive violations of human rights, or even to discrete acts of territorial invasion and plunder, is fuelling both a regionalization of security interests and increasing efforts on the part of individual states to prepare to defend themselves. As the world moves towards the next century, the tensions between classic notions of self-help clash ever more forcefully with the recognition that the security of any state or community cannot be entrusted either to that entity alone or to some universal body. It is in these interstices — between subnational, national, and regional interests — that the art of the politics of security will face its greatest challenge. And it is in these same arenas that it is necessary to ensure that security is not understood merely in the stark traditional terms of military defence, but rather in the more variegated and complex notions of security *for* and *of* as well as security *from*.

The right of governing regimes to employ coercive means — including the military — to maintain civil order and to defend borders has been a principal pillar of the international order developed after the Treaty of Westphalia of 1648. However, the quantitative and qualitative changes in the destructive capacity of weapons have undermined that traditional mode of reasoning. The use of military force against neighbours now has the potential of escalating well beyond the initial theatre of violence. The reach of modern military systems now places entire populations in peril, both of direct attack and of destruction of the basic social, economic, and technological infrastructure of the community. Hence it is increasingly commonplace to hear the term 'regional conflict', as distinct from 'interstate conflict'; the latter implies bilateral dispute, while the former acknowledges the escalatory nature of modern warfare. Furthermore, these factors have been complemented by a growing consensus that human rights, albeit defined and practised differently the world over, have emerged as a new pillar upon which to build a post-cold-war system.

These two factors—the destructiveness of military might and the basic rights of individuals and communities—although still contentious, are the defining characteristics of the emerging global system. The following chapters make it clear that the difficulties these factors pose for the existing order are substantial, and are aggravated by the concomitant demands of state-building, including the legitimization of political processes and the development of economic capacity. Not only is there no simple replacement for the military power that states have tried to accumulate in the face of uncertainty and threat, but neither regional organizations nor the United Nations have histories that instil confidence in states' willingness to relinquish both the right and the ability to engage in self-help practices—that is, to defend by themselves what they see as their best interests. Concerning human rights, whether individually or communally, the norms or laws are still lacking that would provide codified and regularized procedures for determining why, when, where, or how others should or must intervene in the internal affairs of sovereign states. Even when federal states dissolve in violence, as in Yugoslavia, aside from traditional diplomatic initiatives only *ad hoc* measures are undertaken—and then not to stop the violence, but to use foreign military contingents to try to alleviate the suffering of civilians. The efforts to provide humanitarian aid and assistance to the Kurds in northern Iraq set an important precedent, as much for what they were unable to accomplish as for what they did. And even in the case of Somalia, important challenges remain.

Security challenges become more complex when one turns to those issues that may not directly challenge the viability of the state, in traditional terms, but that may nevertheless undermine the sovereignty of the state, compromise its ability to control the penetrability of its borders, and exacerbate relations whether between groups within the polity or between states within the regional or global system. Demographic pressures on land, food, and resources; environmental degradation; illicit movements of populations, technology, information, and drugs; unintended spread of disease and pollution—these are but a few of the factors that increasingly affect the security and well-being of individuals, communities, and states. In various ways and combinations, they can contribute quite directly to violence and other forms of coercion. These factors, probably as much as weapons proliferation and human-rights abuses, pose profound challenges to efforts to build a new global order. These emerging trends in international security must be addressed systematically and with commitment if the world is to succeed in creating a more equitable and secure global commons. We hope that this book will contribute to a more informed discussion, understanding, and analysis of these issues facing all those who would work for a more equitable, just, and compassionate world.

Notes

[1]Compare with Joseph S. Nye, Jr, 'What New World Order?' *Foreign Affairs* (Spring 1992).

[2]For an early pessimistic analysis on the implications of the dramatic events in Europe in the wake of Gorbachev, the collapse of the Berlin Wall, and the rising expectation for a peace dividend, see John Mearsheimer's provocative and perceptive article 'Back to the Future: Instability in Europe After the Cold War', *International Security* 15, 1 (Summer 1990): 5–56.

[3]See, for example, Boutros Boutros-Ghali, *An Agenda for Peace: Preventive Diplomacy, Peacemaking and Peace-keeping*, Report of the Secretary-General pursuant to the statement adopted by the Summit Meeting of the Security Council on 31 January 1992 (New York: United Nations, 1992).

part one

The New International Distribution

of Power

Quo Vadis? The United States' Cycle of Power and its Role in a Transforming World

Charles F. Doran

The rise and decline of states is not simple. This is as true for the global-power situation of the United States, Russia, China, and Japan today as it was for Britain, Austria-Hungary, Russia, and Germany a century ago. This is also why confusion permeates much of the contemporary discussion about the future power and role of the United States and other leading countries. *Concepts* must guide historical interpretation and policy assessment. Unless the concept of change in relative power, and of the trajectory of that power, is sound, interpretation is likely to continue to go awry.

This chapter attempts to put the contemporary debate on US 'decline' into a context that is meaningful for the way Washington addresses policy. First, it examines some of the theoretical questions posed by analysts in the field. Second, it suggests that these questions can be resolved when treated within an analytic framework known as *power-cycle theory*. Third, the chapter looks at the US situation from the power-cycle perspective, and then considers the changes in the Soviet Union that affect the long-term power position of Russia and its affiliated republics. Finally, having demonstrated that the rise and decline of states is not simple, the chapter concludes with an examination of the consequences of all this structural change for policy and world order.

Is the United States 'bound to lead', as Harvard political scientist Joseph Nye argues, or should it accept its 'end of empire' and 'gracefully retreat' from its leadership role, as Yale historian Paul Kennedy advises?[1] What is an appropriate 'grand strategy' for the United States—appropriate both for US interests and, since this is what leadership is all about, for the interests of the international system as a whole? A separate, albeit related, question underlies and further complicates the debate: Does the opportunity exist for American resurgence, as Richard Rosecrance asserts, or is decline so aggravated as to preclude this possibility?[2] A review of the basics of power-cycle analysis illuminates both questions.

Today, foreign affairs in Moscow as well as Washington hinge on seemingly domestic issues. *Perestroika* and the United States' trade and budget deficits symbolize the kind of preoccupations that increasingly affect statecraft. Yet if economics is high politics, high politics is much more than economics. At stake for each polity is its future power, and role, in an international system whose structure and *modus operandi* are changing. The United States and the former Soviet Union, however dissimilar internally and politically, have been struggling to cope with some of the same hard facts regarding shrinking power positions, gaps between foreign-policy ends and means, and the altered power and role expectations of all the major powers. But the Soviet Union collapsed in its efforts to adjust to an admittedly far graver set of problems. Today more than ever, it is the differences between the Soviet (Russian) and American power cycles—differences in level and trajectory, and in how each polity now sees its future position in the system—that hold the key to the stability of the international system and to the strategies that the United States must adopt.

Scholars in Dialogue: Structural Change and its Implications

The debate over US decline is part of a larger scholarly dialogue about the structure of the international system and the dynamics of international politics. Structural theories focus on the distribution of power in the system—the hierarchic order, and the changing relative power (systemic share), of the member states.

Two concepts at the heart both of the debate and of structural theories require preliminary definition. A state's *absolute* power and the rate of growth in its absolute power are observable—for example, the current size of its GNP (or of its armaments base) and the yearly increments in its GNP (or in its armaments). But the state's international political behaviour is conditioned by how its absolute power compares with the absolute power of other states in the system. The state's *relative* power on any indicator is the *ratio* of its absolute power to the absolute power of the other states in the system at that time. Change in the relative power of states in the system is equivalent to change in the structure of the system. This chapter will resolve paradoxes and contradictions in the debate by showing how changes in absolute power create, or set in motion, the changes in relative power described as the rise and decline of states.

At a panel entitled 'Beyond Hegemonic-Stability Theory' at the 1990 American Political Science Association meetings in San Francisco, the debate over American decline sharpened. Supporting the thesis of US decline, hegemonic-stability theory treats the international system as controlled, or governed, by a single dominant state (hegemon) until overcommitments and excessive leadership costs erode its resource base, inviting challenge from a rising state seeking to establish a new system of rules and benefits. Robert Gilpin, author of the theory, reminded the audience that American decline was rooted in the deterioration of the whole liberal trade order. Joseph Nye noted that if the United States were in fact in such severe decline, no other state was poised to take over the US role; the conditions of rivalry between a leader and a challenger that the theory hypothesized were not being met. Moreover, he warned that the proponents of hegemonic-stability theory had exaggerated the control that the United States was able to exercise in the past; power in the international system has always been pluralistic. Robert Keohane suggested that the conclusions reached by Nye and by Henry Nau regarding the capacity of the United States to lead in the last decade of the twentieth century had created a Nye–Nau paradox.[3] How could a state in decline nonetheless be relied upon by many members of the international system for leadership?

The analysis in this chapter begins with my summary response to that question at the conference. A distinction must be made between the assertions of hegemonic-stability theory about decline and the actual dynamic of decline. Agreeing with Nye that hegemonic-stability analyses exaggerate the earlier control and present decline of the United States, I emphasized two facts about the dynamic of decline. First, to unravel the paradox cited by Keohane, analysts must assess the causes of decline, and whether it is absolute and/or relative. US decline is a relative phenomenon caused more by what other states have been able to achieve in the system, especially in Asia, than by extensive (and permanent) deterioration in US absolute economic or military strength. No one in the debate denies the severity of the American trade and budget deficits, the 'hollowing-out' of industrial economies, the strain of NATO and other military commitments on the US economy, the problems of competitiveness in US industry, and the educational and other social ills that continue to constrain the US absolute-growth rate. But the latent base for reinvigorated absolute growth is present, and hence the rate of relative decline could be slowed.

Second, relative decline is measured in decades, not years. US relative decline is still nascent, and thus continued US leadership in fact is not paradoxical. The true paradox is that US relative decline has been so small despite an absolute-growth rate much smaller than that of a number of other leading states. Again, Joe Nye is correct: Who else in the contemporary system could have achieved what the United States did in the face of the Iraqi aggression in Kuwait? Certainly this achievement hardly suggests a state nearing imminent collapse of role. Stephen Krasner added that my overall observation about American power was indeed correct, and that US capability of leadership was to be explained by the high, perhaps historically unique, level of absolute power that the United States enjoyed in the post-1945 period.

In other words, the United States may be past its peak of relative power, but at present it still towers over the system as a whole. Indeed, with the collapse of the Soviet Union, it appears even more to predominate. American leadership remains necessary, and it is still reliable, albeit more burdensome. Moreover, leadership in international relations is in no way equivalent to empire or dominance. The question is not merely whether the United States can 'adjust sensibly to the newer world order' by reducing its leadership function.[4] At issue are the twofold adjustments at the heart of public debate long before the debate about decline started. On the one hand, the United States must get its economic house in order, if it is to prevent further relative decline (a priority underlined by Kennedy's historical study). On the other, the increasingly capable powers, who have not yet gracefully stepped forward to assume even a proportionate share of the financial and operational costs of order maintenance, must adjust sensibly to their increasing responsibility toward their own security and that of the system.

Such analysis of the levels and rates of change in absolute and relative capability and role follows directly from an extensively developed (and empirically tested) conceptualization of international politics that has been labelled *power cycle theory*. Stimulated by 'thought experiments' in 1964 about what drives systemic change (i.e., changing relative power in the system), the principles of the power cycle explain *how absolute-power changes in the system create the rise and decline of states*.[5] In this, power-cycle theory remains unique in the literature. Although many scholars are finally seeking a logic that exposes the non-linear (rise and decline) path of relative-power change, they ultimately must confront the principles of the power cycle that create this non-linearity.[6] Moreover, the power-cycle dynamic invokes a paradigm shift in the understanding of statecraft itself.[7] Much of the confusion about US decline arises, this chapter will show, because seemingly obvious assumptions about relative change are wrong.

Examined in detail in the next section, the principles of the power cycle are principles of changing system structure. The power cycle encompasses the state and the system in a *single dynamic* of relative power change in that system (of changing systemic share). The single dynamic, generalizable across states and across periods of history, expresses structural change at the two analytical levels simultaneously. The principles of the power cycle explain how the given absolute-power levels and growth rates for the individual states translate into the single dynamic of changing systemic share (relative power) for the member states. They explain what sets the cycles in motion and the peculiar properties of relative-power rise and decline. The single dynamic thus results in a graph depicting the various state relative-power trajectories simultaneously—the changing structure of the system. Moreover, each state's future power and role projections in that system are tied to the changing slope of its power cycle. *Vis-à-vis* the decline debate, power-cycle theory explains why a declining United States is 'bound to lead' in the international system for some time to come. The power cycle must be recognized holistically as a cycle of power and role, wherein the inertia in role change is even stronger than the inertia in relative-power change itself.

This observation leads to a second seeming paradox. I assert that the power-cycle notion supports Nye's view of the necessity for American leadership; yet this same notion was apparently regarded by Kennedy, who advised graceful retreat, as a foundation of his notion of state rise and decline.[8] Moreover, power-cycle theory has long been asserting the thesis of US relative decline (albeit nascent, beginning in the mid-1960s) and exploring its policy implications.[9] In other words, both hegemonic-stability theory and power-cycle theory are believed by many to be equivalent to, or to support, the Kennedy thesis. Many concepts and basic arguments of the structural theories are unquestionably apparent in his analysis. But the conclusions of power-cycle theory regarding the future US trajectory, current and future US leadership, and the future trajectories of other leading states are very different from those argued by Kennedy and many structural theorists. Indeed, a correct understanding of the power-cycle concept also yields quite a different interpretation of past historical trends. Kennedy's utilization of the power-cycle paradigm thus *highlights confusions and contradictions within the structural school itself.*

A key problem is that the fundamentally different ideas expressed by power-cycle theory and other hypotheses about changing systems structure have been treated as if they are equivalent. Power-cycle theory has been criticized as 'different jargon . . . used to express the same ideas.'[10] Analysts originally categorized it as a power-transition theory, but subsequently acknowledged that the power-cycle concept is unique in origin and more encompassing: a power transition between two states is just the point at which their power cycles intersect.[11] Other analysts grouped power-cycle theory with other structural theories as sharing a concern with differential growth of states, while ignoring its admittedly important differences; relative-power change was thought to be simple and obvious.[12] But this dismissal of variation in theory and concept has hindered scholarly advancement, for *relative-power change can be insidiously counter-intuitive.* For instance, in hegemonic-stability theory and power-transition theory, expectations about the changing structure of the system are precisely the same as those extrapolated from absolute-power trends, but these expectations (and predictions) are shown to be wrong because of the unexpected non-linearities in relative-power trends.[13]

The concept of relative power, a mainstay of international-relations research, cannot be understood outside the context of the full power-cycle dynamic. Analysis is doomed by an error of fundamental concept. The theoretical problems are confounded when analysts who do not understand the principles of the power cycle use it to depict the trajectory of state rise and decline. John Ruggie has correctly criticized those analysts who would talk of systemic share, or calculate it, without explaining the 'underlying principles that govern the patterning of interactions'.[14] Power-cycle theory provides these generative principles of changing systems structure.

Like those analysts of structural change, Kennedy repeatedly evoked the concept of relative as opposed to absolute power, and he repeated their errors of understanding. In his introduction he sought to distinguish between 'generally valid conclusions' based on the 'historical record' and 'generalizations' based on what he called '*a priori* theories'. He then asserted what he believed to be clear and uncontestable generalizations within the systems-structure school—that changing relative power reflects shifts in the world-power balance; that differential rates of growth and technological change underlie these changes in relative power; that rise and fall in military power closely parallel, albeit with a noticeable lag, rise and fall in economic power; that victory in great-power wars has gone to the power with the more productive economic base—and dismissed the further complexities of the structural analyses as incapable of resolution.[15] However, although Kennedy correctly used power-cycle graphs to depict the trends of history, he did not fathom the conflicting messages and shocking surprises inherent in relative, compared with absolute, changes, *as those trends are being created.* His analysis of the 'shifting balance of world forces' thus revealed that he did not yet comprehend the most important feature of systemic structure and changing relative power (the power-cycle notion): how the bounds of the system cause the 'tides of history' to suddenly and unexpectedly shift against a state.[16]

The shifting tides of history are structural undercurrents that can counter even the strongest growth in absolute-power terms. Power-cycle theory explains why, even with a much lower rate of absolute growth than Japan and China, for example, the US has had a very low rate of relative decline; actual US decline could not begin to approximate the extensive decline of Kennedy's historical analogies. Moreover, notwithstanding the great stress he placed upon assuming the continuation of existing trends, and the reasonableness of this assumption,[17] Kennedy's projections for the future trajectories of other major powers too are flawed by confusion about the power-cycle dynamic. In fact, the trends of relative power can change *even when present trends continue in absolute-power terms.*[18] Hence Japan's rise on its power cycle will not continue in the foreseeable future. In fact, its peaking results from China's more rapid absolute-growth rate, not from competition with the United States. Finally, Kennedy did not explore the strategic subtleties of the relationship between power and role at various points along the cycle, notwithstanding his acknowledgement of the lag effect, so that perhaps the greatest distortion was of power-cycle theory's concept of power-role equilibrium.

Unfortunately, neither concept nor history conforms to the 'reasonable' simplifications that Kennedy brought to his analysis. Structural theorists must finally confront the contradictions inherent in their assumptions about relative-power change. As the next section demonstrates, a correct understanding of the power-cycle concept is necessary to unravel the complexities of structural change occurring today.

Decline on the Power Cycle

Among foreign-affairs analysts, disconsolation over the writings on US decline is understandable. Although no one disagrees that what is at issue is decline in relative power, confusion surrounds its meaning. Much of the commentary does not analyse satisfactorily the *level* of relative power in comparative and contemporary terms. It fails to convey any sense of the *rate* of rise or decline of state power over long time periods, or indeed to distinguish adequately between declining rates of growth and declining levels of relative power. It fails to acknowledge the incremental nature of change on the power cycle of the nation-state, where consequences are measured in decades, not years. There is not even an agreed-upon shorthand for integrating the two primary dimensions of power, economic and military. Instead, uncertainty accompanies the concepts and the data themselves—let alone their interpretation.

The question of comparative *levels* of relative power is readily assessed, since the hierarchies of relative and absolute power are the same. The level of overall US power has exceeded that of the Soviet Union throughout the century. This edge is based upon an economy that was at least twice the size of that of the Soviet Union, combined with a far higher per capita income. On the basis of military considerations alone, however, the Soviet Union was catching up with the United States throughout the 1960-80 interval in both conventional and strategic terms, as a result of military spending that, as a percentage of GNP, was two or more times that of the United States. The Reagan military build-up once again placed the United States in the lead regarding the surface navy and certain areas of advanced weapons, if not in the areas of traditional Soviet strength such as the manned army, tanks, artillery, and size of nuclear weapons. Overall US power continues to exceed that of Russia and its affiliated republics today. The United States is still the leading state in the system, larger than its closest competitors, the newly constituted Russian-led Commonwealth of Independent States and Japan, by a sizeable margin.

Then why all the clamour about American decline? Perhaps the greatest concern stems from the instinctive feeling on the part of policy analysts that the implications of changing relative power for future foreign-policy conduct are not well drawn.[19] While policy analysts readily reject exaggerations about 'end of empire' and mistaken assumptions within the 'graceful retreat' strategy,[20] a clear picture has yet to emerge regarding the consequences for the larger structural situation in which the United States may eventually find itself, and for the strategic policy choices now open to it.

Likewise unsettling is the fact that decline has been given alternative meanings that are quite contradictory. Only when decline in relative power is defined in the context of a correct conceptualization of the power cycle of the nation-state can this problem be eliminated.

Charting nothing more, nor less, than a state's political development as a major power, involving a variety of leadership functions, the power cycle traces that state's changing performance and size relative to other members of the central system over long time periods. It is not a 'law'. Rather, it reflects the fact that a state's power *can* follow a cycle of rise, maturation, and decline relative to the changing performance of other states in the system with regard to a broad mix of economic and military indicators. How long a state remains at any one level, or on any given trajectory, depends on conditions both internal and external to the state during that interval. The power–cycle dynamic is at every moment dependent upon factors immediately affecting each state's absolute and relative capability (see Table 2.1).[21] The limits of the system are no less important than differential levels and growth rates in determining a state's relative-power trajectory.

Relative power is a ratio of one state's capability to that of other states. (When expressed in terms of percentage of systemic share, the ratio is readily interpretable as reflecting the structure of the system.) The numerator reflects what the state does internally, within its own polity; the denominator reflects what others do in theirs. The debate about decline has to do with whether less is being done internally within the United States, or more is being done internally within other states, or both, and by how much. A state's level of relative capability shows its comparative standing in that system. The rate of change in that level shows its current ability to increase share: that is, its degree of competitiveness in that system.

What, then, sets the power-cycle dynamic in motion? At base, the state's competitiveness in a system, and hence the direction of its relative-power trajectory, is a function of how its absolute-growth rate compares with the absolute-growth rate of that system as a whole (see Figure 2.1).[22] Two principles underlie the dynamic of the power cycle. First, a state's relative capability in a system will increase when its absolute-growth rate is greater than the norm for the system. Moreover, a single state growing faster than the systemic norm will initiate a momentum for change on power cycles throughout the system. Second, *even when absolute-growth rates continue unchanged*, a state's relative-capability growth will accelerate only for a time before the limits of the system (at point F in Figure 2.1) require deceleration, leading to a peak and then a turn into relative decline. Similarly, accelerating decline ultimately (at point L) begins to decelerate to a minimum level prior to levelling out or beginning a new upturn. In mathematical terms, point F and point L are *inflection points*. Thus on the state power cycle there are four critical points of sudden, massive, and unanticipated change where the projection of future foreign-policy role very abruptly is proven wrong. Each of these critical points in the power-cycle dynamic—the

Table 2.1.   Some Causes of Decline and their Locus

FACTORS AFFECTING BOTH ABSOLUTE- AND RELATIVE-GROWTH RATES DIRECTLY

a, b	Excessive private consumption (opulence; low savings ratio)
a, b	Excessive public consumption (government overspending)
a, b, c	Military overextension
a, b, c	Foreign borrowing that leads to unfavourable exchange rate
a, b	Loss of technological innovativeness
a, b	Diminution of risk-taking propensity
a, b	Regulatory rigidities that impede efficiency
a, b, c	Capital outflows that are not recovered
a, b, c	Manpower shortages; military, civilian labour
a, b, d	Lower literacy
a, b, c, d	Built-in limits to growth: environment, resources, physical space
a, b, d	Declining net new investment
a, b, d	Reduced competitiveness regarding market share

ADDITIONAL FACTORS AFFECTING ONLY RELATIVE-GROWTH RATES DIRECTLY

d	Past industrializers overtaken by more recent industrializers with larger territorial and population bases
d	Impact of entry and exit of states from central system
★	Impact of upper asymptote on rate of growth in relative power (based on finiteness of systemic shares)

LEGEND:

a:	internal to state in decline
b:	absent or present to lesser degree for other states in system
c:	external environment, including existing economic and political regimes
d:	historical epoch
★:	the dynamic of logistic growth

upper and lower turning points and the inflection points on the rising and declining trajectories — corresponds in the state's experience to the shifting tides of history.

State power thus follows a not-so-simple cycle of rise, maturation, and decline that is best described as a type of logistic growth and decay in a finite system. Such change has many counter-intuitive aspects that greatly complicate the debate about US decline. For instance, a larger state can begin declining in rate of relative growth (competitiveness) long before it enters relative decline itself; but once relative decline sets in, the same absolute-growth rate differentials will yield accelerating decline.

Further confusion in the debate stems from the different meanings attributed to the notion of decline. Decline can legitimately be defined as occurring when the state first begins to feel competition in the system: that is, at point F, where its rate of growth in relative power begins to fall off even as the level of relative power continues to rise. In assessments of absolute growth, economists refer to this as the point where diminishing marginal returns set

**Figure 2.1.   The Dynamics of Absolute and Relative Capability:
Principles of the Power Cycle**

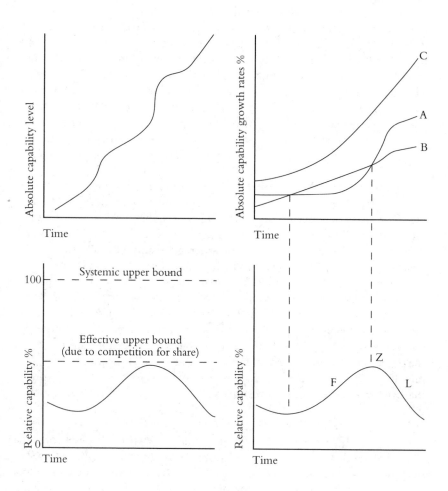

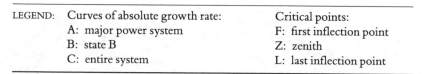

LEGEND: Curves of absolute growth rate: Critical points:
           A: major power system   F: first inflection point
           B: state B   Z: zenith
           C: entire system   L: last inflection point

SOURCE: On the right is a disaggregation of the figure in Doran (1971: 193).

in. Some analysts seem to think of decline in this sense, although it is often unclear whether they are referring to diminishing absolute- or relative-growth rates.[23] But, as noted above, the point of diminishing marginal returns in relative power usually arrives far in advance of any diminishing marginal returns in absolute growth.

For other analysts, decline seems to mean very extensive movement downward on the relative-power curve, perhaps even past the time (second inflection point) when the rate of relative growth once again increases.[24] A more familiar bench-mark is the apex of the relative-power curve, a point that like the others can be identified analytically only after it has been passed. The apex is the point at which a declining rate of growth in relative power can no longer sustain further increases in level of relative capability. In fact, after the apex, declining competitiveness begins to chip away some of the previously held share of relative power. According to our analysis, this is the point that is most relevant to a discussion of decline for either of the super-powers.[25]

Notwithstanding the very artificial period of reconstruction after World War II when American power was inflated (the collapse of Europe and Japan yielded a disproportionately small denominator in the power ratio), and the interval of the Reagan defence build-up that once again boosted the military dimension of US power (though at considerable economic cost), the salient observation is that, when considered across the entire span of US history, US relative power, both economic and military, apparently peaked in the mid-1960s. It is true that in the period 1950-85 some economic indicators even showed absolute decline, such as the share of spending and employment devoted to manufacturing, the savings balance, some measures of industrial competitiveness, and the percentage of gross fixed-capital formation.[26] But the point to be made throughout is not that such absolute decline took place on selected indicators, but that decline occurred in the export *share* of world markets, and in the *share* of investment in GNP relative to Japan, the newly industrializing countries, and even Mexico and Brazil.[27] On average, espe-cially in a phase of rapid world growth (1960-73), but also in slower growth periods (e.g., 1973-80), gross domestic product grew more slowly for the United States than for many of its major trading partners, and more slowly than the average for the advanced industrialized West. On the other hand, the US economy is about twice the size of its nearest competitor, that of Japan. Relative decline in US economic capability is nascent and quite incremental. More than a century was required for the United States to build its position of bipolar dominance, and decades will be required for that position to diminish.

There is indeed a twofold error in the arguments of those looking for another actor to replace the US in its current role. It is an unfortunate misreading of history to depict first Britain and later the United States as dominant powers single-handedly responsible for maintaining world order.[28] Britain was only one member of a five-actor, balance-of-power system, and its doctrine of splendid isolationism meant that it did *not* try to impose order on the continent, but instead relied on a balance of power to prevent war there through shifting alliance relations. Likewise, the United States forwent 'hegemony over its allies', to quote Joseph Nye, and sought instead to increase the productivity and participation of those states weakened by two world wars.[29] The United States has not been the leader, but rather the economic and maritime member of a bipolar system whose other member has been a great Eurasian power capable of exerting enormous influence in Europe, the Middle East, and Asia on its peripheries. To exaggerate the early dominance and extent of subsequent decline for Britain and the United States is to misrepresent the strategic problems of each era, and hence to obscure appropriate paths to their solution.

Likewise, crude dichotomization of analysis into growthist and declinist camps precludes valid explanation. As noted earlier, no one in the debate denies the problems currently confronting the US economy. Nor is the issue merely one of whether the analyst believes the United States is capable of overcoming those problems. The debate was prompted by, and continues to be fuelled by, other aspects of the Kennedy thesis that, according to those analysts, are wrong.

Recall that Kennedy did not say simply that the United States was in decline, but that it was in decline in the same way that Great Britain was at the end of the nineteenth century, and that Hapsburg Spain was at the end of its empire. He sparked the debate with articles such as 'The End of Empire: Can We Decline as Gracefully as Great Britain?'[30] and continued it with such provocative titles as 'Fin-de-Siècle America', with all the historical associations regarding level and irreversibility that such a title conveys.[31] But none of these historical analogies corresponds to the US situation today *vis-à-vis* either the level or the rate of change on its power cycle.[32] Britain at the end of the nineteenth century was confronting a system in which Germany was already an equal in both economic and military power, and several other countries were not far behind.

Movement on the power cycle is slow and incremental; significant change is usually measured in decades, not years. On the other hand, inertia has its effects on the power cycle as it does elsewhere. If steps are not taken to reform educational systems and to increase economic productivity; to harness technological innovation more effectively; to restore the manufacturing base as well as the service economy; and to set the national psyche on a more positive course, in the direction of growth, achievement, and excellence, then eventually decline will so entrap the United States that a reversal would become all but impossible. In the next decade, therefore, when the United States could well face larger relative burdens of leadership, not smaller ones, it may find that its relative power is somewhat diminished, and that it must devote increasing attention to the economic aspects of high politics.

Multipolarity and Other Causes of Decline

What is most puzzling is that any of this should come as a surprise. Warned Henry Kissinger in 1968: 'the age of the superpowers is now drawing to a close.'[33] American policy-makers were almost immediately aware of the constraints on the country's future role, leading at the time to the announcement of the Nixon doctrine of greater self-help for allies. Clearly it is not these facts that are at issue but their implications.

To eliminate distortions in the declinist thesis, some writers have asserted that American power has not declined, but that multipolarity has merely become more pronounced. It is true that the US relative-power position reflects the great increases in capability of other major powers during the past three decades (denominator increasing faster than numerator). But such an increase in multipolarity nonetheless yields a decline in US relative power. That the world share of the semiconductor business going to Japan increased from 30 to 50 per cent over the last decade may result from greater Japanese efficiency and innovativeness, or from reduced American efficiency and innovativeness, or from peculiar conditions affecting trade in semiconductors, such as the exchange rate or third-party competition. In terms of this industrial sector, the effect is the same: US market share has deteriorated. However, those writers are correct in asserting that this rise in multipolarity did not reflect diminished *absolute*-capability growth within the United States — certainly not to the extent argued by the declinists.

If the trend toward multipolarity is taken to mean *only* changes occurring elsewhere in the international system, it surely overlooks important factors contributing to relative decline. Decline in practice often cannot so easily be separated into internal and external causes. In the semiconductor example, lack of capital at competitive rates, inability to market quickly, and shortcomings of technology explain the outcome on the US side. Ironically, both states improved their industrial efficiency, but the diverging rates of improvement had the same effect of declining relative power for the less productive. The onset of multipolarity is not at variance with relative decline for the superpowers; it epitomizes their declining shares of systemic power (albeit at differing rates and from differing internal causes).

One of the most significant internal conditions in regard to a state's future trajectory is its potential for development: that is, the abundance of its natural and human resources. But equally significant is the extent to which a state's internal-power generation is hostage to policies of other states in trade and finance, and the extent to which the costs of leadership drain away resources and future growth potential. Proper identification of causes of relative decline is necessary to determine specific policy remedies.

It is tempting to explain most of a state's decline in terms of external considerations, thus removing responsibility for policy initiative to increase literacy and human skills, to eliminate long-term structural problems in the economy, and to improve the functioning of the market. But a state with a strong resource and technological base can do much to improve the numerator of the relative-power ratio, thereby diminishing the effect of factors outside its control. By running its own economy better, it enhances all of its long-term policy options.

Expectations of Soviet Ascendancy and Parity

The dynamic of structural change created a foreign-policy dilemma for the Soviet Union. The Soviet Union and the United States viewed their two power cycles, and hence their leadership roles in the system, quite differently. Throughout the 1970s and early 1980s, the Soviet Union perceived itself to be in the ascendant and the United States in decline. As far back as 1971, Andrei Gromyko asserted that 'today there is no question of any significance which can be decided without the Soviet Union or in opposition to it.'[34] Despite recognition under Mikhail Gorbachev that actual Soviet means required some realignment of Soviet foreign-policy objectives, Moscow continued to expect a larger role in world affairs based on its estimate of its own relative-power trend. Despite the United States' awareness that its own power might indeed have peaked, it believed such Soviet foreign-policy projections to be pretentious and inflated. After all, in Washington's view, a sizeable disparity in levels of overall power still favoured America.

Across all dimensions of foreign policy, not just the nuclear strategic, the Soviet Union demanded parity with the United States. Soviet historian Stephen Cohen observed that 'whatever else may be characteristic of Soviet leaders, they are intensely proud of their country's great-power status, achieved only in their lifetime and at enormous cost, and thus they are profoundly resentful of any perceived challenge to its international prestige.'[35] Hence, to the Soviets, the 'prerequisite of *detente*' was 'Soviet security and parity in world affairs'.[36]

The Soviet Union was unprepared to admit that, with respect to levels of national capability, the United States still predominated. Trial balloons concerning such notions as 'reasonable sufficiency' — meaning capability to offset one nuclear state but not all possible nuclear states — were from time to time floated, indicating that a vigorous debate was going on within the Kremlin on the issue.[37] Eduard Shevardnadze publicly attacked the premise of some strategists that the Soviet Union 'can be just as strong as any possible coalition of opposing states,' but not the notion of parity with the United States.[38]

Gorbachev's reforms must be interpreted in this light. The purpose of *glasnost* and *perestroika* was to release the stagnating energies of the Soviet people and to get the Soviet economy back on a growth path. *Perestroika* was necessary for the continued ascendancy of the Soviet state.

While Shevardnadze attempted to prepare the Soviet policy élite for difficult choices of adjustment, Gorbachev himself seemed to believe that economic reform under the old system of communism was still feasible. He held out the possibility to the Soviet military and the intelligence services that the Soviet ascendancy in world affairs could continue under the old leadership, abetted by a loyal and more free intelligentsia and a market economy. This was the great mirage of building *perestroika* upon *glasnost*.

The danger was that *perestroika* would not take root, that a market economy would not flourish, because the old élite would not give it the flexibility to do so, and stagnation would replace slow growth. These conditions in turn could topple the floundering Gorbachev regime, and plunge the country into civil violence. Worse from the perspective of world order, the chaos in the Soviet Union could spill over into the international system wherever the one instrument of governmental policy that still worked comparatively well, the Soviet armed forces, might be invited to intervene.

The Trauma of Expectations Forgone

Suppose *perestroika* collapsed under the weight of bureaucratic resistance. What would this mean for the long-term cycle of Soviet power? If economic and political reform failed, the Soviet Union, despite its enormous resource base, potential for scientific research, and huge armed forces, would have reached the apex of its relative power. It would have entered nascent decline, albeit at a much lower level of overall power than the United States.

Historically, reaching the peak of power for any government, especially one bent on a world role, is not insignificant for either that government or the system. All of the foreign-policy expectations that the society has built up for decades suddenly demand rethinking. All projections of future status and security position are at risk. The entire foreign-policy *Weltanschauung* of the state is reoriented in a new direction. A great possibility is that gaps, long in the making, between interests (merely sought or seriously entertained) and the capability to cover those interests, will suddenly become nakedly evident. In short, at this critical point on the state's power cycle, the society and government may perceive themselves to be in crisis.

Hence passing this critical point in Soviet power would not be a trivial experience, either for the Soviet Union or for the other members of the system. Apocalyptic warnings emanating from Moscow periodically revealed some of the anxiety and uncertainty that accompanied this stressful interval. Communist Europe faced 'a danger of destabilization, of a rupture that could be enormously harmful,' admonished Gorbachev, 'not only to the countries in question but to developments in the world, above all the European continent. . . .'[39] Yurii Afanasev of the Moscow Historical Institute put the situation even more poignantly: 'There is no alternative to *perestroika* other than descending into an abyss, and if that occurs, it will not be our internal, national abyss. We will necessarily drag many others behind us.'[40]

Those in the West who were perhaps tempted to discount such statements as morbidly introspective or politically self-serving may have failed to grasp the essential gravity of the situation as seen by the Soviet leadership. Historical evidence carefully gathered and analysed shows that, by the standards of the modern state system, this Soviet anxiety about the prospects for reform, and the possible consequences for change on the cycle of power, was not exaggerated. Traversing a point of sudden reversal of prior power projection — a so-called critical point — has traditionally been an unsettling event. For instance, French relative power peaked prior to 1790, and the Napoleonic onslaught followed the French Revolution. Both earlier historical examples (the Hapsburg Empire and that of Louis XIV of France) and more recent state behaviour reinforce this assessment of the trauma of sudden change in projection of future power and foreign-policy role.[41]

Examining Historical Precedent: The German Case

Based on empirical data with respect to the initiation of major war for nine leading states (1815-1985), a significant statistical relationship emerges between a critical point on a state's power cycle and its involvement in major war.[42] There are four such critical points (with the fifth representing a return to the starting point) on the complete cycle of power for each state. Although they differ regarding the nature of the revised projections of future power and role, each critical point seems to create stress, uncertainty, and difficulty for foreign-policy adjustment, as governments struggle to adapt to new foreign-policy circumstances.

A case study is provided by Germany. Figure 2.2 shows the remarkable association between three critical points on the German power curve and the greatest wars in its history.[43] In each case, with a few years' lag-time for the sudden discovery of declining relative growth and other structural changes to sink into the consciousness of opinion élites, massive political instability and major war followed one of these critical points. Perceived gaps between interests and power, long in the making, surfaced and became apparent at these times of critical change. Bismarck wanted final consolidation of territory in 1870; imperial Germany sought its long-denied place in the sun in 1913; Hitler told the German people in 1938 that they would never again have the opportunity for a world role. Critical change created an atmosphere in which such ideas became thinkable for policy-makers.

But the system was equally responsible for the mismanagement and miscalculation that led to some of these wars. Prior to both world wars, a disproportionate amount of critical structural change occurred for all the leading states (Figure 2.3). These were periods of systems transformation. Rigidities, gaps between interest and power, hesitancies to yield position or to assume new responsibilities — all contributed to the tumult of transformation from the old European balance-of-power system to the new bipolar system.

Inability to accept decline and to move over caused Austria-Hungary, France, and Britain to encircle ascendant Germany and to prevent it from assuming a role commensurate with its increasing strength. For twenty-five years prior to the First World War, foreign-policy contradictions in the system compounded as the states resisted making the adjustments required

Figure 2.2.   War and the Power Cycle: Critical Points of Power Change and War in the German Example[1]

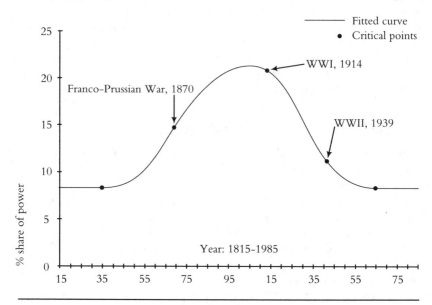

[1]Germany's Share of Central Systemic Power Using a Composite of Five Aggregate Indicators of Power

SOURCE: Doran, 1989.

by the changing power relationships.[44] After that war, when Germany was no longer ascendant, Hitler's promise to avert German decline by force was possible only because the system had not yet established foreign-policy roles commensurate with the new power relationships. For their own respective reasons of isolationism and internal convulsion, the US and the Soviet Union did not immediately assume their roles as the new systemic leaders; instead of curbing aggressive impulses early, they allowed Germany and Japan to upset the international equilibrium.

Contemporary Germany illustrates another important aspect of the power-cycle dynamic: the potential for reversal. Germany certainly seems to have passed the low point on its power cycle and may again be trending upwards, although now at a slowed rate because of its reacquisition of the east. But this bottoming-out is not to be explained as most casual observers may contend.

Some observers of structural change may look to unification as the stimulus for a rebirth of German power, whether fearfully or with anticipation. This judgement would be quite wide of the truth. The German renaissance had already been in the making for a decade at least. It preceded unification on the basis of an upsurgence of economic and military strength in the Federal Republic. Recovery was not the result of unification, but its cause.

Figure 2.3. *Temporal Distribution of Critical Points by Type*

FIVE-YEAR INTERVAL	SUMMARY OF CRITICAL POINTS	CRITICAL POINT	YEAR	COUNTRY
1815	H	H	1814–17	Britain
1820				
1825				
1830				
1835	L	L	1832–37	Prussia/Germany
1840	H	H	1839–44	Austria/Hungary
1845				
1850	I_2	I_2	1851–56	Russia
1855				
1860	H	H	1858–63	Italy
1865	I_1	I_1	1864–69	Germany
1870				
1875				
1880		I_2	1882–87	Austria-Hungary
1885	I_2, I_2	I_2	1884–89	Italy
1890				
1895	L	L	1894–99	Russia
1900	I_2, H	I_2	1900–05	Britain
		H	1902–07	Germany
1905	L	L	1907–12	Italy
1910	L, I_1	L	1910–14	Austria-Hungary
	I_2	I_1	1910–15	US
1915		I_2	1911–16	France
1920				
1925				
1930	I_2, I_1	I_2	1933–38	Germany
1935	I_1	I_1	1934–39	Italy
1940		I_1	1939–44	Japan
1945	L	L	1944–49	China
1950				
1955				
1960		H	1960–65	US
	H, I_1	I_1	1960–65	Soviet Union
1965	$\star L_2, \star I_1$	$\star L_2$	1963–68	Germany (lower plateau, no upturn)
1970		$\star I_1$	1965–70	Japan (return to pre-war trajectory)
1975				
1980				
1985				

LEGEND:
I_1, and I_2 = First and second inflection points.
H = high point.
L = low point.
$\star I_1$ For Japan in 1965–70 is a recovery to its pre-WWII trajectory.
$\star L_2$ For Germany is the calculated *end* of the period of its decline.

Evidence for prior West German recovery can be found in the diplomacy of the period. Although a number of European states plus the Soviet Union attempted to deny German unification or to postpone it, West Germany was able to circumvent these systemic constraints. Admittedly, the United States and some other parties did not support the effort to stymie unification. But even if they had tried, the outcome was probably unstoppable by peaceful means. Germany's economic vitality was too strong, and its resurgence of political will too quietly compelling. The Deutschmark overcame Soviet recalcitrance as effectively as a NATO military challenge.

Recovery of German political vigour was symbolically present at the last moment in the talks with Moscow. Undoubtedly the West had worked out the details of the power transfer in general terms with Bonn. Yet in the final talks the United States was something of a bystander. Bonn negotiated with Moscow alone. This bilateralism testified to Germany's ability to reassert itself *before* unification. Unification could only amplify the trend of Germany's long-term recovery on its power cycle, slow though this probably will be.

Unified Germany is preoccupied with fuller integration in the European Community and a reinvigorated *Ostpolitik*. Each of these efforts will siphon off German energies to some extent, reducing the likelihood of the instability in foreign policy that might otherwise be expected to accompany the lower turning-point on the German power cycle. Furthermore, Germany is still overshadowed by the continent-sized superpowers, and by the giant Asian states. Finally, Germany shows every indication of breaking with its expansionist past. Hence German *revanche* is far from a likely result of the latest passage through the lower turning-point on the power curve. Of course political activism and some restoration of pride in Germany's new status is anticipated and, under the circumstances, no more than is justified in the context of European regional politics.

The international system is once again in transformation, and one of the two superpowers of the bipolar system is confronting the crisis of impending decline. Thus when analysts inside Russia, Eastern Europe, or the West warn of the strain experienced by the leadership in the Kremlin, and the possibility of major political trouble should the reforms fail, or other unspecified political mishaps occur, the United States and its allies should not dismiss these ruminations as idle or empty. Not only are they based on valid current observation of decision stress and uncertainty in Moscow, but they are buttressed by the weight of historical and empirical research as to the gravity of the possible implications for statecraft.

Adjusting to a New Foreign-Policy Projection

Where does the collapse of the Soviet empire leave Russian power? Note that the onset of aggravated relative decline occurred prior to that collapse, not after it. An understanding of the direction of causation is very important both for the development of international-relations theory and for policy assessment. The Soviet Union was in deteriorating economic health well before the dissolution of the federation. In fact, the primary purpose of the political reforms of the late 1980s was to continue the ascendancy on the Soviet power cycle. It is further true that the failure of those reforms to stimulate the economy — indeed, they seemed to have the opposite effect, leading to sudden absolute dips in the Soviet GNP not unlike those experienced in the Depression of the 1930s — contributed to the disintegration of the empire and the Soviet state. Thus feedback loops are operative here. Economic decline precedes overall political collapse; the attempt to stave off further economic decline hastens political collapse, and ushers in a wholly different power trend for the reconstituted Russian state.

The second question is what impact the unravelling of the Soviet Union will have on world power relationships. Much has been made of the fact that the United States is now the sole superpower; at least it is the only Rankean 'great power', defined by that nineteenth-century German historian as the state that can stand alone. Relative to the old Soviet Union, the United States is enjoying a sharp rise in its power position. But because this upward curve is the result of changes in the denominator of the power ratio, not of anything the US has recently done, it is somewhat illusory in the multilateral context of the system. For the Soviet demise had shifted each state's power position upward on the global power hierarchy.

Therefore it is not at all surprising to find the Japanese and Germans acting as if they were now much more salient and influential. They *feel* they are more visible now that the Soviet shadow has been shortened. This in turn means that West-West diplomatic interaction is likely to show greater intensity. The United States will find that other allies are likely to follow its lead on some matters with less alacrity than in the past. Germany has already shown its independence, *vis-à-vis* its own European compatriots, who initially favoured the Yugoslav federal position, and *vis-à-vis* the United States, which was left with an empty telephone receiver on the other end of the oft-used line. Still, this sorting out of status and policy is not the same as a fundamental realignment in security terms. The current shuffling of policy cards is a direct consequence of the new flexibility some of the allies feel after the demise of the Soviet Union, and in the absence of any new policy initiative or assertiveness on the part of the United States. The US of course is not without influence, most likely to be felt when another ally wishes to pick up the telephone to hear a supportive American president. In diplomacy, friends are needed at the most sudden and unexpected intervals — among the democracies, especially at election time.

The third question is, how will Russia emerge in the future? Soviet power is no more, and Soviet communism is dead. But neither development suggests that an international political vacuum has arisen in Eurasia. By decentralizing itself and divesting itself of costly responsibilities in Eastern Europe and even in republics like Ukraine that were a net drain on the Russian economy, Russia hopes to re-emerge phoenix-like in the twenty-first century as a world power as prominent in relative terms as it was in the 1970s. Much will have to happen commercially and financially for such optimism to be warranted. But the human- and natural-resource bases exist, and if they are properly tapped, the resurgence of Russia could well occur. Likewise, less attractively, Russian expansionist tendencies could re-emerge, first with regard to other members of the Commonwealth by centralizing authority more tightly, later with regard to other governments that Russia has traditionally thought to be within its sphere of influence. Russian nationalism has always been less territorial and more mobile than the nation-state nationalism of the West.

As power-cycle analysis warns, the Soviet Union could have responded to the trauma of the upper turning-point as a number of other governments have in the past, by spilling over onto the system in major aggression. Perhaps the aggression in Afghanistan was a limited and abortive movement in the direction of such military activity. Perhaps the presence of Gorbachev and like-minded Russian leaders was crucial to the reversal of such tendencies. Certainly the steadfastness of the West, mixed with the proper conciliation and self-restraint, was also essential to a benign outcome for world order.

Instead, the Soviet Union internalized its frustration and hostility. Collapse was the Soviet Union's response to its inability to accelerate its trajectory in relative-power terms or to adjust to its reduced status and foreign-policy role, and to economic constraint. As with the French Revolution, the Soviet example shows that external aggression is not the only response to a critical point. Another is internal fragmentation and an undermining of internal authority and sense of political direction, when adjustment in more positive ways appears impossible.

Power-cycle theory also emphasizes that, given the latent capability base of the new Russian-led Commonwealth, Russian leaders continue to believe that Russia has another opportunity for ascendancy. The present decline, absolute as well as relative, is considered only temporary, the consequence of a faulty political and economic system: change that system of government, and the prospects for continued relative ascendancy will once again become positive. That is the faith of the current Russian leadership, and the meaning of the USSR's response to its confrontation with the changing tides of history.

Consequences of Structural Change for Policy and World Order

In recent years both the Soviet Union and the United States have faced challenges to their power positions not previously experienced in the post-1945 international system. The Soviet Union collapsed under the weight of the attempted adjustments. This collapse in turn impinged upon the system. For the second time in the twentieth century, the system has entered transformation.

Perhaps the most important aspect of systems transformation is that it involves structural change characterized by a massive, abruptly acknowledged alteration of foreign-policy outlook.[45] In the present system, transformation is brought on by structural change involving not only the Soviet Union, but potentially five actors, each of which will face an alteration of its foreign-policy role.

First, it is entirely possible that Russia and its affiliated states, exploiting a vast undeveloped resource base, will eventually succeed through domestic reform and national commitment in reversing relative decline and accelerating once again. A reduction of external burdens on Russia, and an end to the diversion of funds toward sister republics under the guise of ideology, is certainly a factor in Russian plans for recovery.

Second, awareness in the United States of its new pre-eminence, but also of its new domestic economic and social needs, will bring about a prudent balancing of foreign with domestic priorities. A smaller defence budget should yield some dividends. But an enhancement of America's human-capital base, a greater commitment to saving and investment, and reduction in consumption at all levels would revive the underlying industrial base. The United States in this interval of industrial renaissance will not succumb to isolationism. It will adopt a more prudent foreign policy, assuming responsibilities more selectively. This in turn will allow the flexibility at the top of the system for new role adjustment.

Third, much depends upon what the two Asian giants, Japan and China, are able to achieve industrially and, therefore, ultimately in military terms. Japan is well past its first inflection point; its increase in relative power has slowed down. Yet with a GNP half that of the United States at present, it is still growing at perhaps, on average, twice the US rate. While Japan may never overtake the United States in economic and military terms, it will continue to have an impact upon the system, and will increasingly have to share with the United States the responsibilities of leadership, a proposition far from clearly worked out in practice. Moreover, the question remains: when will Japan's relative-power ascendancy peak, and how will it and the system adjust to that peak?[46]

China, with its enormous but poor population, its great territorial and resource base, and its awkwardly surging economy, is quite a different potential member of the central system. No one can predict the outcome of Deng Xiaoping's initiatives, but few in China are anticipating a return to Maoist policies. China is experiencing a rising level and rate of growth in relative power. Its influence contiguously on the new Russian Commonwealth, and thus indirectly upon all of international politics, is undeniable. This influence will increase significantly, but, relative to the United States, it will be most perceptible within the Asian region itself.

Fourth, Western Europe faces both a problem and an opportunity in terms of global politics. It is too soon to determine whether either the problem or the opportunity will act as a sufficient catalyst to bring about the kind of integration that eventually leads to a single defence policy and a coherent foreign policy. The problem is that as US influence declines, the credibility of extended deterrence wanes; the opportunity is that as Soviet power diminishes, the chance to exert an independent European role, even *vis-à-vis* Eastern Europe (particularly important for Bonn, in the aftermath of unification), becomes far more realizable. Should Western Europe emerge as an autonomous, cohesive actor, the process of transformation will clearly have achieved some form of new multipolar configuration.

Finally, whatever else happens during the forthcoming period of systems transformation, the political distance on the power hierarchy between the two members of the present bipolar system, the United States and the former Soviet Union, and the other members of the international system, is likely to narrow. Accelerated diffusion of power at the top is bound to loosen regional balances of power and stimulate regional competition for new status and new foreign-policy roles. Difficult as it is to speculate on configurational shifts within a new central system, the greatest changes, and those most problematic for assessment, result from the lessened capacity of Russia to intervene on behalf of regional clients. The decision to oppose Iraq in a limited war to defend Kuwait's independence may be less a bellwether of future policy initiatives than a legacy of past ones.

Set against all of these structural changes, raising uncertainties and introducing new unpredictability into world politics, is the matter of how Russia and Germany view their new policy roles in the vastly changed Eurasian setting. Systems transformation is always characterized by just such uncertainties. The rules of the game, what will constitute equilibrium, even the identities of the major players — all are up for revision.

Management and Adjustment Imperatives

Within the next decade, the United States will determine — largely by its internal economic policies and its patterns of military spending — whether it wants to retain its present systemic role, and whether it is capable of doing so. In spectacular fashion, the Soviet Union showed its inability to sustain its world role.

Similarly, if the United States does not revitalize its economy and accelerate its growth in a sustained way, if increasing its means proves impossible, it must slowly yield some of its status and perquisites, transfer responsibilities to ascendant states, tidy up its foreign policy in terms of commitments it cannot meet, and in general bring ends in line with means. It must steer between the appeals of would-be Cassandras who predict imminent decline and catastrophic foreign-policy failure, or who advise retreat from leadership, and the Oedipuses who blind themselves to the existence of the power cycle and its imperatives for prudent foreign-policy conduct. Although obscured by the debate, the direction of that course was outlined long before the debate started. The United States can with some confidence forecast that a middle ground exists for thoughtful refinement of its foreign policy, but that refinement requires co-ordinated foreign-policy changes among the other leading states as well. Ascendant power cannot be artificially halted;

declining power cannot be artificially bolstered. A new equilibrium can emerge only if the United States maintains a balance with the Russian-led Commonwealth of Independent States, while preparing the way for a new, larger central system in which Japan, China, and a potentially more unified Europe may assume larger roles — which will entail assuming a larger share of the costs of leadership and order maintenance, as well as a greater influence in decision-making.

Therein lies a key problem of adjustment, historically as well as in the present setting: rising powers hesitant to assume the responsibilities (financial and operational costs) of leadership even as they anticipate greater influence in the future. In the short run, the greatest rethinking probably involves Japan. Both the United States and Japan find delusion comfortable. Yet smooth adjustment requires that Japan assume somewhat larger systemic responsibilities both in terms of international financial and trade leadership and in terms of its own security.

For both internal and external reasons Japan has been induced to defer foreign-policy gratification. But this deferral does not mean that Japan has given up its appetite for a larger foreign-policy role. It only means that Japan is unwilling to accept a role presently offered by other states on their terms, rather than Japanese terms. It means that Japan may find the role of financial aid-giver, through international institutions, to governments assigned by those institutions, less rewarding than bilateral aid to governments of its own choice who show deference to Tokyo. It means that Japan would rather postpone assuming its world military role until it can do so with greater confidence and less competition from governments that it believes to be in relative decline — namely, the former Soviet Union and the United States — than attempt to push into that role today.

But deferring gratification carries the risk that it may not be attained. To postpone assuming a major role is to increase the state's frustrations when its ascendant power is suddenly halted by the bounds of the system — that is, when it reaches its peak. For history has shown that it is at the hour of a state's greatest achievement in terms of absolute-power gains that it is suddenly and unexpectedly driven into relative decline.

Future systems transformation need not re-enact history. It can be orderly, even if the reality it encompasses is not. The key is to anticipate the kind of adjustments to structural change that are necessary, and to introduce them in timely fashion, not too early and not too late, but *prior to* the onset of tensions that in earlier transformations have led to the conspicuous failure of peaceful change.

Opportunities for the Soviet Union and the US to demonstrate how well they could handle structural change presented themselves, in the late 1980s, in the form of *perestroika* and the twin deficits respectively. The odds were that the United States would do better. It has done so, but to date largely on the basis of Soviet default. Now the United States can concentrate, with fewer distractions, on its own situation. Yet it must still contend with a Eurasia composed of state fragments disgruntled by lost visions of parity with the US and of a world role. The United States must also accommodate other states that are rising but not ready to assume the responsibilities of broader leadership. Herein lies the test of world politics for the next decade.

Notes

[1]Joseph S. Nye, Jr, *Bound to Lead: The Changing Nature of American Power* (New York: Basic, 1990); Paul Kennedy, *The Rise and Fall of the Great Powers* (New York: Random House, 1988); Kennedy, 'The End of Empire: Can We Decline as Gracefully as Great Britain?', *Washington Post*, Outlook section (24 Jan. 1988).

[2]Richard Rosecrance, *America's Economic Resurgence: A Bold New Strategy* (New York: Harper & Row, 1990).

[3]Henry R. Nau, *The Myth of America's Decline: Leading the World Economy into the 1990s* (Oxford: Oxford Univ. Press, 1990). The paradox could be called the Nye-Nau-Rosecrance paradox. For the hegemonic-stability thesis, see Robert Gilpin, *War and Change in World Politics* (New York: Cambridge Univ. Press, 1981), and Robert Keohane, *After Hegemony: Cooperation and Discord in the World Political Economy* (Princeton, NJ: Princeton Univ. Press, 1984). Regarding structural theories, see Kenneth Waltz, *Theory of International Politics* (Reading, MA: Addison-Wesley, 1979), and Robert Keohane, ed., *Neorealism and Its Critics* (New York: Columbia Univ. Press, 1986).

[4]Kennedy, *The Rise and Fall of the Great Powers*, 534.

[5]Power-cycle theory was first published in Charles F. Doran, *The Politics of Assimilation: Hegemony and Its Aftermath* (Baltimore: Johns Hopkins Univ. Press, 1971). The thought experiments that led to the theory are explained in Doran, *Systems in Crisis: New Imperatives of High Politics at Century's End* (Cambridge: Cambridge Univ. Press, 1991), 4; they are demonstrated via seeing-is-believing simulations on pages 65-8. The principles of changing systems structure appear in *The Politics of Assimilation* (193), in *Systems In Crisis* (62, with mathematical proofs in the appendix), and as Figure 2.1 in this chapter.

[6]For instance, in an oral presentation at the 1991 American Political Science Association meeting in Washington, DC, Kelly M. Kadera (Univ. of Illinois) described a differential equation for relative-power change that is equivalent to the logistic equation of power-cycle theory. But she did not explore how differential absolute-growth rates create that non-linearity (principles of the power cycle) and its surprises.

[7]It rejects the traditional view that systems transformation is a structural discontinuity caused by massive war, and the static view of order maintenance, such as that argued in George Liska, *War and Order* (Baltimore: Johns Hopkins Univ. Press, 1968), 59, 65, and in most other structural theories. Rather, it asserts that the non-linearities of systems transformation occurred naturally (as explained by the principles of the power cycle), provoking a discontinuity of perception and expectations that caused the massive war, and that order maintenance 'must be based on observa-

tions of long-term changes in relative power' fine-tuned by the balance of power; Doran, *The Politics of Assimilation*, 1.

[8]Kennedy, *The Rise and Fall of the Great Powers*; for instance, 215ff on the power cycles of Austria-Hungary, Britain, and France; 240-1 on the power cycles for Germany and Russia, including reprint of the graphs; 536 on the theory of the power cycle itself.

[9]For example, Doran, 'Change, Uncertainty, and Balance: A Dynamic View of United States Foreign Policy', *International Journal* 35 (Summer 1980), 563-79, regarding superpower diplomacy; 'War and Power Dynamics: Economic Underpinnings', *International Studies Quarterly* 27, 4 (Dec. 1983), 419-41; *Economic Interdependence, Autonomy, and Canadian/American Relations* (Montreal: Institute for Research on Public Policy, 1983), based on analysis of dependency reversal delivered at the International Studies Association meeting (Toronto, March 1979); 'Theoretical Perspectives on Superpower Conflict: Systems Transformation, the Power Cycle, and US-Soviet Relations', paper presented at the American Political Science Association Annual Meeting (Washington, DC, August 1986).

[10]Lois W. Sayrs, review of Manus Midlarsky, ed., *Handbook of War Studies* (1989), *American Political Science Review* 84, 4 (Dec. 1990): 1453.

[11]For example, William R. Thompson, 'Cycles, Capabilities and War: An Ecumenical View' in Thompson, ed., *Contending Approaches to World Systems Analysis* (Beverly Hills, CA: Sage, 1983), 141-63; Jack S. Levy, 'Declining Power and the Preventive Motivation for War', *World Politics* 35, 1 (Oct. 1987), 82-107; and Woosang Kim, 'Power, Alliance, and Major Wars, 1816-1975', *Journal of Conflict Resolution* 33 (1989), 255-73.

[12]For example, Woosang Kim and James D. Morrow, 'When Do Power Transitions Lead to War?', a paper presented at the Midwest Political Science Association (Chicago, 1990); Daniel S. Geller and Daniel M. Jones, 'The Effect of Static and Dynamic Power Balances on Conflict Escalation in Rival Dyads', a paper presented at the American Political Science Association (Washington, DC, Sept. 1991).

[13]Germany competed with Britain for position at the top of the hierarchy, but it was the faster growth rate of the pygmy Russia—nowhere near a point of transition with Germany—that forced Germany to peak and enter relative decline (experience a critical point). Transition theory and hegemonic-stability theory in actuality deal only with absolute trends and miss the dynamic concerns of statecraft.

[14]John Gerald Ruggie, 'Continuity and Transformation in the World Polity: Toward a Neorealist Synthesis', in Keohane, ed., *Neorealism and Its Critics*, 131-57, 153.

[15]Kennedy, *The Rise and Fall of the Great Powers*, xxii-xxiii.

[16]See Paul Kennedy, 'The First World War and the International Power System', *International Security* 9, 1 (Summer 1984), and the theoretical and empirical rebuttal in Doran, *Systems in Crisis*, chap. 3.

[17]For example, 438-41, 467, 538. Kennedy argues that the projections are 'sensible expectations', merely those it is 'reasonable to assume' based on 'the evidence of existing trends' (440). Hence the epilogue asserts: 'Unless the trends of the past two

decades alter (but why should they?), the *pattern* of world politics looks roughly as follows' (538).

[18]Doran, *Systems in Crisis*, chap. 9 and 10; and Doran, 'Expectations, Shifting Tides, and Asian Power Cycles', *Social Science and Policy Research (Korea)* 12, 3 (June 1991), 19-35, paper delivered at the conference 'The Post-Cold War World Order' (Institute of Social Sciences, Seoul National University, Seoul, Korea, 22 March 1991).

[19]Samuel P. Huntington, 'Coping With the Lippmann Gap', *Foreign Affairs* 66, 3 (1987-8), 453-77; Walt W. Rostow, 'Beware of Historians Bearing False Analogies', book review, *Foreign Affairs* 66, 4 (Spring 1988), 863-68; Joseph S. Nye, Jr., 'America's Decline: A Myth', *New York Times* (10 April 1988); and 'Understanding US Strength', *Foreign Policy* (Fall 1988), 105-29.

[20]At the end of the last century, Britain's graceful retreat from world affairs so as to focus on opposition to Germany was not appropriate strategic policy, for it helped precipitate World War I.See Doran, *Systems in Crisis*, chap. 6.

[21]The table is drawn from chap. 9, ibid.

[22]Doran, *The Politics of Assimilation*, figure on p. 193; Doran, *Systems in Crisis*, appendix and figure 3.1 on p. 62.

[23]Arguments in Mancur Olson, *The Rise and Decline of Nations* (New Haven: Yale Univ. Press, 1983), apply to the period of declining rate of absolute growth after a first inflection in absolute power. That a declining rate (absolute or relative) does not necessarily produce declining level is a point made in Bruce Russett, 'The Mysterious Case of Vanishing Hegemony', *International Organization* 39 (1985), 207-31.

[24]This is the implication in David Calleo, 'The End of Hegemony on the Cheap', *New Perspectives Quarterly* 5 (Spring 1988), 24-35; and in Kennedy, *The Rise and Fall of the Great Powers*.

[25]Doran, *Systems in Crisis*, chapters 8 and 9.

[26]Robert W. Lawrence, *Can America Compete?* (Washington, DC: Brookings Institution, 1984).

[27]George C. Lodge and Ezra F. Vogel, eds, *Ideology and National Competitiveness: An Analysis of Nine Countries* (Boston: Harvard Business School Press, 1987), 307.

[28]E.H. Carr, *The Twenty Years Crisis: 1919-1939* (London: Macmillan, 1939); Gilpin, *War and Change in World Politics*.

[29]Nye, 'Understanding US Strength'.

[30]See note 1 above.

[31]Paul Kennedy, 'Fin-de-Siècle America', *New York Review of Books* (28 June 1990), 31-40.

[32]If Kennedy had emphasized that decline is very incremental and that decline for Britain from peak to trough required some 150 years, the analogy with the United States would not have seemed so sensational: the policy conclusions to be drawn would have been far more meaningful.

[33]Henry Kissinger, *American Foreign Policy* (New York: W.W. Norton, 1974), 56.

[34]Quoted in Vernon V. Aspaturian, 'Soviet Global Power and the Correlation of Forces', *Problems of Communism* (May–June 1980): 1.

[35]Stephen F. Cohen, *Sovieticus: American Perceptions and Soviet Realities* (New York: W.W. Norton, 1985), 142.

[36]Ibid., 138.

[37]S. Blogovolin, head of department of Institute of World Economics and International Relations, *Izvestiia* 18 (1988), 5.

[38]Address at the 19th All-Union Party Conference, *Pravda* (26 July 1988), 4.

[39]News Conference, Paris, 5 July 1989. Reported in James M. Markheim, 'Gorbachev's Vision', *New York Times* (8 July 1989), 1.

[40]Quoted in Cord Meyer, 'Uneasy Stirrings at the Waysides? Nationalist Issues Irk Gorbachev', *Washington Times*, Commentary (3 March 1989), 1.

[41]Doran, *The Politics of Assimilation*.

[42]C.F. Doran and Wes Parsons, 'War and the Cycle of Relative Power' *American Political Science Review* 74 (December 1980): 947–65; Doran, *Systems in Crisis*.

[43]Doran, *Systems in Crisis*, chap. 3, and notes 13 and 46 herein.

[44]Ibid., chap. 5. See also C.F. Doran, 'Systemic Disequilibrium, Foreign Power Role, and the Power Cycle', *Journal of Conflict Resolution* 33, 3 (Sept. 1989), 371–401.

[45]Doran, *Systems in Crisis*, chap. 3 and 4.

[46]Doran (ibid., chap. 9) demonstrates empirically what is happening to the Japanese relative-power trajectory, as predicted by power–cycle theory. The historical parallel for Japan is Germany's sudden peak prior to World War I: the giant's huge increments in absolute power were not sufficient to prevent its peak in relative power. For policy implications see Doran, 'Expectations, Shifting Tides, and Asian Power Cycles', and Doran, 'World Politics at Century's End', paper delivered at the German Studies Association meeting (Los Angeles, Sept. 1991).

chapter three

The Collapse of the USSR and World Security

S. Neil MacFarlane

Introduction

The USSR's period as a contender for global power is over. Its economy is in ruins. Domestic political and economic failure ensured the collapse of the union. Faced with this collapse — and with the failure of its prior approach to foreign policy — the USSR had already largely abandoned its military posture in Eastern Europe and had written off the Warsaw Treaty Organization as a meaningful military alliance. It had given up the global political-military competition with the United States. It was seeking to divest itself in an orderly fashion of non-paying Third World assets. It hoped to integrate itself into — rather than to bury — the Western European and global economies in the hope that this would produce levels of trade, technology transfer, and credit sufficient to rescue it from the legacy of seventy years of economic folly.

The Soviet threat, which was one pillar of the Western alliance system, no longer exists. Of necessity, this will alter the post-war Western alliance system profoundly. At the same time, however, the collapse of the USSR and the implosion of the Soviet empire may yet cause new and different security problems that call for a collective Western or Northern response.

Substantiating the above requires, first, a summary of the traditional role of the USSR in post-World War II world politics. This chapter will then examine the evolution of the contradictions in Soviet politics, economics, and society that ultimately determined the revolutionary transformation of

1985 onward. It will conclude with a discussion of the Soviet response to these problems, and the implications it had for the place of the old USSR in the international order as the world moved beyond the cold war.[1]

The Traditional Soviet Union

The USSR's general foreign-policy orientation in the post-war period may be reduced to the following propositions. Soviet policy-makers for most of the period prior to 1985 perceived the international system to be bifurcated into two camps: that of socialism and progress, and that of imperialism and reaction. Conflict between them was structural and ineradicable until one or the other achieved final victory. This conflict constituted the essence of international politics. Thus the Soviets perceived themselves to be permanently at odds with, and threatened by, the West. At various moments, Soviet leaders took the view that this bipolar and conflictual situation did not preclude intersystemic co-operation in specific areas, as occurred during *détente*. However, this tactical co-operation changed nothing essential. As Leonid Brezhnev put it in 1976:

> Some bourgeois gentlemen show amazement and howl over the solidarity of Soviet communists and the Soviet people with other peoples for freedom and progress. This is either *naïveté* or, more likely, deliberate obfuscation. After all, it could not be clearer that *détente* and peaceful coexistence relate to relations between states. This indicates above all that conflicts between countries must not be settled by war or the threat or use of force. *Détente* does not at all abolish, nor can it abolish or alter, the laws of class struggle.[2]

The essential approach of the USSR to the question of security in this context, with some exceptions (e.g., Nikita Khrushchev's abortive cuts in conventional forces in 1959-60),[3] was to build up its offensive military potential. This unilateral approach to security based itself on the proposition that the West would be deterred from attack or pressure by the threat of defeat should war occur. In this sense, the USSR was secure to the extent that the West felt threatened. This confrontational deterrent posture demanded, among other things, a quest for military superiority and close control of the Eastern European glacis, both as a buffer against Western attack and as a jumping-off point for offensive action.

The necessity of weakening the adversary also dictated efforts to undermine its influence and strategic positions, and to establish Soviet positions in their stead. As the nuclear stalemate descended on the centre, while the Soviet capacity to pursue active policies grew elsewhere, these efforts concentrated in the Third World, where risks and potential costs were lower.

Soviet expansion in the Third World also served the needs of a party and a system whose claim to rule rested on their leading role in interpreting and in promoting communism. The expansion of the 'positions of socialism' and the growing influence of the 'forces of progress' were perceived to enhance the legitimacy of the Soviet Communist party (CPSU). Conversely, because the link between regime legitimacy inside the USSR and the fortunes of socialism abroad was perceived to be so tight, losses were taken very seriously for domestic as well as international reasons. Once a socialist regime was established and recognized as such by the Soviets, the USSR was strongly predisposed to defend it against external challenges (as in Cuba), against its own people (as in Poland), and, if necessary, against itself (as in Czechoslovakia).

The structure of the Soviet political system (i.e., the concentration of political power in the hands of a hierarchically organized, highly disciplined party; the proscription of formal opposition; and the existence of substantial constraints on intra- and extra-party informal opposition) gave the leadership considerable flexibility in resource allocation and in foreign-policy decision. That is to say, domestic political constraints on foreign-policy decision-making were very weak. In short, the Soviet view of the international system was zero-sum in character, military in focus, and relatively unconstrained by the domestic political process.

Stagnation and Crisis in the USSR

In the Soviet Union, and consequently in the West, much was made initially of the role played by Brezhnev and his gerontocratic colleagues in allowing the USSR to drift into serious decline.[4] As time passed, however, Soviet scholars and policy-makers came to the conclusion that this link between the problem of *zastoi* (stagnation) and the previous regime underestimated the seriousness of the problem, and distorted its causes. There is no doubt that the immobilism, sloth, and corruption of the Brezhnev era exacerbated the crisis inherited by Brezhnev's successors. However, the fundamental problems were not linked fundamentally to any particular personality (except perhaps Lenin and Stalin): they were structural in character. The most obvious dimension of the problem lay in the gradual drop in quantitative rates of growth in the Soviet economy through the 1970s and 1980s, to a point in 1985 where by some estimates there was zero or negative growth in GNP. This was linked to a rapid decline in productivity. Again, by 1985 it appeared that the marginal rate of increase in production from additional inputs of labour and capital was negative. A third aspect of the economic problem was the incapacity to generate sustained improvement in the quality of Soviet industrial output.[5]

As the Soviets saw it, these problems reflected the difficulty of achieving the transition from extensive growth (adding ever greater quantities of inputs to production) to intensive growth (increasing the efficiency with which an existing pool of factors of production is used). Such a transition was necessary for two reasons. As growth proceeded and under-utilized factors of production were absorbed, the marginal costs of new inputs increased. As increasing amounts of labour, capital, and other resources were added into production, all other things (including technology) being equal, the output derived from each additional unit of input declined (the law of diminishing returns). Both of these problems called for more effective use of existing factors of production—that is, increasing the output of existing factors of production. This necessitated sustained technological innovation.

The Soviet economy appeared in 1985 to be incapable of generating sustained technological change. This failure was particularly serious in the comparative context, since the advanced industrial economies with which the USSR had to compete relied to an increasing extent on accelerating technological innovation (particularly in the realm of electronics) to sustain growth. In such conditions, the USSR faced the prospect of slipping ever farther behind those states benefiting from technologically driven growth. By the mid-1980s it was clear that in many respects, such newly industrializing countries as South Korea, Taiwan, and Brazil had outstripped the USSR in terms of the technical sophistication of their civilian industrial bases. Without substantial change in the Soviet economic mechanism, the USSR risked being left out of the so-called third industrial revolution.[6]

In addition to affecting Soviet prestige and general economic health, this lag had concrete military implications. New generations of weaponry drew to an increasing extent on the very technologies (electronics, laser optics, computer systems) that the USSR had such difficulty either in developing itself or (given restrictions on the transfer of sensitive technology) in importing. In turn, the USSR's efforts to keep up in the military sphere despite general economic backwardness exacerbated the problem of resource allocation in a period of negligible economic growth.[7]

What were the principal causes of the economic deterioration? In some respects, it could be attributed to specific policies of the Brezhnev era. Brezhnev's policies of resource allocation caused Soviet industrial plants to run down while money was poured into agriculture and the military.[8] It was the principle of stability of cadres that ossified the entire Soviet administrative structure, preventing the movement of more efficient and innovative personnel into positions of responsibility. In part, Brezhnev's (and his colleagues') deep ambivalence about the political consequences of reform precluded any effective effort to address the evolving needs of the Soviet economic mechanism.[9]

Such an analysis is superficial, however. The overinvestment in the military was clear in the Brezhnev era; it was also clear that the consequent underinvestment in other sectors was debilitating. But this pattern was in many respects the continuation of one established by Stalin, as were the distortions associated with it. Both Stalin's system of central planning and the resource-allocation decisions taken in its context were oriented towards the rapid development of a military industrial base and the buildup of military power. The pattern of Soviet growth was one in which heavy industry developed at the expense of other sectors.[10]

Likewise, the overinvestment in agriculture typical of the late 1970s reflected the previous failure of that sector to perform adequately. This failure in turn was a product of prior investment and organizational decisions that, finally, reflected deeper political and economic variables.

At a more profound level, the economic crisis was explicable in terms of structural deficiencies in the Soviet model designed and put into place under Stalin. In the first place, the closely controlled, centralized, and hierarchical decision-making apparatus was a profound impediment to economic rationality, let alone innovation. Those with knowledge of the productive process at the operating level lacked the power to act on their knowledge. Those with the power to act were distant from production, and hence lacked the operational knowledge necessary to guide their decisions. Market mechanisms could not encourage efficiency, since exchange values (prices) were determined centrally, with no necessary relation to use (real) value. The incentive mechanism produced further distortions. The system rewarded producers according to fulfilment of arbitrary plan targets rather than profitability. The worker, meanwhile, had little incentive to perform efficiently: the guarantee of full employment and job security deprived employers of a stick, while the lack of desirable consumer products deprived the system of carrots. The attempt to compensate through ideological or patriotic exhortation grew increasingly ineffectual. As the USSR consolidated the gains of socialism, the millennial promise of communism grew ever more remote.

In a way, these failures point to a basic cultural dimension of the problems that faced the USSR. Seventy years of communist rule—of effort unrewarded and egalitarian slogans masking naked exploitation by an increasingly narrow and closed élite—had produced a profound popular disillusionment and malaise evident in rampant alcoholism (itself hardly a spur to production), declining birth rates in Russia and other ethnically European areas, decaying public health, and rising rates of divorce and juvenile delinquency, but perhaps most directly revealed in the deep cynicism of popular humour:[11]

> Q.: 'What's the difference between capitalism and socialism?'
> A.: 'Under capitalism, man is exploited by man. In socialism, it's the reverse.'
> OR: 'Under socialism, they pretend to pay us and we pretend to work.'[12]

This deep social malaise reflected a crisis of legitimacy in the political system. The Communist party claimed to represent the people, but denied them a voice in their affairs. It claimed to be democratic, but provided a veneer for oligarchic rule. It exhorted the people to sacrifice in the building of socialism, and appropriated the fruit of their labour to create and sustain a closed privileged élite. The party, in short, had in the popular mind expropriated the expropriators in order to replace them.[13]

The crisis inherited by Gorbachev spanned the realms of economics, culture, society, and politics. It was systemic and, to judge from Soviet comment, sufficiently deep as to raise doubts about whether the system could survive, let alone flourish, without fundamental change.

The Attempt at Reform

The initial reform programme revolved around three concepts: *perestroika* (restructuring), *glasnost* (openness), and *demokratizatsia* (democratization). The first, in theory, involved substantial reform of the economic mechanism, including

1. decentralization of economic decision-making away from central ministries and to the level of the individual enterprise;

2. increased self-accountability (*khozraschot*) at the level of the enterprise, where the economic unit would be obliged to show profitability;

3. alteration in resource-allocation priorities, with a large portion of defence spending being converted to civilian use;

4. movement towards a system whereby markets would replace central planning in the allocation of resources;

5. change in property laws to permit expansion of the co-operatives and (eventually) the private sector;

6. flexibility in the pricing of goods, so that price could operate as a market-clearing device.

The basic objectives of these reforms were to curb waste, to enhance efficiency and improve quality, and to stimulate innovation by changing the locus of economic decision-making and the incentive structure of the producer. These reforms were implemented only very partially in the face of persisting ideological inhibitions, the institutional resistance of the bureaucracy, and the fears of the working class about employment security and declining living standards. They were often carried out in a contradictory fashion. As a result, the economic situation deteriorated further. This deterioration—coupled with disappointed popular expectations—stiffened popular resistance to the regime. This resistance was increasingly manifested not only in popular demonstrations but in strike activity resulting in further economic dislocation and loss of output.[14]

A second concept was *demokratizatsia*. The essential instrumental purposes of democratic reform were threefold:

1. to outflank the entrenched party and government apparatuses by creating new decision-making bodies and empowering and restructuring older ones;

2. to rekindle popular support for the state by granting the public real participation in politics;

3. to enhance the efficiency of the state apparatus by devolving power from the centre to local and regional levels, which are in theory more responsive to the needs of the population and of enterprises in their localities.

The essential problem with the dismantlement of traditional organs of control and the creation of new quasi-democratic institutions was that it tangled lines of authority. The political relaxation meanwhile allowed new political forces to emerge whose demands and programmes were not obviously compatible. Moreover, the process of democratization took on a momentum of its own to the extent that the central leadership lost control of it. This in turn raised questions about the survivability of the Soviet state, particularly as the worsening economic situation embittered relations between groups competing over a diminishing pool of resources.

The most prominent form of political struggle was, and remains, the struggle between nationalities. The first five years of Gorbachev showed that seventy years of attempts to draw the various ethnic groups of the USSR into a single Soviet nationality had failed abjectly; that ethnic consciousness had, if anything, grown stronger under Soviet rule; that perceived Russian domination of Soviet politics continued to be deeply resented; and that interethnic rivalries among non-Russian peoples remained as bitter as ever.

In these conditions, the tendency of party and state to relax control from above coincided with increasingly ambitious attempts by the national republics to seize power from below. The result was chaos—a plethora of competing claims to sovereignty over territory (e.g., Nagorno-Karabakh) and resources (e.g., Russian claims to Soviet energy resources), inconsistent federal and republican legislation, republican resistance to Soviet law (e.g., conscription), and a loss of the state's monopoly of force as republics began to create their own autonomous police and military organs. In specific instances—for example, in the Caucasus, where informal militias had acquired considerable amounts of military equipment through raids on police and military installations, and were using them in communal warfare against rivals—the process deteriorated into near anarchy and was marked by considerable bloodshed.[15]

Despite the central authorities' occasional displays of the will to resist disintegration (e.g., in Lithuania), Gorbachev and his colleagues appeared to have little idea of how to cope with the issue of national self-assertion, and little control over the course of events. The Union as traditionally defined—with hierarchical control exercised by a centralized party both directly and indirectly, through a subservient centralized state, over all significant policy issues—had died and could not be resuscitated. However, there was much middle ground between the old fiction of federalism and the dissolution of the Soviet state.[16] And although the desire for autonomy was strong (and indeed irresistible) in certain cases, in others this was balanced by continuing strong interest in retaining some form of federal structure. Some regions benefited from the historical economic tie to Moscow (compare, for example, living standards in Tadzhikistan or Turkmenistan with those in Afghanistan or northern Pakistan). Others facing powerful contiguous ethnic rivals sought to retain the umbrella of federation as insurance. What was clear was that any future central structure governing all or part of the USSR would be much less powerful, and would exercise far looser constraints over its parts, than its predecessor. This had obvious implications for the capacity of the central state to marshal resources for use in foreign and security policy.

The same could be said of the strengthening of legislative organs at the centre. As the Congress of People's Deputies and the Supreme Soviet doled out new powers and developed the institutional mechanisms to enhance their capacities of oversight and legislation, the capacity of the party and the executive to monopolize decision-making correspondingly diminished. Here as elsewhere, representative legislatures were reluctant to sacrifice domestic concerns for the sake of foreign policy unless such policies could be clearly related to issues of domestic import, or to values widely held by their constituents.[17]

The third element of reform was *glasnost*—the opening up of flows of information in Soviet society. Here the purpose was also threefold:

1. to enhance the pace of technological innovation by allowing freer exchange of technical data;

2. to improve efficiency and reduce waste by exposing the incompetent and corrupt to public opprobrium;

3. to create the impression that the state cared about and was prepared to respond to the concerns of the people.

The problem here was that this process too was difficult to control. If the economic situation failed to improve, criticism of specific abuses was likely to evolve into an indictment of the system as a whole. Moreover, although initially the leadership might have preferred to limit open discussion, the manifest inadequacy of the country's economic system, the abusive quality of its politics, and the evident and ubiquitous falsification of its history all invited deeper historical and political analysis, the result of which was the further delegitimation of party rule. One sees this in the progression from the critique of Brezhnev as a historical exception to the indictment of Stalin as the creator of evil, to the increasingly critical and uncomplimentary analysis of Lenin's historical role and of the body of thinking he left to the party.[18] In this way *glasnost* promoted a fundamental challenge to the justifying myth of the CPSU and merged with democratization in destabilizing the political system.

Considerable time has been spent here on the nature of the crisis, and the approach taken by the party to resolving it, for an important reason. In assessing the implications of the domestic situation for the Soviet role in international relations, it is necessary to demonstrate that what was at issue was not merely an adjustment to domestic difficulties, but a profound domestic crisis that threw into question the survivability of the Soviet system. Gorbachev's attempts at reform—which he apparently conceived as a renewal of the Leninist tradition—practically assured the collapse of that system. And one could predict with confidence that, just as Soviet foreign policy traditionally reflected in important respects the nature of the Soviet system, as the internal system transformed itself, the external role of the USSR would be radically redefined.

Environmental Factors and Change in Soviet Foreign Policy

It was not only the transformation of the political and economic situation in the USSR that conduced to a redefinition of its role in international politics. International behaviour is a product of domestic factors, but also of variables in the international system itself. Events and processes in the environment initiate responses that are mediated by domestic political and economic variables. Policy responses are affected also by perceptual processes and structures. Foreign policy is a response not to international events *per se*, but to leaders' perceptions of these events. Perceptions are not random, but reflect the intellectual structures employed by political élites to make sense of the world around them. These structures — or filters — in turn reflect political culture (including ideology) and historical experience. Given that policy-makers rely on these sets of beliefs and assumptions to order their understanding of the nature and significance of events around them, such structures tend to be resistant to change. On the other hand, if traditional patterns of belief and understanding are manifestly inaccurate — if in this sense the filter systematically distorts reality in such a way as to favour dysfunctional policy responses — eventually the dissonance between theory and practice may produce a 'schema transformation', a fundamental restructuring of the beliefs and assumptions informing leadership perceptions of environment and role. Such a transformation occurred in the USSR in 1985-90, and it was prompted by the academic re-evaluation of international relations in the Khrushchev and Brezhnev years.[19]

The generational change associated with the disappearance (by death, incapacitation, or retirement) of the neo-Stalinist leadership removed the more substantial political constraints on the reformulation of official Soviet perspectives on international relations and foreign policy. The emergence into positions of power and responsibility of an élite that had fundamentally different formative experiences (and in particular that was not directly implicated in the excesses of the Stalin era) favoured the consideration of essentially different approaches to international relations.

The development of an increasingly radical critique of the Stalinist system inside the USSR under conditions of *glasnost* legitimized the articulation of the equally radical foreign-policy implications of that critique. Criticism of the command economy and political centralization opened the way to questioning the image of the external enemy, which in part justified these arrangements. It also justified scepticism as to the desirability of replicating the Soviet model abroad. The aforementioned enhancement of the role of representative organs in the formulation of foreign policy, and the corresponding diminution of the role of the Politburo and Central Committee apparatus as determinants of that policy, also favoured change in Soviet perspectives by shifting the locus and broadening the basis of participation in foreign policy. Thus internal political developments conduced to a significant reassessment of the USSR's approach to foreign policy.

But ultimately it was critical assessment of past experience that defined the specific outlines of the revision known as 'new thinking'. At its root lay the fact that by the mid-1980s policies of the Brezhnev era had produced the near complete isolation of the USSR. Relations with the Western European states were problematic in view of their acceptance of Intermediate Nuclear Force (INF) deployment and increases in overall defence spending. Although Eastern Europe was stable at a superficial level, the region was crippled by the deepening debt crisis and its economic implications. These issues — in conjunction with the persistence of nationalism frequently defined (for obvious reasons) in anti-Soviet terms — in turn raised questions about the viability of client regimes sustained there by Soviet military power.[20]

The United States was demonstrably hostile to the USSR, committed to rolling back Soviet gains of the 1970s, to denying it access to the fruits of technological change sweeping the West, and to sustaining a military build-up, the Soviet response to which (as noted earlier) greatly exacerbated the deepening economic crisis in the USSR. Despite several overtures at the highest level, the USSR's relations with China remained frozen as a result of Soviet policies on Kampuchea, Afghanistan, and the militarization of the Sino-Soviet border. Soviet-Japanese relations remained unfriendly as a result of the USSR's inflexibility on the Northern Territories issue and its buildup of the Pacific Fleet. In the Third World, the successes of the 1970s had produced an array of unviable, poverty-stricken clients, all of whom expected more in material terms than the USSR was willing or able to provide. The military adventure in Afghanistan had produced a lengthy, costly, and painful entanglement. In short, there was much evidence in this period of significant domestic change that the previous Soviet approach to foreign policy had produced increasingly unpalatable results.

These results were at least in part the product of flawed assumptions and beliefs about world politics. False perceptions led to policy failure in at least three ways. First, the assumption that the international arena was divided along class lines into two systems, between which conflict was ineradicable and co-operation only a matter of tactical expediency, was a self-fulfilling prophecy. The Soviet adherence to the principle of class struggle threatened other actors in the international system, encouraging them to band together to resist the threat. Western fears also limited Soviet access to international markets and technologies. This in turn reduced the competitiveness of the Soviet industrial base.

Moreover, the perception of a world divided along Manichean lines between the transnational forces of socialism and imperialism tended to divert attention away from the state and the nation as significant variables in international relations. The underestimation of the capacity of states to resist popular pressure against the INF deployment in Western Europe in the early 1980s is one example of the unfortunate implications of this methodological preference. The incapacity of the USSR to develop durable influence in much of the Third World is another. Presumptions about the comparative significance of class as opposed to other groupings led to an inadequate estimation of the devotion of Third World élites to sectional and national interests that had little to do with the world revolutionary process of struggle against imperialism.

A related interpretive problem was the perceived relationship between base and superstructure in international relations, or, to put it another way, the autonomy of politics. Traditional Soviet Marxism posited that just as politics is a superstructural manifestation of forces and relations obtaining in the economic base, the state and its foreign policy narrowly reflected the interests of controlling economic groups. This understanding had a double-edged effect. In the socialist community, it fostered the perception that since these states were dominated by the proletariat and its vanguard, the basis of conflict among them had been eliminated. It may well be that many in the Soviet élite have not believed this for years, given the Soviet-Yugoslav and Sino-Soviet disputes. But this ideologically determined and officially endorsed analytical structure limited the scope for meaningful debate and discussion of those conflicts that did emerge. The result was a tendency to underestimate the potential for conflict among socialist states, a lack of preparation for such events, and an incapacity to focus unfettered analytical attention on these conflicts.[21] Moreover, the proposition that the policies adopted by states are the product of forces and relations of production within them strengthened the Soviet propensity to replicate its own model elsewhere, both in Eastern Europe and in the Third World, with unfortunate results.

In the capitalist world, the traditional Stalinist assumptions (a) that the monopoly bourgeoisie was monolithic; (b) that it was—as a unified class—hostile to the proletariat and to the latter's leading force, the CPSU; and (c) that the governments of capitalist states had no autonomy, being the creatures of 'monopoly capital', favoured an underestimation of these states' capacities to engage the USSR in substantial long-term co-operation. As was noted above, basic assumptions about the hostility of the capitalist world combined with beliefs about the nature of power to produce a unilateralist conception of security, according to which the accumulation of superior force would convince putative adversaries that an attack on the USSR or its allies could only produce defeat. The problem here was that when this perspective on procurement was combined with a heavy emphasis on warfighting (as opposed to deterrence) and on the offensive (rather than defensive) in strategy, it increased the perceived insecurity of the adversary. Whether this was intentional and part of an effort to intimidate other states into submission and compliance with the Soviet agenda of world power, or an inadvertent strategic by-product of the operationalization of an essentially defensive military *doctrine*,[22] it resulted not in the collapse of Western will and cohesion, but in the reverse. In the parlance of the current literature on security, the Western states tended to balance rather than bandwagon in the face of growing Soviet military power.

These cognitive problems were exacerbated by the linkages between assumptions and beliefs about international relations, on the one hand, and the official ideology justifying the party's hold on power at home and the structure the party had imposed on Soviet society, on the other. At a general level, the rule of the party was justified in part by its status as the leading force in a global struggle against imperialism and oppression. If one questioned class as a fundamental organizing principle of world politics and the significance of class struggle in international relations, this had obvious implications for the legitimacy of party rule at home. If one questioned the feasibility of the Soviet model in the comparatively more advanced societies of Eastern Europe, this raised questions about the wisdom of its application inside the USSR.

In the past, resource allocation favouring heavy industry and the military was justified by evoking the image of a permanent enemy committed to the destruction of the USSR and deterred only by Soviet military power. Change in the perception of the external threat, therefore, had fundamental implications for Soviet domestic economic policy. It is for these reasons that official reformulation of basic precepts of foreign policy was predicated upon internal political change. In this sense, *perestroika* permitted the absorption of lessons derived from Soviet experience in foreign policy, an experience suggesting that the previous ideologically determined structure of perception and interpretation had inhibited rational (value-maximizing) behaviour.

The reformulation of Soviet perspectives on international relations may be summarized as follows:

1. the recognition that world politics is a global system: i.e., that it is not dominated by a bifurcation between two distinct and competing socio-political systems;

2. the recognition of a number of issues in which states of whatever social system share transcendent common interests (avoidance of nuclear war, limitation of the arms race, stability, growth, and integration in the world economy, environmental preservation, and Third World development);

3. a reduction in the significance of class as a category of world politics and of class struggle as a basic focus of policy, with an associated increase in the significance of state interest in Soviet policy and of the balance of such interests in relations between states;

4. a growing attention in the latter context to profitability or concrete benefit as a criterion for policy responses to environmental stimuli;

5. increasing attention to the interactive aspects of security, the dominant perspective being a state's perceptions of threat.[23]

This fifth dimension had three important theoretical implications that were recognized and elaborated on in the Soviet literature on security. If the other's sense of threat defines the degree to which one is secure oneself, bilateral (or unilateral) disarmament enhances security. There is no need to insist on symmetry in forces or in arms control. Transparency also enhances security, by reducing the putative adversary's uncertainty about one's capabilities and intentions. Finally, this interactive understanding of security suggests that strategy and force posture should emphasize clearly defensive configurations.

Before discussing the implications of these changes in Soviet perspectives both for Soviet behaviour and for international security, it is useful to summarize this discussion of the sources of change. As will become clear below, Soviet foreign policy on many fronts moved away from previous zero-sum competitive approaches (in which one's gain was assumed to be the other's loss, with the overall sum always zero) to a more collaborative positive-sum role (in which both could simultaneously win) in international relations. This shift reflected

1. the depth of the domestic crisis and the consequent need to reduce external pressure on the USSR in order to reallocate existing resources to domestic economic regeneration;

2. the need to enlist the West in this process of renewal;

3. a profound questioning of past approaches to economic, political, and social modernization;

4. a recognition that past approaches to foreign policy have produced dysfunctional results, isolating the USSR and seriously exacerbating its internal problems.

The depth and structural quality of the domestic crisis suggested that it was likely to endure, as would its foreign-policy implications. The thorough discrediting of the Stalinist form of Soviet Marxism suggested a move beyond mere tactical adjustment. The difficulty of any return to orthodoxy in Soviet ideology and domestic policy suggested an equal difficulty in returning to a more activist foreign policy under the rubric of socialist internationalism. This indicated in turn that a reversal of the learning process in Soviet foreign policy was improbable.

Implications

What were the implications of these changes for international security? A review of changes in Soviet international behaviour from 1987 to 1991 suggests that profound change had occurred in the role that the USSR defined for itself in international relations. In the realm of security policy, the Soviets embraced a degree of unilateral disarmament, as in Gorbachev's announcement of a 500,000-person reduction in Soviet forces in December 1988, and in the 1989 projection of a 35 per cent reduction in the defence budget by 1995. They also abandoned the prior notion of equal security, and accepted asymmetrical reductions in key areas such as intermediate nuclear forces and, in the Paris agreement, conventional forces. The verification clauses of these agreements, moreover, contemplated a degree of transparency well beyond anything previously accepted by the Soviet Union (or, for that matter, the United States). There was good reason to expect agreement on substantial reductions in both strategic weapons and conventional forces in the not-too-distant future.[24]

This reduction was linked to substantial change in Soviet policy in Eastern Europe. Indeed, in this context the Soviets had every reason to pursue substantial multilateral agreed-upon conventional and nuclear reductions in Europe, even if these were deeply asymmetrical. Change in Eastern Europe, and the Soviet abandonment of the Brezhnev doctrine (which asserted a Soviet right to maintain Communist regimes in Eastern Europe through military intervention), effectively destroyed the Soviet military position there. The Warsaw Pact was no longer—if it ever was—a militarily significant alliance structure. Its Eastern European members were disarming and reducing defence spending even faster than the USSR. The Soviet willingness to take the lid off Eastern Europe—in particular, to allow the reunification of Germany—fundamentally altered the security equation. The Soviet threat in Central Europe, as traditionally conceived, evaporated.

This was good news, but it had a number of potentially disturbing implications. As many American proponents of the merits of the now-defunct cold-war system in Europe noted,[25] the systemic function of the USSR in Europe was in many respects one of stabilization. Arguably, one reason for the forty-five years of peace in Europe was that the politics of the continent were controlled by two military hegemons, neither of whom desired (or could afford) war. As the USSR abandoned its hegemony in Eastern Europe, it became clear that few of the problems of that region (either civil or interstate) had been resolved, and that actors in the region were returning to ancient conflictual agendas (namely, Slovak-Hungarian disputes over Southern Slovakia, Hungarian-Romanian tension over Transylvania, Hungarian-Yugoslav tension over the Vojvodina, intra-Yugoslav conflict between Croats, Serbs, Slovenes, and Albanians, and tension between Bulgarians and Turks within Bulgaria, to name but a few). The emergence of intercommunal tensions within the USSR, in the context of ambiguity about the nature of the union, paralleled these Eastern European phenomena. In this sense, Europe was both more and less secure, and there was a need for new security mechanisms to manage the problems previously suppressed under the now-defunct structure of security.

Progress in the dismantlement of the cold-war structure in Europe was accompanied by sustained Soviet efforts to set relations with the United States on a new and more co-operative basis. This was evident in the substantial progress in the realm of arms control noted above. The Soviets also sought a deepening of the bilateral economic relationship (e.g., a trade agreement) and were willing to make substantial concessions in pursuit of it (e.g., the effective abandonment of restrictions on the emigration of Jews). The process of consultation on security issues deepened with frequent meetings between the foreign ministers of the two countries, and with a broadening of contacts between the security establishments at lower levels (e.g., the exchange between the Joint Chiefs and the Soviet General Staff). The effect was to reduce substantially the American perception of threat emanating from the USSR and to initiate a gradual reduction of the American defence establishment. The effect of change in the Soviet approach to foreign policy was to create a situation in which the nature of the superpower relationship had shifted a considerable distance towards co-operation. The role of military issues in these relations was declining and was being challenged to an increasing extent by diplomacy and economic issues. Evolution in Europe and in the Soviet-American relationship and the decreasing salience of their bipolar confrontation called into question just what the US role in world politics was to be. Although the constraints of domestic economic factors were hardly as intense in the United States as they were in the USSR, the Gulf crisis raised some doubt about the capacity of the United States to act as a global power on its own, even should it wish to do so.[26]

Trends in Soviet policy in the Third World were consistent with those discussed above. The Soviets were gradually distancing themselves from traditional, ideologically kindred friends. They were setting their economic relations with Third World states on a basis of profitability and concrete benefit to the USSR. This necessitated some refocusing of Soviet efforts towards states that had things the Soviets wanted (for example, Brazil, the Association of South East Asian Nations, South Africa) rather than states that were ideologically correct. The Soviets were forgoing opportunities for competitive involvement in Third World civil and regional conflict, were attempting to extricate themselves honourably from those in which they were involved, and were seeking to co-operate with other states — and specifically the United States — in the management and resolution of Third World conflict.[27]

In general, change in the USSR produced a profound transformation in global security. The era of confrontational bipolarity had largely ended, and was replaced by a substantial accord on many security issues between the remaining superpower and what was left of its previous rival. The collapse of the USSR's position in world politics did, however, carry some less positive implications, as noted above, in that the removal of the Soviet pillar of the European security system reopened many previously suppressed regional rivalries in Central and Eastern Europe.

Since the spring of 1991 much more has changed. The destruction of old structures of power, authority, and economic organization in the Union of Soviet Socialist Republics and the failure to replace these with viable alternatives continued to deepen the crisis facing the Soviet polity. Gorbachev's hold on power grew increasingly shaky throughout 1991. His weakness in the face of conservative challengers at the union level was evident in the Soviet government's hardening of its stance on economic reform and republican autonomy in December 1990-January 1991. That this had potentially serious implications for foreign affairs was evident in the wavering of the Soviet commitment to the US-led coalition in the Gulf War in January and February of 1991, as war grew near. Although when the chips were down, the USSR continued to support UN action, Gorbachev tried to broker a last-minute peace. This reflected considerable unhappiness within the USSR, but also unhappiness concerning the eclipse of the USSR's influence in global security, made evident by the US role in the international community's response to the Iraqi invasion of Kuwait.

The weakness of the centre as a whole, in the face of increasing republican assertiveness and an economy that by mid-year was in free fall, was clear in Gorbachev's sudden abandonment of the conservatives and his compromise with Yeltsin and eight other republican leaders on a formula for a new union treaty in the spring of 1991.

The imminent signature of that treaty on 20 August 1991, coupled with Yeltsin's decision in July to remove Communist-party organizations from workplaces on Russian territory — both of which would have greatly circumscribed the remaining power of party and central ministerial bureaucrats — resulted in the coup of 19-23 August 1991. That the coup was defeated so easily — as a result not only of the ineptitude of its leadership, but also of serious divisions within those organizations responsible for carrying it out, and the unwillingness of many regional and republican authorities to co-operate in a reimposition of central control — reflected the extent to which the rot had penetrated the central institutions of the Soviet system.

The principal effect of the coup was to delegitimize the institutions inherited from the communist period, while transferring power away from the centre and to the republican authorities — notably to the principal beneficiary of its defeat, Boris Yeltsin. The Russian government took advantage of its victory in suppressing the coup to complete the deconstruction of the principal central instruments of coercive power, through substantial purges of upper levels of the armed forces and the KGB, and the beginning of a substantial restructuring and shrinkage of the latter.

As the centre self-destructed, the outlying pieces of the union began to spin off, with the Baltics' independence being generally recognized in the immediate aftermath of the coup. Strenuous efforts on Gorbachev's part to reconstruct a looser economic and political union failed, as a result of fundamental differences over the division of responsibility between centre and periphery. Ukraine's referendum and subsequent declaration of independence in December of 1991 proved the final straw. At year's end, the leaders of Russia, Ukraine, and Belarus declared the Union of Soviet Socialist Republics to be defunct.

Notes

[1] For a more complete analysis, see my article, 'The Implications of Change in Soviet Strategy', *International Journal* XLVI (Winter 1990-1).

[2] Leonid Brezhnev, 'Report of the CPSU Central Committee and the Policy', *Pravda* (25 Feb. 1976).

[3] See David Holloway, *The Soviet Union and the Arms Race* (New Haven: Yale Univ. Press, 1983), 39-41.

[4] See, *inter alia*, Timothy Colton, *The Dilemma of Reform in the Soviet Union* (New York: Council on Foreign Relations, 1986), in particular 24-9. Colton concludes this section, entitled 'The Loss of Vigor and Dynamism', by noting that Brezhnev and his cohorts settled for 'stultification when imagination was needed'. In citing Colton here, I am not implying that he underestimates the structural causes of crisis in the USSR.

[5] For general discussions of Soviet economic difficulties in the period prior to Gorbachev's accession to power, see Anders Aslund, *Gorbachev's Struggle for Economic Reform* (Ithaca, NY: Cornell Univ. Press, 1990), 13-22; A. Hewett, ed., *Reforming the Soviet Economy* (Washington, DC: Brookings Institution, 1988), 50-93, 153-220; and Friedemann Muller, 'Economic Reforms in the Soviet Union', in Richard Feinberg, John Echeverri-Gent, et al., eds, *Economic Reform in Three Giants* (New Brunswick, NJ: Transaction Books, 1990), 45-50.

[6] The term is from Seweryn Bialer, '"New Thinking" and Soviet Foreign Policy', *Survival* XXX, 4 (July/Aug. 1988), 292.

[7] On the link between economic stagnation and Soviet stature in international relations, see Mikhail Gorbachev, *Izbrannye Rechi i Stat'i* II (Moscow, 1986), 86.

[8] Alec Nove noted in 1980 that investment in agriculture absorbed about 27% of total investment under Brezhnev; Alec Nove, 'Agriculture', in Archie Brown and Michael Kaser, eds, *Soviet Policy for the 1980s* (Bloomington: Indiana Univ. Press, 1982), 172. For a useful account of military spending — and the problems of estimation — in the Brezhnev era, see Holloway, *The Soviet Union and the Arms Race*, 115-17. See also Harry Gelman, *The Brezhnev Politburo* (Ithaca, NY: Cornell Univ. Press, 1984), 92-6.

[9] The spillover of economic reform into political transformation in Czechoslovakia in 1968 dampened whatever enthusiasm the Soviet leadership had for piecemeal reform of the Soviet economy. See Robert Hutchings, *Soviet-East European Relations* (Madison: Univ. of Wisconsin Press, 1987), 52-4.

[10] See, for example, Michael Checinski, 'The Soviet War Economy and Economic Development', in Hans-Joachim Veen, ed., *From Brezhnev to Gorbachev* (New York: Berg, 1984).

[11]On Soviet alcoholism, see Vladimir Treml, *Alcohol in the USSR: A Statistical Analysis* (Durham, NC: Duke Univ. Press, 1982). On Soviet demography, see Ann Helgeson, 'Demographic Policy', in Brown and Kaser, *Soviet Policy*, 118-26. On the deteriorating health situation, see Murray Feshbach, 'Soviet Health Problems', in *The Soviet Union in the 1980s, Proceedings of the American Academy of Political Science* XXXV, 3 (1984), 81-97. Feshbach quite rightly stresses that the decline in Soviet health is a result not only of these issues, but also of the underinvestment in public health facilities that followed from the resource allocation decisions discussed earlier. For a useful and concise summary see also Colton, *The Dilemma of Reform*, 34.

[12]This sentiment was eloquently expressed by a Soviet tractor driver interviewed by the *New York Times* (14 Dec. 1990) on the question of food aid to the USSR: 'You tell America, don't give these communists a kopeck. They're bandits.'

[13]For a more complete discussion, see Aslund, *Gorbachev's Struggle, passim.*

[14]The Soviet/East European Report noted that 'according to Soviet officials, the time lost through strikes in the first six months of 1989 accounted for 2 million man days. That is an average of 15,000 workers on strike each day. Losses for the following six months amounted to 5.5 million man days—that is, an average of nearly 52 thousand workers on strike each day'; 'Workers of the USSR Unite', *Soviet/East European Report* VII, 16 (1 Feb. 1990), 3. In a more recent issue, the same publication reported that the number of man days lost in the USSR in the first six months of 1990 was 10.3 million, suggesting a continuing acceleration. Strike activity in 1990 became more overtly political, and focused on the minority republics, suggesting a strong ethnic dimension; 'Ethnic Conflicts Plague Soviet Industry', *Soviet/East European Report* VIII, 3 (15 Oct. 1990).

[15]As was evident in the pogroms in Sumgait, and in ongoing warfare between Azerbaijan and Armenia.

[16]One example was the draft union treaty. See the description of the treaty and the surrounding discussion in the *New York Times* (18 and 19 Dec. 1990).

[17]This was evident, for example, in the highly acrimonious recent discussions of the wisdom of Soviet foreign-assistance programs. The link between foreign assistance and domestic sacrifice is specifically and critically drawn by, among others, Andrei Kortunov, in a *Moscow News* article from December 1989. The article and the foreign ministry's response are discussed in 'New Directions in Soviet Foreign Policy', *Soviet/East European Report* VII, 14 (20 Jan. 1990), 1.

[18]On Stalin, see, for example, Yurii Afanasev, in *Literaturnaya Rossia* no. 2 (17 June 1988), where Stalin's excesses are compared to those of Pol Pot. For a discussion of Lenin's role in setting precedents for the development of Soviet politics and political economy under Stalin, see V. Selyunin, 'Sources', *Novyi Mir* 5 (1988).

[19]For discussions of the evolving academic literature, see, *inter alia*, Allen Lynch, *The Soviet Study of International Relations* (Cambridge: Cambridge Univ. Press, 1987); Walter Clemens, *Can Russia Change?: The USSR Confronts Global Interdependence* (Boston, MA: Unwin Hyman, 1990), 29-166; Elizabeth Valkenier, *The USSR and the Third World: An Economic Bind* (New York: Praeger, 1983); Neil Malcolm, *Soviet Policy Perspectives on Western Europe* (London: Routledge, 1989); and Margot Light, *The Soviet Theory of International Relations* (Brighton, UK: Wheatsheaf, 1988).

[20]See Karen Dawisha, *Eastern Europe, Gorbachev, and Reform* (Cambridge: Cambridge Univ. Press, 1988), 102-56; and Hutchings, *Soviet-East European Relations*, 136-205.

[21]On this point, see Lynch, *The Soviet Study of International Relations*, 116-24.

[22]On the distinction in Soviet discourse between doctrine and strategy, or more precisely between the political and military technical aspects of doctrine, see Holloway, *The Soviet Union and the Arms Race*, 29.

[23]There is an infinite body of literature elaborating these themes. See in particular Mikhail Gorbachev's 'Politicheskii Doklad Ts. K. KPAA', *Pravda* (26 Feb. 1986), 2-10; 'Theses of the Central Committee to the 19th Party Conference', *Pravda* (10 July 1988); Mikhail Gorbachev, 'Speech to the United Nations' (1988), as reprinted in *Soviet Life* 2, supplement (1989).

[24]An agreement on conventional-force reduction in Europe, involving wildly asymmetrical Soviet reductions, did emerge. In the summer of 1991, the United States and the USSR signed a START agreement.

[25]For an analysis stressing the stabilizing impact of nuclear bipolarity, see John Mearsheimer, 'Back to the Future: Instability in Europe after the Cold War', *International Security* 15, 1 (Summer 1990): 5-56.

[26]Namely, the American reliance on European and Japanese financing of US military operations.

[27]For example, the co-ordinated Soviet-American effort to assist in the mediation of an end to the internal war in Angola between UNITA and the MPLA. See the *New York Times* (13 Dec. 1990), A25.

chapter four

European Security after the Cold War: Issues and Institutions

C.C. Pentland

As revolutions will do, the stunning collapse, from 1989 to 1991, of the post-war European order has magnified expectations of change and put at risk a sense of perspective. No Western observer reflecting on the global retrenchment and domestic breakdown of the Soviet Union, the rush to capitalism and democracy in Eastern Europe, the reunification of Germany, and the dissolution of East-West bipolarity can be completely immune to the sense that a new era has dawned. Issues that divided Europeans for over forty years seem to have been resolved overnight. As the realists remind us, however, and as some romantics learned following the euphoria of 1789, revolutions tend to create, or make worse, as many problems as they resolve. The revolution of 1989 had several causes — economic, ideological, and religious, among others — but any adequate explanation must make some reference to the institutions, policies, and issues of European security, whether it be NATO arms and arms-control policies in the early 1980s, or the unexpected evolution of the Helsinki process after 1975. Similarly, while the revolution will have far-reaching consequences for domestic politics, economic relationships, society, and culture, its most profound impact will likely be in the field of security. It is with the 1989 revolution's consequences for an understanding of Europe's security needs, and of the institutions designed to meet those needs, that this chapter is concerned.

Thinking about the nature and extent of change, with respect to security, calls for a sense of perspective and caution difficult to sustain in times of dramatic change. The sudden end of the cold war challenges understanding of the issues of European security: first, by changing perceptions of Europe; second, by questioning conventional and long-standing definitions of security; and third, by facing governments with unusually complex and difficult issues of institutional adaptation and design. Yet however it is redefined, Europe will find itself still at the centre of world politics; and its security problems, however changed, may not have diminished. As a consequence, shaping the institutions of European security after the cold war will require considerable diplomatic creativity to fashion what is needed out of what already exists. In attempting to design a regional security regime for a new era, Europeans will find themselves once more at the leading edge of global development.

Two cautions are in order. In the first place, Europe's being at the leading edge may not always be comfortable for Europeans, or comforting to others. True, after the Second World War, Western Europe refined the diplomacy of complex interdependence, and became a testing-ground for theories of pacification through democracy and prosperity. On the other hand, an earlier Europe had led the world into the era of total war and genocide. The prospect of a Europe once more at the leading edge should not, therefore, be taken as proof of some progressive view of history. Second, it seems clear that whatever happens with post-Soviet domestic reforms, Eastern European democracy, or the new Germany, there is no going back to the Europe of the cold war: alliance structures and domestic politics will be affected accordingly. By looking at how Europe has been redefined, and the concept of security reconsidered, one can arrive at an understanding of Europe's security needs that in turn clarifies the institutional issues to be resolved. This will not provide a map or a blueprint for the new European security regime, but it may give a general sense of direction.[1]

Redefining Europe

The revolution of 1989 transformed Europe's political identity, power structure, and institutional order. With respect to all three of these, old if often unhappy certitudes have vanished, to be replaced by something more hopeful, albeit still fragile and indeterminate. These radical changes bear directly on the issue of security.

What happened to Europe's political identity from 1989 to 1991? During the cold war Europe was generally perceived in two ways: as a geographical expression it embraced the subcontinent as traditionally understood from the Atlantic to the Urals (the Soviet Union was seen to be both in and of Europe, in this sense, as Canada and the US were not); as a political expression, however, Europe had been successfully appropriated by the nations of its western half that made up the core of NATO and the European Community (EC). In political economy this was particularly evident after 1973 when the EC incorporated Britain, Denmark, and Ireland, and effectively put an end to the European Free Trade Association (EFTA) as a rival. The Community's claim to be the real Europe, at least in economic terms, was reflected in the literature of the 1970s, which referred to the Scandinavians as 'reluctant' Europeans (because they would not join the EC) and to the Eastern Europeans as beset with problems of identity.[2] It is reinforced in Brussels' currently fashionable image of a 'concentric' Europe with the most committed EC members at the core and the rest — EFTA, Eastern Europe, the Mediterranean associates — arranged in orbits of different proximity around it.

In matters of military security, too, the language of political identity was at variance with that of geography. For most of the cold war European security meant the security of West against East, or vice versa, with a handful of neutrals pursuing a different vision again. From the early 1970s on, the Conference on Security and Co-operation in Europe (CSCE) sought to give substance to a collective pan-European concept of security while its 35 participants continued, in varying degrees, to give priority to concepts rooted in national or alliance interests.[3]

The significance of 1989, then, is that it marks the beginning of a truly pan-European era, both economically and militarily. Economically, whether the concentric image is judged to be empirically or normatively well-founded, all of Europe is now oriented toward and dominated by the EC. Militarily, the point of reference for European security has shifted — definitively in the East, still hesitantly in the West — from the respective alliances to something approximating a pan-European security community. Since World War II, European security has been assumed to be a collective matter, but now for the first time the collectivity in question is all of Europe.

For all its importance in redefining Europe, however, the revolution of 1989 has left some issues unresolved. Chief among these is the European status of the successor states of the Soviet Union. Where they fit in Brussels-centred economic Europe is far from clear. The three Baltic states seem to have slipped into the same antechamber as the former members of the Council for Mutual Economic Assistance (CMEA) in Eastern and Central Europe, and it is conceivable that Belarus, Ukraine, and Moldova might join them. On the other hand, the three Caucasian states (Azerbaijan, Armenia, and Georgia) embroiled in political and military turmoil, and the central Asian republics clearly lie outside the most inclusive definition of economic Europe's boundaries. Indeed, EC member-states' denials of Turkey's Europeanness apply to them a fortiori. The problem is Russia. No longer the economic and ideological nucleus of a purported rival bloc to the EC, it is still perceived as too large, unstable, poor, and alien even to join economic Europe, no matter what its leaders might hope or how much it still has in common with the states of Eastern Europe.

In matters of security the pattern and the problems are much the same, except that the most western parts of the former Soviet Union, while included in the CSCE, have few prospects of joining NATO, the security organization at the core of Western Europe. Again, the Caucasus and Central Asia are remote enough that their conflicts need not automatically create a security problem for Europe. The uncertainties once more centre on Russia. A full participant in the CSCE, engaged along with its former Warsaw Pact allies in a security dialogue with NATO,[4] Russia nevertheless retains many attributes of an external threat through its sheer size, its Asiatic reach, its still-impressive nuclear and conventional arsenal, and its domestic volatility. As long as the ambiguous status of the former Soviet Union, especially of Russia, obscures Europe's eastern boundary, the post-revolutionary redefinition of its identity will remain incomplete.

The second important transformation that has occurred since 1989 has been in Europe's power structure. The two principal shifts here have been, first, the decline in the presence and the influence of both superpowers, particularly the Soviet Union, and second, the rise of Germany. What began with Gorbachev's renunciation of the Brezhnev doctrine has developed into a full Soviet and post-Soviet recessional, with forces already out of most Eastern European states and due to be out of the former German Democratic Republic (GDR) by 1994, the Warsaw Pact (and CMEA) wound up, and general force levels due to be reduced in compliance with the agreement on Conventional Forces in Europe. These developments, and mounting domestic preoccupation with political reform, economic disorder, and ethnic upheaval, have made what remains of the Soviet Union a diminished presence on the European stage.[5]

Despite some protestations to the contrary, the United States seems headed in the same direction. The general perception of a diminished threat from the east, the CFE agreement, economic constraints, and congressional pressures all point to a severely reduced American military presence in Europe. Efforts to Europeanize the defence of Western Europe through the EC, the Western European Union (WEU), or a restructured NATO are in fact premised on some reduction in America's military and political commitment to Europe, while seeking to forestall a more extensive withdrawal. In a remarkably short time, then, Europe has seen the end of the dual hegemony in which its two halves, and its collective fate, were subject to the superpowers and the fortunes of their relationship. Europe may still be a stake in US-Russian relations, and hence a central concern for both, but less than ever can either aspire to manage its affairs unilaterally or even bilaterally. In a real sense Europe now controls the agenda; if the US and Russia wish to have a say in its management they must do so in a multilateral European setting.

The other shift in the distribution of power is the re-emergence of Germany in the heart of Europe. The importance of this dramatic development, at least in the short term, does not centre on economic or military capabilities. The former are being severely strained by the unforeseen cost of absorbing the former GDR.[6] The latter will be much reduced under the terms of the unification agreement; in any case the new Germany continues to display a diffidence toward the use of military force that some allies find frustrating, others reassuring. The immediate impact of the power shift is psychological: whatever the real limitations of German power now and in the future, the widespread anticipation of German hegemony has a life of its own, as does a related expectation that however deep its roots in, and stated commitment to, Western integration may be, it will be tempted by the old siren-call of *Mitteleuropa*. Therein lies the prospect of a revival of an old and frequently troublesome pattern of rivalry and accommodation between Germany and Russia.

The third transformation wrought by the revolution of 1989 is in Europe's institutional order. This reflects, in part at least, the shifts in power structure just discussed. The bipolarity of cold-war Europe was represented by the military confrontation of NATO and the Warsaw Pact and the economic confrontation of the EC and CMEA. For most of this period pan-European institutions such as the CSCE or the UN Economic Commission for Europe carried little real weight.

In economic matters, Europe's institutional bipolarity was always something of a sham, as demonstrated by the behaviour of both parties in the long minuet over EC–CMEA relations.[7] Not until the renaissance of Western European integration in the mid-1980s, however, did the economic asymmetry masked by these formalities become really evident. As the EC's drive to a single market by the end of 1992 gathered force, the failings of the Soviet and East European economies were multiplying and the ineffectiveness of social- ist integration through the CMEA was laid bare. Fearful of being excluded from the single market, the Eastern Europeans began to seek, and win, separate deals with the EC. Domestic economic reform and external realign- ment sealed the fate of the CMEA, and marked the end of economic bi- polarity.

These economic forces, plus the cumulative effects of the CSCE's Helsinki process of East-West normalization, arms-control negotiations, and political change in the Soviet Union and Eastern Europe, put increased strain on the institutions of military bipolarity. Their rapid collapse since 1989 has not, of course, been symmetrical. The Warsaw Pact has been formally dissolved,[8] while NATO has undertaken a far-reaching strategic review to ensure its continued relevance to European security. Other Western bodies—the EC and WEU—have advanced claims to a role in the defence of Europe rivalling or complementing that of NATO. Such institutional asymmetry can, however, be deceptive.

It may be correct, assessing the post-Gulf War international system, to proclaim the arrival of a 'unipolar moment',[9] but that language misleads if it is applied to post-1989 Europe. First, if the demise of the Soviet Union has been dramatic and unforeseen in both its haste and its extremity, the eclipse of America's presence is no less real for being gradual and widely anticipated. Second, while Russia may, even before the collapse of its Eurasian empire, have become a negligible player in many parts of the world, it retains immense capabilities in or near Europe and, along with other former Soviet republics, an abiding national interest in what happens there. If there is any region where Russia can and will continue to be a major power, it is in Europe. The prospect of a reduced American commitment, the persistence of Russian concerns and capabilities, and the rise of the new Germany all make nonsense of 'unipolarity' in the European context, however well it might apply elsewhere.

Institutionally, in fact, the new Europe is in transition from bipolarity to multipolarity, the latter represented by the newly formalized and still-developing CSCE. The institutions of the Soviet bloc are gone. Those of the West—the EC, the WEU, the Council of Europe, NATO—are in the throes of taking on new tasks, reforming their structures and looking eastward for new members. They are responding to the recognition that while it may be premature to speak of a 'common European home',[10] the revolution of 1989 has created a Europe marked by a more equitable distribution of power, increased East-West interdependence, and a new freedom to determine its own fate.

Rethinking Security

The traditional concept of security in international relations centres on military measures to protect the sovereignty and integrity of states, and to ensure the physical survival of their people. Challenges to the alleged narrowness or obsolescence of this concept and, in particular, its preoccupation with the use of force both as threat and as response, are hardly a novelty. In the late 1980s, however, no doubt in response to the heightened nuclear anxieties of the early Reagan era and the resurgence of the environmental movement, security revisionism seems to have acquired a new vigour. The end of the cold war has further intensified the debate, particularly with respect to Europe.

One version of the revisionist argument simply seeks to broaden the concept by expanding the range of issues bearing on national and international security. Without claiming that traditional military aspects of security are necessarily diminished, for example, Mathews argues that global developments in the 1980s suggest the need for a 'broadening definition of national security to include resource, environmental and demographic issues'. (The 1970s, she notes, already saw the definition broadened to include international economics.)[11] Sorensen, on the other hand, writing in the wake of the cold war, argues for a reordering of US national-security priorities. '[T]he actual likelihood,' he writes, 'of a threat to our national security from a Soviet invasion of Western Europe or a Soviet nuclear strike . . . ranks far below a host of non-Soviet, and even non-military, threats to that security'. In the new multipolar era, two important national security goals—neither of them primarily oriented toward defence, the Soviet Union, or Europe—should be, in his view, the preservation of 'economic effectiveness and independence' and 'the peaceful enhancement of democracy around the world'.[12]

Going further than Sorensen, who notes the continuing need for defence forces and the persistence of some level of risk in US-Russian relations, are those who claim that the events of 1989-90 solved the problem of European military security and created, virtually overnight, a true 'security community' in which no European state expects to go to war with any other over anything. To the extent that security continues to matter, they argue, it will increasingly take non-military forms.[13] Most lists of such post-cold war security issues for Europe include: (a) economic security, focused on availability of essential raw materials and foodstuffs, access to export markets, control of scientific knowledge and technology, and financial stability; (b) environmental security, focused on industrial pollution of air, water and land; (c) demographic security, focused on growing pressures of migration both within Europe and from poor countries to Europe; and (d) cultural security, focused on the threats posed to indigenous European culture primarily by immigration and American dominance of international media.

Persuasive as this agenda is, however, we should not rush to conclude that Europe's security in the traditional sense is assured. Indeed, it can be argued that the receding of superpower tensions in Europe, like the draining of a swamp, may have created a healthier microclimate in some respects, but has also revealed some unpleasant creatures long submerged. Realists assert that the revival of ethnic conflict and old-fashioned interstate rivalries will soon make us nostalgic for the nuclear bipolarity of the cold war.[14] It is possible, moreover, that every one of the 'new' security issues on the revisionist agenda has been exacerbated, directly or indirectly, by the revolution of 1989, and that the more critical these become the more they are likely to bear on security in the traditional political and military sense. Each of these points needs elaboration.

Consider first what has come to be called the Mearsheimer thesis. This unabashedly realist argument holds that with the hegemonic discipline of the blocs dissipated and nuclear anxiety greatly reduced, those ethnically driven quarrels over wealth, population, and territory that twice this century have made Europe the Balkans of the world will re-emerge with fresh virulence and increased destructiveness. First advanced in the early days of Europe's revolution, when others were celebrating the 'springtime of nations',[15] this seemed to some an implausible and slightly ungracious thesis. It was criticized as an overly dogmatic application of Waltz's long-standing theoretical claims about the virtues of bipolarity.[16] Certainly it challenged liberal beliefs that war in Europe had been made obsolete by widespread conviction as to its horrors, by the spread of economic prosperity and interdependence, and by the flourishing of democracy.

As the consequences of 1989 have unfolded in the former Soviet Union and its successor states, in Yugoslavia, in Hungary, in Romania, and elsewhere in Eastern Europe, the thesis is gaining converts. Not only, it seems, has the collapse of Soviet hegemony and the Russian empire released long-suppressed energies and aspirations, but their very awareness that a new European order is in the making may be pushing groups to assert claims for territory, statehood, and redress of grievances while they can. Several of these claims or counter-claims have already led to the threat or use of force. At a time when Europe has reverted to 'a state system that created powerful incentives for aggression in the past',[17] Eastern Europe, in particular, is witnessing the proliferation of possible national and subnational flash-points for a general conflagration.

The second point concerns the possibility that the events of 1989 will have a negative impact on the revisionists' security agenda. First, with respect to economic security, the very real prospect of a reduced American presence in, and commitment to, Western Europe suggests that in future overseas crises that threaten security of supply in energy, raw materials, or foodstuffs, Europe may be left more to its own devices. Widespread sentiment in Congress and American public opinion that in the Gulf conflict Europe's (particularly Germany's) role was less than its stake might have dictated will surely reinforce this tendency. In addition, it is conceivable that the end of the Soviet threat has reduced the power of appeals to Atlantic solidarity as a restraint on US-European economic conflict. Given the GATT's fragility, the result could be a further deterioration of the multilateral trading system on which Europe's prosperity depends. Finally, it is worth noting—although this effect is expected to be temporary—that German reunification, by diverting German attention toward domestic interests, has increased risks of domestic chaos and instability in Eastern European countries desperate for investment.

Second, with respect to environmental security, the opening up of Eastern Europe has revealed the appalling extent of the ecological destruction wrought by socialist strategies of industrialization. By political and economic default, this burden passes to Western European and other governments, and private investors, as a kind of 'delayed externality' (or additional, unaccounted-for cost) imposed by the departed Soviet-bloc regimes from beyond the grave. This unsavoury inheritance represents, on the one hand, economic costs on a massive if, as yet, undetermined scale and, on the other hand, physical risks, some of which Europeans have been bearing all along, others of which they are now exposed to through increased East-West mobility and exchange.

Finally, demographic (and to some extent cultural) security has been affected by the relaxation of restrictions on the emigration of Eastern Europeans. In recent years, Western Europeans have become increasingly sensitive to the influx of immigrants—legal and illegal—from the Third World. Cultural and racial tensions have become acute, giving rise in many countries to right-wing, xenophobic parties. Eastern Europeans may be less distinctive culturally and ethnically than, say, Africans, but particularly in times of recession they represent competition for scarce jobs, a potential burden on welfare systems, and, for some countries such as Germany or the Benelux states, further congestion of already overpopulated areas. Their potentially large numbers, the inevitable chaos accompanying attempts to control their flow, and the emotions surrounding these movements all make this an explosive issue with a clear connection to national security.[18]

In each of these items on the revisionist security agenda there are elements that go convincingly beyond the traditional understanding of national security. Some may still be defined away by being seen as economic costs — albeit high ones for societies — rather than as risks to sovereignty and survival. But others do persist as challenges to the classic concept of security. On the whole, however, the economic, environmental, and demographic aspects of European security have come forward not because they are the only ones left, but because the end of the cold war has intensified them. And their resolution is likely in many instances to go beyond economic, scientific, and social means to the traditional realms of force and bargaining.

European Security in the 1990s: Issues and Tasks

The revolution of 1989 has created a new Europe whose security agenda has been reordered but not significantly reduced. Most of the items on that agenda are old and familiar, although the degree and kind of threat each represents may have changed; some items are new, or at least have been rediscovered. This section will explore the range of security issues and tasks likely to face Europe in the next decade or so, beginning at the global level, moving then to the European state system, and considering finally a variety of subnational and transnational forces.

The Global System

If the end of the cold war has no other significance, it surely means reduced fears that, on the one hand, superpower rivalries will be played out on the European stage at the price of political repression, diplomatic rigidity, and nuclear anxiety for Europeans, while, on the other hand, European crises risk escalation to global war through alliance linkages and the logic of nuclear strategy. Undoubtedly Europe now represents less of a danger to the rest of the world than it has at any time since the nineteenth century. As the Gulf War has shown, however, the reverse is not true.

An aspiring civilian power that is heavily dependent on trade requires a benign international environment as free as possible of political and military risk, uncertainty, and disruption. European attempts to secure such an environment necessarily involve, first, a broad, indirect and long-term strategy of shaping the international milieu through economic, technological, and cultural diplomacy, and, second, a more direct, immediate strategy of responding to regional crises believed threatening to European interests.

The first of these strategies probably needs little comment. It is based on the old, if unproven, assumption that prosperity and democracy lead to co-operation and peace. Although frequently couched in humanitarian language, this strategy expresses the enlightened self-interest of an essentially satisfied group of nations. They may pursue it through UN multilateral agencies concerned with the management of international trade and finance, or with economic development, through collective European action targeted at particular groups of states, or through unilateral diplomacy. Whatever the medium, the purpose is to deploy the assets of the civilian power to minimize the risks to Europe's global interests inherent in the underdevelopment and instability of the international system. It is primarily through such a strategy, in fact, that environmental and demographic security — the revisionist agenda — must be pursued.

The more direct, immediate approach has to do with development of Europe's collective capacity to intervene in out-of-area conflicts that endanger its security or that of its friends. The decade of wars and crises in the Gulf and American criticism of the EC's response has, of course, placed this issue near the top of the security agenda. The Gulf is one of a handful of regions — principally in Western Asia and Africa — where Europe has significant historical and economic reasons for keeping the peace. The historical reasons are largely political and cultural legacies of empire, while the economic interests centre on assured access to raw materials, energy, and export markets. European intervention to defend or police these regions, or specific governments in them, may not always appeal to all, although France, for example, may find it prudent to seek, and invoke, collective EC support for unilateral actions in Africa. Multilateral actions, on the other hand, may not always be exclusively European: if the 'new world order' proclaimed by President Bush means strengthening the United Nations' capacity for genuine collective security (peace enforcement) and preventive diplomacy (peace-keeping) in Third World regions, one might expect enthusiastic endorsement from Europe.[19]

For many, however, the real question about out-of-area security is whether Europe itself will be willing and able to develop its own collective capabilities, perhaps through a European defence entity such as the WEU, or in partnership with the US and Canada in a revised NATO. Pooling resources, spreading the risk, and showing the European flag abroad are real incentives for collective action. More important in future could be a lack of confidence in a continued American commitment to lead, or even participate in, exercises along the lines of the Gulf War. The relaxing of Europe's cold-war alliances, then, and the acceleration of the EC's integration have increased pressures for an indigenous European out-of-area capability.

The Soviet Union and its Successors

Until the end of 1991 the Soviet Union stood alone in an ambiguous, hybrid category of potential threats to European security. As a global superpower, geographically and demographically only part-European, it was seen by some as an external threat; yet as a nation whose history and overall orientation is European, it was internal to the regional state system encompassed by the CSCE. However they categorized the Soviet Union as a power, and however they assessed the prospects of new thinking, Europeans could not assume it had ceased to represent a potential threat to their security. Now that Gorbachev is out of power, and the former Soviet Union is passing through the purgatory of the CIS en route to complete dissolution, one must ask how much of this analysis still holds.

In the first place, Russia has inherited from the Soviet Union not only its UN Security Council seat and a lot of its nuclear weapons, but also many of its ambiguities as a major European power with most of its territory in Asia. In this respect it is both an external contributor to Europe's security problem and an institutionalized part of the solution. Fears that Gorbachev's reforms might fail, that he and his supporters would be removed, and that the Soviet Union would revert to some semblance of its hardline, paranoid former self, were transformed, in 1992, into anxiety about Yeltsin and his programme in the face of domestic Russian backlash. A reactionary Russia seeking to recreate the Union through coercion, and to reimpose its will on its neighbours, would pose a security problem for the rest of Europe in a way that Gorbachev's occasional attempts to hold the Union together by repression never did.

It is, however, conceivable that Yeltsin and his supporters can stay the course and their economic and political reforms begin to bear fruit. Gorbachev's aim in launching *perestroika* was to make the Soviet Union a modern, efficient, and productive superpower worthy of the name,[20] and there is no reason to believe that Yeltsin's objectives for Russia are any different. However open, democratic, and 'new-thinking' the new Russia might prove to be, it would still be an immense presence whose influence the rest of Europe, not least its former sister republics and allies, would need to counter.

A third possibility is that there will be no decisive resolution of Russia's domestic economic and political problems, either through reaction or through modernization, and that it will continue instead to stagger along from crisis to crisis. Such a neighbour would be dangerous enough to the rest of Europe through the threat of economic disruption and the pressure of political and economic refugees. In addition, however, with all its domestic problems, Russia remains a massive military power; the effect of the CFE agreement, the new strategic arms treaty, and the division of former Soviet forces among the independent republics will be to relocate, diffuse, and reduce those forces, but hardly to eliminate them as a factor in the European security calculus.

Another scenario focuses not on Russia as heir to the Soviet Union, but on the consequences of the Union's dissolution for regional conflict. Fears of a war of secession leading to calls for European intervention have, since the end of 1991, been succeeded by concern that the violent ethnic and territorial conflicts in the Caucasus are but the prelude to a plague of such confrontations among the former republics. Some of these, such as that over the

Crimea, will have Russia as a party to the dispute. Others may see Russia attempting to enforce the peace. Both will raise questions about the responsible use of Russian power in the region, and will have wider implications for European security.

All these possibilities point to the need for the rest of Europe to have the capacity to deter and defend against the threat or use of force. The awkward point here is that a CSCE-type collective security system probably will not suffice for this purpose (although it might serve the need for mediating or peace-keeping forces). What is needed is an extended NATO-type collective defence—preferably with the US, necessarily with nuclear weapons—that has developed the strategy, force structure, and command systems to defend Europe against a range of threats from the East. In effect this would amount to an adaptation of the present system of Western European defence—extended eastward, possibly at lower force levels with a revised strategic doctrine, and with an uncertain degree of trans-Atlantic support.

Germany

Reactions to the precipitous unification of the two Germanies, completed in October 1990, ranged from celebration tinged with disbelief, especially among German and trans-Atlantic observers, to resignation tinged with apprehension, especially among Germany's immediate neighbours.[21] The central event of the European revolution, German unification, heralds the emergence of a formidable presence—a potential hegemon—in the heart of Europe. Once the unexpectedly complex and costly tasks of reforming, industrializing, and integrating the former East German economy are complete, the united Germany—with 78 million people, the world's third-largest economy, and, even after the coming reductions, armed forces of 370,000—will dominate Europe. Whether such dominance necessarily constitutes a security problem for the rest of Europe is a vital question, difficult to answer.

There is, of course, history. Any German who thought that 45 years of exemplary behaviour might have normalized Germany's image among its neighbours must have been disabused by the Poles' reaction to Chancellor Kohl's long hesitation in affirming the eastern boundary, by French President Mitterrand's studied coolness and verbal ambiguities about the unification process, and by the bluntly expressed prejudices of a British cabinet minister.

But while it would be wrong to downplay the psychological and political force of memory, or of anxiety about the future, it remains unclear precisely what kind of potential threat to Europe's security the united Germany is believed to constitute. There seems little genuine concern about renewed military adventurism or revanchism, since Germany is widely accepted to be domestically stable and democratic, satisfied and conservative with respect to the balance of forces in the European system, and successful in substituting economic expansion and competition for other more political and military activities. Rather, anxieties centre on (a) the use of German economic and financial power to shape a European economic-political order serving primarily German interests, possibly at the expense of smaller states' autonomy; (b) in this connection, revival of traditional hegemonic aims in Central and Eastern Europe; and (c) reflecting the general resurgence of 'tribalism' in Europe, a revived German nationalism that, at the expense of global multilateralism, Atlanticism, and Europeanism, begins to reassert border claims, old territorial grievances, and ethnic affinities with German-speaking peoples outside the Federal Republic.

These anxieties, listed in order of decreasing plausibility, have led to two types of response, likely to remain the pattern for the future. The first is to harness and contain German dynamism, in a multilateral European or Atlantic framework, directed to a common task. This was the political rationale of Jean Monnet, Robert Schuman, and Konrad Adenauer's European Community, and it is at the moment the principal argument for retaining NATO.[22] (It is worth noting that German governments have been among the keenest proponents of this view.) The second response is to create a European system of countervailing power to deter German expansion. The great-power coalitions assembled at various times in the last hundred years did not deter Germany, but had to defeat it, at huge cost. The critical question now is whether the CSCE collective security system, with a potential directing coalition of the US, Russia, France, Britain, and, of course Germany itself, can provide an effective deterrent to any such ambitions that might arise in future.

Interstate Conflict

If Mearsheimer and his fellow pessimists are correct, coping with old-fashioned interstate rivalries will be an increasing burden on any post-cold war system of European security. To judge by the present, most of its business is likely to come from the East. The conflicts between Greece and Turkey, Turkey and Bulgaria, Hungary and Romania, Albania and Yugoslavia, Czechoslovakia and Hungary, and among the successor states of the Soviet Union, are about territory, populations, resources, and status—issues of a kind Europe seemed, for most of the cold war, to have suppressed or put behind it. With the possible exception of the Irish question, such disputes have indeed pretty much disappeared from Western Europe. This may be a consequence of prosperity, interdependence, and democracy, but since a further test of that hypothesis must await the establishment of all three conditions in Eastern Europe, more immediate security measures may be advisable.

The most obvious need here is for institutions of genuine collective security, designed to deal automatically and impartially with a threat to the peace arising anywhere in the European state system. Such a system would have to make available the classic instruments of conflict resolution and peace enforcement, ranging from investigation and good offices through mediation and conciliation to arbitration and possibly judicial settlement, with provision for sanctions and police action should these fail. The institutional framework for such a system would ideally be pan-European and hence inclusive, true to the classic form of collective security. If it had sufficient leverage, however, an organization to which the disputing parties did not necessarily belong might be able to intervene effectively, offering rewards, threatening punishment, or simply providing a neutral third party to facilitate communication and negotiation.

Ethnic Conflict

The cold war was generally less successful in suppressing the claims of subnational ethnic groups than it was in controlling interstate rivalries; nevertheless, its termination has seen a resurgence of domestic ethnic conflict, again more dramatically in the East than in the West.[23] Examples include the revolt of the Baltic republics, Moldova, and Ukraine against the Soviet state, and the complex post-Soviet hostilities in the Caucasus. In Central and Eastern Europe there are domestic conflicts centred on Czechs and Slovaks, the Hungarian minority in Romania, Bulgarian Turks, and virtually all of what used to constitute federal Yugoslavia. In two of these, the Caucasus and Yugoslavia, ethnic conflict has descended into bitter civil war. If the violent Azeri-Armenian dispute might be perceived as marginal to European security, raising doubts as to whether some form of collective European peace-keeping force could, or should, replace the Russians, there is no question about the centrality of the former Yugoslavia and the inevitability of European involvement. Through arms and through international pressure, Slovenian and Croatian secession was secured rapidly, in the former case fairly clearly, in the latter with a difficult aftermath of further ethnic violence within the new territory. The immediate European ramifications of these conflicts were limited to creating tensions between Germany and its EC partners over the balance to strike between recognition of the breakaway states and attempts at even-handed peace-keeping; however, the threat of spillover from the conflicts besetting what remains of Yugoslavia is more serious. The crises in Macedonia, Kosovo, and Bosnia-Herzegovina all risk drawing in neighbours in support of beleaguered minorities.

The problem posed by domestic ethnic conflict for a European security system is, primarily, how to prevent it from developing, through secession and appeals for support, or through irredentism, into interstate conflict and war. If, in order to forestall this, Europe acquires a collective capacity for third-party intervention into domestic conflicts, Yugoslavia has served as a reminder of the difficult questions that then must be asked about timing, domestic jurisdiction, humanitarian aims, impartiality, recognition, and sanctions. Most of these cases also illustrate how domestic ethnic disputes can build to great intensity below the perceptual horizon of a security system necessarily preoccupied with interstate conflict. Here is where an early detection and diagnosis mechanism seems to be of most potential value.

Ethnic conflicts in Western Europe seem somewhat less dangerous and potentially destabilizing to the state system than Eastern European disputes, but this may be misleading. Ethnicity is generally on the rise as a political force, and it clearly has a demonstration effect. Events in Yugoslavia, therefore, may quicken ethnic rivalries and nationalist movements in Belgium, France, the United Kingdom, and elsewhere. It is not at all clear that democracy and prosperity have a pacifying effect on such movements. Indeed, the reverse may sometimes be true: in Spain and Yugoslavia the most prosperous regions with the strongest democratic traditions have historically been the most bent on secession. The view that the European Community itself is potentially a framework for giving expression to, but also containing, such nationalist movements does not seem sustainable unless member governments are willing to restructure it to give them representation. Whether Western European governments would ever permit the CSCE's conflict-management machinery to play a role in their domestic ethnic conflicts is equally problematic.

The Revisionist Agenda: A Final Note

It was argued earlier that for Europeans economic, ecological, and demographic security is indeed at issue, and that the end of the cold war has in fact made this revisionist security agenda more troublesome. It was also suggested that European multilateral actions aimed at securing a benign global environment addressed this agenda both directly, through out-of-area interventions aimed at securing economic lifelines, and indirectly, through development programmes to create more prosperous trading partners and stem the flow of immigration.

A similar logic is at work at the European regional level. A good part of the argument for extending massive official aid and private investment eastward is that it will harness the underdeveloped resources and human capital of Eastern Europe to the long-term economic benefit of the whole continent. In the process, it is expected, pressures for westward migration will ease, and environmental damage will be reduced. It is further assumed that development, in this broad sense, and increased interdependence with the West will secure democracy and stabilize the pan-European state system. Although these assumptions seem reasonable, they deserve the same close critical scrutiny that similar claims about the applicability of Marshall Plan models of assistance to the successors of the Soviet Union have begun to receive. It may indeed be the case that serious economic and political reform in Eastern Europe—the prerequisite for starting work on the revisionist security agenda—must await the resolution of many of the interstate and ethnic conflicts discussed above.

European Security in the 1990s: Institutions

Two forces will shape the institutional landscape of European security in the next decade and beyond. One is the emergent order of priority, as measured by immediacy and magnitude, of the potential threats to Europe's security discussed in the previous section. The other is the capacity of existing institutions to adapt to the post-cold-war world, taking on new roles and manoeuvering among rivals in the turf wars likely to ensue. With the exception of some demolition on the eastern side, the Europeans are in the business of adapting and extending institutions, rather than clearing the site and rebuilding from the ground up. On much of the architecture there is a surprising degree of consensus among the planners. In some of the more important areas, however, the ultimate design is far from clear, and the principals have strong, and different, views. The following pages explore the developing interplay of new security needs and existing institutions, paying particular attention to where difficult issues are likely to emerge.

Consider, first, security institutions with a global mandate. At this level, it has been argued, Europe's interest is in a benign international environment, to be sought both through a long-term programme of economic development and democratization ('peace-building', to use an old expression) and a more immediate improvement in the world's capacity for regional peace-keeping and enforcement. As wealthy, trade-dependent countries with old and extensive ties to the Third World, Western European states have been strong supporters of United Nations economic development programmes and specialized agencies and, with some notable exceptions, of multilateralism generally. Support for and participation in peace-keeping and enforcement has, on the other hand, been somewhat inconsistent. Small and middle powers such as Ireland, Sweden, Finland, Austria, and Poland have been more enthusiastic than the major European states such as Britain and France, with their historically based reservations, and Germany, a late-comer with constitutional inhibitions. Europe's collective disarray over the Gulf was instructive, if unsurprising, in that light.

The fact is that at the global level many Europeans, like the Americans, are often attracted to unilateral or multilateral action outside UN auspices. For the longer-term pacification of its environment, for instance, the European Community clearly sees more value in creating privileged and institutionalized trade and aid relationships with selected Third World states, as under the Lomé Conventions.[24] As for out-of-area enforcement actions, Chad and the Falklands are reminders that European unilateralism—albeit with appeals for Community backing—is not out of fashion. The prospect of genuinely collective European intervention seems more distant. Neither the EC nor the WEU (or a combination of the two) is likely to acquire, in the near future, the political support and institutional capacity needed to project European power abroad in this way. Two other alternatives are to stay at home and leave it to the Americans, or to play only a supporting role in essentially American shows, possibly (and preferably) through the UN or NATO. Neither Americans with memories of the Gulf nor Europeans with their eye on global status are likely to find much in those options. The most attractive, and perhaps the most likely, option is for Western Europe to put its collective weight behind an enhanced UN peace-keeping and enforcement system (possibly with standing forces and a reactivated Military Staff Committee) and a reconstituted NATO extending membership, or at least protection, to the East, while developing an out-of-area mandate and capability. To do this would be to take seriously, and pursue constructively, American notions of a 'new world order', while giving them a genuinely multilateral character.

The second institutional context of European security is the Atlantic, meaning of course NATO. Debate here has centred, surprisingly quickly, not on whether NATO should still exist but on what it should do. Recognition of a new threat from the East — not invasion but instability — and replacement of one set of German questions by another have kept alive the argument for some American military involvement in Europe, and hence for NATO. Indeed, former Warsaw Pact states and Soviet republics, including Russia, are asking NATO for membership, or at least for protection, although they have so far been denied formal guarantees. Although NATO has not intervened in the Yugoslav civil war, the ineffectiveness of the CSCE and the mixed reviews of EC initiatives have tended to strengthen the alliance's claim to primacy as a European security organization.

NATO has, in fact, shown an impressive ability to adjust to its new circumstances. Within a year it radically revised its military doctrine and its political strategy toward the Soviet Union and Eastern Europe, and it has continued to revise them after the former's collapse. It has reduced and restructured its forces, replaced 'forward defence' with lateral mobility and defence in depth, and de-emphasized (but not eliminated) early reliance on nuclear weapons. NATO's political strategy now embraces the long-dormant 'Canadian' Article 2 (stressing economic and functional collaboration), and emphasizes opening dialogue and friendship with the former Warsaw Pact states.[25] Creation of the North Atlantic Co-operation Council in November 1991 is the first step in institutionalizing that dialogue. Whether these changes go far enough is not yet clear. NATO remains unambiguously an organization for collective *defence*; any serious attempt to move into the business of collective *security* and conflict management may have been pre-empted by developments in the CSCE. In any case, major issues in the alliance remain unresolved — the extent of French participation, the prospect of German nuclear sharing, the role of the 'European pillar', and the continuation of the North American commitment. They may not be resolvable without further adjustments to doctrine and strategy, and a major overhaul of military commands and political institutions.[26] Contrary to some claims, NATO does seem to have a future, but subject as it is to pressures for an effective West European 'pillar' on the one hand, and a pan-European mandate on the other, it is bound to undergo further evolution. In that process, its relations with narrow Western European and broader pan-European institutions will be critical.

There are two exclusively Western European institutions whose aspirations to a security role have been widely debated. From the mid-1980s onward, both the WEU and the EC began to advance rival claims to be the legitimate expression of Western Europe's defence identity, whether within or distinct from the Atlantic framework. With the end of the cold war, what had sometimes looked like a zero-sum turf war began to shade into a debate over competing forms of inter-institutional co-existence and co-operation, while the horizons of the prospective mandate extended eastward to embrace all of Europe. The roles of each institution and the division of labour between them were clarified considerably in the provisions for a common European foreign and security policy negotiated at Maastricht in December 1991. It is far from certain, however, that the major issues have been settled.

Virtually dormant since its creation in 1954 as an organization for regional defence and arms control, the WEU began finally to attract some serious attention in the early 1980s.[27] Its membership, consisting of the EC less Denmark, Ireland, and Greece, has made it attractive to some as a potential European defence entity; in effect, it is a European NATO without a number of states whose geography or defence postures make them peripheral or problematic to the alliance. And the overlap with the EC (nine of the Twelve after 1986) has given it some claim to be that organization's military counterpart. In the words of its Secretary-General, the WEU 'stands at the crossroads of Atlantic and European co-operation. It aims to be both the European pillar of the Atlantic Alliance and the security dimension of European integration'.[28] In the Intergovernmental Conference on Political Union preparing for the Maastricht summit, the WEU's advocates pursued these aims, albeit with differing views as to the appropriate weight of the Atlantic component.

Since the early 1980s the strongest advocates of a revitalized WEU have been France and Germany. The French have promoted the WEU as an avenue for reintegrating into a Western defence system without necessarily rejoining NATO's command structure, and for steering European defence toward an intergovernmental form of organization, out of reach of the supranationally inclined European Community. The Germans, on the other hand, have looked to a more formalized relationship between the WEU and both NATO and the EC. Both value the WEU — the only Western European organization with a treaty-based defence and security role — as giving substance to Franco-German defence co-operation as sketched in the 1963 bilateral treaty, but virtually ignored for some twenty years.[29] All its members point to the WEU's success in co-ordinating European naval operations in the Gulf as an indication of its potential as an operational arm of European security.

None of its supporters argued that the WEU should operate independently of, or compete with, NATO or the Community. Its own official preference was to move in with the EC under the intergovernmental roof of the European Council (the summits of EC heads of state or government) while retaining its own structure and mandate.[30] Other proposals called for a merger of the WEU and European Political Co-operation (EPC), the EC members' vehicle for foreign-policy co-ordination.[31] In the run-up to Maastricht, however, even these relatively modest schemes met with some resistance, principally from the US, Britain, and others who worried lest an institutionalized European pillar further weaken trans-Atlantic links. The genius of the compromise reached at Maastricht is that it appears to incorporate the WEU as an integral part of the development of the new European Union while on the one hand containing it in a distinct, intergovernmental pillar out of reach of the EC Commission (which is nevertheless to be fully associated with it), and on the other reaffirming 'the necessary transparency and complementarity' between this 'emerging European security and defence identity' and the Atlantic alliance. The WEU's task, within this framework, is to 'formulate common European defence policy and carry forward its concrete implementation through the further development of its own operational role.'[32]

The Maastricht document underlines the importance of synchronization, harmonization, and consultation between the various institutions of the WEU and the European Union, as well as NATO, and sets out wide-ranging operational objectives for the WEU with respect to planning, logistics, transport, training, and strategic surveillance. There is reference to the eventual creation of a 'European armaments agency' and a European Security and Defence Academy. All these provisions, most of which will be put into place gradually, are to be reviewed in 1996. Whatever the progress made by that time, however, it is unlikely that the institutionalization of the WEU as the bridge between the European Union and NATO will be seriously challenged. In that respect, at least, some of the long-standing issues of Europe's security architecture seem to have been resolved. Others remain, however, particularly those centred on British-French nuclear co-operation, Germany's nuclear future, the role of the United States and Canada, and the need for greater congruence of membership among the WEU, the European Union, and European NATO.

If the WEU's place in European security now seems more assured than at any time in its history, what are the implications of Maastricht for the EC? The idea that European integration should encompass defence and security is, of course, as old as the Community itself, going back to early post-war federalism and the abortive scheme for a European Defence Community. Against those federalists who argued that economic integration would, and should, spill over into political and military integration have stood governments — principally but not exclusively the French — who insisted that foreign policy and defence were too central to national sovereignty ever to be entrusted to a supranational body. The 1970 Davignon Report, reflecting this position, led to the creation of EPC, an intergovernmental system of foreign-policy coordination parallel to, but institutionally separate from, the EC. Its mandate, however, did not embrace defence. Indeed the only route by which Community member states could approach collaboration in security issues was through industrial policy, which covered arms industries and defence-related science and technology.[33]

These arrangements, pragmatic and reasonably effective but frustrating to advocates of the EC as an integrated European defence entity, have persisted for two decades. A series of studies and reports, and continuous adaptation, has, however, strengthened the institutions and processes of EPC. Moreover, the once-rigid distinction between EC external (economic) relations and EPC foreign-policy co-ordination, long criticized as doctrinaire and unworkable, has in practice become usefully blurred. And since the early 1980s pressure has been building to bring all common foreign policy, including defence, under a single EC roof.[34] The Intergovernmental Conference on Political Union was handed the daunting task of resolving these matters.

The EC's security role can be expected to develop in three main ways over the next few years. First, at a minimum, the full fruition of the 1992 project (and of high-technology collaborative schemes such as ESPRIT and EUREKA) in the remainder of this decade should see the emergence of a genuinely European defence-industrial base. Second, while the Maastricht agreement falls short of finally integrating EC external economic relations and EPC — in fact perpetuating the formal distinction through its provisions for a common foreign and security policy under Title V[35] — the close involvement of the EC Commission and Parliament, the more permissive provisions for qualified majority voting in the Council, and the continuation of the European Council's governing role atop both the economic- and the foreign- and security-policy pillars all promise more effective co-ordination of economic and political foreign policy. Will this enhance the capacity of the existing twelve-member Community to act as a civilian power, using its economic weight to influence events abroad—in the Middle East, Africa, the Mediterranean—that might affect European security? The EC's attempt to mediate in Yugoslavia, reinforcing its efforts at conflict-resolution with explicit economic threats and promises in the classic manner of the civilian power, does not seem to augur well. This may, however, be a comment more on the futility of economic weapons in the face of atavistic ethnic passions than on the EC's emergent structures.

The third and most far-reaching development, which the Yugoslavia experience can only have spurred on, is to bring security and defence policy in under the common roof of the new European Union, as set out in the Maastricht document. The Intergovernmental Committee eschewed the federalist ideal—supported by some governments—of a single Community with revised institutions and new political functions (including foreign policy and defence) in favour of the more conservative model of parallel communities (or 'pillars') under the intergovernmental European Council. As noted above, the security and defence function within the foreign and security policy pillar is to be performed by the WEU, which also represents a bridge to NATO.[36] This arrangement does seem to provide for a useful division of labour between the Community and the WEU, but whether the latter, in its bridging role, can mitigate the continuing stresses within the EC between Atlanticists and Europeanists while preventing further erosion of the American commitment to European defence remains to be seen.

The prospect, in the late 1990s, of the EC's enlargement to include the EFTA countries and most of Eastern Europe further complicates the security picture. First, as mentioned, a number of these aspiring members are neutrals. Although the end of the cold war has called into question the rationale for neutrality in Europe, the tradition has deep cultural and historical roots in many of these states. Drawn by the EC's economic magnetism, they are at best ambivalent about its political and military aims. What might be finessed if only Ireland were at issue could prove more difficult if, while developing its defence and security identity, the EC was admitting new members of whom most were not members of the alliance to which it is linked through the WEU. Second, the more its membership comes to embrace all of Europe, the more the EC's security mandate is likely to overlap or compete with that of the CSCE. To the extent that its destiny is pan-European rather than West European, then, the EC's coexistence with NATO and CSCE is likely to be troubled.

Finally, there is the pan-European context of security. As noted, a major consequence of the revolution of 1989 has been to infuse pan-Europeanism with real meaning and, among other things, to press Atlantic and West European security institutions to extend themselves eastward. More significantly, it has endowed the CSCE, as the framework of pan-European security, with new power and legitimacy.

The CSCE, or the Helsinki process, is intimately related to the European revolution of 1989 both as source and as beneficiary. This is not the place to assess its precise contribution to the transformation of Eastern Europe. Suffice it to note, first, the series of negotiations on confidence-building and other military-security measures under Basket I, significant as process as much as for substance; second, the growing importance, signalled by the 1990 Bonn economic conference, of East-West links under Basket II; and third, the dramatic and unforeseen cumulative effects—not least via the Review Conferences—of pressures under Basket III for the free movement of people and ideas. Some long-standing reservations about the CSCE still persist, particularly in the US and the UK.[37] In Europe generally, however, it has achieved an unprecedented stature, drawing legitimacy from a recognition of its achievements, and credibility from its congruence with the new pan-European order of things.

The Paris Charter of November 1990, transforming the CSCE from a process to an organization, was thus both a logical culmination of its work and a recognition that security had for the first time become a genuinely pan-European concern, requiring a corresponding institutional response. That response included a commitment of Heads of State or Government to meet at all follow-up meetings beginning in 1992 (these to be held every two years, as a rule); establishment of a Council of Foreign Ministers to meet regularly, at least once a year, to provide the central forum for political consultations, and of a Committee of Senior Officials to serve the Council; and creation of a Secretariat, based in Prague. Among the more innovative provisions are a Conflict Prevention Centre, to be based in Vienna, a Dispute Settlement Mechanism (worked out in early 1991 at Valletta), an office for Free Elections, in Warsaw, and plans for the development of a parliamentary assembly.[38]

This rapid proliferation of institutions reflects most member states' ambitions for the CSCE's future, centred on a comprehensive vision of European security. Beyond a commitment to build on the agreements on Conventional Forces (signed by the 22 NATO and Warsaw Pact states) and on Confidence and Security Building Measures (a CSCE document), the Charter of Paris calls for a broad range of co-operative measures dealing with the human dimension (human rights, democracy and rule of law, freedom of movement for people and ideas), economic and social development (market economies, integration, science and technology), the environment and culture (protection, promotion, and exchange). On the one hand, the new Europe provides unprecedented opportunities and incentives for such co-operation. On the other hand, co-operation is clearly seen not as an end in itself but in functionalist terms, as the foundation of lasting security, or a 'working peace system'.

It is nevertheless certain that any claim for the CSCE as the prime security institution of the new Europe will stand or fall on its performance in managing and resolving interstate and ethnic conflict. There is, as noted earlier, no shortage of potential flash-points, especially in the East. There is, as well, something of an institutional vacuum in Europe with respect to this type of conflict. With the ambiguous exception of Cyprus, there is really no precedent or enthusiasm for UN involvement in intra-European conflicts. Excluded for forty-five years by East-West nuclear bipolarity, the UN seemed to have become, in European eyes, an organization appropriate for collective security and preventive diplomacy in the Third World, but either superfluous or troublesome if introduced closer to home. Its peace-keeping role in Yugoslavia, following the apparent exhaustion of all European regional alternatives, may represent a dramatic recantation of this doctrine. On the other hand, it may just be a reflection of the temporary weakness of the regional institutions. NATO has as yet neither the instruments nor the standing to play such a role beyond its own members' territory; even its few attempts to mediate in conflicts among its members (again, Greece and Turkey) have not seen much success. The EC certainly has the economic weight to mediate in some Eastern European conflicts, but until its economic, political, and security policy-making has become effectively integrated under one roof, achieving consensus and implementing decisions on the substance of security policy among the Twelve will be difficult. An optimistic view of this situation is that by throwing a harsh and humiliating light on the inadequacies of these European institutions, the Yugoslavian crisis may push their members to concert their actions more effectively.

From that perspective the CSCE has both opportunity and potential as a collective security system for Europe.[39] Its membership is comprehensive, embracing all of Europe (including, soon, Albania) as well as Canada and the US. It has at last acquired institutions that could provide it with the means to detect and react quickly to conflict. Its prestige and legitimacy are high across most of Europe. On the other hand, to have a real chance at succeeding, the CSCE will need a greater commitment from the major European powers, and more enthusiasm from Washington, than it has been accorded thus far. Its institutions are still rudimentary, and it has no provisions for the collective use of force to keep the peace. And as the League of Nations showed, prestige, legitimacy, and, most important, confidence are fragile creatures, vulnerable to inaction or failure. Their collapse could herald a return to a system of self-help and alliances reminiscent of the 1930s.

Conclusion

The best insurance against such a reversion would be the sort of rough division of labour among co-existing and overlapping institutions towards which Europe may currently be groping its way. No system of security is likely to endure unless it has these four characteristics: it must be genuinely collective in purpose, diverse in means, capable of flexibility and innovation, and free of interorganizational friction. Being genuinely collective means that conflict anywhere in Europe is of concern to all, and that institutions for managing and resolving it must be designed on a basis of universality and impartiality. Diversity of instruments and a capacity for flexibility and innovation are necessary responses to the expanding agenda of European security, and the number and variety of possible flash-points. The reduction of duplication and rivalry among security institutions can only enhance their collective authority and credibility.

At present, NATO has military power and the American commitment, but its relationships with the eastern states — solemnly declared no longer to be adversaries[40] — remain unclear, while its new strategy is still taking shape. The EC has economic power and a sense of eventual pan-European destiny, but it has an uneven record in making and implementing common foreign policy and is by no means assured — even after Maastricht — of acquiring the wherewithal to do better in future. The CSCE has legitimacy, comprehensive membership, and some new institutions, but whether it can develop procedures to make decisions, and can marshal the military and economic means that may be needed to implement them, remains to be seen.

Taken together, however, these three organizations, as each of them evolves, may go some distance toward meeting the four criteria for an effective security arrangement. Perhaps the greatest uncertainty surrounds the question of interorganizational rivalry. Until recently most of the jostling has been among NATO, the WEU, and the EC, although the issues have not all proven as intractable as many believed.[41] For the next few years, however, as NATO adapts to its new environment by seeking new roles, and as the EC expands eastward, equipped with new competence in foreign and defence policy, the prospects for overlap with the CSCE are considerable. This may not always be a bad thing; some overlaps may amount to complementarity or mutual reinforcement (e.g., NATO's supplying peace-keeping forces under CSCE auspices). But it would be prudent to expect a decade or more of competitive manoeuvering and adaptation among these three organizations as Europe works through the unfolding consequences of its revolution.

Notes

[1] The revolution of 1989 has already given rise to a flourishing literature on Europe's emergent security arrangements. See, for example, Barry Buzan et al., *The European Security Order Recast: Scenarios for the Post-Cold-War Era* (London and New York: Pinter, 1990); Richard Ullmann, *Securing Europe* (Princeton: Princeton Univ. Press, 1991); Nicholas Rizopoulos, ed., *Sea-Changes: American Foreign Policy in a World Transformed* (New York: Council on Foreign Relations, 1990), esp. the articles by Ronald Steel, 'Europe after the Superpowers', 7-21; Robert Tucker, '1989 and All That', 204-37; and Stanley Hoffmann, 'A New World and Its Troubles', 274-92; and John Lewis Gaddis, 'Toward the Post-Cold War World', *Foreign Affairs* 70, 2 (Spring 1991), 102-22.

[2] Toivo Miljan, *The Reluctant Europeans* (Montreal: McGill-Queen's Univ. Press, 1977); André Liebich, 'Six States in Search of an Identity', *International Journal* 43, 1 (Winter 1987-8), 1-17. See also William Wallace, 'Introduction: The Dynamics of European Integration' in Wallace, ed., *The Dynamics of European Integration* (London and New York: Pinter, 1990), esp. 12-19.

[3] The history of the CSCE is explored in R.A. Spencer, ed., *Canada and the Conference on Security and Cooperation in Europe* (Toronto: Centre for International Studies at the University of Toronto, 1984), and Victor-Yves Ghebali, *La Diplomatie de la détente: La CSCE 1973-1989* (Bruxelles: Bruylant, 1989).

[4] 'Friends, Not Allies', *Economist* (15 June 1991), 49-50.

[5] Coit Blacker, 'The Collapse of Soviet Power in Europe', *Foreign Affairs* 70, 1 (1990-1), 88-102.

[6] See, for example, the estimates of François-Georges Dreyfus, 'L'Europe et la question allemande', *Etudes Internationales* 21, 4 (décembre 1990), 802.

[7] John Pinder, 'Integration in Western and Eastern Europe: Relations between the EC and CMEA', *Journal of Common Market Studies* 18, 2 (1979), 114-34; and Avi Shlaim and George Yannopoulos, eds, *The EEC and Eastern Europe* (Cambridge: Cambridge Univ. Press, 1978).

[8] The military structure was dissolved in April 1991, with last rites administered in July (almost simultaneously with those for CMEA).

[9]Charles Krauthammer, 'The Unipolar Moment', Foreign Affairs 70, 1 (1990-1), 23-33.

[10]It is worth, even after the author's political demise, reviewing Mikhail Gorbachev's formulation of this much-cited concept. See Perestroika: New Thinking for Our Country and the World, updated ed. (New York: Harper and Row, 1988), 80-4.

[11]Jessica Tuchman Mathews, 'Redefining Security', Foreign Affairs 68, 2 (Spring 1989), 162.

[12]Theodore Sorensen, 'Rethinking National Security', Foreign Affairs 69, 3 (Summer 1990), 7.

[13]For a careful exploration of this position see Boyce Richardson, Time to Change: Canada's Place in a World of Crisis (Toronto: Summerhill, 1990).

[14]John Mearsheimer, 'Back to the Future: Instability in Europe after the Cold War', International Security 15, 1 (Summer 1990), 5-56. See also his 'Why We Will Soon Miss the Cold War', Atlantic 266, 2 (August 1990), 35-50.

[15]Michael Howard, 'The Springtime of Nations', Foreign Affairs 69, 1 (1989-90), 17-32. While celebrating 1989 as an annus mirabilis, Howard anticipates many of Mearsheimer's anxieties, drawing pointed historical analogies with earlier revolutionary years (1789 and 1848) or proclamations of 'new world orders' (1919).

[16]Kenneth Waltz, 'The Stability of a Bipolar World', Daedalus 98, 3 (Summer 1964), 881-909.

[17]Mearsheimer, 'Why We Will Soon Miss the Cold War', 36. For the ensuing debate on Mearsheimer's thesis see the correspondence from Stanley Hoffmann, Robert Keohane, and Mearsheimer in 'Back to the Future, Part II: International Relations Theory and Post-Cold War Europe', International Security 15, 2 (Fall 1990), 191-9; and from Bruce Russett, Thomas Risse-Kappen, and Mearsheimer in 'Back to the Future, Part III: Realism and the Realities of European Security', International Security 15, 3 (Winter 1990-1), 216-22. See also the well-developed rejoinder to Mearsheimer by Stephen Van Evera, 'Primed for Peace: Europe after the Cold War', International Security 15, 3 (Winter 1990-1), 7-57.

[18]For a careful overview of this issue see Nicholas Eberstadt, 'Population Change and National Security', Foreign Affairs 70, 3 (Summer 1991), 115-31.

[19]Bruce Russett and James Sutterlin, 'The UN in a New World Order', Foreign Affairs (Spring 1991), 69-83, focuses on US-Soviet consensus as the essential requisite of effective UN peace enforcement.

[20]Blacker, 'The Collapse of Soviet Power in Europe', 88-9.

[21]For a sample of reassuring comment, see Karl Kaiser, 'Germany's Reunification', Foreign Affairs 70, 1 (1990-1), 179-205; and Theo Sommer, 'Germany: United but not a World Power', European Affairs 5, 1 (Feb./March 1991), 38-41. On the French reaction see David Yost, 'France in the New Europe', Foreign Affairs 69, 5 (Winter 1990-1), 107-28.

[22]Wolfram Hanrieder, 'Germany in the New Europe', International Journal 46, 3

(Summer 1991). See also his *Germany, America, Europe* (New Haven: Yale Univ. Press, 1989).

[23]For a prescient analysis of Soviet and Eastern European ethnic issues, see Zbigniew Brzezinski, 'Post-Communist Nationalism', *Foreign Affairs* 68, 5 (Winter 1989-90), 1-25.

[24]An authoritative treatment of the Lomé agreements, which now embrace the EC and some 60 African, Caribbean, and Pacific (ACP) countries, is Carol Cosgrove Twitchett, *A Framework for Development: The EC and the ACP* (London: Allen and Unwin, 1981).

[25]*Declaration of NATO Heads of State and Government* (London, 5-6 July 1990). This declaration set in motion the alliance's strategic review.

[26]For proposals along these lines see Douglas Bland, *The Military Committee of the North Atlantic Alliance: A Study of Structure and Strategy* (New York: Praeger, 1991).

[27]The WEU emerged from the transformation of the 1948 Brussels Treaty through the accession of West Germany and Italy, and the addition of new political and military functions. For details see Political and Economic Planning, *European Unity* (London: Allen and Unwin, 1968), chapter 9.

[28]Willem van Eekelen, 'The WEU: Europe's Best Defense', *European Affairs* 4 (Winter 1990), 9-10.

[29]David Haglund, *Alliance Within the Alliance? Franco-German Military Cooperation and the European Pillar of Defense* (Boulder, CO: Westview, 1991), esp. chapters 1 and 7.

[30]Van Eekelen, 'The WEU', 11.

[31]This proposal, really amounting to a takeover of the WEU by EPC, was made by the Italian Foreign Minister in the fall of 1990. See David Buchan, 'Italian Foreign Minister Proposes Military Dimension for EC', *Financial Times* (17 Sept. 1990). For a more elaborate argument along these lines, which goes on to dismiss possible American objections to the EC's playing the role of 'European pillar' in NATO, see Jacques Delors' speech to the International Institute for Strategic Studies (London, 7 March 1991), and *European Community News* NR 91, 14 (11 March 1991).

[32]*Treaty on European Union*, 'Declaration on Western European Union I: Declaration on the Role of the Western European Union and its Relations with the European Union and the Atlantic Alliance', signed at Maastricht, 7 Feb. 1992 (*Europe Documents* 1759/60 [7 Feb. 1992], 55-6).

[33]On EPC see William Wallace, 'Political Cooperation: Integration through Intergovernmentalism' in Helen Wallace, William Wallace, and Carole Webb, eds, *Policy-Making in the European Community*, 2nd ed. (New York: Wiley, 1983), 373-402.

[34]The EC's Single European Act, which came into force in 1987, takes a major step toward this end. See Commission of the European Communities, *The Single European Act*, Bulletin of the European Communities Supplement 2: 86 (Luxembourg, 1986). An excellent commentary is in Jean de Ruyt, *L'Acte unique européen* (Bruxelles: Editions de l'Université de Bruxelles, 1987); chapter 10 covers EPC and defence.

[35] *Treaty on European Union*, Title V, *Europe Documents* 1759/60, 31-3.

[36] On the fortunes of this originally French idea, see 'In the Beginning was the Word, and the Word was Defence', *Economist* (18 May 1991), 59.

[37] For a reflection of these Anglo-American doubts, see *The Economist*'s editorials of 7 April 1990, 'The Dream of Europax', and 14 July 1990, 'Beware the Organization of European Unity'.

[38] 'Charter of Paris for a New Europe', *NATO Review* 38, 6 (Dec. 1990), 27-31.

[39] Gregory Flynn and David Scheffer, 'Limited Collective Security', *Foreign Policy* 80 (Fall 1990), 77-101; and Berndt Goetze, 'The CSCE: Alternative for European Security?', *Canadian Defence Quarterly* 20, 1 (Autumn 1990), 27-31.

[40] See the 'Joint Declaration of Twenty-Two States', signed in Paris along with the CFE agreement (19 Nov. 1990), and *NATO Review* 38, 6 (Dec. 1990), 26.

[41] An excellent account of the interorganizational turf-wars is Haglund, *Alliance Within the Alliance?* See also Robbin Laird, *The Europeanization of the Alliance* (Boulder, CO: Westview, 1991), and Mathias Jopp, Reinhardt Rummel, and Peter Schmidt, eds, *Integration and Security in Western Europe* (Boulder, CO: Westview, 1991).

chapter five

The Third World in the Changing Strategic Context

Mohammed Ayoob

The Superpowers and Third World Conflict

The dramatic changes that have taken place during 1989-91 in US-Soviet relations and in the political landscape of Central and Eastern Europe have thrown into disarray some of the most cherished assumptions of a whole generation of strategic pundits. The collapse of the Soviet Union has further confounded the strategic community. These changes have also had an impact on the way scholars and analysts of international relations perceive the Third World, and are prompting them as well to look afresh at the relevance of many of their premises regarding the role (and particularly the future) of the Third World within the international system. This is especially true in the field of Third World security studies, because of the significant impact that the global strategic context, in particular the nature of superpower relations, has had during the post-war decades on the security environments of Third World states and regions.[1]

However, even though the most highly visible facet of the latest Third World crisis, namely that in the Gulf, had its international dimension, it is still valid to argue that in the 1990s the security problems in the Third World will continue to have their origins—defined both as causes and as beginnings—in the intrastate, interstate, and region-wide dynamics of conflict and co-operation in various parts of the Third World. Even the crisis over

Iraq's invasion of Kuwait conforms to this pattern. It is true that the most dramatic manifestation of the crisis was the American decision to confront Iraqi ambitions by landing troops in Saudi Arabia. It is also true that the immediate provocation for the Iraqi attack on Kuwait was related to the internationally relevant oil factor, in particular Kuwait's initial defiance of OPEC pricing policy, as well as its reluctance to share its fabulous oil wealth with its more populous and war-devastated neighbour. However, Iraqi ambitions regarding Kuwait date back to the founding of the Iraqi state in the aftermath of World War I, as one of the Arab successor states to the Ottoman Empire. The Ottomans had traditionally claimed sovereignty over Kuwait, even during the period after 1899 when Kuwait had been proclaimed a British protectorate. In recent times, Baghdad had twice revived its claims to Kuwait: first in 1961, when the British granted formal independence to the Sheikhdom; and again in 1973, when it moved its troops into northern Kuwait in an abortive attempt to force the latter to cede the strategically important Bubiyan and Warbah islands to Iraq. Both these attempts at annexing or subordinating Kuwait were based on the technicality that until World War I the Ottomans had claimed formal authority over Kuwait, and aspired from time to time to bring it under their control, which was to be exercised from the Ottoman *vilayet* (or province) of Basra, the region that now forms the southernmost part of Iraq.

Furthermore, the Iraqi annexation of Kuwait in 1990 was also linked to Iraqi ambitions of leadership both in the Gulf (particularly in its Arab littoral) and within the wider Arab world. It was this complex interplay of the region's boundaries inherited from colonial days, Iraqi irredentism, inter-Arab rivalry, Baghdad's quest for predominance in the Gulf, its desperate search for greater resources in the wake of the war with Iran, and the issue of oil pricing and production, that provided the basic motivation for the Iraqi invasion of the oil-rich emirate. While the American reaction globalized the crisis, it was basically just that — a *reaction* to a crisis that was fundamentally grounded in regional realities.

The primacy of internal and regional factors in defining the contours of Third World interstate relationships in general, and regional conflicts in particular, has as its corollary the assumption that the great powers' calculations of advantage *vis-à-vis* each other have played, and will continue to play, a secondary, though often important, role in determining the level of regional conflict and/or co-operation in different parts of the Third World. The secondary nature of the great-power equation in this regard is likely to become even more evident in the context of the current superpower situation. Therefore, while analysts of Third World international relations cannot afford to be oblivious to great-power involvement — whether unilateral, bilateral, or multilateral, co-operative or adversarial — in conflictual situations in the Third World, such involvement and intervention should not become the centre-piece of the paradigms they construct to explain the fundamental reasons for regional conflict and co-operation in different parts of the Third World. That status must be reserved for factors and dynamics intrinsic to the states and regions of the Third World, although great powers may often be able to influence to varying degrees the intensity and levels of conflict in particular regions.

The high level of violence and conflict in the Third World as compared to the developed countries is, above all, related to the process of state-making, and is the direct product of the state élites' preoccupation with the task of 'primitive central state power accumulation'[2] that lies at the heart of this process during the early stages of state-making.[3] Since such attempts entail the extension of state power over demographic and territorial space on a state's periphery, often subject to territorial and demographic claims by one or more neighbouring states usually engaged in the same process, the raw ingredients of interstate and intrastate conflict are both present within this unfolding process. Often enough, in fact, they translate into overt interstate wars, as well as into civil wars ranging from inter-ethnic riots to wars of secession. These realities of Third World state-making and conflict are not about to change just because the nature of great-power relationships within the international system has changed.

Of course, if superpower (and other great-power) actions and interactions are not able fundamentally to determine the sources of conflict and violence within the Third World, this does not mean that they do not possess the capacity to exacerbate or alleviate conflict and insecurity there. During the four-and-a-half decades of the post-war era, the workings of the international system in general, and the policies adopted by the superpowers in particular, tended to exacerbate conflict in the Third World. They did so largely by manipulating the individual and collective weaknesses — political, economic, military, and technological — of the newly emerging Third World states, and by attempting to use them as pawns and proxies (although far from unwilling ones in most cases) in the new 'great game' between the United States and the Soviet Union that began to be played almost immediately after the end of the Second World War. At the same time, however, both superpowers clearly distinguished between regions of vital importance to them for both strategic and economic reasons — primarily the industrial and technological powerhouses of North America, Europe, and Japan, where interstate conflict was ruled out in the epoch of nuclear weaponry — and the grey areas of the globe, the Third World, where violent conflict was permissible because it did not vitally affect the management of the dominant global relationship and was marginal to the maintenance of the central balance of power. This is one reason why, as one author has pointed out, 'All interstate wars since the end of World War II have taken place in the Third World, although there have been industrialized country participants in some of these conflicts.'[4]

Some analysts have even argued that conflict in the Third World during the post-war decades was actively encouraged by superpower policies largely aimed at testing one another's political will and power projection capabilities in areas of the globe peripheral to the vital concerns of the superpowers themselves.[5] This *de facto* division of the globe, roughly corresponding to the core-periphery dichotomy of the world-system theorists,[6] while allowing for the exportation of the developed world's conflicts to the Third World, effectively insulated the core of the international system from the intramural conflicts and internal instabilities prevalent within the Third World. It comes as no surprise, therefore, that during the post-war era, 'the Third World has been a principal arena of East-West rivalry. From Southeast Asia to the Middle East, from Southern Africa to Central America, the superpowers have found themselves on opposing sides of regional conflicts, locked in global competition for influence.'[7] The very fact that the superpowers chose the Third World as the arena where they could afford to be 'locked in a global competition for influence' in the thermonuclear age demonstrates the low priority they attached to gains and losses in the Third World, and the vast distance that separated their Third World concerns from their vital interests, which were protected by the nuclear balance of terror. This state of affairs increased the insecurity of Third World states and regimes, which suffered from a feeling of dual impotence: unable to prevent the penetration of their polities and regions by superpower rivalries and conflicts, they were equally unable to affect, except marginally and in selected cases, the global political and military equation between the two superpowers and their respective alliances.

Although the end of the cold war may help alleviate some of these insecurities among Third World states, it does nothing to address the basic issue of their marginality as states (rather than as oil fields or copper mines) to the system of states. This peripherality results, on the one hand, from their multiple weaknesses in the fields of economics, technology, and military might and, on the other, from their relatively low level of stateness as measured by their lack of 'unconditional legitimacy'[8] among their populations and their lack of adequate 'infrastructural power',[9] which is crucial to the management of state-society relations. As a result they are, although to varying degrees, both vulnerable to pressure from and highly dependent upon the advanced industrial powers in almost every important sphere of state activity. Sources of insecurity are fundamentally related to the collective marginality of Third World states to the multidimensional power structure within the international system as a whole.[10] This, in turn, is directly the result of the weakness of the Third World states individually and collectively *vis-à-vis* what Robert Gilpin has termed the two organizing principles of contemporary international social life: the (sovereign) state and the (international) market.[11]

The main purpose of this chapter, however, is to explore the likely effects of the changing strategic context in the 1990s on the security of Third World states and regions, and the future role that these states are expected to play in the shaping of the international security agenda now that the potential for global superpower confrontation and conflict has seemingly vanished. The rest of the chapter will therefore concentrate on these questions rather than the more fundamental issues of Third World state-making, its impact on the level of violent conflict in Third World regions, the vulnerability of Third World states to external systemic forces, and the consequent effects of these weaknesses on the security of Third World states and regions.

The Re-orientation of the Soviet Union

The revolutions in Europe and in the former Soviet Union and the new position of the US will all have important effects on the international dimension of the security picture in the Third World.[12] The former Republics' preoccupation with internal issues, above all the restructuring of their economies and the management of international relations among themselves, has already led to a discontinuation of involvement in the Third World, a trend perhaps most dramatically foreshadowed by the Soviet military withdrawal from Afghanistan in early 1989.

The inevitability of this withdrawal from the Third World had, in fact, been discernible in Soviet thinking from the beginning of the last decade, and antedates Gorbachev's ascension to power by several years.[13] However, it was only with the launching of the twin policies of *perestroika* and *glasnost* under Gorbachev, and the subsequent impact of these policies on Moscow's foreign relations, that a perceptible shift in Soviet policy toward the Third World became evident. While the withdrawal of Soviet troops from Afghanistan was the most visible proof of this new policy, it had been reflected in many other areas of the Third World as well, especially where major regional conflicts had been in progress. As Stephen Larrabee argued before the collapse: 'While Moscow has by no means given up on the Third World, it has become much more selective and cautious about its involvement. . . . [T]he Soviets have begun to take a new and more constructive approach toward regional conflicts. . . . Rather than exploiting these conflicts militarily, they now seem more intent on finding political solutions to them.'[14] The new Soviet policy had been reflected to varying degrees and in different mixes in later Soviet stances toward almost all major regional conflicts in the Third World, including those in Central America (Nicaragua), Southern Africa (Angola, Namibia), the Horn of Africa (Ethiopia), the Middle East (Arab-Israeli), the Persian Gulf (Iran-Iraq), and Southeast Asia (Cambodia). It was most dramatically visible in the Soviet approach to the latest crisis in the Gulf.

What will Russia's relationship be to the Third World? Moscow has over the last four decades made major political, military, and economic investments in selected Third World countries and regions. Some of these relationships, like the one with India, were considered very valuable in both political and economic terms by Gorbachev and other policy-makers around him. Following the de-ideologization of Soviet foreign policy, the importance of large, geopolitically important and economically viable states like India increased at the expense of ideologically compatible but economically weak and politically vulnerable states that had been a steady drain on the Soviets' increasingly scarce financial resources.[15]

The Re-orientation of the United States

The changing nature of Soviet policy toward Third World conflicts also brought about shifts in American strategies in this traditional arena of super-power competition. However, American policy toward the Third World has continued to be subject to contrary pulls and pressures—both ideological and strategic. Therefore, even while reacting to shifts in Soviet policy under Gorbachev, American policy was not as clear-cut in its sense of direction and in its ultimate goal as its Soviet counterpart appeared to be during the last few years.[16] One set of pressures emanated directly from the perceived retrench-ment of Soviet power and the consequent dramatic change in the super-power equation. Proponents of this view argued that the Third World was important—if it was important at all—to US strategy primarily, if not exclusively, in the context of superpower competition. They further argued that once the Soviet threat to the West had been dramatically reduced, Washington should not be overly concerned with events in the Third World, including Third World conflicts, which in any case have autonomous origins and dynamics subject to only minimal and marginal influence by the United States.

On the other hand, some argued that the Third World—or at least certain regions therein, like the Persian Gulf—is of major intrinsic significance to US security irrespective of any superpower equation, and hence that the US should maintain—in fact, increase—its interventionist capability vis-à-vis at least certain selected regions of the Third World. Some even argued that in the changed strategic context, the Third World should replace the Soviet Union as America's leading security concern. This argument received added strength in 1990 from the Iraqi invasion of Kuwait, the consequent perceived threat to Saudi and other Gulf oil reserves, and the impact of the whole episode on oil prices and output and, therefore, on the Western industrialized economies in general and the American economy in particular.

This argument was made most succinctly by Steven David, who, just before the unravelling of the Soviet sphere in Eastern Europe, had argued: 'The Third World matters [to the United States] because of the strategic-military threat from the Soviet Union and, *more importantly, because of the threat from the Third World states themselves.*'[17] David had then concluded with a foresight corroborated by the events of 1990: that 'American allies in Japan and Western Europe are threatened far more by developments in the Persian Gulf than by any direct threat against these allies themselves. . . . It is . . . far more likely that any call upon the United States to defend its interests in Western Europe and Japan will be in response to threats in the Persian Gulf, rather than to a Soviet invasion of its allies.'[18]

Michael Desch provided the rationale for selective, yet major, American strategic concern for certain areas in the Third World by arguing that 'there are areas outside the homeland that have little intrinsic value, but are nonetheless strategically vital because they contribute to the defence of the homeland or of other intrinsically valuable areas. A great power must protect its interests in such areas, i.e., control them, have access to them, or be able to deny them to an adversary . . . These areas have what I term *extrinsic* value.'[19] He concluded:

> To defend intrinsically valuable areas such as Western Europe, the Persian Gulf, and Northeast Asia, the United States must also integrate other areas into its grand strategy. The Caribbean, the Indian Ocean littoral, and a base in the Western Pacific have extrinsic value because of their proximity to important lines of communication, because of the nature of current anti-shipping and transportation technology, and because forward defense is currently the best strategy for US defense of intrinsically valuable areas of the world.[20]

The crisis in the Gulf in 1990-91, which led to the deployment overseas of the largest number of American military personnel since the Vietnam war, augmented this school's arguments and conclusions that parts of the Third World are of intrinsic importance to the United States irrespective of the existence of a Soviet threat, and that American interventionist capabilities in relation to these regions should not be drawn down in response to the end of the cold war.[21]

Implications for Third World Conflict

The end of cold war, however, may not turn out to be an unmixed blessing for the Third World. It may prompt the United States to act more cavalierly as far as the security and the vital interests of Third World states and peoples are concerned, and to attempt to subordinate their economic and political concerns to its own economic and political agenda. It is instructive to note in this context that Arab criticisms of Washington's insensitivity to Arab concerns in the formulation of American responses to the Gulf crisis were heard from the very beginning, when the United States had just begun to deploy its troops in and around Saudi Arabia.[22] The United States may be tempted to undertake unilateral military intervention if developments in what Washington considers to be strategic regions of the Third World, such as the Gulf or Central America, are not to its liking. Important Third World state élites, in the absence of a balancing power that could neutralize in some measure the dominant superpower's interventionist proclivities, may begin to feel more vulnerable and insecure. This was already evidenced in the ambiguous reactions of many Third World state élites to the changing nature of US-Soviet relations in the 1980s. While many of them, as demonstrated by the numerous resolutions passed at successive meetings of the Non-aligned Movement, welcomed superpower *détente* in principle, they were alarmed at the terms on which the US-Soviet *rapprochement* has been achieved. They felt that with the Soviet Union abdicating its superpower status and abjuring its global responsibilities, the international system was entering a unipolar phase, at least in the strategic-political arena. The Soviet decision by and large to endorse American actions, and play second fiddle to Washington in the Gulf, augmented the Third World's sense of unease at the transformed superpower relationship. Many Third World leaders seemed to believe that in the long run this might have serious adverse consequences for Third World states individually as well as collectively, because it would seriously limit their manoeuverability *vis-à-vis* the West in general and the United States in particular.[23]

On the other hand, if the disengagement from the Third World by the now defunct Soviet Union is matched by a genuine reduction in American political and strategic involvement in arenas of tension and conflict in the Third World (which may well be the case except in relation to strategic regions like the Gulf), it may create problems of another kind. Such disengagement is likely to remove significant restraints on the conflictual behaviour of major Third World states whose aggressive, or at the very least assertive, potential was constrained in the past by the apprehension that it might draw negative political and even military reactions from one, or both, of the superpowers, and thereby end up tipping the regional balance against them. As a result, US disengagement now from Third World regions may lead to greater assertiveness on the part of regionally pre-eminent powers interested in translating their pre-eminence into hegemony, or at least into a managerial role within their respective regions.

Iraqi President Saddam Hussein's decision to invade Kuwait in August 1990 seemed to have been based at least in part on his perception that— given the relaxed nature of superpower relations and, consequently, the reduced motivation for them to view events in the Third World as having strategic significance for their bilateral relationship—his move into a small neighbouring country would not be viewed by Washington as marking a major shift in the bipolar balance of power in favour of the Soviet Union (as would have been the case a few years ago) and would not, therefore, invite severe economic and military reprisals on the part of the United States and its Western allies. It was unfortunate for him that Iraq and Kuwait happened to be located within a region defined by American strategists as one of intrinsic import to American security irrespective of the state of superpower relations. Had such an episode taken place in a less strategically important region of the Third World, and had it involved countries without the oil reserves controlled by Kuwait, Iraq, and Saudi Arabia, the outcry in the United States would have been far less, and the outcome would almost certainly have been very different. In this context, it may be instructive to speculate about a hypothetical future crisis in South Asia involving an Indian move into Bhutan, and to predict the likely American reaction to such a venture. One wonders if the US reaction to such a crisis in South Asia would bear any resemblance to its response to the Iraqi invasion of Kuwait.

The Gulf crisis also pointed to another trend, in some ways the opposite of the disengagement discussed above. This is the possibility of co-ordinated great-power policies and actions aimed at managing, if not resolving, regional crises in the Third World. The Kuwaiti crisis demonstrated that such a co-ordinated effort will probably be aimed at restraining the hegemonic ambitions of the pre-eminent regional power.[24] However, this need not always be the case. If in certain hypothetical future situations the great powers jointly or separately came to the conclusion that their individual or combined interests were better served by supporting the hegemonic ambitions of a regionally predominant power willing to safeguard, or even promote, their economic or other interests, there is nothing to prevent them from pursuing such a course of action in either co-ordinated or at least parallel fashion. Many important Third World countries are unlikely to view this prospect favourably, however. They would see it as a concert of industrialized powers attempting to maintain what is already perceived as an iniquitous distribution of power within the international system. As a consequence, the term 'neocolonialism' could experience an instant revival and acquire greater credibility than it has had at any time during the past two decades.

The disappearance of the Soviet threat to the Western allies, combined with the growing economic muscle of Western Europe and Japan, may in fact fundamentally reshape relations between the great powers, dramatically change their foreign-policy priorities, and rewrite the global agenda by radically shifting the emphasis to economic rather than military concerns in fields of co-operation and conflict alike.[25] In such a scenario, the importance of the US to the maintenance of the global political and economic order would diminish, and the country's major problems in the 1990s would emanate from its competition with Europe and Japan for a fair share of the global economic cake.

In this context Third World crises such as the one in the Gulf serve a useful American purpose. They help to refocus attention on the variable of military power and its continuing need and utility, in particular, to assure the industrialized countries' access at reasonable prices to scarce commodities like oil. They also help to demonstrate that the United States is the only major power with both the will and the military wherewithal to perform this role of policing for the developed world, and that without its global military reach and its decisive political leadership, Europe and Japan would be left at the mercy of Third World extortionists like Saddam Hussein. The Kuwaiti crisis helped remind Europe and Japan of the continuing need for the US shield, if not against the Soviet Union, then against future Third World predators. It has thus performed a very valuable function for Washington—namely, that of decelerating the almost inevitable shifts of power within the Western alliance—and has for the moment allowed the United States to remain in control of Western strategic and security concerns, both generally and in relation to the Third World in particular. It has also strengthened the oft-repeated American case for burden-sharing among the Western allies, which would shift some of the financial if not military load of global policing to other industrialized economies, and thus help partially reduce the American budget deficit.

Arms-transfer Insecurities

The changing strategic context may well have other effects on the Third World, especially in the security arena. For example, conventional arms-control pacts between the superpowers may have opened the way for increasing sales of redundant weapons to the Third World; indeed, the collapse of the Soviet Union has made this quite likely, thus reversing the trend toward diminishing arms sales that was visible through most of the 1980s.[26] As it is, during the last two decades the transfer of modern weapons and weapons technology from the industrialized countries to various parts of the Third World, especially the contiguous regions of the Middle East, the Persian Gulf, and, to a lesser extent, South Asia, has 'produc[ed] new configurations of power and contribut[ed] to the intensity and duration of regional conflicts'.[27] The prime example of this phenomenon was the Iran-Iraq war, which raged for eight years, wreaking human and material damage on a scale unseen since the Second World War.

Although, by and large, weapons are mainly of instrumental value and are not in themselves the cause of war, the possession of increasingly sophisticated weapons systems that tend to become quickly obsolete, and hence often give a Third World state only temporary technological superiority over a regional rival, can become a crucial factor in the calculations of decision-makers, who may escalate disputes to a point where war becomes a distinct possibility. Furthermore, since almost all Third World countries that possess the capacity to wage major wars are dependent to some degree on the importation of sophisticated weapons and weapons technology from the industrialized countries, this dependence has become 'the defining characteristic of post-colonial North-South military relations'.[28]

The nature of this dependence can be expected to be augmented by the increasing availability of sophisticated surplus armaments from the arsenals of major powers. Sales to interested countries in the more conflict-prone regions of the Third World are likely to be justified on the basis of hard-currency requirements (a particularly important consideration for the former Soviet Republics), the necessity to shore up friends and allies (especially those with immense oil reserves and surplus petro-dollars, or with links to important domestic constituencies in the United States) by making them more self-reliant in terms of hardware, and the need to find alternative sources of profitable returns for domestic arms industries. The projected increase in such arms transfers would add to the insecurity of Third World states, both by providing regional rivals with deadlier weapons, and by strengthening the military-technological dependency of important (and some not-so-important) Third World states on the industrialized countries.

Nuclear Proliferation and Missile Technology Transfer

The problem of nuclear proliferation is a subset of the problems connected with the transfer of weapons technology. It is, however, the most dramatic of these problems, because it is the only one that ties Third World security concerns to those of global security. This is why, even at the height of the cold war, the superpowers collaborated in an attempt to institutionalize international controls on Third World behaviour through the Nuclear Non-Proliferation Treaty (NPT). Aimed at delegitimizing and thus preventing horizontal proliferation beyond the five established members of the nuclear club, the NPT was opened for signature in 1968, and came into force in March 1970. In combination with the safeguards administered since the 1950s by the International Atomic Energy Agency (IAEA), it was considered to be the most effective method of keeping in check the nuclear ambitions of certain important Third World states that were on the verge of attaining the technical capability to begin manufacturing nuclear weapons.

Anxious to maintain their autonomy of decision on nuclear matters, however, important states in the Third World with nuclear-weapons potential refused to adhere to the NPT. Leading members of this group — Israel, India, Pakistan, and South Africa foremost among them — have in fact attempted to circumvent the controls imposed by the nuclear club, both through the medium of the London Suppliers' Group of countries with nuclear technology and materials and otherwise, in order to build up their actual or potential nuclear capabilities to varying degrees.[29] Furthermore, their policies regarding the acquisition of nuclear-weapons capability have been cloaked in deliberate ambiguities (although some of these are more transparent than others) in order to keep in suspense both regional adversaries and the international nuclear establishment. Such unacknowledged but nonetheless credible instances of nuclear (or near-nuclear) proliferation pose more than the abstract problems of managing a world with a dozen or so nuclear powers. They also pose the far more acute problem of the likely nuclearization of some of the most sensitive and conflict-prone regional environments in the Third World, because the four de facto nuclear powers mentioned above have all been engaged in protracted conflicts with their neighbours.[30] Although the superpowers' experience has demonstrated that nuclear powers tend to act with great responsibility, and that mutual nuclear deterrence prevents the outbreak of shooting wars, sceptics believe that such restraint may not apply equally in Third World contexts, for a number of reasons. First, a situation of nuclear deterrence and relative symmetry does not exist in the most volatile region of the Third World, the Middle East, where Israel monopolizes nuclear-weapons capability and has made it clear — not merely verbally, but with its 1981 attack on the Iraqi nuclear reactor suspected of contributing to Baghdad's nuclear aspirations—that it will not allow any Arab country to attain that capacity.[31] Such a situation of nuclear monopoly is extremely dangerous, because in a time of acute crisis, when vital interests appear to be threatened, it is likely to provide the major incentive and justification for the unleashing of nuclear weaponry on a non-nuclear adversary that may temporarily appear to be in a position of advantage in terms of conventional power.[32] It is also dangerous in the sense that non-nuclear adversaries of such a nuclear monopolist would be tempted to take grave risks to acquire nuclear capability themselves. Iraq's attempt to circumvent IAEA restrictions, in order to acquire nuclear-weapons capability to match Israel's, provides adequate testimony to this fact.

But even an ostensibly balanced instance of nuclear proliferation, like the one projected in South Asia between India and Pakistan, carries risks of miscalculation and/or adventurism that may end in catastrophe. It does so because of the fundamentally unstable and asymmetrical nature of the India-Pakistan nuclear and conventional balance; serious doubts about the two parties' second-strike capabilities, even after they overtly acquire first-strike capacity; and the highly charged emotional atmosphere that surrounds their bilateral disputes, principally that over Kashmir.[33]

The prospect of nuclear-weapons proliferation (even if covert or ambiguous in nature), especially in the most volatile and conflict-prone regions of the Third World, has in the last decade given rise to greater concern in light of the simultaneous proliferation of ballistic-missile technology in the same regions and among many of the same countries that aspire to possess nuclear weapons.[34] Foremost among these regions is the Middle East. As one analyst has pointed out,

> Within a setting . . . inherently unstable . . . ballistic missiles . . . accentuate insecurities by undermining long-standing deterrent postures, and by emphasising the benefits of pre-emptive counter-force action. The virtual certainty that enemy ballistic missiles will penetrate defensive systems may lead to conclusions that first-strike attacks aimed at destroying opposing missile forces are preferable to absorptive and second-strike strategies. Regional crisis stability may be further jeopardized, and the preference for pre-emptive assault transformed into a strategic imperative, should fears arise that enemy missiles may be used to deliver nuclear or chemical warheads. In the Middle East, this concern is real as the spread of surface-to-surface systems has in some countries been accompanied, and in others predated, by an interest in nuclear, chemical and bacteriological weapons.[35]

The intensity of this problem in the Middle East is underscored by the fact that, according to a study carried out by the US Congressional Research Service, nine of the seventeen Third World countries considered to be in possession of, or in the process of developing or procuring, ballistic missiles are located in the Middle East.[36] Israel's possession of an all-but-acknowledged nuclear arsenal, and the known Iraqi possession and use of chemical weapons — which Egypt, Israel, Libya, Syria, and Iran are also suspected of possessing — makes the possession of missile technology an extremely destabilizing factor in the political and military equations in the Middle East.

The South Asian region is not far behind in this field. India demonstrated its capacity to develop sophisticated delivery systems most dramatically by test-firing in May 1989 its first domestically produced Intermediate Range Ballistic Missle (IRBM), *Agni*, capable of delivering a payload of 1000 pounds to a distance of 1500 miles.[37] While the Indian ballistic-missile programme is primarily a delayed response to the development of IRBM capacity by China, Pakistan has undertaken its own missile-development programme in response to the buildup of Indian capabilities in this field. It may have done so with the help of China, whose sales to Iran and Saudi Arabia have made it one of the leading missile exporters.

Efforts to check the uncontrolled transfer of missile technology have been mounted through the Missile Technology Control Regime (MTCR), announced in April 1987 after four years of negotiations, and based on a voluntary agreement among the leading Western industrial powers. The MTCR has been limited in its success, because of the non-participation of the Soviet Union, China, and Third World missile producers like Brazil and Argentina in that regime. (For a full analysis see Chapter 15.)

The proliferation both of chemical weapons themselves and of the political will to use them in defiance of international conventions (as demonstrated by the Iraqis in their war with Iran and against the Kurdish insurgents in Iraq) has provided a terrifying weapons alternative for many Third World countries that are not in a position, either technologically or financially, to launch a serious nuclear-weapons programme. Furthermore, given the high cost and cumbersome nature of the protective gear essential to defend against a chemical attack, a pre-emptive, first-strike counterforce strategy might appear attractive to policy-makers on one or both sides in conflicts involving two countries known to possess such weapons. Combined with short and medium-range missile capability, therefore, such weapons may not only wreak havoc on civilian populations, but also destabilize local balances and make Third World crises more difficult to manage. Once again, it would be extremely difficult to enforce a ban on such weapons in vast parts of the Third World, because the relatively simple technology required to manufacture such weapons is readily available.

Conclusion

Several conclusions emerge from this analysis. First, while the fundamental determinants of state and regional security in the Third World are primarily rooted in the intrastate and regional dynamics within the Third World, the global strategic context does play an important role in determining the level, intensity, and duration of conflicts in various regions of the Third World.

Second, the global strategic environment in the post-war era has, by and large, exacerbated rather than alleviated conflict in the Third World.

Third, there is some reason to believe (although the evidence on this is not conclusive) that this pattern may be reversed following the demise of the Soviet Union.

Fourth, however benign the effects of this demise may be, it is likely to have only a limited impact on the level of security enjoyed by states and regions in the Third World, since its effects will be confined to the distribution of power and polarity — only one of several international systemic variables that impinge upon Third World security.

Fifth, this demise may in fact exacerbate insecurity within certain strategically important Third World regions, because it is likely to permit a greater degree of unilateral political, economic, and military action on the part of a US no longer constrained by concern for a hostile Soviet Union.

Sixth, powerful Third World states with ambitions of regional hegemony may feel emboldened to undertake political and military ventures that they would have hesitated to undertake during the heyday of superpower competition and high involvement in Third World affairs. This trend could be strengthened in the event of escalating unilateral US intervention in regions of the Third World considered strategic by Washington, since other regions, considered less important, could be left largely on their own and hence increasingly subject to the hegemonic ambitions of pre-eminent regional powers.

Seventh, overt nuclear capabilities in the Third World may be expected to increase as antagonistic regional powers calculate that the global restraints formerly imposed by superpowers are reduced, and they are forced to find countervailing strategies against each other on their own.

Eighth, the proliferation of sophisticated weapons technology in the Third World, including ballistic missiles as well as nuclear, chemical, and biological weapons, has reached a point where it cannot be reversed; this points to escalating costs, both human and material, in any future Third World conflict — a trend already foreshadowed by the devastation of the Iran-Iraq war.

Finally, the frequency and intensity of intra- and interstate conflicts in the Third World are unlikely to diminish just because the cold war has ended. Because they are linked primarily to state-making and nation-building — processes entailing the accumulation and consolidation of state power over territorial and demographic space that is often contested by multiple political entities or ethno-linguistic or ethno-religious groups — such conflicts are only marginally amenable to external influence and control.

Notes

[1]For a more detailed analysis of the Third World's security problematic and its relationship to issues of global and great-power security, see Mohammed Ayoob, 'The Security Problematic of the Third World', *World Politics* 43, 2 (1991), 257-83.

[2]Youssef Cohen, Brian R. Brown, and A.F.K. Organski, 'The Paradoxical Nature of State Making: The Violent Creation of Order', *American Political Science Review* 75, 4 (1981), 902.

[3]For details of this argument, see Mohammed Ayoob, 'The Security Predicament of the Third World State: Reflections on State-Making in a Comparative Perspective', in Brian Job, ed., *The Insecurity Dilemma: National Security of Third World States* (Boulder, CO.: Lynne Rienner, 1992).

[4]Nicole Ball, *Security and Economy in the Third World* (Princeton, NJ: Princeton Univ. Press, 1988), 33.

[5]For example, see Sisir Gupta, 'Great Power Relations and the Third World', in Carsten Holbraad, ed., *Super Powers and World Order* (Canberra: Australian National University Press, 1971), 125.

[6]For details of the core-periphery dichotomy, see Johan Galtung, 'A Structural Theory of Imperialism', *Journal of Peace Research* 8, 2 (1971), 81-117, and the various works of Immanuel Wallerstein.

[7]Robert S. Litwak and Samuel F. Wells, Jr, 'Introduction', in Litwak and Wells, eds, *Superpower Competition and Security in the Third World* (Cambridge, MA: Ballinger, 1988), ix.

[8]I have explained elsewhere that the 'late development of modern state structures has meant that they still lack legitimacy . . . in large parts of the Third World. Defined, as they have been, primarily by boundaries drawn by the colonial powers for the sake of administrative convenience or in some form of trade-off with colonial competitors, these structures have not yet developed the capacity to ensure the habitual identification of their populations with their respective states and the regimes that preside over the post-colonial structures within colonially dictated boundaries' (Ayoob, 'Security in the Third World: The Worm about to Turn?' *International Affairs* 60, 1 [1983-4], 45). For an insightful analysis of the colonial inheritance and its impact on Third World stateness, see Joel Migdal, *Strong Societies and Weak States: State-Society Relations and State Capabilities in the Third World* (Princeton, NJ: Princeton Univ. Press, 1988).

[9]Infrastructural power has been defined by Michael Mann as 'the capacity of the state actually to penetrate civil society, and to implement logistically political decisions throughout the realm' (Mann, 'The Autonomous Power of the State: Its Origins, Mechanisms and Results', in John A. Hall, ed., *States in History* [Oxford: Basil Blackwell, 1986], 113).

[10]Some of these issues have been dealt with in greater detail in Mohammed Ayoob, 'The Third World in the System of States: Acute Schizophrenia or Growing Pains?', *International Studies Quarterly* 33, 1 (1989), 67-79. For a relatively comprehensive and up-to-date discussion of the major sources of insecurity in the Third World, see Yezid Sayigh, *Confronting the 1990s: Security in the Developing Countries; Adelphi Papers, 251* (London: International Institute for Strategic Studies, 1990).

[11]Robert Gilpin, *The Political Economy of International Relations* (Princeton, NJ: Princeton Univ. Press, 1987), 10.

[12]For an forthright account by a senior Soviet academic of the origins of change

within the Soviet Union, see Oleg T. Bogomolov, 'The Origins of Change in the Soviet Union' in *The Strategic Implications of Change in the Soviet Union, Part I; Adelphi Papers 247* (London: International Institute for Strategic Studies, 1989-90), 16-28. For an explicit account by a senior Soviet academic (and close confidant of, and policy adviser to, Gorbachev) of the impact of the new Soviet thinking on Soviet policy towards the Third World, see Yevgeni Primakov, 'USSR Policy on Regional Conflicts', *International Affairs* (Moscow, June 1988), 3-9.

[13]For details, see Elizabeth Kridl Valkenier, 'New Soviet Thinking about the Third World', *World Policy Journal* 4 (1987), 651-74; also, David E. Albright, 'The USSR and the Third World in the 1980s', *Problems of Communism* 38 (1989), 50-70.

[14]Stephen F. Larrabee, 'Regional Conflict: Cooperation and Competition: Paper II', in *The Strategic Implications of Change in the Soviet Union, Part II; Adelphi Papers 248* (London: International Institute for Strategic Studies), 63.

[15]Francis Fukuyama, 'Patterns of Soviet Third World Policy', *Problems of Communism* 36 (1987), 7. Yevgeni Primakov extends this logic to the arena of Third World conflicts: 'The main point . . . is that self-restraint by the external forces, the Great Powers above all, backed up by their joint or parallel action, is a necessary condition for eliminating regional conflicts on a just and lasting basis. The Soviet Union is prepared for such cooperation' (Primakov, 'USSR Policy', 9).

[16]The contending philosophies that have attempted to shape America's Third World policy have been lucidly presented in two articles with self-explanatory titles that are essential reading for all analysts interested in this subject: Robert H. Johnson, 'Exaggerating America's Stakes in Third World Conflicts', *International Security* 10 (1985-6), 32-68, and Steven R. David, 'Why the Third World Matters', *International Security* 14 (1989), 50-85. For two additional perceptive articles on the same subject, see Charles William Maynes, 'America's Third World Hang-ups', *Foreign Policy* 71 (1988), 117-140, and Michael C. Desch, 'The Keys that Lock Up the World: Identifying American Interests in the Periphery', *International Security* 14 (1989), 86-121.

[17]David, 'Why the Third World Matters', 61. Emphasis added.

[18]Ibid., 77, 78.

[19]Desch, 'The Keys that Lock Up the World', 98, 99. Emphasis in original.

[20]Ibid., 121.

[21]For a theory of alternating American and Soviet surges of activism in the Third World, see Samuel P. Huntington, 'Patterns of Intervention: America and the Soviets in the Third World,' *National Interest* 7 (1987), 39-47. However, Huntington's conclusion that 'If past patterns hold true, improved relations with the U.S. plus Gorbachev's consolidation of power could lead to greater Soviet activity in the Third World' (47) appears to run contrary to trends so far visible in superpower patterns of activity around the Third World and elsewhere. For one of the few balanced accounts of Soviet involvement in the Third World written in the United States during those days of heightened American concern about Soviet intentions and capabilities, see Rajan Menon, *Soviet Power in the Third World* (New Haven: Yale Univ. Press, 1986).

[22]For one example, see Kamel S. Abu Jaber, 'Once More, the U.S. Misreads the Arab World', *New York Times* (10 Aug. 1990), A25.

[23]Some of these fears were expressed by Julius K. Nyerere, former President of Tanzania, in an interview on an American television program 'Like It Is' broadcast on WABC TV, New York, on 30 Sept. and 7 Oct. 1990. Third World political leaders in office are understandably reticent about expressing such sentiments in public and for the record.

[24]For an analysis of the remarkable degree of American and Soviet co-operation during the early crucial period of the Kuwaiti crisis, see Bill Keller, 'U.S. and the Soviets as Allies: It's the First Time Since 1945', *New York Times* (8 Aug. 1990), A1, A8.

[25]For one example, see Theodore C. Sorensen, 'Rethinking National Security', *Foreign Affairs* 69 (1990), 1-18.

[26]For details of this argument, see Robert Pear, 'Prospects of Arms Pacts Spurring Arms Sales', *New York Times* (25 March 1990), 12. For trends in arms transfers to the Third World during the 1980s, see Richard F. Grimmett, *Trends in Conventional Arms Transfers to the Third World by Major Suppliers, 1982-1989* (Washington, DC: Congressional Research Service, Library of Congress, 1990), especially 1-3.

[27]Michael T. Klare, 'The Arms Trade: Changing Patterns in the 1980s', *Third World Quarterly* 9, 4 (Oct. 1987), 1257.

[28]Andrew L. Ross, 'Arms Acquisition and National Security: The Irony of Military Strength', in Edward E. Azar and Chung-in Moon, eds, *National Security in the Third World: The Management of Internal and External Threats* (Aldershot: Edward Elgar, 1988), 156.

[29]For a recent comprehensive overview and assessment of the leading threshold powers' nuclear capabilities, see Leonard S. Spector and Jacqueline R. Smith, *Nuclear Ambitions: The Spread of Nuclear Weapons 1989-1990* (Boulder, CO: Westview, 1990).

[30]For a prospective scenario on the Indian subcontinent, see Leonard S. Spector, 'India-Pakistan War: It Could Be Nuclear', *New York Times* (7 June 1990), A23. For the Middle East, where a situation of *de facto* nuclear monopoly prevails, see Helena Cobban, 'Israel's Nuclear Game: The U.S. Stake', *World Policy Journal* 5 (1988), 415-33.

[31]For the latest account of Israeli nuclear capability, see Seymour M. Hersh, *The Sampson Option* (New York: Random House, 1991). Hersh has asserted that Israel has many more nuclear warheads than previously suspected—he mentions 300— including nuclear artillery shells and 'low-yield neutron warheads capable of destroying large numbers of enemy troops'. Hersh has also asserted that, in addition to its Arab neighbours, a principal potential target for Israel's impressive nuclear arsenal was the Soviet Union. Also, see Spector and Smith, *Nuclear Ambitions*, 149-74.

[32]It is commonly acknowledged that Israel was contemplating the use of nuclear weapons during the initial stages of the October War of 1973. This view is corroborated by Hersh, *The Sampson Option*.

[33]The case for continuing asymmetry and instability in the India–Pakistan nuclear relationship has been best put forth by a perceptive Pakistani scholar: 'The development of operational nuclear weapon systems in South Asia might not produce a stable strategic environment as advocated by the proponents of the bomb option in both India and Pakistan. The outdated NATO doctrine of massive retaliation and nuclear option to augment meager conventional defence sources is hardly relevant in Pakistan's case because of the vast and unbridgeable disparities in the conventional and assumed nuclear capabilities of the adversaries' (Rasul B. Rais, 'Pakistan's Nuclear Program: Prospects for Proliferation', *Asian Survey* 25 [1985], 472).

[34]For details, see Janne E. Nolan, *Trappings of Power: Ballistic Missiles in the Third World* (Washington, DC: Brookings Institution, 1991).

[35]Martin S. Navias, 'Ballistic Missile Proliferation in the Middle East', *Survival* 31 (1989), 225.

[36]*Missile Proliferation: Survey of Emerging Missile Forces*, Congressional Research Service Report 88-642-F (3 Oct. 1988), quoted in ibid., 226.

[37]For details of India's missile development programme, see Nolan, *Trappings of Power*, 38–48.

part two

The New Transnational Processes

chapter six

The Dynamics of Military Technology

Andrew L. Ross

The role of technology in the conduct of and preparation for war is ubiquitous. Technology pervades every aspect of war. Technological change has exerted a strong independent influence on warfare. Technology generates offensive, defensive, and deterrent capabilities, and determines the interface among offence, defence, and deterrence. It exerts an independent influence on force modernization and, perhaps more than strategy, is at the centre of national defence-policy debates and force-structure decisions. Peacetime readiness and the wartime sustainability of forces in the field are dependent on technology. It has served as a force multiplier, providing the qualitative edge thought to compensate for quantitative inferiority, and is critical to strategic warning and intelligence. Military research and development efforts have as their objective the advancement of technology. And the production of war materiel is highly dependent on modern technology.

The significance of military technology has not been eclipsed by the end of the cold war. With the end of that struggle between the United States and the Soviet Union, and the West and the East, and the disintegration of the internal Soviet empire, the military technological competition embedded in the seemingly perpetual arms race that once symbolized the superpower rivalry has come to an end. The history of military technology, however, has not ended. International politics and military conflict will continue to be shaped by the patterns and dynamics of military technological development.

There is no indication that the end of the cold war and the demise of the Soviet Union have eroded the desire of the world's remaining superpower to maintain the military technological superiority demonstrated in Operation Desert Storm and squander its 'unipolar moment' (Krauthammer, 1990-1). While, in the absence of a perceived global threat from a power such as the former Soviet Union, the pursuit of technological superiority will require fewer resources and allow for at least selective cancellation of planned investments in modernization, US defence planners are busy devising post-cold-war rationales for cold-war programmes such as the Strategic Defense Initiative (SDI). The United States, of course, will not be alone in its pursuit of technological advantage. Other powers, or aspirants to power, will attempt to develop and produce indigenously or to acquire from abroad the conventional and unconventional military technologies thought to enhance security or bolster efforts at regional and even global ascendance.

The dynamics of military technology evident during the relatively brief historical phase known, and by some beloved, as the cold war both preceded and survived that interregnum of American predominance and Soviet challenge. It is the enduring dynamics of military technology that will be focused upon here: the dynamics and patterns of revolutionary and evolutionary technological change; the relationship between offensive and defensive technology; the balance between spin-on and spin-off; the interaction between autonomous and mastered development; the constant emergence of new technologies; and the continuing global diffusion of modern conventional and unconventional weapons and technologies. The following attempt to differentiate what is believed to be known from what remains to be known about military technology and its dynamics begins by drawing upon the literatures on technology and technological change, international relations, and international security to examine the concepts of technology and military technology. This necessary conceptual discussion is followed by an effort to synthesize and distil the primary concerns of the vast literature on the dynamics of military technology. The historical as well as the contemporary dynamics of military technology are of interest here. Military technology, like technology itself, must be placed in historical context to distinguish what is new and different from what is constant and enduring.

The Concepts of Technology and Military Technology

Discussions of the development and impact of technology, especially military technology, are all too frequently unencumbered by conceptual clarity. Analysts typically neglect to define (or perhaps more accurately, avoid defining) the term 'technology'. Conceptual ambiguity consequently surrounds the widespread use of the term.

The apparently pervasive notion that technology is simply applied science, as conveyed by standard dictionary definitions,[1] is clearly inadequate. Historically, as Basalla (1988: 27) notes, technology preceded science. In addition, technology and technological innovation were not in the past and are not now dependent upon scientific understanding. The case of gunpowder is illustrative: 'Gunpowder . . . was known and used in Europe at least from the early part of the fourteenth century, but the purpose served by the nitrate in it, which is to provide oxygen for the quick combustion of the other components, was not fully understood until nearly five centuries later' (Brodie and Brodie, 1973: 8).

Basalla's (1988: 30) concept of technology as artifact, and the centrality of artifact to technology and artifactual change to technological change—'the artifact as the primary unit for study' in the understanding of technology and technological change—is no more satisfactory than the view of technology as applied science. An artifact is merely 'hardware', a particular manifestation or embodiment of technology. The concept of technology must encompass 'software' as well as hardware.

The distinction between technology and engineering made by Arnold Pacey (1990) in his most recent work reinforces the point that the conceptualization of technology should not be limited to applied science. Yet while Pacey provides an intriguing historical analysis of the dialectics between universal and specific, survival and baroque, fantastic and practical technologies, and of technological exchange or dialogue within and across societies, an explicit discussion of the concept of technology is absent in this work. In an earlier work, however, Pacey (1983: 6) did provide an explicit definition of technology, one intended to encompass the cultural and organizational as well as the technical aspects of technology, or what he then termed 'technology-practice' and subsequently, more broadly (Pacey, 1990), the 'technology complex'. This conceptualization advances beyond the view of technology as applied science to include not only the artifactual, or hardware, aspect, but also the software, or organizational and process aspects of technology. Similarly, Robert Merrill (1968: 576-7) conceives of technology as 'bodies of skills, knowledge, and procedures for making, using, and doing useful things,' as 'techniques, means for accomplishing recognized purposes', and as processes.[2]

Though students of international relations and international security affairs frequently employ the terms 'technology' and 'military technology', they rarely assign adequate meanings to these terms. Similarly rare are efforts to draw systematically, or even selectively, from the broader literatures on technology and technological change. In one early volume on technology and international relations, meaning is given to particular technologies, but not to technology generally (Ogburn, 1949b).[3] In a more recent collection of essays (Hieronymi, 1987), the editor and contributing authors neglect to explicitly attach precise meaning to 'technology', though one of the contributors (King, 1987: 9), apparently as much for the sake of expediency as for any legitimate analytical rationale, dismisses the experiential distinction between science and technology, arguing that 'the two are symbiotically related, interactive and inseparable'. Snow (1991), in an otherwise useful piece, abstains from definitional considerations. Though his usage appears to equate technology with applied science and the development component of research and development, Skolnikoff (1967: 16-19), in a brief definitional discussion of science and technology in which he notes the problematical nature of distinguishing between activities—such as basic and applied research—that are located on a continuum, opts out by electing to use 'science' as a generic covering term. Basiuk's (1977: 8) concept of technology is essentially limited to 'physical tools', or hardware. His conceptualization also features a novel attempt to subsume the impact of technology, which for most analysts is reasonably distinct from technology, within the concept of technology itself. In the introduction (Keatley, 1985: 8) to a collection that appeared under the auspices of the American National Academy of Sciences, the National Academy of Engineering, and the Council on Foreign Relations, technology is left undefined, though 'the innovative process' is identified as including research, development, manufacture, and distribution. Ramo (1985: 13), in the same collection, did (parenthetically) define technology as 'products and know-how', and Cooper and Hollick (1985: 228) used the term to mean 'the systematic application of human and financial resources toward the development of useful knowledge'. Sanders (1983: 28), in a utilitarian volume intended to demonstrate the importance of technology in international affairs, maintains the distinction between science and technology and usefully defines technology as 'a body of knowledge and devices by which things are commonly done or made'. For Sanders (1983: 28, 29), 'Technology means more than tools and machines; it includes techniques that enable people to perform tasks,' and encompasses product, know-how, and 'product with know-how imbedded'. In another useful work, Szyliowicz (1981: 7) distinguishes between scientific know-why and technological know-how, and includes in his conceptualization of technology both hardware and software: 'machines and tools of all kinds . . . methods, routines and procedures . . . patterns of organization and administration.'

The conceptual ambiguity and imprecision that pervade all too much of the work on technology and international relations are also evident in the international security literature on military technology. A recent American Association for the Advancement of Science volume with the promising title *New Technologies for Security and Arms Control* features discussions of a variety of new military technologies, but not even the semblance of a discussion of the concepts of technology and military technology (Arnett, 1989). An International Institute for Strategic Studies volume on new and emerging military technologies is similarly devoid of any unifying concept of technology (O'Neill, 1985), as is another volume edited by Pfaltzgraff, Ra'anan, Shultz, and Lukes (1988). Nor does Hans Günter Brauch (1989), in his edited collection on military technology, provide a discussion. In what was apparently intended to be an analytical survey of the literature 'On Science, Technology, and Military Power', Bellany (1989) fails to mount a serious effort either to delineate and differentiate between science and technology or to explore the relationship between the two, offering instead a rambling discourse marred by conceptual imprecision. Thee (1985) similarly neglects to provide a definitional discussion of the concept of military technology.

In an otherwise sophisticated, theoretically informed discourse on military technology and international security, Buzan (1987: 7) at one point appears to equate military technology with 'the instruments of force'. Clark (1989: 16), in an introduction to a collection on *Defence Technology*, usefully distinguishes between technology as output and technology as content, with output 'embodied in the production of material objects or the creation of procedural systems designed to expand human capabilities' and content 'embodied in the knowledge and methods used in making these objects or procedures'. The generic characteristics of technology, furthermore, are said to include systemic embeddedness, complexity, ubiquity, and diffuseness (Clark, 1989: 6-18). Technology is indeed ubiquitous and diffuse, in non-military as well as military arenas. However, it need not be embedded in a system, nor is it necessarily complex. Van Creveld, in an illuminating account of the historical development of military technology, correctly notes that technology is more than hardware. Yet its non-hardware characteristics are left to the somewhat fuzzy suggestion that 'Technology is perhaps best understood as an abstract system of knowledge, an attitude towards life and a method for solving its problems' (Van Creveld, 1989: 312). Tsipis (1989: 6) briskly and concisely defines technology as 'the ability to make something useful'. In identifying 'new technology' as 'the ability to devise a process or manufacture a device that can either perform a new task or do an existing one more cost-effectively, more easily, or better', Tsipis (1989: 7) recognizes the distinction between hardware and software. This distinction is also evident in Williams (1987: 280): 'technology is perhaps best understood as the final product of scientific and engineering research and development . . . it clearly encompasses not simply weapons but also the capabilities for command, control, and communication. . . .' However, the recognition that technology is not simply applied science is not evident in Williams's discussion. By distinguishing among basic, component, generic, and functional military technologies, Kincade (1987: 69-70) contributes a potentially useful classification scheme, though he explicitly rejects the opportunity to become mired in the 'metaphysics' of technology.

Military technology, clearly, is merely a particular form and expression, a particular subset, of technology. Technology itself is essentially benign. It can be employed for non-military or military, peaceful or warlike, productive or destructive purposes. Both militarized and non-militarized forms of technology are prior to science. Even though contemporary military technology is derived overwhelmingly from science, military technology cannot, historically, be reduced to the application of science to military objectives. Military technology also cannot be reduced to military hardware. Military technology, like technology generally, encompasses both hardware and software. It includes not only the actual instruments or artifacts of warfare, but the means by which they are designed, developed, tested, produced, and supplied — as well as the organizational capabilities and processes by which hardware is absorbed and employed.

Technological Change: Continuity or Discontinuity? Evolution or Revolution?

Historical and historically informed analyses of the impact of technology on the conduct of and preparations for war tend to underscore either the continuities inherent in evolutionary processes of technological development or the discontinuities apparent in revolutionary technological leaps. Conflicting accounts are the norm. Historical periods characterized by some analysts as singularly lacking in technological fecundity are lauded by others for their technological fruitfulness. Revolutionary change apparently takes place along a continuum ranging from days, months, or perhaps years to several centuries. And analysts systematically neglect to differentiate clearly between technological continuity and discontinuity, incremental and nonincremental, and evolutionary and revolutionary change.

Buzan, for one, writes of the slow pace of technological change and the prevalence of technological continuity and incremental, evolutionary change and the infrequency of transformational, revolutionary change prior to the nineteenth century. As he sweepingly observes (1987: 18):

> The military technology of the Roman legions changed little in the six centuries between the conquest of Greece and the fall of Rome. The galleys used by the Ottomans and the Christians during their Mediterranean wars as late as the sixteenth century were quite similar to those used by the Greeks against Xerxes in 480 BC. The ships of the line that fought at Trafalgar in 1805, and even as late as the Crimean War (1854-6), were easily recognizable as the same class of ship pioneered by Henry VIII in the first half of the sixteenth century.

The refrain of pre-nineteenth-century technological continuity is evident as well in Smoke's (1984: 11) minimization of the technological disparities between the militaries that fought in the Thirty Years War and the Napoleonic Wars. With the Industrial Revolution of the nineteenth century, however, technological continuity gave way to discontinuous technological change, and continuous change became the norm that it remains today. Only with the Industrial Revolution was cumulative, self-sustaining technological advance launched (Landes, 1969: 3). The quantitative and qualitative changes integral to the mechanization and industrialization of warfare initiated during the Industrial Revolution are evident in the large number and increasing frequency of technological innovations, and the ability not only to improve upon existing capabilities but to create new ones. Buzan (1987: 19-26) points to revolutionary advances in fire-power, protection, mobility, communications, and intelligence. Smoke (1984: 11-12) notes nineteenth-century shifts from wooden to iron naval vessels and from sails to steam, rapid advances in riflery and artillery, and the new-found strategic mobility afforded by railroads. This emphasis on pre-nineteenth-century/ Industrial Revolution continuity in military technology and rapid, revolutionary metamorphosis concurrent with and subsequent to the Industrial Revolution is also evident in Brodie's (1973) classic account of the development of military technology,[4] Osgood's (1957: 61-119) and Osgood and Tucker's (1967) interpretive historical analyses of limited and unlimited war, Dupuy's (1984) account of the evolution of weapons and war, and, even though military technology is not his primary focus, Howard's (1976) short history of European warfare.[5]

Yet discontinuous technological change is not solely a function of the nineteenth-century mechanization and industrialization of war. Revolutionary innovations have appeared even during periods thought to be the embodiment of technological stagnation, such as the Middle Ages, when in the eleventh century the construction of stone castles inaugurated an enduring predominance of defensive over offensive technology. Geoffrey Parker (1988) writes of how the revolutionary technological developments stemming from the Industrial Revolution of the nineteenth century were preceded by the military revolution of 1500-1800. This early modern European revolution, which according to Parker mirrors the even earlier military revolution that followed the decline of China's Chou dynasty in the eighth century BC, featured qualitative improvements in artillery and fortifications, heightened reliance on fire-power, and a non-incremental expansion in the size of military forces—advances that enabled a relatively small and resource-poor Europe to dominate the rest of the world (and in the process diffuse advanced European military technology to Africa, Asia, and the Americas).

William McNeill (1982: 9), in a magisterial analysis, 'detect[s] in the historic record a series of important changes in weapons-systems resulting from sporadic technical discoveries and inventions that sufficed to change preexisting conditions of warfare and army organization.' These erratic technological advances pre-date the Industrial Revolution, as does the industrialization of war. The first three transforming advances identified by McNeill occurred during antiquity: the Mesopotamian introduction of bronze weapons and armour (around 3500 BC); the invention of two-wheeled chariots (about 1800 BC); and the development of iron weapons in eastern Asia Minor (about 1400 BC) (McNeill, 1982: 9-13). These sporadic changes continued with the early invention of gunpowder (by AD 1000) and guns (about AD 1290) by the Chinese, and during the subsequent (but pre-Industrial Revolution) commercialization and bureaucratization of war. During the eighteenth century, the cumulative 'inventions of scores of experts and technicians . . . prepared the way for the revolutionary expansion in the scale of warfare' that engulfed Europe after 1789 (McNeill, 1982: 161).

In his ambitious treatise on *Technology and War*, Van Creveld (1989) identifies four historical periods: the age of tools, from before 2000 BC to about

AD 1500, when military technology was driven by organic power and evolved extremely slowly; the age of machines, from the Renaissance to about 1830, when organic power was displaced by non-organic power, and the rate of technological change accelerated; the age of systems, from around 1830 to 1945, when technology was subjected to organizational systemization, and innovation became institutionalized; and the age of automatization, from 1945 to the present, marked by exponentially increasing rates of technological change. If Van Creveld's historical interpretation is accepted, the Industrial Revolution of the nineteenth century was not so much a watershed event in the development of military technology as another, though distinct, stage in a continually accelerating process. By emphasizing historical technological continuity rather than discontinuity and the predominance of technological follow-on over revolutionary breakthrough, and even discounting the impact of the technological changes stemming from the Industrial Revolution on nineteenth-century warfare, Archer Jones (1989) even more fundamentally questions the notion of the nineteenth century as a technological watershed.

The contrasting emphases on technological continuity and discontinuity and on evolutionary and revolutionary, incremental and non-incremental, change that are evident in the historical literature are also apparent in analyses of the impact of technological change upon the contemporary conduct of and preparations for war. Analyses emphasizing the revolutionary nature of technological change are most evident in work on the impact of nuclear weapons (see Brodie, 1959; Jervis, 1984, 1989; Mandelbaum, 1979, 1981). While there are also analyses emphasizing the revolutionary nature of selected advances in non-nuclear weapons technology, especially PGMs (precision-guided munitions), much of the literature on post-World War II technological developments tends to underscore the incremental, evolutionary, rather than the non-incremental, revolutionary, nature of military technological change.

This emphasis is evident in the literatures on Soviet and American weapons research, development, and acquisition (see Ross, 1989b: 100-4, for a more complete review and synthesis of these literatures). In the Soviet Union, a multitude of state and party actors participated in an acquisition process shown by Alexander (1978-9: 24-30) to be marked by conservatism, bureaucratization, departmentalism, and secrecy. The products of the Soviet procurement process reflected the nature of the process: 'Soviet designers have shown a marked preference for simple designs; for the common use of subsystems and components in different weapons systems; and for incremental or evolutionary technological change' (Holloway, 1983: 147). Though attempts have been made to contrast the American and Soviet military research and development styles, with American research and development characterized as innovative and radical, and Soviet as incremental and evolutionary, when US research and development is examined in the context of the characteristics of the American weapons acquisition process, it is apparent that the contrast is overblown. In addition to the well-known uncertainties resulting from the unpredictable outcomes, costs, and schedules inherent in defence research and development efforts (Hitch and McKean, 1960: 247-9; Peck and Scherer, 1962: 17-54), the nature of the US acquisition process itself hampers innovation and radical progress. Gansler (1980: 105) argues that 'the high visibility and accountability of the R&D decision-makers places them in a position in which they feel they must minimize the risk associated with a particular R&D program. Thus there is a tendency to give the business to large, well-established firms, and to select conventional ideas for development.' In addition, the large firms in which military research and development are concentrated emphasize risk minimization rather than the pursuit of innovative, revolutionary technological departures (Gansler, 1980: 101).

An emphasis on the incremental, evolutionary character of military technological change is also apparent in those literatures situated by Buzan (1987: 94-104) in the context of a domestic-structure model.[6] Kurth's (1973, 1989) economic explanation of the follow-on imperative, for instance, focuses on a practice embedded in the US weapons-acquisitions process: the awarding of a contract for a new weapons system to a firm as it phases out production of an old system. This follow-on imperative yields evolutionary rather than revolutionary change: 'the new contract is for a system which is structurally similar while technically superior to the system being phased out' (Kurth, 1973: 40). The bureaucratic politics of weapons development and acquisition similarly gives rise to a process of military technological change marked by continuity rather than discontinuity.[7]

Several flaws are evident in these efforts to characterize either specific military technologies or military technological change during particular historical periods as evolutionary or revolutionary. First, the distinction apparent in the preceding sentence is typically obscured. It is conceivable that a radical breakthrough could occur during a period that was otherwise technologically stagnant. A particular revolutionary leap does not a revolutionary period make. Second, analysts, as previously noted, have systematically neglected to differentiate sharply between technological continuity and discontinuity, between incremental and non-incremental change, and between evolutionary and revolutionary change. Third, analysts have failed to recognize that technological continuity and discontinuity, incremental and non-incremental change, and evolutionary and revolutionary change are dichotomies located on continuums: recognition that one is operating in the realm of the relative rather than the absolute may assist in differentiating between them. Fourth, analysts have failed to distinguish between the improvement of existing military capabilities and the development of new ones. The ability to do something (such as fly) that could not be done previously is more likely to be the result of revolutionary military technological change than a better way of doing something one could already do. Fifth, it is necessary to differentiate between revolutionary military technology and the employment of such technology. It is conceivable that a revolutionary technology may be employed to do not something that could not be done previously, but something that could already be done (though perhaps not as well). Nuclear weapons, for instance, were used by the United States against Japan to do what the US had done repeatedly during World War II: bomb cities.

Offensive and Defensive Military Technology

The interaction of offensive and defensive military technology periodically draws the attention of international-security analysts.[8] Whether it is evolutionary or revolutionary, generated by incremental or non-incremental processes, military technology clearly is employed for offensive or defensive purposes. Indeed, analysts often say that the offensive or defensive employment of weaponry is determined as much (if not more) by the technology embodied in weaponry as by tactics, doctrine, and strategy. Propositions about the consequences of interaction between offensive and defensive military technology and offensive or defensive dominance rest upon the differentiation between offensive and defensive military technology that lies at the heart of efforts to identify the technological determinants of offence-defence interaction.

Generally, as in Van Evera (1990-1) and Jervis (1978), it is thought that the likelihood of war is heightened and the security dilemma worsened by offence dominance, while the likelihood of war is diminished and the security dilemma ameliorated by defence dominance. Under conditions of offence dominance, 'when offence appears easy and conquest seems feasible', the perceived indefensibility of existing boundaries promotes territorial expansion, pre-emptive and preventive wars become more attractive, diplomatic risks that increase the likelihood of war are more lightly assumed, and the heightened secrecy that shrouds military capabilities spawns misperceptions and miscalculations (Van Evera, 1990-1: 11-12). According to Jervis (1978: 187), when the offence is dominant 'it is easier to destroy the other's army and take its territory than it is to defend one's own.' Offence dominance encourages status-quo states to behave as expansionist aggressors, strike first, maintain large arsenals, engage in destabilizing arms races, and perceive the behaviour of others as aggressive, thereby deepening the security dilemma (Jervis, 1978: 187-90). When the defence has the advantage, however, 'it is easier to protect and to hold than it is to move forward, destroy, and take' (Jervis, 1978: 187). Defence dominance increases the cost of war and dampens aggression, first-strike incentives, and arms races. If sufficient, defence dominance renders military force unusable and aggression ineffective. It allows one state to enhance its security without diminishing that of others, thereby offering the possibility of an escape from the security dilemma. Quester (1977), in an insightful, carefully argued analysis of the historical interaction of offence and defence that reveals much about the causes of war, similarly argues that offence dominance yields war and empire, while defence dominance fosters independence and peace.[9]

Since technology is postulated to be one of the primary determinants of the relative dominance of offence or defence (Jervis, 1978: 194), analysts have attempted to distinguish between technologies that are offensive or defensive (see Jervis, 1978; Quester, 1977; Wright, 1965: 808-10; and, for a review of the relevant literature, Levy, 1984). Primary among the characteristics of offensive weaponry that have been identified are mobility, vulnerability, and striking power. Jervis (1978: 205) adds that weapons dependent on the element of surprise tend to be offensive while Quester (1977: 4) includes as offensive weapons those that are 'potent only for temporary durations'. Defensive weapons are said to have considerable holding power and to be fixed and invulnerable.[10] Thus while fixed fortifications, trenches, land mines, fixed anti-aircraft emplacements, and short-range interceptors, for instance, are generally thought to be defensive, weapons such as long-range bombers, unhardened land-based ballistic missiles, tanks, and mobile heavy artillery tend to be categorized as offensive.

Though an apparently rich source of generalizations about the impact of military technology on the likelihood of war, such efforts to differentiate between offensive and defensive military technologies and to advance propositions regarding the consequences of offensive or defensive dominance are theoretically underdeveloped, insufficiently rigorous, and non-cumulative. They do, however, offer greater promise than suggested by Levy's (1984) critical, even harsh, evaluation of the literature on the interaction of offensive and defensive military technology. Yet several problems must be addressed before the full potential of these efforts can be realized.

First, the ambiguity of the distinction between offensive and defensive military technology is theoretically and empirically untenable. It must be reduced to more manageable proportions. Even some who have employed the distinction have questioned its validity (see Wright, 1965: 806). Conceptual ambiguity is reflected in empirical efforts at operationalization, which have been anything but systematic. Contradictory identifications of the characteristics of offensive and defensive military technology, as in Wright's (1965: 808) classification of holding power and protection as offensive rather than defensive characteristics, preclude cumulative research.

A second problem that must be confronted is that of unclassifiable military technologies. A larger proportion of military technology than most analysts would prefer to admit is dual-use. As Levy (1984: 225) notes, striking power, rapidity of fire, and range are characteristics that are not inherently offensive or defensive. In addition, other military technologies thought to be classifiable as offensive or defensive are actually context-dependent. The characteristics of military technologies must be situated in the context of the tactics, doctrine, and strategy according to which they are employed and interact. Anti-tank weapons (and tanks) may be used for offensive or defensive purposes. Defensive forces (such as fixed coastal fortifications) may be used to protect offensive forces (such as commerce-raiding naval vessels). Greater effort must be devoted to differentiating systematically among the offensive, defensive, and dual-use technologies embodied in weaponry, and to examining the implications of dual-use military technologies—both those inherent in the technologies embodied in weapons and those that are context-dependent—for the interaction of offensive and defensive military technologies and propositions regarding the consequences of offensive or defensive dominance.

Another problem that requires attention is the impact of nuclear weapons on the interaction of offensive and defensive military technologies. Efforts both to differentiate between offensive and defensive technologies and to develop propositions about the consequences of offensive or defensive dominance have been confounded by the nuclear revolution. Analysts have, of course, acknowledged the confounding impact of nuclear weapons. Yet neither those who affirm the revolutionary impact of nuclear weapons nor those who would treat nuclear weapons as evolutionary have produced valid propositions regarding the consequences of offensive or defensive dominance.

A fourth significant problem evident in the literature is the absence of systematic empirical support for propositions about the consequences of offensive or defensive dominance. The use of selected anecdotal data that lend credence to generalizations has advanced, but that is not enough. The illustrative use of data is most evident in Jervis (1978). Quester (1977) at least provides a comprehensive narrative, analytical survey of the interaction of offensive and defensive military technologies from the time of the Persians and Greeks to the nuclear age; yet even he did not systematically collect and analyse the historical data in the way that practitioners of quantitative international political analysis or structured, focused comparison do (George, 1979). Cumulative research requires the systematic collection and analysis of empirical data, both historical and contemporary, not merely selected illustrations or even informed but non-replicable historical interpretation.

Finally, the offensive and defensive characteristics of military technology are seldom linked to other dimensions of military technology. Among the questions that might be raised are the following: What is the relationship between offence and defence and evolutionary and revolutionary technological change? Are periods of offensive or defensive dominance the result of evolutionary or revolutionary technological change? Are offensive and defensive technologies predominantly the product of spin-on from commercial research and development programmes, or do they tend to be generated primarily by programmes indigenous to the military? Are offensive or defensive military technologies favoured by discovery-push or demand-pull processes?

Spin-On or Spin-Off?

The relationship between military and civil technologies has seldom been the subject of sustained, systematic inquiry.[11] The thought that has been given to this subject is generally unidirectional. Since the Second World War, defence analysts have tended to stress the presumed benefits of military technology spin-offs for the civil, commercial sector.[12] The following passage from a well-regarded text by Smoke (1984: 19) is representative of the conventional wisdom:

> . . . with the exceptions of the automobile and the radio, most of the technology we take for granted today had its source and/or much of its development in the pursuit of national security.
>   . . . All the basic research and development for television, jets, and atomic energy took place during World War II. The first civilian jetliner, the Boeing 707, was largely derived from a U.S. Air Force bomber of the early 1950s, the B-47. Subsequent commercial airplanes, as well as the air traffic control systems that make high-volume air travel possible, have also drawn heavily from aeronautical and electronic technology first developed for military uses.

Recently, however, analysts have come to the belated recognition that the relationship between civil and military technologies is not unidirectional: not only has military innovation contributed to the civil sector, but civil, commercial innovation has contributed to the military sector. To the well-known phenomenon of spin-off from the military to the civil sector must be added the phenomenon of spin-on. As Welch (1990: 112) notes, 'in the technology environment of today and tomorrow, civilian technology results in an ever-more recognizable "spin-on" benefit for military use. Ministries of defence have a growing dependence on spin-on as the most sophisticated technologies are found increasingly in the civilian marketplace. Nations gain years of leadtime over adversaries and friendly competitors by way of spin-on.'[13]

The emerging technology of photonics provides a good example of spin-on. Photonics involves the use of light waves instead of electronic signals for the transmission and processing of data. According to Hughes (1990: 24), the lagging military photonic computing effort means that 'the challenge for military researchers will be to take off-the-shelf commercial products and adapt them for military use.' An earlier example of how 'fundamental advances used by the military have often originated in the private sector' (Hughes, 1990: 24) can be found in the invention and development of the integrated circuit.

Implicit in this recognition of the importance of the spin-on transferral of technology from civil to military sectors is a recognition of the vital role of dual-use technology in contemporary military equipment. The capabilities of modern military equipment, especially aircraft (including the much-vaunted American stealth aircraft), must be attributed as much to this dual-use technology as to technology that is exclusively military.

Defence analysts, again, appear to have rediscovered the wheel. Indeed, the wheel itself provides an early example of spin-on. Though its development was influenced by military requirements, its genesis was not. The same must be said of aircraft. The modern mechanization and industrialization of war were by-products of the Industrial Revolution. Even the atomic bomb was a spin-on product of a discovery-push process that began with basic research in nuclear physics.

Discovery-Push or Demand-Pull?

As Szyliowicz (1981: 8) observes, two conceptual models purporting to explain the emergence of new technologies have been developed: discovery-push and demand-pull. Discovery-push — or what Kincade (1987: 75) terms 'autonomous technology' and Cooper and Shaker (1988) call 'technology push' — emphasizes the central role of basic research, the relative autonomy of the technology development process, and the likelihood that the process will yield unexpected results. Szyliowicz (1981: 8) schematically portrays the discovery-push process as follows:

$$\underset{\text{research}}{\text{Basic}} \rightarrow \underset{\text{research}}{\text{Applied}} \rightarrow \underset{\text{and testing}}{\text{Development}} \rightarrow \text{Production} \rightarrow \text{User}$$

Demand-pull, termed 'command technology' by Kincade (1987: 74) and 'requirements-pull' by Cooper and Shaker (1988), stresses 'the specific need that exists to be filled' (Szyliowicz, 1981: 8) and 'the determinative role of intentions in technological evolution' (Kincade, 1987: 74). The demand-pull process was schematically illustrated by Szyliowicz (1981: 8) as follows:

User need	→	Pool of knowledge	→	Awareness of solution	→	Match solution to need solution	→	Critical evaluation of technological	→	Development, testing, production

Discovery-push, as Szyliowicz (1981: 8) notes, creates its own demand in the market, while demand-pull responds to market demands. Some seventy per cent of all technological innovation, Szyliowicz (1981: 8) reports, is attributable to the demand-pull process. This process tends to yield what have been referred to here as incremental or evolutionary technological advances, rather than the non-incremental, revolutionary, or what Szyliowicz (1981: 8-10) terms 'breakthrough', advances that tend to be the result of the discovery-push process. Demand-pull, then, can generally be equated with technological continuity, and discovery-push with technological discontinuity.

Discovery-push and demand-pull should be viewed as complementary rather than mutually exclusive processes. One need not rule out or negate the other. The two processes may also operate simultaneously, though it would be difficult to integrate them effectively. A country's armed forces, or specific services, may well draw on discovery-push and demand-pull concurrently.

Cooper and Shaker (1988) argue in a brief analysis that the United States Air Force tends to emphasize discovery-push, the Army relies primarily on demand-pull, and the Navy has shifted from an earlier emphasis on demand-pull to a more recent emphasis on discovery-push. According to this account, therefore, the Air Force and Navy are engaged in the pursuit of revolutionary technological breakthroughs, while the Army is content to pursue incremental, evolutionary progress. Given the cursory nature of Cooper and Shaker's analysis, however, more extensive empirical research is required before such a generalization about the US military can be accepted, and comparative empirical investigation is needed before it can be universally extended.

The distinctiveness of the discovery-push and demand-pull processes is widely appreciated, as are their respective implications for the autonomy and mastery of technological innovation. However, the analytical potential of the discovery-push and demand-pull models has not yet been fully exploited. In addition to acknowledging and utilizing the seemingly mundane yet analytically significant recognition that discovery-push and demand-pull bracket a continuum, analysts would do well to determine the conditions that foster discovery-push and demand-pull and that assign predominance to one over the other. Also worthy of attention, and thus far largely untreated in the literature, is the relationship between discovery-push and demand-pull processes and the other dimensions of the dynamics of military technology.

Emerging Technologies

The rapid pace of military technological development since World War II has enabled modern militaries to deploy a wide array of enhanced ground, air, and naval capabilities (Deitchman, 1983; Miettinen, 1983: 52-6). Contemporary artillery fires at a faster rate and over a greater range, is more accurate, and can be highly mobile (in the air as well as on the ground). Multiple rocket launchers enable ground forces to deliver high concentrations of a variety of advanced munitions with great accuracy. Main battle tanks such as the American M1 Abrams feature greater fire-power, the improved protection provided by multiple-layer armour, increased mobility, digital fire-control computers, laser range-finders, stabilized day/night sights, and thermal-imaging night vision optics. Military aircraft have greater speed, range, and payloads, night and all-weather capabilities, and electronic surveillance, warning, target identification, fire control, and countermeasures systems. They are armed with not only gravity bombs but radar-guided and heat-seeking air-to-air and air-to-ground missiles. Today's large aircraft carriers can accommodate air wings of eighty-five to ninety aircraft. Surface vessels are equipped with land-attack, anti-aircraft, and anti-ship missiles, anti-submarine torpedoes, phased-array air-search and fire-control radars, and radar jamming and deception systems. The speed and endurance of submarines have been increased, and their vulnerability reduced, by nuclear propulsion. Extremely accurate cruise missiles have been deployed on land, air, and sea platforms. At the core of many of these enhanced capabilities, especially sensing, guidance, and information-processing, have been rapid, even revolutionary, advances in electronics technologies.

The constant, continuing process of technological development has yielded a plethora of what analysts have identified as new or emerging technologies with military potential. These new or emerging technologies, which have been variously characterized and categorized, range from techniques and materials to components, subsystems, and systems. Major trends in the development of technology include increasing miniaturization; improved accuracy; greater fungibility of systems; improved surveillance, data processing, and information and communications technologies; and the development of exotic technologies such as plasma weapons, X-ray lasers, and railguns (Williams, 1987: 280-3). For Boskma and van der Meer (1986: 23), the primary characteristics of emerging technologies are automation, cybernation, and integration. In an earlier piece (Burt, 1981: 47-53), the most significant technological developments were identified as occurring in precision guidance (seeker and correlation guidance and precision positioning); remote guidance and control; munitions; target identification and acquisition; command, control, and communications (C^3); and electronic warfare. Walker (1986) focused on emerging technologies for surveillance, guidance, and warhead design. Martin (1986) identified new military research and development initiatives as including the Advanced Integrated Propulsion System (AIPS) for land-combat vehicles, closed-cycle electric torpedo propulsion, metal-matrix composites, short take-off and landing (STOL) aircraft, the all-composite helicopter, the Very High Speed Integrated Circuits (VHSIC) project, Ada software, artificial intelligence, robotics, biotechnology, and digital architecture. New and emerging technologies such as microelectronics, ceramics, composite and crystalline materials, and infrared, visible, and radar sensors are contributing to the development of products such as new computers, signal processors, guidance and intelligence-gathering sensors, and battle-management and expert systems (Tsipis, 1989: 8-26). Among the subsystems and systems already generated by new technologies are precision guided munitions (PGMs), remotely piloted vehicles (RPVs), Doppler target acquisition radar, remote sensors, area weapons, image intensifiers and thermal sights, and military cybernetics (Miettinen, 1983: 56-64).

These and other new and emerging technologies are expected to find a variety of applications. Mission areas in which they are likely to be utilized range from strategic to tactical offence and defence (see O'Neill, 1985). Tsipis (1989: 29-46) notes that at the strategic level, new technologies may enhance the counterforce capabilities of land-based ballistic missiles; further improve the accuracy of submarine-launched ballistic missiles (SLBMs) and the ability to command, control, and communicate with SLBM platforms; ensure the continuing ability of long-range bombers and cruise missiles to penetrate air defences; and benefit area defence, point defence, anti-submarine warfare, and air defence efforts. At the tactical, battlefield level, new technologies may lead to improvements in the weaponry, sensors, and battle-management systems employed in ground, air, and naval operations (Tsipis, 1989: 46-61). Specific tactical applications are expected (Moodie, 1989: 42-57) in the areas of reconnaissance, surveillance, and target acquisition, fire-power (both accuracy and range), C^3, mobility, concealment (through low observable or stealth technology), and protection (as provided, perhaps, by reactive armour).

Despite the occasional confident forecast, the implications of new and emerging technologies for military strategy, doctrine, force planning, operations, and tactics are not readily apparent. The difficulties inherent in discerning the potential impact of new and emerging technologies are evident in efforts to categorize them as offensive or defensive. Herolf (1988), for instance, argues that new technology bolsters defensive strategies and postures. Burt (1981: 57, 58), however, suggests that while 'it is tempting to conclude that the defence stands to gain over the offence', it is possible that 'the attacker could use the defensive capabilities of the new technologies for offensive ends'; the offensive or defensive character of new technologies, therefore, is context-dependent. Yet Welch (1990: 118) asserts that 'the either-or of offence-defence superiority is blurred by technology and becomes a neither-nor.'

In spite of pervasive fascination with the performance-enhancing capabilities of the new and emerging technologies, they have not been greeted with universal enthusiasm. Boskma and van der Meer (1986: 23) caution that new and emerging technologies may fuel degenerative action-reaction arms races. For Drell and Johnson (1989: 97-100), the new technologies portend a less stable strategic environment marked by counterforce capabilities and war-fighting strategies. They contribute to the erosion of the distinction between nuclear and conventional weapons, thereby blurring the nuclear threshold (Welch, 1990: 114; Williams, 1987: 284). It has been suggested (Boskma and van der Meer, 1986: 23-5; Miettinen, 1983: 65-6; Moodie, 1989: 58-61) that at the tactical, operational level, in addition to compelling the integration of land, air, and sea operations, technology is broadening the scope and increasing the fluidity and lethality of the battlefield, compressing reaction time, and increasing logistical support requirements. Williams (1987: 283) fears that despite the 'illusion of controllability' fostered by improved C^3I (Command, Control, Communication and Intelligence) and more discriminate weaponry, 'control is likely to become increasingly tenuous', and 'conflict may become less manageable.' New and emerging technologies also contribute to the spiralling costs of modern weaponry and the increasing capital intensity, and hence depersonalization, of the military and war. And the continuing diffusion of these technologies has potentially far-reaching implications for global and regional order and stability.

Diffusion of Military Technology

The diffusion of military technology is a phenomenon as old as military technology itself. Though it is too seldom the subject of sustained inquiry by historians, broad historical overviews, focusing primarily on the diffusion of military technologies among European countries and from them to Africa, Asia, and the Americas, are provided by Cipolla (1965), McNeill (1982), and Parker (1988). A recent account of the spread of European military technologies and techniques to, and their role in military reforms carried out by, Russia, the Ottoman Empire, Egypt, China, and Japan from 1600 to 1914 is provided by Ralston (1990). The utilization of superior arms by imperialist European powers in the subjugation of Africa and Asia during the nineteenth century, depicted by Headrick (1981), resulted not only in the introduction of European military technology to those regions, but also in its assimilation by the indigenous inhabitants integrated into colonial militaries, and its eventual use against colonial occupation forces. In an extremely insightful contribution, Krause (1990) drew on the historical literature to examine the process of military technology diffusion through material, design, and capacity transfers in an evolving international arms-transfer system among three tiers of core, semi-peripheral, and peripheral producers, and material transfers between producers and consumers, since the emergence of the European state system.

Far more analytical attention has been focused on the contemporary spread of military technology. There are essentially two dimensions to the post-world-wars diffusion of military technology: the conventional and the unconventional. The conventional dimension encompasses the diffusion of aircraft, armoured vehicles, missiles, and naval vessels, while the unconventional dimension encompasses the diffusion of the NBC (nuclear, biological, and chemical) weapons of mass destruction.

Diffusion of these capabilities has proceeded simultaneously since 1945. The spread of weapons of mass destruction, as evident in the alarm generated during late 1990 and early 1991 by Iraq's chemical, biological, and emerging nuclear capabilities, has commanded a large share of the analytical attention devoted to the contemporary diffusion of military technology. Yet it is the horizontal proliferation of conventional weaponry that has provided ever more actors in the international system with fungible military capabilities.

Diffusion of Conventional Military Technology

The diffusion of conventional military technologies has involved flows of a range of types and forms of military technologies, both among the advanced industrial countries of the North and from those countries to the developing countries of the South. Transfers of military equipment and design and production technologies were concentrated among the advanced industrial countries during the emergence of the post-World War II international arms market. The United States emerged as the predominant source of military technology. Its new NATO allies absorbed the bulk of American military exports through the 1950s, though the share of exports directed to select friends and allies in the developing world, especially in East Asia and the Middle East, increased gradually.

Soviet military technology transfers evolved in a similar manner. While the United States supplied its NATO allies, the Soviet Union armed what became its Warsaw Pact allies. And though the preponderance of its military technology transfers went to its East European clients, as indicated by the initiation of military transfers to North Korea in 1949, Egypt in 1955, and Iraq in 1958, the proportion of Soviet transfers flowing to developing countries also increased gradually. Yet the Soviet Union, unlike the United States, was a relatively minor source of military exports for nearly two decades after World War II. Not until the mid-to-late 1960s did the Soviet Union become a major supplier, and not until the 1970s did it rival the United States as a source of military technology. Of the other future major suppliers, only Britain was an important source of military technology exports during the early post-war years.

The economic recovery of Europe and the decolonization of Africa and Asia contributed to supply- and demand-side changes in the international arms market that dramatically altered the early patterns of the diffusion of conventional military technologies analysed by Catrina (1988), Harkavy (1975), Leiss, Kemp, Hoagland, Refson, and Fischer (1970), and the Stockholm International Peace Research Institute (SIPRI; 1971). On the supply side, France, the Federal Republic of Germany, and Italy joined the United States, the Soviet Union, and Britain as major sources of military technology. On the demand side, the newly independent developing countries of Africa and Asia, plus the not so newly independent developing countries of Latin America, emerged as the primary recipients of conventional military technology transfers. Indeed, as indicated by Catrina's (1988: 21) presentation of US Arms Control and Disarmament Agency (ACDA) arms-transfer data, developing (rather than advanced industrial) countries have absorbed at least fifty per cent of the world's annual conventional military-technology imports every year since 1965. From 1970 to 1986, developing countries imported an annual average of 72 per cent of global military-technology transfers (derived from data presented in Catrina, 1988: 21).

As advanced industrial countries were displaced by developing countries as the principal recipients of conventional military-technology transfers, transfers burgeoned. From 1963 to 1984, when they peaked, the value of global transfers increased fivefold—from $9.9 billion in 1963 to $50.1 billion in 1984. The value of transfers to developing countries alone increased almost ninefold—from $4.5 billion to $39.2 (values in constant 1984 US dollars; derived from ACDA transfer data presented in Catrina, 1988: 21).

This dramatic, near-exponential increase in the value of transfers was accompanied by, and in part the result of, an increase in the sophistication of the military technology transferred. The rapidly rising value and volume of transfers represented not the surplus, often obsolescent, World War II-era equipment transferred during the late 1940s and the 1950s, but advanced, frequently state-of-the-art, and consequently more expensive, military hardware that, as Catrina (1988: 26-7) notes, narrowed the technological gap between supplier and recipient. The massive transfer of military capabilities from advanced industrial countries to the developing countries of Africa, Asia, and Latin America that occurred during the 1970s and 1980s provided the developing world with sophisticated military hardware that included super- and subsonic combat aircraft, helicopters, main and medium battle tanks, tracked and wheeled armoured fighting vehicles, guided and ballistic missiles, major and minor surface warships, guided-missile patrol boats, and submarines.[14] Some developing countries, such as Iraq and North and South Korea, built up large inventories of imported military equipment.

The diffusion of conventional military technologies from advanced industrial to developing countries has resulted from the transfer of military production capabilities as well as hardware. Developing countries have not been content simply to acquire off-the-shelf military hardware from foreign suppliers. In an attempt to reduce, if not eliminate, the vulnerabilities and constraints inherent in dependence on foreign arms suppliers, increasing numbers of developing countries have exploited the often intense competition among suppliers in the international arms market to acquire, through compensatory trade agreements (also known as offsets), the know-how needed to build indigenous military production capabilities and substitute domestically manufactured for imported weaponry. Offset packages, now a familiar feature of arms-transfer agreements (see Klare, 1983; Neuman, 1985), have provided for the transfer of military production technology to Third World importers, often in the form of assembly operations, co-production, licensed production, and subcontractor production.

Technology thus acquired has permeated the development of military industrial capabilities, which typically evolve in a five-stage process (Ross, 1988: 167; 1991: 82-3). In the first stage, equipment is imported in the form of prefabricated components and is simply assembled in-country. The foreign supplier assists in setting up assembly operations and provides technical training, including instruction in the utilization of equipment employed in weapons inspection, evaluation, and testing, as well as instruction in assembly operations. Actual production begins during the second stage, when weapons components are manufactured under licence agreements with foreign suppliers. Although the entire weapon or system is not yet produced, an increasing number of components are fabricated domestically. In the third stage, foreign weapons are produced under licence. Technological skills and manufacturing capabilities developed in earlier stages are utilized to modify, redesign, or reproduce foreign weapons in the fourth stage. Domestically designed arms are produced in the fifth stage. Typically, production during this last stage progresses from production based on domestic research and development that still incorporates components designed or produced abroad, to production founded on autonomous indigenous research and development without significant imported inputs.

Building on foreign technology, fifty-three developing countries, according to SIPRI data (Brzoska and Ohlson, 1986a: 16; 1986b: 305-49), had developed the capability to manufacture either small arms and/or ammunition, or one of the four major types of conventional weapons—aircraft, armoured vehicles, missiles, and naval vessels—by the mid-1980s. Thirty-five of the fifty-three were manufacturing at least one of the four types of major weapons. Eight—Argentina, Brazil, Egypt, India, Israel, South Korea, South Africa, and Taiwan—had proven across-the-board capabilities, and another eight were developing such capabilities. In 1950 the only developing countries producing any of the four types of major conventional weapons were Argentina, Brazil, Colombia, and India (Neuman, 1984: 172).

A particular manifestation of the continuing diffusion of military technologies that has recently captured the attention of policy-makers and analysts alike is the spread of ballistic missiles to the developing world. Though generally classified as conventional weapons (Nolan, 1989b), ballistic missiles, like other delivery systems, can be used to deliver nuclear, biological, and chemical warheads as well as conventional explosives over long distances. The US Director of Central Intelligence, in testimony before the Committee on Foreign Relations of the US Senate in 1989, forecast that 'by the year 2000, at least fifteen developing countries will be producing their own ballistic missiles' (Webster, 1989: 30). Eleven developing countries with deployed ballistic missiles and eight countries with a total of eighteen ballistic-missile development programmes were included among the sixteen developing countries identified by the US Arms Control and Disarmament Agency (1989) as either possessing or developing ballistic missiles in 1989. According to a more recent count (Carus, 1990: 1), 'Twenty-two countries in the Third World currently possess ballistic missiles or are actively attempting to acquire them. Thirteen of these countries have programs to design and build ballistic missiles, and at least fifteen have operational missile forces.' Additional compilations of ballistic-missile capabilities in the developing world have been provided by Hackett (1990), Karp (1988, 1989, 1990), Navias (1990), Nolan (1989a), Nolan and Wheelon (1990), and Shuey et al. (1989). The number of developing countries identified by these analysts either as having deployed ballistic missiles or as engaged in active ballistic-missile development projects varies. Yet it is clear that ballistic-missile technology is spreading to an increasing number of countries in the developing world—despite the Missile Technology Control Regime (MTCR) established by Britain, Canada, France, the Federal Republic of Germany, Italy, Japan, and the United States in 1987.

Aided and abetted by the adverse market conditions confronting the major arms suppliers, their own industrialization, and the developmental role of the state in the Third World, an increasing number of developing countries are finding that the military industrialization that has provided them with indigenously manufactured missiles and other conventional weaponry is enabling them to nationalize arms acquisition and reduce their dependence upon imported arms. His empirical analysis of the relationship between arms imports and military industrialization led Looney (1989: 19) to the finding that 'arms producers have been able to significantly reduce their levels of, and dependence on, external sources of arms'. Indeed, pervasive attempts by developing countries to substitute domestically produced for imported weaponry, in combination with deteriorating economic conditions, especially high levels of foreign indebtedness, and the often large stockpiles of weapons accumulated during the Third World's arms-buying spree of the 1970s, contributed to the declining demand for imported arms and the consequent stagnant international arms market of the 1980s. And with the transition from import substitution to export promotion, already well under way for, among others, Brazil, Israel, and South Korea, arms producers in the developing world have entered the export market in an attempt to challenge the market dominance of their former suppliers (Ross, 1989a).

Diffusion of NBC Technologies

The diffusion of unconventional military technologies — the nuclear, biological, and chemical weapons of mass destruction — has been both less extensive and less driven by market forces than the diffusion of conventional military technologies. Fewer countries possess NBC weapons than conventional weapons. The spread of NBC technologies that has occurred has been largely clandestine, in black or grey markets outside the legitimate international markets in which conventional military (and non-military) goods and services are generally exchanged, and in contravention of national and international export guidelines.[15] NBC weapons technologies are not openly traded in the international market. Their diffusion, consequently, has been more difficult to monitor. Yet it has also been more amenable to supplier control.

A large and expanding literature, surveyed by Buzan (1987: 57-65) and Potter (1989), has been generated by widely held concerns about the potentially adverse consequences of nuclear proliferation. In contrast to the vertical proliferation of nuclear weapons, however, their horizontal proliferation has proceeded relatively slowly. Contrary to early projections of the future number of nuclear armed countries — the Nth (or additional nuclear-armed) country problem — that forecast the presence of perhaps dozens of nuclear powers by 1980 (National Planning Association, 1958: 41), the nuclear club remains rather small. In addition to the first nuclear power, the United States, only the former Soviet Union, Britain, France, and China have both deployed and demonstrated nuclear capabilities. While Israel, India, Pakistan, and South Africa have been identified as de facto nuclear states, and Iran, Iraq, Libya, North Korea, Taiwan, Brazil, and Argentina are on the watch list

(Spector, with Smith, 1990), the Non-Proliferation Regime, which encompasses a variety of formal and informal multilateral, bilateral, and unilateral codes and arrangements, such as the International Atomic Energy Agency and the Non-Proliferation Treaty (Nye, 1981; Smith, 1987; Ward, 1987), apparently has effectively stemmed, if not halted, the spread of nuclear weaponry, despite the variety of political, military, and economic incentives (reviewed by Potter, 1989) to acquire nuclear weapons. Of the twelve countries identified by the National Planning Association (1960: 28) as on the nuclear threshold in 1960, only three—China, France, and India—have actually exercised the nuclear option. Since the United States dropped atomic bombs on Hiroshima and Nagasaki in 1945, nuclear proliferation has occurred at a rate of only one new nuclear power about every eleven years, if just those countries with deployed and demonstrated capabilities are counted, and one about every six years if the de facto nuclear powers listed above are included as well. Perhaps most important, 140 countries, by signing and ratifying the Non-Proliferation Treaty, have formally elected to maintain their nuclear innocence and not exercise the nuclear option. And the diffusion of nuclear capabilities, unlike the spread of conventional military technologies, has not yet provided states with military power employable on the battlefield.

Though they are more readily available, and perhaps more usable, than nuclear weapons, the diffusion of biological and chemical weapons has, until recently, received far less attention than the proliferation of nuclear weapons. Despite the Geneva Protocol of 1925, which prohibited the use of both chemical and bacteriological agents, and the Biological Weapons Convention of 1972, which banned the development, production, stockpiling, acquisition, and transfer of biological agents and toxins, and required the destruction of such agents and toxins and their means of delivery upon entry into force of the convention (US Arms Control and Disarmament Agency, 1990: 129-41), 'the world is presently witnessing a disturbing and dangerous trend in the increasing efforts by states to acquire biological weapons' according to the testimony of the US Assistant Secretary of State for Politico-Military Affairs before the Senate Governmental Affairs Committee and its Permanent Subcommittee on Investigations (Holmes, 1989: 43). The US Director of Central Intelligence (Webster, 1989: 30) in 1989 stated that 'at least 10 countries are working to produce both previously known and futuristic biological weapons.' In the developing world, according to data compiled by McCain (1990: 265), four countries—Iran, Iraq, Syria, and North Korea—possessed biological weapons stocks; six were engaged in significant research and development and/or acquisition efforts; and another eight were pursuing low-level research and development and/or acquisition efforts in 1990.

Even more countries are working to acquire chemical weapons. The Director of Central Intelligence, again, stated in 1989 that 'we believe that as many as 20 countries may be developing chemical weapons, and we expect

Brodie, Bernard (1976). 'Technological Change, Strategic Doctrine, and Political Outcomes'. Pp. 263-306 in Klaus Knorr, ed. *Historical Dimensions of National Security Problems*. Lawrence, KA: Univ. Press of Kansas, for the National Security Education Program.

Brodie, Bernard, and Fawn Brodie (1973). *From Crossbow to H-Bomb: The Evolution of the Weapons and Tactics of Warfare*, revised and enlarged ed. Bloomington: Indiana Univ. Press.

Brzoska, Michael, and Thomas Ohlson (1986a). 'Arms Production in the Third World: An Overview'. Pp. 7-33 in Brzoska and Ohlson, eds (1986b).

Brzoska, Michael, and Thomas Ohlson, eds (1986b). *Arms Production in the Third World*. London: Taylor & Francis, for the Stockholm International Peace Research Institute.

Brzoska, Michael, and Thomas Ohlson (1987). *Arms Transfers to the Third World 1971-85*. Oxford: Oxford Univ. Press for the Stockholm International Peace Research Institute.

Burt, Richard (1981). 'New Weapons Technologies: Debate and Directions'. Pp. 46-77 in Jonathan Alford, ed. *The Impact of New Military Technology*. Westmead: Gower, for the International Institute for Strategic Studies.

Buzan, Barry (1987). *An Introduction to Strategic Studies: Military Technology and International Relations*. New York: St Martin's.

Buzan, Barry, and Guatam Sen (1990). 'The Impact of Military Research and Development Priorities on the Evolution of the Civil Economy in Capitalist States'. *Review of International Studies* 16, 4: 321-39.

Carus, W. Seth (1990). *Ballistic Missiles in the Third World: Threat and Response*. The Washington Papers 146. New York: Praeger, for the Center for Strategic and International Studies.

Catrina, Christian (1988). *Arms Transfers and Dependence*. New York: Taylor & Francis, for the United Nations Institute for Disarmament Research.

Cipolla, Carlo M. (1965). *Guns, Sails and Empires: Technological Innovation and the Early Phase of European Expansion 1400-1700*. New York: Pantheon.

Clark IV, Asa A. (1989). 'The Role of Technology in U.S. National Security: An Introduction'. Pp. 3-20 in Asa A. Clark IV and John F. Lilley, eds. *Defense Technology*. New York: Praeger.

Cooper, Earl D., and Steven M. Shaker (1988). 'The Military Forecasters'. *The Futurist* 22, 3: 37-43.

Cooper, Richard N., and Ann L. Hollick (1985). 'International Relations in a Technologically Advanced Future'. Pp. 227-65 in Keatley (1985).

Deitchman, Seymour J. (1983). *Military Power and the Advance of Technology: General Purpose Military Forces for the 1980s and Beyond*. Boulder, CO: Westview.

Drell, Sidney D., and Thomas J. Johnson (1989). 'Technological Trends and Strategic Forces'. Pp. 85–115 in Asa A. Clark IV and John F. Lilley, eds. *Defense Technology*. New York: Praeger.

Dupuy, Trevor N. (1984). *The Evolution of Weapons and Warfare*. Fairfax, VA: Hero Books.

Evangelista, Matthew (1988). *Innovation and the Arms Race: How the United States and the Soviet Union Develop New Military Technologies*. Ithaca: Cornell Univ. Press.

Gansler, Jacques S. (1980). *The Defense Industry*. Cambridge, MA: MIT Press.

George, Alexander L. (1979). 'Case Studies and Theory Development: The Method of Structured, Focused Comparison'. Pp. 43–68 in Paul Gordon Lauren, ed. *Diplomacy: New Approaches in History, Theory, and Policy*. New York: Free Press.

Gummett, Philip, and Judith Reppy, eds (1988). *The Relations between Defence and Civil Technologies*. Dordrecht: Kluwer Academic Publishers.

Hackett, James T. (1990). 'The Ballistic Missile Epidemic', *Global Affairs* 5, 1: 38–57.

Harkavy, Robert E. (1975). *The Arms Trade and International Systems*. Cambridge, MA: Ballinger.

Harris, Elisa D. (1989–90). 'Stemming the Spread of Chemical Weapons'. *Brookings Review* 8, 1: 39–45.

Headrick, Daniel R. (1981). *The Tools of Empire: Technology and European Imperialism in the Nineteenth Century*. New York: Oxford Univ. Press.

Herolf, Gunilla (1988). 'New Technology Favors Defense'. *Bulletin of the Atomic Scientists* 44, 7: 42–4.

Hieronymi, Otto, ed. (1987). *Technology and International Relations*. New York: St Martin's.

Hitch, Charles J., and Roland N. McKean (1960). *The Economics of Defense in the Nuclear Age*. Cambridge, MA: Harvard Univ. Press.

Holloway, David (1983). *The Soviet Union and the Arms Race*. New Haven: Yale Univ. Press.

Holmes, H. Allen (1989). 'Biological Weapons Proliferation', *Department of State Bulletin* 89, 2148: 43–5.

Howard, Michael (1976). *War in European History*. Oxford: Oxford Univ. Press.

Hughes, David (1990). 'Defense Dept. Must Exploit Commercial Technology'. *Aviation Week & Space Technology* (24 Dec.): 23–5.

Jacobsen, Carl G., ed. (1987). *The Uncertain Course: New Weapons, Strategies and Mind-Sets*. Oxford: Oxford Univ. Press for the Stockholm International Peace Research Institute.

Jervis, Robert (1978). 'Cooperation Under the Security Dilemma'. *World Politics* 30, 2: 167–214.

Jervis, Robert (1984). *The Illogic of American Nuclear Strategy*. Ithaca: Cornell Univ. Press.

Jervis, Robert (1989). *The Meaning of the Nuclear Revolution: Statecraft and the Prospect of Armageddon*. Ithaca: Cornell Univ. Press.

Jones, Archer (1989). *The Art of War in the Western World*. Oxford: Oxford Univ. Press.

Karp, Aaron (1988). 'The Frantic Third World Quest for Ballistic Missiles'. *Bulletin of the Atomic Scientists* 44, 5: 14-20.

Karp, Aaron (1989). 'Ballistic Missile Proliferation in the Third World'. Pp. 287-318 in Stockholm International Peace Research Institute. *SIPRI Yearbook 1989: World Armaments and Disarmament*. Oxford: Oxford Univ. Press for the Stockholm International Peace Research Institute.

Karp, Aaron (1990). 'Ballistic Missile Proliferation'. Pp. 369-91 in Stockholm International Peace Research Institute. *SIPRI Yearbook 1990: World Armaments and Disarmament*. Oxford: Oxford Univ. Press for the Stockholm International Peace Research Institute.

Keatley, Anne G., ed. (1985). *Technological Frontiers and Foreign Relations*. Washington, DC: National Academy Press.

Kincade, William H. (1987). 'New Military Capabilities: Propellants and Implications'. Pp. 69-77 in Carl G. Jacobsen, ed.

King, Alexander (1987). 'Science, Technology and International Relations: Some Comments and a Speculation'. Pp. 9-24 in Hieronymi, ed. (1987).

Klare, Michael T. (1983). 'The Unnoticed Arms Trade: Exports of Conventional Arms-Making Technology'. *International Security* 8, 2: 68-90.

Klare, Michael T. (1986). 'Global Arms Transfer Patterns in the 1980s: The State of the Trade'. *Journal of International Affairs* 40, 1: 1-21.

Klare, Michael T. (1988). 'Secret Operatives, Clandestine Trades: The Thriving Black Market for Weapons'. *Bulletin of the Atomic Scientists* 44, 3: 16-24.

Klare, Michael T. (1988-9). 'Deadly Convergence: The Perils of the Arms Trade'. *World Policy Journal* 6, 1: 141-68.

Krause, Keith (1990). 'The Political Economy of the International Arms Transfer System: The Diffusion of Military Technique via Arms Transfers'. *International Journal* 45, 3: 687-722.

Krauthammer, Charles (1990-1). 'The Unipolar Moment'. *Foreign Affairs* 70, 1: 23-33.

Kurth, James R. (1973). 'Why We Buy the Weapons We Do'. *Foreign Policy* 11: 33-56.

Kurth, James R. (1979). 'The Political Consequences of the Product Cycle: Industrial History and Political Outcomes'. *International Organization* 33, 1: 1-34.

Kurth, James R. (1989). 'The Military-Industrial Complex Revisited'. Pp. 195-215 in Joseph Kruzel, ed. *American Defense Annual 1989-1990*. Lexington, MA: D.C. Heath.

Landes, David S. (1969). *The Unbound Prometheus: Technological Change and Industrial*

Development in Western Europe from 1750 to the Present. Cambridge: Cambridge Univ. Press.

Leiss, Amelia C., Geoffrey Kemp, John N. Hoagland, Jacob S. Refson, and Harold E. Fischer (1970). *Arms Transfers to Less Developed Countries*. Cambridge, MA: Arms Control Project, Center for International Studies, MIT.

Leopold, George (1991). 'Technology Impetus Flows From Civilian to Military'. *Defense News* 29 (2 Dec.).

Levy, Jack S. (1984). 'The Offensive/Defensive Balance of Military Technology: A Theoretical and Historical Analysis'. *International Studies Quarterly* 28, 2: 219-38.

Looney, Robert (1989). 'Have Third-World Arms Industries Reduced Arms Imports?'. *Current Research on Peace and Violence* 10, 1: 15-26.

Lundin, S.J. (1990a). 'Chemical and Biological Warfare: Developments in 1989'. Pp. 107-40 in Stockholm International Peace Research Institute. *SIPRI Yearbook 1990: World Armaments and Disarmament*. London: Oxford Univ. Press.

Lundin, S.J. (1990b). 'Multilateral and Bilateral Talks on Chemical and Biological Weapons'. Pp. 521-44 in Stockholm International Peace Research Institute. *SIPRI Yearbook 1990: World Armaments and Disarmament*. London: Oxford Univ. Press.

Mandelbaum, Michael (1979). *The Nuclear Question: The United States and Nuclear Weapons, 1946-1976*. Cambridge: Cambridge Univ. Press.

Mandelbaum, Michael (1981). *The Nuclear Revolution: International Politics before and after Hiroshima*. Cambridge: Cambridge Univ. Press.

Martin, Edith (1986). 'New Initiatives in Defense R&D'. Pp. 3-11 in Stephen J. Andriole, ed. *High Technology Initiatives in C³I*. Washington, DC: AFCEA International Press.

McCain III, John S. (1990). 'Proliferation in the 1990s: Implications for US Policy and Force Planning'. *Military Technology* 14, 1: 262-7.

McNeill, William H. (1982). *The Pursuit of Power: Technology, Armed Force, and Society since A.D. 1000*. Chicago: Chicago Univ. Press.

Merrill, Robert S. (1968). 'The Study of Technology'. Pp. 576-89 in David L. Sills, ed. *International Encyclopedia of the Social Sciences* 15. New York: Macmillan and the Free Press.

Miettinen, Jorma K. (1983). 'The Effect of New Military Technology on Future Battlefield Tactics and the Structure of Armed Forces'. Pp. 51-73 in William Gutteridge and Trevor Taylor, eds. *The Dangers of New Weapon Systems*. New York: St Martin's.

Milward, Alan S. (1977). *War, Economy and Society 1939-1945*. Berkeley: Univ. of California Press.

Moodie, Michael (1989). *The Dreadful Fury: Advanced Military Technology and the Atlantic Alliance*. The Washington Papers, 136. New York: Praeger, for The Center for Strategic and International Studies.

National Planning Association (1958). *1970 Without Arms Control: Implications of*

Skolnikoff, Eugene B. (1967). *Science, Technology, and American Foreign Policy*. Cambridge, MA: MIT.

Smith, Roger K. (1987). 'Explaining the Non-Proliferation Regime: Anomalies for Contemporary International Relations Theory'. *International Organization* 41, 2: 253-81.

Smoke, Richard (1984). *National Security and the Nuclear Dilemma: An Introduction to the American Experience*. Reading, MA: Addison-Wesley.

Snow, Donald M. (1991). 'High Technology and National Security: A Preliminary Assessment'. *Armed Forces & Society* 17, 2: 243-58.

Snyder, Jack (1984). *The Ideology of the Offensive: Military Decision Making and the Disasters of 1914*. Ithaca: Cornell Univ. Press.

Snyder, Jack (1985). 'Civil-military Relations and the Cult of the Offensive, 1914 and 1984'. Pp. 108-46 in Steven E. Miller, ed. *Military Strategy and the Origins of the First World War*. Princeton, NJ: Princeton Univ. Press.

Spector, Leonard S., with Jacqueline R. Smith (1990). *Nuclear Ambitions: The Spread of Nuclear Weapons 1989-1990*. Boulder, CO: Westview.

Stockholm International Peace Research Institute (1971). *The Arms Trade with the Third World*. London: Paul Elek.

Szyliowicz, Joseph S. (1981). 'Technology, The Nation State: An Overview'. Pp. 1-39 in Szyliowicz, ed. *Technology and International Affairs*. New York: Praeger.

Thee, Marek (1985). *Military Technology, Military Strategy and the Arms Race: Their Interaction*. Oslo: International Peace Research Institute.

Tsipis, Kosta (1989). *New Technologies, Defense Policy, and Arms Control*. New York: Harper & Row.

United States Arms Control and Disarmament Agency (1989). 'Ballistic Missile Proliferation in the Developing World'. Pp. 17-20 in United States Arms Control and Disarmament Agency, *World Military Expenditures and Arms Transfers 1988*. Washington, DC: United States Arms Control and Disarmament Agency.

United States Arms Control and Disarmament Agency (1990). *Arms Control and Disarmament Agreements: Texts and Histories of the Negotiations*. Washington, DC: United States Arms Control and Disarmament Agency.

Van Creveld, Martin (1989). *Technology and War from 2000 B.C. to the Present*. New York: Free Press.

Van Evera, Stephen (1985). 'The Cult of the Offensive and the Origins of the First World War'. Pp. 58-107 in Steven E. Miller, ed. *Military Strategy and the Origins of the First World War*. Princeton, NJ: Princeton Univ. Press.

Van Evera, Stephen (1990-1). 'Primed for Peace: Europe After the Cold War'. *International Security* 15, 3: 7-57.

Vernon, Raymond (1971). *Sovereignty at Bay: the Multinational Spread of U.S. Enterprises*. New York: McGraw-Hill.

Walker, Paul F. (1986). 'Emerging Technologies and Conventional Defence'. Pp. 27–43 in Frank Barnaby and Marlies ter Borg, eds. *Emerging Technologies and Military Doctrine: A Political Assessment*. New York: St Martin's.

Ward, Barclay (1987). 'Nuclear Proliferation'. Pp. 147–64 in Paul F. Diehl and Lock K. Johnson, eds. *Through the Straits of Armageddon: Arms Control Issues and Prospects*. Athens, GA: Univ. of Georgia Press.

Webster, William H. (1989). Statement of Hon. William H. Webster, Director of Central Intelligence. Pp. 29–120 in *Chemical and Biological Weapons Threat: The Urgent Need for Remedies*. Hearings of the Committee on Foreign Relations, United States Senate, 101st Congress, 1st Session. Washington, DC: US Government Printing Office.

Webster's Third New International Dictionary of the English Language (1981). Springfield, MA: Merriam–Webster.

Welch, Thomas J. (1990). 'Technology Change and Security'. *Washington Quarterly* 13, 2: 111–20.

Williams, Phil. (1987). 'Emerging Technology, Exotic Technology and Arms Control'. Pp. 279–93 in Carl G. Jacobsen, ed.

The Uncertain Course: New Weapons, Strategies and Mind-Sets. Oxford: Oxford Univ. Press for the Stockholm International Peace Research Institute.

Winner, Langdon (1977). *Autonomous Technology: Technics-out-of-Control as a Theme in Political Thought*. Cambridge, MA: MIT.

Wright, Quincy (1965). *A Study of War*, 2nd ed. Chicago: Univ. of Chicago Press.

Zysman, John (1991). 'US Power, Trade and Technology'. *International Affairs* 67, 1: 81–106.

chapter seven

Production and Security

Robert W. Cox

Production and security, the linked themes of this chapter, are not to be thought of as independent and dependent variables. Their relationship is reciprocal or dialectical. Furthermore, the relationship of these two terms should be understood as taking place within a third term: the changing structures of world order. This chapter sketches a framework for thinking about these relationships in structural terms by placing the contemporary world in its historical dimension. It offers not an empirical study but some linked hypotheses that may be suggestive for more empirical investigation.

Fordism and Post-Fordism

What is the relationship of 'production' to military power and world order? Two critical thresholds in the contemporary history of production are separated by about one hundred years.[1] During the last decades of the nineteenth century, a new system of production was initiated, which (with a certain anachronism in naming) is now called Fordism. Following a similar break in the dominant pattern of production, the era of post-Fordism is being initiated now, in the last decades of the twentieth century.

Fordism is a complex phenomenon.[2] In purely technological terms it is based on mass production, the assembly line, and the replacement of the skilled worker under factory discipline by a large proportion of semi-skilled, quickly trainable workers in Taylorized production systems. This new structure of production was linked to new structures of economic organization, consumption and income distribution, welfare, and the consolidation of the territorial basis of state power. Fordism meant the concentration of economic power in large corporations and the adoption of employment, wage, and welfare policies that would enable mass consumption of standardized goods to sustain mass production.

From its early stages, Fordism encouraged measures of economic nationalism to protect national labour and product markets. In its later stages, Keynesian demand-management policies helped to sustain an alliance of corporate management and organized labour with the state, based on full employment and welfare. Fordism was part and parcel of the world order of rival imperialisms that displaced the putative liberal order of the mid-nineteenth century; and it was consistent with the state system of the mid-twentieth century. Fordism was the basis for international economic relations, the interstate arrangements to regulate transactions among national economies. Fordism was also an integral part of the military security system of the mid-twentieth century: it produced the material basis of military power, provided a model for military organization, and was essential to the national interests of the states constituting the interstate system.

Fordist production began to give way to a new kind of production organization, particularly in the technologically most advanced sectors, following the economic crisis of 1973–74. Business became concerned about restructuring capital, so as to become more competitive in world markets, and pressed its concern upon governments. The international economic relations of the Fordist era were gradually displaced by the emergence of a world economy of transnationalized production and finance that could either escape interstate regulation or become self-regulating with the support or connivance of states.[3]

Post-Fordism meant a shift away from large plants mass-producing standardized goods, towards shorter-run production for a greater variety of more specialized markets. No longer were large numbers of semi-skilled workers to be brought together in big plants. The need now was to combine the outputs of a large number of smaller production units according to shifting demands. The high overhead cost of plant-employed labour and inventory was to be minimized in favour of greater flexibility in staffing and sub-contracting. Post-Fordism is built upon a segmentation of labour markets. It has been accompanied by a weakening of organized labour (whose strength lay very largely in the mass-production industries) and an attack on the welfare state (regarded by business as a cost, obstructing international competitiveness).

Post-Fordist production lends itself to international production: i.e., to linking groups of producers and plants in different territorial jurisdictions in order to supply markets in many countries. It is promoted and sustained by an international financial system that is global in scope, with focal points in major cities—New York, Tokyo, London, Frankfurt. Post-Fordism is the production mode congruent with interdependence within a global economy, just as Fordism was congruent with the system of rival state sovereignties. Whereas Fordism encouraged the organization of national economies under state management, post-Fordism encourages the internationalizing of the state: making the state an instrument for adjusting national economies to the exigencies of world-economy expansion. This has, of course, implications for world order and for the concept of military security.

Today, two concepts of world order stand in conflict: the territorial concept and the globalization concept.[4] Of course, this opposition puts the question more starkly than reality will admit. These are two tendencies rather than two completed structures. And they are not just opposed, but also interrelated. The globalizing economy requires the backing of territorially-based state power to enforce its rules.

Globalization results in a realignment of powers. The United States has assumed the pre-eminent role in the promotion and enforcement of its conception of a global economy that is largely self-regulated by the interactions of private economic agents. Most other states, especially those that are economically more dependent, are constrained to apply internally the adjustment mechanisms that will integrate their economies more fully into this kind of world economy. The United States, however, cannot alone determine the rules and practices of the global economy, and must try to negotiate these with other major economic powers—Europe and Japan notably, and perhaps also China. These other major economic powers hedge their bets between the globalizing and the territorial principles of world order. Their economic practice is conditioned by a higher degree of state involvement. Enforcement of the rules of economic globalization is thus problematical, because there is no firm agreement concerning these rules and probable conflicts of interest among the major powers over particular instances of enforcement.

If observers take a longer historical perspective than the one hundred years of the contemporary era, stretching it backward to two hundred years, then Fordism and its related social and political structures can be seen as a reaction to the socially polarizing effects of what Karl Polanyi (1957) called the self-regulating market. In *The Great Transformation*, Polanyi analysed how the British state used its legal force to create free markets in goods, money, land, and labour. For Polanyi as an economic historian and anthropologist, the self-regulating market was never a natural phenomenon, but the artificial creation of coercive power in the pursuit of a Utopian idea. In response, traditionalists, moralists, and the newly-deprived subaltern classes supported political efforts to counteract the market, and to build through the state and state-supported institutions, like collective bargaining, the means of social protection. 'Fordism' was the ultimate shape of this response.

What happened on the scale of the national economy during the nineteenth century could be repeated on the scale of the global economy in the twenty-first century. By polarizing the satisfied and the deprived within and among national societies, and indeed across territorial boundaries in an increasingly global society, post-Fordism could well arouse a reaction among the disadvantaged and the dispossessed with support from a segment of the competing dominant groups. This could revive the aim of regulating the global economy with the interests of these groups more clearly in mind —a revival of the aim of the New International Economic Order that was on the global agenda in the mid-1970s—and of organizing local economies with a view to social equity.

If and when this reaction occurs, it is likely to have one or more territorial bases that will take steps to insulate themselves from world-economy pressures. Such secessionist territorial powers would use their authority to control finance, trade, investment, production, and access to their country's resources in the interests of explicit national goals.[5] Various names may be applied to such state forms: state capitalism, socialism, and corporatism are some of the well-worn terms that may be replaced by new ones. The common factor is rejection of the notion of the state as serving world-economy exigencies, as being the agency that ensures that global market pressures operate without constraint. This reaffirmation of the territorial principle of economic and social organization will be perceived as challenging the structures of global economy, and will thus encounter the hostility of the territorial power that stands as the military bulwark for globalization.

Fordism and Military Power

There is no inevitability in the course of history. If analysts can discern patterns in the past that can serve as indicators for future possibilities it is because, while outcomes are unpredictable, there are powerful pressures that shape the circumstances in which the future is decided. Knowing these pressures can help distinguish the feasible from the impractical, and thus may enable observers to try to channel events in whichever of the feasible directions appear to be desirable.

In this vein, there was no inevitability in the transformation of manufacture into mass production. In the more industrially-advanced European countries, a craft tradition of high-quality manufacture was well entrenched in the small manufacturing of Birmingham, the steel of Sheffield, and the silk of Lyons, all of which produced varieties of goods for segmented markets. The major factors encouraging mass production were, in the first instance, the American market, which was ready for mass consumption of standard goods; and, in the second, military demand for standardized weapons and munitions.[6] The Singer sewing machine, the Colt, and the Winchester were the harbingers of a new industrial era. In retrospect, the American Civil War provided the necessary threshold and stimulus for future economic organization.

Economies of scale gave mass production of consumer articles a cost advantage over shorter-run specialized manufacture, which guaranteed the spread of mass production. The military demand was particularly important, since, once it was established, any country without a mass-production industry would be vulnerable. Both factors can be assimilated to competition: competition for shares of consumer markets and competition between states. Competition led not to greater differentiation and choice, but to greater uniformity, to homogenization. This effect of competition among capitalist powers was extended in an unlikely manner through the adoption of Fordist production organization by Lenin and the Bolsheviks in Russia.

The social correlates of mass production were also perceived as essential to national security. A modern industrial state could sustain its world-power position only to the extent that it could counter the Communist Manifesto's appeal for the workers of the world to unite, by binding them through loyalty and interest to the state. Bismarck was among the first national leaders to understand that the new industrial working class had to be incorporated within the nation in order to enhance state power. He made overtures to the nascent German socialist movement, introduced a whole series of social insurance measures, and formulated a concept of corporatism, linking workers and employers with the state, as a basis for his drive for German unification and primacy in Europe. Bismarck's approach was closely followed by conservative statesmen in Britain, France, and Italy.[7] The success of this line of policy was demonstrated at the outbreak of World War I when the national labour movements of the Western and Central powers came to the defence of their respective states.[8] The same broad tendency, through national corporatism or tripartism, culminated in the welfare states of the post-World War II period. The Fordist contribution to national security was the integration of industrial labour into the pursuit of national goals.

If military demand was a driving force behind Fordism, productive capacity even more than population became the basis for measuring military capability. Paul Kennedy has recently argued the point in his *The Rise and Fall of the Great Powers* (1987). Kennedy advances a cyclical theory: economic and productive capacity is the basis for developing military power, but beyond a certain point overinvestment in military means becomes a drag upon the nation's economy. A great power whose military might is disproportionately great in relation to its economic performance is on the verge of decline.

The Kennedy thesis can be read into the latter-day Reagan cold-war strategy. The Reagan administration's determination to build up US military force and pursue the Strategic Defense Initiative (SDI) increased the competitive pressure on the Soviet Union to what in retrospect must have been an intolerable level. With a smaller productive capacity, the Soviet Union had to devote a much larger proportion of its capacity than the United States to military consumption, and it had fewer external resources on which to call for its effort. In the final analysis, the outcome of the political–ideological contest was conditioned by economic–productive capacity to sustain high levels of military expenditure.

In the relationship between productive and military capabilities, military demand was for a long time the stimulant of new ways of organizing production. The case of munitions requirements as a shaper of mass production in the early stages of Fordism has been paralleled in more recent times in the development of nuclear power and space technology. The 'great powers' (to employ the term Kennedy borrowed from von Ranke) have subsidized research and development in these fields, and these subsidies have had spin-offs in civilian industrial production. It would be difficult to estimate the full extent to which the direction of technological development since the mid-twentieth century has been determined by military demand, but it is not unreasonable to accord it the status of a primary determinant.

In more recent years, however, the direction of technological flow has become more ambiguous. Military innovations have become more and more dependent upon the progress of civilian technologies. The flow has to a considerable extent been reversed. Military demand is still important, but military R&D now has to draw heavily upon civilian technological development. Nowhere is this more clear than in the aerospace field, and in the relationship between the United States and Japan in this field.

One major industry that did not develop in Japan after World War II was the aircraft industry. The base for aircraft production in those few countries that supply the world market for civilian aircraft has been the demand from their states for military aircraft. Article 9 of Japan's post-war constitution limited Japan's military force to self-defence and precluded the export of arms, so there was no basis for an aircraft industry.

The initiative towards the introduction of an aircraft industry came only in the 1980s; and it was prompted by changes in the civilian economy rather than security considerations. Those large corporate enterprises that were to become the centres of Japan's aerospace industry had until then been the leaders in steel and heavy machinery, industries that were coming under growing competition from the Newly Industrializing Countries (NICs). The need to adjust to a changed world-market environment suggested aerospace as potential new territory. This coincided with US pressure on Japan to circumvent article 9 (which had originated under US dictation), so as to allow Japan to assume a larger share of defence costs. The Japanese initiative in aerospace took advantage of these changed political circumstances, but was precipitated by an oncoming global crisis of Fordism: the spread of labour-intensive heavy industries into the lower-cost labour zones of the NICs. Aerospace offered Japan a chance to break into a world market from which it had hitherto been excluded; and to enter this market, the military point of access was indispensable.

The complexity of the United States-Japan security arrangement enters the picture here. Japan depended upon US military protection. US military aircraft development was, however, becoming less and less able to advance on the basis of its own technological resources alone; it was more and more dependent upon being able to mobilize foreign contributions to its technological growth. The aircraft industry's problem was part of a broader problem, illustrated as well by US efforts to secure foreign participation in the SDI project. The US government and US industry accordingly sought Japanese technology, but at the same time wished to bind any Japanese technological contribution within the framework of security secrecy. The United States also wished (for balance-of-payments reasons) to remain the chief military supplier for the aircraft needs of the Japanese self-defence force. A nascent Japanese military-industrial complex, for its part, envisaged independent Japanese aircraft development, drawing upon existing US technology, as the foundation for a civilian aircraft industry. Japan would do in aircraft what it had already done in automobiles (and what Europe was doing with the Airbus).

The result of these conflicting goals was a compromise. For Japan to 'go it alone' would have provoked a furor in the US Congress and run the risk of a protectionist attack on Japanese access to the US market. Instead, Japan is producing a Japanese development of a US design of a fighter aircraft with a US component of production, and with US access to the new Japanese technology built into the new design.[9] One can see this compromise as leading either to a continuation of a highly integrated US-Japanese aerospace industry or as a step towards a more autonomous Japanese aerospace industry, one whereby Japan can expand its production capacity and technology in this sphere. Both Japan and the United States have military and commercial interests in mind, but for the Japanese the commercial motive may be the dominant consideration for the future.

This sketch has suggested several propositions concerning the relationship between production and security in the Fordist era:

1. Military demand, along with the opening of broad-based civilian markets, was a major determinant of the shift from manufacture to mass production;

2. Fordist social and economic organization created the political basis for sustaining national security interests;

3. Military subsidizing of R&D acted as a major stimulus to the development of civilian production;

4. Overinvestment in military consumption became a drain on the economic capabilities of the great powers;

5. In the most dynamic economies, i.e., in countries whose strength lay in the economic, rather than in the military, field, civilian technologies took the lead in innovation so that further development of military technologies became dependent upon the development of civilian production.

Security Implications of Post-Fordism

A general crisis in Fordism began with the economic downturn in the world economy of the mid-1970s, which stimulated a restructuring of production organization. Broadly speaking, the large, integrated plant mass-producing standardized articles ceased to be the model for the most advanced industries. Markets became more fragmented and specialized and production technologies shifted to supplying shorter runs and greater diversity. This required a more flexible type of production organization based on a relatively small core of permanent workers with polyvalent skills, able to adapt themselves to shifting product design and demand, and a larger proportion of ancillary workforce that could be linked into the production system according to need.

This ancillary workforce—peripheral in relation to the integrated core workforce—is fragmented (or segmented in the terminology of labour economists).[10] Some have less secure jobs in core plants; some are in subcontracted maintenance jobs or temporary employment; some are employed by subcontracting suppliers, or as putting-out workers, or in the underground economy. Frequently, to the fragmentation of production tasks corresponds a fragmentation of group identities: for example, on an ethnic or gender basis.

Post-Fordist production organization thus generates social relations that contrast with those of Fordism. Fordism concentrated workers from different origins in a common mass, providing a basis for strong industrial trade unions. Post-Fordist production organization takes a core of skilled, stably employed workers and integrates them with capital in a relatively privileged status; and it fragments the larger proportion of peripheral workers into a mix of often competing identities. Post-Fordism thereby undermines the strong industrial trade unions that were a force in the making of state policy. The class struggle of post-Fordism is latent, but it is there.

This new pattern of social organization of production has become characteristic of the technologically most advanced sectors. It has also begun to change public-service employment, with the contracting-out of some government services (e.g., franchising of postal work), increasing recourse to private consultants, etc. It is accompanied by some geographical shifts in production within countries, mainly the shift of labour-intensive work to areas where union organization is weak. It is also accompanied by the growth of international production systems based on labour-intensive, energy-intensive, and polluting operations in low-wage countries.

Post-Fordism is congruent with the globalization trend towards greater interdependence not only among countries, but in the operations of individual production organizations. (Globalized production organizations include not only multinational corporations, but also production systems constructed *ad hoc* to link many individual producing units in different countries providing components and assembly of a particular product.) It thus implicitly contradicts the territorial principle that was congruent with Fordism.

Along with this transnational mixing of producing units comes a greater mixing of peoples. A large-scale migration from South to North is in progress, from the Third World to the old core areas of the world economy. This migration obviously generates new social tensions that reinforce the fragmenting tendency of production relations, while obstructing the possibility of a coherent articulated viewpoint on the part of peripheral workers. There is frustration, but no effective outlet for it in social demands. The politics of distant regions surface within the countries of immigration. Local politics come to have a global reach.

The environment becomes an issue. The old Fordist industries were polluters. Post-Fordism cleans up pollution in the core areas, but it generates more pollution in the peripheries. The energy-intensive as well as labour-intensive (usually the same) operations are located in areas less able or willing to defend their interests. Resource extraction proceeds apace in zones that are politically unprotected. Petroleum and other mineral reserves, the trees of the forests, and the fish of the seas are appropriated by the relatively rich without much concern for ecological consequences. The environmental power relationship of exploiters and exploited is charged with a conflict that is only beginning to be articulated—most notably by indigenous peoples, from the Amazon to northern Canada.

The post-Fordist complex is dismantling the welfare state that Fordism built. Together, the erosion of organized labour's strength and capital's insistence that welfare costs are a burden upon international competitiveness overturn the tripartite alliance of government, big labour, and big industry upon which the welfare state and Keynesian demand-management of the economy were grounded. Government now acts to provide internationally oriented business with the best possible conditions, and conspires to obstruct labour's demands. The symbolic signal was given by President Reagan in his action against the air-traffic controllers; but any number of actions by any number of governments could be cited as following that lead.

In the leading capitalist powers, post-Fordist employment structures and politics have left a large part of the population relatively satisfied, while another large part has been economically and socially marginalized, fragmented, and, in effect, depoliticized.[11] Here again, conflict is largely submerged. The alternative to post-Fordist politics has not been formulated and articulated. Fordism thrived in cohesive national societies intent upon embracing all effective social forces within the nation. Post-Fordism deprives the national entity of its social unity; ideologically, it can substitute only a jingoism empty of social content.

The security implications of post-Fordism thus become clear:

1. Greater international interdependence in sophisticated production processes makes these processes the more vulnerable to disruption, whether to supplies of energy or of technological components;

2. Greater international mingling of populations creates potential for dissent by minorities from state goals and, at the extreme, for political use of hostages;

3. New sources of conflict are generated by the core-periphery structuring of production, some identified as centring on ethnicity, some on gender, some on environmental issues, all of which undermine the concept of national identity;

4. Jingoism may produce a momentary psychological impact in an economically fragmented population, but cannot have much staying power in public opinion where it has no material foundation (the late nineteenth-century British worker and the US hard-hat during the Vietnam era were both beneficiaries, in a way, of their countries' imperial strategies, but the peripheral worker of post-Fordism is not);

5. There is a contradiction inherent in post-Fordism: the globalizing interdependence principle is strengthened as the territorial national principle is weakened; but ultimately the security of globalization depends upon military force with a territorial basis.

The United States and Global Security

US Secretary of State James Baker was reported as saying that the Persian Gulf crisis that began in the summer of 1990 was the first crisis of the post-cold-war world. It was a perceptive comment, even if the crisis was not favourable for the future world order projected by the US administration. The US intervention in the Gulf did, however, reveal in action the structure of world power underpinning globalization in the post-Fordist era.

The conflict began at the regional level between forces based on the territorial principle challenging forces deeply embedded in globalizing interdependence. Iraq's goals were to use territorial power to secure economic resources for its own economic recovery from the Iran-Iraq war, and for consolidation of a strong Middle East territorial power that could control resources (oil) required by the world economy, and thereby extract from the world economy a rent that could be used to further its own developmental and security goals. Palestinian claims for statehood are an extension of that goal. (Post-revolutionary Iran's goals, while distinct and potentially conflicting, are also territorially oriented: i.e., to use its economic resources and to control its economic links to the outside world in the interests of nationally determined priorities.)

Kuwait, Saudi Arabia, and the other Gulf states are fully integrated into the interdependent world economy. Indeed, these states are more analogous to large holding companies than to territorial states. The revenues they derive from oil are invested by their rulers through transnational banks into debt and equities around the world. Within the territories of these countries, the workforce is multinational. The region thus contains the elements of conflict between territorial and globalizing principles, both struggling to align themselves with the other major sources of conflict. In this struggle, the territorial principle has the advantage of being more readily able to mobilize the demands of the poor versus the rich, and the claims of cultural specificity versus the homogenizing tendencies of globalism.

The trigger to the conflict was Iraq's effort to constrain Kuwait, through OPEC and other negotiations, to restrict its deliveries of oil to the world market so as to raise the world price of oil. This would have benefited Iraq's goal of reconstruction and development. The issue pitted territorial development against world-economy stability. When Kuwait resisted, Iraq asserted historical claims to Kuwait as an excuse for occupation and annexation. The United States responded as the principal guarantor and enforcer of the globalizing world economic order and, in that role, rallied support from other states deeply concerned about the stability of the world economy.[12]

The role of principal enforcer has, however, evolved as one beset by some basic contradictions. US projection of military power on the world scale has become more salient, while the relative strength of US productive capacity has declined.[13] As a consequence, US military power in defence of world-economy interests has become a *quid pro quo* for foreign support of the US economy.

Two main means of coercion are available to enforce compliance with the exigencies of a globalizing world economy: financial and military. These two have become intertwined, particularly since the mid-1960s. The Vietnam War was a turning point in their relationship as concerns the United States. President Lyndon Johnson proved able to choose *both* guns and butter — both a substantial military commitment abroad and the Great Society programme at home. He was able to do this because foreigners paid for the war. Foreign central banks bought US Treasury bills to roughly the same extent that the US government spent on the war. The US national debt became increasingly a debt held by foreigners, a trend that has continued ever since.[14]

At that time, President de Gaulle of France objected that an unrestrained accumulation of payments deficits by the United States constituted an abuse of the special privilege inherent in the dollar's status as the principal international currency. He signalled his unwillingness either to finance a US war in Indochina that France did not support or to assist in a US takeover of European businesses by accepting an unlimited supply of dollars. France had some leverage at the time in its ability, under the rules of the Bretton Woods system, to exchange dollars for gold, at a time when dollars held by foreigners had come to exceed the value of US gold reserves. The rules then prevailing placed some restraint upon US policy, at least potentially.

Although it shared the French concern over undisciplined US monetary behaviour, West Germany was in effect a US military protectorate. In the mid-1960s, the United States was able to make German acceptance of US public debt the *quid pro quo* for the US military presence in the heart of Europe as a counter to a perceived Soviet threat.[15]

By the 1980s, the rules of the Bretton Woods system, which had some potential for restraint on US policy, ceased to be operative. The link of the dollar to gold was severed in the summer of 1971, and from 1973 the exchange rates of the major world currencies were afloat. Management of the dollar became a matter of negotiation among the treasuries and central banks of the chief industrial powers, and in these negotiations the military power and world role of the US could not but be factors. Under the Reagan presidency, the build-up of US military strength contributed to growing budget deficits. A US trade deficit had also appeared during the 1970s, and it continued to grow apace during this period. The US economy was consuming far beyond its ability to pay.

The accumulating gap continued to be bridged by borrowing from foreigners. At the end of 1981, the United States was in a net world creditor position of $141 billion. By the end of 1987, it had become the world's biggest debtor nation, to the tune of some $400 billion,[16] and the debt has remained high ever since. In the interplay of political pressures among the industrial states, US military power and commitments to allies became counterweights to the compliance of allies with US financial needs. Whereas in the post-war world, US hegemonic leadership had been the means of reviving the economies of the other non-communist industrial countries, now military power could be seen as the justification for exacting tribute. A hegemonic system was becoming transformed into a tributary system.

There is a striking contrast between the US situation as the greatest debtor nation and the situation of other debtor nations. While the United States has been able to attract, cajole, or coerce other nations' political leaders, central bankers, and corporate investors to accept its IOUs, other countries become subject to the rigorous discipline imposed by market forces and by the agencies of the world economy, notably the IMF. Under the euphemistic name of 'adjustment programmes', they are required to impose domestic austerity with the effect of raising unemployment and domestic prices, which fall most heavily on the economically weaker segments of the population. Through the financial mechanism, these debtor states are constrained to play the role of instruments of the world economy, opening their national economies more fully to external pressures. By acquiescing, they contribute to undermining the territorial principle: i.e., the possibility of organizing collective national self-defence against external economic forces. Any show of resistance in favour of an alternative developmental strategy can be met by a series of measures beginning with a cut-off of foreign credit, and progressing through political destabilization, to culminate in covert and ultimately overt military attack.

The uniqueness of the US position in relation to debt cannot be attributed solely, or perhaps even primarily, to wilful policy. It results from a structural inability of the US polity to change certain parameters of the military-debt relationship. Americans have been able to enjoy, through debt, a higher level of consumption than their production would otherwise permit, because foreigners were ready to accept a flow of depreciating dollars. Part of the debt-causing US deficit is attributable to military expenditure (or military-related spending, i.e., payments to client states that provide military staging grounds, like Egypt or the Philippines); and part is attributable to domestic-transfer payments (so-called entitlement programmes), which by and large benefit the American middle class.

The peace dividend anticipated as a result of the end of the cold war seems a much less likely prospect since the Gulf crisis has underscored the US role as enforcer in the world economy. Domestic political resistance to cuts in the entitlement programmes is on a par with resistance to tax increases. Public funds on an unprecedented scale can be taken to cover a government-business scandal in the savings and loan sector, but the rising price of oil resulting from the Gulf conflict effectively precluded any increase in fuel tax that might have been a gesture towards alleviating the deficit. American politicians cannot confront their electors with the prospect of a necessary reduction in their living standards when the Middle East confrontation has been presented as the defence of the American way of life. With no relief in the deficit, there can be no prospect of Washington's undertaking the massive investment in human resources that would be necessary in the long run to raise productivity by enabling the marginalized quarter or third of the population to participate effectively in the economy, so that the US might gradually move out of its dependence on foreign debt sustained by military power. All elements of the military-debt syndrome conspire to prevent an American initiative to transform it.

The structural obstacles to change extend outside the United States, but not quite so obstinately. Those foreigners who hold US debt are increasingly locked in as the exchange rate of the dollar declines. They would suffer losses by shifting to other major currencies; and their best immediate prospect may be to exchange debt for equity by purchasing US assets. In the longer run, however, foreigners may weigh more seriously the option of declining to finance US debt; and if this were to happen it would force the United States into a painful domestic readjustment. Indeed, it is probably the only thing that could precipitate such an adjustment. But there are serious risks for the rest of the world in forcing the world's pre-eminent military power into such a painful course. They are the risks inherent in assessing self-restraint in the use of military power.

Japan is in a particularly delicate position as the major financier of the US deficit. There is a commercial incentive for Japan to hold US debt. By continuing to subscribe to US Treasury bills, Japan maintains access to the US market and appeases the protectionist proclivities of the US Congress. On the other hand, resistance to the conversion of debt into equity has arisen within the United States. There is evidence of intolerance in US domestic opinion for increased Japanese ownership of US assets. (Such intolerance does not arise in the same way, for example, regarding British or Dutch ownership of US assets, which is also considerable.)

Japan, like West Germany, has also been subject to the US *quid pro quo* of financial support for military protection. This incentive is reduced, as dependence on US military cover seems less significant for Japan now that the cold war has ended and the sense of Soviet, now Russian, threat has weakened. By contrast, Japan's security would be seriously threatened by a prolonged disruption in the flow of oil from the Persian Gulf. It is not surprising that influential voices are raised in Japan to criticize the lack of discipline in US domestic and economic policy, to urge Japan to diversify economic relations away from dependence upon the US market, and to advocate an independent political-military position.[17] The risks are, however, still considerable for Japan. The asymmetry in the relationship of the two powers (Japan's relative economic dynamism and the US preponderance of military power) brings to the back of the mind the spectre of Japan as America's Kuwait.

Conclusion

This sketch of the structural model of a crisis in world power relations grounded in the relationship of production to military power is uncomplicated by debate about the motives of actors and moral judgement on their behaviour. There are no good guys or bad guys in this realist model. Indeed, the model is not so much concerned with actors as with the objective forces that condition actions.

The basic distinction around which these forces cluster is that between the territorial and the globalizing principles of world order. This chapter argues that although the globalizing principle is now dominant, the contradictions within it are likely to lead, not next year or even during the present decade but in the course of several decades, to a different kind of world order produced by the interaction of the two principles.

The United States stands at the heart of the contradiction between these two principles: it is the champion of globalization, yet its role as military enforcer is territorially based. Within the US state, the globalizing policies and ideology of the executive branch and the big corporations and banks are contested by territorial protectionism in the Congress, the states, and a sector of domestic business and labour.

The Japanese and European economies have become globalized in practice without entirely sacrificing the territorial principle, retaining it as a safeguard and insurance against risk. Neither (with the exception of Britain in Europe) has assimilated the ideology of globalization to the degree common in the United States. The tradition of a corporatist relationship of state to productive forces remains strong in Europe and Japan. In their economies, aggressive economic expansionism in world markets coexists with social protectionism at home.[18] Russia and China aspire to globalization (or at any rate to further integration into the world economy), but, in the light of their past, find it difficult to dismantle the controls over external economic forces affecting them.

Those countries with the least defences against the socially and economically polarizing consequences of globalization are the Third World countries and the NICs. For them, assertion of the territorial principle is the only means of undertaking an alternative development strategy; and only a few — those with valuable natural resources — can have a chance to survive if they were to pursue such a strategy. When Iraq tried to seize this chance, its action threatened the globalizing world economy's reliance on cheap oil, and its fragile financial structure. It also threatened the balance of domestic forces determining US policy. The Iraqi action accordingly provoked military confrontation.

The Middle East crisis showed the kind of conflict situation that could become characteristic of the transition from globalization to a post-globalization world order. The conflict had the external features of a territorial confrontation; but its implications lie in the transformation of societies through the spread of new production relations, the disturbance and mixing of peoples that has unleashed an affirmation of suppressed identities (ethnic, religious, gender), and the challenge this poses to existing forms of state. This challenge, most visible now in parts of the Third World and in the disintegration of the Soviet empire, will in due time appear within the most powerful centres of the world economy. When it does, the ability of military force to obstruct change will itself be challenged. Power in the world system will become fragmented, and the possibility of culturally diverse alternatives to global homogenization will become more real.

Notes

[1] The usage 'contemporary history' is borrowed from Geoffrey Barraclough (1967). He meant by 'contemporary' a structural shape of the world that is recognizable in its main features today, and that he dated from the last decades of the nineteenth century.

[2] Antonio Gramsci (1971), in his prison notebooks of the early 1930s, used the term 'Fordism' to designate a particular technological–economic–social–moral–political organization of production. It has been adopted by economists of the French regulation school, e.g. Alain Lipietz (1987), and by some American political economists, e.g. Charles Sabel (1982).

[3] On the distinction between international economy and world economy see Madeuf and Michalet (1978).

[4] The point has been argued in Rosecrance (1986).

[5] Hymer (1972) discussed the grounds of conflict between two forms of economic organization: the multinational corporation and national planning, or, in our terms, the globalizing and territorial principles of organization.

[6]Sabel (1982: 44); Landes (1969: 308).

[7]E.H. Carr (1945); Borkenau (1942); Cox (1987: chap. 6). Bismarck, it may be noted, was consistent with Clausewitz, who understood that the French Revolution had created a threshold beyond which military power had to be based upon the solidarity of a nation's people, and could no longer, as in eighteenth-century Europe, be the activity of a military caste employing mercenaries, i.e., distinct from the nation. See Paret (1976).

[8]The exception was Italy, where the socialist movement split, and only that fraction led by Mussolini rallied to the defence of the state.

[9]Packard (1987); Samuels and Whipple (1988); Toshiyuki Toyoda (1988).

[10]Gordon, Edwards and Reich (1982); Wilkinson (1981); Cox (1987: chap. 9).

[11]There is an ideological current within the rich countries that argues for a degree of depoliticization as being essential to the 'governability' of Western-style democracies. Too active participation, in this argument, would place demands upon governments that would preclude the possibility of their carrying out the economic policies required to adjust their countries to the world economy (Crozier, Huntington and Watanuki, 1975). This can be read as a premonition of the coming 'Polanyi effect' discussed above.

[12]It has been objected that Iraq could hardly embody the territorial principle, because it violated the territorial integrity of another state, Kuwait; also that Iraq's economy could not be taken as an example of Fordism, since Iraq's economy relies on oil exports, not manufacturing. These points are quite apart from this chapter's argument. My point is that Iraq's strategy has been to consolidate territorial power within which control of oil could be used as a basis for development of economic and military strength; and that these territorial aims threatened a sensitive sector of global economic organization. There is nothing in the territorial principle of economic organization that implies respect for boundaries. Indeed, respect for the sanctity of boundaries, by removing territorial matters from conflict, favours the globalizing principle of economic organization.

[13]There is a burgeoning literature debating the question of US decline. Suffice it to mention two contributions giving opposing views: Kennedy (1987) and Nye (1990). There is very little disagreement on the basic facts: the decline of US productivity relative to European and Japanese productivity; and the extent of functional illiteracy and non-participation in economically productive work among the US population. The debate is mainly between optimists and pessimists as to whether these conditions can be reversed (Kennedy, 1990).

[14]Hudson (1977).

[15]Calleo (1982: 51-6); Hudson (1977: 53-4).

[16]Peterson (1987).

[17]Morita and Ishihara (1989); also Cox (1989).

[18]This was aptly argued in Stoffaes (1978).

References

Barraclough, Geoffrey (1967). *An Introduction to Contemporary History*. Harmondsworth: Penguin.

Borkenau, Franz (1942). *Socialism, National or International*. London: George Routledge.

Calleo, David P. (1982). *The Imperious Economy*. Cambridge, MA: Harvard Univ. Press.

Carr, Edward Hallett (1945). *Nationalism and After*. London: Macmillan.

Cox, Robert W. (1987). *Production, Power, and World Order: Social Forces in the Making of History*. New York: Columbia Univ. Press.

Cox, Robert W. (1989). 'Middlepowermanship, Japan, and Future World Order'. *International Journal* 44 (Autumn).

Crozier, Michel J., Samuel P. Huntington, and Joji Watanuki (1975). *The Crisis of Democracy: Report on the Governability of Democracies to the Trilateral Commission*. New York: New York Univ. Press.

Gordon, David M., Richard Edwards, and Michael Reich (1982). *Segmented Work, Divided Workers: The Historical Transformation of Labor in the United States*. Cambridge: Cambridge Univ. Press.

Gramsci, Antonio (1971). *Selections from the Prison Notebooks*. Ed. Quintin Hoare and Geoffrey Nowell Smith. New York: International Publishers.

Hudson, Michael (1977). *Global Fracture: The New International Economic Order*. New York: Harper & Row.

Hymer, Stephen (1972). 'The Multinational Corporation and the Law of Uneven Development'. In Jagdish N. Bhagwati, ed. *Economics and World Order: From the 1970s to the 1990s*. London: Macmillan.

Kennedy, Paul (1987). *The Rise and Fall of the Great Powers*. New York: Random House.

Kennedy, Paul (1990). 'Fin-de-siècle America'. *New York Review of Books* (28 June).

Landes, David S. (1969). *The Unbound Prometheus: Technological Change and Industrial Development in Western Europe from 1750 to the Present*. Cambridge: Cambridge Univ. Press.

Lipietz, Alain (1987). *Mirages and Miracles*. London: Verso.

Madeuf, Bernadette, and Charles-Albert Michalet (1978). 'A New Approach to International Economics'. *International Social Science Journal* 30, 2: 253-83.

Morita, Akio and Shintaro Ishihara (1989). *The Japan that Can Say 'No'*. Tokyo: Kobunsha.

Nye, Joseph S., Jr (1990). *Bound to Lead: The Changing Nature of American Power*. New York: Basic Books.

Packard, George R. (1987). 'The Coming US-Japan Crisis'. *Foreign Affairs* 66, 2: 348-67.

Paret, Peter (1976). *Clausewitz and the State*. Oxford: Clarendon Press.

Peterson, Peter G. (1987). 'The Morning After'. *Atlantic Monthly* (October).

Polanyi, Karl (1957). *The Great Transformation: The Political and Economic Origins of Our Time*. Boston: Beacon Press.

Rosecrance, Richard (1986). *The Rise of the Trading State: Commerce and Conquest in the Modern World*. New York: Basic Books.

Sabel, Charles (1982). *Work and Politics: The Division of Labor in Industry*. Cambridge: Cambridge Univ. Press.

Samuels, Richard J., and Benjamin C. Whipple (1988). 'Defence Production and Industrial Development: the Case of Japanese Aircraft'. From *MIT-Japan Science Technology Program*.

Stoffaes, Christian (1978). *La Grande Menace industrielle*. Paris: Calman-Levy.

Toyoda, Toshiyuki (1988). *A Study on Military R & D: Concerns About Japan's Participation in the Strategic Defense Initiative*. Yokohama: PRIME.

Wilkinson, Frank, ed. (1981). *The Dynamics of Labour Market Segmentation*. London: Academic.

chapter eight

Global Communications, Culture, and Values: Implications for Global Security

David V.J. Bell

Introduction

This ambitious subject poses daunting problems for research and analysis. Nevertheless, this chapter will attempt to address the following questions:

1. Does communication have the ability to transform international consciousness: i.e., is it likely to lead to a world that is less nationalistic, or more?

2. Are some technologies likely to be more conducive to consciousness transformation than others?

3. How genuinely global is the spread of integrated communications networks and systems?

4. Has the communications revolution empowered citizens *vis-à-vis* their states, or states *vis-à-vis* their citizens?

5. Are there any breakthrough technologies in communications that might have a major impact on international security in the coming decade?

These questions cut to the heart of scholarly debates that have raged for decades (if not centuries) without resolution. What shapes consciousness? What is the relative importance of ideational factors, structural change, and technology? To these questions, around which have formed whole schools of thought associated with figures like Hegel, Marx, and Weber, the present concern for international security—at a time when unprecedented changes are occurring both in global geopolitics and in the conceptualization of security itself—adds new dimensions. Moreover, some of these questions ask for more than a report on the way the world is now: they also call for prophecy as to what it might become in the future.

For the ancient Greeks, the gift of prophecy—the ability to foresee the future—was given as compensation for the loss of normal vision. The prophet could see what lay ahead but could *not* see what lay around, for he or she was by necessity blind. At the risk of total loss of vision, this chapter confines its attempts at prophecy to a brief section at the end.

The Impact of Media on Cultural Dynamics

Communications, culture, and values are related in fascinating ways. Marshall McLuhan captured one dimension of this relationship in his unforgettable aphorism 'the medium is the message'. The media through which people communicate affect profoundly the content of communication, and also the way in which content is interpreted. Media are not transparent vessels that carry meanings between people. On the contrary, they help to shape meaning, and thereby exert an important influence on both culture and values.[1] Indeed, communications scholars use the term mediation (or mediatization) to refer to 'the impact of the logic and form of any medium involved in the communication process' (Altheide, 1989: 416).

McLuhan's ideas about communications were largely derived from the work of Harold Adams Innis, who saw communications as the material base of culture. His remarkable studies of the historical development of civilization led him to the conclusion that the mode of communication available to a society conditions its approach to both space and time, thereby giving rise to unique cultural epochs and political formations. Thus Innis distinguished oral from written cultures, and identified the invention of the printing press as the necessary and sufficient precondition for the emergence of modernity (Couch, 1990; Lang, 1989).

Innis also saw political institutions as shaped and limited by the available means of communication. He distinguished types of polities on the basis of their relationship to both space and time, and this crucial relationship depended in turn on how the available modes of communication permitted society to adapt to and manipulate these two dimensions. Media that were heavy and permanent (such as clay tablets) favoured time over space, and generated small, compact polities that cherished history and tradition. Lighter media that could be transported easily (e.g., parchment) permitted polities to expand their boundaries over large areas, thus making possible the emergence of vast empires. Developments in the technology of communication (e.g., the invention of the printing press) in his view had enormous effects on culture and political forms. Indeed, the printing press ushered in the modern age of politics, permitting the expansion of political participation to the masses, challenging the narrow hierarchies of both church and state, and underpinning the emergence of political ideologies.[2]

Innis's brilliant insights at first escaped the notice of most American political scientists[3] (although they were soon picked up by students of communication). One exception, however, was Karl Deutsch, whose own work made several contributions to the emerging field of political development.

Deutsch's first major publication was *Nationalism and Social Communication*.[4] Like many other scholars, Deutsch was concerned with the impact of nationalism on global political geography in the post-World War II period. In several of his writings he adopted a communications perspective to unravel the mystery of nationalism and its political consequences: 'If we look upon nations and governments as communications systems, impersonal, verifiable evidence can be obtained to check general descriptive or qualitative assertions about nationalism, about sovereignty, and about the merger of states' (Deutsch, 1964: 49). Accordingly, Deutsch operationalized communication variables in an attempt to understand the relationship between subjective and structural changes. In his seminal 1961 article 'Social Mobilization and Political Development', he formulated a series of hypotheses linking structural change with political and cultural modernization conceptualized as social mobilization.

Deutsch later went on to study political change (specifically integration) in the advanced industrial societies of Western Europe. At this point his work moved from comparative politics into the domain of international relations. Deutsch examined the relationship between patterns of flow of communications, trade, population, and capital *between nations*, and analysed how these flows affected both international political structures and political consciousness. Deutsch's assessment of the prospects of creating an international political community was much more sophisticated than the rather naïve McLuhanesque slogans about the capability of communications to transform the world into a global village.

In fact, however, Deutsch's writings seemed to point in two different directions at the same time. Modern communications helped to achieve social mobilization and accelerated the breakdown of parochialism. This in turn facilitated the growth of nationalism and the strengthening of the nation-state. At least this appeared to be the outcome in the Third World. In the advanced industrial societies of Western Europe, however, communication across state boundaries was helping to break down these boundaries and facilitate supra-national political organization. Could both these outcomes really stem from the same source? Is communication the underpinning of both nationalism and internationalism?

This apparent paradox seems to reflect the ambivalent implications of modern communications, which like a double-edged sword can cut in two different directions, depending at least in part on the general stage of social, economic, and political modernization. Wilbur Schramm, one of the pioneers of modern communications research, underscores two key points. First, the development of modern mass media began five centuries ago, and has involved several epochal changes in the past fifty years. Second, these developments have been drastically foreshortened in Third World countries, which have been hit all at once with changes that occurred much more gradually in the developed world. For them, 'the media tumble over one another as they grow, rather than following the historical pattern of print, picture, sound, motion, and electronics' (Schramm, 1973: 221). These media have a spectacular impact on traditional life. They change the bases of political power, world outlook, individual aspirations, and the common stock of knowledge. (See Lerner in Pye, 1963). Understandably, such changes are not universally welcomed. But they are nonetheless significant and influential. For instance, Schramm (1973: 222) estimates that '[w]ithout the profound changes that have taken place in communication, sixty new countries would not be in existence today.'

Given the wide divergences found around the globe in regard to modernization, it is not surprising that changes in communications are simultaneously generating both nationalism and internationalism; and depending on the geopolitical setting, stage of economic development, and historical context, the results include both integration (as in Europe) and disintegration (as in Canada, where regionalism and separatism appear to be increasing, and in the former Soviet Union, whose disintegration they contributed to).[5] Increased communication and the spread of modern mass media can lead either to co-operation or to conflict. In this respect, the medium is *not* the message. Modern media can help disseminate a variety of different cultural contents, including both global and local culture. Indeed, these two kinds of culture are in heavy competition with each other.

This paradoxical conflict between global culture and local culture is interpreted differently by scholars from different countries and varying ideological persuasions. Those at the centre of the global cultural empire take a sanguine view:

> At present what seems to be at work is a complex interaction between a much more dynamic, but not yet clearly institutionalized, international system and the individual nation-states that we have traditionally viewed as relatively autonomous. Sovereignty still prevails in some domains, but a host of international or transnational forces are simultaneously at work, affecting how people act in what were once considered to be domestic affairs, and above all, impinging on the priorities of government. All governments are put under pressure by the increasingly significant flows of international trade, finance, and communications; by the effects of contemporary science and technology; and by all the other elements that make up what we imprecisely call modernization. But the authoritarian regimes are the most vulnerable and are therefore being seriously undermined (Pye, 1990: 6).

Those on the periphery have a different perspective. They see modernization and the spread of global culture as a threat to the survival of their own indigenous culture. This is a sentiment with which Canadians can identify. To Canadians, and many others, so-called global culture is really American culture (Nordenstreng and Schiller, 1979). Lester Pearson voiced concern about Canadian autonomy and sovereignty *vis-à-vis* our southern neighbour. What worried him most was neither the military nor the economic threat, but instead the pervasion of American ideas, the northward flow of American attitudes, American entertainment, the American approach. This fear has animated much conflict between the two countries over regulation of magazine advertising, cable transmissions, film rights, and a host of other issues.[6] American culture has a world-wide appeal because it is mass culture in a very advanced stage. Canadians are not alone in fearing it. *Time Magazine* is the leading magazine in the Arab countries in the Middle East.

Global-cum-American culture is also closely tied in with capitalist consumerism. Indeed, this is its defining characteristic. Although the countries of Eastern Europe can scarcely contain their enthusiasm for capitalist forms of development, in the West capitalism is under attack from a variety of perspectives. Despite its world-wide appeal, it is considered problematic by those who are concerned with such global issues as environmentalism, and by the left, which has traditionally fought to mitigate the underside of capitalist development in terms of its effect on both class and region.

In an important book, *National Sovereignty and International Communication*, Nordenstreng and Schiller (1979: xii) argue vigorously that

> the preservation of national sovereignty may be understood best as a step in the larger struggle to break the domination of the world business system. In this ongoing effort, international communication has been an extremely effective and direct agent of the market system. . . . [T]he overseers of the system have insisted that communications are not only neutral but that they are beneficial to receiver societies and individuals everywhere. This, in brief, is the rationale of those who have pressed the *free flow of information doctrine* on the world community since the early 1940's [emphasis added].

Against the free-flow-of-information advocates, led by the United States, a number of countries urged the adoption of prior consent concerning international broadcasting and communications:

> The advocates of the principle of prior consent argue that the principle of sovereignty gives to a state the right freely to select and develop its own political, social, economic, and cultural systems. The concept of exchange implies that the flow should be bilateral and not in one direction only. States have uneven opportunities of using the direct broadcasting technology and this factor strengthened the need to ensure that activities in this area are conducted on the basis of prior consent. The opponents of the prior consent principle [argue] . . . that it would legitimize international censorship and stifle technological progress . . . (Signitzer, 1976: 79, quoted in Nordenstreng and Schiller, 1979: 116).

Similarly, the West's domination of news and information[7] generated a counter-movement of Third World and socialist countries committed to creating the New World Information Order (NWIO). Patterned after the New International Economic Order, the NWIO (also referred to by some authors as a New Information Order or the New World Information and Communication Order) represented an attempt by Third World and other nations to organize against the hegemonic control of the West. Its emergence coincided with the attack on the 'developmentalist' paradigm by advocates of the 'dependency' perspective and those interested in world-systems theory (Smith, 1985; Wiarda, 1985; Chilcote, 1984; So, 1990). Drawing on Marxist-Leninist theories of imperialism, students of dependency argue that the plight of the Third World is comprehensible only when seen as part of the development of global capitalism, which favours the imperial centres of finance and systematically drains resources from the peripheral, dependent states of the Third World. Instead of spreading prosperity to all regions of the world, capitalism enriches the wealthy nations at the expense of the poor.

But alongside inequalities in wealth must now be placed inequalities in access to and control over information. As Hamelink points out:

> Particularly after the Second World War the international flow of messages was expected to bring the nations of the world to a better understanding of each other and to the respect for the sovereignty of individual countries. Meanwhile, sufficient documentation has been amassed to show that the international flow is in fact one sided, ethnocentric, and unequally accessible to the nations (1985: 146).

Western control of the global mass media inspired a growing concern in the Third World with 'cultural imperialism'. This concern expressed itself in a number of international conferences in the 1970s, and led to various efforts to 'decolonize' information.[8] 'The new international information order can be defined as the negotiation of an international agreement for a system of relationships between the subjects and objects of international communication' (Oledzki, 1981-2: 163; see also Argumedo, 1981-2).

Technological developments in satellite broadcasting make global communication easy to achieve and difficult to prevent. As Lucian Pye (1990: 8) elaborates:

> The revolution in communications has gone far beyond the impact of radio, which Daniel Erner . . . saw as a key instrument for modernization. The invention of microchips and satellites has meant not only that authoritarian rulers find it harder to isolate their countries from the intellectual and cultural trends sweeping the world but that their own actions are instantly played back to them and to their people. Thus, Ferdinand Marcos made his politically fatal mistake of promising an election while on US television. The Chinese leaders were initially inhibited in taking instant action against the demonstrating students in Tiananmen Square because of the world wide television coverage of Gorbachev's visit to Beijing. The Chinese students demonstrating for

democracy were receiving each day faxed copies of the editorials and news reports of the *New York Times, Washington Post, Boston Globe, Los Angeles Times,* and the *San Francisco Chronicle* only minutes after they reached the streets of US cities. Indeed, the miracle of satellite television made the dream of Tiananmen Square a superspectacle that enthralled and then dismayed a worldwide public for nearly two months and made the Deng-Li clique's attempt at the Big Lie so obscene, so impossible to get away with.

In many respects, it does indeed appear that 'the global information revolution . . . is fuelling democratic movements around the world' (Pilat and White, 1990: 89-90). Paradoxically, however, the health of democracy in countries like Canada and the United States is rather problematic. Voter apathy and political cynicism seem to be epidemic. In the 1988 US elections, for example, only 71.1 per cent of the voting age population registered to vote, and of that group only 70.6 per cent actually voted. In the 1990 mid-term elections, the proportion of the population that actually voted fell to 36 per cent.

Furthermore, whatever its effects on democratic movements, international communication itself requires democratization, according to one scholar. Echoing observations noted above, Waterman (1990: 78) writes that 'international capitalism is shifting into an "informational mode of development"', and that 'inter-state relations are increasingly a matter of communication or culture', and calls for the development of '"internationalist communication" to give direction and dynamism to the struggle against the dominant international communications media and culture'. Waterman notes that there has been considerable growth in democratic or alternative communication globally in the form of intercourse among various environmental, peace, women's, human rights, etc. movements. These new social movements (NSMs) could become the 'political force for the development of internationalist communication'[9] (Waterman, 1990: 84; see his '10 propositions').

Consciousness Transformation

According to Innis, all major developments in the technology of communication will have an impact on consciousness. While many communication scholars agree, few have been able systematically to prove his contention in any satisfactory way. Most would agree, however, that of all recent media innovations television has had the biggest impact. Indeed, some have gone so far as to claim that if the first great communications revolution was effected by Gutenberg's invention of the printing press, television has ushered in the second (Kidder, 1986). Those in the West certainly live in a video culture, as Kidder calls it. The impact on our individual and collective consciousness is rather difficult to gauge. Among television's effects is the tendency to favour 'movement over stillness, simplification over complexity, specificity over abstraction, personality over conceptualization, and the present over both past and future' (Kidder, 1986: 60). According to Meyrowitz (1985: viii), television and other electronic media 'have altered the significance of time and space for social interaction'. Echoing Innis's analysis of media as extensions of the human sensory organs, Kurt Lang (1989: 409-10) observes:

> The audio-visual media are leading the return to a new orality. . . . Their mere existence also makes obsolete the book, the medium most closely linked to intellectual progress. On both these counts, the ear seems once again to be beating the eye. But without some assistance from the available technical apparatus, the spoken word does not suffice to re-establish a real dialogue across the cultural schisms that divide nations and classes. In bringing the world closer, they have allowed, or actually condemned, all of us to live much of our lives at a distance. They have come between us and the rich fabric of meaning that goes with direct experience.

Lang's nostalgia for the age of 'direct experience' may seem a trifle unrealistic if not atavistic. The world is clearly not likely to go back from the age of 'new orality' ushered in by modern electronic media. But where is it going? What lies ahead? How will the communications revolution affect the relative balance of power between states and citizens? How will it affect international security?

Communications and Empowerment

The development of modern mass media has had an ambivalent impact on political power. Early theorists of 'mass society', such as C. Wright Mills, believed that modern media would lead to public apathy and the destruction of democracy. The town meeting, the hallmark of American democracy, allowed two-way communication between leaders and citizens. Everyone could *listen and speak* as issues of common concern were debated in small gatherings. According to Mills, broadcasting changed all this forever, because it afforded 'tremendous opportunities for mass hearing, but not mass participation'. Instead it created huge audiences 'where citizens are mere spectators or auditors of the elite few who speak' (Peters, 1989: 214).[10]

Mills's critics rejected his lament for democracy, arguing that he had ignored the actual pattern of social interaction found in so-called mass society. Challenging the view of media as a giant hypodermic needle injecting information into a passive mass society, theorists of the 'two-step' model claimed to have discovered that people really interact face-to-face in small groups guided by opinion leaders who are well informed by the mass media. 'The media could therefore be seen not as usurpers of the public space (as Mills and a whole range of mass-society critics saw them) but as contributors to it: the media provided material for discussion via the first step of the two-step flow' (Peters, 1989: 215).

If theorists disagreed about the impact of mass media on democracy, they were much nearer consensus that these media would enhance the power of authoritarian regimes.[11] The availability of the means of mass persuasion and control had facilitated the appearance of a new form of tyranny called totalitarianism, about which much was written in the years following World War II. Perhaps the most influential of these works, George Orwell's *1984*, prophesied a grim society in which The Party (personified by Big Brother) used the then futuristic technology of television as an instrument of surveillance and total control. 'Big Brother is watching you' was a by-word of this terrifying future world. At regular intervals, dutiful subjects would be summoned to huge TV screens where Big Brother's image and voice would boom out, shaping the thoughts and emotions of his defenceless, pathetic audience.

Neither Orwell nor Mills could have anticipated the subsequent development of television as a medium of entertainment and commercialization. Its impact on politics has followed these primary tendencies, resulting in the commercialization of electioneering and the trivialization of political debate. But television has also had a more subtle impact on political culture that *is* best captured in McLuhan's overworked but underdeveloped notion of the global village. Horrible images from the Vietnam war broadcast daily into millions of American homes ultimately eroded the legitimacy of American involvement.[12] Images of Western affluence projected into homes in Eastern Europe ultimately ignited the liberalization movement of 1989. Hesse (1990: 355) describes the impact of television in terms of the achievement of electronic unification:

> In divided Germany in recent years an 'electronic reunification' took place in front of the TV sets day-by-day. People in the German Democratic Republic (GDR) received information and entertainment from the western media. For the GDR rulers, this created difficult problems. The collapse of the Honecker regime had many sources of course; but an important factor in the process of political change was the influence of West German TV, which has an excellent image in East Germany, for the quality and credibility of its news and current affairs programmes. East Germans shaped their picture of the world under the continuous influence of western TV.[13]

Thus television has not always reinforced the power and influence of established political regimes. Nor have other modern media. According to Di Norcia (1990: 354): 'Power and Knowledge meet in communications media. They both encode knowledge and mediate the struggle for social supremacy. User-friendly interpretive codes and easily accessible media abet democratic groups; difficult codes and less accessible media facilitate elite control.' Photocopying technology made possible the publication of the Pentagon Papers and countless other sensitive secret documents. The fax machine allowed sympathizers around the globe to communicate precise information to the Chinese students who were occupying Tiananmen Square. The slogan 'Fax the truth to China' was heard from Hong Kong to London. Modern media have been as often instruments of liberation as of enslavement. They have allowed the people to talk back to their would-be rulers, and to see and talk to each other around the world.[14]

Integrated Communications Networks

The capability of using the same communications network to transmit a variety of types of information or data—for example, voice, computer data, and printed material—has given rise to the development and diffusion of integrated communications networks. Such networks are spreading throughout the globe, virtually wherever telephone linkages exist. Geographical barriers are easily transcended, because most long-distance telephone connections are now made via satellite.[15] The fax machine and modem allow individuals to make sophisticated connections virtually instantly, and have facilitated access to computer-based data banks and decision centres. This access, moreover, is two-way. The remote user can tap into these sources for financial, scientific, or even military information. The clever user can also input information, and in some instances manipulate the source itself by breaking through security codes. Numerous examples of the work of computer hackers have been documented in court cases, and fictionalized in novels and films. The rather terrifying possibility of breaking computer security, for nefarious personal or political purposes, obviously has implications for international security.

Integrated communications networks and the consequent ability to transmit information around the globe almost instantly affect international economics as well as politics. According to Walter Wriston, former chairman of the board of Citibank: 'An individual sitting anywhere in the world before his [sic] PC can command in microseconds incredible amounts of information stored in the data base of the world. Information . . . is becoming the new capital' (quoted in Barfield and Benko, 1985: 11).

With regard to trade and economics, McCracken and Esch (1985: 3) refer explicitly to the North-South discussion, but their question applies more generally as well: 'Can the developed and the developing countries agree on international communication and information systems that provide the open infrastructure needed for trade and commerce to flourish across boundaries, while protecting individual rights and the sovereignty and security of nations?'

Whenever economic and financial concerns are raised, political and military considerations cannot be far behind. In a careful assessment of the plethora of international policy problems posed by the communications revolution, Barfield and Benko (1985: 18-19) emphasize the following:

Privacy and data protection. Concern about the potential Orwellian misuse of advanced computer technologies led many nations to adopt privacy and data protection measures in the late 1970s and early 1980s. In 1980 the Organization for Economic Cooperation and Development (OECD) also passed its guidelines on the Protection of Privacy and Transborder Flows of Personal Data in an attempt to establish some universally agreed upon principles to promote the harmonization of national privacy laws. . . .

Economic and national sovereignty restrictions. Most nations view economic power as a key component of national power and therefore consider economic restrictions in the interest of national sovereignty. All barriers to the flow of information that result from government monopolization of the national communications network, for example, can be construed as economic restrictions, since PTTs [Post, Telephone and Telegraph monopolies] themselves are justified in such terms. . . .

National security. National security controls include the obvious restrictions on the flow of strategically sensitive military information. Included in this category is the information embodied in some high-technology goods and services. . . . Foreign countries are [also] designating an expanding list of data bases and types of information as vital to the national security and, as a consequence, requiring that this information be stored within the country's borders and that certain operations on, and manipulations of, these data bases be localized and monitored.

Cultural restrictions. Nations impose restrictions on transborder data flows to preserve the 'cultural integrity' of their society. The developing nations . . . call for restrictions on the flow of information from the industrialized North, in all its forms, to halt 'cultural imperialism'. They also seek strict control over the information leaving their borders, ostensibly to stop the allegedly biased press of the industrial world from perpetuating myths about the less-developed countries.

Each of these four policy areas has enormous implications for international security, because each could generate friction and conflict between nation states.

'Breakthrough' Technologies and Future Changes in International Security

Social scientists distinguish several different types of statements about the future, including *prediction*, literally an attempt to say what lies ahead, usually based on an explanatory model or theory: *projection*, literally a throwing ahead of recent trends and developments; and *forecasting*, a rather ambiguous term that derives from meteorology. In international politics, these methods are even less reliable than in weather.[16] In the area of communications, two shortcomings in theory and analysis leap out. First, communication theorists did not anticipate the development and diffusion of the technologies that have become so important in the 1980s: the fax, VCR, personal computer, etc. Second, even had they anticipated these technologies, theorists could not have predicted how they appear to have affected societies around the globe.

In light of the enormous, virtually unpredictable changes in global geopolitics, it is not surprising that the concept of 'security' itself is changing. The realist approach to security, which has remained the dominant conception for over two centuries, emphasizing power-based competition among countries, has been seriously challenged. For some, this challenge has reflected the more global view — graphically illustrated by pictures of Earth taken from outer space — that sees all Earthlings as sharing a common stake in global survival. All are in the same boat in many respects. No one can make his or her end of the canoe more stable by trying to make the other end more tippy, as the noted US scholar Roger Fisher has put it.

Nor is security a simple, straightforward matter of defence and military strategy. Threats to security are seen increasingly in non-military areas, especially in humans' relations with the fragile world ecosystem, and in the patterns of global economic development that have proved so damaging to the environment. The link between these crises occasioned the establishment of the World Commission on Environment and Development, headed by Gro Harlem Brundtland, whose 1987 report was called *Our Common Future*.

Brundtland had been a member of the group established by fellow Scandinavian Olof Palme, who popularized the parallel notion of common security five years earlier in the 'Report of the Independent Commission on Disarmament and Security Issues'. In the prologue to the Palme report, Cyrus Vance (1982: vii) wrote:

> There is one overriding truth in this nuclear age — *no nation can achieve true security by itself*. . . . The fact is that there are no real defenses against nuclear armed missiles — neither now nor in the foreseeable future. To guarantee our own security in this nuclear age, we must . . . work together with other nations to achieve common security [emphasis added].

In his introduction, Palme outlined the implications of this overriding truth. The doctrine of mutual assured destruction, with its corollary requirement of an ever-expanding arsenal of weapons and the resulting nuclear balance of terror, must be repudiated in favour of a conception of international security based on 'a commitment to joint survival rather than on a threat of mutual destruction' (xiii). This in turn requires a reversal of the arms race, in fact 'a downward spiral in armaments', including conventional arms as well as weapons of mass destruction.

The development of military technologies of mass destruction has made total war unthinkable as a rational instrument of statecraft and has necessitated a reconceptualization of security itself. The notion of common security was propounded to address both the military and the broader economic and environmental aspects of security. In a follow-up report written in 1989, several years after the death of their chairman, Palme commission members expressed the hope that ultimately 'common security could evolve from a concept intended to protect against war to a comprehensive approach to world peace, social justice, economic development, and environmental protection.'

One fairly safe prediction regarding international security in the coming decade is that this expanded definition of the concept will achieve much greater currency. Environmental and economic concerns will be juxtaposed with military concerns. Furthermore, problems associated with cultural security will also achieve greater salience. All of these issues, which are clearly international collective goods of one kind or another, entail a strong imperative of multilateralism, which Barfield and Benko (1985: 19) insist 'remains the best hope for solving emerging problems in the international . . . system.'

Conclusion: Implications for International Security

What are some other implications of the developments described above? How will they affect international security now and in the foreseeable future? Notwithstanding the dangers of prophecy, it is possible at least to speculate about future developments. As noted by Ithiel de Sola Pool (1990), modern communications systems are indeed 'technologies without boundaries'. They therefore pose difficult challenges to the integrity and sovereignty of traditional nation-states, which define their very existence in terms of boundaries that can somehow be 'secured'. For example, traditionalists define Canadian national security as 'surveillance and control over land, sea and air approaches to Canada'. But, as Choucri and North so eloquently point out later in this volume, all contemporary nation-states have displayed massive incompetence in controlling the flow of goods, services, human beings, and effluent across their boundaries. In this age of satellites and fibre optics, communications and data must be added to this list of things that are flowing across national boundaries with little surveillance and even less control.[17] Thus modern communications appear to have the potential to undermine national security.

But perhaps this is too facile. To appreciate more fully the impact of communications on security, it is helpful to recall Kenneth Waltz's 'three images' of the causes of international war. Waltz (1965) identified three distinct foci for theories of war and peace: human nature, political regimes within states, and the state system itself. Each of these images derives from a different assumption about the root cause of war. The first image explains war in terms of 'human nature' — the natural propensity to aggression and violence that is deeply engrained in the human psyche.[18] To eliminate war one must transform human nature, according to this perspective. The second-image theorists argue (as did Immanuel Kant in *Perpetual Peace*), that wars are caused not by human nature, but by autocratic rulers who act irresponsibly to commit their subjects to war. Kant believed that once all states were democratized, wars would disappear because 'the people' would never choose such a painful and costly course of action for solving conflict. Finally, the third-image theorists assume that war is a product of the state system itself. Sovereign states, irrespective of their form of government, will inevitably clash violently with one another, because they lack a higher sovereign power to keep them 'in awe', to enforce agreements, and to punish transgressors (to borrow from Thomas Hobbes's unforgettable analysis of the 'State of War'). To eliminate war one must either eliminate international anarchy by introducing some form of world government; or eliminate nation-states and revert to smaller, less dangerous and powerful political units; or perhaps abolish and eliminate weapons, the means of warfare.

Bearing in mind that the conceptualization of security now extends far beyond the narrow traditional focus on war, can one adapt this framework to explore the impact of modern communications on mass publics, political élites, and the state system? Looking ahead to the future, how will modern communications affect (a) the attitudes of mass publics towards international security; (b) the élite attitude toward war and broader aspects of security; and (c) the nature of the international system of sovereign states?

Communication and Mass Publics

In Third World countries (perhaps including the republics of the former Soviet Union) communications will increase 'social mobilization'.[19] This may either expand national power or accelerate fragmentation through heightened regional or ethnic conflict, depending on the particular circumstances. The world is living through a period of extraordinary national and subnational consciousness and conflict. Instead of eroding cleavages based on these 'primordial' affiliations, modernization and industrialization seem to be sharpening them. Thus 'most of the multilingual, bi-national, or bi-religious states that have persisted for many decades, if not centuries, have faced turmoil in recent years' (Lipset, 1985: 336). This generalization applies to East and West, North and South.

In addition to exacerbating social cleavages and antagonisms in advanced Western countries, modern communications appear to be (a) fragmenting audiences, by permitting the expansion of specialized media and programming; (b) eroding national boundaries, because of the impossibility of regulating the flow of communications across boundaries; (c) increasing political cynicism, by exposing government action (and inaction) to public scrutiny; and (d) raising consciousness about issues like environmental degradation that cut across national boundaries (Pool, 1990: 262). It is unclear whether, on balance, communications have served to empower citizens or states. Probably they have the potential for empowering both. In any given situation, the outcome will be a function of leadership, will, and skill in using communication systems.

One communications-related development that has definitely strengthened the voice of the people is the technology of public-opinion surveying, which has become perhaps the foremost instrument of democracy. Governments use surveys on a regular basis to take the pulse of publics on issues and policies.[20] This practice is so advanced that Wriston (1990) identifies as the three participants in political communication politicians, the media, and the mass public speaking through polls. Insofar as public policy (especially in

engines of change propelling humankind into this new age is the electronic revolution and its transformation of communications and information technology. Rosenau calls on students of international polities to break out of the old paradigms and become aware of the realities of this new second world of world politics, whose structure and process are distinctive in numerous ways.

Robert Cox, in this volume, sounds a similar note in his discussion of the impact on territorial states of various global forces that characterize the emergence of a 'post-globalization world order', which might entail the 'possibility of culturally diverse alternatives to global homogenization'. And even Alvin Toffler has written on the power shift that has made access to electronic knowledge, not wealth or military might, the key factor in the new world order. The 'world of world politics' has obviously become dramatically more complex. New structures have appeared at levels both above and below that of the nation-state. The idea that territoriality is a defining characteristic of political association (i.e., statehood) may be overtaken by new types of political associations based on shared communications (no longer dependent on geographical propinquity).

Will the development of global markets, global actors, global structures, and global problems be accompanied by a new global consciousness? Such a development is probably a precondition to a harmonious new world order. As Karl Deutsch once remarked, 'nothing more is required for world government than that the people of each country have as much concern for each other as the people of Alabama have for the people of Massachusetts.' But, he went on to add, 'nothing less is required also' (personal communication to the author, 1968).

If any medium has the potential of producing some form of humane global consciousness, it must surely be television. Because it is primarily a visual medium, its impact can transcend language. Everyone in the world can see the same image, and can do so simultaneously. Moreover, there is emerging for the first time in history a 'video generation'. By the time individuals graduate from high school in advanced Western societies, they have spent more time in front of a television set than they have spent in school. For them television—not the family, not the educational system, not religion, not books and newspapers—has become the primary agency of political (and general) socialization. Youngsters growing up in the age of satellites have the potential to experience a truly *global* television upbringing. Members of this video generation are not yet in charge of major social, scientific, economic, or political institutions. But they soon will be. The present élite, whose 'first culture' (cf., 'first language') is print—which reinforces (indeed helped create) the conception of the territorial nation-state and the paradigms of realism and neo-realism—will soon be displaced by an élite whose first culture is video—which is tied in with other global forces; which transcends language; which dissolves history and tradition; which is increasingly the dominating force in both popular culture (through soap operas, TV dramas and sit-coms) and political communication (through news and public-affairs programming).

The hope for the future lies in the possibility that in the twenty-first century both élites and masses will experience a cultural mutation that will lead to a new global consciousness—and sense of global citizenship and responsibility—capable of sustaining human existence and the world environment on which it depends.[25]

But the likelihood of this creative transformation is slight at best. There is a move to a new world order, to be sure. But it is a world order of unipolar militarism sustained by financial tribute (i.e., OPM—other people's money) and dominated by the military might of the United States operating under the guise of the United Nations. Despite staggering global developmental problems, there seems to be a further huge investment in military weaponry and technology. The war in the Gulf is but the first example of the phenomenon of Third World War.

In 1989, the *New York Times* wrote an obituary for the New World Information Order. The NWIO died not of natural causes, but as a result of a relentless series of attacks, amounting to a war, conducted by the US under the banner of freedom of information. The US succeeded in labelling the NWIO as communist-inspired anti-democratic censorship. At the same time, the US was advancing the cause of 'freedom' through what it called a Strategic-Communications Initiative. The new world order envisioned by George Bush will feature a sophisticated use of state-of-the-art communications technology, put to the service of global imperial interests. Through SCI the United States may achieve successes beyond the wildest dreams of the supporters of SDI. They may succeed in creating a new Military Information Society (Mosco, 1991).

Pax Americana is undoubtedly preferable to a number of alternative futures. But it represents the defeat of a more hopeful vision of a world order based on decreased militarism, increased mutual understanding, and a global commitment to tackling seriously the problems of the environment, of poverty and starvation: a world order built on technological developments that are life-sustaining rather than life-destroying.

Notes

[1]See Altheide (1989: 417): 'media are more than a neutral conduit of information transmission; they are concrete action agents that come to represent or stand for the location and establishment of various kinds of meanings.'

[2]See Di Norcia (1990: 344): 'Books encouraged the rise of secular knowledge and new scientific, literary and political elites. It [*sic*] also facilitated the victory of the absolute state over religion in the sixteenth century struggle for social supremacy.'

[3]Kurt Lang (1989: 408-9) points out that the Italian sociologist Franco Ferrarotti 'is one of the few sociologists to take Innis as a point of departure and to break new

ground by incorporating elements of his conceptual scheme into their analysis of the television age.'

⁴Looking back at this work a decade after it was published, Deutsch (1964: 46) observed: 'Students of international affairs have spent years trying to find out why people insist at certain times upon having a sovereign state of their own which occupies a sharply bounded area of the world. They also have been occupied with the motivation of the rank and file of the population, who often show extreme resistance to their country's being amalgamated or merged with other governments.'

⁵James Laxer traces these developments to economic factors, specifically the creation of large economic trading blocs: 'Today, because so many decisions have moved beyond them, nation states are becoming less effective in shaping the socio-economic conditions in which their citizens live. The consequence is the rapid growth in the importance of two levels of identity—identity at the supranational level and identity at the regional level—both of which are undercutting the loyalty once directed to the nation-state' (Laxer, 'Global Forces Leave Canada at U.S. Whim', *Toronto Star*, 9 Oct. 1990, A13). Cf. also Rosenau (1988: 333): 'the dynamics of post-industrialism are simultaneously fostering centralizing and decentralizing tendencies in world politics, some of which cancel each other out but many of which progressively circumscribe nation-states and the international system they have sustained for several centuries.'

⁶The security implications are obvious, if the term security is expanded to include culture as well as military considerations. In this regard, it is interesting to contrast the duties of the Canadian Secretary of State (charged in many recent cabinets with responsibility for cultural matters) with the American Secretary of State, whose duties entail a more traditional conception of national security. For a fascinating case study of Canada by a leading academic who has also served as chairman of the Canadian Radio-Television and Telecommunications Commission, see Meisel (1986).

⁷The extent of this domination is indicated by the fact that of the 1200 or so news agencies operating in the world, the four largest Western agencies—Reuters, Agence France Presse (AFP), Associated Press (AP), and United Press International (UPI)—together 'put out 34 million words per day and claim to provide nine-tenths of the entire foreign news output of the world's newspapers and television stations [as of the late 1970s]' (Lorimer and McNulty, 1987: 232). According to Hudson (1986: 322), 'Access to information, and to the facilities to produce, store, and transmit information is now considered vital to development, so that the classifications information rich and information poor may mean more than distinctions based on GNP or other traditional development indicators.'

⁸Oledzki (1981-2) notes that a parallel concern animated American reactions to the dominant position of European news agencies in the early 1900s.

⁹Soedjatmoko (1986: 68-9) offers a more cautious assessment: 'People's movements, organized or unorganized, positive or negative, are significant forces in both the North and the South. Some display a grand generosity of spirit such as the Band-Aid fundraising concerts. . . . In stark contrast to these are the quasi-fascistic

movements that have revived racism, xenophobia, and anti-immigrant sentiment in the industrialized countries.'

[10]Cf. also Couch, 1990: 'All information technologies are, in McLuhan's terms, extensions of man. One of the extensions provided by the mass media is procedures whereby one person can communicate to a multitude. Print extends the ability of a person to communicate to a multitude via discursive visual symbols; radio extends the ability of a person to communicate to a multitude via discursive symbols and evocative auditory symbols; television extends the ability of a person to communicate to a multitude via discursive symbols, evocative auditory symbols, and evocative images.' By the same token, audience and viewer ratings (such as the Nielsen ratings) allow the many to send a message back to the few who decide what programs will be aired.

[11]This theme is repeated by Couch (1990: 125): 'Hitler's totalitarianism was bolstered by his access to and effective use of the radio to establish and maintain a state structure infused with charisma. More recently Khomeini effectively used television to establish and maintain a totalitarian regime infused with charisma.'

[12]Some scholars argue that the print medium, particularly newspapers, played an even larger role in delegitimating US involvement in Vietnam.

[13]Cf. also his conclusion: 'Western TV in East Germany has a "soma effect", as in Aldous Huxley's *Brave New World*: Short-term satisfaction through relaxation provided by Western TV. The long-term effects of Western TV, however, were not system stabilizing. Western TV regularly conveyed another world. This was not only a dream-world, which facilitated escape from everyday life, but was also a spur to compare realities and act on them. In October 1989 the people of the GDR decided that the time for action had come. This "October Revolution" would not have happened at that time and in that way without the presence of Western media, in particular Western TV.'

[14]Several scholars have pointed out that television may facilitate two-way communication between the political élite and the mass public, if certain recent technological innovations are encouraged. Video text (and other recent equivalent technologies) now make it possible for the opinion of the silent majority to be systematically monitored, thus permitting the development of teledemocracy. (See, *inter alia*, Kidder, 1986; Becker, 1981).

[15]'Currently, two modes of transfer for international telecommunications exist — satellite and submarine cable. Global satellite communication operations are governed by INTELSAT, a 110-nation organization that owns and operates the fifteen-satellite system. INTELSAT carries about two-thirds of the world's transoceanic communications traffic and almost all international television transmission' (Barfield and Benko, 1985: 17).

[16]Cf. Lipset (1985: 329), who points out that 'social scientists cannot possibly anticipate specific outcomes because they are still in a situation comparable to that of the meteorologists — they can describe what is happening to produce a cold wave or a drought; they can look at yesterday's weather and predict tomorrow's; but they do not understand enough about the complex relations among the many forces that produce diverse weather to make reliable long-term predictions.'

[17]'Trans-border data flow' (TBF) is a recognized problem in international security. See, *inter alia*, Meisel (1986).

[18]Theorists who endorse the first image usually argue that aggression is a biological (i.e., innate) rather than a cultural (i.e., learned) behavioural disposition. Many argue further that its biological basis makes aggression impossible to eliminate.

[19]As of 1990, only 67% of Soviet households had radios, 35% televisions, and a mere 15% telephones. At best, the former Soviet Union would have been placed near the bottom of the list of 'modernized' societies as far as communications are concerned.

[20]For a strong critique of the limitations and distortion this entails, see Fletcher (1990).

[21]The security dilemma at the international level is held to be analogous to the Hobbesian state of war, where every man fears every man. It is a painful aspect of gender relations in modern society, where despite the achievement of 'peace, order, and good government', every woman lives in fear of every man.

[22]As the world approached the deadline of 15 January 1991, when the United Nations sanction for military action against Iraq took effect, public opinion in all countries actively involved in the conflict, though divided, was broadly supportive of war, and yet concerned about the potential costs in human lives and material destruction.

[23]Cf. Meisel (1986: 328): 'As telecommunications becomes increasingly fundamental to the national interests of developing countries, and as the basic components of the infrastructure become more affordable, global competition for orbit and spectrum resources will become more intense. If this prospect brings about changes in values and foreign policies, then collective solutions may be found. If not, competition may well lead to intense conflict.'

[24]Cf. Soedjatmoko (1986: 72): 'In short, modern technologies of communication and transportation, to say nothing of a pervasive commercial culture, have added a new stratification of the world; people [are divided] into transnational classes that share very little information, experience, or common concern. The psychological distance between the strata is in imminent danger of reaching the point where the only form of discourse between top and bottom is violence, punctuated by occasional spasms of charity.'

[25]Cf. Boulding (1988), who uses the concept 'global civic culture' to refer to a similar type of cultural mutation.

References

Altheide, David L. (1989). 'The Elusive Mass Media'. *Politics, Culture and Society* 2, 3 (Spring).

Argumedo, Alcira (1981-2). 'The New World Information Order and International Power'. *Journal of International Affairs* 35, 2 (Fall-Winter).

Barfield, Claude E., and Robert Benko (1985). 'International Communications and

Information Systems: The Impact on Trade'. *AEI Foreign Policy and Defence Review* 5, 4.

Becker, Jorg (1982). 'Communication and Peace: The Empirical and Theoretical Relation Between Two Categories in Social Sciences'. *Journal of Peace Research* XIX, 3.

Becker, Ted (1981). 'Teledemocracy: Bringing Power Back to People'. *The Futurist* (December).

Beitz, Charles R. (1979). *Political Theory and International Relations.* Princeton, NJ: Princeton Univ. Press.

Bell, Daniel (1968). *Toward the Year 2000: Work in Progress.* Boston: Beacon.

Bell, David V.J. (1990). 'What is Common Security?'. *Peace Magazine* VI, IV (August).

Blatherwick, David E.S. (1987). *The International Politics of Telecommunications.* Berkeley, CA: Institute of International Studies.

Boulding, Elise (1988). *Building A Global Civic Culture.* New York: Teachers College Press.

Brundtland, Gro, et al. (1987). *Our Common Future.* New York: Oxford Univ. Press. *A World at Peace* (1989).

Burt, Richard (1986). 'The Security Implications of Slow and Uneven Growth'. *Washington Quarterly* 9, 4 (Fall).

Caruso, Andrea (1987). 'The Shrinking Earth — Communications Through Space'. *NATO's Sixteen Nations* 32, 3 (June).

Chilcote, Ronald H. (1984). *Theories of Development and Underdevelopment.* Boulder, CO: Westview.

Chilton, Paul, and George Lakoff (n.d.). 'What Is Security?'. Unpublished mimeo.

Choucri, Nazli, and Robert C. North (1993). 'Population and (In)Security: National Perspectives and Global Imperatives', in this volume.

Couch, Carl J. (1990). 'Mass Communications and State Structures'. *Social Sciences Journal* 27, 2. ·

Cowhey, Peter F. (1990). 'The International Telecommunications Regime: The Political Roots of the Regimes for High Technology'. *International Organization* 44, 2 (Spring).

Deutsch, Karl (1953). *Nationalism and Social Communication: An Inquiry into the Foundations of Nationality.* New York: John Wiley and Technology Press of M.I.T.

Deutsch, Karl (1961). 'Social Mobilization and Political Development'. *American Political Science Review* LV, 3.

Deutsch, Karl W. (1964). 'Communication Theory and Political Integration'; 'The Price of Integration'; 'Integration and the Social Structure: Implications of Functional Analysis'. Three chapters in Philip E. Jacob and James V. Toscano, eds. *The Integration of Political Communities.* Philadelphia: Lippincott.

DiNorcia, Vincent (1990). 'Communications, Time and Power: An Innesian View'. *Canadian Journal of Political Science* 23, 2: 335-57.

Dordick, Herbert S. (1986). *Understanding Modern Telecommunications*. Toronto: McGraw-Hill.

Douglas, Steven M. (1979). 'Technology and the New International Order'. *Journal of International Affairs* 33, 1 (Spring-Summer).

Eckhardt, William (1983). 'War/Peace Attitudes, Events and Values'. *Bulletin of Peace Proposals* 14, 2.

Finlay, Marik (1987). *Powermatics: A Discursive Critique of New Communications Technology*. London: Routledge and Kegan Paul.

Fischer, Dietrich (1982). 'Invulnerability Without Threat: The Swiss Concept of General Defense'. *Journal of Peace Research* XIX, 3.

Fletcher, Fred (1990). 'Polling and Political Communication: The Canadian Case'. Unpublished paper presented at the International Association for Mass Communication Research Conference. Lake Bled, Yugoslavia.

Guttenplan, Barry (1981). 'Space Communication Enters a New Stage'. *Dialogue* 52 (21 Feb.).

Habermas, Jurgen (1977). 'Hannah Arendt's Communications Concept of Power'. *Social Research: An International Quarterly of the Social Sciences* (Spring).

Haglund, David G., and Michael K. Hawes, eds (1990). *World Politics: Power, Interdependence and Dependence*. Toronto: Harcourt Brace Jovanovich.

Hamelink, Cees J. (1985). 'International Communication'. In Teun A. Van Dijk, ed. *Discourse and Communication: New Approaches to the Analysis of the Mass Media Discourse and Communication*. New York: Walter de Gruyter.

Hamelink, Cees J. (1986). 'Is There Life after the Information Revolution?'. In Michael Traber, ed. *The Myth of the Information Revolution*. London: Sage.

Hassner, P., David P. Calleo, et al. (1990). *Europe and America Beyond 2000*. New York: Council on Foreign Relations.

Hesse, Kurt R. (1990). 'Cross Border Mass Communication from West to East Germany'. *European Journal of Communication* 5, 2-3 (June).

Hollins, Harry B., Averill L. Powers, and Mark Sommer (1989). *The Conquest of War: Alternative Strategies for Global Security*. London: Westview.

Hopkins, Frank Snowden (1981). 'Communication: the Civilizing Force'. *Futurist* XV, 2 (April).

Hudson, Heather (1986). 'New Communications Technologies: Policy Issues for the Developing World'. *International Political Science Review* 7, 3 (July).

Independent Commission on Disarmament and Security Issues (1982). *Common Security: A Blueprint for Survival*. New York: Simon and Schuster.

Keohane, Robert O., and Joseph S. Nye (1977). *Power and Interdependence: World Politics in Transition*. Boston: Little Brown.

Kidder, Rushworth M. (1986). 'The Impact of Video Culture'. *Dialogue* 2, 72.

Lang, Kurt (1989). 'Mass Communications and Our Relation to the Present and the Past'. *Politics, Culture and Society* 2, 3 (Spring).

Lasswell, Harold. D., et al. (1979). *Propaganda and Communication in World History Volume III: A Pluralizing World in Formation*. Honolulu: Univ. Press of Hawaii.

Lerner, Daniel (1958). *The Passing of Traditional Society: Modernizing the Middle East*. New York: Free Press.

Letwin, Shirley Robin (1979). 'Politics and Language: Why There Are No "Authoritarians"'. *Policy Review* (Spring).

Lipset, Seymour Martin (1985). 'Predicting the Future: The Limits of Social Science'. *Consensus and Conflict: Essays in Political Sociology*. New Brunswick, NJ: Transaction.

Lorimer, Rowland, and Jean McNulty (1987). *Mass Communication in Canada*. Toronto: McClelland and Stewart.

Malitor, Graham T. (1981). 'The Information Society: The Path to Post-Industrial Growth'. *Futurist* XV, 2 (April).

Martino, Joseph P. (1979). 'Telecommunications in the Year 2000'. *Futurist* XIII, 2 (April).

Matthews, Robert, and Charles Pentland, eds (1987). 'The Politics of International Telecommunications'. *International Journal* XLII, 2 (Spring).

McCormack, Thelma (1989). 'The Southam Lecture: The Texts of War and the Discourse on Peace'. *Canadian Journal of Communication* 14, 1 (Winter).

McCracken, Paul W., and Marvin L. Esch (1985). 'Introduction' to 'The International Environment for Trade'. *AEI Foreign Policy and Defense Review* 5, 4.

McLuhan, Marshall, and Bruce R. Powers (1989). *The Global Village: Transformations in the World Life and Media in the 21st Century*. New York: Oxford Univ. Press.

Meisel, John (1986). 'Communications in the Space Age: Some Canadian and International Implications'. *International Political Science Review* 7, 3 (July).

Meyrowitz, Joshua (1985). *No Sense of Place: The Impact of the Electronic Media on Social Behavior*. New York: Oxford Univ. Press.

Mosco, Vincent (1991). 'Whose Media? Whose New World Order?'. *Peace Magazine* VII (May), 24-5.

Mowlana, Hamid (1971). *International Communication: A Selected Bibliography*. Dubuque, IA: Kendall/Hunt.

Nordenstreng, Kaarle, and Herbert I. Schiller, eds (1979). *National Sovereignty and International Communication*. Norwood, NJ: Ablex.

Oledzki, Jerzy (1981-2). 'Polish Perspectives on the New Information Order'. *Journal of International Affairs* 35, 2 (Fall-Winter).

Oliver, Robert T. (1962). *Culture and Communication: The Problem of Penetrating National and Cultural Boundaries*. Springfield, IL: Charles C. Thomas.

Palme report (1982). See Independent Commission on Disarmament and Security Issues (1982).

Pearce, W. Barnett, (1989). *Communication and the Human Condition*. Carbondale: Southern Illinois Univ. Press.

Pearson, Geoffrey (1986). 'East-West Relations: Values, Interests and Perceptions'. *Points of View* 1 Canadian Institute for International Peace and Security (March).

Pearson, Lester B. (1970). 'At the Liberal Leadership Convention'. *Words and Occasions*. Toronto: Univ. of Toronto Press.

Pierce, John R. (1965). 'Communications Technology and the Future'. *Daedalus* 94, 2 (Spring).

Pilat, Joseph F., and Paul C. White (1990). 'Technology and Strategy in a Changing World'. *Washington Quarterly* (Spring).

Pool, Ithiel de Sola (1990). *Technologies Without Boundaries: Telecommunications in a Global Age*. Cambridge, MA: Harvard Univ. Press.

Pye, Lucian W., ed. (1963). *Communications and Political Development*. Princeton, NJ: Princeton Univ. Press.

Pye, Lucian W. (1990). 'Political Science and the Crisis of Authoritarianism'. *American Political Science Review* 84, 1 (March).

Roche, Douglas (1986). *Building Global Security: Agenda for the 1990's*. Toronto: N.C. Press.

Rosenau, James (1988). 'Patterned Chaos in Global Life: Structure and Process in the Two Worlds of World Politics'. *International Science Review* 9, 4.

Samuels, Michael A., and William A. Douglas (1981). 'Promoting Democracy'. *Washington Quarterly* 4, 3 (Summer).

Schramm, Wilbur (1973). 'Mass Communication'. In George A. Miller, ed. *Communication, Language and Meaning: Psychological Perspectives*. New York: Basic.

Slater, Ian (1975). 'Orwell, Marcuse and the Language of Politics'. *Political Studies* XXIII, 4.

Smith, Tony (1985). 'Requiem or New Agenda for Third World Studies'. *World Politics* (July).

So, Alvin (1990). *Social Change and Development*. Beverly Hills: Sage.

Soedjatmoko (1986). 'Values in Transition'. *Washington Quarterly* 9, 4 (Fall).

Varis, Tapio (1990). 'Peace and Communication: An Approach by Flow Studies'. *Journal of Peace Research* XIX, 3.

Vollmer, C.D. (1990). 'The Future Defense Industrial Environment'. *Washington Quarterly* 13, 2 (Spring).

Waltz, Kenneth N. (1965). *Man, the State, and War: A Theoretical Analysis*. Boulder, CO: Colorado Univ. Press.

Waterman, Peter (1990) 'Reconceptualizing the Democratization of International Communication'. *International Social Science Journal* (February).

Weiner, Myron, and Samuel P. Huntington, eds (1987). *Understanding Political Development*. Toronto: Little, Brown.

Welch, Thomas. J. (1990). 'Technology, Change and Security'. *Washington Quarterly* 13, 2 (Spring).

Wiarda, Howard J. (1985). *Ethocentrism in Foreign Policy: Can We Understand the Third World?* Am. Enterprises.

Wriston, Walter B. (1990). *The Twilight of Sovereignty: How the Information Revolution is Transforming Our World*. New York: Macmillan.

chapter nine

Global Environmental Change and International Security[1]

Thomas F. Homer-Dixon

Is the New Environmentalism Just a Fad?

On 23 June 1988, Dr James Hansen, a leading atmospheric scientist, sat down to testify before the Senate Energy Committee in Washington, DC. It was a stifling day in the American capital, and North America was in the midst of a severe, crop-devastating drought. Hansen spoke about his climate-modelling efforts at NASA; based on the results of his and other general circulation models, he declared he was 'ninety-nine per cent' certain the string of warm years in the 1980s was the first signal of human-induced greenhouse warming. 'It is time to stop waffling so much,' he said, 'the evidence is pretty strong that the greenhouse effect is here.'

The next day, the *New York Times* capped its front page with the headline 'Global Warming has Begun, Expert Tells Senate'.[2] There followed a wave of media reports, and suddenly global change was in the spotlight.[3] A host of environmental problems quickly jumped to the forefront in public policy and public consciousness. This sudden salience was aided by the declining ideological and military confrontation between the superpowers, which opened a space for other issues in public discourse in Western societies. Many politicians moved to exploit this opening by presenting environmental problems as an arena for a new era of national action and international collaboration.

These factors that helped generate this environmental awareness were largely circumstantial, and many sceptics have concluded that this new environmentalism is just another fad generated by opinion-makers and the media. Indeed, if these were the only factors at work, one could expect that environmental issues would soon lose prominence in the public mind, only to return years in the future when the media and public noticed such problems once again. But there is another factor at work: during the last decade there has been a genuine shift in the scientific community's perception of global environmental problems. The environmental system, in particular the earth's climate, used to be regarded as relatively resilient and stable in the face of human insults. But now it is widely believed to be in many respects chaotic and hence unpredictable, with many non-linear relationships between variables, and multiple local equilibria that are not highly stable.[4] In 1987, for example, geochemist Wallace Broecker reflected on recent polar ice-core and ocean-sediment data: 'What these records indicate is that Earth's climate does not respond to forcing in a smooth and gradual way. Rather, it responds in sharp jumps which involve large-scale reorganization of Earth's system. . . . We must consider the possibility that the main responses of the system to our provocation of the atmosphere will come in jumps whose timing and magnitude are unpredictable.'[5]

A dramatic and paradigm-shattering example of such non-linear (or threshold) effects in complex environmental systems was the discovery of the Antarctic ozone hole in the mid-1980s.[6] The scientific models of ozone depletion used to that point had, for the most part, assumed a rough linear relationship between chlorofluorocarbon (CFC) emissions and ozone depletion. Atmospheric scientists had not even remotely anticipated the ozone-destroying catalytic process that occurs on the surface of stratospheric ice crystals when certain temperature and light conditions interact with particular concentrations of water, nitrogen compounds, and CFCs. If the conditions are right, it turns out, this destruction can occur at lightning speed, stripping the ozone from multi-kilometre-thick layers of the stratosphere in a matter of days. The Antarctic ozone hole was startling evidence of the instability of the environmental system in response to human inputs, of the capacity of humankind to affect significantly the ecosystem on a global scale, and of humans' inability to predict exactly how the system will change.

The altered perception of the nature of the environmental system has percolated out of the scientific community into the policy-making community.[7] It may also, in various subliminal ways, be influencing the broader public's view of environmental problems. Scientists, policy-makers, and lay people are beginning to interpret data about environmental change in a new light: progressive, incremental degradation of environmental systems is not as tolerable as it once was, because no one is sure any longer that the systems humans live within still have substantial buffering capacities. No one knows where and when humanity might cross a threshold and move to a radically different and perhaps highly undesirable system. Suddenly, many have the uneasy feeling that things are out of control.

If the first factors mentioned above accounting for the renewed salience of environmental issues were circumstantial, this one clearly is not: it is rooted in a mature understanding of natural systems and of the global damage that humans can do to them. This understanding will likely endure and, along with it, the strong concern about the environment. Over the next fifty years there will be no shortage of increasingly ominous data to interpret through this new paradigm. There will almost certainly be a global population approaching nine billion; a decrease in rich, adequately irrigated agricultural land; the loss of much of the remaining virgin forests and the abundance of species they sustain; the widespread depletion and degradation of aquifers, rivers, and other water resources; and the decline of many fisheries. Significant climate change and further ozone depletion are also probable. Even if there are no dramatic, non-linear shifts in the ecosystem (and the probability of some kind of surprise may be quite high), environmental problems will become increasingly severe, and will remain prominent on the scientific, policy, and public agendas.

Current Thought on Environmental Change and Security

A number of scholars have recently asserted that these environmental pressures may seriously affect national and international security.[8] However, although experts have proposed interesting and important arguments about possible links between these variables, most of their work has been preliminary. Some have proposed that environmental change may shift the balance of power between states either regionally or globally, producing instabilities that could lead to war.[9] Or, as global environmental damage increases the disparity between the North and the South, poor nations may confront rich ones for a fairer share of the world's wealth.[10] Conflict may also arise from frustration with hold-out or free-rider states that impede agreement to protect the global commons.[11] Warmer temperatures could lead to contention over new ice-free sea-lanes in the Arctic,[12] and over more easily harvested resources in the Antarctic. Bulging populations and land stress may lead to waves of environmental refugees,[13] often spilling across borders with destabilizing effects on both the recipient's domestic order and international stability.[14] Countries may fight among themselves over dwindling supplies of water and the effects of upstream pollution.[15] In developing countries, a sharp drop in food-crop production could lead to internal strife along urban-rural and nomadic-sedentary cleavages. Moreover, if environmental degradation makes food supplies increasingly tight, exporters may be tempted to use food as a weapon.[16] And the ultimate consequence of environmental change could be the gradual impoverishment of societies in both North and South, which could aggravate class and ethnic cleavages, undermine liberal regimes, and spawn insurgencies.[17] In general, many scholars have the sense that environmental degradation will ratchet up the level of stress within national and international society, increasing the likelihood of many different kinds of conflict and impeding the development of co-operative solutions.

While some of these scenarios seem more plausible than others, it is not immediately clear which are more plausible and why. This chapter will review the major environmental problems that might threaten security and propose some general, system-wide hypotheses about the likely links between environmental change and severe conflict. It uses examples from a variety of cases to support and illustrate these hypotheses; they should eventually be thoroughly tested using both historical and contemporary data at the regional and societal levels.

In brief, the chapter argues that poor countries will in general be more vulnerable to environmental change than rich ones; therefore environmentally induced security threats are likely to arise first in the developing world. In these countries, a range of atmospheric, terrestrial, and aquatic environmental pressures will in time probably produce, either singly or in combination, four main, causally interrelated social effects: reduced agricultural production, general economic decline, population displacement, and disruption of regular and legitimized social relations. These social effects, in turn, may cause several specific types of severe conflict, including scarcity disputes between countries, clashes between ethnic groups, and civil strife and insurgency (with potentially serious international repercussions).

The causal links between these variables are by no means always tight or deterministic. As anti-Malthusians have argued for nearly two centuries, there are numerous intervening factors—physical, technological, economic, and social—that may permit great resilience, variability, and adaptability in humans' relations with their environment.[18] A number of these factors are examined in this chapter; in particular, the free-market mechanisms that may permit developing countries to minimize the negative impacts of environmental degradation. As the human population grows and environmental damage progresses, however, there will be less and less capacity to intervene to keep this damage from producing serious social disruption, including conflict.

A Schema for the Analysis of Environmental Change and Conflict

A careful review of the work cited above on environmental change and conflict indicates that researchers exploring this issue have commonly encountered a number of difficulties, some arising from the analytical approach taken, and others from the demanding nature of the topic itself.[19] For example, researchers have often emphasized atmospheric change (including human-induced greenhouse warming and ozone depletion) to the neglect of severe terrestrial and aquatic environmental problems (such as deforestation, soil degradation, and fisheries depletion). Such problems may in fact interact with atmospheric change to multiply its effects; they deserve immediate attention, because they are already seriously threatening the well-being and cohesion of many societies.

In addition, some of the most widely cited recent writing on the links between environmental change and security is quite anecdotal. In it, the analysis of the mechanisms by which environmental change could lead to conflict remains embedded in analysis of the regions susceptible to particular kinds of environmentally derived conflict. But if researchers are to identify useful generalizations about mechanisms, they need to clearly separate the *how* question (how will environmental change lead to conflict?) from the *where* question (where will such conflict occur?).

This chapter focuses on the *how* question, and will begin by dividing it into two independent questions:

1. What are the important social effects of environmental change?

2. What types of severe conflict, if any, are most likely to result from these social effects?

The context of these two questions can be illustrated with a simple causal diagram. Figure 9.1 shows that the total effect of human activity on the environment in a particular ecological region is a function of two main variables: first, the product of total population in the region and physical activity per capita; and second, the vulnerability of the ecosystem in that region to those particular activities. Activity per capita, in turn, is a function of available physical resources (these include, in addition to non-renewable resources such as minerals, renewable and ecological resources such as water, forests, and agricultural land) and ideational factors (including institutions, social relations, preferences, and beliefs).[20] The figure also shows that environmental effects may cause certain types of social effect that in turn could lead to particular kinds of conflict.[21] For example, the degradation of agricultural land might produce large-scale migration, which could create ethnic conflicts as migratory groups clash with indigenous populations. There are important feedback loops from social effects and conflict to the ideational factors, and thence back to activity per capita and population. Thus ethnic clashes arising from migration could alter the operation of a society's markets, and hence its economic activity.

Figure 9.1 schematically represents an analytical framework in which to address the possible links between environmental change and conflict. This and subsequent causal diagrams thus provide the basis for a detailed causal-path analysis of these links.[22] Not only can such an analysis bring some order into the profusion of data and predictions concerning these issues, but it can also assist researchers to address several of the impediments to research mentioned in the previous section. Most notably, it can help them to gauge the causal power of distant environmental forces, identify potentially important interactions of simultaneous environmental problems, specify intervening variables, and identify causal links across levels of analysis. Furthermore,

Figure 9.1. Environmental Change and Acute Conflict

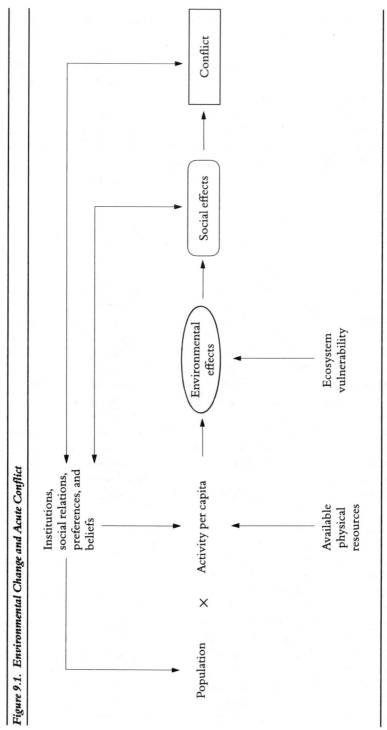

NOTE: In this and all subsequent diagrams, main environmental effects are distinguished by oval outlines, social effects by rounded rectangles, and conflict types by rectangles.

by promoting awareness of a broad range of social effects of environmental change, the causal-path approach should encourage researchers to draw on theories of conflict outside the 'realist' perspective.

The first part of the *how* question above asks about the nature of the causal arrow in Figure 9.1 between environmental effects and social effects, while the second asks about the arrow between social effects and conflict. To focus on these two causal linkages is not to deny the importance of the other variables and linkages in the figure. One must be aware of the role of population growth, demographic structure, and patterns of population distribution.[23] And one must understand the effect of the ideational factors at the top of the diagram. This social and psychological context is immensely broad and complex. It includes patterns of land and wealth distribution; family and community structures; the economic and legal incentives to consume and produce goods (including the system of property rights and markets); perceptions of the probability of long-run political and economic stability; beliefs of people in government, industry, and academe about the economic and social costs of environmental degradation; historically rooted patterns of trade and interaction with other societies; the distribution of coercive power within and among nations; the form and effectiveness of institutions of governance; and metaphysical beliefs about the relationship between humans and nature.

Without a full understanding of these intervening factors one cannot begin to grasp the true nature of the relationships between human activity, environmental change, social disruption, and conflict. Recognition of the role of these factors distinguishes simplistic environmental determinism[24] from sophisticated understandings of the nature of the environmental threat posed to humankind. And it is principally these factors that determine the vulnerability and adaptability of a society when faced with environmental stresses.[25] There is historical evidence that certain societies have technological, institutional, or cultural characteristics that make them very resilient in such circumstances. There is a need not only to identify the thresholds beyond which given societies cannot respond effectively when confronted with particular environmental stresses, but also to determine why some societies respond better than others.

Figure 9.1 clarifies this part of the research agenda. On the one hand, to understand a society's capacity to prevent severe social disruption (where the preventive action could be either mitigation of or adaptation to the environmental stress), one needs to understand the arrows between the ideational factors at the top of the figure and the population, activity per capita, and social effects along the main spine of the figure. On the other hand, if one wishes to understand a society's propensity to exhibit conflict behaviour (given certain social effects caused by the environmental stress), one needs to understand the arrow between the ideational factors and conflict. When sufficiently advanced, this research should help identify key intervention points where policy-makers might be able to alter the causal processes linking human activity, environmental degradation, and conflict. These interventions will fall into two general categories: those that seek to prevent negative social effects and those that seek to prevent the conflict that could result from these social effects. The following pages refer to these as first-stage and second-stage interventions.

The Range of Environmental Problems

Relative to rich countries, developing countries are likely to be affected first and worst by environmental change. By definition, they do not have the financial, material, or intellectual resources of the developed world; further-more, their social and political institutions tend to be fragile and riven with discord, which hinders their ability to develop co-ordinated responses to environmentally induced scarcity and dislocation. It is probable, therefore, that developing societies will be less able to apprehend or respond to environmental disruption.[26]

There are seven major environmental problems (i.e., the environmental effects in Figure 9.1) that might be expected to contribute to conflict within and among developing countries: greenhouse warming, stratospheric ozone depletion, acid deposition, deforestation, degradation of agricultural land, overuse and pollution of water supplies, and depletion of fish stocks. The first three of these problems involve atmospheric change, the next two are terrestrial, and the last two concern water resources. They can all be crudely characterized as large-scale, human-induced problems, with long-term and often irreversible consequences, which is why they are often grouped together under the rubric 'global change'.[27]

Actually, however, these problems vary greatly in spatial scale: the first two involve genuinely global physical processes, while the last five involve regional physical processes, although they may appear in locales all over the planet. These seven problems also vary in time scale: for example, while a region can be deforested in only a few years, and severe ecological and social effects may be noticeable almost immediately, human-induced greenhouse warming will probably develop over many decades, and may not have truly serious implications for humankind for half a century or more after the signal is first detected. In addition, some of these problems (for instance, deforestation and degradation of water supplies) are much more advanced than others (such as greenhouse warming and ozone depletion), and are already starting to produce serious ecological and social disruption. This variance in tangible, empirical evidence for the existence of these respective problems contributes to great differences in our certainty about their severity, and how they will develop. The uncertainties surrounding greenhouse warming are thus far greater than those for deforestation.[28]

Many of these seven problems are causally interrelated. For instance, acid deposition damages agricultural land, fisheries, and forests. In addition, greenhouse warming may contribute to deforestation by moving northward the optimal temperature and precipitation zones for many tree species, by increasing the severity of windstorms and wildfires, and by expanding the range of pests and diseases. (The release of carbon from these dying forests would, of course, reinforce the greenhouse effect.) The increased incidence of ultraviolet radiation because of the depletion of the ozone layer will probably damage trees and crops. And this radiation may also damage phytoplankton at the bottom of the ocean food chain.[29]

Finally, in considering the social effects of environmental change, especially of climate change, one should be especially aware of changes in the incidence of *extreme* environmental events. Wigley notes that social impacts result 'not so much from slow fluctuations in the mean, but from the tails of the distribution, from extreme events'. For instance, while a mean global warming of 2 to 3°C might not seem too significant, in itself, for agricultural production, it may produce a large increase in crop-devastating droughts, floods, heat waves, and storms, even if it does not force the climate system to a completely new equilibrium. Since the probability distributions for most climate variables describe a bell curve, Wigley calculates that 'a change in the mean by one standard deviation would transform the 1-in-20 year extreme to something that could be expected perhaps 1 year in 4, while the 1-in-100 year extreme becomes a 1-in-11 year event.'[30]

Four Principal Social Effects

In addressing the first part of the *how* question above, one realizes that environmental degradation may cause countless, often subtle, changes in developing societies. These range from the increasing need to cook communally as fuel-wood becomes scarce around African villages, to the worsening poverty of Filipino inshore fishermen whose once-abundant grounds have been destroyed by trawlers and industrial pollution.

Which of these social effects are important? What are the crucial links between environmental change and acute conflict? Only certain types of social effect (making up a small proportion of the full range of types) are likely relevant. Clearly, to identify these one must use the best current knowledge and theory about environmental change and its potential social effects; but in addition one must draw on the best knowledge about the nature and causes of social conflict. One can then use this combined information to judge the plausibility of various environment-conflict scenarios (and in turn, of course, identify the relevant social effects). To generate environment-conflict hypotheses, therefore, one must work from both ends towards the middle of the causal chain, and should address the two parts of the how question simultaneously, not consecutively.

Application of this procedure suggests that four principal social effects may, either singly or in combination, substantially increase the probability of acute conflict in developing countries: decreased agricultural production, economic decline, population displacement, and disruption of legitimized and authoritative institutions and social relations.[31]

Agricultural Production

Decreased agricultural production is often mentioned as potentially the most worrisome consequence of environmental change.[32] Figure 9.2 presents some of the causal scenarios frequently proposed by researchers. This illustration is not, of course, intended to be exhaustive: the systemic interaction of environmental and agricultural variables is far more complex than the figure suggests.[33] Moreover, no one region or country will exhibit all the indicated processes. But Figure 9.2 indicates that the current literature identifies many routes by which environmental change may influence food production.

The case of the Philippines provides a good illustration of deforestation's impact (as can be traced out in the figure).[34] As recently as the Second World War, about half the area of the Filipino archipelago was forested. Since then, logging and the encroachment of farms have reduced the virgin and second-growth forest from about 16 million hectares to between 6.8 and 7.6 million hectares. At the turn of the century, the Philippines had about 10 million hectares of virgin forest; now less than a million hectares remains, and it seems certain that almost all of this will be gone by early in the next century. Across the archipelago, especially on the island of Luzon, logging and land-clearing have accelerated erosion, changed regional hydrological cycles and precipitation patterns, and decreased the land's ability to retain water during rainy periods. The resulting flash floods have damaged irrigation works while plugging reservoirs and irrigation channels with silt. This may seriously affect crop production. One study suggests that by 2007 only about half of the projected 36,000 hectares of irrigated farmland on the island of Palawan will actually be irrigable, because of the hydrological effect of decreased forest cover.[35]

Figure 9.2 also highlights the importance of the degradation and decreasing availability of good agricultural land. Currently, total global cropland amounts to about 1.5 billion hectares. Optimistic estimates of potentially arable land on the planet range from 3.2 to 3.4 billion hectares, but nearly all the best land has already been exploited. What is left is either less fertile, insufficiently rain-fed or easily irrigable, infested with pests, or harder to clear and work. Experts generally describe a country as 'land scarce' when 70 per cent or more of the potentially arable land is under production. In Asia about 82 per cent of all potential cropland is cultivated. While the percentages are lower in Africa and Latin America, the poor quality of the remaining land and its inequitable distribution suggest that the previously high rates of cropland expansion cannot be maintained.

For developing countries during the 1980s, cropland grew at just 0.26 per cent a year, less than half the rate of the 1970s. More important, arable land per capita dropped by 1.9 per cent a year.[36] In the absence of a major increase

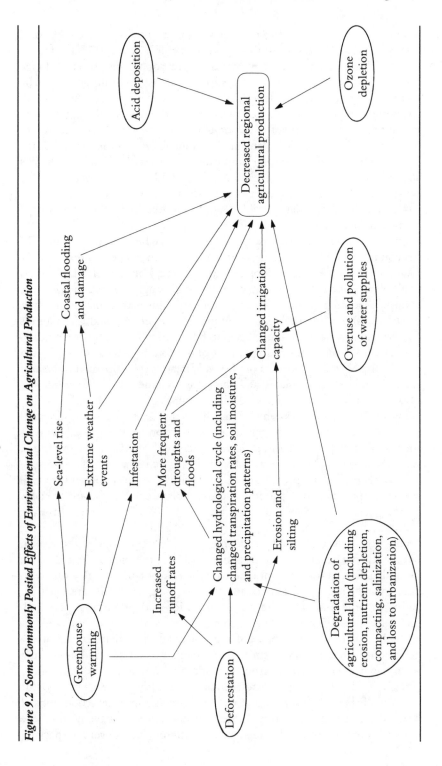

Figure 9.2 Some Commonly Posited Effects of Environmental Change on Agricultural Production

in arable land in developing countries, experts anticipate that the world average of 0.28 hectares of cropland per capita will decline to 0.17 hectares by the year 2025, given the current rate of world population growth.[37] Large tracts of land are being lost each year to a combination of urban encroachment, erosion, nutrient depletion, salinization, waterlogging, acidification, and compacting. The geographer Vaclav Smil, who is generally very conservative in his assessments of environmental damage, estimates that two to three million hectares of cropland are lost annually to erosion, with perhaps twice as much land going to urbanization and at least one million hectares abandoned because of excessive salinity.[38] In addition, about one-fifth of the world's cropland is suffering from some degree of desertification. He concludes that, in all, the planet will lose about one hundred million hectares of arable land between 1985 and 2000.[39]

Smil gives a startling account of the situation in China. From 1957 to 1977 the country lost 33.33 million hectares of farmland (30 per cent of its 1957 total), while it added 21.2 million hectares of largely marginal land. He notes that 'the net loss of 12 million hectares during a single generation when the country's population grew by about 300 million people means that per capita availability of arable land dropped by 40 per cent and that China's farmland is now no more abundant than Bangladesh's — a mere one-tenth of a hectare per capita!' About 15 per cent of the country's territory is affected by erosion. Severe soil loss on the Loess Plateau 'makes the region the area with the lowest grain yields and the poorest standard of life', while the Huanghe river annually carries 1.6 billion tonnes of silt to the sea.[40]

Figure 9.2 also outlines some of the effects that greenhouse warming and climate change may have on agricultural production.[41] Cropland in countries such as Bangladesh and Egypt is extremely vulnerable to storm surges, which will be more common and devastating as global warming progresses, storms increase in intensity, and sea levels rise. The greenhouse effect will also change precipitation patterns and soil moisture; while this may benefit some agricultural regions, others will suffer. The World Resources Institute contends that 'the impacts on agriculture could be double-edged: by altering production in the main food-producing areas, climate change could weaken our ability to manage food crises, and by making growing conditions worse in food-deficit nations, it could increase the risk of famine.'[42] Regions with little capital to fund substantial adjustments in agricultural infrastructure, and with large imbalances between population and agricultural potential, may be at special risk from climate change.

Lately, much has been made of the potentially beneficial effects of the greenhouse effect on agriculture: many plants grow faster and larger in a warm environment rich in carbon dioxide, and they often use water more efficiently.[43] However, optimistic estimates of greatly increased crop yields have usually been based on laboratory experiments under ideal conditions of water and nutrient availability. In general, the estimates have ignored the influence on yields of a higher incidence of extreme climate events (especially droughts and heat waves), increased pest infestation, and the lower nutritional quality of crops grown in a carbon-dioxide-enriched atmosphere (due to an increase in the carbon-nitrogen ratio in the plant tissue).

Economic Decline

Perhaps the most important potential social effect of environmental degradation is the further impoverishment it may eventually produce in developing societies. Figure 9.3 summarizes some of the most important links between environmental change and the capacity of developing nations to produce wealth. It shows that this capacity may be influenced directly by environmental disruption, or indirectly via other social effects, such as decreased agricultural production. (Thus the node labelled 'decreased regional agricultural production' represents all the causal processes indicated in Figure 9.2.)

Figure 9.3 shows that a great diversity of factors may affect the production of wealth. For example, the increase in ultraviolet radiation caused by stratospheric ozone depletion will likely raise the rate of disease in humans and livestock, which may have serious economic consequences. Logging for export markets — as in the Philippines, Indonesia, Honduras, and many other countries — may produce short-term economic gain for a developing country's élite, but the resulting deforestation can greatly reduce the country's longer-term productivity. The increased runoff can damage roads, bridges, and other valuable infrastructure; and the extra siltation may reduce the transport capacity of rivers and their usefulness for generating hydroelectric power. In addition, as forests are destroyed, wood becomes scarcer and more expensive, and it absorbs an increasing share of the household budget for the poor families using it for fuel.[44] Again, while few developing countries or regions will exhibit all causal links indicated in Figure 9.3, most will exhibit some.

Agriculture is the source of a large share of the wealth generated in developing societies. Food production has soared in many regions over the last decades, because capital inputs and new agricultural technologies have more than compensated for declining soil productivity. But some experts believe this economic relief will be short-lived. Jeffrey Leonard writes: 'Millions of previously very poor families that have experienced less than one generation of increasing wealth due to rising agricultural productivity could see that trend reversed if environmental degradation is not checked.'[45] Damage to the soil is already producing a harsh economic impact in some areas. Commenting on Indonesia, Robert Repetto notes: 'With erosion, farm output and income have fallen in some regions without major changes in farm practices; other farmers have been induced to change cropping patterns and input use; and in extreme cases, erosion has led to the complete withdrawal of land from cultivation. . . . As erosion becomes more severe, rice is replaced by peanuts; and on nearly depleted soils only cassava is grown.'[46]

Figure 9.3.   Some Posited Effects of Environmental Change on Economic Productivity in Developing Countries

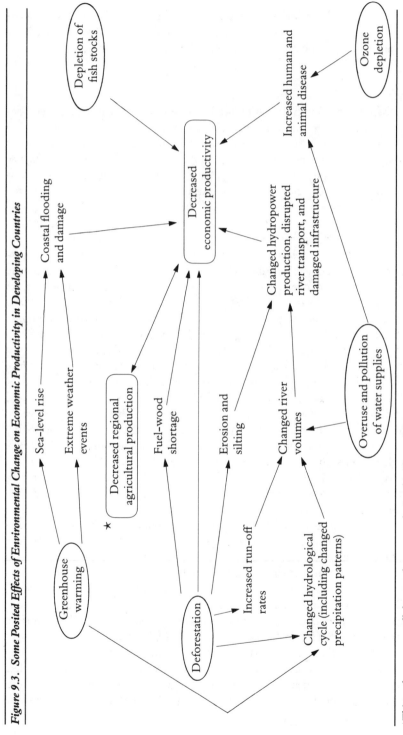

*This node represents all the causal processes depicted in Figure 9.2.

Unfortunately, gauging the actual economic cost of land degradation is not easy. Current national income accounts do not incorporate measures of resource depletion. Repetto comments elsewhere: 'A nation could exhaust its mineral reserves, cut down its forests, erode its soils, pollute its aquifers, and hunt its wildlife to extinction — all without affecting measured income.'[47] Such inadequate measures of economic productivity reinforce the perception that there is a policy trade-off between economic growth and environmental protection; this perception, in turn, encourages societies to generate present income at the expense of their potential for future income.

After a careful and extensive analysis of soil types, cropping practices, logging, and erosion rates in Indonesia, Repetto concludes that the country's national income accounts 'significantly overstate the growth of agricultural income in Indonesia's highlands'.[48] The true economic cost of soil degradation is 'the present value of losses in farm income in current *and* future years.' Using a 10 per cent discount rate, Repetto calculates the one-year cost of erosion in Indonesia to be $481 million. He concludes:

The *one-year* costs of erosion are about 4 percent of the annual value of dryland farm output, and in the same order of magnitude as annual recorded growth in agricultural production in the uplands. Thus despite apparently healthy growth, upland farming on Java has been on a treadmill: each current increment in production is offset by an equal but unrecorded loss in soil productivity. . . . Nearly 40 cents in future income is sacrificed to obtain each dollar for current consumption.[49]

He also estimates that off-site costs, including the higher expense of clearing waterways and irrigation channels of silt, come to $30 to $100 million a year.

Population Displacement

Environmental degradation may produce vast numbers of environmental refugees. For example, sea-level rise may drive people back from coastal and delta areas in Egypt; spreading desert may empty Sahelian countries as their populations move south; and Filipino fishermen may leave their depleted fishing grounds for the cities. The term 'environmental refugee' is somewhat misleading, however, because it implies that environmental disruption will be a clear, proximate cause of certain refugee flows. Usually this disruption will be only one of a large number of interacting physical and social variables that may ultimately force people from their homelands.

The West Bengal-Bangladesh-Assam region in South Asia may provide an important example of environmentally linked population displacement. Over the last two decades, there has been large-scale migration from Bangladesh to Assam. Many specialists believe this movement is a result, at least in part, of a rapidly growing population, unsustainable agricultural practices, and consequent shortages of adequately fertile land. In the future, people may be driven from the region by other environmental problems, including rising sea levels coupled with extreme weather events (which may both result from climate change), and by flooding caused by deforestation in watersheds upstream on the Ganges and Brahmaputra rivers.[50] Norman Myers writes: 'In Bangladesh particularly, the combined effects of population growth, poverty, landlessness, climate change, and inadequate supplies of food will surely generate pressure for mass migration into neighbouring areas of India.'[51]

Disrupted Institutions and Social Relations

The fourth social effect is the disruption of institutions and legitimized, accepted, and authoritative social relations. In many developing societies, this fabric of custom and habitual behaviour will likely be torn by the three social effects described above. Dropping agricultural output may weaken rural communities through malnutrition and disease and by encouraging people to leave; economic decline may corrode confidence in the national purpose, and undermine financial, legal, and political institutions; and mass migrations of people into a region may disrupt labour markets, shift class relations, and upset the traditional balance of economic and political authority between ethnic groups.

These four social effects will often be causally interlinked, sometimes with reinforcing relationships. For example, the population displacement resulting from a decrease in agricultural production may further disrupt agricultural production. Or, economic decline may lead to the flight of people with wealth and education, which in turn could eviscerate universities, courts, and institutions of economic management.

The Capacity of Developing Countries to Respond

First-Stage Interventions

Can developing countries respond effectively to environmental problems, thereby preventing severe and ongoing hardship? In other words, can these societies employ first-stage policy interventions to avert the social effects described here? The example of agricultural production offers reason for optimism. Between 1965 and 1986, many developing regions suffered some combination of the environmental problems outlined above, including land erosion, salinization, nutrient depletion, and land loss to urbanization. Yet during this period cereal production increased at 3 per cent a year, and root-crop output grew at a rate of 0.8 per cent. Meat and milk output increased 2 per cent annually, while the rate for oil crops, vegetables, and pulses was 2.5 per cent. At the regional level, increased food production kept ahead of population growth except in Africa. Regional shortfalls were alleviated by exports from countries with huge surpluses, including the United States, Canada, and Australia. One might therefore conclude that developing countries (with intermittent assistance from Northern grain exporters) have sufficient capacity to respond to these problems.

But the aggregate figures — although undoubtedly useful — are often misleading, because they hide significant disparities in food availability among developing countries. In 1985, for example, average caloric intake was insufficient for health, growth, and productive work in 46 countries. Similarly, there are often large disparities within developing countries. Indonesia is frequently cited for its dramatic success in boosting food production during the last two decades;[52] but while the Javanese lowlands produce huge quantities of rice, falling demand for labour in these areas has forced large numbers of people to pursue subsistence farming in the uplands, where densities are as high as 2,000 per square kilometer, most households own less than 0.4 hectares, and soil degradation is very grave. And while it may be true that the percentage of hungry people in the world has declined, the absolute number is still increasing, and is now variously put between 500 million and 1 billion people.

Moreover, even the aggregate figures may not be as promising as they once were: the effect of the green revolution has passed through the agricultural system in many developing countries, and the rate of increase in global cereal production has declined since the 1960s.[53] In 1988 global stocks fell below the Food and Agriculture Organization's minimum threshold for food security, set at 17 per cent of annual consumption.[54] For three successive years — from 1987 through 1989 — estimated global cereal consumption exceeded production. While bumper grain crops were again harvested in 1990, carryover stocks can be depleted rapidly. The world is always within one or two years of a global food crisis.

Over the long term, whether developing countries can respond effectively to the effects of environmental change on agriculture will depend on the complex interactions within each society of the factors indicated in Figure 9.1, including population growth, available resources (such as soil fertility), ecosystem vulnerability, institutions, social relations, beliefs, and preferences. In particular, one must examine the society's prevailing land-use practices and technologies, land distribution, the social structure of wealth, and market mechanisms within the agricultural sector. This latter factor is especially relevant today. Soviet-led socialism in Eastern Europe has collapsed, and the economies of developing countries that followed the socialist path have generally performed dismally in terms of material consumption. This has helped discredit interventionist economic policies, and has catalyzed a move toward economic liberalism. Numerous developing countries are now relinquishing state control over the marketplace, reducing government spending and allowing unimpeded foreign investment.

Economists often contend that — in a market economy with an efficient price mechanism — environmentally induced scarcity will encourage conservation, technological innovation, and resource substitution.[55] Julian Simon, in particular, has an unwavering faith in the capacity of human ingenuity to overcome scarcity when spurred by self-interest. He notes that developing countries applying market policies have been able to achieve remarkable gains in crop yields per hectare, in spite of declining soil quality, through the use of new semi-dwarf varieties of grains and dramatic increases in capital inputs such as fertilizers and pesticides (these increases are, essentially, a substitution of a petroleum resource for a degraded-land resource). Population growth, by this analysis, is not necessarily a bad thing; in fact it is quite possibly helpful, because it increases the labour force and the potential reservoir of human ingenuity. Boserup, for instance, claims that 'the growth of population is a major determinant of technological change in agriculture.'[56] It may even be true that population growth aids environmental protection by allowing a society to implement certain kinds of labour-intensive soil conservation practices that would otherwise be impossible (such as terracing and the construction of extensive soil-retaining levees).

This is a powerful argument that leads to clear policy recommendations not unlike those (for market liberalization and 'structural adjustment') currently promoted by international financial and lending institutions, such as the IMF and World Bank. It deserves close analysis, as many experts say that a liberal-economic approach offers developing countries the best hope for effectively responding to environmental scarcity.

Cornucopians and Neo-Malthusians

Often, it seems, debates between 'cornucopians' such as Simon, on one hand, and neo-Malthusians such as Paul and Anne Ehrlich on the other reflect deep personal orientations to the world more than empirical evidence.[57] Holsti notes that social scientists face multiple realities when considering such issues; it is possible to build a thoroughly supported case for any of a number of points of view. He asserts: 'My impression is that many of the theoretical arguments about the fundamental contours of our discipline are really debates about optimism and pessimism, our very general outlooks toward the world in which we live.'[58]

To move beyond such biases, one should keep in mind a useful distinction: when speaking of renewable or ecological resources, environmental scientists now often distinguish between resource capital and the income derived from that capital. The capital is the resource stock that generates a flow (the income) that can be tapped for human consumption and well-being. A sustainable economy, using this terminology, is one that leaves the capital intact and undamaged so that future generations can enjoy an undiminished income stream. The cornucopians have a much more flexible conception of ecological capital than the neo-Malthusians. Cornucopians do not worry much about protecting the stock of any single resource, because of their faith that market-driven human ingenuity can always be tapped to allow the substitution of more abundant resources to produce the same end-use service. Extreme cornucopians say that eventually all material scarcities will be reduced to energy scarcities (since, given sufficient energy, we can transmute one element into another and create any compound), and that human ingenuity will, in time, identify a boundless source of energy. In this case, we do not have to worry at all about sustaining our ecological capital.

In contrast, the neo-Malthusian notion of ecological capital is much more rigid. If, for example, average topsoil creation on farmed land is about 0.25 millimeters per year (or about 3.25 tonnes per hectare), then sustainable agriculture should not, on average, produce soil loss greater than this amount. This is a limit on human activity that should rarely be breached: topsoil is a resource essential to human well-being; human beings cannot create it themselves; and petroleum-based substitutes such as fertilizers and pesticides are only short-term remedies. Neo-Malthusians are much more cautious about the capacity of human ingenuity to develop new technologies and to discover possibilities for inter-resource substitution.

Historically, cornucopians have been right to criticize the idea that resource scarcity places fixed limits on human activity. Time and time again humans have found their way around scarcities, and neo-Malthusians have often been justly accused of crying wolf for declaring that doom was just around the corner. But cornucopians go too far in assuming that the experience of the past will pertain to the future. They overlook seven points.

First, whereas serious scarcities of critical resources in the past usually appeared singly, now we are facing multiple scarcities that may exhibit powerful interactive, feedback, and threshold effects. An agricultural region may, for example, be simultaneously affected by degraded water and soil, greenhouse-induced precipitation changes, and increased ultraviolet radiation. This makes the future highly uncertain for policy-makers and economic actors; tomorrow will be full of extreme events and surprises.[59] Furthermore, as numerous renewable and non-renewable resources become scarce simultaneously, there will be fewer abundant resources to substitute for scarce ones; that is, it will be harder to identify substitution possibilities that produce the same end-use services at the costs that prevailed when scarcity was less severe.[60]

Second, in the past the scarcity of a given resource usually increased slowly and incrementally, allowing time for social, economic, and technological adjustment. But human societies now suck in and expel staggering quantities of material, because populations are much larger and the activities of individuals are, on average, more resource-intensive than those of yesteryear.[61] This means that debilitating scarcities often develop much more quickly than before: whole countries are deforested in a few decades; most of a region's topsoil can disappear in a generation; and critical ozone depletion may occur in as little as twenty years. In the future, there will likely be a progressive decrease in the length of time between the first appearance of serious scarcity of a given resource and the arrival of a full-blown resource crisis, leaving societies and markets with far less time to respond.

Third, consumption today has far greater momentum than in the past, because of the size of the consuming population, the sheer quantity of material consumed by this population, and the density of its interwoven fabric of consumption activities. The countless individual and corporate economic actors making up human society are heavily committed to certain patterns of resource use (such as energy production from fossil fuels); and the ability of markets to adapt may be sharply constrained by these entrenched, vested interests.

In the not too distant future, these first three factors will combine to produce a daunting syndrome of environmentally induced scarcity: humankind will face multiple resource shortages that are interacting and unpredictable, that grow to crisis proportions rapidly, and that will be hard to address, because of powerful commitments to certain consumption patterns.

The fourth reason that cornucopian arguments may not apply in the future is that the free-market price mechanism provides a highly imperfect gauge of scarcity. This is especially true for resources that are not fungible—that is, resources that cannot be divided into functionally equivalent units and exchanged for money in the marketplace (such as the atmosphere or biodiversity), and whose scarcity, therefore, cannot be directly reflected by any market mechanism. In the past, many such resources seemed endlessly abundant, and hence not a source of worry. But now they are being degraded and depleted. Moreover, even when the market effectively reflects the scarcity of certain resources, it does not give a good estimate of the decreased or changed quality of life that often accompanies resource substitution and other market adjustments. In addition, the market encourages actors to adopt short time horizons, because future costs and benefits are usually discounted at the expected long-term interest rate.[62] Yet today's economic activities may produce environmental scarcities only decades in the future, because of the long lead times of the physical and social processes involved. Finally, market mechanisms inadequately reflect true resource scarcity, since many economic actors cannot participate in market transactions, because they either lack the resources or are distant from the transaction process in time or space.

The fifth reason is that market-driven adaptation to resource scarcity is most likely to succeed in wealthy societies. Abundant reserves of capital, knowledge, and talent will help economic actors invent new technologies, identify conservation and substitution possibilities, and make the transition to new production and consumption activities. But many of the societies that will confront environmental problems in the coming decades will be poor. Even if they have put in place efficient markets, lack of capital and know-how will hinder their response to these problems. For instance, shifts in precipitation patterns because of greenhouse warming might increase potential food production in certain areas. While some of this new potential might be exploited by certain countries, in general poor countries will be unable to build the new transportation, irrigation, and storage infrastructure necessary to capitalize on the changes. This problem will be worsened if Northern aid budgets are further restricted, as seems likely. Additionally, many environmental problems and scarcities can be addressed only through advanced science and technology. The knowledge and resources for this activity are almost exclusively located in the North, and in general will be used to serve Northern interests.

Sixth, cornucopians have an anachronistic faith in humankind's ability to unravel and manage the myriad processes of nature. There is no *a priori* reason to expect that human scientific and technical ingenuity can always surmount all types of scarcity. Human beings may not have the mental capacity to understand adequately the complexities of environmental-social systems. Even if they do have the capacity, it may simply be impossible, given the physical, biological, and social laws governing these systems, to redress all scarcity or repair all environmental damage. Moreover, the chaotic behaviour of such systems may render them forever beyond prediction and manipulation. Humans may thus never be able to anticipate fully the possible unintended consequences of various adaptation and intervention strategies.[63] Also, the time available to solve these problems is limited. Yet scientific and technical knowledge is cumulative; it must be built incrementally — layer upon layer — and its diffusion in usable form to the broader society often takes decades. Technical solutions to environmental degradation and scarcity may arrive too late to prevent catastrophe.[64]

Seventh and finally, future environmental problems, instead of inspiring the wave of ingenuity predicted by cornucopians, may actually reduce the supply of ingenuity available in a society. The success of market mechanisms depends on an intricate and stable system of institutions, social relations, and shared understandings (the ideational factors in Figure 9.1). Cornucopians often overlook the role of *social* ingenuity in producing this complex legal and economic climate in which *technical* ingenuity can flourish. Policy-makers must be clever social engineers to design and implement effective market mechanisms.[65]

Unfortunately, though, the above-mentioned syndrome of multiple interacting, unpredictable, and rapidly changing environmental problems will increase the complexity and pressure of the policy-making setting. It will also generate numerous social stresses, or increased 'social friction', as élites and interest groups squabble over resources and try to protect their prerogatives. The ability of policy-makers to be good social engineers — for example, to construct efficient markets, to anticipate and internalize external costs, and to mobilize factors of production, including capital and technical ingenuity — will likely decrease as these decision-making complexities and social stresses increase.

The Scarcity-Ingenuity Race

What do the above seven points say about the ability of developing countries to respond effectively to future environmental degradation and scarcity?

This depends on the effect of one other factor: population growth. In many developing countries, population growth gives great impetus to complex processes of environmental change. It operates in conjunction with key social and technological factors, in particular the inequitable distribution of land and inappropriate agricultural modernization. Simon and Boserup are correct: in combination with certain social structures and technologies, population growth has no negative effect on the environment; and if a society's social and technical engineers are very clever, population growth might even alleviate environmental problems. But population growth is often the 'forcing factor' behind environmental degradation; that is, as Figure 9.1 shows, total population is the causal variable changing most rapidly and ominously in the environmental-social system.

Consequently, many developing countries are trapped in a race between population growth (and the climbing consumption and environmental damage it entails, given prevailing technologies and social structures), and their social and technical ingenuity to sustain per capita output (by reforming the social structure, changing technologies, reducing population growth, and lessening or compensating for environmental damage). Most poor countries will need ever-increasing social and technical ingenuity to keep abreast of their population growth and the multiple environmental scarcities it often engenders.

In many developing countries, ingenuity seems likely to lose the race. For one thing, population growth is not slackening quickly enough. In fact, the growth rates of some of the world's most populous countries—including India and China—are hardly declining at all.[66] India's rate has levelled off at around 2.1 per cent (17.9 million people) per year, while China's has stalled at around 1.3 per cent (14.8 million) per year. During the 1970s and early 1980s family size in many countries dropped dramatically from six or seven children to three or four. But demographers and family planners have discovered that it is much more difficult to persuade mothers to forgo a further one or two children to bring family size down to replacement rate. These developments have recently led the United Nations to revise its medium estimate of the globe's population when it stabilizes (predicted to occur towards the end of the twenty-first century), raising it from 10.2 to 11 billion, which is over twice the size of the planet's current population.

Thus the race between ingenuity, on one hand, and consumption and environmental degradation, on the other, is likely to be of longer duration than was anticipated just ten years ago, when population growth rates were falling dramatically. Many countries will have to keep boosting their agricultural production by 2 to 4 per cent per year, well into the next century, to avoid huge food imports.[67] But, for the seven reasons discussed above, the social and technical engineers in these countries may not be able to deliver the ever-increasing ingenuity required over this extended period.

For instance, green-revolution technologies—including new grain varieties, chemical inputs, and wider irrigation—have already been almost fully exploited. There is no new generation of agricultural technologies waiting in the wings to keep productivity rising. Although genetic engineering may eventually help scientists develop nitrogen-fixing, salinity-resistant, and drought-resistant grains, the widespread use of such crops in developing countries is undoubtedly decades in the future. The use of biotechnology to develop new plants is only just beginning and, even if successful, the course of this research will be long, painstaking, and marked by many reversals and mistakes. Moreover, the world will likely need not one but multiple independent technological breakthroughs, and the probability of achieving the whole set may be very small. Finally, the diffusion of the resulting technologies to farmers in developing countries — which would not be rapid even under the best of circumstances — will be hampered by the social friction and lack of resources discussed above.

Without slipping into environmental determinism, in regard to the poorest countries on this planet, one should not invest too much faith in the potential of human ingenuity to respond to multiple and interacting environmental problems once they have become severe. Growing population, consumption, and environmental stresses will increase social friction. This will in turn reduce the capacity of policy-makers in developing countries to intervene as good social engineers, in order to chart a sustainable development path — and to prevent acute social disruption. Neo-Malthusians may underestimate human adaptability in *today's* environmental-social system, but as time passes their analysis may become ever more telling.[68]

Increasingly, the optimism of cornucopians, and others who put great faith in the potential of human ingenuity when spurred by need, seems forced, self-deceptive, and imprudent. The path suggested by cornucopians involves taking a huge gamble. Should it turn out, in the end, that market-driven ingenuity cannot deal with the host of environmental stresses that humankind faces, there is no return to the world of today. The soils, waters, forests, and climate will not repair themselves in a time-span relevant to human societies. In fact they may never return to their current state.[69]

Types of Conflict

It seems likely that first-stage policy interventions will not be fully successful in preventing the four principal social effects posited above. In that case, what types of conflict will result? Specifically, if agricultural production drops, if developing societies slide further into poverty, if large numbers of people are forced from their homelands, and if institutions and social relations are disrupted, what kinds of conflict will develop?

At present the empirical evidence is limited. This may be partly because environmental and population pressures have yet to pass a critical threshold of severity in many developing countries; also, there has been little case-study research on environment-conflict linkages. What follows, therefore, is an attempt to define issues for further research.

Three Theoretical Perspectives on Conflict

In the absence of abundant empirical evidence, scholars must rely on theories on the nature and etiology of social conflict. Few scholars of social conflict adhere to only one type of theory; instead, they tend to combine them in light of the goals of their research and the specific nature of the conflict they are investigating. Three general types of theory — one each at the individual, group, and systemic levels of analysis — are particularly important in light of the four general social effects identified above.

Frustration-aggression theories use individual psychology to explain civil strife — including strikes, riots, coups, revolutions, and guerrilla wars. They suggest that individuals become aggressive when they feel frustrated by something or someone they believe is blocking them from fulfilling a strong desire. Theorists often couple this with the idea of relative deprivation: people are said to become frustrated and aggressive when they perceive a widening gap between the level of satisfaction they have achieved and the level they believe they deserve (satisfaction is often defined in economic terms). Alternatively, some theorists suggest that aggression may arise because of absolute deprivation: that is, the failure to receive a certain minimum amount of food, shelter, or recognition of such things as national or cultural identity.[70]

Group-identity theories use social psychology to help explain conflicts involving nationalism, ethnicity, and religion. The focus here is on the way groups reinforce their identities and the we-they cleavages that often result. Individuals may have a need for a sense of camaraderie or we-ness that can be satisfied in a group when it discriminates against or attacks another group; similarly, a person's sense of self-worth may be strengthened when his or her group's status is enhanced relative to that of other groups. By attacking outside groups, leaders may try to exploit these needs in order to increase their political power within their own groups, but this behaviour makes intergroup divisions deeper and more acrimonious.[71]

Structural theories, which are often grounded in the assumptions of micro-economics and game theory, explain conflicts arising from the rational calculations of actors in the face of perceived external constraints. For a given actor, the structure of his/her social situation is the perceived set of possible interactions with other actors and the perceived likely outcomes of these interactions. This structure can be determined by physical factors such as the number of actors, resource limits, and barriers to movement or communication; by social factors such as shared beliefs and understandings, rules of social interaction, and the set of power relations between actors; and by psychological factors, in particular the beliefs and preferences of other actors. The structure of a social situation can thus also be understood as these physical, social, and psychological constraints.[72]

Structural theories can be roughly divided into those used to explain conflict in general and those used to explain civil strife. General theories suggest that external constraints can encourage or even compel actors to engage in conflict.[73] Domestic theories hold that civil strife will be more likely if there are well-organized groups within a society that can quickly channel, articulate, and co-ordinate discontent. In particular, these theories suggest that insurgency is a function of the 'opportunity structure' confronting groups challenging the authority of élite groups. This opportunity structure depends on the relative power and resources of challenger and élite groups, on the power of groups that might ally themselves with challenger and élite groups, and on the costs and benefits that groups believe will accrue to them through different kinds of collective action in support of, or in opposition to, élite groups.[74]

These theories suggest that severe environmental degradation will produce three principal types of conflict. These should be considered ideal types: they will rarely, if ever, be found in pure form in the real world. As shown in Figure 9.4, the correspondence between the above types of theory and the posited types of conflict is almost one-to-one.

Simple-Scarcity Conflicts

These are explained and predicted by general structural theories. They are the conflicts one intuitively expects when state actors rationally calculate their interests in a zero-sum or negative-sum situation, such as might arise from resource scarcity. Such conflicts have arisen often in the past; they are easily understood within the realist paradigm of international-relations theory; and they therefore are likely to receive much attention from current security scholars. Figure 9.4 suggests that simple-scarcity conflicts will arise over three types of resource in particular: river water, fish, and agriculturally productive land. These renewable resources seem particularly likely to spark conflict because their scarcity is increasing rapidly in some regions, they are often essential for human survival, and they can be physically seized or controlled. There may be a positive feedback relationship between conflict and reduced agricultural production: for example, a reduction in food supplies caused by environmental change may lead countries to fight over irrigable land, and this fighting could further reduce food supplies.

The current controversy over the Euphrates river illustrates how simple-scarcity conflicts can arise. On 13 January 1990, Turkey began filling the giant reservoir behind its new Ataturk dam in southeastern Anatolia. Turkey announced that for one month it would hold back the main flow of the Euphrates river at the dam, and this effectively cut the downstream flow within Syria to about a quarter of its normal rate. By early in the next century, Turkey plans to build a huge complex of over twenty dams and irrigation systems along the upper reaches of the Euphrates. This $21 billion Great Anatolia Project, if fully funded and built, will reduce the annual average flow of the Euphrates within Syria from 32 billion cubic metres to 20 billion. Moreover, the water that passes through Turkey's irrigation systems

Figure 9.4. Some Posited Types of Conflict Likely to Arise from Environmental Change in the Developing World

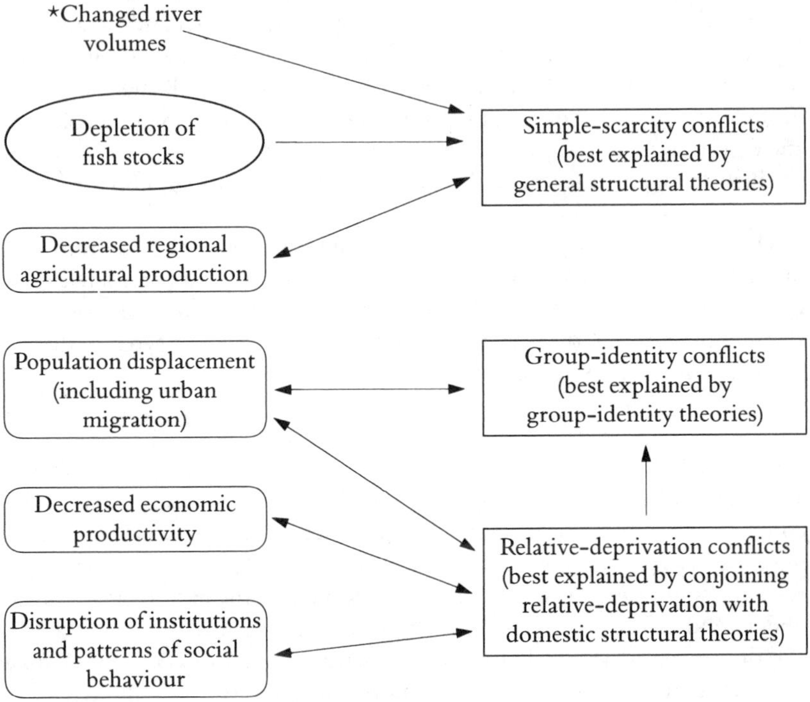

★Changed river volumes

Depletion of fish stocks

Decreased regional agricultural production

Simple-scarcity conflicts (best explained by general structural theories)

Population displacement (including urban migration)

Decreased economic productivity

Disruption of institutions and patterns of social behaviour

Group-identity conflicts (best explained by group-identity theories)

Relative-deprivation conflicts (best explained by conjoining relative-deprivation with domestic structural theories)

★In terms of Figure 9.1, only one of the three posited causes of simple-scarcity conflicts (i.e., decreased regional agricultural production) is a 'social effect'. Depletion of fish stocks is an 'environmental effect', and changed river volumes is a physical variable intermediate between environmental and social effects.

and on to Syria will be laden with fertilizers, pesticides, and salts. Syria is already desperately short of water, with an annual water availability of only about 600 cubic metres per capita.[75] Almost all of the water for its towns, industries, and farms comes from the Euphrates, and the country has been chronically vulnerable to drought. Furthermore, Syria's population growth rate — 3.7 per cent per year — is one of the highest in the world.

Turkey and Syria have exchanged angry threats over this situation. Syria gives sanctuary to guerrillas of the Kurdish Workers Party (the PKK), which has long been waging an insurgency against the Turkish government in eastern Anatolia. Turkey suspects that Syria might use these separatists to gain leverage in bargaining over Euphrates water. Thus in October 1989, then Prime Minister Turgut Ozal suggested that Turkey might impound the river's water if Syria did not restrain the PKK. Although he later retracted the threat, by the spring of 1993 the tensions have not been resolved, nor have high-level talks on water-sharing taken place.

Group-Identity Conflicts

These are explained and predicted by group-identity theories. They will likely arise from the large-scale movements of populations brought about by environmental change. As different ethnic and cultural groups are propelled together under circumstances of deprivation and stress, intergroup hostility with a strong identity dynamic will rise. The aforementioned situation in the Assam-Bangladesh region may be a good example of this process; Assam's ethnic strife over the last decade has apparently been catalyzed by immigration out of Bangladesh.[76] In Africa, migration from drought and famine-stricken areas in the Sahel and the Horn of Africa has contributed to the ethnic strife in the region.

As population and environmental stresses grow in developing countries, there will also be surging immigration to the developed world. People will seek to move from Latin America to the US and Canada, from North Africa and the Middle East to Europe, and from South and Southeast Asia to Australia. This migration has already shifted the ethnic balance in many cities and regions of developed countries, and governments are struggling to contain a xenophobic backlash. Such racial strife will probably become much worse.

Relative-Deprivation Conflicts

This type of conflict may turn out to be the most common and serious type to arise from environmental change. Relative-deprivation theories suggest that as developing societies produce less wealth because of environmental problems, their citizens will probably become increasingly discontented by the widening gap between their actual level of economic achievement and the level they feel they deserve. The rate of change is very important here: the faster the economic deterioration, the greater the discontent. Lower-status groups will be more frustrated than others, because élites will use their power to maintain, as best they can, access to a constant standard of living, despite a shrinking economic pie. At some point, the discontent and frustration of some groups may cross a critical threshold, and they will act violently against those groups perceived to be the agents of their economic misery, and/or those thought to be benefiting from a grossly unfair distribution of economic goods in the society.

Relative-deprivation theories are often contrasted with domestic-structural theories of civil strife. This is unfortunate because, as suggested by Figure 9.4, these points of view can be usefully combined. As noted above, domestic-structural theories emphasize the opportunity structure that confronts potential challenger groups. The idea of opportunity structure is important here, because a principal social effect of environmental change in developing countries is likely to be the disruption of institutions and regular, legitimized social relations. Thus, it seems, environmental problems will not only increase the frustration and anger within developing societies (through increased relative deprivation); in addition, by disrupting institutions and social relations they may open up structural opportunities for challenger groups to act on their anger and overthrow existing authority. McAdam writes:

> *Any* event or broad social process that serves to undermine the calculations and assumptions on which the political establishment is structured occasions a shift in political opportunities. Among the events and processes likely to prove disruptive of the political status quo are wars, industrialization, international political realignments, prolonged unemployment, and widespread demographic changes.[77]

In sum, the relative-deprivation and domestic-structural perspectives together suggest that severe civil strife is likely when (1) there are clearly defined and organized groups in a society; (2) some of these groups regard their level of economic achievement—and in turn the broader political and economic system—as wholly unfair; and (3) these same groups believe that all peaceful opportunities to effect change are blocked, yet regard the balance of power within the society as unstable—that is, they believe there are structural opportunities for overthrowing authority in the society.[78]

Figure 9.4 reflects these two theoretical perspectives: relative-deprivation conflicts are jointly caused by decreased economic productivity and disrupted institutions. These causal relations are proposed to be reciprocal. In addition, the figure proposes that the arrival of refugees in an area—even if the event does not reduce total economic productivity—will likely result in a dilution of existing resources, and aggravate a sense of relative deprivation in the indigenous population. This stress may also manifest itself as inter-ethnic tension. Thus there are causal arrows from population displacement to relative-deprivation conflicts, and from these conflicts to group–identity conflicts.

The probability of civil strife is also strongly influenced by whether challenger groups have the organizational and leadership capacity to provide themselves with adequate information and co-ordination. Leaders are particularly important in producing the firm belief among the members of a challenger group that the group's situation should and can be changed. McAdam calls this a group's 'cognitive liberation'. Leaders set up and define the categories through which challenger groups see their situations and themselves. By developing and exploiting a particular theory of the social good, leaders can shift the preferences of the members of a challenger group, so they come to view their situation as illegitimate and intolerable (thus increasing their sense of relative deprivation). In addition, by altering group members' self-perceptions, their understandings of the nature of power, and their assumptions about the possible means to achieve change, leaders can instil the belief that their group will succeed in a contest for power (thereby changing the perceived opportunity structure).

The Filipino Insurgency

There is strong evidence that environmental damage is an underlying cause of civil strife in the Philippines.[79] The country's population growth rate of 2.5 per cent is among the highest in Southeast Asia. This growth, combined with the expansion of large-scale lowland agriculture for the export market, has displaced many traditional farmers and swelled the numbers of landless agricultural labourers. Many have migrated to the Philippines' steep and ecologically vulnerable uplands, where they have cleared land or established plots on previously logged land. This has set in motion a cycle of erosion, falling food production, and further clearing of land. In the Filipino uplands, even marginally fertile land is becoming hard to find in many places, and economic conditions for the peasants are often dire.

It is in these peripheral areas, largely beyond the effective control of the central government, that civil dissent is rampant. Although the country has suffered from serious internal conflict for many decades, resource stresses and environmental degradation appear to be increasingly powerful forces driving local discontent. During the 1980s, the National Democratic Front (NDF) and the New People's Army (NPA) found upland peasants very receptive to revolutionary ideology, especially where coercive practices of landlords and local governments appear to leave them little choice but to rebel or starve. In a vivid description, Gregg Jones highlights the connection between deforestation, land degradation, and civil unrest:

> 'The magnitude of the land problem can be summed up here,' the Communist Party official said, gesturing around us toward the bare, rocky mountains where *kaingeros* (slash-and-burn farmers) were losing their fight to scrape a living from the tired soil. 'Look at these people, trying to cultivate this rocky hillside. They have no other place to go.'
>
> We were sitting in an NPA camp in the Cordillera Mountains of Nueva Vizcaya province in 1988 with a bird's-eye view of the desperate plight of Filipino peasants in this rugged corner of the northern Philippines. In all directions, the mountains had been almost entirely stripped of trees by logging companies owned by powerful politicians. Erosion was cutting deep grooves into the severe slopes and carrying away the thin remaining layer of precious topsoil. By night, the mountainsides twinkled with the orange glow of fires set by *kaingeros* as they prepared plots wrested from the hardscrabble for June planting. By day, an acrid pall of smoke and haze hung above the treeless hills, which shimmered like a desert mirage in the baking tropical sun.[80]

The Filipino insurgency is motivated by the relative deprivation of the landless agricultural labourers and poor farmers displaced into the uplands where they try to eke a living from the failing land; it exploits structural opportunities in the country's hinterland provided by the crumbling of the central government's authority; and it is facilitated by the creative leadership of the cadres of the NPA and the National Democratic Front (NDF). Building on indigenous understandings and social structures, these revolutionary groups help the peasants define their situation and focus their discontent, and they assist the peasants in extracting concessions from landlords. Hawes conducted in-depth interviews in these peripheral areas, and he describes how the NDF and NPA have changed the peasants' understandings of their situation:

> According to the farmers, they did not think about struggling to change their situation before the comrades came. They felt it was enough just to work and eat. Although they believed they had a right to own land, the legal concept of private property had penetrated deeply; it was, to them, a right to *buy* the land. The cadres taught them how to struggle, how to petition for changes, and how to confront the landlord. Now they feel they have a right to land even if they cannot afford to buy it. Their vision of acceptable patterns of landholding has changed, as has the ability to implement their vision.[81]

This example suggests that to assess the likelihood of civil strife arising from environmental degradation in a particular society, one must have a thorough understanding of the social relations, institutions, and beliefs of the people and groups in that society. One needs to know its class, ethnic, religious, and linguistic structure; the culture of leadership in these groups and in the society as a whole; and the theories of the social good that motivate challenger and élite groups. In technical terms, one needs to use the techniques of anthropology, ethnomethodology, and interpretivism to develop a detailed internal understanding of these societies.[82] Since the analysis must, therefore, be so specific to each case, at this point one cannot hope for more than very rough, probabilistic generalizations about the relationship between environmental degradation, economic decline, and civil strife.

Conflict Objectives and Scope

Table 9.1 compares some attributes of the principal types of acute conflict that may result from environmental change. The table lists the objectives

Table 9.1. Comparison of Conflict Types

CONFLICT TYPE	OBJECTIVE SOUGHT	CONFLICT SCOPE
Simple-scarcity	Relief from scarcity	International
Group-identity	Protection and reinforcement of group identity	International or domestic
Relative-deprivation	Distributive justice	Domestic (with international repercussions)

sought by actors involved in these conflicts. There is strong normative (what 'ought' to be) content to the motives of challenger groups involved in relative-deprivation conflicts: these groups believe the distribution of rewards is unfair. But such an 'ought' does not necessarily drive simple-scarcity conflicts: one state may decide that it needs something another state has, and then try to seize it, without being motivated by a strong sense of unfairness or injustice. The table also shows that the predicted scope of conflict differs. Although relative-deprivation conflicts will tend to be domestic, one should not underestimate their potentially severe international repercussions. Wilkenfeld finds that the links between civil strife and external-conflict behaviour depend on the nature of the regime and on the kind of internal conflict it faces. For example, highly centralized dictatorships threatened by revolutionary actions, purges, and strikes are especially prone to engage in war and belligerent activities directed at external societies. In comparison, less-centralized dictatorships are more prone to war and belligerence when threatened by guerrilla action and assassinations.[83] External aggression may also result after a new regime comes to power through civil strife: Skocpol suggests that regimes born of revolution, for example, are particularly good at mobilizing their citizens and resources for military preparation and war.[84]

While environmental stresses and the conflicts they induce may encourage the rise of revolutionary regimes, other results are also plausible: these pressures may, for instance, overwhelm the management capacity of institutions in developing countries, inducing praetorianism[85] or even widespread social disintegration. They may also weaken the control of governments over their territories, especially over the hinterland (as in the Philippines).[86] The regimes that do succeed to power in the face of such disruption are likely to be extremist, authoritarian, and abusive of human rights. Moreover, the already short time horizons of policy-makers in developing countries will be further shortened. These political factors could seriously undermine efforts to mitigate and adapt to environmental change.

If many developing countries evolve in the direction of extremism, the interests of the North may often be directly threatened. Of special concern here is the growing disparity between rich and poor nations that may be induced by environmental change. Heilbroner notes that revolutionary regimes 'are not likely to view the vast difference between first class and cattle class with the forgiving eyes of their predecessors'. Furthermore, these nations may be heavily armed, as the continued proliferation of nuclear and chemical weapons and ballistic missiles suggests. Such regimes, he claims, could be tempted to use nuclear blackmail as a 'means of inducing the developed world to transfer its wealth on an unprecedented scale to the underdeveloped world'.[87] Ullman, however, believes this concern is overstated. Third World nations are unlikely to confront the North violently because of the 'superior destructive capabilities of the rich'.[88] The discussion in this chapter suggests that environmental stress and its attendant social disruption will so debilitate the economies of developing countries that they will be unable to amass sizeable armed forces, conventional or otherwise. But the North would surely be unwise to rely on impoverishment and disorder in the South for its security.

Second-Stage Interventions

There are many factors that could break the causal links between the four main social effects identified earlier in this chapter and the three types of conflict described in the previous section. Some of these factors could be open to intentional manipulation by policy-makers and would therefore qualify as potential second-stage interventions.

To focus first on domestic conflict, it appears that regime repressiveness is a critical variable. Muller and Seligson, for instance, find that semi-repressive regimes are more vulnerable to insurgency induced by income inequality than either highly repressive or democratic regimes. In semi-repressive societies, dissident groups can develop 'relatively strong organizations', but 'opportunities to engage in nonviolent forms of collective action that effectively exert influence on the political process are limited.'[89] This underscores the importance of a society's opportunity structure.

Another critical variable is the perceived legitimacy of the regime — that is, its perceived fairness, appropriateness, and reasonableness. Lipset shows that this variable mediates the relationship between economic crisis and political instability: economic crisis must first lead to a crisis of legitimacy before widespread civil strife can occur.[90] A perception that the political and economic system is legitimate will moderate a citizen's sense of relative deprivation, and will hinder the mass mobilization of discontent. Through various techniques of persuasion and distraction, policy-makers may be able to sustain a perception of legitimacy even in the face of environmentally induced economic decline.

Finally, there is the role of *politics* in shaping a society's response to social stress. For example, analysing the varied effects of the Depression on European societies in the 1930s, Zimmermann and Saalfeld emphasize the explanatory importance of coalitions between politically powerful groups such as agrarian classes, labour, the bourgeoisie/business class, and the state. They argue that 'the key to understanding the political implications of the Depression is the forging of new coalitions or reaffirmation of older ones which either defended democracy or led to its collapse.'[91] The propensity for stabilizing coalitions is influenced by a host of factors, some quite idiosyncratic, including political culture, the nature and extent of socio-economic cleavage, the 'channels and procedures' for political bargaining, and (as emphasized previously) political leadership.

In the area of international conflict, several variables might offer opportunities for second-stage policy intervention. For example, the spread of liberal democracy in the developing world might reduce the chance that environmental stress and its social effects will cause interstate conflict.[92] Similarly, increased trade between states could increase their economic interdependence, and thereby strengthen disincentives to engage in conflict.[93] Also important are the nature and rate of change of power relations among states. These factors may be affected by environmental degradation, yet they may also be open to independent manipulation by political leaders. Numerous scholars of international relations, especially those of the realist school, have claimed that shifting power relations can prompt war. 'According to realism,' Gilpin writes, 'the fundamental cause of wars among states and changes in international systems is the uneven growth of power among states.' He suggests that war may be started by a dominant state suffering declining power, while Organski and Kugler contend the initiator will usually be a weaker state gaining in power and challenging the hegemon.[94] Whichever view is more accurate, these theories suggest that statesmen might hold in check the risk of interstate conflict despite the effects of environmental change, if they can keep power relations among states relatively stable.

Conclusions

This chapter sets out a research agenda for studying the links between environmental change and acute conflict. This agenda is structured by the two parts of the 'how' question, by the analytical schema in Figure 9.1, and by the diagrammatic method of causal-path analysis that helped identify possible routes to conflict.

Current theories and data make it difficult to go much further than the preliminary analysis offered here. There is a need for case studies of specific societies, focusing on the *where* question: Where are the different kinds of environmentally derived conflict most likely to occur? Research so directed will help answer the *how* question and at the same time reveal important things about real societies in the real world.

There are numerous intervening variables (including institutions, technologies, and market mechanisms) that humankind might influence in order to change the course of environmental-social systems. Hope for avoiding widespread conflict could rest with such variables. Research may show that there are real opportunities for intervention; hardship and strife are not preordained. But it seems likely that, as environmental degradation proceeds, not only will the size of the potential social disruption increase, but the capacity to intervene to prevent this disruption will decrease. It is, therefore, not a reasonable policy response to assume societies can intervene at a late stage, when the crisis is at hand. Developing countries, in concert with the North, should act now to address the forces behind environmental degradation.

Notes

[1] A longer version of this chapter was prepared as a paper for the Global Environmental Change Committee of the Social Science Research Council in New York. Portions have appeared in 'Environmental Change and Economic Decline in Developing Countries', *International Studies Notes* 16, 1 (Winter 1991), 18-23; 'Environmental Change and Human Security', *Behind the Headlines* 48, 3 (Toronto: Canadian Institute for International Affairs, 1991); and 'On the Threshold: Environmental Changes as Causes of Acute Conflict', *International Security* 16, 2 (Fall 1991), 76-116. For their helpful comments, I am very grateful to Peter Cebon, William Clark, Daniel Deudney, Peter Gleick, Ernst Haas, Fen Hampson, Sean Lynn-Jones, Vicki Norberg-Bohm, George Rathjens, James Risbey, Richard Rockwell, Thomas Schelling, Eugene Skolnikoff, Martha Snodgrass, Janice Stein, Urs Thomas, and Myron Weiner. The Royal Society of Canada provided some initial financial support for this research, while the Donner Canadian Foundation sponsored the preparation of an early version of the paper.

[2] Philip Shabecoff, 'Global Warming Has Begun, Expert Tells Senate', *New York Times* (24 June 1988), A1 and A14.

[3] This incident and its media aftermath are well-described by Stephen Schneider in chapter 7 of *Global Warming: Are We Entering the Greenhouse Century?* (San Francisco: Sierra, 1989).

[4] A chaotic system has non-linear and feedback relationships between its variables that amplify small perturbations, thereby rendering accurate prediction of the system's state increasingly difficult, the further one tries to project into the future. Chaos should not be confused with randomness: deterministic causal processes still operate at the microlevel and, although the system's state may not be precisely predictable for a given point in the future, the boundaries within which its variables must operate are often identifiable. See James Crutchfield, J. Doyne Farmer, and Norman Packard, 'Chaos', *Scientific American* 255 (Dec. 1986), 46-57. A popularized account is James Gleick, *Chaos: Making of a New Science* (New York: Viking, 1987).

[5] Wallace Broecker, 'Unpleasant Surprises in the Greenhouse?' *Nature* 328 (9 July 1987), 123-6. See also James Gleick, 'Instability of Climate Defies Computer Analysis', *New York Times* (20 March 1988), 30. Clark has made a similar point about interlinked physical, ecological, *and* social systems. See William Clark, *On the Practical Implications of the Carbon Dioxide Question* (Laxenburg, Austria: International Institute of Applied Systems Analysis, 1985), 41.

[6] J.C. Farman, B.G. Gardiner, and J.D. Shanklin, 'Large Losses of Total Ozone in Antarctica Reveal Seasonal ClO_x/NO_x Interaction', *Nature* 315 (16 May 1985), 207-10. Significant depletion of ozone over Antarctica began in the 1970s but was not identified until the 1980s, because ozone-measuring satellites had been programmed to discard anomalous results. See Schneider, *Global Warming*, 226.

[7] See, for example, the speeches on the floor of the US Senate by Senators Nunn, Gore, and Wirth (28 June 1990), *Congressional Record — Senate*, S8929-37.

[8] See, for example, Janet Brown, ed., *In the U.S. Interest: Resources, Growth, and Security*

in the Developing World (Boulder, CO: Westview, 1990); Neville Brown, 'Climate, Ecology and International Security', Survival (Nov./Dec. 1989), 519-32; Peter Gleick, 'Climate Change and International Politics: Problems Facing Developing Countries', Ambio 18 (1989), 333-9; Gleick, 'The Implications of Global Climatic Changes for International Security', Climatic Change 15 (1989), 309-25; Ronnie Lipschutz and John Holdren, 'Crossing Borders: Resource Flows, the Global Environment, and International Security', Bulletin of Peace Proposals 21 (June 1990), 121-33; Jessica Tuchman Mathews, 'Redefining Security', Foreign Affairs 68 (1989), 162-77; Norman Myers, Not Far Afield: U.S. Interests and the Global Environment (Washington, DC: World Resources Institute, 1987); Myers, 'Environment and Security', Foreign Policy 74 (Spring 1989), 23-41; Michael Renner, National Security: The Economic and Environmental Dimensions, Worldwatch Paper 89 (Washington, DC: Worldwatch, 1989); Richard Ullman, 'Redefining Security', International Security 8, 1 (Summer 1983), 129-53.

[9]David Wirth, 'Climate Chaos', Foreign Policy 74 (Spring 1989), 10.

[10]Robert Heilbroner, An Inquiry into the Human Prospect (New York: W.W. Norton, 1980), 39 and 95; William Ophuls, Ecology and the Politics of Scarcity: A Prologue to a Political Theory of the Steady State (San Francisco: Freeman, 1977), 214-17.

[11]Daniel Deudney, 'The Case Against Linking Environmental Degradation and National Security', Millennium 19 (1990), 473-74.

[12]Fen Hampson, 'The Climate for War', Peace and Security 3 (Autumn 1988), 9; Ian Cowan, 'Security Implications of Global Climatic Changes', Canadian Defence Quarterly (Oct. 1989), 47.

[13]Jodi Jacobson, Environmental Refugees: A Yardstick of Habitability, Worldwatch Paper 86 (Washington, DC: Worldwatch Institute, 1988).

[14]Population stress is often indicated as the cause of the brief Soccer War between El Salvador and Honduras in 1969. See P. Ehrlich, A. Ehrlich, and John Holdren, Ecoscience: Population, Resources and Environment (San Francisco: Freeman, 1977), 908. For a more sophisticated appraisal, see William Durham, Scarcity and Survival in Central America: The Ecological Origins of the Soccer War (Stanford, CA: Stanford Univ. Press, 1979). On the disparity in population growth between the North and the South, see Nathan Keyfitz's review of Alfred Sauvy, L'Europe submergée: Sud → Nord dans 30 ans (Paris: Dunod, 1987), in Population and Development Review 15 (June 1989), 359-62. See also Alfred Sauvy, A General Theory of Population (New York: Basic, 1969).

[15]Gleick, 'Climate Change', 336; Malin Falkenmark, 'Fresh Waters as a Factor in Strategic Policy and Action', in Arthur Westing, ed., Global Resources and International Conflict: Environmental Factors in Strategic Policy and Action (New York: Oxford Univ. Press, 1986), 85-113.

[16]Peter Wallensteen, 'Food Crops as a Factor in Strategic Policy and Action', in Westing, ed., Global Resources, 146-55.

[17]Ted Gurr, 'On the Political Consequences of Scarcity and Economic Decline', International Studies Quarterly 29 (1985), 51-75.

[18]In his classic formulation, the economist Thomas Malthus claimed that severe

human hardship was unavoidable, because human population grows geometrically when unconstrained, while food production can only grow arithmetically; Malthus, *An Essay on the Principle of Population* (New York: Penguin, 1970), 70-1.

[19] A review of these difficulties can be found in Thomas Homer-Dixon, *Environmental Change and Violent Conflict*, Occasional Paper 4 (Cambridge, MA: American Academy of Arts and Sciences, 1990), 4-7.

[20] Over short and medium terms, activity per capita is also a function of the economy's current capital stock, which reflects the society's prevailing level and type of technological development. Over the long term, one can assume that a society's technology is a result of two components of Figure 9.1: certain ideational factors (most importantly, beliefs about the nature of physical reality held by particular knowledge-oriented groups in the society) and available physical resources. The adjective ideational is used to emphasize that factors such as institutions, social relations, and beliefs are products of the human mind.

[21] Numerous writers, especially those considering the social impact of climate change, have generated similar diagrams. See in particular the excellent survey article by Richard Warrick and William Riebsame entitled 'Societal Response to CO_2-Induced Climate Change: Opportunities for Research', *Climatic Change* 3 (1981), 387-428. All the figures in this chapter represent a compromise emphasizing visual accessibility and explanatory power.

[22] Each variable in Figure 9.1 clearly aggregates many specific subvariables. For example, activity per capita encompasses subvariables ranging from the extent of cattle ranching to the rate of automobile use. Consequently, an arrow in Figure 9.1 may represent either a positive or a negative causal relation, depending on the specific subvariables considered. In subsequent diagrams, which identify more specific variables, all arrows represent positive causal relations.

[23] Experts still vigorously dispute the effects of population growth on the environment, economic well-being, and social organization. Julian Simon, for example, is relentlessly optimistic in *The Ultimate Resource* (Princeton: Princeton Univ. Press 1981), while Paul and Anne Ehrlich reiterate their well-known pessimism in *The Population Explosion* (London: Hutchinson, 1990). The question is thoroughly surveyed by Geoffrey McNicoll in 'Consequences of Rapid Population Growth: An Overview and Assessment', *Population and Development Review* 10 (June 1984), 177-240. See also Robert Repetto, 'Population, Resources, Environment: An Uncertain Future', *Population Bulletin* 42 (July 1987); Peter Hendry, 'Food and Population: Beyond Five Billion', *Population Bulletin* 43 (April 1988); and M. Mamdani, *The Myth of Population Control* (New York: Monthly Review, 1973).

[24] Neville Brown, for example, implies that climate change was an important and proximate cause of social upheaval in Europe in the late 1840s, the imperial expansion between 1850 and 1940, the cold war, and the 1974 Ethiopian coup. This article is perhaps the most egregious example of neo-environmental determinism in the environmental security literature. See Brown, 'Climate, Ecology and International Security', 532-4.

[25] These two issues are the focus of much research and thought. For a survey, see Warrick and Riebsame, 'Societal Response'. For a summary of the conditions and

variables that seem to be important in determining vulnerability, see Diana Liverman, 'Vulnerability to Global Environmental Change', in *Understanding Global Environmental Change: The Contributions of Risk Analysis and Management*, report of an international workshop, Clark University, 11-13 October 1989, Roger Kasperson et al., eds (Worcester, MA: Clark University, 1989), 32-3.

[26]Gurr, 'Political Consequences of Scarcity', 70-1. See also Liverman, 'Vulnerability', 32; Ian Burton et al., *The Environment as Hazard* (New York: Oxford Univ. Press, 1978); and Warrick and Riebsame, 'Societal Response', 401.

[27]Readers interested in technical detail should consult *World Resources 1990-91* (New York: Oxford Univ. Press, 1990), and *World Resources 1988-89* (New York: Basic, 1988). This publication is produced biennially by the World Resources Institute in collaboration with the United Nations Environment Programme and other organizations. It is widely regarded as the most accessible, accurate, and comprehensive source of information on global change issues. The more popular *State of the World* report published annually by the Worldwatch Institute is useful, but sometimes selective and tendentious. Also helpful are *The State of Food and Agriculture* published yearly by the Food and Agriculture Organization of the United Nations, and William Clark et al., 'Managing Planet Earth', *Scientific American*, Special Issue 261 (September 1989).

[28]Determining the exact extent of deforestation in a region is, however, often very difficult. There are different kinds and degrees of forest degradation, and it is often not clear whether a particular hectare should be included in the category deforested. Furthermore, forests frequently recover through planting and natural regeneration, which also tends to blur category boundaries. Finally, satellite images are far less precise than often thought in allowing researchers to determine the extent of forest damage. The images usually have to be supplemented with detailed ground inspections. See Vaclav Smil, *Energy, Food, Environment: Realities, Myths, Options* (Oxford: Oxford Univ. Press, 1987), 231-37.

[29]Robert Worrest et al., 'Potential Impact of Stratospheric Ozone Depletion on Marine Ecosystems', in John Topping, Jr, ed., *Coping with Climate Change: Proceedings of the Second North American Conference on Preparing for Climate Change* (Washington, DC: Climate Institute, 1989), 256-62.

[30]T.M.L. Wigley, 'Impact of Extreme Events', *Nature* 316 (1985), 106-7.

[31]While these four effects deserve special attention, they are not exactly comparable. First, population displacement and decreased agricultural productivity involve environmental and social systems narrower in scope than economic decline or disrupted institutions. Second, one understands and analyses these four effects using concepts and methods from sharply different disciplinary paradigms. For instance, the disruption of social relations caused by environmental change is perhaps best grasped using an internal or interpretive approach to social understanding; but assessing economic decline often involves quantitative evaluation of output using the tools of modern econometrics. Third, as Warrick and Riebsame point out, agricultural systems are best thought of as intermediate systems implicating both physical and social variables; on the other hand, economic, institutional, and habitat systems are more purely social, and are therefore perhaps more

flexible and resilient in the face of environmental shock; Warrick and Riebsame, 'Societal Response', 393-4.

[32]See, for example, Lester Brown, 'Reexamining the World Food Prospect', in *State of the World 1989* (New York: W.W. Norton, 1989), 41-58.

[33]Useful discussions include World Commission on Environment and Development, 'Food Security: Sustaining the Potential', in *Our Common Future* (Oxford: Oxford Univ. Press, 1987), chapter 5, 118-46; *World Resources 1988-89*, 18-21, 51-68, and especially 215-34, 271-84; *World Resources 1990-91*, 5-6, 83-100; Food and Agriculture Organization, *The State of Food and Agriculture 1989*, 65-74.

[34]The principal works on the Philippines used in this chapter are Gary Hawes, 'Theories of Peasant Revolution: A Critique and Contribution from the Philippines', *World Politics* 42 (Jan. 1990), 261-98; Gregg Jones, *Red Revolution: Inside the Philippine Guerrilla Movement* (Boulder, CO: Westview, 1989); Myers, *Not Far Afield*; Gareth Porter and Delfin Ganapin, Jr, *Resources, Population, and the Philippines' Future: A Case Study*, WRI Paper 4 (Washington, DC: World Resources Institute, 1988); World Bank, *Philippines: Environment and Natural Resource Management Study* (Washington, DC: World Bank, 1989).

[35]Christopher Finney and Stanley Western, 'An Economic Analysis of Environmental Protection and Management: An Example from the Philippines', *The Environmentalist* 6 (1986), 56.

[36]Nafis Sadik, *The State of the World Population 1990* (New York: United Nations Population Fund, 1990), 8.

[37]*World Resources 1990-91*, 87. Nearly 73 per cent of all rural households in developing countries are either landless or nearly landless. Using this figure, Leonard estimates that '935 million rural people live in households that have too little land to meet the minimum subsistence requirements for food and fuel. These data exclude China, which could add as many as 100-200 million more people to the category'. See Jeffrey Leonard, 'Overview', *Environment and the Poor: Development Strategies for A Common Agenda* (New Brunswick, NJ: Transaction, 1989), 13.

[38]Smil, *Energy, Food, Environment*, 230. The World Resources Institutes cites a figure of 6 to 7 million hectares, which is 'more than twice the rate in the past three centuries'; *World Resources 1989-90*, 217. The Food and Agriculture Organization (FAO) calculates that nearly half the 92 million hectares of irrigated cropland in the developing world needs reclamation, because of salinity and poor drainage; Food and Agriculture Organization, *Agriculture: Toward 2000* (Rome: FAO, 1987), 257.

[39]Experts give desertification a variety of meanings. In general, it implies a complex syndrome of very low soil productivity, poor rain-use efficiency by vegetation, and consequent adverse changes in the hydrological cycle. It can therefore encompass several of the variables identified in Figure 9.2. See Michel Verstraete, 'Defining Desertification: A Review', *Climatic Change* 9 (1986).

[40]Smil, *Energy, Food, Environment*, 223, 230.

[41]There is widespread scientific debate about the likely magnitude, rate, and timing of greenhouse warming, and about its climatic, ecological, and social impacts. The current consensus is summarized in the reports prepared by Working Groups I and

II of the Intergovernmental Panel on Climate Change under the auspices of the World Meteorological Organization and the United Nations Environment Program. The complete report of Working Group I has been published as *Climate Change: The IPCC Scientific Assessment*, J.T. Houghton et al., eds (Cambridge: Cambridge Univ. Press, 1990). A very useful general resource on the greenhouse effect, climate change, and its impacts is Mark Handel and James Risbey, *An Annotated Bibliography on Greenhouse Effect Change* (Cambridge, MA: Center for Global Change Science, MIT, 1990).

[42]Some experts are much more optimistic. See Thomas Schelling, 'Climatic Change: Implications for Welfare and Policy', National Research Council, *Changing Climate: Report of the Carbon Dioxide Assessment Committee* (Washington, DC: National Academy Press, 1983), 477.

[43]See, for instance, Richard Adams et al., 'Global Climate Change and US Agriculture', *Nature* 345 (17 May 1990), 219-24.

[44]The FAO estimates that up to 3 billion people in the developing world will face acute fuel-wood shortages by the year 2000; Food and Agriculture Organization, 'Fuelwood Supplies in the Developing Countries', *FAO Forestry Paper 42* (Rome, 1983).

[45]Leonard, *Environment and the Poor*, 27.

[46]Robert Repetto, 'Balance-Sheet Erosion — How to Account for the Loss of Natural Resources', *International Environmental Affairs* 1 (Spring 1989), 129.

[47]Robert Repetto, 'Wasting Assets: The Need for National Resource Accounting', *Technology Review* (Jan. 1989), 40.

[48]Ibid., 42.

[49]Repetto, 'Balance-Sheet Erosion', 129-32.

[50]Wigley and Warrick, *Effects of Climate Change*; Lester Brown and John Young, 'Feeding the World in the Nineties', in *State of the World: 1990* (Washington, DC: Norton, 1990), 59-78.

[51]Norman Myers, 'Environmental Security — the Case of South Asia', *International Environmental Affairs* 1 (Spring 1989), 150.

[52]See, for example, Peter Timmer, 'Indonesia: Transition from Food Importer to Exporter', *Food Price Policy in Asia: A Comparative Study*, Terry Sicular, ed. (Ithaca, NY: Cornell Univ. Press, 1989), 24-64; also Nathan Keyfitz, 'An East Javanese Village in 1953 and 1985: Observations on Development', *Population and Development Review* 11 (Dec. 1985), 695-719.

[53]From 1962 to 1972, global cereal production increased at an annual rate of 3.7 per cent; from 1972 to 1982, at 2.5 per cent; and from 1982 to 1986, at 2.1 per cent. See Pierre Crosson and Norman Rosenberg, 'Strategies for Agriculture', *Scientific American* 261 (Sept. 1989), 130.

[54]*The State of Food and Agriculture 1989*, 13. The lower global harvest of 1988 was the result, in large part, of drought in the United States. Also important were US

programmes setting aside farm acreage to support grain prices and conserve marginal lands.

[55]Most people, when they hear the term 'resource scarcity', think of non-renewable resources such as petroleum or iron ore. Economists, however, see scarcity as a central fact of human existence, and they therefore tend to regard environmental problems as instances of such scarcity. But in these cases the scarce resource may be renewable (e.g., the atmosphere, soil, or forests).

[56]E. Boserup, *The Conditions of Agricultural Growth: The Economics of Agrarian Change Under Population Pressure* (Chicago: Aldine, 1965), 56.

[57]Paul Ehrlich et al., *Ecoscience*; Paul and Anne Ehrlich, *The Population Explosion.* Warrick and Riebsame describe and contrast four important theoretical perspectives on social vulnerability to environmental problems: the perceptual, the environmental/ecological, the economic, and the social-structural perspectives. The second and third in this list roughly correspond to the neo-Malthusian and cornucopian views discussed here; Warrick and Riebsame, 'Societal Response', 398-401.

[58]K.J. Holsti, 'The Horsemen of the Apocalypse: At the Gate, Detoured, or Retreating?' *International Studies Quarterly* 30 (Dec. 1986), 356.

[59]M.L. Parry, *Climate Change, Agriculture and Settlement* (Folkstone, UK: Dawson, 1978); see also Clark, *On the Practical Implications*, 40-1.

[60]For instance, as petroleum becomes scarcer and more expensive, developing countries will find it less feasible to substitute fertilizer for degraded soil. Between 1950 and 1984, annual world fertilizer use increased from 14 to 125 million tons. On a per capita basis, the increase was from 5 to 26 kilograms. See Brown, 'Reexamining the World Food Prospect', 52. On the relationship between modern intensive agriculture and fossil-fuel consumption see John Gever et al., *Beyond Oil: The Threat to Food and Fuel in the Coming Decades* (Cambridge, MA: Ballinger, 1986).

[61]The resource intensity of economic activity in most developing countries is rising very rapidly. However, in industrialized countries the 1970s saw a reversal of this trend. Per capita consumption of many basic industrial materials — such as steel, cement, aluminum, and paper — began to decline. But the drop has been relatively small compared to the growth this century. In the US, for example, steel consumption per capita increased from about 90 kilograms in 1890 to about 500 kilograms in 1972, and then declined to a modern low of 360 kilos by 1983. See Jose Goldemberg et al., *Energy for a Sustainable World* (Washington, DC: World Resources Institute, 1987), 38.

[62]If the rate is 6 per cent, it is not economically rational to invest more than $5 today to prevent $100 of environmental damage (in constant dollars) fifty years from now. While the market may encourage such discounting, there is evidence that normal cognition does not actually follow this principal of economic rationality. See Shel Feldman, 'Why Is It So Hard to Sell "Savings" as a Reason for Energy Conservation?' in *Energy Efficiency: Perspectives on Individual Behaviour*, Willet Kempton and Max Neiman, eds (Washington, DC: American Council for an Energy-Efficient Economy, 1987), 27-40.

[63]Our interventions and substitutions might be actually increasing the probability of dramatic threshold effects in environmental social systems; Roy Rappaport, 'The Flow of Energy in an Agricultural Society', *Scientific American* 224 (1971), 130.

[64]Some scholars claim that the rate of scientific and technical progress may soon slow. See, for example, Gunther Stent's thoughtful discussion in *Paradoxes of Progress* (San Francisco: Freeman, 1978). Contributing factors might include the declining interest and faith in science in developed countries, and the rapidly increasing expense of basic research. Furthermore, the growing knowledge base makes it ever harder for one person to master anything more than a narrow discipline, which may increasingly impede the cross-disciplinary fertilization often vital to scientific creativity.

[65]Development experts dispute the extent to which such social engineering is possible. See James Bradford De Long, 'The "Protestant Ethic" Revisited: A Twentieth Century Look', *The Fletcher Forum of World Affairs* 13 (Summer 1989), 229–41; and Clive Hamilton, 'The Irrelevance of Economic Liberalization in the Third World', *World Development* 17 (1989), 1523–30. On the difficulties of rapid and directed cultural change, see Harry Eckstein, 'A Culturalist Theory of Political Change', *American Political Science Review* 82 (September 1988), 789–804.

[66]Sadik, *The State of World Population 1990*; Griffith Feeney et al., 'Recent Fertility Dynamics in China: Results from the 1987 One Percent Population Survey', *Population and Development Review* 15 (June 1989), 297–321.

[67]Assuming the necessary foreign exchange or financial aid is available, such imports might seem a reasonable way to compensate for Southern shortfalls, even over an extended period. However, a dependence on agricultural areas in the North will make importers vulnerable to vagaries of climate, economics, and politics in the exporting countries. As the redundancy of food-growing regions is reduced, the likelihood of a sudden and catastrophic global shortfall increases.

[68]While cornucopian policies are unlikely to prove successful in the long run, their failure will occur in different ways and at different rates in different societies. Notably, some rapidly industrializing societies — such as Thailand, South Korea, and Indonesia — seem to have successfully shaped their social, economic, and political structures to promote the production of material wealth. As this development is often at stunning cost to the environment, it represents in part a massive conversion of current and future ecological wealth to current economic wealth, in the form of physical and intellectual capital and materials for consumption. This wealth may give these countries greater ability to respond and adapt to environmental change, thus weakening the force of the fifth reason above. But the other six factors will still have force, which suggests that these societies are only postponing the crisis, not escaping it.

[69]See Nicholas Georgescu-Roegen, *The Entropy Law and the Economic Process* (Cambridge, MA: Harvard Univ. Press, 1971); Herman Daly, ed., *Toward a Steady-State Economy* (San Francisco: Freeman, 1973); and Ilya Prigogine, *Order Out of Chaos* (New York: Bantam, 1984).

[70]John Dollard et al., *Frustration and Aggression* (New Haven: Yale Univ. Press, 1939); Leonard Berkowitz, *Aggression: A Social Psychological Analysis* (New York: McGraw-

Hill, 1962); Neil Smelser, *Theory of Collective Behaviour* (New York: Free Press of Glencoe, 1963). On relative deprivation, see James Davies, 'Toward a Theory of Revolution', *American Sociological Review* 6 (1962), 5-19; Ted Gurr, *Why Men Rebel* (Princeton, NJ: Princeton Univ. Press 1970); Ted Gurr, *Comparative Studies of Political Conflict and Change: Cross National Datasets* (Ann Arbor: ICPSR, 1978); and Ted Gurr and Raymond Duvall, 'Civil Conflict in the 1960s: A Reciprocal Theoretical System with Parameter Estimates', *Comparative Political Studies* 6 (1973), 135-69. A version of a theory of absolute deprivation and conflict is offered by John Burton in chapter 3 of *Deviance, Terrorism and War* (New York: St. Martin's, 1979), 55-84.

[71]See M. Sherif, *Group Conflict and Cooperation: Their Social Psychology* (London: Routledge and Kegan Paul, 1966); Henri Tajfel, ed., *Differentiation between Social Groups* (London: Academic, 1978); Henri Tajfel, *Human Groups and Social Categories: Studies in Social Psychology* (Cambridge: Cambridge Univ. Press, 1981); Edward Azar and John Burton, *International Conflict Resolution: Theory and Practice* (Sussex: Wheatsheaf, 1986); Lewis Coser, *The Functions of Social Conflict* (London: Free Press, 1956); Donald Horowitz, *Ethnic Groups in Conflict* (Berkeley: University of California Press, 1985).

[72]As Wendt notes in his excellent review of the agent-structure debate, the view of structure as constraint is only one of three possible positions on the issue. Structure can also be thought of as generating the actors rather than constraining them, or structure and actor can be seen as dialectically related — that is, as generating but not reducible to each other (as Giddens suggests); Alexander Wendt, 'The Agent-Structure Problem', *International Organization* 41 (1987), 335-70; Anthony Giddens, *The Constitution of Society: Outline of the Theory of Structuration* (Cambridge, UK: Polity Press, 1984).

[73]Those scholars who emphasize such constraints usually also acknowledge the causal importance of internal factors, such as the actor's particular interests and beliefs. See Ernst Haas's discussion of structuralism and the mechanical metaphor in 'Words Can Hurt You; Or Who Said What to Whom about Regimes', *International Organization* 36 (Spring 1982), 45-52. By stressing power relations almost exclusively, perhaps Waltz comes closest to presenting a purely structural theory of international behaviour and war. De Mesquita contends that the geographic proximity of actors is an important structural determinant of international conflict, while Choucri and North emphasize differences in states' resource endowments. See Kenneth Waltz, *Theory of International Politics* (Reading, MA: Addison-Wesley, 1979); Bruce Bueno de Mesquita, *The War Trap* (New Haven: Yale Univ. Press, 1981); and Nazli Choucri and Robert North, *Nations in Conflict* (San Francisco: Freeman, 1975).

[74]See in particular Doug McAdam, *Political Process and the Development of Black Insurgency, 1930-1970* (Chicago: University of Chicago Press, 1982); and Charles Tilly, *From Mobilization to Revolution* (Reading, MA: Addison-Wesley, 1978).

[75]Peter Gleick, 'Climate Change and International Politics', 333-9.

[76]Myron Weiner, 'The Political Demography of Assam's Anti-Immigrant Movement', *Population and Development Review* 9 (June 1983), 279-92.

[77]McAdam, *Political Process and the Development of Black Insurgencies*, 41.

[78] A wealth of literature exists on the theoretical and empirical relationships between economic deprivation and civil strife. Mark Lichbach provides a survey in 'An Evaluation of "Does Economic Inequality Breed Political Conflict?" Studies,' *World Politics* 41 (July 1989), 431-70. Also noteworthy are the numerous articles by Muller and Opp applying rational-choice theory to explain rebellious collective action. See Edward Muller and Karl-Dieter Opp, 'Rational Choice and Rebellious Collective Action', *American Political Science Review* 80 (June 1986), 471-88; and George Klosko, Edward Muller, and Karl-Dieter Opp, 'Controversy: Rebellious Collective Action Revisited', *American Political Science Review* 81 (June 1987), 557-67.

[79] See especially Porter and Ganapin, *Resources*.

[80] Jones, *Red Revolution*, 175.

[81] Hawes, 'Theories of Peasant Revolution', 282.

[82] See Hugh Mehan and Houston Wood, *The Reality of Ethnomethodology* (New York: John Wiley, 1975); and Clifford Geertz, *The Interpretation of Cultures* (New York: Basic, 1973). Such an internal understanding is also essential if we are to estimate the potential for group-identity conflicts between ethnic groups propelled together by environmental decline. The cultures and belief systems of some groups may allow them to coexist reasonably peacefully with other groups, even in situations of stress, while certain ethnic combinations may be explosive.

[83] Jonathan Wilkenfeld, 'Domestic and Foreign Conflict Behaviour of Nations', *Journal of Peace Research* 5 (1968), 56-69.

[84] Building on Huntington's views, Skocpol claims that revolutions produce a 'special sort of democratization' understood as the 'enhancement of popular involvement in national political life.' See Theda Skocpol, 'Social Revolutions and Mass Military Mobilization', *World Politics* 40 (1988), 147-68; and Samuel Huntington, *Political Order in Changing Societies* (New Haven: Yale Univ. Press, 1968).

[85] 'Praetorian' is a label used by Huntington (*Political Order*, 196) for societies in which the level of political participation exceeds the capacity of political institutions to channel, moderate, and reconcile competing claims to economic and political resources.

[86] Jose Goldemberg and Eunice Ribeiro Durham, *The Amazonia and National Sovereignty*, draft paper presented to the workshop 'Our Changing Atmosphere: Sources of Stress and Challenges to Cooperation', Cambridge, MA: American Academy of Arts and Sciences (1989).

[87] Heilbroner, *An Inquiry into the Human Prospect*, 39 and 95. These North-South disputes would be the international analogues of domestic relative-deprivation conflicts.

[88] See Ullman, 'Redefining Security', 143.

[89] Edward Muller and Mitchell Seligson, 'Inequality and Insurgency', *American Political Science Review* 81 (June 1987), 425-52.

[90] See Seymour Martin Lipset, *Political Man: The Social Bases of Politics* (Garden City, NY: Doubleday, 1959); and Mitchell Seligson and Edward Muller, 'Democratic

Stability and Economic Crisis: Costa Rica, 1978-83', *International Studies Quarterly* 31 (Sept. 1987), 301-26.

[91]Ekkart Zimmermann and Thomas Saalfeld, 'Economic and Political Reactions to the World Economic Crisis of the 1930s in Six European Countries', *International Studies Quarterly* 32 (Sept. 1988), 326.

[92]The argument that democracies are less inclined to war is often traced to Kant. For a thorough discussion, see Michael Doyle, 'Liberalism and World Politics', *American Political Science Review* 80 (Dec. 1986), 1151-70. This kind of second-stage intervention may be particularly difficult here, because environmental change may reduce the prospects for success of democratic regimes.

[93]See Richard Rosecrance, *The Rise of the Trading State* (New York: Basic, 1986).

[94]Robert Gilpin, *War and Change in World Politics* (Cambridge: Cambridge Univ. Press, 1981), 94 and 191; A.F.K. Organski and Jacek Kugler, *The War Ledger* (Chicago: Univ. of Chicago Press, 1980); and Jack Levy, 'Research Note: Declining Power and the Preventive Motivation for War', *World Politics* 40 (Oct. 1987), 82-107.

chapter ten

Population and (In)security:
National Perspectives and Global Imperatives[1]

Nazli Choucri and Robert C. North

This chapter examines some of the complex interconnections between demographics and security on the national, international, and global levels. 'Security' refers broadly to a feeling or condition of being secure, or 'safe'. But two questions are also crucial: Secure from what? And how much security is enough? For the purpose of this chapter it is assumed that human beings seek security both from want and from harm in the form of threats or acts of oppression, forced deprivation, and/or violence, including crime, military attack, invasion, and conquest.

This discussion focuses on three issue areas of particular relevance to the cold-war and post-cold-war eras: (1) wars of decolonization; (2) migrations of large populations (with particular attention to war-generated movements of refugees); and (3) the impacts of growing numbers of people (in close conjunction with rapid technological development and resource availabilities) on the security of social and natural environments within the global system. Towards this end, this chapter draws upon a conceptual framework and analytical approach developed in the authors' earlier studies of international conflict and war and recently applied to interrelationships among national, international, and global environments —natural and social.

Dimensions of Security and Insecurity

In both academic and policy-making communities, prevailing views of security have been shaped by three distinct conceptions of what it means to be 'secure'. These perspectives owe their intellectual origins and analytical foundations to different disciplinary bases; they proceed from different premises, establish different priorities, and generate different types of predictions. So far there has been little agreement as to what 'overall' security really means, and progress towards integrating the different approaches has remained limited.

Three Views

In general, academic perspectives on security have developed in three phases. The first is the conventional view that defines the security of states in terms of strategic military defence and global security in terms of the prospects for resolving conflicts and avoiding (or winning) wars. Thus the academic field of 'strategic studies' in the United States and elsewhere addresses issues of the 'high politics' of war and peace and focuses almost exclusively on military considerations. A recent review of the field (Nye and Lynn-Jones, 1988) summarizes and reinforces such tendencies. This conventional perspective defines the 'security dilemma' as an inadvertent outcome of national interactions whereby a move designed by one state to ensure its security is construed by others as hostile, thereby contributing to *in*security on both sides and commonly leading to arms races, international crises, and sometimes war.

As described by Richard Ullman (1983), a second, revisionist phase in the development of security studies widens the frame of reference to include a number of different approaches. But it leaves basic assumptions, concepts and functions undefined and provides no criteria or procedures for bounding the security concept.

In a third phase of such studies the national-security phenomenon is seen as inherently multifaceted. This approach attempts to integrate the conventional and revisionist views by bringing their characteristic features together in an internally consistent framework and linking security issues across the three interconnected levels of *structural*, *regime*, and *strategic* security. This approach recognizes that a state can be threatened from 'below' (by individualistic or organizational pressures on the regime, revolution, civil war, and the like); from 'above' (by oppressive or otherwise threatening governmental initiative, policy, or action); or strategically, from outside (by the expansionist or other antagonistic activities of other states).

In the structural realm, many activities that are economically, politically, strategically, or otherwise 'normal' and constructive (e.g., manufacturing, certain types of agriculture, disposal of medical wastes) can be environmentally threatening. Environmental costs rise with (a) population size (numbers of 'consumers' or claimants); (b) levels of technology (knowledge, skills, capacities for obtaining, transforming, and 'consuming' resources); and (c) resource access and availability.

At the structural level, security is defined as a viable balance or ratio between the size of a state's population and the demands of that population relative to the level and characteristics of its technology, economic performance, and resource endowments; in other words, the structural dimension refers to a country's economic foundations. Similarly, security at the regime level is defined in terms of the capacity of a government to protect itself from domestic disorder or revolt. And strategic security is identified as the ability of the state to defend itself from external coercion, attack, or invasion. A state is insecure to the extent that any of these dimensions of security is threatened or eroded. Indeed, insecurity in one area inevitably means insecurity in others: for example, regime security is undermined to the extent that a government is unable to manage either structural or strategic security.

A Multidimensional Perspective

The theoretical foundations of this integrated view of security were first advanced in broad theoretical terms by North (1990) and then in a set of case studies (Choucri, Brown, and Haas, 1990). A detailed study of the three dimensions of security for Egypt, a country where threats to security are complex and diverse (Choucri, forthcoming), shows that the population variable (interacting with technology and resource availabilities) is critical, since population is a basic denominator for any socio-economic, political, or strategic variable contributing to national power and performance. Central to the integrated view, therefore, are demographic factors and their interaction with technological change and resource access in shaping actions, reactions, and patterns of international conflict and violence (Choucri, 1974, 1984).

The economic, political, and strategic interactions among states can be viewed in terms of 'offensive' and 'defensive' bargaining and leveraging (threatening, punishing or otherwise negative exchanges) within and between states (North, 1990: 11-19, 42-8; Choucri, North, and Yamakagi, 1992). The problem of 'governance' within and between states can be defined as one of consensus formation and the management of contending pressures and strains.

Concepts of security and insecurity are further complicated when the concept of environmental security is introduced. All human activities, from the individual to the state, international, and global levels, can be seen as taking place within a nest of Chinese boxes — that is, people act within state environments (natural and social); states (and their populaces) act within the international environment; and the international system operates within global environments (planetary and social). Within this intensely interactive world, the ability of states to regulate natural forces and, to a lesser but considerable extent, movements of people is limited, and for this reason the definition of security in terms of states and their regimes (governments) is inadequate.

It is not easy to devise scalable indicators of happiness or security for purposes of comparison between individuals or groups or nations. By contrast, it is quite easy to identify countable phenomena that make individuals (groups, nations) feel more, or less, *un*happy or *in*secure. Almost any indicator of serious loss — numbers of refugees, war dead, dangerous pollutants of the earth's atmosphere — can be expected to aggravate feelings of insecurity. This suggests the analytic utility of *in*security measures in addition to whatever security indicators may be available.

As the twentieth century draws to a close, a major challenge is how to identify linkages that connect in persuasive ways the many individual needs, demands, and activities undertaken for personal reasons that in the aggregate, over large populations, contribute to unintended — and sometimes undesirable — outcomes: that is, to national, international, or global insecurity. Under such circumstances, the treatment of security/insecurity phenomena in strictly national terms can be misleading; it may also be disruptive within the international and global systems. Crucial steps in constraining such tendencies include the integration of security/insecurity theory and analysis within broader international and global frameworks.

In principle, a carefully calibrated *balance* between (a) demographic and economic growth and (b) development of effective, efficient, and adaptive knowledge, skills, and resource applications could provide a key to the future sustainability of planetary life forms. But pervasive unevennesses in population growth, resource availability, and technological development tend to shape the ways people — from individuals to large corporations and whole nations — interact with each other and with the planet and its resources.

Framing the Master Variables

Population — interacting with technological advancement — directly affects the sustainability of a society's resource base (and overall environment) under the pressures of its needs, wants and demands. Although *sustainability* may be defined in many ways, the basic criteria were put forward by the World Commission on Environment and Development (and were central to the deliberations of the United Nations Conference on Environment and Development): A sustainable society is one that meets the needs of present generations without compromising the ability of future generations to meet their own needs.

The *master variables* within and between states — *population, technology* (knowledge and skills), and access to *resources* — are so interactive that they are analytically inseparable. Nevertheless, a legitimate case can be made for the recognition of *population* as the critical variable, since without people the other two master variables — technology and resource availability — would be (for our purpose) meaningless. Although there are no populations anywhere without some knowledge and skills, and no people anywhere who could survive without some minimal level of resources (food, water, shelter), the demographic variable is clearly dominant. From this perspective, then, the second and third master variables can be viewed as attributes of the population (demographic) variable. To the extent that knowledge/skills and resource applications (including consumption) differ from individual to individual and from organization to organization (including states), it becomes analytically appropriate to treat population and the technology and resource attributes as co-independent and intensely interactive variables. The larger the population in a community or society, the greater is the aggregate demand for energy and other resources.

Technology enhances the capabilities of people to obtain and transform resources. Historically, however, the greater the advances in knowledge and skills, the greater has been the demand for energy and other resources. The greater the population growth and the more rapid the technological development of a country, the greater is likely to be the expansion of its activities and interests beyond home borders.

In order to achieve co-operatively what they cannot accomplish individually, people seek to influence the decisions and actions of others by bargaining and leveraging ('influencing') each other (and their organizations, institutions) interactively and establishing coalitions in support of their preferred behaviours and outcomes. Such activities contribute to organizational decisions, policies, and actions, but to the extent that such leverages are perceived as negative (threatening, punishing, violent) they often fuel escalations of competition, conflict, and war. These outcomes are not 'inevitabilities', although they are often treated as if they were.

Unevenness in the interactive growth and development of the master variables within and across societies contributes to unevenness in the size, development, and capabilities of such societies, to differential capabilities among them, and to competitions, conflicts, and disasters on playing (and survival) fields that are not easily rendered level.

The central figure within this framework—the only relevant thinking, feeling, deciding, acting, goal-seeking actor in the system—is the individual human being, whose demands and capabilities combine to produce action. In this context 'demand' refers to potential as well as actual claims exerted by people on the regime, or government, and the overall political system. These claims can be wide-ranging, including symbolic as well as material concerns.

Kenneth Boulding (1956) has identified individual decision-making as an effort to narrow or close a gap between fact and value or, more simply, between 'what is' and 'what ought to be'. Similarly, Richard Cyert and James March (1963) have defined group decision-making processes on organizational levels in terms of bargaining and leveraging within a leadership élite and the achievement of a winning coalition in support of a particular outcome.

A somewhat different 'decision-making' process is evident in the uneven growth and development of states. Here the 'decision-making' is a long-term, more or less gradual and unintended or inadvertent process with a 'social-steering' effect. In practice, such 'deep-level' decisions are driven by whole populations of individuals seeking to close their personal (or group or organizational) 'is'/'ought to be' gaps. In the increasingly global society as it (unevenly) grows and develops today, the ubiquitous 'decision' to procreate is among the more fateful outcomes of this 'deep' social-steering function.

Integrative Propositions

The main threads of the preceding discussion—the three master variables, the unevenness among them, and the various types of decision-making—are integrated in the following propositions:

1. Insofar as the growth of a population accelerates relative to technological advancement, demands for energy and other resources may be expected to increase and development to be constrained.

2. To the extent that technology (knowledge and skills) is accelerated in advance of population growth, one may expect development to be enhanced and resource availabilities to expand (through exploration, 'discovery', territorial conquest, or trade) and demand for energy and other resources to accelerate—along with resource depletion, pollution, and other manifestations of degradation. Environmental costs are constrained, however, to the extent that resource and technological applications become more efficient.

3. In general, the rising demands associated with population growth, combined with commensurate technological development, tend to generate 'lateral pressure': i.e., a disposition to expand activities and interests outward—beyond national borders—in terms of imports, exports (including new markets) and strategic security.

4. When the expanding activities and interests of two or more countries experiencing high lateral pressure intersect, their relationships commonly 'get out of hand' and lead to previously unintended consequences.

5. A critical inference, therefore, is that behavioural inertias generated by uneven growth and development processes can shape decision- and policy-making and action on organizational (including state), international, and global levels in ways that neither leaders nor rank-and-file citizens (including voters) are likely to comprehend or even recognize. Commonly, in fact, the decisions and activities of individuals applying their own values (how many children to have, for one clear example) in pursuit of their personal objectives aggregate to 'steer' whole societies in unintended or inadvertent directions (e.g., overpopulation on a rapidly depleted resource base) and create paradoxes and policy dilemmas that can immobilize or grievously distort subsequent decision and policy-making and outcomes at higher organizational

(including state, international and global) levels and invite 'irrational', undesirable, or even disastrous outcomes.

Lateral Pressure and the Rise and Fall of Empires

Collisions of the lateral pressures of two or more countries often contribute to the 'war/peace paradox' wherein a 'defensive' move by one side may be construed as an offensive move by the other side, and a conciliatory move by one side may be interpreted by the other as either a sign of weakness or an opportunity that it should take advantage of. Thus, each in pursuit of its own security — or responding to feelings of insecurity — two parties to a conflict commonly exacerbate their differences and create 'inextricable' crises that lead them into war.

World history between the early seventeenth century and the outbreak of World War I provides many examples of lateral pressure as European nation-states — characterized by rising populations, advancing technologies, and spiralling demands for resources — expanded their activities, interests, and territorial holdings into South, Southeast, and Eastern Asia, the Americas, and eventually Africa. In search of treasure — whether spices, gold, 'heathen' souls, furs, farmlands, or timber — several of these countries rapidly transformed themselves from nation-states into intensely competitive commercial and later industrial empires, as distinct from the older agrarian empires of China, the Ottoman Turks, Austro-Hungary, and the Russian Tsars.

Consistent with the propositions in the lateral-pressure theory, the expanding activities and interests of these new empires (and subsequently the German and Japanese upstarts of the late nineteenth century) led to nearly four centuries of bitter competition, rivalry, and war.

Colonial and Collision Wars

Throughout the era of colonial expansion, two kinds of war were widespread. First were *colonial* wars, which amounted to force exerted for purposes of colonial subjugation or for the incorporation of contiguous, often sparsely populated land directly into the territorial domain of the imperial state (e.g., the Mexican and Indian wars of the United States).

Second were wars of *collision* between the expanding activities and interests of the imperial states themselves (Portugal and Spain, Spain and England, England and Holland, England and France, France and Russia, etc.) in competition for colonial jurisdictions or in defence of their territories and trade routes. Competition for colonial territories and trade routes was not necessarily the only factor in warfare between great powers, but it tended to become the major issue whenever the interests and activities of powerful states collided. In many, if not most, conflicts and wars, moreover, it has been commonplace for states or empires competing for land and other resources, markets, trade routes, and so on to incite and 'mobilize' ethnic, religious, and nationalistic emotions and loyalties, which are then invoked to rally domestic support for external activities and interests. A religious, patriotic, or nationalistic war may often reflect a territorial, commercial, or other more tangible interest. Expansionism and war tend to be 'multi-causal'.

Historically, great empires have always collapsed, or at least shrunk to more manageable size, sooner or later. The fall of the Roman empire is only one example: the empires of ancient Egypt, Assyria, China, and India, of the Incas, Mayas, Aztecs, and many others have all suffered similar fates. Over time, uneven growth and development, expansion, colliding activities and interests, together with accumulating domestic inefficiencies and contradictions, have led to the decline and eventual disruption or dismemberment of over-extended states and empires—the case of the USSR being only the most recent example.

Twentieth-Century Cases

Early in the twentieth century the ancient Chinese empire collapsed, in large part under its own weight. World War I contributed to the demise of the Austro-Hungarian, Ottoman, and Tsarist empires, although those of China and Russia were retrieved from the historical dust-bin, however temporarily. After two succeeding decades dominated by the imperial aspirations of Mussolini and Hitler, World War II destroyed these two upstarts and their empires, and in its aftermath contributed, in turn, to the relatively voluntary dissolution of the vast commercially based empires of Great Britain, France, Belgium, the Netherlands, and Portugal. (The Spanish empire of the sixteenth, seventeenth, and eighteenth centuries had already collapsed by the wayside.)

Following World War II both the USSR and the US expanded their territorial and industrial activities. The lateral pressures exerted by the former amounted to a revitalization and continuation of Tsarist expansionism. US lateral pressures, on the other hand, were continuations of British expansionism under a new flag and a new constitution—from the Atlantic seaboard across the Alleghenies, the Great Plains, and the Rockies to the Pacific (all Indian country) south and southwestward into the Caribbean and Mexico, westward to Hawaii and the Philippines, and northward to Alaska (the only territory actually paid for).

The notion of *national* security is difficult to identify in these empires. There is ample evidence that among imperial leaders, the distinction between nation and empire was often obscured as threats to colonial holdings were interpreted as threats to the empire and hence to the nation. Clearly the security concept may be twisted to mean whatever one wants.

Empirical Framework for Global Analysis

To facilitate the empirical investigation and analysis of states and their growth and relationships through time, this section presents an empirically derived global framework in which the three master variables—population, technology, and resources—may be examined in conjunction with an open-ended array of intervening and conditioning variables that can be introduced as the problem under scrutiny requires.

Profile Groups

In accordance with all possible combinations of unevenness in the growth and development of the three master variables through time, any state may be categorized as belonging to one of six empirically identifiable and defined configurations or groups (see Table 10.1).

Table 10.2 presents the empirical referents for each group. These figures define the profile of each nation in the six groups, providing a 'snapshot' of its growth and development configuration or structure. Through time, however, each country can be envisaged as making its own way down a broad growth and development *pathway* or trajectory shared with other nations in its group.

Dynamics of Change

Since the rates of change and changes in rates of change of each master variable (or indicator) of each nation are likely to be different (uneven growth and development), there is always the possibility that within a time series analysis one or more countries may be transformed at some point from one profile group into another. Such transformational trends can be analysed and (within margins of error) projected by at least two strategies: calculating the rates of change of the variables themselves; and/or calculating the (changing) gaps between each of all possible pairs of all the master variables through time.

The social, economic, and political activities and public policies that shape such transformations can be ascertained in two primary ways: (a) the conventional decision- and policy-making activities undertaken by heads of state and their advisers who are charged with governing the country; and (b) the aggregate outcomes of all the bargaining, leveraging, and other activities of the populace and their coalitions and coalitions of coalitions in pursuit of interests affecting the growth and development of their country. Such 'deep' decision- and policy-making, however difficult to identify, commonly affects the trajectories of a nation's master variables in complex ways.

The table indicates major differences among states in terms of their population/technology/resource-access ratios and characteristics and their overall capabilities. Individual states tend to be constrained or empowered by their individual population/technology/resource-access ratios. Thus countries with radically different profiles—Bangladesh or Burundi, for example, as contrasted to France or the United States—differ substantially in terms of their domestic capacities and dispositions for resource distribution, allocation, or 'sharing'. Something similar can be observed within countries as well: that is,

Table 10.1. Profile Definition

Group I:	Resources	>	Population	>	Technology
Group II:	Population	>	Resources	>	Technology
Group III:	Population	>	Technology	>	Resources
Group IV:	Resources	>	Technology	>	Population
Group V:	Technology	>	Resources	>	Population
Group VI:	Technology	>	Population	>	Resources

NOTE: For *operational* purposes, groups have been defined as follows. For every country, each master variable was computed as a share of the *global* total for that variable. The variables in each group definition were then arranged in proportional terms. Thus the group profiles were determined by relative shares. This simple method provides information about (1) relative size of master variables within states and (2) relative constraints among the master variables within states. The same information is provided (3) across states within each profile and (4) across states and across profiles. Following Kindleberger (1962), we use area as a rough indicator of resources; as an indicator of technology, following Kuznets (1966), we use GNP.

SOURCE: Choucri and North, 1993.

who among the populace of any one of these states (individuals, ethnic or national minorities, social and/or economic classes, warlords, or, in some instances, clan chiefs) gets what, when, and how (Lasswell, 1958). These internal phenomena lie close to the heart of rebellions, revolutions, and civil wars.

Uneven Growth and Development: Implications for War

Wars, which have been ubiquitous throughout written history, have been analysed and explained in many ways. The linkages among growth, development, and the natural environmental and their conflictual and ecological impacts appear increasingly compelling. But there is a major definitional problem. At what point does a coup, mass murder, uprising, crisis, or series thereof become a war? And is there a reliable distinction between revolutions and civil wars? Or between a major power's provision of loans, weapons, intelligence, military advisers and other assistance to a nation at war and active participation as a combatant? How much difference does it make to draw such a distinction? This analysis has set 1,000 casualties as the threshold between other forms of violence and war — and established the commitment of troop units to battle as the threshold for formal participation.

Lateral Pressures and Wars of the Cold War

At least two phenomena set cold-war lateral pressures apart from previous manifestations. Associated with one of these were the pervasive idiosyncrasies of Marxist-Leninist strategies and tactics — ideological, psychological, political, and strategic — that to one degree or another induced antagonists to

Table 10.2. Growth and Development (1986)

	POPULATION (% global)	AREA (% global)	GNP (% global)	GNP ($US)	POP. DENSITY (sq. km)
GROUP I					
Brazil	2.837	6.469	1.655	1,810	16
Iran	0.935	1.252	0.571	1,895	28
Argentina	0.635	2.103	0.481	2,350	11
Algeria	0.459	1.810	0.383	2,590	9
Cameroon	0.215	0.361	0.063	910	22
Sudan	0.463	1.904	0.048	320	9
Kenya	0.434	0.443	0.042	300	36
Tanzania	0.471	0.718	0.038	250	24
Jordan	0.074	0.074	0.037	1,540	37
Colombia	0.594	0.866	0.236	1,230	25
Peru	0.406	0.977	0.143	1,090	15
Zimbabwe	0.178	0.297	0.036	620	22
Ethiopia	0.892	0.929	0.034	120	36
Angola	0.184	0.948	0.031	522	7
Bolivia	0.135	0.835	0.026	600	6
Afghanistan	0.316	0.492	0.020	200	24
Mozambique	0.291	0.609	0.020	210	18
Nicaragua	0.070	0.099	0.018	790	26
Congo	0.041	0.260	0.013	990	6
Somalia	0.113	0.485	0.010	280	9
Chad	0.105	0.976	0.005	160	4
Laos	0.076	0.180	0.004	178	16
GROUP II					
China	21.602	7.266	2.089	300	110
India	16.015	2.499	1.497	290	238
Indonesia	3.410	1.458	0.539	490	87
Nigeria	2.113	0.702	0.436	640	112
Turkey	1.055	0.594	0.378	1,110	66
Thailand	1.078	0.391	0.281	810	102
Iraq	0.338	0.331	0.264	2,424	38
Egypt	1.019	0.761	0.250	760	50
Pakistan	2.033	0.611	0.229	350	123
Philippines	1.174	0.228	0.212	560	191
Malaysia	0.330	0.251	0.195	1,830	49
Syria	0.221	0.141	0.112	1,570	58
Bangladesh	2.115	0.109	0.109	160	717
Morocco	0.461	0.340	0.088	590	50
Vietnam	1.297	0.251	0.082	196	192
Tunisia	0.150	0.125	0.055	1,140	45
Guatemala	0.168	0.083	0.050	930	75

Table 10.2 — *Continued*

	POPULATION (% global)	AREA (% global)	GNP (% global)	GNP ($US)	POP. DENSITY (sq. km)
Burma	0.779	0.514	0.050	200	56
Sri Lanka	0.330	0.050	0.043	400	244
Ghana	0.271	0.182	0.034	390	355
Dominican Rep.	0.135	0.037	0.031	710	135
Uganda	0.312	0.179	0.023	230	64
Burundi	0.098	0.021	0.008	240	171
GROUP III					
S. Korea	0.851	0.074	0.650	2,370	423
Portugal	0.209	0.070	0.152	2,250	111
N. Korea	0.428	0.092	0.126	909	173
GROUP IV					
USSR	5.761	17.024	15.571	8,384	13
Canada	0.525	7.581	2.388	14,120	3
Australia	0.328	5.842	1.260	11,920	2
Libya	0.080	1.337	0.132	5,128	2
Oman	0.027	0.228	0.043	4,980	2
GROUP V					
US	4.952	7.115	27.90	17,480	26
GROUP VI					
France	1.135	0.416	3.924	10,720	101
UK	1.162	0.186	3.323	8,870	231
Spain	0.793	0.384	1.243	4,860	77
Netherlands	0.299	0.031	0.967	10,020	356
Belgium	0.203	0.024	0.604	9,230	319
Greece	0.205	0.100	0.243	3,680	76
Israel	0.088	0.016	0.176	6,210	205
Kuwait	0.037	0.014	0.165	13,890	100

SOURCE: Choucri and North (1993)

improvise rough countermeasures (leverages, 'dirty tricks') of their own. The other—perhaps in the long run overriding—phenomenon was the development of nuclear weapons and the missiles for transporting them.

Some Empirical Evidence

The introduction of these two cold-war phenomena into the minefield of post-World War II 'decolonization' conflicts was deadly. In effect, nearly half a century of colonial 'disinvestment' wars fought by the last great empires

Table 10.3. Summary of Wars (1945-91)

LOCATION	WARS	INT'L	DECOLON.	CIVIL	DEAD
Europe, North America, Australia	5	3	0	2	0.2 mil.
Middle East/Islamic	37	10	4	23	5.3 mil.
Africa	26	2	7	17	4.5 mil.
Asia	46	14	5	27	17.0 mil.
Latin America	27	6	0	21	0.6 mil.
	141	35	16	90	27.6 mil.

SOURCE: Adapted from Sullivan, 1991: 34

including the United States (by 'association' and also in view of its own expansionist tendencies) presented to the USSR, several of its satellites, and the People's Republic of China what amounted to open invitations for intrusions of their own — whether through ideological and organizational subterfuge, or by supplying military advisers and weapons to rebelling colonies (or fractions of colonial populations).

Because of definitional differences, available listings of wars fought since the end of World War II differ substantially. As of 1992, according to the criteria used here, 94 wars have been fought since 1 September 1945. In contrast, Michael Sullivan (1991: 34-42) cites 141 international, colonial and civil wars over roughly the same period. Of these, only 5 were fought on European soil; of the remainder, 26 were fought in Africa, 27 in Asia, and 27 in Latin America (Table 10.3).

For the world, Sullivan (1991: 27) reported a cumulative total of 25 million war deaths during the period 1945-90. This aggregate is accounted for by 17 million war deaths in Asia, 4,500,000 in the 'Islamic zone', 650,000 in Latin America, and 200,000 in Europe.

Colonial Wars

Of the 94 wars since 1945, 46 were associated, directly or indirectly, with colonies or former colonies of the recent past. The former colonial empires (excluding the United States) involved in these conflicts were Spain (1), Portugal (2), Netherlands (2), Belgium (1) France (9) and the United Kingdom (13). Other conflicts were wars either with or by colonies of the past. Thus the wars between the two Koreas (a former Japanese colony) and the two Vietnams (formerly French-held) were in part, at least, consequences of the expanding influence of the USSR in eastern Asia.

A typical pattern of 'decolonizing' warfare (see Table 10.4) was commonplace during the 1950s and 1960s when countries in Groups IV (the USSR, Canada, and Australia), V (the US) and VI (the UK, France, Belgium, the Netherlands, and Spain) intervened — on opposing sides — in numerous countries of Groups I (Angola, Algeria, Panama, Afghanistan, etc.), II

Table 10.4. Wars of 'Decolonization'

Indonesia (I)	vs	Netherlands (VI), UK (VI)	1945–46	5,000
Indochina	vs	France (VI)	1946–54	600,000
Kenya (I)	vs	UK (VI)	1952–53	15,000
Tunisia (II)	vs	France (VI)	1952–54	3,000
Morocco (II)	vs	France (VI)	1953–56	3,000
Algeria (I)	vs	France (VI)	1954–62	1,100,000
Cameroon (I)	vs	France (VI), UK (VI)	1955–60	35,000
Angola (I)	vs	Portugal (III)	1961–65	50–75,000
Mozambique (II)	vs	Portugal (III)	1966–88	30–60,000
Zimbabwe (I)	vs	Rhodesia	1972–79	19,500
Guinea-Bissau	vs	Portugal (III)	1962–74	15,000

SOURCE: Adapted from Sullivan, 1991: 34–8

(Morocco, Indonesia, Vietnam, etc.), and III (North and South Korea, Hungary, and Lebanon). The anomalous country was Portugal, a former colonial empire with a Group III profile.

In these and other conflicts involving former colonies, old empires were not rigidly opposed to decolonization, but they were inclined either to retain some measure of dominion with respect to former colonies (as was achieved in the cases of Canada and Australia) or otherwise to influence the 'direction' that independence movements might be 'persuaded' to take in a cold-war world, where local communist movements, backed by the USSR or China, were preparing to take over wherever they could.

In human terms, one of the costliest of these wars was the Korean War of 1950–53 during which four empires of the past (United Kingdom, France, Belgium, and the Netherlands), two former British colonies by settlement (Canada and Australia) and Greece joined the United States in support of South Korea against the North, which received arms, other military equipment, and 'advice' from the Group IV USSR and active troop support from Group II Communist China (like the Soviet Union, a Marxist-Leninist empire transformed from an empire of the old order). Total casualties numbered some 3,000,000. At that time, or within a few years thereafter, the British, French, Belgians, and Dutch were all involved in their own 'private' decolonization conflicts.

By the early 1950s highly organized, highly effective revolutionary movements were threatening in French Indochina, Dutch Indonesia, and many other former colonies in various parts of the world. Following the US assumption of responsibility in Vietnam (Indochina) from the French, fighting there exacted up to 2,300,000 casualties by the mid-1970s. Lower levels of carnage continued for years after the US withdrawal.

Despite continued disagreement over the 'causes' of this nearly worldwide conflict, the uneven growth, development, and lateral-pressure dynamics that contributed interactively to colonization of various expanses of the earth and to the uneven growth (including population growth) and development (including 'modernization') of the former colonies still operate, but from a new, continually changing base. The consequent activities and expectations of the new states — including expectations of security in whatever forms they imagine it — are exerting unprecedented impacts upon the world and social and natural environments. But new problems — and many old ones — create serious obstacles.

Of the 94 wars since 1945, 31 were wars of decolonization and 58 were civil wars (see Table 10.5 for the major ones). Small alterations in criteria, however, would change these distributions considerably. In fact, few of these 'civil' wars were entirely internal or 'domestic': many, if not most of the combatants were supplied, or even actively supported, by external countries, movements, or agencies like the CIA or KGB, or were targets of intervention by 'insecure' and/or opportunistic neighbours. (See Table 10.6 for the major international wars.)

'Civil' Wars and Self-Destruction

Presided over by often ruthless, sometimes uncertain, occasionally bewildered leaders of poverty-stricken, often unruly, in some instances starving, populations, the 'new world order' has been characterized less by stability, equilibrium, and security than by *in*stabilities, *dis*equilibria, and *in*securities that appear to be better explained by *chaos* theory than by conventional rational-actor assumptions. Overall, if World Wars I and II, putting an end to empires, seemed to make the world safe for liberated *nation-states* (if not true democracies), then the cold war's termination has caused numbers of nations to shatter into smaller and smaller pieces.

The self-destruction of the USSR and its East European satellites was hastened, if not 'caused', by the gross misappropriation of human and material treasure of a large and rich resource base. The unexpected termination of the cold war and four-and-a-half decades of almost unconstrained military growth and development also left the United States with stubborn disturbances in its domestic economy and unprecedented national indebtedness. Just as World War II liquidated the 'old order', so the cold war destroyed the 'new order' of the superpowers including military, political, and economic bonds forged, sustained, and justified by incongruous alliances in fear of shared destruction. Group III Yugoslavia (population > resources > territory) provides depressing evidence of a country that rapidly tore itself apart once its regime was sufficiently weakened.

Notably, of the 94 wars, 75 were fought by developing countries — largely colonies or former colonies — in Groups I and II. The number of consistently 'peaceful' countries in these two groups is extremely small. Insofar as some of these wars were actively participated in by major powers of Groups III, IV, V, or VI, they have been categorized above as wars of decolonization. Most of the remaining wars fought by countries of Groups I and II are domestic wars

Table 10.5. Civil Wars (1945-92) with 100,000 Deaths or More, Ranked by Numbers of Deaths

Nigeria	1963-70	2,000,000
Bangladesh vs gov't (Pakistan)	1971	1,000,000
China: CCP vs KMT	1946-50	1,000,000
China: land reform	1950-55	1,000,000
Indonesia: gov't vs communists	1956-66	600,000
Ethiopia: gov't vs Tigreans	1978-91	570,000
Sudan: gov't, SPLA/SPLM	1983ff	505,000
China: Cultural Revolution	1967-68	500,000
Uganda: Idi Amin massacres	1971-78	300,000
Colombia: gov't vs left rebels	1949-72	120,000
Burundi: gov't vs Hutus	1972	110,000
Iraq: gov't vs Kurds	1961-70	105,000
Algeria: gov't vs rebels	1954-62	100,000
China: gov't vs Tibet	1956-58	100,000

SOURCE: Compiled by Robert C. North from various sources.

—revolutionary or civil—generated in large part by the grossly uneven growth, development, and resource distributions among the populace.

Refugees 'Produced' by War

Among the side-effects of the cold war was the dislocation of large populations and the dispersion of refugees beyond national borders—a unique manifestation of lateral pressures (Table 10.7). This phenomenon persisted and in some regions was exacerbated with the collapse of the USSR and its satellites.

Table 10.6. International Wars (1945-92) with 100,000 Deaths or More, Ranked by Numbers of Casualties

N. Korea, China vs S. Korea, US, and allies	1950-53	3,000,000
N. Vietnam vs S. Vietnam, US, and allies	1955-65	2,000,000
Afghanistan gov't vs Mujahideen, USSR	1978ff	1,300,000
Mozambique gov't, MNR, S. Africa, Zimbabwe	1978ff	1,050,000
Bangladesh, India vs Pakistan	1971	1,000,000
Iran vs Iraq	1980-89	500,000
Sudan, Arab North vs Black South, Egypt	1963-72	500,000
S. Vietnam, US vs Viet Cong, N. Vietnam	1960-65	300,000
Lebanon vs Israel, Syria, US, UK, and allies	1975ff	180,000
Cambodian gov't vs Khmer Rouge, N. Vietnam	1970-75	156,000
E. Timor vs Indonesia, Portugal	1975ff	159,000
Persian Gulf, Iraq vs Kuwait, US, and allies	1990-91	100,000
Guatemala left vs right, US	1966ff	140,000
Katanga (Congo/Zaire) vs Belgium, US	1960-65	100,000

SOURCE: Compiled by Robert C. North from various sources.

Table 10.7. Refugees Crossing Borders[1]

COUNTRIES OF ORIGIN		COUNTRIES OF ASYLUM	
Afghanistan (I)	6,027,100	USA (V)	1,355,858
Mozambique (I)	1,427,500	Canada (V)	287,225
Ethiopia (I)	1,066,300	France (VI)	186,957
Iraq (II)	529,700	Australia (IV)	172,623
Sudan (I)	499,100	Sweden (V)	108,315
Somalia (I)	454,600	Germany (VI)	84,960
Angola (I)	435,700	Spain (VI)	38,196
Kuwait (VI)	585,500	Denmark (VI)	28,733
Kampuchea (II)	344,500	Switzerland (VI)	21,487
Sri Lanka (I)	228,000	Austria (VI)	20,521
Iran (I)	211,100	Netherlands (VI)	20,171
Rwanda (II)	203,900*	Norway (V)	17,911
Burundi (II)	186,200	UK (VI)	13,797**
Vietnam (II)	165,000	New Zealand (IV)	10,988
China (II) (Tibet)	114,000		
Bangladesh (II)	75,000		
Laos (I)	67,400		
Mauretania	60,100		
Guatemala (II)	57,400		
Burma (II)	50,800		
Zaire (I)	50,700		
Nicaragua (I)	41,900		
S. Africa (I)	40,000		
El Salvador (III)	37,300	*sources vary	
Chad (I)	34,400	**statistics for 1975-81 unavailable	

[1]These cumulative data (to the late 1980s) are strongly illustrative but lack sufficient rigour for formal analysis.

SOURCE: Compiled by Robert C. North from various sources.

A distinction needs to be made between *refugees*, who, fleeing political persecution, revolution, or civil war (Richmond, 1988: 111) are 'forced' to seek asylum beyond the borders of their own countries, and *migrants*, who move —temporarily or permanently—to a foreign country for economic reasons. Individuals or whole families in both categories affect their countries both of origin and destination in various ways—socially, economically, politically, and environmentally. Refugees and voluntary migrants alike can be viewed as producers, consumers, and polluters whose effects are subtracted from the country of origin and added to the country of destination. If the latter is more highly developed than the former, the migrants—with luck or foresight—may be expected to produce more, earn more, consume more, and probably pollute more after they move than before. The plight of the refugee is likely to be more problematical.

For the better part of four decades following World War II, the cold war, together with the Third World proxy battles it spawned, was a major producer of refugees throughout many parts of the globe. With the termination of the cold war in 1989-90, hopes for a more peaceful future rose around the world.

Before the first year was over, however, 'several developments, revelations, and trends were muddying the waters of earlier prognostications' — first of all a lag between the ends of wars and possibilities for refugee peoples to return home, and second, and more disruptive, 'the absence of the Cold War framework' that, for all its evils, had kept the lid on many lesser conflicts and had served as 'a great simplifier' which 'made [US] foreign policy a great morality play of good and evil.' Later, freed from this framework, 'ethnic hatred, nationalism, and other forces' (including newly generated pressures on and competitions for resources) ran wild without 'the discipline of the old framework' (Winter, 1991: 2).

As the twentieth century draws to a close, sending and receiving countries alike are experiencing rapid technological, economic, and social changes that influence migrations in complex, often indirect and unprecedented ways that in turn contribute to and reflect environmental changes that are also complex, often indirect, and normally unprecedented.

Statehood and Refugeeism

The production of refugees has been identified as an outcome of the state-building process. The reasoning is that since nationalistic homogeneity does not guarantee consensus on other issues such as economic or constitutional functions, the new economic and political distributions emerging from the creation of a state may be achieved by revolution or civil war, producing refugees in large numbers. It is thus no accident that new states tend to be the leading producers of refugees (Keely, 1991: 22).

Refugee movements can be viewed as manifestations of lateral pressure — the expansion of a society's activities and interests (see Choucri, 1974). Refugees have been identified more specifically as 'those who flee in fear of immediate violence resulting from conflict . . . between state and civil society, between opposing armies, or among ethnic groups or class formations that the state is unable or unwilling to control (Zolberg et al., 1989: 208). In recent decades, 'most refugee-producing conflicts have involved the newly independent states and have been based on issues of internal nation building, revolutionary change, or conflicts with neighbours' (Stein, 1991: 15).

Population Movements and State Profiles

Such population movements can pose threats to sending and receiving countries alike, as well as to their interactions. They may threaten the environment not only of the latter but — less directly, but not uncommonly — of the former. Or they can create demands and claims on the society that were unintended or unanticipated. Unintended effects can occur even when there is a policy of allowing, encouraging, or forcing people to move across territorial boundaries. Three cases—Europe after World War II, and Japan and the Middle East today—point to the negative long-term consequences of short-term policies pertaining to the importing of labour.

Among the most serious political consequences over time is the fact that, as people migrate, they influence not only the labour market in the receiving country, but the structure of political demand, environmental pressures, and the social contract. In effect, migrants from a Group I or Group II country may be expected to demand and consume more, in the long run (essentially as much as a native-born person) than they did in the country of origin. This means that a Group V or VI country with a population growth rate of 0.8 per cent (US), 0.4 per cent (France), or 0.0 per cent (Belgium), may find itself a destination for migrants from countries where the population growth rates range between 3 per cent (doubling time 23 years) and 4 per cent (doubling time 18 years). To the extent, therefore, that migrants and refugees in host countries of Groups V or VI can be expected to remain there for good (or to be replaced if they repatriate), issues of economic, political, social, and environmental integration remain salient.

The oil-producing countries of the Middle East present special demographic problems because the opportunities for employment there have attracted migrants. As a Group II country, Iraq, with a population growth-rate of 0.35 per cent (and associated domestic and external pressures), is less an anomaly than some of the others whose oil-based economies have been targets for migrants. A more striking example is provided by Group VI Kuwait, which has grown 'oil-rich', but with a 3.5 per cent population growth (prior to the Iraqi invasion) that is uncharacteristic of Group VI countries.

In principle, Group IV Oman and Saudi Arabia have the advantage of territories that are large relative to their populations, but with arid resource bases and current (early 1990s) population growth rates of 3.8 per cent and 4.0 per cent they might do well to take the conditions for a demographic transition under early advisement. The same could be recommended to Group IV Libya (3.7) and Group I Yemen (3.7).

The *World Refugee Survey* reported the global total of refugees in May 1991 at 18,355,400. The principal receiving countries for the world's refugees are in Groups IV, V, and VI. The United States leads with a cumulative total (1973-89) of 1,355,858, with Canada (268,225) and France (186,957) placing second and third (Table 10.7). Most of these refugees were produced by states in Groups I and II, poor countries where individuals, families, classes, and ethnic communities commonly compete for limited, often exceedingly scarce resources (and distributions thereof) and where warfare is likely to be almost endemic.

It will be recalled that Group I countries have territory and/or resources that are extensive in relation to the size of their populations and thus appear to possess good potential for population growth and technological development. At the same time, however, their technologies are often so poorly developed that access to those resources is limited and reliance on imports (and the exports to pay for them) is heavy.

If, under these circumstances, the growth rate of these relatively sparse populations should accelerate in relation to existing knowledge, skills, and resource accessibility, many countries in Group I could find themselves in serious difficulties. Currently, some of them still have annual per capita GNPs in the low hundreds of dollars, combined with relatively high rates of population growth: for example, Chad (2.5 per cent), Ethiopia (2.7 per cent), Laos (2.8 per cent), Somalia (3.3 per cent) and Botswana (3.7 per cent) are already referred to as 'basket cases'.

Countries in Group II are characterized by populations that are large and growing relative to area (domestic resource base) and GNPs that are low relative to both population and area. Most, if not all, countries in this group are former Group I societies with rising birthrates that have 'outgrown' their previous earlier profiles. That is, they have been unable to hold their population densities reasonably constant while accelerating technological advancement. Thus they have locked themselves into a profile from which escape is likely to become increasingly difficult.

Many countries in Group I suffer from combinations of drought (or seasonal flood and drought), famine, and warfare that exacerbate trends toward starvation, disease, and death. Those who compete ineffectively in these countries are vulnerable whichever way they seek to turn.

Group II countries are often no better off, but the implications of their plights are different: whereas many Group I nations can still seize upon the possibility of constraining population growth and accelerating technological advancement, only drastic measures can rescue Group II countries from the 'lock-in' of high population levels exerting heavy pressures on an already damaged and depleted resource base in combination with low and inefficient levels of technology.

Many Group II countries possess extensive territories, but the sheer numbers of people overburden their natural environments with fundamental and justifiable demands. The soil, forests, water, and other resources are already in serious jeopardy; yet for lack of a sufficiently advanced technology, sufficient resources cannot be extracted, transported, processed, or in some instances even located in sufficient quantities to satisfy basic human needs. China was considered resource-poor (only limited supplies of low-grade coal and oil were known until new technologies and expanded exploration located wholly new reserves under the Maoist regime). Despite (or because of) the political oppression of the Chinese regime and the casualties inflicted during the Great Leap Forward and the Cultural Revolution, the People's Republic has produced relatively few refugees.

A few countries, including India and China, have made efforts to curb birthrates and steer toward a Group VI profile by accelerating technological advancement well in advance of population growth and high levels of exports to pay for the importation of resources that the domestic resource base cannot supply. In effect, the intention is to emulate modern Japan—as distinct from the 'overpopulated' Japan of the late nineteenth and early twentieth centuries. This is a long pathway for an overpopulated country to travel, however, in view of China's 1987 density of 110 persons per sq. km and per capita GNP of $300 (or India's 238 per sq. km density and $299 per capita GNP) as compared with Japan's density of 327 persons per sq. km and per capita GNP of $12,840.

In recent years, not without high costs in terms of civil rights, China's Draconian birth-control measures have been relatively successful, but in view of the country's huge population base, it is not surprising that the numbers of people continue to increase, albeit at a considerably lower rate (1.5 per cent) than in the not too distant past. India (2.1 per cent) has a longer way to go in this respect.

Population and the Global Environment

Profile Groups and Global Environmental Change

The by-products of population growth and technological advancement—generally toxic in nature and bearing on issues of security and insecurity—are so diverse and widespread that this chapter will confine itself to the issue of climate change, specifically global warming.

US Senator Timothy Wirth in 1987 referred to the 'greenhouse effect' as 'a challenge as compelling and as imperative as nuclear arms control. Unfortunately,' he continued, 'we cannot negotiate with the planet. Instead, the nations of the world must make choices, unilaterally and collectively, to adapt their behaviour to maintain existing climatic conditions.' He then identified 'high rates of population growth' — together with energy-efficient technologies and resources and preservation of forests—as critical policy issues that had 'been passed from the world's scientists to its public policy makers' (Wirth, 1987: xiii–xv). The director of the Institute for International Economics, C. Fred Bergsten, in his preface to a more recent book (Cline, 1992: ix) referred to global warming as 'the quintessential international economic problem'—transcending national borders, involving 'irreversible change and the risk of major adverse surprise', confronting 'international policy with the need to make decisions in the face of considerable uncertainty', and calling for 'a coordinated and multi-faceted response from a large number of countries'.

Table 10.8 shows the CO_2 emissions of some of these countries within their respective profile groups. Countries in Groups I to VI generate quite different levels of CO_2 and other greenhouse emissions, but that production tends to be relatively uniform within profile groupings. One can draw from these

Table 10.8. Growth, Development and Carbon Emissions

	POPULATION (% global)	AREA (% global)	GNP (% global)	GNP ($US)	POP. DENSITY (sq. km)	CO_2 (% global)	CO_2 (m.t. per cap.)
GROUP I							
Brazil	2.837	6.469	1.655	1,810	16	5.882	2.807
Iran	0.935	1.252	0.571	1,895	28	0.472	0.884
Argentina	0.635	2.103	0.481	2,350	11	0.398	0.869
Algeria	0.459	1.810	0.383	2,590	9	0.234	0.690
Cameroon	0.215	0.361	0.063	910	22	0.070	0.159
Sudan	0.463	1.904	0.048	320	9	0.052	0.040
Kenya	0.434	0.443	0.042	300	36	0.017	0.054
Tanzania	0.471	0.718	0.038	250	24	0.009	0.024
Jordan	0.074	0.074	0.037	1,540	37	0.037	0.684
Zimbabwe	0.178	0.297	0.036	620	22	0.053	0.406
Ethiopia	0.892	0.929	0.034	120	36	0.009	0.013
Angola	0.184	0.948	0.031	522	7	0.009	0.069
Bolivia	0.135	0.835	0.026	600	6	0.017	0.172
Afghanistan	0.316	0.492	0.020	200	24	0.065	0.051
Mozambique	0.291	0.609	0.020	210	18	0.005	0.023
Nicaragua	0.070	0.099	0.018	790	26	0.009	0.168
Congo	0.041	0.260	0.013	990	6	0.007	0.023
Somalia	0.113	0.485	0.010	280	9	0.005	0.054
Chad	0.105	0.976	0.005	160	4	0.001	0.011
GROUP II							
China	21.602	7.266	2.089	300	110	8.393	0.526
India	16.015	2.497	1.497	299	238	2.685	0.227
Indonesia	3.410	1.457	0.539	490	87	3.333	1.329
Nigeria	2.113	0.702	0.436	640	112	1.099	0.704
Turkey	1.055	0.593	0.378	1,110	66	0.520	0.667
Thailand	1.078	0.390	0.283	810	102	0.520	2.063
Iraq	0.335	0.264	0.264	2,424	38	1.643	0.555
Egypt	1.017	0.760	0.250	760	50	0.301	0.400
Pakistan	2.031	0.611	0.229	350	123	0.247	0.132
Philippines	1.173	0.228	0.212	560	191	0.248	1.148
Malaysia	0.330	0.251	0.195	1,830	49	0.458	0.572
Syria	0.221	0.141	0.112	1,570	58	0.127	0.779
Bangladesh	2.112	0.109	0.109	160	717	0.047	0.030
Morocco	0.261	0.339	0.088	590	50	0.076	0.223
Vietnam	1.296	0.251	0.082	196	192	0.622	0.649
Tunisia	0.149	0.125	0.055	1,140	45	0.050	0.452
Guatemala	0.158	0.093	0.050	930	75	0.015	0.123
Burma	0.778	0.514	0.050	200	56	0.799	1.389
Sri Lanka	0.330	0.054	0.043	400	244	0.015	0.063
Ghana	0.270	0.182	0.034	300	390	0.036	0.055

Table 10.8. — *Continued*

	POPULATION (% global)	AREA (% global)	GNP (% global)	GNP ($US)	POP. DENSITY (sq. km)	CO$_2$ (% global)	CO$_2$ (m.t. per cap.)
GROUP II — *Continued*							
Dominican							
Rep.	0.135	0.037	0.031	710	135	0.027	0.272
Uganda	0.311	0.179	0.023	250	64	0.003	0.014
Burundi	0.098	0.021	0.008	240	171	0.001	0.009
GROUP III							
S. Korea	0.840	0.074	0.650	2,370	423	0.687	1.094
Portugal	0.020	0.070	0.152	2,250	111	0.123	0.797
N. Korea	0.477	0.092	0.301	909	173	0.608	0.881
GROUP IV							
USSR	5.754	17.014	15.574	8,354	13	15.303	1.094
Canada	0.524	7.577	2.389	12,120	3	1.593	4.110
Australia	0.328	5.838	1.260	11,920	2	0.495	3.829
Libya	0.080	1.337	0.163	5,128	2	0.126	2.142
Oman	0.027	0.228	0.453	4,900	2	0.110	4.229
GROUP V							
US	4.952	7.115	27.900	17,480	26	18.192	4.974
GROUP VI							
France	1.135	0.416	3.924	10,720	101	1.489	1.775
UK	1.162	0.186	3.323	8,870	231	2.516	2.931
Spain	0.793	0.384	1.243	4,860	77	0.755	1.285
Netherlands	0.299	0.031	0.967	10,020	356	0.531	2.402
Belgium	0.203	0.024	0.604	9,230	319	0.402	2.631
Greece	0.205	0.100	0.243	3,680	76	0.243	1.603
Israel	0.088	0.016	0.176	6,210	205	0.110	1.691
Kuwait	0.037	0.014	0.165	13,890	100	0.124	4.563

SOURCE: Choucri and North (1993)

data some inferences that may be pertinent to global insecurity and security. (See Schneider, 1989: 19–23, for a scientific discussion.)

The contributions of bottom and middle Group I countries to carbon emissions and other globally threatening effluents tend to be low, but to the extent that such effluents generated by the Group as a whole are globally aggregated, their low–level resource depletions, pollutants, and other degradations cannot be discounted — especially (and paradoxically) as such countries manage to grow and develop.

Top countries in Groups I and II often suffer from some of these same problems, but numbers of them have achieved substantial industrialization and accompanying forms of development that provide higher living standards for many of their people and new possibilities for technological advancement. Since biogeochemical cycles do not respect territorial boundaries, one state's actions and degradation cannot be prevented from affecting the natural environment of another state. Industrial countries are characterized by high levels and rates of technological advancement combined with access to resources. They exhibit high levels of consumption, emit high levels of CO_2, generate extensive wastes, and produce a high volume of greenhouse gases. Then, often transported by air currents and other natural forces, these effluents contribute to global warming and degradation of the planetary environment.

Carbon Emission and Growth

The global distributions of energy use and carbon emissions carry a compelling message: at one end of the spectrum are states with large or growing populations and relatively limited basic technology, contributing low carbon emissions per capita. And at the other end are the industrial states, which currently generate more effluents and threaten the global balances more than do the developing states.

Although states all over the world generate many of the same effluents — carbon dioxide (CO_2), methane (CH_4), nitrous oxide (N_2O), chlorofluorocarbons ($CFCs$), and a host of others — they do so in different ways and in varying amounts. The differences are shaped by population, levels of technology, and resource availabilities — and also by geographical location (climate zone) and policy priorities. Not all the pollutants are traceable to industrial smokestacks. Carbon dioxide, for example, comes also from biomass burning, which can be traced in part to deforestation in Brazil, Indonesia, New Guinea, the Philippines, and other parts of the tropics as well as along the northwestern coast of North America (Canada and the United States, including Alaska).

Similarly, CH_4 — methane — is generated by cattle and rice fields as well as by landfills and fossil-fuel production. Traceable in part to biomass burning — slash-and-burn agriculture and, in Brazil and a number of other countries, the burning of timber-cutting refuse in the preparation of forest land for agriculture — are carbon monoxide (CO), and nitrous oxide (N_2O) gases.

The fundamental issues for countries of Groups I and II pertain to their future growth and development. It is here that the growth/development $\longleftrightarrow$ environmental sustainability paradox (and policy dilemma) emerges most starkly. For their future stability as nations and the survival of many of their less-favourably situated people, countries in these two groups *must* grow and develop with dispatch; but if their populations continue to grow, and if they rely for their development upon the technologies prevailing in Groups IV, V, and VI, they will be in deep trouble. Specifically, a number of developing countries need to accomplish by new means (energy-efficient technologies and resources that the industrialized countries are still seeking) what countries of Groups IV, V, and VI achieved with coal, oil, and 'dirty' technologies over the better part of a century. As these nations industrialize, however, their large populations will make them significant contributors. China's CO_2 emissions per capita are only 0.5 m.t./yr, but in the aggregate it is already the world's third largest contributor of global CO_2. Imagine China with the US per capita GNP (1986) of $17,480 and the US share of automobiles, then factor in its reserves of coal and oil—China's most readily available energy resources—and one can begin to imagine its future in the event that current modes of growth and development persist.

The level at which the future world population is expected to stabilize (estimated at 10-14 billion persons) will have radically different impacts on the global carbon budget, depending on the level of development worldwide. If the highest possible global population is reached at a global development level equivalent to that of Bangladesh (with almost trivial carbon emissions) the impact on the environment will obviously be very different from what it would be if the development level were that of Iran (the country that demarcates the global median in CO_2 emissions per capita), or Italy (close to the global per capita average; for details see Choucri 1992).

Sustainability and Security

From a systems perspective, a sustainable society is one that 'has in place informational, social and institutional mechanisms to keep in check the positive feedback loops that cause exponential population and capital growth. This means that birthrates roughly equal death rates, and investment rates roughly equal depreciation rates, unless and until technical changes and social decisions justify a considered and controlled change in the levels of population or capital.' In terms of general welfare and quality of life, such a society would have to be 'configured so that the material standard is adequate and secure for everyone'—worldwide (Meadows, Meadows, and Randers, 1992: 209). And to be physically sustainable, 'the society's material and energy throughputs would have to meet economist Herman Daley's three conditions':

- Its rates of renewable resources use do not exceed their rates of regeneration.

- Its use of nonrenewable resources does not exceed the rate at which sustainable renewable substitutes are developed.

- Its rates of pollution emission do not exceed the assimilation capacity of the environment (Meadows, Meadows and Randers, 1992: 209, citing Daley, 1971: 237).

In the terms of this chapter, sustainability also requires maintenance of a country's population/ resource ratio at a socially defined and acceptable level beyond the minimum requirements for survival in terms of food, water, space, and shelter. Population serves as the denominator in both the equation for structural security (or minimal insecurity) and the basic sustainability ratio. Since structural security refers, in turn, to the broad context and viability of the society, its absence will be manifested in 'crumbling' of the state as a result of internal strains, and inability of the state and government to contain (manage, regulate, diffuse, or export) the pressures on its resource base and/or to find external sources of needed resources. In the latter case, the resort to external resources always involves some cost in the form of transport, debt, debt service, barter arrangements, political exchange, and so forth. These costs will be determined by the access, the scarcities in question, and the relative capability of the parties to the exchange.

If those in the 'favourably situated' groups do not lead the way—in demographics, technology and efficient use of resources—nations in the other groups, and in due course the global system itself, may well be doomed to persisting insecurity. It is therefore necessary to begin immediately with a world-wide strategy of (1) population constraint; (2) acceleration of technology (knowledge and skills, both 'mechanical' and organizational) within the bounds of (3) efficiency in applications of technology and natural resources —with some optimal security for each and all as a guiding beacon. To be acquired globally, a reasonable quality of life and level of security must be achieved locally—and vice versa.

Note

[1] The editors are responsible for the version of this paper that is presented here. For a more complete account see Choucri and North (1993).

References

Boulding, Kenneth E. (1956). *The Image*. Ann Arbor: University of Michigan Press.

Choucri, Nazli (1974). *Population Dynamics and Local Conflict: A Cross National Study of Population and War: A Summary*. Cambridge, Mass.: MIT Center for International Studies, C/74-9.

Choucri, Nazli, ed. (1984). *Multidisciplinary Perspectives on Population and Conflict*. Syracuse, NY: Syracuse University Press.

Choucri, Nazli (1991). 'Population and the Global Environment.' In Jefferson W. Tester, David O. Wood, and Nancy A. Ferrari, eds. *Energy and the Environment in the 21st Century*. Cambridge, MA: MIT Press.

Choucri, Nazli (forthcoming). *Challenges to Security: Population and Political Economy in Egypt*. London: Routledge.

Choucri, Nazli, Janet Welsh Brown, and Peter M. Haas (1990). 'Dimensions of National Security: the Case of Egypt'. In Janet Welsh Brown, ed. *In the U.S. Interest: Resources, Growth and Security in the Developing World*. Boulder, CO: Westview.

Choucri, Nazli, Robert C. North, and Susumu Yamakagi (1992). *The Challenge of Japan Before World War II and After*. London: Routledge.

Choucri, Nazli, and Robert C. North (1993). 'Growth, Development, and Environmental Sustainability: Profile and Paradox'. In Nazli Choucri, ed. *Global Accord: Environmental Challenges and International Responses*. Cambridge, MA: MIT Press.

Cline, William R. (1992). *The Economics of Global Warming*. Washington, DC: Institute for International Economics.

Cyert, Richard M., and James G. March (1963). *A Behavioral Theory of the Firm*. Englewood Cliffs, NJ.

Daley, Herman (1971). In John Harte and Robert Socolow. *Patient Earth*. New York: Holt, Rinehart and Winston.

Keely, Charles P. (1991). 'Filling a Critical Gap in the Refugee Protection Regime: The Internally Displaced'. *World Refugee Survey*, Washington, DC: US Committee for Refugees.

Kindleberger, Charles (1962). *Foreign Trade and the National Economy*. New Haven: Yale University Press.

Kuznets, Simon (1966). *Modern Economic Growth: Rate, Structure, and Spread*. New Haven: Yale University Press.

Lasswell, Harold D. (1958). *Politics: Who Gets What and How?*. New York: McGraw-Hill.

Loescher, Gil (1991). 'Mass Migrations as a Global Security Problem'. *World Refugee Survey*. Washington, DC.: US Committee for Refugees.

Meadows, Donella, Dennis L. Meadows, and Jurgen Randers (1992). *Beyond the Limits: Confronting Global Collapse, Envisioning a Sustainable Future*. Post Mills, VT: Chelsea Green.

North, Robert C. (1990). *War, Peace, Survival*. Boulder, CO: Westview.

Nye, Joseph S., and Sean M. Lynn-Jones (1988). 'International Security Studies: A Report of the Conference on the State of the Field'. *International Security* 12, 4: 5–27.

Richmond, Anthony H. (1988). 'Social-Cultural Adaptation in Immigrant-Receiving Countries'. *International Migration Today* 2.

Schneider, Stephen H. (1989). *Global Warming: Are We Entering the Greenhouse Century?* San Francisco: Sierra Club.

Stein, Barry N. (1991). 'Repatriation under Conflict'. *World Refugee Survey*. Washington, DC: US Committee for Refugees.

Sullivan, Michael J. (1991). *Measuring Global Values: The Ranking of 162 Countries*. New York: Greenwood.

Ullman, Richard H. (1983). 'Redefining Security'. *International Security* 81, 1: 129–53.

Winter, Roger P. (1991). 'The Year in Review'. *World Refugee Survey*. Washington, DC: US Committee for Refugees.

Wirth, Timothy E. (1987). 'Introduction'. In Dean E. Abrahamson, ed. *The Challenge of Global Warming*. Washington, DC: Island Press.

Zolberg, Aristide R., Astri Suhrke, and Sergio Aquayo (1989). *Escape from Violence: Conflict and the Refugee Crisis in the Developing World*, New York: Oxford University Press.

part three

The New Institutions of

Global Governance

chapter eleven

Opportunities and Obstacles for Collective Security after the Cold War

Thomas G. Weiss and Laura S. Hayes Holgate

With the end of the 45-year cold war and the 45-day Gulf War, international politics has been transformed. No student of international politics, no matter how clever or astute, could have been adequately prepared for the events from 1989 through 1991. Everything, in both theory and practice, that had been taught about the international system seems to have acquired an antique aspect.

Nowhere is this more obvious than in the regional conflicts of the Third World.[1] And nowhere have the possibilities for new or enhanced forms of multilateral co-operation increased more than at the United Nations, which, in his final report on the work of the organization, the cautious outgoing Secretary General Javier Pérez de Cuellar characterized as experiencing a renaissance.[2] Bipolarity appears to some to have given way to unipolarity, if only temporarily. Whereas many observers, particularly in the Third World, had initially worried about a superpower 'condominium', in which the United States and Soviet Union would jointly manage the world, the Soviet Union has now disappeared. Russia and the Commonwealth of Independent States are unable to counterbalance the United States on the international chess-board. The central organizing notion of superpower confrontation has dissolved during what Charles Krauthammer has aptly dubbed this 'unipolar moment',[3] thereby exposing old conflicts and making space for new ones.

The world has retreated from the midnight of nuclear annihilation, but the Gulf War proved that non-nuclear wars are also fearsome and perhaps now more likely. At the same time, new approaches to solving and preventing violent conflicts are now also possible. The growing international confidence in the United Nations—first evident in Mikhail Gorbachev and Eduard Shevardnadze's 'new thinking', but also having had a visible impact even on such cold warriors as Ronald Reagan and Margaret Thatcher—raises the question of what new opportunities exist for the founders' vision of the UN's ultimate contribution to international peace: collective security. The first-ever summit of the Security Council, in January 1992, indicated how pertinent this question has become for heads of state and government.[4]

Inis Claude long ago rued the misappropriation of the term 'collective security' (or, alternatively, 'peace enforcement') to describe virtually any international arrangement whose aim is peace.[5] An explicit definition is in order: collective security rests on the assumption of all against one; it is a set of commitments and institutions that ensure that aggression by any state will automatically be met with the combined power of the rest of the world to repulse that aggression and restore the *status quo ante*.

The concept of peace enforcement was developed in opposition to classical balance-of-power and alliance politics. Collective security does not permit the designation in advance of a putative enemy, as is the case with defensive alliances. It differs from alliances in that it is directed against all aggressors, not merely a particular foe.[6] War under collective-security arrangements is waged in the name of the entire community of nations against an aggressor that is genuinely perceived to threaten them all, whereas alliances by their nature not only exclude certain nations, but also may be aggressors themselves. With collective security, the greater force is always on the side of the victim. Aggression against any member of a collective-security organization will be met by the preponderant force of all other members.

In spite of the enthusiasm for the coalition's military efforts against Iraq,[7] the most successful peace-enforcement system would rarely need to resort to the use of international military force; the mere existence of such a system acts as a damper on unacceptable behaviour. Its power would lie both in an enhanced respect for the rule of law and in the assurance that aggressors would encounter universal opprobrium and the certainty of a worldwide reaction. The logic of collective security resembles that of nuclear deterrence in that the unilateral use of force would be prevented by fear of a forceful riposte. Collective security shares with nuclear deterrence an assumption of rationality and the promise of overwhelming force. Fear is not the only factor, of course, since the acceptance of rules as just and secure is the critical factor behind the international community's willingness to respond to aggression. Nonetheless, success depends to a significant degree on the credibility of the deterrent threat.

Further research on collective security is required not only because of the dramatic changes that have taken place in the international environment, but because the subject has received almost no scholarly attention in the last three decades. Most of the scholarly literature was produced in the first two decades after the end of the Second World War and consists mainly of historical analyses of the League of Nations and the United Nations;[8] theoretical inquiries into the differences between balance-of-power, alliance, and collective-security systems;[9] and endeavours to evaluate the feasibility of collective security.[10] It is thus time for a fresh look.[11]

This chapter begins by tracing the theory of collective security as a method for the maintenance of international peace, and by recalling the peace-enforcement aspects of the League of Nations and the United Nations. Its second section examines how, as the Persian Gulf War demonstrated dramatically, the world without the cold war resembles that of 1945, even though the current international system is also quite different from that envisioned by the UN Charter's architects. The third section examines the implications of this simultaneous change and continuity for collective security, as well as obstacles to change within the UN system. Several proposals are offered for adjustments to the United Nations that would emphasize collective security, and the challenges facing those proposals are discussed. The final section assesses the possibilities for expanding the limited space for action to mobilize support for a functioning United Nations collective-security system.

Evolution of the Concept, Ideas, and Theories of Collective Security

Contrary to conventional wisdom, the multinational military effort is not a purely modern phenomenon. The Western literary tradition began with Homer's version of the *just* war waged collectively against Troy. Crusades and holy wars fought by forces from multiple states or principalities abound in historical records.

Moreover, collective security is not a new idea. Traces of the concept can be found in a number of peace plans and discussions of international politics beginning in the 1300s. Early discussions of the use of force to impose collective decisions were inescapably intertwined with European power politics and the question of unification, with the development of the modern state system, and with the tension between pacifism and coercion for peace. One fourteenth-century student of international affairs, Pierre DuBois, proposed a Common Council, composed of the sovereigns of Christian Europe, that would agree to use sanctions and war against those who flouted Council decisions.

The sixteenth century saw the rise of just-war theory, which was regarded by some as authorizing the use of arms to enforce collective decisions, but which offended pacifists. Collective-security ideas were submerged in a variety of seventeenth-century peace frameworks but reappeared in a number of eighteenth-century plans. The discussions of these plans saw the first recognition of the dilemma of achieving peace through the threat of war, for many proposals included arrangements for the joint use of force against rogue states. Fears that international groupings would undermine sovereignty were eased by appeals to the greater domestic power of sovereigns in a peaceful world.

Grotius built on these intellectual frameworks and developed a law regulating the conduct of relations between states. On the basis of this so-called 'inter-national law', Vattel and Wolff[12] debated in the eighteenth century whether society should be internationally or nationally based. The defeat of Wolff's *civitas maxima* ('great republic') meant a change of emphasis away from the collective and toward the parts. Thus followed the rise in importance of pursuing collective security against transgressors, and in the absence of collective security, the pursuit of alliances and the balance of power.

A variety of philosophers grappled with these issues. Jean-Jacques Rousseau and Immanuel Kant agreed that a rigid federation of states was the only road to peace, but they differed on the need for enforcement and on the role of conflict itself. Rousseau advocated force as a guarantor of the federation, but was pessimistic about the achievement of such a federation in the face of the severe conflicts between states. Kant saw those conflicts as the means to progress toward improved international law, but rejected the enforcement of international law through arms. Jeremy Bentham and John Stuart Mill agreed on the importance of informed public opinion as a motive force behind international law, but Mill dismissed Bentham's sympathy for possible joint uses of force against aggressor states.

In the early nineteenth century, the problem of uniting Europe was conflated with the problem of ending war, and collective security was overwhelmed by the organizational questions of unification. By the late 1800s, military sanctions and peace enforcement resurfaced in plans put forward by relative newcomers to the peace community — political scientists, diplomats, and international lawyers.

Collective-security ideas were represented only peripherally in the Concert of Europe, the first prototype of international organization. Its forerunner, the Congress of Vienna, was unable to guarantee united armed action, but its goals were reproduced in looser form in the Concert of Europe. The latter was without a capacity for peace enforcement, and was primarily a power-balancing arrangement, but the great powers co-operated to prevent wars, maintain the territorial status quo, and impose their decisions on lesser powers.[13]

The League of Nations embodied the first full-blown promise of the institutional structure necessary for a working system of collective security, at least on paper. Political conditions, however, prevented its realization. The lack of will is visible both in the provisions of the League's Covenant and in their application. The Covenant embodied the 'principle of concern' that the use of force offends all nations and peace should be preserved through joint action. It contained the first detailed attempt to banish war and a pledge of joint sanctions — economic and eventually military — against aggressors.

The League's constitution did not eliminate the right to wage war, but restricted it to cases in which the dispute had been submitted to its Council and the combatants (both the alleged aggressor and the defender) had waited three months after the Council's ruling, or in which war was waged by a non-member.[14] In the absence of an absolute ban on the use of force, war persisted as a legitimate method of international relations. The lack of effective mechanisms for prompt decision and action further doomed the implementation of collective-security measures. The League's rule of unanimity ensured failure in that both parties to a dispute, as well as the rest of the member nations, had to agree that the Covenant had been violated.

The League's provisions, faulty though they were, represented an ambitious attempt to curb unilateral violence. And its shortcomings were not attributable solely to its members. The US Senate refused to approve membership in the organization, despite the efforts of President Wilson in formulating the collective-security concept, because of objections to the very definition of the ideal contained in article 10 of the Covenant, the obligation of every state 'to respect and preserve as against external aggression the territorial integrity and existing political independence of all Members of the League'. Without the US, the League was incapable of carrying out its own guarantees. Subsequent meetings of the member states proceeded to reduce those guarantees further, through constant challenges to article 10 and diminutions in the immediacy and universality of imposed sanctions. League members were eventually reduced to calling for bilateral treaties of mutual assistance, regardless of their obligations under the Covenant. This schizophrenic response was the result of widespread insecurity among European states combined with a refusal to accept the obligations of a collective-security regime.

Reflecting these shortcomings of will and means, the League focused increasingly on reconciliation and persuasion rather than coercion of any type. Only in the case of the Italian attacks on Ethiopia in 1935 did the League invoke economic sanctions, which came close to crippling Italy despite the tendency of member states unilaterally to opt out of the partial blockade. More and more marginalized, the League observed the opening skirmishes of the Second World War without significant debate about a response. Leaders at the time implicitly attacked the idea of collective security by refusing to see in German or Japanese aggression any justification for taking action themselves in defence of Austria or China.

The experiment added a certain legitimacy to the concept, if not the practice, of collective security. In fact, the very nature of the League's shortcomings with respect to peace enforcement laid the foundations for the post-World War II agenda for the new United Nations.

After the shock of the second of the two world conflicts 'to end all wars', the farthest-reaching collective-security arrangement to date began with the signing of the UN Charter. Against the backdrop of the ineffectiveness of the League of Nations, the mechanisms for the pacific settlement of disputes (chapter VI) and collective enforcement (chapter VII) took centre stage. The projection of military might under international control to enforce international decisions against aggressors was to distinguish the United Nations from its predecessor. Peace-enforcement mechanisms were explicitly spelled out in chapter VII: renunciation of the use of force as national policy; authority to impose economic sanctions; rights to use force to maintain international peace and security; commitments to set terms of member-state forces for UN actions; the establishment of a great-power Military Staff Committee to plan and advise on the joint use of international military forces to back up binding decisions from the Security Council.

Though more ambitious in its goals and more universal in its membership, the United Nations almost immediately suffered the effects of political realities similar to those experienced by its predecessor. The combination of the great-power veto with the deepening cold war rendered many measures inoperable. The 1949 victory of the Chinese communists made the permanent seat of Taiwan an additional source of discontent. The formation of the North Atlantic Treaty Organization (NATO) and the Warsaw Treaty Organization (WTO) as peacetime alliances exposed the hollow shell of UN collective security.[15]

Apart from the fundamental rift among the permanent powers, which upset the basic logic of the UN Charter system, still other objections surfaced from governments about the challenges to national sovereignty posed by foreign troops, and possible limitations on future actions in an uncertain world. While states might have been willing to forswear the unilateral use of force for the near term, the great powers were reluctant to commit themselves to arrangements that would have constrained future foreign-policy decisions.[16] The great-power veto ensured that any collective-security actions would be limited to those cases in which the vital interests of the permanent five members were not at issue. While the cold war prevented the establishment of a standing force, it is not clear what kind of force could have been approved by the Security Council in any event. Not only was there an unwillingness to turn over command and control responsibilities for a country's troops to the world organization, but the prospect of foreign armies under UN command occupying their own states was also more than many diplomats from lesser powers—including the newly independent countries of Africa and Asia that joined the world organization beginning in the mid-1950s—were willing to bear. As a result, during the first 40 years of the UN, no effective Military Staff Committee was convened, Security Council resolutions on issues of international security were routinely ignored by the parties in question, and no true United Nations collective-security force was ever mounted. In the place of the Charter's collective-security regime sprang up the improvisation of United Nations peace-keeping, and the two anomalies of Korea and Iraq.

Claude explains collective security in terms of objective and subjective conditions. Among the latter are worldwide acceptance of the basic premise that 'a breach anywhere threatens disintegration everywhere';[17] advance commitment of nations to a certain set of responses to the aggression of any other nation; renunciation of unilateral resort to force; willingness to fight for the status quo; and confidence in the fairness and competency of the collective-security system. Full acceptance of these subjective conditions would amount to an extraordinary surrender of national sovereignty. Objective prerequisites include rough equality of several great powers, universal membership, partial disarmament, universal economic vulnerability, and an institutional structure to implement the principles of collective security.

Given these conditions, the lack of a functioning collective-security system is understandable. In the case of the League of Nations, only great-power equilibrium and economic interdependence obtained, together with a general vague acceptance of the idea that any aggression threatened the peace of all. Despite its rhetoric, the League's practice indicated the clear unwillingness of states to accept the accompanying limits on sovereignty, and its Covenant lacked the concrete organizational mechanisms for peace enforcement.

The United Nations improved upon the experience of the League in its universal membership; and the UN began at a time when the world was characterized by an emerging economic interdependence and relatively diffuse power. The rise of atomic superpowers, however, soon destroyed the broad power distribution. Subjectively, the UN benefited from a slightly stronger belief in the indivisibility of peace, but the veto symbolized the refusal of great powers to bind themselves to specific courses of action regardless of circumstances.

Change and Continuity in the 'New World Order'

Recent changes in the international landscape seem to indicate that more of Claude's subjective and objective conditions may now exist than at any moment in the recent past. For example, the precipitous demise of the Soviet Union and the need of the United States to address domestic and budget problems broaden the disposition of power. The waning of zero-sum approaches to international relations may mean less frequent use of Security Council vetoes and more space for UN actions. Great powers may begin to favour maintenance of the territorial status quo as pressures on international boundaries grow in the former Soviet Union, Eastern Europe, and Middle East. These trends could bring about a greater willingness among the great powers to commit themselves to limited collective-security arrangements.

While the post-cold-war world resembles in some ways that of the UN Charter's framers, whose design for preserving international peace and security was premised on great-power collaboration, the approximation of the world of 1945 applies to the 'high' politics of peace and security far more than 'low' politics of economic and social affairs. If borders have become more porous, this has been much more the case for trade and economic affairs than for military security. Moreover, new aspects of the international security scene have been inadequately reflected in UN structures, or even in the intellectual frameworks used by many observers, diplomatic and scholarly, of the world organization. It is to the relative balance between change and continuity in the international system that this chapter now turns.

Change

Changes in the level of violence, in the number and power of states, in weapons and communications technology, and in the internal nature of conflict have left the UN somewhat out of date. In particular, the international system at the dawn of the twenty-first century will no doubt be characterized by levels of violence and unrest not imagined when the Charter was drafted. In the words of former UN Undersecretary General Brian Urquhart:

> We are entering a period of great instability, characterized by longstanding international rivalries and resentments, intense ethnic and religious turmoil, a vast flow of arms and military technology, domestic disintegration, poverty and deep economic inequities, instantaneous communications throughout the world, population pressures, natural and ecological disasters, the scarcity of vital resources, and huge movements of population.[18]

Beyond the possible substantive limitations of the Charter for the world now emerging, there also is the question of adequate representation of states in the world organization. The rise of such new Western financial powers as Japan and Germany and of such Third World political giants as India, Brazil, Nigeria, and Egypt indicates serious structural shortcomings. At the same time, the proliferation of microstates — whose votes in the General Assembly bestow influence out of all proportion to power resources, however defined — has also led to calls to reconsider the one-nation/one-vote principle. Even if Charter reform is unlikely, the credibility and operability of the United Nations may depend on the discovery of creative solutions to questions of appropriate governance and representation.

Technological changes — in weapons, communications, and other areas — have also outstripped the UN's abilities to operate. The disarmament provisions of the Charter have been honoured more in the breach than in the execution. The proliferation of nuclear and other weapons beyond the great powers has added dangerous new dimensions to international politics. Swelling volumes of conventional armaments, often combined with unstable and repressive regimes or insurgents, have raised both the incidence and the levels of violence, increasing the disruptive power of previously low-level disputes. So-called advances in weapons technology have also had important influences on the trend in political violence toward insurgency, terrorism, and other non-state activities that are beyond the UN's capacity to address constructively.

The much-heralded communications revolution, credited for everything from world-beat music to the lightning revolutions in Eastern Europe, poses new technological challenges for the United Nations. The speed with which ideas and images can travel the globe has increased while the UN secretariat and institutions throughout the UN system have not kept pace. Some would even argue that these organizations have actually grown more cumbersome and less responsive.

While the Office of Research and Collection of Information (ORCI) was founded to help provide the Secretary General with better intelligence and early warning, the paucity of human and financial resources make it impossible for the Secretary General and senior staff to act with anything like the timeliness and information required. The Gulf War and the subsequent humanitarian crisis in Kurdistan indicated the stark reality that breaches of the peace occur with great immediacy, often catching the Security Council by surprise and defying the comfortable pace of deliberations and diplomatic discourse set in the past. These trends offer both challenges to traditional UN activities and structures and opportunities for new approaches to international security.

The evolution in contemporary conflicts toward insurgency and intrastate violence creates more ambiguity and complexity than were ever envisioned by the Charter. The emergence of subnational conflicts has raised a number of challenges for the UN system that do not fit easily into the Charter's framework: undeclared wars between major powers and regimes, or rebel groups in developing countries, often fought by proxies or through aid to indigenous groups; civil wars, many with interventions by neighbours; terrorist campaigns; holy wars; and mercenaries in ministates.[19] Many of these types of conflicts were known to the drafters; some are as old as humankind. Yet in spite of the Charter's opening words — 'We, the peoples of the United Nations' — non-state actors were not seen as fitting into the Charter or international law.

Designed to represent states, and not peoples or factions, the UN lacks mechanisms to acknowledge or represent the claims of internal combatants, and the organization is by its own Charter prohibited from interfering in the internal affairs of states, as Knight and Yamashita indicate in the following chapter. New approaches are needed to account for the real impact of these internal disputes on international peace and security. For example, international assistance to implement the peace process to end the Cambodian civil war may demand enforcement measures beyond the traditional, essentially defensive peace-keeping approach initially employed. UN forces in both Yugoslavia and Somalia have recognized the likelihood that dangers will increase and they must be ready to remain, whether or not the parties to the conflicts agree. It is highly unlikely that the approval of the various factions can be assured for the duration of the UN's involvement, and significant military force may be required to back up an internationally-brokered agreement.

These changes mandate improvements in existing UN capacities and expansion of the UN's traditional set of tasks. While the United Nations has long pursued peace-making and sanctions under less than ideal administrative procedures, improved approaches and a new rationale are now more feasible at the end of the cold war. The provisions leading to the peaceful settlement of disputes, for instance — explicitly outlined in chapter VI of the UN Charter — remain fairly haphazard in their application. The Security Council often does not take up a particular conflict before it reaches an advanced stage, and the pronouncements of the General Assembly often exacerbate rather than temper disagreements. Furthermore, questions have long been raised about the difficulties of settling underlying disputes once UN peace-keeping forces restore relative calm, as in Cyprus or Lebanon.

Economic sanctions are the first step on the path to peace enforcement outlined in chapter VII of the Charter. But the experience of the Gulf War demonstrated some of the weaknesses of UN procedures for establishing and enforcing sanctions. Whether the war would have been unnecessary had sanctions and diplomacy run their course is a rich subject for speculation. At a minimum, however, improved information on international trade and more effective monitoring could make sanctions a more potent tool of international persuasion. Particularly in view of the destruction inflicted by the Gulf War, governments will no doubt wish sanctions to be pursued thoroughly before authorizing 'all necessary means'.

Among the new tasks that have emerged as a result of the renaissance of the United Nations is that of providing oversight by a third party. For example, the negotiations toward an international ban on chemical weapons require an international cadre of arms-control verification specialists: putting such teams under UN auspices may be the only acceptable means of carrying out increasingly intrusive verification. UN experience in disarming the Nicaraguan *contras* and in investigating Iraqi capacities for weapons of mass destruction is particularly relevant here.

Recent increases in requests for outside monitoring of elections in fledgling democracies indicate a growing need for trained UN teams to provide technical assistance and represent the international concern for free and fair elections. The 1990 elections in Namibia, which called for such assistance, indicated the need for this capacity on a large scale, and smaller undertakings in Nicaragua and Haiti could be harbingers of growing UN involvement in domestic elections, breaking a long taboo.

Other trends in the nature of modern conflicts indicate a need for combined humanitarian assistance and military protection, as in Kurdish Iraq and the Horn of Africa.[20] A UN peace-keeping-type force with a humanitarian element, or perhaps a back-up enforcement force for civilian aid officials, could be more palatable for states needing this kind of assistance than the national armies used in Iraq.[21] In fact, the inability of the international community to provide an adequate safety net in Kurdistan led to a proposal to establish standing international groups of military and civilian personnel in UN Humanitarian Assistance Teams (UNHAT).

Continuity

Not only must the UN account for these important changes in the international system, but in addition several traditional sets of issues will pose new challenges to UN structures and activities. There are three long-standing characteristics of the international scene that are also changing in important ways.

First, sovereignty has always circumscribed the activities of international organizations. Even though eroded in some aspects, sovereignty remains the defining element of the existing international order. Collective security poses a paradox: states must release some sovereignty over their military policy in order to enter into collective-security arrangements; but the concept depends upon, and defends, national sovereignty. The rationale for the pursuit of the Gulf War was, after all, the defence of the territorial integrity of Kuwait.

At the same time, alterations in the traditional conceptions of sovereignty are facilitating international intervention for humanitarian reasons, for disarmament, and for reparations. The world is beginning to recognize that some non-military activities are morally equivalent in severity to armed aggression. The UN can take advantage of this growing consensus to expand its activities into areas formerly considered out of bounds because of their supposedly internal nature.

The use of US, British, French, and Dutch marines in pursuit of Security Council Resolution 688 to establish havens for Kurdish refugees and displaced persons illustrates most dramatically how the international community's increasing stake in human rights may alter, and eventually transcend, traditional notions of sovereignty. Former Secretary General Pérez de Cuellar, ever cautious about his choice of words, commented on this matter. After noting that article 2 (7) prohibits intervention in domestic affairs, he asked 'whether certain other texts that were later adopted by the United Nations, in particular the Universal Declaration of Human Rights, do not implicitly call into question this inviolable notion of sovereignty.' He concluded that '[w]e are clearly witnessing what is probably an irresistible shift in public attitudes toward the belief that the defence of the oppressed in the name of morality should prevail over frontiers and legal documents.'[22]

The second seemingly stable element in the debate over the proper scope of UN action is the definition of security. Almost everywhere, national security is still conceived primarily in military terms. This too, however, is subject to change. A host of visible international commissions headed by Willy Brandt, Olof Palme, Gro Harlem Brundtland, and Julius Nyerere have argued that far more comprehensive approaches are necessary.[23] The 1970s saw a growing cry to expand the definition of security to include economic security, and the 1980s brought exhortations to add environmental security to the mix.[24] These demands were then picked up in Soviet 'new thinking' under the label of 'comprehensive security'.

The debate continues. Traditional security scholars reject the dilution of the term by those who would apply it to virtually every issue on the international agenda, while economic and environmental advocates appeal for the resources and attention traditionally enjoyed by the proponents of the military aspects of security. Others, including some environmentalists, argue against broadening the definition on the grounds that the structures and concepts of traditional military security—competition, zero-sum games, mutually assured destruction, hierarchical organizations—are poor tools to address global economic and environmental problems.[25]

Since collective security as spelled out in chapter VII of the UN Charter envisions economic and/or military reactions to military aggression, it may appear that security is defined somewhat narrowly in this context. As disputes over economic affairs, access to resources, and environmental disruption will continue, and no doubt in some cases result in violent conflicts, these aspects of international relationships are de facto elements of national security, and therefore of concern in a system of collective security. To address the sources of these conflicts they must be assigned a priority similar to that given to military security in the past. This wider approach is not yet conventional, but older and narrower conceptions are clearly on the wane. In fact, the new approach is being championed by the so-called Stockholm Initiative, a high-level international group composed of prominent participants from earlier, more specialized commissions.[26]

A third persistent element of collective coercion concerns operational necessities. The institutional dimension is critical, because coercion requires the subordination of command and control of sovereign armed forces to a centralized instrument, authorized to act by the larger community in the event of aggression. The deterrent threat of collective-security measures will not be credible without the subordination of foreign policies and military command to an international organization. These requirements strike, of course, at the very essence of the responsibilities of national governments.

Such an operational arrangement would essentially remove from individual nations the discretion to distinguish between small- and large-scale aggression, or to permit democratic consideration of each decision to employ international coercion. Persuading nations to choose, and remain in, such a system has never been easy. In fact, the great powers have generally been among the most reluctant to go beyond rhetoric and make the necessary commitments to a collective-security system.

However, here too there are indications of movement. After four and a half decades of refusal to agree to the details of articles 43 through 47 of the Charter (dealing with the implementation of enforcement decisions), discussions are at least taking place about the feasibility and desirability of an enhanced international military capacity.[27] If the current leading powers were to realize that these articles could serve their interests, and press for agreement on the details, other nations would be much more likely to join in meeting the essential obligations of a collective-security system. The operations under discussion at the beginning of 1992 — 30,000 troops to serve in Yugoslavia and Cambodia, at an additional annual cost of at least $1.5 billion —illustrate the urgency of such a realization. The summit meeting of the Security Council in January 1992 was at least a rhetorical step in this direction.

Thus several current trends encourage many prominent observers to argue for the vigorous implementation of the components of a collective-security regime.[28] However, there are several significant obstacles to strengthening the United Nations.

Obstacles to Change in the UN System

The rapidity of the international change witnessed in the last three years may complicate rather than ease international commitments. Uncertainty has always been a reason for nations to resist policies that restrict future options. And in many ways uncertainty is now greater than ever, with governments wary about limiting their options by premature commitment to multilateral security mechanisms. There is almost a nostalgia for the predictability of the cold war since Europe, the former Soviet Union, the Middle East, and South Africa are simultaneously on the edge of changes that will probably be as breath-taking as the revolutions of 1989 and have consequences for the rest of the world. In such an atmosphere, states may be unwilling to accept the deep obligations required by collective security. Four obstacles should be singled out as constraints on governments.

First and foremost, the August 1991 coup attempt in the Kremlin and the rush toward independence of several republics in what had been the Soviet Union were vivid reminders of the enormous uncertainty surrounding the transition of that former superpower. Disturbances in the central government and unanswered questions about governance exacerbated the significant challenges posed by production, transportation, distribution, communication, and other perennial problems of the economy and society. The sheer size of the former USSR and the distribution of its nuclear arsenal among several republics give the entire world a stake in its reorganization. The unknown impact of domestic chaos on the foreign policy of this permanent member of the Security Council creates wariness about long-term commitments by other governments to multilateral security arrangements.

A second critical element contributing to uncertainty is unbridled nationalism in separatist warfare, in popular coups, and in short-lived victory celebrations in such places as Croatia or Eritrea. There may be a demand for Cyprus-like partitions as substate nationalism overwhelms other trends. This may create more demands for UN services.[29] But new states are likely to be especially sensitive about transferring their newly won sovereignty to a collective-security system, in much the same way that the newly independent countries of Africa and Asia were sensitive about their prerogatives in the heyday of North-South vitriol.[30]

A third factor exacerbating nationalist trends and continuing uncertainty is the high level of armaments used, and stockpiled, in regional conflicts as well as internecine battles. Despite the important progress made in US-USSR arms-limitation efforts, conventional arms manufacturing and global transfers continue apace.[31] While arms expenditures are slightly down from the one trillion dollars spent worldwide in 1988, far deeper reductions are necessary for a system of collective security to succeed. Paradoxically, states are not likely to disarm until after such a system is in place, and solving this conundrum will take more creativity and leadership than has been apparent following the Persian Gulf War. It is not without irony that what made recent UN military operations and the Gulf War itself necessary were arms transfers to governments and insurgents by the permanent members of the Security Council.

A final obstacle to strengthening the UN's role in world affairs lies in the comprehensiveness of the solutions required for many new security issues. For example, the only respect in which the battles against drugs and terrorism resemble traditional interstate and less traditional intrastate conflicts is in levels of violence. Halting the drug trade entails not only interdiction by military force, but also the provision of economic alternatives in supplier countries, as well as demand reduction and treatment for users in consumer countries. Inconsistent national policies and relative ease of movement only benefit terrorists, while the eradication of wide-scale terrorism requires serious treatment of the conditions that spawn it: political frustration, individual alienation, and availability of the means of violence. The comprehensiveness of these requirements points to a constructive role for the United Nations, but past activities by international organizations offer few models.

Proposals for the Post-Cold-War Era

The global tendencies described above, together with the prevailing uncertainty, call for measures to improve the integration and operational effectiveness of the United Nations. While implementation of the proposals presented here would hardly constitute a collective-security system, it would represent a significant step toward an improved international structure to deal with threats to international peace. Four areas in particular require attention if the preconditions for successful co-operative security arrangements are to be created: information, decision-making, management, and expanded activities.

Information

Improved information resources are critical to provide a credible, authoritative basis for international action. Better information and an early warning capacity are crucial to a more effective United Nations. A collective-security system requires that the Security Council develop the capacity to be a serious world-crisis monitoring centre, to constitute a kind of global watch, while its central official, the Secretary General, should be among the first to know about conflicts in order to launch preventive diplomacy.

Some have suggested the creation of a UN intelligence network, including satellites and electronic communications.[32] Short of such a massive undertaking, measures for improved sharing of national intelligence data with the world body (as the US shared its information on Iraqi nuclear capabilities and, since 1977 the exact disposition of Egyptian and Israeli forces in the Sinai) would improve the quality of information available to the Security Council and the Secretary General. Having the permanent members pool intelligence data through a revitalized Military Staff Committee is also an idea worth exploring. Satellite monitoring and aerial reconnaissance could also be combined with greater use of more traditional measures such as fact-finding missions and regional meetings at the foreign-minister level to keep abreast of tensions and, when possible, forestall conflicts. Moreover, if 'open skies' (in which overflights of each other's territory are permitted by potential belligerents) became a routine rather than an unusual procedure, the UN would be in a better position to have its own global intelligence network.

Decision-making

Strictly speaking, widespread acceptance of the idea of collective security would guarantee responses against aggression and obviate the need for a discussion of decision-making; however, this remains an idea ahead of its time. Since action does not occur automatically and without discrimination, the nature of international decision-making procedures is clearly relevant.

A lack of political will, and not just a lack of information, is of course responsible for inaction; and once information is received, the Security Council must still decide on appropriate responses. The great-power veto has often stymied Security Council initiatives. While removal of this roadblock is one likely outcome of US-Russian *rapprochement*, in many instances member states will persist in wishing the Security Council to remain aloof so that they may pursue their own perceived interests. In order to overcome the present shortcomings, three types of improvement should be considered.

First, various trigger mechanisms should be considered that would automatically activate deliberations by the Security Council. While decisions would not be guaranteed, members could at least be embarrassed into admitting that they lacked the interest or ability to deal effectively with a festering crisis. For example, in the area of humanitarian emergencies,[33] it has been suggested that an independent monitoring group, or perhaps a sub-unit of the International Court of Justice, could track such matters as the number of persons affected (either in absolute numbers, or as a percentage of population), the severity of threats to human life, the generation of refugees, or the abuse of human rights. When conditions reached agreed thresholds, the Security Council would have to be convened.

Second, consideration should be given to allowing the Secretary General to launch preventive measures that would engage the Security Council. The Secretary General should have the authority to introduce a small but truly multinational UN force, for example, to a disputed border or into an area with an incipient conflict as part of preventive diplomacy. Not only would potential aggressors be deterred, but the Security Council would have to respond to any violation of the UN's positions. Such actions would of course put UN forces at risk, for they would involve not peace-keeping but more dangerous tasks intended to deter the use of force. While soldiers would probably have to be recruited independently for use in these assignments, threats to nationals of a particular country would still mobilize sufficient domestic support to elicit vigorous action in the Security Council should problems arise.

The third area of improved decision-making concerns the composition and procedures of the Security Council. Reductions in American and Russian use of the veto may also create new dynamics in which China is perhaps the most likely spoiler. Moreover, a more collegial approach to decision-making on international security points directly to the questionable legitimacy of Security Council decisions reached without adequate representation of such major powers as Japan and Germany in the North, as well as India, Nigeria, Egypt, and Brazil in the South. If the UN were established today, its structural model would be very different from that outlined in the 1945 Charter. The Security Council is unlike much of the UN system, which has been characterized by unplanned growth; but it is similar in that it was conceived to meet specific problems under political circumstances very different from those of today.

There have been several suggestions to expand the Security Council to include the above countries as permanent members without veto, or to have the European Community and Japan replace Britain and France. The Non-Aligned Movement at its 1991 summit called for the expansion of the Security Council, and Italy, on behalf of at least a portion of the European Community, raised the issue during the forty-sixth session of the General Assembly. Third World countries and middle powers such as Canada[34] have begun to worry about the strength of their voices, a concern that is logical as they 'have no pretense at world leadership and need a strong international organization'.[35]

Any alteration would require unanimity among the current permanent five—unlikely, with Russia, Great Britain, and France clinging to their Security Council seats as among the few remaining symbols of their former status as great powers. However, the end of the cold war, the growing importance of the United Nations in security affairs, and the public stances by many countries have moved this issue onto the international agenda and made debate over it inevitable.

In the absence of juridical changes in the Security Council's structure, its decision-making procedures must elicit the widest possible support. One approach would be to seek consensus in the context of strong leadership by the permanent members. Consensus need not be defined as unanimity. One of the advances of the United Nations over the League of Nations was its institution of majority voting, so that sovereign states must accept decisions that they have voted against. However, making the compromises necessary to obtain the widest possible political support, as was the case during the Gulf War, is preferable to gaining narrow majority votes on matters of international peace and security. Consensus could be informally institutionalized if the permanent members announced that no action would be pursued should there be more than two dissenting votes among the eleven rotating members.

Another option might be the creation of an intermediate status between the permanent and rotating representatives: that is, an informal agreement that other geopolitically important countries would share a fixed number of quasi-permanent seats. These latter adjustments would not require Charter amendment. And although they raise a host of questions — who protects the have-nots? who revolves off? — they would still be a step in the right direction, and less likely than a Charter amendment to encounter the opposition of the permanent members.

Management

Imperative for the timely and accurate execution of Security Council decisions relating to international security and ultimately peace enforcement are improved management and implementation procedures at the secretariat level. There are many proposals for improving the professionalism of secretariat operations in the field of peace and security.[36] Observers within and outside the UN agree that improvements are urgently needed to strengthen the technology, autonomy, and expertise available to the Secretary General and his staff. Making the UN capable of meeting the challenges of an increased demand for its military forces will require a variety of measures, including adding qualified military personnel to headquarters; instituting a 'peace room' for monitoring operations; coming to terms with the need for a standing reserve force; and taking a more entrepreneurial approach to such new tasks as monitoring internal elections and human-rights abuses, as well as the delivery of humanitarian assistance in war zones.

Among the proposals that might be revived is one that seeks to address both the weaknesses of the secretariat and the decision-making difficulties of the Security Council: the creation of a Security Council Commission.[37] This working-level body would operate under the political direction of the Security Council; but it would remain in constant operation, have a technical orientation, and lack veto privileges for permanent members. The objective is to resolve the dilemma of maintaining the benefits of compact size and unanimity of rule while ensuring more effective operations. The UN secretariat would answer both to the Commission and to the Secretary General, and assist them in their activities. The Commission's depoliticized atmosphere and secret voting could help it implement and oversee broad Security Council decisions on information-gathering, peaceful settlement of disputes, economic sanctions, support for regional collective-security agreements, military enforcement and peace-keeping procedures, and parallel disarmament negotiations.

The 1991 election of the Secretary General began with discussions on improving the international community's aberrant selection process for its chief executive officer.[38] But it also revived calls for leadership and openness to imaginative risk-taking by the Secretary General in pursuing peace-making and preventive diplomacy. The realization is growing that the major powers will need to permit and even urge the Secretary General to use his powers to the full to move toward a working collective-security system.

The election of Boutros Boutros Ghali as the sixth Secretary General opens up the possibility that these options may be pursued with vigour. One of his first decisions was to streamline the undersecretaries general, in line with some controversial proposals about restructuring the secretariat. He also moved ahead forcefully to propose that the Security Council abandon its usual practice of consent by the parties in sending UN troops to Yugoslavia, and to consider humanitarian-motivated military action in Somalia.

Expanded Activities

For collective security to operate effectively, the tools of economic and military coercion must be prepared in advance for invocation on extremely short notice. According to one observer, a major lesson of the Gulf crisis was that it 'wasted the most promising opportunity the United Nations has ever had to determine whether it could function as intended: forcefully against aggression but with a minimum of violence'.[39] While begging the question as to whether sanctions would eventually have led Saddam Hussein to abandon his expansionist adventure, the experience with economic sanctions against Iraq highlighted the need for greater efforts at implementation and greater knowledge.[40] Among the issues that arise are immediate and universal application, improved co-ordination among states and other relevant entities, compensation for those societies suffering undue economic hardship, naval capacity required for enforcement, and measures against states or others found breaking the sanctions. The UN's effectiveness would be enhanced if pre-planned sanctions were available. For instance, had guidelines existed for economic sanctions, and had sanctions been a standard operating procedure against aggressors before 1990, they might have led to different calculations by Saddam Hussein; they would almost certainly alter those of other potential aggressors whose regimes are more subject to domestic pressures.

As for a UN military force, there has been a renewed interest in the idea proposed long ago by Clark and Sohn for an international peace force-in-being with appropriate reserves stationed around the world and ready to enforce Security Council decisions.[41] Economic limitations on the size of such a force, however, make it far more practicable in a world with drastically reduced levels of conventional arms. Until disarmament is achieved, collective security depends on the certainty of overwhelming applications of military force, a promise that could be strengthened by merging contingents from national forces under a single UN command. Toward this end, member states should negotiate their force commitments as originally anticipated under article 43 of the Charter. Each member should back up these commitments with training and deployment in modes appropriate to joint action under UN command, and should consider establishing its own permanent UN peace-keeping force, or at a minimum, earmarking troops for immediate deployment, as the Nordics and Canadians have done for years. The moribund Military Staff Committee should be rejuvenated by inviting new contributors of peace-keeping troops to supply international military experts who have appropriate operational experience to help oversee planning and operations, and also to provide military advice to the Secretary General, upon his request.

It is unthinkable to call for a standing UN force powerful and massive enough to take action in a crisis involving such a major power as Iraq. Yet it is quite reasonable to foresee standing or earmarked UN forces capable of deployment in one hundred or so countries. At the January 1992 Security Council summit, France took a step in this direction by offering to make available 1,000 soldiers on a day's notice, and an equal number within a week to meet a crisis.

In fact, one main advantage of institutionalizing UN forces would be the creation over time of what we might call 'UN wards'. The UN could take responsibility for the security of small countries, providing the type of guarantee that would relieve them of the burden of maintaining armed forces that drain precious human and financial resources.[42] These countries would then be in a position to undertake the type of disarmament that would not only free up local funds for development, but also reduce the clout of national military organizations, which are often major threats to democracy in small countries.

For activities short of large-scale peace enforcement, an élite rapid-response team of UN personnel could address terrorism, or other unconventional threats, on behalf of countries without the capacity to mount their own specialized units. Such a team could even be considered when a coup like Haiti's in October 1991 removes an elected government. Such a force, along with many of the other reforms mentioned above, would also enhance the professionalism of traditional UN peace-keeping, which will continue to be in great demand. In fact, classic interstate aggression as practised by Saddam Hussein is likely to be rare. Thus peace-keeping—the traditional reactive work that the UN has usually done so well—may well be the most useful approach to improve international peace and security.

Furthermore, peace-keeping mandates are apt to broaden to include regular activities for disarmament and delivery of humanitarian aid, as well as electoral and human-rights work, as has already been the case in the Gulf and Central America. While many analysts and diplomats have bemoaned the inability of the Special Committee on Peacekeeping Operations to develop agreed guidelines for UN peace-keepers, no two peace-keeping efforts have been alike. Without abandoning the flexibility of the current *ad hoc* approach, the UN must distinguish between tailoring individual operations to local conditions and mere improvising, which can mean a lack of professionalism and readiness.[43]

In this context, the present guidelines were formulated in 1973 to meet the exigencies of the cold war, and they require updating to reflect the contemporary state of international affairs and the resulting new contingencies and possibilities. In any case, greater planning for the supply and training of national forces earmarked for peace-keeping operations would improve the timeliness and effectiveness of all UN actions. Adequate financing for peace-keeping must also move beyond the unreliable case-by-case approach to include assurances of sufficient and timely payments by all member states, whether or not they approve a particular action.[44] The possibility of nearly quadrupling the peace-keeping budget in 1992 to meet the needs of proposed operations in Yugoslavia and Cambodia makes it imperative to take decisive action in this area. This increase comes at a time when the world organization is owed about $1 billion in unpaid regular budget and peace-keeping dues.

The tasks of peace-keepers and peace-enforcers would be substantially eased by reductions in arms transfers. Iraq would probably not have invaded Kuwait had it not for decades been building up its arms supplies—with considerable help from the five permanent members. In addition to helping build a system of security guarantees for disarmed small states, the United Nations must further facilitate multilateral arms-control discussions and binding agreements, to be verified and enforced by UN personnel and agencies.

As the era emphasizing nuclear arms-control by the superpowers draws to a close, more intense UN involvement is plausible in three areas: chemical weapons, nuclear proliferation, and conventional arms. Agreement on chemical disarmament under UN auspices is already tantalizingly close; once achieved, it will mean unprecedented intrusive monitoring and actual destruction of vast stockpiles. Already the experience gained by the UN in determining Iraq's arsenal of weapons of mass destruction and overseeing its destruction has demonstrated the utility of entrusting such duties to objective international monitors, rather than self-interested suppliers.

Moreover, the successful completion of work on the Chemical Weapons Convention could provide a model for additional efforts at multilateral nuclear-arms control to augment the Non-Proliferation Treaty (NPT). Progress by the United States and the former Soviet Union in reducing nuclear weaponry was advanced somewhat at the July 1991 summit, and later accelerated by unilateral announcements of cut-backs on both sides.

The inclusion of significant superpower reductions in a world-wide agreement on nuclear arms could answer many of the Third World concerns traditionally raised during NPT reviews; perhaps the positive moves by Argentina, Brazil, and South Africa to eliminate their nuclear weapons programs are harbingers of a more co-operative approach by other significant Third World dissenters. Similarly, the 1990 Paris Treaty to reduce conventional forces in Europe could point the way to agreements to reduce conventional arms and forces elsewhere.

Such reductions could be expedited if international financial aid and investment to developing countries were tied to reductions in military expenditures; among the advocates of this new 'conditionality' is Robert McNamara.[45] The 1991 G-7 summit in London called for linking resource flows from the World Bank and the International Monetary Fund, as well as from bilateral donors, to reductions in the percentages spent on armaments. These measures should be combined with policies aimed at reducing substantially arms exports and security guarantees for smaller countries. The construction of a workable collective-security regime would help weak nations feel protected enough to participate in disarmament, and incremental steps in one area could facilitate progress in others.

Developments outside universal organizations could also further the construction of a viable collective-security system. While chapter VIII of the Charter foresaw the critical importance of strong regional organizations, their performance in the Third World has been particularly disappointing in the security realm. Lacking both resources and political will, the Organization of African Unity, the Organization of American States, and the Arab League have simply not been able to be effective in (respectively) Chad, Panama, and Lebanon. The 1990 military operation in Liberia by the Economic Community of West African States was hardly more encouraging.

A comparative advantage may, however, exist for regional organizations to pursue certain tasks as part of a more comprehensive system of collective-security measures. For example, monitoring of human rights or democratic reform might be undertaken more widely and easily if it were not seen as being orchestrated mainly from neo-colonial outposts in Geneva or New York. Still other tasks (for example, diplomatic arm-twisting of the kind used in Central America or Cambodia) may be quite effective when conducted by neighbours in close co-operation with UN military forces. The record of the Conference on Security and Cooperation in Europe has provided a new impetus for regional-security co-operation in the next decade, an example that might well spill over into the Third World. The European experience cannot simply be copied; but confidence-building measures, agreements on arms limitations and reductions, and zones free of particular types of weaponry could be tried elsewhere. As one observer has suggested, 'the 1990s should be a decade in which the construction of regional collective security organizations is inaugurated.'[46]

Conclusion

These reforms and adjustments depend on the continued interest of the permanent members in pursuing their foreign-policy goals through the United Nations, and in providing leadership to galvanize widespread support for their initiatives. For France, the United Kingdom, and Russia, the Security Council may provide greater political power than they can command elsewhere, and they may therefore look increasingly to the UN to make their international marks. For China, the Security Council is the primary contact with the West, and China will remain an active participant, if only to ensure that attention is paid to its domestic priorities and interests in exchange for support or abstention in votes on Western initiatives.

After the demonstration of the unquestionable dominance of American military forces in the Gulf War, some might be excused for expecting the United States to exercise unilateral power in the new unipolar world. The very fact that it was judged necessary to apply overwhelming force under UN authority would seem to indicate otherwise. And the renewed American interest in the United Nations is likely to continue, as the end of East-West conflict and the demise of the former Soviet Union increases US capability to shape outcomes through multilateral diplomacy.[47] In fact, the visibility of the United Nations and its utility for American interests has rarely been higher.[48]

Establishing a UN standing force, with great-power participation, as a credible deterrent to aggression is no longer relegated to the realm of idealism. As Lawrence Freedman has written: 'The sweeping victory in the Gulf undermined any notion that the Third World can now compete with the West in the military sphere.'[49] The demonstration of resolve by the Security Council in the Gulf War should help impede future aggressors. Had multilateral diplomacy been more firm before 1990, it is even conceivable that Saddam Hussein might have calculated differently about the likelihood of getting away with his blatant annexation of Kuwait.

The United States would be wise to expand its commitment to work for a collective-security regime under United Nations auspices now, while it exerts significant influence over the multilateral process. The jury is still out on the nature of US decline (see Doran's chapter in this volume), but American primacy can only wane, and future discussions and decisions will be less amenable to US influence. As the world moves toward a greater diffusion of economic power, the US is likely to see a decrease in its ability to control events—whether unilaterally or through multilateral arm-twisting. US interests, as viewed from Washington, may be better served by giving up some prerogatives now, in order to secure the commitment of other emerging powers to participate fully in a multilateral collective-security system that is shaped by the US. Working in the interests of all concerned, what has been called mutual security in the central theatre of Europe[50] could also serve US interests in the construction of a better system to foster international peace and security.

While a true collective-security system is not imminent, incremental steps toward chapter VII of the UN Charter (spelling out peace-enforcement mechanisms) can ease the transition and garner credibility for the concept, with radical implications for international politics. Most of the suggestions outlined earlier in this chapter would apply mainly to Third World conflicts (although Yugoslavia provides a potential illustration of the UN's universal utility). Over time, however, the dynamics of international co-operation might crystallize sufficiently to permit the selective application of international monitoring to the great powers, and perhaps even tempt the permanent members to forgo the exercise of their veto. Meanwhile, the goal for the next decade should be to enlarge the limited space for action by improving existing mechanisms and professional capabilities for peace-keeping and peace-making and, in certain instances, for peace enforcement.

Notes

The authors are grateful to Kurt M. Campbell and Jarat Chopra for comments on earlier drafts.

[1] For a discussion of this overall landscape, see Thomas G. Weiss and Meryl A. Kessler, eds, *Third World Security in the Post-Cold War Era* (Boulder, CO: Lynne Rienner, 1991); and for more specific case studies, see Thomas G. Weiss and James G. Blight, eds, *The Suffering Grass: Superpowers and Regional Conflict in Southern Africa and the Caribbean* (Boulder, CO: Lynne Rienner, 1992).

[2] 'Report of the Secretary-General on the Work of the Organization', Document A/46/1 (6 Sept. 1991), 2.

[3] Charles Krauthammer, 'The Unipolar Moment', *Foreign Affairs: America and the World 1990/91* 70, 1 (1991), 23-33.

[4] 'New Risks for Stability and Security', unanimous declaration issued by the Security Council on 31 January 1992; *New York Times* (1 Feb. 1992), 4.

[5] Inis L. Claude, Jr, *Swords Into Plowshares* (New York: Random House, 1971), 247.

[6] For a further discussion of this distinction, see Edward Gulick, *Europe's Classical Balance of Power* (Ithaca: Cornell Univ. Press, 1955).

[7] For some reflections that are not celebratory, see three essays by Stephen Lewis, Clovis Maksoud, and Robert C. Johansen, 'The United Nations After the Gulf War', *World Policy Journal* 8 (Summer 1991), 537-74.

[8] See, for example, Gilbert Murray, *From the League to the U.N.* (London: Oxford Univ. Press, 1948); and Roland Stromberg, *Collective Security and American Foreign Policy: From the League of Nations to NATO* (New York: Praeger, 1963).

[9] In addition to Inis Claude, see, for example, Hans Morgenthau, *Politics Among Nations* (New York: Knopf, 1960); Arnold Wolfers, ed., *Discord and Collaboration* (Baltimore: Johns Hopkins, 1962); and Quincy Wright, *The Study of International Relations* (New York: Appleton, 1955).

[10]See, for example, John Herz, *International Politics in the Atomic Age* (New York: Columbia Univ. Press, 1959).

[11]See a set of essays by scholars and practitioners in Thomas G. Weiss, ed., *Collective Security in a Changing World* (Boulder, CO: Lynne Rienner, forthcoming in 1993).

[12]See Philip Allott, *New Order for a New World* (Oxford: Oxford Univ. Press, 1990), paragraphs 13.105 to 13.111.

[13]This discussion of the history of collective security was based on F.H. Hinsley, *Power and the Pursuit of Peace* (Cambridge: Cambridge Univ. Press, 1963), 1–238. For a discussion of the early frameworks of peace, see also Thomas G. Weiss, *International Bureaucracy* (Lexington, MA: D.C. Heath, 1975), 3–32. A discussion of both aspects, along with some suggestions for instructors, is found in Thomas G. Weiss and Jarat Chopra, *Peacekeeping: Teaching and the State of the Field* (Hanover, NH: Academic Council on the United Nations System, 1992).

[14]The prohibition of war *per se* was encapsulated in article 1 of the General Treaty for the Renunciation of War, 1928, sometimes known as the 'Pact of Paris' or the 'Kellogg-Briand Pact'. The UN Charter was subsequently to outlaw the 'threat or use of force' in article 2(4).

[15]The distinction between alliances and collective security is mistakenly not always maintained by analysts, as for example in the subtitle of Stromberg's *Collective Security and American Foreign Policy: From the League of Nations to NATO*.

[16]Julius Stone, *Conflict Through Consensus: United Nations Approaches to Aggression* (Baltimore: Johns Hopkins, 1977), 12–13.

[17]Claude, *Swords*, 250–61.

[18]Brian Urquhart, 'Learning from the Gulf War', *New York Review of Books* (7 March 1991), 36. See also James Rosenau, *Turbulence in World Politics: A Theory of Change and Continuity* (Princeton: Princeton Univ. Press, 1990); Augustus Richard Norton, 'The Security Legacy of the 1980s in the Third World', in *Third World Security*, 19–34; and Thomas M. Franck, 'Who Killed Article 2(4)?' *American Journal of International Law* 64 (1970), 809.

[19]This categorization was formulated by Edward C. Luck, 'Renewing the Mandate', in *A Successor Vision: The United Nations of Tomorrow*, ed. Peter Fromuth (New York: United Nations Association, 1988), 122.

[20]See Thomas G. Weiss and Kurt M. Campbell, 'Military Humanitarianism', *Survival* 30 (Sept./Oct. 1991), 451–65.

[21]See Leon Gordenker and Thomas G. Weiss, eds, *Soldiers, Peacekeepers and Disasters* (London: Macmillan, 1991).

[22]'S.G. Pérez de Cuellar Sees Change in Basic Noninterference Doctrine', *Diplomatic World Bulletin* 22 (6–13 May 1991), 1.

[23]The reports of these commissions are, respectively: *North-South: A Programme for Survival* (London: Pan Books, 1980); *Common Security* (New York: Simon and Schuster, 1982); and *Our Common Future* (London: Oxford Univ. Press, 1987). See also the arguments made by a group of Third World intellectuals under the chair-

ship of Julius Nyrere, *The Challenge to the South* (New York: Oxford Univ. Press, 1990).

[24] See Jessica Tuchman Mathews, 'Redefining Security', *Foreign Affairs* 68 (Spring 1989), 162-77.

[25] Daniel Duedney, 'Environment and Security: Muddled Thinking', *Bulletin of the Atomic Scientists* 47 (April 1991), 22-8.

[26] See *Common Responsibility in the 1990s* (Stockholm: Prime Minister's Office, 1991).

[27] See, for example Benjamin Rivlin, *The Rediscovery of the UN Military Staff Committee* (New York: Bunche Institute Occasional Paper IV, May 1991).

[28] See 'Toward Collective Security: Two Views', *Occasional Paper* 5 (Providence: Thomas J. Watson Jr. Institute for International Studies, 1991), for the perspectives of Brian Urquhart and Robert S. McNamara.

[29] See Kurt M. Campbell and Thomas G. Weiss, 'The Third World in the Wake of Eastern Europe', *Washington Quarterly* 14 (Spring 1991), 91-108.

[30] See Thomas G. Weiss, *Multilateral Development Diplomacy in UNCTAD* (London: Macmillan, 1985).

[31] See Richard F. Grimmett, *Trends in Conventional Arms Transfers to the Third World by Major Suppliers, 1982-1989* (Washington: Congressional Research Service, Library of Congress, June 19, 1990); and Michael T. Klare, 'The Arms Trade: Changing Patterns in the 1980s', *Third World Quarterly* 9 (October 1987), 1257-81.

[32] See Michael Krepon and Jeffrey P. Tracy, 'Open Skies and UN Peacekeeping', *Survival* 32 (May/June 1990), 251-63; and Thomas E. Boudreau, *The Secretary-General and Satellite Diplomacy* (New York: Council on Religion and International Affairs, 1984).

[33] See Larry Minear et al., *Humanitarianism Under Siege: A Critical Review of Operation Lifeline Sudan* (Trenton, NJ: Red Sea, 1990).

[34] See, for example, Stephen Lewis, 'A Promise Betrayed', *World Policy Journal* 8 (Summer 1991), 539-50; and Bernard Wood, *World Order and Double Standards: Peace and Security 1990-91* (Ottawa: Canadian Institute for International Peace and Security, 1991), 22-6.

[35] Marc Nerfin, 'The Future of the United Nations System', *Development Dialogue* 1 (1985), 1.

[36] See Augustus Richard Norton and Thomas G. Weiss, *UN Peacekeepers: Soldiers With a Difference* (New York: Foreign Policy Association, 1990); and a special issue of *Survival* 32 (May/June 1990).

[37] See David Steele, *The Reform of the United Nations* (London: Croom Helm, 1987), 111-32.

[38] See Brian Urquhart and Erskine Childers, *A World in Need of Leadership: Tomorrow's United Nations* (Uppsala: Dag Hammarskjöld Foundation, 1990); and Thomas G. Weiss, 'Round Up the Usual Suspects: Selecting the Next UN Secretary-General', *Peace and Security* 6 (Fall 1991).

[39]Robert C. Johansen, 'Lessons for Collective Security', *World Policy Journal* 8 (Summer 1991), 562.

[40]For an extensive analysis of this issue from the point of view of US foreign policy, see David A. Baldwin, *Economic Statecraft* (Princeton: Princeton Univ. Press, 1985); and Gary Clyde Hufbauer, Jeffrey J. Schott, and Kimberly Ann Elliott, *Economic Sanctions Reconsidered* (Washington, DC: Institute for International Economics, 1990).

[41]Grenville Clark and Lewis Sohn, *World Peace Through World Law* (Cambridge: Harvard Univ. Press, 1966).

[42]This idea was put forward in *Vulnerability: Small States in the Global Society* (London: Commonwealth Secretariat, 1985). It reflected earlier efforts by the Brandt Commission to devise appropriate strategies for reforms in the global security system that could enhance the survival and viability of small states.

[43]Henry Wiseman, 'Peacekeeping in the International Political Context', in *The United Nations and Peacekeeping*, ed. Indar Jit Rikhye and Kjell Skjelsbaek (London: Macmillan, 1989), 50.

[44]See Susan R. Mills, 'The Financing of United Nations Peacekeeping Operations: The Need for a Sound Financial Basis', *Occasional Paper* 3 (New York: International Peace Academy, 1989).

[45]See Robert S. McNamara, 'The Post-Cold War World and Its Implications for Military Expenditures in Developing Countries', in *Toward Collective Security*, 21-42.

[46]Daniel N. Nelson, 'Security in a Post-Hegemonic World', *Fletcher Forum of World Affairs* 15 (Summer 1991): 35. For a more extended argument of this perspective, see William T. Tow, *Subregional Security Cooperation in the Third World* (Boulder, CO: Lynne Rienner, 1990).

[47]See Leon Gordenker, 'International Organization in the New World Order', *Fletcher Forum of World Affairs* 15 (Summer 1991), 73.

[48]See, for example, Bruce Russett and James S. Sutterlin, 'The U.N. in a New World Order', *Foreign Affairs* 70 (Spring 1991), 69-83.

[49]Lawrence Freedman, 'The Gulf War and the New World Order', *Survival* 33 (May/June 1991), 202.

[50]See Richard Smoke and Andrei Kortunov, eds, *Mutual Security: A New Approach to Soviet American Relations* (New York: St Martin's, 1991).

chapter twelve

The United Nations' Contribution to International Peace and Security

W. Andy Knight and Mari Yamashita

Introduction: Why Evaluate the UN's Peace and Security Function?

It has by now become a truism to say that the international system is undergoing an unprecedented transformation. The outcome of this period of major structural upheaval will not be known for some time. One of the major uncertainties is the role the United Nations will play in future world governance, particularly in the maintenance of international peace and security. This chapter presents a historical and empirical account of the United Nations' contribution in this area since 1945, with a view to furthering our understanding of how the UN might function as an agent of security governance in future.

Whether or not one believes that conflict among states is natural, the clash of interests has gone on for millenia, and is likely to continue—whether among states or whatever entities might replace them. Throughout the centuries, there have been several attempts to devise regulatory mechanisms to control, and in some cases eliminate, conflict. So-called 'peace plans' were designed by such thinkers as Dante, Pierre DuBois, Emeric Crucé, the Duc de Sully, William Penn, the Abbé de Saint-Pierre, Rousseau, Bentham, and Kant.[1] Actual experimentation with mechanisms to regulate conflict can be traced back to the Congresses of Vienna, Paris, and Berlin, respectively in 1815, 1856, and 1878; the London conferences of 1871, 1912, and 1913; the

Berlin congress of 1884-85; the Algeciras conference of 1906; the Hague conferences of 1899 and 1907; the Concert of Europe system; and the League of Nations, which emerged from the Versailles peace conference in 1919. The United Nations is an embodiment of this historical and evolutionary experimentation.

Until quite recently, it was fashionable to criticize the UN's inability to perform several tasks assigned to it under its Charter. Given especially that the organization's central role has been to maintain international peace and security, its performance has been judged primarily in relation to its ability to prevent war, reduce international conflicts, and encourage dialogue among member states. Critics have even dismissed the UN as irrelevant, at least in the field of international peace and security, either because it was so often bypassed by certain member states who favoured unilateral or bilateral approaches to resolving conflicts, or because regional organizations and other institutions not only competed with the world body for influence, but, in the critics' opinion, actually did a more effective job of resolving international disputes.

Even some well-meaning observers, sympathetic to the UN, have lamented the organization's inability to maintain the peace function as the framers of the Charter had intended.[2] It is now generally acknowledged and accepted among this group that the inability stemmed from, *inter alia*, the post-World War II, cold-war environment; excessive use of the veto by the permanent members of the Security Council; management failings; poor leadership; excessive rhetoric and politicization in the UN's primary organs; competing ideological visions of the UN's purpose and goals; passage of useless and irresponsible resolutions; excesses in the Secretariat; graft and incompetent staff; and financial withholding by some member states of assessed contributions.[3]

Recently, however, public criticism of the UN has subsided, though perhaps only temporarily. There are at least two reasons for this. First, since 1986 there has been a gradual revitalization of the Security Council occasioned, in part, by the recommitment of the permanent five (United States, Britain, France, Russia, China) to principles of multilateralism, peace-keeping, peace-making, conflict resolution, and collective security. Second, UN action taken against Iraq during the recent Gulf War silenced those critics who claimed, for valid reasons, that the Council had been incapable of functioning in the way the Charter had envisaged. The 1991 American-led UN intervention in the Iraq-Kuwait conflict was the first time a UN-sanctioned, collective-security and/or enforcement measure had been launched since the Korean War in 1950.

This chapter seeks to squelch the myth that the UN has been ineffective in fulfilling its primary purpose: maintaining international peace and security. To be sure, the UN is not and never has been the sole contributor to this task in the post-war era. The Charter is quite explicit on the need for regional arrangements to resolve disputes between states, and to maintain the peace between them. It is our view that with the broadening conceptualization of security, it is increasingly likely that the UN will make significant contributions to the new collective-security order outlined in the preceding chapter. Our purpose here is chiefly to provide the historical context for thinking about the UN and the issue of security governance in the 1990s.

Ideological Roots and Conception of Role

The UN system is in some sense a mixed product of idealistic hopes, pragmatic realism, and social-engineering ideology. It was envisioned that through this organization succeeding generations might be saved from the scourge of war. If wars could not be entirely eliminated through fundamental changes in the attitudes and beliefs of humankind, the UN founders imagined that they could at least be reduced through social engineering and the creation of 'correct' political, functional, and legal institutions. In the event that deviant states persisted in waging war, collective security and self-defence would be invoked to check them in their paths.

When the Charter of the United Nations was signed on 26 June 1945, the intent was that the organization play the lead role in maintaining international peace and security. Determined not to repeat the same mistakes that had led to the demise of the League of Nations, the UN founders produced a document that although idealistic in part, was firmly grounded in 'realities' of the international system at the time. Thus the Charter reflected a conception of security predicated on great-power consensus and on the expectation that those powers—the permanent five members of the Council—would combine efforts to enforce peace globally. In one sense, this arrangement was simply an extension of the wartime alliance into the post-1945 peacetime.[4]

Within the Charter, provision was made for a variety of approaches to securing and maintaining international peace and security. Among these were collective security; peaceful settlement of disputes; disarmament; preventive diplomacy; debate and discourse; judicial settlement; trusteeship; and functional activity.[5] The Security Council was vested with responsibility for immediate threats to international peace and security, while the remainder of the UN system was left to offer functional long-term solutions to international security problems.

The means given to the Council reflected an attempt to reconcile two contradictory visions of how international peace and security governance should work. The first embodied the ideal of 'pacific settlement' (chapter VI of the Charter), presumably reflecting the utopianism left over from the failed League of Nations. The second embraced the idea of 'peace enforcement' through collective action (chapter VII), and represented the attempt of 'realists' to ensure that this new organization would not suffer the fate of the League.

It was generally believed by the Charter framers that one of the principal sources of chronic global instability was the militarization of human society expressed in the increase in armaments levels and defence budgets in several countries. While the Charter itself made few references to disarmament, the theory undergirding its disarmament provisions was based on the simple belief that by removing the means of waging war, war itself could be eliminated. Therefore Charter framers conferred on the Security Council and the General Assembly specific responsibilities for arms limitation and disarmament. The latter body would, according the article 11 of the Charter, consider 'principles governing disarmament and the regulation of armaments' and make recommendations to member states or to the Security Council, or both, regarding the implementation of such principles. For its part, the Security Council, according to article 26 of the Charter, 'in order to promote the establishment and maintenance of international peace and security with the least diversion for armaments of the world's human and economic resources', was made directly responsible for 'the establishment of a system for the regulation of armaments'.

While these provisions placed less emphasis on the problem of disarmament than had the League Covenant, they nonetheless signalled an evolving concern with devising ways eventually to eliminate weapons. At the very least, they conveyed the message to member states that they ought to rely less on the destructive instrumentalities of warfare for the resolution of disputes.

Charter Provisions for the Use of Force

In spite of its disarmament provisions, the Charter stopped short of renouncing war as a technique for settling international disputes. Recognizing that from time to time there might well be deviants in the international system, the Charter drafters felt it wise to legitimize the use of force under certain conditions: (1) for collective action authorized by the Security Council; and (2) for individual and collective self-defence.

Collective security was expected to replace the old balance-of-power system of the nineteenth century. As Inis Claude explains, it involved the establishment and operation of

> a complex scheme of national commitments and international mechanisms designed to prevent or suppress aggression by any state against any other state, by presenting to the potential aggressors the credible threat and to potential victims of aggression the reliable promise of effective collective measures, ranging from diplomatic boycott through economic pressure to military sanctions, to enforce the peace.[6]

The collective security device envisaged in the Charter did not evidently require ideological consensus to function. The only precondition was that 'member countries . . . make provision to restrain and/or punish, through cooperative or coordinated action, any country that attacks another with military aggression or help in a collective security action authorized by the system.'[7] But as the League members found out, collective security can be problematic at best. Thus the UN founders felt the need to preserve the basic principle of self-help in the event that collective security failed.

The Charter's self-defence provision is found in article 51. This allows any member state to use force in self-defence, until the Security Council has had a chance to adopt the necessary measures to restore peace and security. Any self-defence measures would have to be reported immediately to the Security Council. The question of whether or not this provision allows anticipatory self-defence has never been resolved by UN members.[8] The traditional meaning of the right to self-defence is limited to those cases when an attack 'is instant, overwhelming, and leaving no choice of means, and no moment for deliberation'. Under such circumstances, the countervailing use of force must be 'reasonable' and 'proportional'.[9]

However, with the development of high-technology weapons a strong case can be made for anticipatory self-defence. Oscar Schachter, for instance, argues that 'there may well be situations in which the imminence of an armed attack is so clear and the danger so great that defensive action is essential for self-preservation.'[10] In this he is obviously alluding to pre-emptive strikes. When Israel attacked the Iraqi Osiraq nuclear reactor under construction in 1981, the action was justified by the Israeli government as legitimate anticipatory self-defence. Similarly, when the US bombed key targets in Libya in 1986, in response to terrorist activities, that same justification was advanced. Despite the intent that collective security be the means of dealing with deviant states, article 51 does suggest to the member states that they cannot expect to base their security wholly on the organization's disarmament schemes or its collective measures.

Charter Provisions for Peaceful Settlement of Disputes

The institutionalization of mechanisms for the pacific settlement of international disputes can be traced back to the Hague conference of 1899,[11] which adopted the Convention on the Pacific Settlement of Disputes with the support of 26 countries, including the United States. This Convention obligated members to settle international disputes through such legal means as commissions of inquiry and arbitration panels. A permanent Court of Arbitration was set up, a precursor to the International Court of Justice. The second Hague conference, in 1907, expanded both the concept of pacific settlement and the number of contracting parties to the convention.[12]

An impetus for the increasing focus on instruments of pacific settlement came with the advent of nuclear weapons. The realization that modern warfare had become far too costly, destructive, and unpredictable a technique for settling international disputes forced the international body to consider preventive and mediatory measures. But even prior to the atomic age, the UN Charter, in chapter VI, had called on its members to 'settle their international disputes by peaceful means in such a manner that international peace and security, and justice, are not endangered'; and to 'refrain in their international relations from the threat or use of force against the territorial integrity or political independence of any state, or in any manner inconsistent with the purposes of the United Nations'.[13] Parties to a dispute should first try to settle their differences by 'negotiation, enquiry, mediation, conciliation, arbitration, judicial settlement, resort to regional agencies or arrangements, or other peaceful means of their own choice.'[14]

When dispute cases are brought to the General Assembly they are generally placed on the agenda for debates, which tend to be emotional, ideological, and politically charged. General debate in the Assembly has served to highlight the dangers of nuclear weapons, expose the wrongs of colonialism and apartheid, reveal the strength of neutralism and nationalism, demonstrate the sensitivities of newly emergent states, and aid the Secretary General in identifying 'hot spots' around the globe. In addition, the General Assembly elaborates broad principles that may govern the process of pacific settlement. It can also recommend action in this regard, or establish *ad hoc* committees or subsidiary organs do so.

Should all pacific-settlement tools be used and the matter remain unresolved, appeals can then be made directly to the Security Council by individual member states, non-member states, the General Assembly, or the Secretary General.[15] Matters involving litigation may be referred to the International Court of Justice (ICJ), the UN's principal judicial organ.

If it is still determined that a threat to international peace and security is imminent, the insertion of a 'UN presence' in the troubled region may be considered. Such intervention can range from sending representatives of the Secretary General's office to the potential hot spots as observers, to deploying a number of diplomatic and/or military personnel supplied by member states into the area in question. The purpose is primarily to buy time so that disputing parties can find a face-saving way out of physical confrontation.

Given the experiences of the World Wars, the framers of the Charter detailed specific procedures to be followed and means to be used in dealing with possible defections from the pacific-settlement norm. Should disputing parties fail to resolve their differences using appropriate procedures or methods of adjustment suggested by the Charter, the Security Council has been given the authority to recommend, in the last resort, enforcement action.[16]

Charter Provisions for Enforcement Action

The Security Council was designed to be the pivotal organ for post-war security governance. Chapter VII of the Charter was expected to become the 'muscle' for enforcement action by the Council. Article 42 authorizes it to take action 'with respect to threats to the peace, breaches of the peace, and acts of aggression'. Article 43 calls on the members of the UN to co-operate in such actions. To advise the Council on force deployment and strategy, the Charter provided for the creation of a Military Staff Committee (MSC) to consist of the Chiefs of Staff of the permanent members or their representatives.

In theory, the Security Council holds the primary responsibility for international peace and security, and all members agree to 'accept and carry out the decisions' of the Council pertaining to enforcement measures.[17] The possible range of enforcement action, on a graduating scale, is as follows: (1) demanding that conflicting parties comply with certain provisional measures (e.g., ceasefires and armistices); (2) calling on member states to apply non-military measures or sanctions, such as complete or partial interruption of economic relations; similar interruptions of rail, sea, air, postal, telegraphic, radio, and other communication means; and cutting off of diplomatic ties; (3) using demonstrations, blockades, or other military operations by the air, naval, or ground forces of member states; and (4) authorizing and utilizing military force as a last resort.

In practice, however, the above actions can be taken only with the support and co-operation of member states, particularly those with substantial military and economic capabilities. Since there was no provision for a permanent standing UN security force as such, the Security Council could only hope that member states would agree to make readily available to it contingents of armed forces and military facilities.[18] Any such agreement, however, must first be ratified by the signatory states after approval from their respective domestic constitutional bodies, and this is by no means an automatic, or 'rubber-stamping', procedure. In any case, UN enforcement action has not always been within the sole purview of the Council: the General Assembly, under certain circumstances, has been called upon to play a significant role in this.

The separation of powers of the Security Council and the General Assembly was a firm underlying concept of the framers of the Charter. The Assembly, as the supreme representative body of the world, was to establish the principles on which global peace and solidarity must rest. The Security Council was to act in accordance with those principles and with all speed necessary to prevent any attempted breach of international peace and security. In other words, the former is a creative body and the latter an organ of action.[19] In reality, however, the competence of the Assembly has extended to discussion of any international issue or agenda item, including those relating to international peace and security, with only two exceptions: those matters that are essentially within the domestic jurisdiction of states (article 2 [7]), and international peace and security matters that are under consideration by the Council (article 12).

The great influx of new states into the organization between 1945 and 1966 resulted in a dramatic change in the Assembly's political complexion and role.[20] Initially, the US could galvanize majority support among these new member states and use that voting majority in the Assembly to circumvent Soviet intransigence on the Council. The new Third World states, which were essentially left out of the creation of the principles, rules, and decision-making procedures that governed the UN, saw a perfect opportunity to acquire a greater say in matters of regional and international security that pertained to them. Accordingly, they employed their majority to bring about what amounted to a power shift, away from the Council and toward the Assembly.

Because of the cold war and the resulting stalemate on the Council, the Assembly quickly etched out a larger role for itself in international peace and security. In 1950, the American-engineered Uniting for Peace Resolution was adopted by the Assembly, virtually empowering that body to do what the Council had to that point failed to do. This resolution allowed the Assembly to discuss and recommend appropriate measures in response to breaches of the peace, including the use of armed forces, in situations (e.g., Korea) that threatened international peace and security, should the Council fail to act.[21] Filling the void created by the Security Council's inaction, the General Assembly utilized the Uniting for Peace Resolution to devise a peace-keeping function for the United Nations, something that had also not been envisioned in the Charter.

The office of the Secretary General also shares some responsibility for enforcement action. The Charter provisions that refer to the role of the Secretary General are articles 97 to 99, under chapter XV. Article 97 establishes the Secretary General as the chief administrative officer of the organization, one whose political responsibilities are spelled out in the two following articles. Article 99 provides the core of the Secretary General's political role, and must be considered in any analysis of this official's relationship with both the Assembly and the Council, and particularly of his or her role in the maintenance of international peace and security. Taken together with article 98, it establishes that the position of the Secretary General should approximate that of a sixteenth member of the Council, albeit one without a vote. Nevertheless, the Secretary General has at least the possibility of exercising some moral suasion when decisions are being made to utilize force.

Article 99 exists primarily for crisis situations. In such situations the Secretary General must have ample evidence that the matter warrants the attention of the Council: i.e., that it is a question of an immediate or potential threat to international peace and security. The use of article 99 therefore represents the highest use of the Secretary General's political initiative, and places that official at the centre of the UN system whenever interventionary action is needed to prevent, or forcefully repress, a conflict threatening global security.

False Assumptions, Dashed Hopes, and Obstacles

The UN Charter is widely thought to have been an advance over previous plans for international organization. However, the optimism that accompanied the drafting of the Charter at Dumbarton Oaks in 1944, and its eventual endorsement by 50 states at the San Francisco conference in 1945, was short-lived.[22] Why was this the case? First, many of the assumptions upon which the Charter was based proved false, and second, the organization encountered several obstacles in its attempt to accomplish its peace and security mission.

In 1945 it was generally expected that the victorious wartime powers would remain united in their fight to preserve a stable international security environment, and would collectively punish defectors. This assumption proved false when the leading powers, the Soviet Union and the United States, drifted apart in a cold-war environment. East-West tensions and rivalry quickly dominated international affairs.

The ideological competition between the capitalist US and communist USSR was played out in the UN arena. It soon became obvious that when any of the great powers became involved in a conflict, the Council would likely not be involved in its resolution (examples include the Soviet veto of attempts by the UN Security Council to address the Berlin blockade issue in the early cold-war period, and the US refusal to allow the organization to provide solutions to the Vietnam conflict). As a result, during this period the UN resembled more a battlefield than a place where international disputes could be settled amicably.

While North-South rhetorical battles resulting from the decolonization phenomenon were being waged in the General Assembly, the East-West ideological and political divide became increasingly pronounced in the Security Council and throughout the UN system. Apart from the propaganda wars in the Council and the Assembly, the greatest evidence of this schism was manifest in the exercise of their veto power by the permanent five members of the Council—particularly the US and the USSR. The decision to give veto power to the five permanent members seems to have been based on the dominant thinking of the immediate post-war period that the UN would be effective only if great-power unanimity existed, and if all the major powers maintained their membership in the organization. While the veto was a contentious issue at Dumbarton Oaks, it is clear that both superpowers and the other permanent members wanted, at the very least, the right of veto over substantive resolutions coming before the Council. As Cordell Hull recorded in his memoirs, the US would not have remained a member of the UN if it had been denied the veto.[23]

It is certain that the veto privilege did much to hinder the organization from accomplishing its peace and security tasks. Initially, the veto was utilized more often by the USSR than by any of the other permanent powers. But the Western powers later increased their frequency of use. In 205 substantive issues raised at the Council between 1946 and 1987, the USSR cast 121 vetoes, the US 58, the UK 27, China 22, and France 16. The fact that the Soviet Union cast more vetoes than any other state does not absolve the others from the charge of abuse and ultimate devaluation of the veto through excessive use. Several issues were never even raised at the Security Council level, because of the threat by one of the permanent five to utilize the veto. Because these threats were generally not made public, it is difficult to document them. There also exists what some call the hidden veto. Permanent members have used this strategy in the past to persuade enough Council members to abstain, or cast a negative vote on an issue, so that a resolution on a substantive matter would fail to secure the required nine votes.

While veto use over the years can rightly be considered excessive, it is important to remember that this power was vested in the permanent members of the Council because it was deemed important for them to be able to reach consensus on matters that might require the mobilization of the organization's collective-security mechanisms. It is because of their failure to achieve consensus on ways of handling most of the international conflicts brought before the Council during the cold war that the collective-security provisions of the Charter remained, for all intents and purposes, a dead letter.

The major failure, then, of the UN's experience in the peace and security realm was its inability to implement collective security. Ideally, in the case of a breach to the peace that threatens the security of the entire international community, UN member states must be willing collectively to apply sanctions, including military sanctions, against the peace-breakers if asked to do so by the Council. In reality, states have been reluctant to set their national interests aside to meet the requirements of this kind of collective security. Only a very few states, like Canada and the Nordic countries, have earmarked a portion of their national forces for UN use over the years, and even in their case the mission has been peace-keeping, not collective security.

The UN collective-security device was intended as an instrument to limit, if not eliminate, unilateral action on the part of the great powers. Spheres of influence and balance-of-power concepts should have been abolished if the collective-security concept had worked as it was intended. But almost immediately after World War II, the cold war rendered it ineffectual. Rather than eliminate the balance of power, spheres of influence, military alliances, and unilateral action by the major powers, the cold-war climate fostered them.

Under such conditions UN collective security was inoperable. Some commentators suggested that the UN's collective-security quest would be hopeless unless the organization modified its approach to consensus-building.[24] In the two cases in which UN collective security was invoked there was some measure of qualified consensus within the Council. But in each case there is some reason to doubt that the operations could truly be labelled collective-enforcement ones.

The UN assembled a force to repel North Korean aggression in 1950; in reality, this response was little more than a US action draped in the United Nations flag. While it is true that the concerted military measure was sanctioned by the Security Council, this was made possible only by the absence from the Council of the former Soviet Union—a mistake that would never be repeated.[25] Not only was there no genuine consensus supporting enforcement action, but the Council's enforcement measures were not directed by the Military Staff Committee (MSC), as stipulated by the Charter, but rather by the American Joint Chiefs of Staff. The so-called UN Unified Command was almost identical in structure to the US Far East Command headed by General Douglas MacArthur, who in theory took his orders from neither the Security Council nor the MSC, but from President Harry S Truman.

The other case in which UN collective-enforcement measures were taken was the 1990-91 action against Iraq over the annexation of Kuwait.[26] This time, all five permanent members were present during the Council deliberations, and there was very little disagreement about the illegality of Iraq's aggression; nor was there any negative vote on the resolutions calling for enforcement action. But here again, a true consensus did not emerge since China abstained on the crucial motions. There was also no non-aligned solidarity on the Council, with Cuba and Yemen voting against the resolution to use force against Iraq, and Colombia and Malaysia supporting it.

Like the Korean operation, the Gulf initiative was American-led. The decision to eject Iraq from Kuwait had been taken by President George Bush and British Prime Minister Margaret Thatcher, and was made without reference to the UN. Having made their decision, the two leaders solicited UN support, and unexpectedly received it with little difficulty. The Allied forces throughout Operation Desert Storm were commanded by the American Generals Norman Schwarzkopf and Colin Powell, in consultation with Allied military leaders, and not the MSC. Several thorny questions remained after the Gulf War, but on two matters clarity reigned: this was the first time in its 45-year history that the UN was politically in a position to employ all of its mandated authority to enforce international peace and security; and Desert Storm was not a collective-security operation in the true sense of the term, since the MSC was not given responsibility for its command and control.

That the MSC had been moribund since its establishment was the result of the impasse on the Council. Under those conditions, the Charter vision of a standing army never could have materialized. Another obstacle to the UN's involvement in conflicts has been article 2 (7) of the Charter, which states that nothing in the Charter 'shall authorize the United Nations to intervene in matters which are essentially within the domestic jurisdiction of any state . . .'. In several instances this clause has been invoked by states anxious to prevent UN involvement in matters with certain consequences for the international community.

Technically, several of the conflicts in which the UN did not become involved fell within the jurisdiction of particular states. In most of these instances lives were lost, human rights were violated, and there were calls for outside intervention from those suffering within the state or territory. Yet members of the UN chose to uphold article 2 (7) while disregarding or minimizing the equally important human-rights provision of the Charter. The non-intervention provision, therefore, has acted as a major hindrance to the UN's peace and security role.

Nevertheless, the situations in Yugoslavia and Cambodia suggest how the preoccupation with the non-intervention principle might be overcome in the future. In these cases, the UN indeed intervened in civil conflicts to facilitate either state devolution or state building. Half a dozen years beforehand this kind of intervention simply would not have been thought possible. The UN intervention in Iraq is another example of this trend; the UN response to the plight of the Kurds in northern Iraq after the Gulf War has been unprecedented. However one chooses to approach this action, 'it constitutes a direct interference in the sovereignty of a member state . . .'. This direct intervention into the internal affairs of Iraq sets a precedent that may have long-term consequences both for the international community and for the way in which the UN will handle its maintenance of international peace and its security role in the future.[27]

There is a growing belief within the international community that groups within a state must be protected against other groups within that state, and that acts of genocide and massacre resulting both from indiscriminate acts and civil wars can no longer be tolerated by the international community.

The UN and Arms Limitation

A major contribution made by the UN to peace and security has been in the realm of armaments limitations. The first imaginative initiative in this area occurred with the advent of nuclear weaponry. Immediately after the bombing of Hiroshima and Nagasaki, the UN became preoccupied with developing means to reduce or eliminate the threat posed to international peace and security by these weapons of mass destruction.

The first step in this quest began in 1946, when the General Assembly adopted a resolution establishing an Atomic Energy Commission. The terms of reference for this Commission addressed the question of eliminating all atomic and other weapons of mass destruction. The Commission was expected, concurrently, to ensure that atomic energy would be used for peaceful purposes only. In some circles, particularly among the Soviet delegation at the UN, this US-sponsored proposal was seen as an attempt by Washington to monopolize atomic-energy technology and to block other countries from attaining atomic weapons, since the US was the first country to manufacture and deploy such weapons. While this motive may have been present initially, once the Soviets too had developed the technology to produce these weapons of mass destruction, it became more apparent why such an international authority might be important and necessary.

From 1946 on, the UN seriously tackled disarmament issues. The primary bodies designated to address disarmament issues have been the Security Council, the General Assembly, the First Committee, the Military Staff Committee, and the Disarmament Commission. Other UN bodies were also established to deal with questions of disarmament and arms limitation. For example, in 1957 the International Atomic Energy Agency (IAEA) was established to ensure, through the application of safeguards, that nuclear materials and equipment intended for peaceful use were not diverted to military purposes. This task has been accomplished through basic nuclear-material accountancy during on-site verification checks. The IAEA also regulates the safe transport of radioactive materials.[28]

From time to time the Assembly has established *ad hoc* bodies to address specific disarmament concerns. For instance, in 1955 the UN Scientific Committee on the Effects of Atomic Radiation (UNSCEAR) was struck to explore the means of ending nuclear-weapons tests. It examined and disseminated information concerning the observed levels of ionizing radiation and the effects of such radiation on the planet. An *ad hoc* Committee on the Indian Ocean meets occasionally to evaluate the progress made in meeting the objectives of the 1971 UN Declaration of the Indian Ocean as a zone of peace. In 1972 the General Assembly passed Resolution 2930 (XXVII), establishing a Special Committee on the World Disarmament Conference, and in 1973 a similar measure, Resolution 3183 (XXVIII), set up an *ad hoc* Committee on the World Disarmament Conference.

The Secretariat is also involved in the quest to control and limit arms. The Department for Disarmament Affairs, formerly called the Centre for Disarmament, is headed by an undersecretary general. This department is based in New York with a branch in Geneva and three regional centres in Africa, Asia, and Latin America. It assists meetings of UN disarmament bodies; helps the Secretary General in preparing reports requested by the Assembly on disarmament-related topics; carries out and follows up on Assembly resolutions pertaining to disarmament and arms limitation; and facilitates and directs activities of the World Disarmament Campaign.

Several of the specialized agencies are committed to various aspects of the UN's work in the field of disarmament and arms limitation. The UN Educational, Scientific, and Cultural Organization (UNESCO) is involved with studies of the causes of the arms race and its implications. The World Health Organization (WHO) has done a series of studies on arms control and related issues as they pertain to the medical profession and practice. The International Labour Organization (ILO) has undertaken research and released information regarding the socio-economic benefits that could be derived from the freeing up of funds currently spent on the procurement of arms. The United Nations Environmental Program (UNEP) collaborates with the Stockholm International Peace Research Institute (SIPRI) of Sweden to study the effects of military activity on the environment. The World Meteorological Organization (WMO) decided in 1983 to use its World Weather Watch global telecommunications system to transmit data for the detection and identification of seismic occurrences as a means of developing verification procedures for a comprehensive test-ban treaty. Finally, the UN Food and Agricultural Organization (FAO) works closely with the IAEA on research that examines the extent of atomic radiation in food and agriculture.

The Conference on Disarmament (CD), although an autonomous body not bound by UN decisions, takes into account the recommendations of the General Assembly and the agenda items submitted by the Secretary General.

The secretary of the CD is an appointee of the Secretary General and there-fore acts as his representative. The CD submits regular reports to the General Assembly. The text of agreements worked out by that body is also submitted to the UN member states for ratification and signature. Since 1963 the CD membership has grown to 40, which makes it far too unwieldy to be a truly effective drafting body.

A succession of UN resolutions on arms limitation began with the 1959 call for general and complete disarmament. In 1961 another significant resolution was passed by the Assembly, which asked states to refrain from the transfer or acquisition of nuclear weapons. This formed the basis for the 1968 Non-Proliferation Treaty (NPT) signed by 136 states as of May 1990.

In 1963 the UN declared that the use of nuclear weapons would be consid-ered not only a violation of the Charter but a crime against humanity. As a result both China and the USSR subsequently proclaimed a no-use policy. By 1978 a Special General Assembly on Disarmament had elaborated and agreed on general principles for disarmament and developed priorities for an action programme that included measures to be taken both within and outside UN bodies to address this problem. A second special session, held in 1982, was less successful than the first in terms of specific recommendations and plans, but did garner world-wide attention. In June 1982, about 750,000 people marched in New York City in support of efforts to eliminate weapons of mass destruction. A third special session devoted to disarmament was held in New York in June 1988; present were all UN member states along with more than 1,500 representatives of non-governmental organizations and research institutes. Many of the proposals made at these special sessions were subsequently adopted at the next regular session of the General Assembly.

The UN has also used a number of studies on disarmament and arms control to educate member-state representatives, as well as the general pub-lic, about the extent and nature of the nuclear threat to the international community. Many of these studies have been followed by concrete action. Their purpose has been to assist ongoing arms-limitation negotiations, iden-tify specific topics that might result in the initiation of new negotiations, provide general background information regarding current deliberations and negotiations, and promote public awareness of the continuing arms race.

The UN approach to disarmament issues has evolved over the years. This evolution has corresponded to changing political realities, the altered super-power relationship, and general shifts in global technological and scientific developments. From 1945 to the mid-1950s, the preference was to encour-age the regulation, limitation, and balanced reduction of all armed forces and armaments through a comprehensive and co-ordinated programme. This comprehensive approach, however, met with little support from member states. As a result, by 1959 the UN was proceeding with a partial approach while maintaining its long-term objective of general and complete disarma-ment. The emphasis in this second phase was on reducing the spread of certain kinds of weapons and eliminating nuclear-weapons testing. This would be accompanied by confidence-building measures that could create a climate for further arms reductions.

Beginning in the 1960s, a network of a dozen or so major nuclear-arms control agreements, fostered by a period of superpower *détente*, came into effect. While some of these agreements were negotiated outside UN framework and bodies, they nevertheless 'reflected pressures arising out of debates, resolutions, and conferences of the United Nations demanding controls on nuclear weapons and an end to the nuclear arms race.'[29] This two-track approach seems to have borne fruit in the 1960s and 1970s with a number of specific UN instruments and measures in the area of disarmament being adopted and respected by the majority of member states.

The 1959 Antarctic Treaty was the first treaty to adopt and put into practice the concept of a nuclear-weapon-free zone. This set a precedent that was later applied to Latin America (1967 Treaty of Tlatelolco) and the South Pacific (1985 Treaty of Rarotonga), the seabed, and outer space. The intent behind such treaties has been to prohibit any military manoeuvres, weapons tests, construction of installations, and disposal of radioactive materials from the designated zone. In the case of the seabed and outer space, while the UN General Assembly has repeatedly passed resolutions calling for a comprehensive test-ban treaty, it has been successful only in adopting a Partial Test-Ban Treaty in 1963.

The Treaty on the Non-Proliferation of Nuclear Weapons (NPT) was the result of over ten years of pressure from the General Assembly to stem horizontal proliferation. Its primary aims were to limit the spread of nuclear weapons from nuclear to non-nuclear countries, and to promote the disarmament process in states that possessed nuclear weapons, while at the same time developing strategies that would allow all countries to benefit from peaceful nuclear technology. A basic problem with the NPT is that while it prohibits a large number of states from possessing weapons of mass destruction, it nevertheless tolerates the retention of such weapons by a small group of other states.

The problem of international arms transfers is still very much on the agenda of the UN Disarmament Commission. While there are no official figures for the international transfer of armaments, it is estimated that global arms transfers, measured in constant 1985 dollars, grew from US $34.1 billion in 1984 to a peak of US $39.5 billion in 1987.[30] The permanent members of the Security Council all share responsibility for supplying many Third World countries with military hardware in the past three decades.[31] Most of them privately view arms transfers as influence tools and benefit substantially from them.

The 1972 Convention on the Prohibition of the Development, Production, and Stockpiling of Bacteriological (Biological) and Toxin Weapons and on Their Destruction (the Biological Weapons Convention) was the first international agreement that provided for genuine disarmament, that is, the destruction of an existing class of weapons. But, like the NPT, this convention has been ignored by several states. In the Middle East, for instance, Syria, Israel, Egypt, Iran, Iraq, and Libya have all manufactured such weapons, and some have actually used them in warfare.

The most significant arms-control negotiations have been held among the major powers outside the UN. Many of them (such as the Anti-Ballistic Missile Treaty [ABM], Strategic Arms Limitation Treaty I [SALT I], and Inter-mediate Range Nuclear Force [INF] Treaty) were negotiated between the governments of the US and the USSR. Others were agreed on by regional organizations. But it is also important to remember that many of the non-UN treaties were concluded within the general context of UN reminders of the obligation of the superpowers or regional bodies to reduce conventional and nuclear weapons. The treaty between the United States and the Soviet Union on the elimination of their intermediate-range and shorter-range missiles, for example, was welcomed by the UN and accompanied by resolutions at the 45th session of the General Assembly calling on both governments to 'spare no effort in seeking the attainment of all the agreed objectives in the negotiations.'[32]

The UN has not been very successful in arresting the arms race.[33] In fact, the number of states officially recognized to possess nuclear weapons has increased from one in 1945 to at least eight today, with the dissolution of the Soviet Union. An additional six or seven states may already have nuclear capability or may be hovering on that threshold. Global military expenditures have quadrupled since the 1950s; today, expenditures on arms and military establishments world-wide are estimated to be well over $900 billion annually.

While criticism of the UN's performance in the field of arms control and disarmament may be valid, it is also evident that the organization has made a contribution to this aspect of international peace and security. At the very least, it has kept this crucial issue on the agenda of the international community and has provided a forum in which disarmament and arms-limitation debates have been prominent. In doing so, it has also facilitated the codification of international principles governing the control of a major source of threat to the maintenance of international peace and security, i.e., weapons of mass destruction.

In many respects, the UN has been able to set goals for disarmament negotiations, and has served as an important source of information and education for the general public around this issue. With the dismantling of the Soviet Union, one might expect more arms-limitation and control issues to be resolved through multilateral organs and processes.

Peace-keeping and Preventive Diplomacy

Peace-keeping, the substitute form of collective security, not only survived the difficulties posed by the cold war but proved to be one of the UN's most indispensable innovations. Lester Pearson, one of the originators of the concept of peace-keeping, aptly described it as an intermediary technique between 'merely passing resolutions and actually fighting'.[34] This *ad hoc* conflict-management technique can be described as the employment, under UN auspices, of military, paramilitary, or even non-military personnel or forces in an area of political conflict. Its immediate purpose is to separate and disengage disputing parties long enough to allow negotiations to take place between them.

UN peace-keeping operations have had three essential characteristics: (1) their *non-enforcement* aspect, based on principles of consent and the limited use of weapons for self-defence only; (2) the *neutral* nature of their operations (permanent members of the Council have, as a general rule, been excluded from the composition of the forces, although they generally contribute financially and materially); and (3) their *voluntary and international composition*. UN peace-keeping forces must operate under the direct command of the United Nations. Operations have traditionally been divided into two categories: peace-keeping forces, and observer or fact-finding missions. The former consist of lightly armed infantry units with logistical-support elements, while the latter usually comprise officers who are almost invariably unarmed.[35]

The UN's first use of military personnel took place in 1947, when it set up the Special Committee on the Balkans. A similar body called the Consular Commission was instrumental in facilitating a disengagement of Dutch forces from Indonesia. These missions might be considered peace-keeping, but they were not *United Nations* peace-keeping operations, since the special forces worked under the authority of member states rather than the Secretary General or Security Council. The first UN peace-keeping operation was the Truce Supervision Organization (UNTSO) set up in Palestine in 1948. A year later, the UN Military Observer Group in India and Pakistan (UNMOGIP) was dispatched to Kashmir to separate India and Pakistan, and help to arrange terms of a settlement between the two countries. The observer mission remains in that region today, since a settlement did not prove attainable.

One criticism of UN peace-keeping is that it tends to inhibit settlement rather than facilitate it. For instance, UN forces in Cyprus have been used to protect and shore up an abnormal status quo on the island, thereby reducing any sense of urgency for a political solution to the stalemate.[36] Similar charges have been directed against the UN Emergency Force in the Middle East (UNEF).[37] Despite such criticisms, increasing numbers of international actors do rely on the UN's peace-keeping functions. As the international system shifts into a new era of uncertain developments there is more interest in UN peace-keeping than at any other time in the organization's history.[38]

Inis Claude has remarked that if the UN has contributed anything new to the maintenance of international peace and security, it must be the 'development of the theory and practice of preventive diplomacy'.[39] This concept has come to be associated with Dag Hammarskjöld's imaginative leadership in the same way that collective security was linked to Woodrow Wilson. Preventive diplomacy was devised as a means of overcoming the obstacles of the cold war. Initially, Hammarskjöld restricted its practice to areas in which the superpowers were not directly involved.

Preventive diplomacy has taken many different forms, from commissions of inquiry to military observation and truce supervision. But one of its most important uses is in the settlement of actual or potential disputes. The instruments for pacific settlement (e.g., mediation, negotiations) require inquiry into the relevant facts. The Office of the UN Secretary General has established this as an independent and preliminary procedure that is indispensable to the resolution of conflict. But the Council and the Assembly have also initiated investigative procedures in order to determine the 'true' facts surrounding specific events and disputes.

Fact-finding embraces a variety of activities including collection of information, interpretation, judgement, inquiry, interrogation, observation, analysis, area surveys, and inspection, as well as the writing of reports and recommendations. Whether fact-finding, mediation, or negotiation is involved, preventive diplomacy is indeed one of the most flexible instruments available to the UN organization. It is particularly useful in the hands of the Secretary General.

Oran Young has observed that 'there appears to be a growing body of international expectations according the Secretary-General a significant role in a wide range of disputes and crisis situations.'[40] The primary reason for this seems to be the recognition by the majority of states within the UN system that the Secretary General's office is relatively impartial and highly independent of individual state pressures. Using the discretionary powers of article 99, the Secretary General can mobilize UN machinery and personnel fairly quickly for preventive-diplomacy purposes.

Growing numbers of states within the General Assembly have been agitating for an expanded role for the Secretary General, particularly since the Manila conference on the Peaceful Settlement of Disputes held between 1972 and 1973, and the subsequent successes of past Secretaries General. Javier Pérez de Cuellar scrupulously maintained a position of impartiality. He worked closely with the Security Council and particularly with the permanent five members of the Council, and understood that none of his initiatives could get very far without the backing of those states. Although not the most exciting or articulate advocate for the organization, he nevertheless was considered a quintessential diplomat, someone who knew 'how to use his functions as an honest broker to nudge belligerent parties closer together, to find a path of common interest' where none appeared to be present.[41] At the same time he attempted to serve as a true executive officer, launching into reform of the administration of the organization to try and make it more efficient and lean.

Perhaps more than any other Secretary General since Hammarskjöld, Pérez de Cuellar was successful in utilizing article 99 for peace-making purposes. Consider, for instance, his role in the UN's successful monitoring of a democratic election and turnover of government in Nicaragua; its supervision of elections in Namibia and aid in drafting a constitution and completing the independence struggle of that country; successful mediation and termination of the decade-long conflict between Iraq and Iran; supervision of the withdrawal of Soviet troops from Afghanistan following the conclusion of the Geneva Accords; supervision of the withdrawal of foreign troops from Angola; monitoring of elections in Haiti; monitoring of human rights in El Salvador and northern Iraq; progress on the Greek-Turkish issue in Cyprus; and co-ordination of plans for the Western Sahara mission and the beginning of the Cambodia one. These acts of peace-making can in part be credited to the Secretary General's diplomatic skill and hard work in projecting the UN as a neutral and legitimate intermediary.

The Secretary General's peace-making role has been facilitated by a more co-ordinated approach to information-gathering and early warning. The need for an effective diplomatic and information management system that could provide the office with early alert and comprehensive coverage of potential threats to international peace and security stimulated the creation of the Office of Research and Collection of Information (ORCI) in 1987. Prior to ORCI there was no organized or systematic means of early warning for the Secretary General's office. ORCI in effect consolidated a variety of functions that had been performed in a number of offices across the UN system.[42]

Unfortunately, the new Secretary General, Boutros Boutros Ghali, seems to have reduced the importance attached to the UN's information-gathering and early-warning function. Effective 29 February 1992, ORCI, along with eleven other UN offices and departments, was discontinued as a separate entity.[43]

While the dismantling of ORCI flies in the face of General Assembly resolutions indicating the importance of its research and information-collection function, it is too early to tell whether this move will have a detrimental impact on the Secretary General's early-warning capabilities or ability to prevent conflict. At least some of ORCI's activities likely will continue in some form, but probably with fewer resources and staff to carry them out.

Mechanisms to Facilitate Decolonization

One other peace-making innovation was the development of UN machinery to cope with the end of the colonial era. Decolonization became the most significant international development, apart from the cold war, that demanded the attention of the UN. Not only was the task of maintaining international peace and security magnified in the 1950s, 1960s, and 1970s as approximately 50 per cent of the world's population altered its international legal status, but with the transformation came increases in the numbers of national armies and the quantities of armaments, as well as the numbers and varieties of conflicts. The numerous tribal and internecine civil disputes, in particular, were not fully anticipated by the framers of the Charter. But the Charter did obligate member states holding responsibility for dependent territories to facilitate the progress of these territories toward self-government and eventual independence.

As more and more former colonies became independent, the organization admitted them and expanded its machinery to facilitate the process further. The Trusteeship Council, which was initially set up under chapter XIII of the UN Charter with built-in advantages for the colonial powers, became instead a body that in many ways expedited the independence process. It was difficult for the status-quo powers to deny the Charter principle of 'equal rights and self-determination' to those forces demanding it.

The 1960 Assembly Declaration on the Granting of Independence to Colonial Countries and Peoples called for a speedy end to colonialism. This proclamation of emancipation for dependent peoples around the world was followed in 1961 by the establishment of a Special Committee on Colonialism (now known as the Committee of 24) to examine the way in which the declaration was being applied, and to make suggestions on how it should be implemented.

During the following two decades the General Assembly adopted a series of action plans that further expedited the progress toward independence for many states, and also passed a number of resolutions decrying apartheid, racism, and various forms of colonialism. Over that period, more than 60 territories, inhabited by more than 80 million people, have attained their independence and become sovereign members of the UN body. By facilitating this process of transition, the UN has arguably contributed to the maintenance of international peace and security.

Changing World, Changing UN

The ending of the cold war, which led to a climate of relaxed tension within much of the international community, has had a profound impact upon the UN system. Co-operation between the superpowers outside the UN quickly became translated into co-operation within the Security Council.[44] As two analysts noted in 1990: 'The Security Council has been reinvigorated and functions as a collegial body as anticipated in the Charter rather than as a battleground for great and not-so-great powers to score cheap rhetorical victories.'[45]

The turning point, according to one member of the UN Secretariat, occurred some time before the Revolution of 1989. In October 1986, at a luncheon of the permanent five organized by the ambassador of the United Arab Emirates, it was pointed out that a window of opportunity existed for the five finally to act as an executive body for the organization. Of the group, only China seemed to have reservations about the exercise of greater control over the rest of the organization, and the shift of power away from the General Assembly. But Chinese leaders needed Western aid to bolster their economy, and were also looking for a way to further integrate their country into the global economy. The Chinese ambassador to the UN, following his government's direction, went along with the proposal to try to reach informal consensus among the permanent members of the Council. The US played no small role in this endeavour, the US ambassador to the UN travelling to all the other permanent members' capitals to shore up support for this executive leadership role.

Once China had committed itself, one began to witness major successes for the Security Council in several long-standing conflicts around the globe. Some of these must be attributed to the co-ordinated efforts of both the permanent five and the Secretary General. For example, in 1987 the former, with the latter's help, were able to secure a cease-fire between Iran and Iraq after a decade of bitter conflict. Other successes can be attributed to individual permanent members in collaboration with interested non-members of the Security Council. For instance, in the Afghanistan situation, the USSR, Pakistan, and the US hammered out a deal outside the framework of the Security Council, and then brought their agreed-on proposal to the Council for approval.

In the fall of 1988, UN peace-keepers were awarded the Nobel Peace Prize. Since then, new peace-keeping operations have been dispatched to several theatres of conflict around the world. It seemed as if the UN had finally begun to operate in the way its founders intended; almost overnight, the much maligned organization was being credited with major accomplishments. As two students of the UN have written, the primary basis of this series of successes lay in the 'agreement among the five Permanent members of the Security Council on the principle that the processes and instrumentalities of the United Nations can and should be used in efforts to halt conflicts in third world regions'.[46]

To arrive at this new consensus, subtle reforms to the procedures of the Council were informally introduced. These included regular informal meetings of the big five outside formal Council meetings, which tend to be dominated by the US; regular informal consultations between the permanent five and the Secretary General; and agreement by the permanent members to avoid using the veto and instead try to persuade non-permanent members (through such unorthodox techniques as the prodding and cajoling at which US Ambassador to the UN Thomas Pickering so excelled) to support their positions before formal Security Council deliberations. The job of persuading the non-permanent members of the Council to acquiesce was made easier with the breakup of the non-aligned caucus on the Council.

While it has been argued that these informal changes reduced public posturing at Council sessions and led to more behind-the-scene consultations, which set a new tone on the Council and improved its effectiveness, they also helped to marginalize some of the heretofore influential non-permanent members of the Council. According to James Jonah, UN Undersecretary General for Special Political Affairs, these Council reforms produced charges of secrecy, lack of accountability, and rubber-stamping from non-permanent Council members who felt left out of the process. While more than a few of these non-permanent members' representatives may officially and publicly deny making the charge of marginalization, privately they have complained about not being consulted by the five permanent members on key Council issues.

New Directions for Peace-keeping

The year 1986 marked a turning point for the UN and its role in the maintenance of international peace and security. In the half-decade since then, the UN's most tangible contributions to international peace and security have been ten additional peace-keeping operations and observer missions. It was actually in 1989 that UN peace-keeping operations experienced their most significant shift. The operation in Namibia marked the culmination of 70 years of political pressure by the international community, successively through the League Assembly and the UN General Assembly's resolutions and condemnations, to bring a peaceful settlement to the Namibian people. The United Nations Transitional Assistance Group (UNTAG) operation in Namibia was established by the Security Council, and extended beyond traditional peace-keeping. Its mandate transcended simply keeping warring factions apart and arranging a cease-fire, to include such operations as monitoring the local police force in Namibia; supervising and controlling an election; and promoting and conducting a process of rapid political and structural change, resulting in a formal severance of Namibia from the clutches of South Africa on 21 March 1990.

What was peculiarly different about UNTAG, compared with other UN peace-keeping operations, was the extent to which it was involved with political engagement and the process of change. This operation paved the way for future UN peace-keeping efforts that have been, and will be, called upon to perform similar tasks.

On 17 March 1992 the Security Council voted unanimously to begin peace-keeping efforts in Somalia. The situation was considered so urgent that a 24-member team was dispatched immediately to the region. It was primarily humanitarian reasons that prompted the UN to devise a plan to secure a cease-fire in the country, after years of turning a blind eye to its conflict. This may be a sign that the organization was finally beginning to address the gulf between aspiration and fact in the area of human rights. As in Somalia, many of the conflicts around the world have been the result of human-rights abuses. In the past, article 2 (7) restrained the UN from getting involved in any systematic way in addressing these concerns. However, as former Secretary General Pérez de Cuellar has argued, public opinion now seems to demand that in instances where human rights are being violated in systematic fashion and on a massive scale, the intergovernmental machinery of the UN must stop being simply a helpless witness, and become an active and effective agent of redress: 'To promote human rights means little if it does not mean to defend them when they are under attack.'[47]

It is likely that there will be more UN peace-keeping activity in countries where human-rights abuses continue. Operations in Haiti, Somalia, and Iraq demonstrate that the UN, and by extension the international community, may be revising its normative policy with respect to intervention in the internal affairs of states.

Finally, the United Nations Observer Group in Central America (ONUCA) facilitated the ending of a number of protracted conflicts in Central America. ONUCA was deployed in December 1989 to verify compliance with the security arrangements agreed to by the governments of Costa Rica, El Salvador, Guatemala, Honduras, and Nicaragua. The UN was brought in along with the Organization of American States (OAS) to monitor elections, and to participate in an International Verification and Follow-up Commission to ensure that the commitments of the Esquipulas agreement were being fulfilled. This Commission comprised the UN Secretary General, the Secretary General of the OAS, the foreign-affairs ministers of the Central American countries (El Salvador, Nicaragua, Costa Rica, Honduras, Guatemala), the Contadora Group (Panama, Mexico, Colombia, Venezuela), and a support group consisting of Argentina, Brazil, Peru, and Uruguay.

ONUCA had been established by Security Council resolution 644.[48] It did not have static observation posts, as do most other UN peace-keeping operations; indeed, the terrain and large bodies of water in the region forced the establishment of mobile teams of 260 unarmed military observers (as well as crews and support personnel) who patrolled the area by road vehicles with cross-country capability, by patrol boats, light speedboats, fixed-wing aircraft, and helicopter. Command of the operation was exercised by a chief military officer, Major-General Agustín Quesada Gómez of Spain, who operated under the authority of the Secretary General and Security Council. He was responsible for overseeing five liaison offices, three operational posts, and fourteen verification centres in the five countries. The operation was later enlarged to include an infantry battalion contributed by Venezuela and a naval verification centre at San Lorenzo, Honduras; it would eventually cost more than $50 million US.

Peace-keeping tasks have not only increased in number since 1986, they have also broadened to include election monitoring, human-rights verification, safe repatriation of refugees, and, as will be the case in Cambodia, complete responsibility for running a country's bureaucracy and major governmental departments (defence, the interior, foreign affairs, and finance), as well as all constabulary functions. In the aftermath of the Iraq-Kuwait crisis, the UN was asked to perform tasks that also went beyond traditional peace-keeping. Among these tasks were demarcation of the Iraq-Kuwait boundary line; elimination of the mass-destruction capability of Iraq through the International Atomic Energy Agency; management of a compensation fund; and arranging the return of Kuwaiti property that was seized by the Iraqis.

The diversification of UN peace-keeping has become a reality. This has meant the deployment of large numbers of UN civilian personnel to aid in such operations as election monitoring, and the creation of civilian government in some countries. One restructuring move by the new Secretary General may serve to redefine the new UN peace-keeping functions and strengthen existing ones; it at least should bolster the capacity of the Secretary General in the area of peace-keeping. On 1 March 1992, a new UN Department of Peacekeeping Operations came into existence, into which has been incorporated the Office of Special Political Affairs, all under the direction of distinguished diplomat Marrack Goulding of the United Kingdom, who holds the title of Undersecretary General.

This move indicates the importance the organization, particularly the permanent five, places on dealing with a number of outstanding and brewing conflicts around the world. It has become obvious that in order for UN peace-keeping to be successful, certain elements must be present. First, there must be a clear, practicable but flexible mandate. Second, the co-operation and consent of the Security Council, particularly of the permanent five, are vital. Third, sufficient funds must be allocated for each operation, as peace-keeping operations are very costly.[49] Perhaps now that several countries have decided to reduce their military spending, with the end of the cold war, it may be possible for a portion of this saving to be allocated to multilateral efforts aimed at preserving and maintaining the peace.

Conclusion

The first-ever Security Council summit-level meeting was held on 31 January 1992 in New York, to address ways in which the preventive mechanisms of the UN could be further enhanced.[50] The heads of state at this meeting considered such subjects as apartheid, Iraq, the Middle East peace process, and international terrorism. The vast majority of the time, however, was devoted to UN peace-keeping. This seems to indicate that in the aftermath of the Gulf War, and because of the recent UN successes in resolving long-standing conflicts, peace-keepers will be asked increasingly to do more. The size of the Cambodia operation is staggering, but it could become a model for future peace-keeping efforts.

As a result of the summit, the Secretary General forwarded to member states on 1 July 1992 his analysis and recommendations on ways to strengthen, and make more effective within the framework of the Charter, the capacity of the UN for preventive diplomacy, peace-keeping, and peace-making. His report covered the role of the UN in identifying potential crises and areas of instability, and the contributions to be made by regional organizations in accordance with chapter VIII of the Charter. This report also dealt with the financial and material resources that would be needed in any expanded UN role in the above areas, as well as with ways in which the organization could more effectively plan when called upon to perform these peace and security functions.

In addition, the summit provided three other important clues about the direction in which future UN contributions to the maintenance of international peace and security might go. First, there now appears to be official recognition by Security Council members of the indivisibility of peace and prosperity. They came to the conclusion that lasting peace and stability cannot exist unless there is international co-operation to eradicate poverty and promote human rights, justice, and fairness. But one wonders if these state leaders really understand the significance of this conclusion.

To recognize the importance of so-called 'low politics' to the preservation of peace is to accept a new definition of security. This might mean embracing the concept of common security over national security. Or it might mean accepting definitions of security other than the dominant Eurocentric one. It seems no longer sufficient to assume that maintaining international peace and security should involve only arms limitation, pacific settlement, preventive diplomacy, peace-keeping, and collective security. None of the above should be done at the expense of justice and fairness. It will be important for the Security Council, and especially the permanent five members of the Council, not only to recognize that fact, but to act on it.

The second clue arising out of the summit meeting is the possibility that the UN will make another attempt at resurrecting article 43 of the Charter, which calls for a standing army. However, several questions come to mind. Where would it be stationed? Who would pay for it? Who would control it? Who would command it? Under what conditions would the troops be deployed? Who would be responsible for training? Would it really be an improvement over the current situation? Perhaps this idea has been clouded by the recent Gulf experience and the suggestion that the international system has entered into a 'new world order' in which massive global deployment of military might to enforce a Pax Americana will become the norm. If this thinking is being applied to the concept of a UN standing army, the idea ought to be abandoned.

The final observation is that the members of the Security Council recognize the need for some reform of the Charter. However, representatives of the permanent five are reluctant to engage the possibility of a change to the current membership of the Council. It is becoming more obvious that the current composition of the Council does not reflect today's international system. The only justification for the current makeup of the permanent five is the fact that they were mostly the victors of World War II. It is becoming more and more difficult to imagine a permanent component of the Council with both Japan and Germany absent. Any reform of the situation would of course require at least the unanimous agreement of the permanent five, and it is very unlikely that any of them will relinquish their seat. What may be more realistic is an increase in the number of permanent seats to include at least Japan and Germany (recognizing the importance of economic power as a means of addressing the current global problems), and possibly Brazil, India, and Nigeria (reflecting the necessity of bringing some redistributive justice to the organization and the international system). The truth is that the UN may no longer be in a position to cling to cozy familiar structures. To do so could mean weakening the Council's ability to adapt to the changing conditions of the international political and security environment.

As this chapter has indicated, the United Nations has made many meaningful contributions to the maintenance of international peace and security since 1945. Clearly the UN is not the only player in the international governance regime; in some cases it may not even be the central player. However, it is a significant player, and its potential contributions to the preservation of a peaceful world remain numerous.

Notes

[1] See S. Hemleben, *Plans for World Peace through Six Centuries* (Chicago: Univ. of Chicago Press, 1943).

[2] For an example, see Maurice Bertrand, *Some Reflections on Reform of the United Nations* (Geneva: Joint Inspection Unit, 1985).

[3] See Donald Puchala and Roger Coate, *The State of the United Nations, 1988* (New York: Academic Council of the United Nations System, 1988); Amos Yoder, *The Evolution of the United Nations System* (New York: Crane Russak, 1989), 190–4; Adam Roberts and Benedict Kingsbury, eds, *United Nations, Divided World* (Oxford: Clarendon Press, 1989); Thomas Franck, *Nation Against Nation: What Happened to the UN Dream and What the US Can Do About It* (New York: Oxford Univ. Press, 1985); and Brian Urquhart and E. Childers, *A World in Need of Leadership: Tomorrow's United Nations* (Uppsala: Dag Hammarskjöld Foundation, 1990).

[4] Brian Urquhart, 'The Management of Change: The Role of the UN', in *Canada and the United Nations in a Changing World*, Report of a UNA Canada Conference held in Winnipeg (12–14 May 1977), 43.

[5] See Inis Claude, *Swords Into Plowshares: The Problem and Progress of International Organization*, 4th ed. (New York: Random House, 1984), 215–410.

[6] Ibid., 247.

[7] Seymon Brown, *The Causes and Prevention of War* (New York: St Martin's, 1987), 154–61.

[8] See Louis Henkin et al., *International Law: Cases and Materials* (St Paul: West, 1980), 929–38.

[9] 'The Caroline', *Digest of International Law* 412 (1906).

[10] Oscar Schachter, 'The Right of States to Use Armed Force', *Michigan Law Review* 1620 (1982), 1633–5.

[11] The concept of judicial settlement of disputes actually dates to ancient Greece. City-states at that time adopted principles of arbitration and mediation in the

handling of disputes between them. See J. Scott, *Law, the State, and the International Community* (New York: Columbia Univ. Press, 1939), 264–5.

[12]See Yoder, *Evolution of the United Nations System*, 94.

[13]Article 2 (3) and (4).

[14]Article 33 (1).

[15]Article 35 (1) and (2).

[16]Article 36 (1).

[17]Chapters VI, VII, VIII, and XII of the UN charter set out the specific powers granted to the Council.

[18]Article 43 calls on all member states to work out agreements with the Security Council that could 'govern the number and types of forces, their degree of readiness and general location, and the nature of the facilities and assistance provided.'

[19]*The United Nations Conference on International Organization: Selected Documents* (New York: United Nations Information Organization, 1945-6), 706.

[20]The membership in the UN increased from 51 states in 1945 to 114 in 1965.

[21]The Uniting for Peace Resolution provided for emergency sessions for the Assembly, establishment of a Peace Observation Commission, earmarking of national contingents for service with the UN, and establishment of a Collective Measures Committee.

[22]Brian Urquhart, 'Problems and Prospects of the United Nations', *International Journal* 44 (Autumn 1989), 804.

[23]See Claude, *Swords Into Plowshares*, 143.

[24]Bertrand, *Some Reflections on Reform*.

[25]Moscow had withdrawn its representative from the Security Council in protest against the exclusion of Communist China from UN membership. Ever since July 1950, the Soviets maintained a representative at Security Council meetings without interruption; see Otto Pick and Julian Critchley, *Collective Security* (London: Macmillan, 1974), 37.

[26]'Kuwait: The Crisis— Iraqi Invasion and Annexation Evoke Historic Response from Security Council', *UN Chronicle* (Dec. 1990), 5-7.

[27]Janice Gross Stein, 'International Security and Conflict Management', in *Peacekeeping, Peacemaking or War: International Security Enforcement*, ed. Alex Morrison (Toronto: Canadian Institute of Strategic Studies, 1991), 86.

[28]Note also the two major IAEA international conventions: the Convention of Early Notification of a Nuclear Accident (27 Oct. 1986) and the Convention on Assistance in the Case of a Nuclear Accident or Radiological Emergency (26 Feb. 1987). After Chernobyl and recent discussions about the possibility of similar nuclear accidents in the territories of the former Soviet Union, one can understand the increased importance of these two conventions.

[29]Yoder, *Evolution of the United Nations System*, 93.

[30]The value of these transfers is much higher if one considers transactions that minimize direct claims on foreign exchange reserves by concessional prices, loans, offset arrangements, reciprocal sales, licensing agreements, and defence-production sharing arrangements. See *Disarmament Facts 70* (New York: United Nations, 1989), 6-7.

[31]See J. Hurewitz, ed., *Soviet-American Rivalry in the Middle East* (New York: Praeger, 1969); and *The Middle East Military Balance* (Jerusalem: Jerusalem Post, 1990). According to Keith Krause, the market share of traditional arms suppliers has been slipping recently; Krause, *International Trade in Arms*, Background Paper (Ottawa: Canadian Institute for International Peace and Security, March 1989), 3.

[32]See UN Doc. A/45/100, 173, and UN GA Resolution 44/116 B.

[33]For a good discussion of arms transfers see Keith Krause, 'Military Statecraft: Power and Influence in Soviet and American Arms Transfer Relationships', *International Studies Quarterly* 34 (1991).

[34]Lester B. Pearson, 'Force for the UN', *Foreign Affairs* 35 (April 1957), 401.

[35]United Nations, *The Blue Helmets*, 2nd ed. (New York: United Nations, 1990), 8.

[36]James Stegenga, *The United Nations Force in Cyprus* (Columbus: Ohio State Univ. Press, 1968), 186.

[37]See Abraham Yeselson and Anthony Gaglione, *A Dangerous Place* (New York: Viking, 1974).

[38]United Nations, *Report of the Secretary-General on the Work of the Organization* (Sept. 1991), UN Doc. A/46/1.

[39]Claude, *Swords Into Plowshares*, 312.

[40]Oran Young, *The Intermediaries: Third Parties in International Crises* (Princeton: Princeton Univ. Press, 1967), 265.

[41]John Tessitore and Susan Woolfson, eds, *Issues Before the 45th General Assembly of the United Nations* (Lexington, MA: Lexington Books, 1991), 1.

[42]Thomas Boudreau, *Sheathing the Sword: The UN Secretary-General and the Prevention of International Conflict* (New York: Greenwood, 1991), 116.

[43]The other offices and/or departments being discontinued were the Office of the Director-General for Development and International Economic Cooperation; the Office for Political and General Assembly Affairs and Secretariat Services; the Office for Ocean Affairs and the Law of the Sea; the Department of Political and Security Council Affairs; the Department for Special Political Questions, Regional Cooperation, Decolonization, and Trusteeship; Department for Disarmament Affairs; Department of International Economic and Social Affairs; Department of Technical Cooperation for Development; Centre for Science and Technology for Development; United Nations Centre on Transnational Corporations; and the Department of Conference Services.

[44]Donald Puchala and Roger Coate, *The Challenge of Relevance: The United Nations in a Changing World Environment* (New York: Academic Council on the United Nations System, 1989), 9.

[45]Augustus Norton and Thomas Weiss, 'Rethinking Peacekeeping', in *The United Nations and Peacekeeping Results, Limitations and Prospects: The Lessons of 40 Years of Experience*, ed. I. J. Rikhye and K. Skjelsbaek (London: Macmillan, 1990), 23.

[46]Puchala and Coate, *Challenge of Relevance*, 14.

[47]United Nations, General Assembly, *Report of the Secretary-General on the Work of the Organization*, UN Doc. A/46/1, (6 Sept. 1991), 9.

[48]The contributing countries were Brazil, Canada, Colombia, Ecuador, India, Ireland, Spain, Sweden, and Venezuela. Argentina provided four fast patrol boats and crew. The Federal Republic of Germany contributed a civilian medical unit and a fixed-wing aircraft and crew. Canada provided a helicopter unit.

[49]In 1989 the peace-keeping budget was approximately equal to that of the UN's regular budget.

[50]It was attended by the leaders of the US, UK, China, France, Russia, Venezuela, Ecuador, Cape Verde, Japan, Belgium, India, Austria, Hungary, Zimbabwe, and Morocco.

chapter thirteen

Bound to Leave? The Future of the NATO Stationing Regime in Germany

David G. Haglund and Olaf Mager

Introduction

The cold war may be dead, but the consequences of its ending are very much alive. While few serious students of international relations question the fundamental and perhaps even irreversible changes in the international strategic environment since the mid-1980s, there is no consensus on the ultimate meaning of these changes. As with most momentous developments in international security, the ending of the bipolar adversarial relationship between the East and West has triggered a great debate. On the one hand, there are those who argue that the tendency to rejoice over the ending of the cold war is, at best, misguided. Writers such as John Mearsheimer have boldly pronounced that the future of European security — both Eastern and Western — is imperilled by the demise of the bipolar structure that, for all its flaws, was responsible for what another writer has labelled Europe's 'long peace'.[1] To Mearsheimer and other structural realists, it has been the existence of a bipolar bloc system, a state of relative military parity between the blocs, and the centrality of nuclear weaponry to European security that has kept the peace. Now, they believe, with the disintegration of the Warsaw Pact and, more importantly, of the Soviet Union itself, accompanied by progressive loss of faith in the political as well as military utility of nuclear weapons, the future of European security will be but a repetition of a pattern begun long ago.

Standing against this bleak view is that of another group who argue that the future of European security has never looked so bright now that the bloc-to-bloc confrontation has ended, the light of freedom has penetrated the darkest caverns of Eastern Europe, and the spectre of nuclear extinction has been banished. To these analysts, political, economic, and sociocultural transformations of such profundity have occurred in Europe as to render the prospect of interstate warfare between Europeans an effective impossibility.[2] Ethnic unrest and national conflict persist, and are aggravating, in Eastern and Southeastern Europe, it is true; nevertheless, for the optimists Europe as a whole remains 'primed for peace'.[3] Although the causes of Europe's new-found peacefulness remain open to dispute even among the optimists, there does appear to be agreement on certain basic aspects of the transformation. Democracy, social levelling, historical learning, the market economy, the rule of law — all of these are seen to have made it possible for most of Europe to overcome its legacy of armed conflict.

The most prominent governance features of the cold-war era were the institutionalized military arrangements, both conventional and nuclear, that had dominated all other facets of the East-West struggle. Alone among the myriad of institutions that came into being during the cold war, alliances had pride of place. Central to both their purposes and their functioning was the concentration of sizeable units of foreign forces at the point where the blocs met. This, of course, was Germany, the most important prize in the struggle for geopolitical supremacy, as well as the most heavily fortified theatre of political, and potentially military, conflict. As late as 1990, there were in West Germany alone more than 900,000 soldiers, nearly half of whom were from Allied countries. In the former German Democratic Republic (GDR) were to be found nearly 600,000 troops, two-thirds of whom wore Soviet uniforms.[4] It comes, then, as no surprise that an immediate and critical consequence of the demise of the cold war should be a thorough reassessment of the significance and sustainability of the previous stationing regime.[5]

To the pessimists like Mearsheimer, the future of Allied forces in Germany is in no doubt: they will (regretably) be withdrawn, as their *raison d'être*, namely the defence of the West against a predatory Soviet Union, has been lost.[6] For their part, the optimists too see a diminishing rationale for Allied troop stationing in Germany or anywhere else in Europe; indeed, to the most extreme optimists, economic interdependence and democracy alone can provide the necessary basis for the preservation of peace and security throughout the continent.[7] To be sure, not all optimists are willing to dismiss the need for a continuing, albeit residual, Allied (especially US) military presence in Germany and other parts of Europe; it is simply that they find it increasingly difficult to produce a compelling answer to one question: Why should Allied forces remain stationed in a united Germany in a post-cold-war era?

This question is the animating focus of this chapter. Situated in neither the pessimistic nor the optimistic camp, it argues that the adversarial relationship between West and East, while obviously of great importance, should not be taken as the sole justification for the presence of foreign forces in Germany or elsewhere in Europe. Thus the ending of the cold war need not, and does not, constitute an irrefutable argument against the continuation of foreign stationing. Obviously, there has been a predominant emphasis in the past decades on the strictly military rationale for that stationing, and in this sense the cold war's demise has indeed complicated matters for those who would prefer a Europe, and by extension an Atlantic system, in which Allied forces remained relevant elements in security governance. In the absence of compelling military rationales, it will be necessary for those seeking the continuation of the stationing regime to supply persuasive political ones. Perhaps this would require some variant of future-casting, in which new purposes for the Alliance—for example, collective security—might be invoked to satisfy the need for a continuing stationing regime. Alternatively, what might be required is simply a reassessment of the historical consequences— if not indeed the purposes—of the Allies' decisions to create multilateral security structures in the trans-Atlantic context.

The 'Structural Context' of Stationing

Any discussion of the future of stationed forces in Germany must begin with an analysis of past and current circumstances relating to German, European, and trans-Atlantic security interests and requirements.

Here it is useful to recall the various political functions fulfilled over the decades not only by Western troops (foremost among whom were the Americans), but also the forces deployed in East Germany by the Soviet Union. According to Helga Haftendorn, these troops performed three basic roles: (1) they were guardians of the German Question, which meant that they would prevent a re-emergence of German militarism; (2) they were at the same time guarantors, in a competitive fashion, of the security of the divided Germanies; and (3) they were balancing agents in the global contest for geopolitical advantage that was so characteristic of the cold-war era.[8] Although in many ways the consequences of foreign-troop stationing might be regarded as independent of the purpose of the particular alliances it undergirded, in some critical respects, such as the political and legal arrangements associated with the respective blocs' stationing, the differences did outweigh the similarities. For example, the Western stationing powers, even during the early occupation period following the military collapse of the Third Reich, began to work, however grudgingly, in a multinational fashion that would eventually become the most fundamental organizational precept of the Alliance, endowing it with a legitimacy that never could be attained by the now-defunct Warsaw Pact. By contrast, the stationing pattern in the East failed to make the quantum leap from occupation to security partnership, with all that this implied for its long-term sustainability. This can be illustrated by the bilateral understanding reached between the Soviet Union and Germany in July 1990, in which the former agreed, not without some inducements, to leave the expiring GDR by the end of 1994. The Soviet Union was unable to condition its total withdrawal upon a demand for a corresponding, and symmetrical, removal of Western stationed forces. To the contrary, the government in Bonn actually indicated a strong preference that Allied forces remain stationed in the country, including in Berlin.

Numerous politico-legal arrangements gave substance to the Western (and to an extent Soviet) military presence in Germany. Among the most important of these was the June 1945 Four Power declaration that effectively stripped Germany of all its sovereignty. Ranking next in significance would have to be the Treaty on the Final Settlement with Respect to Germany, of September 1990, which fully restored it. In between these critical juridical brackets could be found the legal foundation of each alliance's stationing rights in the two Germanies. For NATO, the relevant document was the 1955 Convention on the Presence of Foreign Forces in the German Federal Republic; for the Warsaw Pact, it was the 1955 Treaty on Relations between the USSR and the GDR. Although Russian forces in the former GDR will leave by 1994, according to an agreement reached by Bonn and Moscow in 1990, NATO stationing countries have been asked by Bonn to stay on.[9] Whether they do so, however, will be a function of their own assessment of interest in being in Germany, as well as the evolving debate in Germany on stationing.

The politico-legal transformation of German sovereign status occurred, of course, because of a dramatic and likely irreversible set of upheavals in the political and military universe of the former Soviet empire in Eastern Europe. While not the only factor responsible for this substantial strategic transformation, the diminishing Soviet military threat must surely rank as the most important one. Indeed, in the aftermath of the failed *coup* and the collapse of the Soviet Union, it is hard to recall the impact that Soviet unilateral measures in foreign and defence policy had upon the East-West strategic relationship in the last years of the 1980s. These measures were rooted as much in economic necessity as in political opportunity. Without wishing to denigrate the undeniable spirit of innovation characterized by the Gorbachev revolution in Soviet foreign policy, one must nonetheless acknowledge the seminal part played by economic constraint in propelling the Soviets to adopt a new defence doctrine, which as the *putsch* of August 1991 indicated, was hardly universally accepted.

Of course, major questions remain regarding those Soviet military reforms. There was a clear link between the reforms and the state of disarray in Soviet military ranks even prior to the ending of the 1980s. It was the perception of a gradually disappearing Soviet threat, first evidenced in Germany, that would become so important to the continued existence of the Allies' own stationed forces in that country. This perception had a solid basis in reality, and was not a figment of the imagination of some high-level officials in the German foreign ministry.

Collectively, the developments that took the name of the Revolution of

1989, coupled with the subsequent implosion of Soviet power, permitted—indeed, obliged—the Western Alliance to undertake the most thorough-going reconsideration of its defence strategy in its history. It took some time, but eventually defence planners in all of the Allied deploying countries would move closer to the assessment of the Soviet threat that had been championed with such singularity in Bonn. Whereas 'Genscherism' (as this German approach was known) was often taken in Washington and other policy centres to constitute, in the latter years of the 1980s, a failing of either the intellect or the spirit, by the early 1990s all defence planners had become, to one degree or another, Genscherites—in that they entertained a decidedly more benign view of Soviet intentions or capabilities (or both).

Although at one time it appeared that Germany was far out in front of the other Allies in seeking accommodation with the Soviets, in the aftermath of the August *putsch* the United States itself seemed to be surging ahead of its Allies in its bid to forge a new relationship, perhaps even security partnership, first with the residual Soviet power base and shortly thereafter with the all-important Russian republic.[10] But the Alliance was not very far behind, and as its November 1991 summit revealed, was reforming itself in dramatic ways. Among the most important of these was the strategy review, which began in the summer of 1990, was in part made public in May 1991, and was adopted by NATO leaders at Rome.[11] Alliance strategists have been grappling with the need to present a compelling and comprehensive rationale for the maintenance of a collective defence system in the trans-Atlantic context—an endeavour that bears a strong resemblance to the task faced by those who would seek legitimate reasons to sustain the stationing regime. This is hardly surprising, given the linkage between Alliance survival and the durability of stationing. To put it differently: should the Alliance fail in its effort to come up with a strategy that is at once operationally credible and politically convincing, it can be safely assumed that the future of Allied forces in Germany will be short. The fate of the new NATO strategy underlines the challenges and opportunities facing member states as they move into a new strategic era in Europe.

Will the Alliance be able to make the required transition? To do so, NATO will have to come to terms with the issue of Europe's new political structure, a matter that is itself indeterminate. Somewhat less uncertain is another issue bearing on the viability of long-term stationing in Germany: in future the Alliance must place much greater emphasis upon the twin concepts of multinationalism and reciprocity—the latter meaning that other countries and not just Germany have to be willing to host Allied forces on their territory.

Whatever the Alliance and its strategists produce, and notwithstanding the intrinsic importance of their efforts, it is obvious that the future of Allied forces in Germany will in large part (but not exclusively) be determined by the preferences of the German government, conditioned as the latter will be by public opinion. But for the new NATO strategy to appeal to the Germans, it must demonstrate a decidedly greater commitment to avoiding their 'singularization' than did the stationing pattern of the cold-war era. What this, in turn, means is that Germans must be convinced that the benefits of Allied stationing outweigh the associated burdens, and that Germany is no longer singularized as the only country hosting non-American forces — that is, that it not be isolated among the *European* Allies. The ultimate danger of a collapse of the stationing regime arguably inheres in the prospect of a 'renationalization' of European defence.

At NATO headquarters, a conviction has developed that multinationalism might become an effective antidote against German stationing fatigue. Although many analysts seem to regard the multinational aspiration as being something new under the Alliance sun, it is in fact a concept whose existence dates to the very beginnings of NATO. Indeed, it was the basis of the extraordinary degree of co-operation that has enabled the Allies to overcome a seemingly endless series of crises over the years. To be sure, multinational defence has long made sense from both a political and an operational perspective, but the unprecedented novelty of the current strategic environment requires a further evolution of multinationalism.

Although it is still in an early stage, certain features of the new multinationalism have already become visible. Perhaps the most dramatic of these is the fundamental reorganization of Allied defences in Germany. Instead of the former layer-cake deployment pattern, which interspersed national corps in West Germany the length of the border with the communist countries, the new strategy of the Alliance calls for the creation of an innovative Rapid Reaction Corps, backed up by Main Defence and Augmentation Forces, many of which will be multinational.[12]

The North American Stationing Countries

Much work remains to be done to integrate the Alliance's new strategy with the force structures and policies of the North American and European stationing countries. The possible emergence of a security partnership (in embryo) between the US and the Russian authorities is perhaps best glimpsed in the Madrid conference on the Middle East peace process. Although the most dramatic military instance of this new quest for partnership was President George Bush's announcement, made in late September 1991, that the US would be eliminating its land- and sea-based tactical nuclear weapons in Europe and Asia, as well as taking its strategic bombers and Minuteman II missiles off alert, the effects of the quest will hardly be confined to the nuclear arena.[13] While the US may, for reasons related to its own fiscal woes, be unable or unwilling to mount a major Marshall Plan for the former Soviet republics, one unavoidable consequence of the most profound reassessment of the 'threat' that has ever been undertaken in post-war Washington will be an unremitting pressure on the US troop presence in Germany and other European countries.[14]

If the Germans have been experiencing 'stationing fatigue' of late, for all the deploying Allies, with the possible exception of the Netherlands, there is a well-developed mood of stationers' fatigue. This mood is not yet as pronounced in the US as in Canada or Belgium. But the American troop deployment in Germany has been particularly significant militarily and symbolic politically: as the US stationing presence goes, therefore, so goes that of the Alliance. It is helpful, in thinking about the 48-year history of US troops in Germany, to draw upon Wolfram Hanrieder's contention that they have had two principal purposes: first to contain Germany, then to contain the Soviet Union.[15] Quite apart from the explicit and implicit purposes, there has been a major consequence associated with the American military commitment to Europe, namely the creation of the foundations of a security community in Western Europe itself. Thus, even in the event of a total disappearance of the Soviet threat, there might still be a good reason for the maintenance of a US troop presence in Europe, and in Germany: to avoid instability in general and the renationalization of European defence in particular.

It does appear that official US planning documents, which in 1992 were envisioning some 150,000 American troops in Europe by 1995, will turn out to have been overstatements; more probably there will be no more than 80,000 US troops in Germany by 1997, and no fewer than 50,000. More importantly, it is likely that longer-range trends within the trans-Atlantic security relationship, coupled with certain fiscal and demographic realities in the US, will lead Americans in the coming few years to question the wisdom and sustainability of their military commitment to Europe. The mood in the US during the 1992 presidential campaign, reflected in a surprising inattentiveness to foreign policy, favoured a turn inward, and betrayed a public conviction that the Bush Administration had been too committed to foreign and defence activism.[16]

Another North American country whose troop deployments in Germany have stirred debate is Canada. Although an early and important participant in the fighting against Hitler's Germany, Canada did not take up significant occupation duties at the end of the war. Instead, it rapidly demobilized armed forces that had made it, by V-J Day, the fourth strongest military power on earth. But the country's absence from Europe was short-lived, and when Ottawa decided, in 1951, again to commit military assets to the old continent, it did so in an impressive manner. Canada took seriously indeed the job of helping to secure Western Europe against possible Soviet aggression, committing to the task an armoured brigade (initially for deployment with the British Army of the Rhine) and, perhaps more important, an air division of 12 squadrons of F-86s, each with 16 aircraft. Moreover, Canada provided the European Allies with mutual aid in the amount of $1 billion by 1956.

When Canada deployed its forces to Germany, it was, like the United States, of the opinion that sooner or later the Europeans would be able to look after their own security without a North American troop presence.

Indeed, at certain moments during the past two decades, the temptation to leave Europe has appeared, in some circles in Ottawa, to be almost irresistible. However, strong counter pressures have been brought to bear by European Allies, who succeeded for some time in modifying the Canadian inclination to depart completely. But what no Ally, not even the United States, could do was to prevent an erosion both in Canadian troop levels in Germany (6,400 by the end of 1991) and in the amount of money allocated to defence spending in general. In February 1992 the Mulroney government announced that Canada would remove all its stationed forces from Germany rather than leave 1,100 ground forces in Europe, as it had indicated only a few months previously, in September 1991.[17]

Although policy-makers in National Defence Headquarters were quick to proclaim that the ending of stationing would not weaken the country's commitment to either NATO or Europe—and pointed to the large Canadian contingent slated for peace-keeping duties in what used to be Yugoslavia as proof—the immediate reaction from the European Allies was a sense of abandonment and panic, stemming from a fear that as Ottawa went, so too would Washington.

The European Stationing Countries

Some have claimed that the Allied stationing regime could not exist in the absence of an American troop presence in Europe (ideally in Germany), a thesis that appears to be borne out by the British experience. Like the Americans, the British had pursued a traditional policy of avoiding permanent stationing on the European continent. To be sure, the British did, for obvious reasons, join the US, USSR, and France as original occupying powers in conquered Germany, but it was far from settled in 1945 whether there would be a long-standing British military role there. By the mid-1950s, especially following the débâcle of the European Defence Community, British leaders became convinced that their country, through its military deployments in Germany, could play an important role in ensuring a continuing American presence. Ever since that time, it has been an article of faith of the country's planners that the defence of its European, or continental, security interests could be assured only through a meaningful trans-Atlantic defence partnership. It is likely that a continuing British troop presence in Germany will be highly contingent upon a continuing American one.

At most (during the Korean War years), Britain deployed some 100,000 military personnel in Germany, mainly in the British Army of the Rhine (BAOR) and the RAF (Germany). The cold war's demise has meant, for Britain as for other Allies, a significant downsizing; for the Rhine Army, this translates into a 50-per-cent cut in effectives, from 55,000 to 27,000 soldiers; RAF (Germany) will also be pruned, according to British planning.[18] There has been a sense in which Britain itself is 'singularized' on the question of stationing, for apparently it is the only Allied country with forces in Germany that is legally constrained from withdrawing troops unless it has the approval of the Western European Union (WEU); escape clauses have existed to modify somewhat this singularity. Also setting Britain apart has been the fact that its troop presence has had an operational and symbolic importance second only to that of the US among the Allies in Germany. Given this importance, it is noteworthy that Britain has decided to leave a significant armed force in Germany, one moreover that has been given some apparent, if still unspecified, operational credibility by dint of its being vested with both the command of and a leading role in the new Rapid Reaction Corps (RRC) that is a product of the NATO strategy review.

The situation of French forces in Germany, by contrast, bears little sustained comparison with that of either the US or the British contingents stationed there. France, having withdrawn from NATO's integrated military command in 1966, has never subscribed, at least in explicit declaratory policy, to the former twin tenets of NATO strategy, flexible response and forward defence. Instead, the *Forces françaises en Allemagne* (FFA), though nearly as numerous as the BAOR, have been assigned reserve roles, surrounded by no little ambiguity, in the event of war in Europe. Above all, the French have held strongly to the conviction that there could be no automaticity of response in the event of aggression; whether French forces would be involved in fighting, it was always maintained, would depend solely upon the decision of the president of the Republic.

Much has altered since the 1990s began, and it is a commonly held view — and not only in France — that the fundamental changes in the European strategic context have made it obligatory for France to reassess radically the presence of its forces in Germany. In July 1990 President François Mitterrand indicated, to the dismay of the German government, that the coming of German unification would render illogical any further French armed presence in Germany, with one exception — the French units composing the joint Franco-German brigade, based at Boblingen in southwestern Germany.[19] As things then stood (although the situation would subsequently change), France intended withdrawing the FFA in their entirety by 1995, in two stages: by the end of 1992, some 20,000 of the FFA's 46,000 soldiers were to have been brought back to France; once the last Soviet soldiers had left the former GDR, in 1994, the remainder were to have been repatriated. With Mitterrand's announcement, France stood out among the Allies in rejecting the related concepts of multinationalism and reciprocity; the first it saw as little more than a cloak for a continued American dominance of European security, the second it regarded as lacking operational sense. However, with the announcement in May 1992 of a decision to create a Franco-German corps of 35,000 soldiers, to which other European Allies were invited to contribute, it is apparent that sizeable French units will remain deployed in Germany, and that German headquarters staff will be stationed in France, in Strasbourg.[20]

Whatever the many differences between the stationing histories and policies of the Allied 'Big Three', on one matter there has been consistency: the US, the UK, and France all began to deploy forces in Germany even before the Second World War had ended, and they kept troops in the country as occupying powers after the war. No such uniformity characterizes the stationing record of the remaining Allied countries with a military presence in Germany: Belgium and the Netherlands. It is true that the Belgians participated unequivocally in the occupation regime, more or less as hitch-hikers in the British zone. But not until the early 1960s did the Netherlands commit itself to the stationing of troops in Germany, a function of a felt need to counter Soviet expansionary tendencies.

The Belgian Corps arrived in Germany in March 1946 at the invitation of the British, who offered to *share* their occupation zone with a Belgium that was keenly interested in containing German militarism and Soviet expansionism, as well as in cementing a secure military bond with Britain. For a relatively small country, Belgium has had, over the decades, a rather large military presence in Germany: by the end of 1946 some 33,000 Belgian soldiers were occupying a portion of the British zone more than half the size of Belgium itself. As late as 1991, Belgium continued to deploy more than a quarter of its entire army in Germany. The nearly 25,000 personnel assigned to the 1 (BE) Corps represent a higher ratio of German-deployed troops to total ground forces than has been the case for any other Allied deploying country with the exception of Britain.

Like the British, the Belgians will be reducing their forces in Germany over the next few years. Unlike Britain, however, Belgium is committed to such a deep cut in personnel — from 25,000 down to 3,500 by 1995 — that it can only be a matter of time before Belgium will find itself with hardly any units at all left in Germany.[21] While strategic calculations have played some part in the recent restructuring of the Belgian army, the most important factor in the reductions appears to have been the budgetary one. Belgium has, by far, the most onerous national debt burden of all the Western deploying countries — worse even than the load carried by the fiscally precarious North American powers, the US and Canada. As a result, there will be only one Belgian brigade, the 17th PsBde, in Germany by mid-decade. Belgium will not leave NATO, but it appears more and more likely that its forces will not remain in Germany for very long after the Russians have left that country.

The Netherlands was the last Allied stationing country to deploy troops in Germany on a quasi-permanent basis. Not until the Berlin Crisis of 1961 would the Dutch begin their long-term stationing of a brigade in Germany, although some air units had been doing temporary duty there since the early 1950s. Dutch stationing policy has, since the beginning, been characterized by clear political objectives as well as military ones. For a series of Dutch governments, NATO has been the pivotal element of foreign and security policy. This has meant, in turn, that the Dutch saw their military commitment to Germany as accomplishing two political and security functions: it has helped bind

Germany to the West by reassuring that country it would not be left alone to face the Soviets; and it has demonstrated to the Americans that the Dutch were willing to bear their share of the West's defence burden, thus contributing to keeping the US in Europe. These twin concerns, of binding both the Germans and the Americans into an integrated Western European defence ensemble, continue to guide Dutch foreign and security policy.

Notwithstanding the durability and consistency of the country's stationing policy, there have been in the Netherlands (as in other Allied countries) resource constraints. The effect has been to so condition the country's force structure that successive governments have never been able to increase the Dutch stationed forces' size to the divisional strength seemingly necessary to complete their operational effectiveness. This problem never did get resolved during the cold war, and it would take the latter's demise to render it, at long last, irrelevant.

Hardly irrelevant, however, is the manner in which the Netherlands conceptualizes the continuing need for stationed Allied forces in Germany and other parts of Europe. Ironically, in view of the fact that the Dutch were the last Allied power to station forces in Germany, the entire future of the stationing regime may depend upon the degree to which certain other countries follow the Dutch model. Their defence white paper has committed the country's armed forces to the norm of multinationalism, with an explicit recognition of the peril awaiting Western Europe in the event of a renationalization of defence.[22] Importantly, the Dutch will not be reducing their ground presence in Germany, even if the 41st Brigade, stationed at Seedorf, will shed its heavy armour and become a light brigade. Current long-term Dutch plans envision a Dutch-German multinational corps, under Dutch command, consisting of two Dutch divisions and one German one. Over the shorter term, the Dutch intend to make available to the ACE Rapid Reaction Corps an airmobile brigade. Finally, and reflective of the principle of reciprocity, the Dutch intend to continue hosting German units at Budel (on the frontier between the provinces of North Brabant and Limburg), where for nearly 30 years German Air Force personnel have trained.

It may turn out that for the stationing regime to persist in Germany, greater emphasis will be required both on multinationalism and on reciprocity. If that is so, then it appears the political contribution of Dutch forces to the Alliance may far outweigh their military contribution.

What Do the Germans Want?

The conditions for a continuing, albeit modified, stationing regime will, during the post-cold-war years, in large measure depend upon the attitude of Germany. Government policy statements have indicated continuing support for Allied forces on German territory. Bonn has actively tried to preserve intact the stationing regime, even if at the same time it has welcomed the substantial reductions in Allied military personnel in the country.

While Bonn apparently could not instantaneously reverse France's 1990 decision in favour of a complete withdrawal, it nevertheless drew attention, even before unification was completed, to the continuing need for an Allied presence during the coming transitional period.[23] The other stationing states with the exception of Canada have agreed to maintain the stationing regime for the time being. Indeed, until the failed Soviet coup of August 1991 rendered the issue less salient, Allied forces had constituted a powerful symbol of Western determination to see the Soviets leave the former GDR. With the coup's failure, the newly established Soviet state council agreed to accelerate the withdrawal of forces from Germany, as well as give assurances that there remained no nuclear or chemical weapons stored at Soviet bases in the country. Shortly afterwards, there was no longer a Soviet Union.

If Germany retains its outspoken interest in playing host to a (much reduced) Allied presence in Europe, it has equally developed an interest in extinguishing those elements of the stationing regime that have, for better or worse, overemphasized the Federal Republic's part. After obtaining its unrestricted sovereignty, and following some considerable public pressure from those *Länder* mostly affected by the coming Allied troop withdrawals, the German government invited the stationing countries to review the Supplementary Agreement to the Status of Forces Agreement. The purpose of these negotiations, which began in September 1991, is to adapt the Supplementary Agreement in a way that does not question the regime as such but, taking into account the new status of Germany, tightens the conditions of stationing for the remaining Allied forces. The negotiations will cover such diverse issues as jurisdiction, training and manoeuvre activities, reinforcements, and base closures. Major agenda items will include whether the stationing countries should continue to train their forces (including units brought in from outside) extensively in Germany. Bonn would like to reduce the burdens that military training imposes on German society, while the stationing countries are interested in preserving the highest possible level of operational readiness. Environmental issues will also require resolution, given that the cleanup of former military areas has already proven extremely costly.

These negotiations, which will be time-consuming, obviously could have a profound impact upon the willingness of the stationing states to keep the regime alive. For Germans, they can be expected to highlight once again the general and specific burdens of playing host to Allied forces, and could generate a consensual, if tacit, understanding that Germany should no longer bear the brunt of the burdens and risks associated with troop stationing.

Until the mid-1990s, however, the current stationing pattern should not pose serious problems from the perspective of German society — at least, not the sort of problems that would lead to a loss of legitimacy for stationing. Indeed, the majority of cities and regions where Allied forces have been stationed are rather concerned about the impact of troop withdrawals on local economies and, most importantly, on the employment market. But once the withdrawal of former Soviet armed forces from Eastern Germany is complete, likely before the end of 1994, it is highly probable that the media will increasingly direct public attention towards questioning the rationale of the continued stationing of Allied forces in Germany. Since general elections in Germany will take place at the latest by December 1994, it is easy to forecast that stationing will become a topic in the election campaign. It can also be envisioned that proponents of the stationing regime will encounter substantial difficulties justifying the continued deployment of *European* armed forces in Germany, if a modification of the stationing pattern cannot be agreed upon. A continued American troop presence should be less difficult for Germans to accept, if only because the US did not 'singularize' Germany in the way the European stationing powers did. After all, the US has maintained a significant number of air, ground, and naval units, and other military installations in nearly all the European NATO member states.

Germany's security requirements can be expected, in the medium and long term, not to differ from those of its European NATO partners. Thus there seems to be no compelling reason why Germany alone should continue to carry a disproportionate burden, albeit a reduced one, of Allied stationing with all its various risks and responsibilities. As long as the NATO front line ran through Germany it *was* reasonable for the stationing states to argue that it would be much more advantageous to defend their national integrity, and Germany's, on the latter's soil rather than on their own. With the end of the cold war, this argument can no longer be made.

NATO's new emphasis on multinationalism and rapid reaction forces is a first important step toward modifying the previous stationing pattern, one that paves the way for a second step: the enhancement of a more thoroughly integrated Atlantic collective-defence system. The need to review the Allied stationing regime will become ever more urgent. From the German perspective, the principle of equality must be the conceptual foundation for a modified stationing regime. However, it is difficult to establish a unified European stationing pattern that would simultaneously be operationally effective and cost-efficient, and, most important, enjoy popular support among European publics. To be sure, it would be simplistic and probably counter-productive to insist that the principle of reciprocity be construed primarily in quantitative terms; not only would this be operationally feckless, it would also hardly be reasonable, given that the requirements of reciprocity could be fulfilled in a rather more symbolic fashion. Moreover, the numbers of troops envisaged by the mid-1990s will probably be even lower than current estimates indicate. Since NATO already announced a new force posture in May 1991 featuring predominantly multinational corps, it would not be too difficult to imagine a stationing pattern characterized by the deployment of multinational units along, and perhaps on either side of, the respective borders of participating states.

Some German units will become integrated elements in the planned multinational corps; they could be stationed to some extent, and for a certain period (or even permanently), on a rotational basis on the territory of other

European stationing countries. This would not represent a totally new departure, for the deployment of some German air, ground, and naval forces in all the stationing states has been a common feature in recent decades, admittedly for training purposes.

Such aspects of Alliance co-operation have not received much public attention. More emphasis on the exchange of army, air force, and naval units, as well as an exchange programme for individual soldiers to serve in the armed forces of an Ally, might be arranged in order to demonstrate the already established extent of mutual co-operation, something that has been a significant feature of the working partnership within the Alliance for some time.

For instance, basic flight training in both the United States and Britain dates back to the earliest years of the *Luftwaffe* and German naval aviation. Missile units of the army and the air force train in El Paso, Texas, and Fort Sill, Oklahoma. Low-level flying and air-defence practice has been undertaken at Goose Bay, Labrador; Decimomannu, Italy; and Beja, Portugal (although the Germans are leaving the latter). Missile and anti-aircraft units train at the NATO missile range at Souda on the island of Crete. As well, the *Luftwaffe* exercises basic military training for a considerable portion of its annually drafted conscripts in Budel, the Netherlands. German heavy armoured units have carried out large-scale firing exercises at the battalion level, initially in Mourmelan, France (1962) and later in Castlemartin, Wales, as well as at Shilo, Manitoba. Naval units have routinely trained at the Royal Naval Training Centre at Portland, England, and in the waters surrounding Scotland, as well as at Guantanamo, in Cuba. Missile-firing exercises take place on a regular basis in the Bay of Biscay and south of Toulon, France. Finally, units of the German armed forces participate in most of NATO's multinational exercises, and Germany has contributed on a permanent basis to NATO's multinational reaction forces.

The mutually beneficial aspects of this training co-operation could be extended to the domain of stationing, and could further enshrine those aspects of Alliance activity that might be more properly regarded as collective security instead of collective defence. To repeat: one of NATO's consequences, even if it has not been one of its stated missions, has been to constitute a reassurance mechanism for the Western Europeans, including the European Community.[24] The stationing of German armed forces on the territory of Allies would confirm that Germany had become and would remain fully recognized as a trustworthy and predictable security partner. The actual size of deployed German forces would be less relevant than their *symbolic* value. In addition to minimizing fears derived from history and reawakened, if only in part, by the recent experience with German unification, foreign stationing would impose a much greater responsibility on Germany itself, strengthening its post-war democratic traditions and dispelling any aspirations toward a dominating position among the European Allies.

A modification of the current stationing regime, along with the incipient reinforcement of the multinational norm, would enable more of the Alliance's members to participate in and benefit from the collective-security dimension of NATO. While there may be no apparent need to extend the sway of Alliance-based reassurance, the degree of co-operation, understanding, and, consequently, confidence and trust among those states that do participate in the Western stationing regime remains much higher than among those that remain apart.

There is no compelling reason why other European countries should maintain their foreign-stationed armed forces exclusively in Germany. For example, some of the remaining British ground forces on the continent might well be deployed in the Netherlands or in Belgium. Given recent attempts to create a stronger European defence identity, a modification and extension of the stationing regime could improve the reciprocal understanding of diverging security requirements, and at the same time strengthen the sense of equality among NATO members. Some institutional changes within the command structure of NATO would, of course, be required.

The American Commitment in Question

The future of the stationing regime depends in large measure on one condition: that Germany no longer be singled out as the one state that plays host to *European* armed forces. Although Germany might, over the short run, accept the stationing status quo, it is unlikely to do so over the long term. There is a prospect that the Social Democrats (SPD) could form the next government: it is worth recalling that this party opposed Germany's rearmament in the 1950s, and has more recently been critically assessing the rationale underlying the country's major security arrangements.

But Germany is only one of the major question marks regarding the longevity of the stationing regime. Also of extreme importance will be the future military role of the United States in Europe. The US military presence has, in effect, been the corner-stone of the stationing regime: both Canadian and European contributions towards Western defence have been predicated on an American military presence in the old continent. Thus Washington remains in a position to influence the degree to which Europe may be able to arrange its *own* defence requirements — even though the US military presence will be scaled down considerably. The emergent order of post-ideological politics in Europe will compel the United States to decide whether it wants to remain a viable player in European security affairs, and if so, how it should do this. The US has yet to debate its own place in the new Europe. So far, US declaratory policy in post-cold-war Europe has displayed remarkable consistency: Washington remains prepared, despite the changes in the strategic environment, to continue to guarantee its European Allies' security, and is apparently determined to exercise its leadership position within the Alliance as a whole, as if convinced that it alone must be 'bound to lead'.[25]

In the short term, although there will be a deepening of the domestic debate on the size of the US defence budget and hence on the scope of the US military presence in Europe, the risk of a complete withdrawal remains remote — notwithstanding the conviction of many analysts that America has declined, largely because of imperial, or hegemonial, overstretch.[26] For the Bush Administration, maintaining an American leadership role in European security remained essential to US interests, and this in turn required keeping a military presence in Europe. For all the rhetoric in support of a stronger European pillar within the Alliance, the US has tended to discourage all security-related initiatives that could, in the long run, erode the coherence of NATO and, as a result, challenge US leadership.[27] Illustratively, Washington maintained a position at the Vienna arms-control negotiations on Conventional Forces in Europe (which focused on manpower ceilings [CFE Ia]) that displayed a determination to preserve its operational manoeuverability in Europe. Suggested ceilings were so much higher than actual force levels on the spot that they have undermined the credibility of the negotiating approach, and raised concern among America's European Allies. Clearly, had the US taken the decision to pull out of Europe, such a negotiating stance would not be easily explicable.

The nuclear disarmament initiatives between the US and the former USSR following the failed coup will likely have an impact on the future size of the US military presence, which probably will not be much greater than 50,000 troops by the mid-1990s. The possibility of a complete withdrawal of Short Range Nuclear Forces (SNF), namely the airborne ones, cannot be excluded; if it comes to pass it will doubtless be a factor further reducing the size of US conventional forces in Europe. With the old threat vanished and a new one at best inchoate, Congress will surely question more closely the operational logic of stationing sizeable numbers of US military personnel (without adequate nuclear protection) in Europe. Congress may come to acknowledge the prospect that residual risks on the southern and eastern peripheries of Europe might serve as a substitute of sorts for the old threat. But US policy toward the Yugoslavian civil war indicates that neither Congress nor the Executive is hankering to concoct substitute threats.[28]

The prospect of a return to something like isolationism over the long term cannot be dismissed. Recent demographic trends suggest a continued drift of America away from Europe in the societal sense, and the apparently irresolvable fiscal crisis of the US leaves open the door to a similar drift in the politico-military domain. Although a total US disengagement from Europe is by no means foreordained, if Americans cannot understand why they should remain in Europe in coming years, it is unlikely that they will do so. It is sometimes argued that US troops will remain based in Europe if only so that they can avail themselves of their forward staging area to move into hot spots on the periphery, especially in the Middle East. One reading of the lessons of the Gulf War is that the US military would be very reluctant to give up the operational advantages of its military bases in Europe. This lesson, however, is dubious for two reasons. First, the European Allies, the Germans in particular, would hardly be amenable to hosting troops intended for a part of the world that Germany continues to regard as not of vital interest to it. Second, and more important, the US itself could not be expected to keep in place an expensive Europe-based tail whose sole justification was to service a Gulf-deployed tooth. Surely more economic forms of force projection could be conceived than to deploy soldiers *in* Europe who were not regarded as being militarily relevant *to* Europe.

Conclusion: Does Stationing Matter Anymore?

Since the inception of the current stationing regime, the Soviet military threat had been the most influential factor affecting its size, scope, and structure. But one need not leap to the conclusion that an obviously eliminated Soviet military danger must in turn undermine the very existence of that regime. To the contrary, the reduced significance of stationing's *military* rationale can be expected to highlight those rationales of the regime that had previously been either overlooked or simply overshadowed by the sheer urgency of the need to deter the Soviet Union. In reassessing the consequences of the stationing regime, one must go back to its origins in the years when West Germany joined NATO, and in so doing began to contribute to the defence of the West by building up its own armed forces and fully integrating them into the Alliance.

Those who have called for symmetrical reductions, and finally a complete withdrawal of US and other foreign armed forces from Germany — and there have been some in the West — apparently have failed to recognize that NATO was not established merely to deter the Soviet Union from extending its political and military influence across the former Iron Curtain; whatever the postulated *justification* for the Alliance may have been, it has had other functions. Quite apart from the felt need to provide a defence organization that could accommodate American involvement in European security in view of the nascent cold war, NATO established the basis for the military integration of the Federal Republic of Germany into the West. This integration, to be sure, was seen as a military necessity, especially by Washington, given that the Soviet war machine remained relatively intact after 1945, and Moscow's foreign-policy intentions were, at the very least, somewhat unpredictable in those early post-war years. Ways and means needed to be found to lessen the financial burden carried by the former Western occupying powers, all of whom eventually came to recognize that the exposure of West Germany to Soviet influence would constitute a serious threat to their own national security.

The establishment of the Allied stationing regime in West Germany, with active German support, was also intended to reassure the country's European neighbours that it would not succumb again to the temptations of a militarized foreign policy. Thus Bonn's rearmament programme was circumscribed by the Western European Union, whose intent was to serve as an early warning system in the event that things went wrong again with German foreign policy.

However, the objective need for reassurance by stationing forces in Germany — that is, the need to contain Germany — has clearly lost applicability in recent decades, notwithstanding the alarums and excursions in some Western European capitals over the unexpectedly rapid pace of unification, or the ensuing spate of neo-Nazi thuggery. Few have been prepared to argue explicitly that continued stationing is justified by a need to keep tabs on Germany.[29] Germany's foreign-policy record would suggest the opposite. The reduction of the combined armed forces of the *Bundeswehr* and the former *Nationale Volksarmee* to 370,000 by the mid-1990s; the country's long-standing commitment to the Non-Proliferation Treaty; and its equally noteworthy restatement of Konrad Adenauer's undertaking not to produce or acquire nuclear, biological, or chemical weapons (in Article 3 of the 'Final Settlement with Respect to Germany') are just a few indications of the country's intention to remain a trustworthy, reliable, and predictable ally within both Europe and the Alliance.[30] Yet there is probably no way Germany can ever totally dispel perceptions associated with dreadful historical experiences. Thus the preservation of arrangements that counter and limit these perceptions — even if the perceptions are without *current* empirical basis — seems to make sense, at least as long as they do not openly singularize one member of the Alliance.[31]

From a pragmatic point of view, there is value in retaining a (modified) stationing regime, one that preserves the psychological advantages associated with states' continuing to work closely together in such a sensitive area of high politics. The aspect of *reassurance* is in no way diminished even though the actual size of the stationed forces shrinks, for the good reason that the latter are not really militarily so important any longer, in the absence of a precise military threat. They do, however, have significant political value, which tends to be overlooked by those who do not take historical experiences into account when thinking about the stationing regime. Why should reassurance continue to matter in Western Europe?

First, Germany's unification did come as a surprise to its neighbours. Many political and media commentators clearly felt uneasy with a less constrained (at least from the juridical standpoint) and united Germany. Admittedly, the impact of unification on German foreign policy remains difficult if not impossible to establish at this early moment, all the more so because Germany's understanding of its status and role in Europe has simply not altered in a way that would allow anyone to argue that a united Germany must become a new source of instability in the heart of Europe. Bonn's keen interest in preserving the continuity of the stationing regime stems in part from a desire to dispel the fears of its neighbours; it also stems from a wish to maintain the security arrangements that guaranteed Germany's political, economic, and even moral recovery after World War II, and its territorial integrity during the cold war.

Second, it remains to be seen whether the European Community, the Western European Union, the Conference on Security and Cooperation in Europe (CSCE), or any newly established European Security Council will be able to provide Europe with a military capability that could generate the same degree of reassurance for Germany and its neighbours as has NATO and its stationing regime.

What would happen if the stationing regime were to collapse as a result of a complete withdrawal of US forces from Europe? It is possible that nothing of great moment would result. If the optimists are correct, Europe has by now learned its lessons, and can be counted upon to sort out its own security affairs without outside tutelage. Indeed, it could well develop that the new Franco-German 'Euro-Corps' might serve as an effective replacement for the NATO-generated stationing regime.

But the optimists may not be correct. Should the US unilaterally pull its forces out of Germany, it would be doubtful whether the other stationing states, France aside, would continue their own conventional commitments towards the remaining Alliance. While it might be argued that the American withdrawal would trigger a new impetus towards enhanced security co-operation (or even integration) among the European stationing states, and possibly among all the European NATO members, the odds are against this. European countries would have to demonstrate the political will to permit significant transfers of sovereignty in the sensitive area of defence to viable security institutions, unless of course it can be assumed that a harmony of interests would keep their age-old security dilemma in check. But where is the evidence to lead one to imagine that a Europe that cannot even agree to shed farm subsidies can, somehow, design a mechanism for achieving genuine security co-operation?

It is at least as likely, possibly more likely, that a US withdrawal would set in train the gradual disintegration of the military co-operation that has been so characteristic of the relationships among most, if not all, the European stationing states. One consequence of the collapse of the stationing regime could easily be a heightened tendency on the part of important states to rely on their own devices to ensure security. Ultimately, one might expect to witness the renationalization of European defence policy, with all that this would imply for the very continuation of the European Community.

Innocuous though it may sound, it is necessary to be clear on what renationalization implies. At the very least, it would remove the trust and confidence built up in the long years of close and intensive co-operation under the NATO aegis, and contribute to a profound reversal of the ongoing efforts to increase the level and degree of confidence-building measures among the CSCE members. A renationalization of European defence policies might also end any number of arms-control and disarmament initiatives, since the states involved could scarcely be expected to let down their guard before threats whose magnitude would become much harder to assess. In this regard, the experience of the former Soviet republics engaged in a madcap dash to renationalize defence might be instructive; one thinks in particular of Ukraine's determination to field the second largest army in all of Europe.[32]

No one can see into the future. Perhaps the spectre of renationalized European defences is exceedingly alarmist. Still, the case for *not* discarding the stationing regime is a strong one. Even with the complete demise of the Soviet Union, it should not be imagined that the need for reassurance will become obsolete. Surely security co-operation in Western Europe can and should remain an end in itself, and not be allowed to become precariously dependent upon the existence of a once clearly identifiable, but now evanescent, adversary. The central question, which no one can answer now, is whether America's troops constitute an irreplaceable, or merely a convenient, element of the European stationing regime.

Notes

[1]John J. Mearsheimer, 'Back to the Future: Instability in Europe After the Cold War', *International Security* 15 (Summer 1990), 5-56; idem, 'Why We Will Soon Miss the Cold War', *Atlantic Monthly* (Aug. 1990), 35-50; John Lewis Gaddis, 'The Long Peace: Elements of Stability in the Postwar International System', *International Security* 10 (Spring 1986), 99-142.

[2]Jean-Baptiste Duroselle, 'Western Europe and the Impossible War', *Journal of International Affairs* 41 (Summer 1988), 345-61.

[3]Stephen Van Evera, 'Primed for Peace: Europe After the Cold War', *International Security* 15 (Winter 1990-91), 7-57.

[4]*The Military Balance, 1990-1991* (London: International Institute for Strategic Studies/Brassey's, 1990).

[5]In choosing to refer to the stationing 'regime', we do not necessarily intend to claim that the Allied troops deployed in Germany have constituted what many contemporary theorists of international relations — particularly of international political economy — term a regime. On the other hand, we do see some affinity between the principles, norms, rules, and processes of Allied stationing and the IPE notion of regimes, namely as intervening variables with a certain capacity to condition outcomes in international politics. Frankly, we believe more research needs to be done on the topic before 'regime' can be used here other than as a loose synonym for pattern. For a discussion of the more ambitious usage of 'regime', see Stephen D. Krasner, ed., *International Regimes* (Ithaca, NY: Cornell Univ. Press, 1983); Robert O. Keohane, *After Hegemony: Cooperation and Discord in the World Political Economy* (Princeton: Princeton Univ. Press, 1984); and James F. Keeley, 'The Latest Wave: A Critical Review of Regime Literature', in David G. Haglund and Michael K. Hawes, eds, *World Politics: Power, Interdependence & Dependence*, (Toronto: Harcourt Brace Jovanovich, 1990), 553-69.

[6]Mearsheimer, 'Back to the Future', 44-7.

[7]The Kantian vision of a Europe structurally at peace with itself has attracted supporters from a variety of perspectives. As examples, see policy statements of the German Social Democratic party (SPD), and the controversial article by Francis Fukuyama, 'The End of History?' *National Interest* 16 (Summer 1989), 3-18.

[8]Helga Haftendorn, 'Foreign Troops in a Changing Europe and Germany: A Structural View', in David G. Haglund and Olaf Mager, eds, *Homeward Bound? Allied Forces in the New Germany* (Boulder, CO: Westview, 1992), 19-40.

[9]These legal arrangements are thoroughly detailed in ibid.

[10]See Marshall Brement, 'U.S.-U.S.S.R.: Possibilities in Partnership', *Foreign Policy* 84 (Fall 1991), 107-24; and Fred Charles Iklé, 'Comrades in Arms: The Case for a Russian-American Defense Community', *National Interest* 26 (Winter 1991-92), 22-32.

[11]Joseph Fitchett, 'NATO Must Prepare to Open Membership to the East, U.S. Says', *International Herald Tribune* (8 Nov. 1991), 1, 4.

[12]Michel Fortmann, 'NATO Defense Planning in a Post-CFE Environment: Assessing the Alliance Strategy Review (1990-1991)', in *Homeward Bound?*, 41-62.

[13]'Bush Announces Major Nuclear Arms Initiatives', US Embassy (Ottawa), *Text* (30 Sept. 1991); Michael Gordon, 'Trust Without Verifying', *New York Times* (29 Sept. 1991), 1.

[14]'You Can't Go Home', *Economist* (28 Sept. 1991), 15-16.

[15]Wolfram F. Hanrieder, *Germany, America, Europe: Forty Years of German Foreign Policy* (New Haven: Yale Univ. Press, 1989).

[16]Richard Nixon, 'We Are Ignoring Our World Role', *Time* (16 March 1992), 72.

[17]See Government of Canada, Department of National Defence, *Canadian Defence Policy* (Ottawa, April 1992), 8-9; and 'Statement of the Honourable Marcel Masse, Member of Parliament for Frontenac and Minister of National Defence at the National Press Theatre' (Ottawa: Department of National Defence, 17 Sept. 1991).

[18]Olaf Mager, 'The Continental Commitment: Britain's Forces in Germany', in *Homeward Bound?*, 179.

[19]Jacques Isnard, 'Près de la moitié des 46,000 militaires français stationnés en Allemagne rentreront en France avant deux ans', *Le Monde* (20 Sept. 1990), 1.

[20]William Drozdiak, 'Bonn and Paris to Deploy Euro-Corps by 1995', *International Herald Tribune* (23-4 May 1992), 1, 4; 'Qu'est-ce qu'on fait? Ich weiss nicht', *Economist* (23 May 1992), 51-2.

[21]Luc De Vos, 'The Scutum Belgarum: The 1 (BE) Corps in Germany, 1945-1991', in *Homeward Bound?*, 199-212.

[22]Dutch Ministry of Defence, *Defensienota 1991* (The Hague, 1991), 21.

[23]Karl-Heinz Bender, 'Die französischen Truppen in Deutschland: überlegungen

zus Frage ihres Abzugs', *Dokumente* 47 (June 1991), 196–8; Jean-Paul Picaper, 'Bonn veut conserver des forces armées occidentales', *Figaro* (6 Sept. 1991).

[24]See Josef Joffe, *The Limited Partnership: Europe, the United States, and the Burdens of Alliance* (Cambridge, MA: Ballinger, 1987), chap. 5: 'Conclusion: Alliance as Order'; and Uwe Nerlich, 'Western Europe's Relations with the United States', *Daedalus* 108 (Winter 1979), 87–111.

[25]For insight into the advocacy for a continued US managerial role, see Joseph S. Nye, *Bound to Lead: The Changing Nature of American Power* (New York: Basic, 1990). For US declaratory policy, see 'U.S. Security Tied to All States of Europe', *Text*, US Embassy, Ottawa (2 April 1992), 1.

[26]This is the thesis of Paul Kennedy's widely debated *The Rise and Fall of the Great Powers: Economic Change and Military Conflict from 1500 to 2000* (New York: Vintage, 1987). It has been restated more recently by Alan Tonelson and Ronald A. Morse, 'Outdated Alliance Strategies', in Clyde V. Prestowitz, Jr, Ronald A. Morse, and Alan Tonelson, eds, *Powernomics: Economics and Strategy After the Cold War* (Lanham, MD: Madison, 1991), 241–56.

[27]Alan Riding, 'U.S., Wary of European Corps, Seeks Assurance on NATO Role', *New York Times* (20 Oct. 1991), 20; 'Return Fire', *Economist* (19 Oct. 1991) 54.

[28]Anthony Lewis, 'Yugoslavia: A Curious U.S. Silence', *International Herald Tribune* (5 Nov. 1991), 4; Jenonne Walker, 'The Wordy West Fiddles While Ex-Yugoslavia Burns', ibid. (21 May 1992), 8.

[29]One official who did so argue is General Robert C. Oaks, commander of US air forces in Europe, who told a *Washington Post* reporter that Germans needed a US military presence to keep them in line. The Supreme Allied Commander in Europe John Galvin was not amused by this comment. See 'Galvin Rebukes a U.S. General Over Interview', *International Herald Tribune* (22 Oct. 1991), 2; and Barton Gellman, 'U.S. Commanders See New Challenge: Slowing Retreat From Europe', *Washington Post* (15 Oct. 1991), A16.

[30]German policy toward the non-proliferation regime is discussed in Wolfgang Kütter and Harald Müller, 'Germany, Europe & Nuclear Non-Proliferation', *PPNN Study* 1 (Southampton, UK: Programme for Promoting Nuclear Non-Proliferation, 1991).

[31]This reassurance logic is deftly treated in Elizabeth Pond, *After the Wall: American Policy Toward Germany* (New York: Priority, 1990), 43; and Barry Buzan et al., *The European Security Order Recast: Scenarios for the Post-Cold-War Era* (London: Pinter, 1990), 238.

[32]Fred Hiatt, 'Nuclear Tug-of-War: Ukraine's Eager Defiance', *International Herald Tribune* (24 Oct. 1991), 1; Serge Schmemann, 'In Earnest, Ukraine Tackles Statehood', ibid. (31 Oct. 1991), 2.

chapter fourteen

The Seven-Power Summit as a New Security Institution

John Kirton

Introduction

In the past two decades, one of the more significant developments in world politics has been the emergence of a new system of international institutions centred around the annual summit of the world's seven largest industrial democracies and the European Community. This summit system was created in 1975 as the major Western powers, following the failure of the existing United Nations and Atlantic organizations, searched for an effective institution to manage a concentrated succession of severe threats to the existing international order. Some of these threats came in the economic domain, in the areas of exchange rates and macro-economic policy (with the collapse of the Bretton Woods regime in August 1971), multilateral trade (with the stalling of the Tokyo Round of Multilateral Trade Negotiations launched in 1973), and energy and North-South relations (following the OAPEC oil embargo of October 1973).[1] Others came equally in the political realm, in the areas of democratic governance (with the spread of Eurocommunism in Italy, Portugal, and Spain in the mid-1970s), nuclear proliferation (with the Indian nuclear explosion in 1974), and regional and/or global security (with the ultimate American defeat in Vietnam in April 1975).[2] This comprehensive assault on the existing international order created for all major industrial democracies the new domestic challenges of 'stagflation' in the economic sphere and a larger 'crisis of governability' in the political realm.

From its visibly modest beginning as a low-key, one-time event in November 1975, the summit quickly acquired a highly institutionalized character, even if it was not organizationally entrenched. During its second seven-year cycle, beginning in 1982, it spawned an ever growing network of subordinate ministerial-level institutions in the fields of trade, foreign policy, and finance, and official-level bodies in these and other subject fields. From its debut as an overtly economic summit, focused on the central ongoing issues of macro-economic policy co-ordination, trade, and North-South relations, it moved to address openly major global issues in the micro-economic, political, and security realms, with a particular emphasis on the new issues on the international security agenda. With its growing institutional depth and policy breadth, the summit soon became an increasingly efficacious forum for setting agendas, arriving at agreements, implementing activities, and adjusting the practices of constituent and outside national governments and international organizations.

In acquiring this important role in shaping global order, the seven-power summit system converged with, complemented, and competed with an impressive array of older, organizationally grounded international institutional systems. The oldest and most entrenched was the United Nations family of institutions created from 1945 onward, with the Security Council at its core, the General Assembly beneath it, and the Bretton Woods and other specialized agencies arrayed around. The second major system was the Atlantic family of institutions started in 1949 and centred upon the North Atlantic Treaty Organization, the Organization for Economic Cooperation and Development, and such separate functional agencies as Intelsat and the International Energy Agency.[3]

Explaining the Summit's Success

In searching for relevance and a role within this dense pre-existing network of institutional collaborators and competitors, the nascent seven-power summit system was devoid of the standard array of assets possessed by international organizations: formal charters embedded in intergovernmental agreements, routine calls on significant national budgetary allocations, and a vast, dedicated international bureaucracy with a fixed secretariat and established support networks within the polities of its member states. What, then, accounts for the ability of the seven-power summit system to flourish for nearly two decades in an international institutional landscape dominated by much more venerable and apparently powerful galaxies of international institutions? Most scholars addressing this question have acknowledged the substantial and increasingly effective role the summit has played in managing international order. They have, however, offered a variety of conflicting explanations for the summit's effectiveness.

Despite the continuing scepticism of journalists, there is a consensus among scholarly observers on the performance of the summit as an international institution. The first generation of reflections on the summit, inspired primarily by the desultory record of the first half of the 1980s, converged on the view that the summit's ability to produce meaningful international policy co-ordination was at worst 'episodic' and 'random', and at best 'very mixed' or highly variable, with the meetings of the 1980s less successful than those of the 1970s.[4] While the summit system, in its seminal economic functions, was useful as an instrument of co-operation, it remained fragile as an instrument of co-ordination, and could be credited only with preventing the global economic situation from becoming worse than it did.[5] As a political institution for the overall management, or governance, of the international system, it posed no threat to the communist East or developing South, or to the existing network of international institutions. Only an increased level of institutionalization in the summit would 'reduce the effectiveness of, and the interest in, such bodies as the OECD or the IMF or others (even the Atlantic Alliance if political and strategic matters are increasingly dealt with)'.[6]

More recent studies, focusing on the experience of the later 1980s and early 1990s, have assigned the summit system a far more potent role. In its core economic functions of exchange-rate management and macro-economic policy co-ordination, analysts have conceded its ability to have a substantial impact on markets in ways both unfavourable and beneficial.[7] Those sensitive to the concerns of the South have asserted that the 'recent past has witnessed a major erosion of the authority of the multilateral institutions charged with the governance of the world economy' as 'key decisions, whether on the debt problem, the setting of international exchange rates or global macroeconomic policy coordination, are taken within a limited group of developed countries, the inner core of which consists of the G-5/G-7 countries.'[8] Most recently, it has been argued that the 'G-7-1/2' (i.e., the G-7 with partial Russian participation) has become the central forum for the overall political management of the post-cold-war era as 'neither the U.N. Security Council, NATO, nor the Conference on Security and Cooperation in Europe (CSCE) can offer similar scope in terms of including the key players, though they and other organizations will continue to play important roles in certain issues'.[9]

Beneath this evolving and still-contested consensus about the summit's enhanced effectiveness, deep disagreements remain as to the causes of its success and the proper route to achieving improved performance. Those highlighting structural factors suggest that summit success reflects the need of the US for strong support from one other key country; or the need for the big three (the US, Germany, and Japan) to act jointly to ensure macro-economic co-ordination; or the ability of five major powers (the G-5) to dominate the world economy; or the need to replace the leadership of a declining US with that of a collectivity of principal countries, including notably Japan.[10] Those emphasizing the institutional characteristics of the summit argue both that the flexibility of the heads to set their agenda and their freedom from bureaucratic constraints in arriving at agreements are responsible for the forum's effectiveness, and, conversely, that this very informality, independence of major multilateral economic institutions, and lack of ongoing organizational support prevent the summit from achieving reliable policy co-ordination.[11]

Others offer explanations based on interdependence, suggesting that the new economic interdependence in the world economy in the 1970s, and political interdependence in the 1980s, required better mechanisms for collective management than the existing international institutions provided, especially at times of slowdown in the world economy, or when policy failures prompted dominant ideas to be replaced by economic ideologies focused on shared interests.[12] Finally, those favouring explanations grounded in domestic politics point to the willingness of the United States to lead, and the domestic bargaining and coalition-building that permit it to do so; national political pressures for strong personal forms of leadership; and the personalities of the leaders themselves.[13]

Building upon earlier analyses of the summit system's rising effectiveness as the central institution for managing world order, this chapter examines the reasons for the summit's predominance and assesses the institution's record to date.[14] It suggests that, in relation to the institutional galaxies of the alternative United Nations and Atlantic systems, the summit system has the advantage of a newly minted modernity that allows it to assemble the powers and address the policy areas that predominate in the world of the 1970s and onward, as opposed to those of the 1940s. More specifically, it argues that the system was created with, and has increasingly developed, a set of structural and institutional characteristics — those of an embryonic international concert — that permit it to play a dynamic role as the leading international forum for shaping international order in general, and addressing the new global security agenda in particular.

The Concert Principle

Four characteristics of the concert principle embodied in the summit institution are of decisive importance. The first is concentrated power: the overall capability represented in a group whose members collectively possess over half the world's GNP and other critical resources ensures that national governments and other international organizations will look to this group for authoritative action, and adjust to its agreements. The second is constricted participation: the small size of the body reduces potential veto points, lowers transaction costs, and increases transparency, thus making it more likely that its members will arrive at timely and meaningful agreements. The third is the common purpose among its members, whose shared attributes and values as major industrial, democratic powers make it more likely that similar problems and perspectives will be focused upon, and that strong agreements will be reached. The fourth is its character as a politically controlled rather than organizationally confined body: its direction by heads of state and government and its freedom from intergovernmental bureaucracy give it a unique flexibility to address, define, and legitimize emerging issues on the global security agenda, and to act on them in ways that individuals in the member governments find more difficult to resist. This unique combination of concentrated power, constricted participation, common purpose, and political control endows the seven-power summit system with an unusually high centrality and effectiveness in defining, addressing, and managing the new global security challenges.

As the seven-power summit system has increasingly acquired these characteristics of a concert, it has developed correspondingly greater institutional depth, policy breadth, and authoritative reach. This progression can be seen in the three phases through which the summit has passed. During its first phase, from 1975 to 1981, the summit served primarily to reinforce the existing international institutions under assault from new shocks, and confined its efforts towards the creation of an institutionalized world order to new issues on the economic and security agendas. During the second phase, from 1982 to 1988, it grew to rival the existing international institutions as the primary source of political direction for an expanding array of economic and security issues, both old and new. And during the third cycle, from 1989 to the present, it has moved to replace the existing international institutional systems as the leading source of governance of a new international order. This leadership has been particularly evident in regard to those 'new' international security issues that the older international institutional systems are not flexible enough to handle.

To explore this progression, this chapter first defines the international security agenda in a way that distinguishes between old, new, and emerging security issues. It goes on to identify the four central criteria for an international concert, indicate how the summit system meets these criteria in ways that the United Nations and Atlantic systems do not, and examines how these features enhance the summit's effectiveness. The chapter then reviews the summit's development as an international institution, to demonstrate its increasing institutional desire and capacity to undertake this broad leadership role, and follows with an examination of the summit's expanding security agenda, to demonstrate how far its ambitions have reached into the security domain. Finally, it outlines the summit's agenda-, agreement-, action-, and adjustment-setting functions, and explores in a preliminary way how effective the summit system has become in reliably determining the shape of the new security order.

The International Security Agenda

Since the end of the new cold war of the early 1980s, and the ensuing disintegration of Soviet power and settlement of several Third World conflicts, it has become fashionable for practitioners and analysts of international politics to turn their attention to a host of non-traditional subjects under the rubric of the new international security agenda. This tendency to label as a new security threat every fashionably discomforting feature of world politics, beyond the familiar cold-war conflict in its East-West axis and North-South extension, is understandable. However, to assess the ability of alternative international institutional arrangements to manage the international security order in the post-cold-war — or, more accurately, post-World War II era — requires a more disciplined conception of which of the multitude of new issues are genuine security threats.

This analysis thus divides the security agenda of post-1945 international politics into the three broad categories of old, new, and emerging security threats. In all cases a security threat consists, by definition, of any directly death-causing physical penetration from abroad against which national governments can provide protection. The distinctions between old, new, and emerging varieties of security threats are based on the four dimensions in which a process in international politics may constitute a clear internationally originating threat to the security of citizens within a nation-state: the directness with which death is inflicted, on a widespread basis, on citizens within a polity; the physical nature of the death-causing agent; the transborder penetration of such physical objects; and the ability of the national government to protect its citizenry from these physically penetrating objects from abroad.

In the case of the old or traditional security threats, these dimensions had a distinctly military cast. Citizens' lives were disrupted and taken by the direct application of armed force on the part of the military services of a foreign government intruding into their territory, or that of an ally. The home government responded with military force, either through border measures (against invasion or incursion) or through action abroad, including multilateral policy co-ordination (such as forming and contributing to alliances and despatching troops to distant theatres). In short, nationally organized armed forces served as the primary instruments and institutions of both the transborder threat and the national protection against it.

In contrast, the new security threats have an overwhelmingly non-military character, in that armed force plays a minimal role. Although transborder intrusions of this kind do directly cause widespread death, they often do so in an incremental and invisible way that distinguishes them from invasions. Second, the physical agents of the new security threats range from terrorist bombs to toxic wastes and atmospheric chemical reactions to drugs and viruses. Third, their transborder trajectories are often unplotted: the originators neither know nor care who gets killed. Finally, they do not arise from specific sources abroad (known enemy countries) that can be directly countered, but have multiple, often-changing, global origins, which means that they can flow from anywhere to anywhere, and be far more difficult to defend against.

Emerging security threats share with new ones the non-military character of their physical agents and their unknown, unintended transborder trajecto-ries. They differ, however, in the nature of their impact in the recipient country, and their origins in the initiating locations outside. Although emerging secu-rity issues may in the future represent large, direct death-causing threats (and are for that reason worrisome in the present), they currently constitute a threat not to human life itself, but to other national values (e.g., economic prosperity, international competitiveness, plant and animal life, historic social and linguis-tic balances). Second, efforts to protect against them can be, and often are, directed against the particular locations from which they emanate; these may include attempts to alter conditions within the originating societies to prevent their transborder export. The deathly threat is thus both indirect (logically and temporally) and distant (spatially).

Using these distinctions, the issues most central to the post–1945 security arena can be categorized as follows. The old security agenda has at its core the East-West conflict (including armed defence, non-military sanctions, arms control, and other confidence-building and conflict-resolution measures). It includes regional security issues, whether or not those are linked to the East-West cleavage, involving the actual or threatened use of armed force. It also embraces, on both the East-West and North-South axes, the issues of hori-zontal arms proliferation (including nuclear, missile, chemical, biological, and dual-use technological measures, and recent efforts to control relative military capabilities through linkage of international development assistance to national defence spending).

The new security agenda as defined above includes four central threats. The first and most familiar is terrorism (including air hijacking and diplo-matic hostage-taking), with the novelty of these venerable threats coming from the instruments and agents used. The second is the transborder trans-port of several items on the global environmental agenda, notably hazardous waste, chlorofluorocarbons, and other substances directly causing human death (but arguably still excluding carbon dioxide). The third is the interna-tional flow of addictive and death-causing narcotics. And the fourth is the international transmission of diseases such as AIDS.

The emerging security agenda consists of a long list of potential concerns. For example, among the 'transborder physical penetrations' that may, but do not yet directly, cause death to home-country citizens are refugees and migrants. Efforts to prevent such potentially threatening flows by altering conditions in the originating country include such agenda items as demo-cratic governance, human rights, and various assistance programmes (targe-ted to both East and South) aimed at alleviating international conflict causing poverty, disease, and death.

The Summit as an International Concert: Implications for Effectiveness

Management of the security agenda—old, new, and emerging—has long been the business of the major institutional systems for governing world politics, notably the broadly universal United Nations, the multilateral Atlantic family of institutions (occasionally with its minority of extra-regional members), and, more recently, the plurilateral summit system of the seven major industrial democracies and the European Community. These three institutional systems differ not only in the number and geographic reach of the members they embrace, but, equally important, in the historic principles of international organization that they each — in improved modern versions — represent. Thus the United Nations embodies the collective-security principle manifest in the League of Nations; the Atlantic family, the collective-defence principle at the core of the dual-entente and triple-alliance systems of the early 1900s; and the seven-power summit system, the concert principle embedded in the Concert of Europe that, for at least half a century following its creation in 1818, prevented general war in the global (if Euro-centric) system.[15]

It is the summit system's character as a contemporary international concert that has given it an increasingly central role in the efficacious management of the international security order.[16] This process has unfolded with growing force, as shifts in relative capability among the major powers since 1975 have increasingly made a concert system the most effective means for shaping international order, and have increasingly concentrated capability within the particular powers represented in the summit. More specifically, the latter's increasing centrality has flowed from its four particular characteristics as a concert system: (1) its concentration of power; (2) its compression of participation; (3) its commonality of purpose; and (4) its political control by heads of state and government.

The first and most fundamental of these features is the structural concentration of power. In comparing the performances of the UN, Atlantic, and summit systems on this criterion, it is important to note that each of the three systems, new and old, is in practice dominated by an inner group, or directorate, of leading countries. In the case of the UN system, this group is formally established, consisting of the five permanent members of the Security Council with individual veto power: the US, the UK, France, Russia, and China. In the case of the Atlantic system, it is the 'Berlin Dinner' four: the US, the UK, France, and Germany. For the summit system it is the seven major powers (the full membership except for the European Community, which claims and is accorded little competence in the security field): the US, the UK, France, Germany, Japan, Italy, and Canada.

Assuming that the international security order is most effectively guaranteed by a group representing the maximum and at least over fifty per cent of capability in the international system, the effects of these variations in management membership are clear. While all three international institutional systems share the same common core of the US, Britain, and France, the UN system uniquely adds the capability of the USSR (since 1992, Russia) and, since the 1970s, the People's Republic of China. NATO adds the capability of Germany. The seven-power summit adds the capabilities of Japan, Germany,

Italy, and Canada. In 1975, at the inception of the summit, it was clear that the United Nations had a significant advantage in security-relevant capability, given the post-Vietnam, pre-Afghanistan relative strength of the USSR, the recent addition of the real China, the absence of East Germany from NATO and the summit, and the absence of Canada from the summit. By 1992, however, the balance-of-capability advantage had shifted strongly to the summit, with the disappearance of the USSR and its replacement by a much weaker Russia, the post-Tiananmen isolation of China, the unification of Germany, and the rapid relative-capability growth of Germany, Italy (which overtook Britain in GNP), Canada, and, above all, Japan.[17]

Although the Russia-China combination still wields superior capabilities to those of the Germany-Italy-Canada-Japan combination in some areas of the traditional security agenda (notably, in-place deliverable nuclear weapons, and size if not projectability of standing armies), the latter combination represents vastly superior capability both overall and in the specialized areas most relevant to the new security agenda of the 1990s. This advantage will only increase if and as Russia continues to associate itself with the summit, and as its relative capability declines. It will be eroded only in the unlikely event that reform of the Security Council brings Japan, Germany, and possibly Italy (perhaps in the name of a European Community seat) onto that body as permanent veto powers, or if Russia and Japan associate themselves with NATO.

This concentration of power has several effects on the capacities of the institution in which it is embedded. First, that institution's preponderance of power helps ensure the effective implementation of any agreements throughout the international system as a whole (both by mobilizing the resources and by ensuring policy adjustments on the part of actors required to realize them). Second, it reduces the probability that any major powers will be left outside, and discourages those that are from developing a rival institutional system of remotely comparable capability and influence. Third, its preponderance of power induces members and outsiders alike to bring their agenda items and appeals to the institution itself, in the knowledge that this is the locus of the resources required to deal with them.

The second fundamental structural feature of the summit as concert is the compression of its core participants. The deployment of overall capability, however overwhelming, by international management groups depends critically on their ability to mobilize for timely and decisive action. Such mobilization is relatively easy in a group in which a single country, or smaller group of countries, has sufficiently superior capabilities to dominate. In a unit-veto system (which the Security Council always was, and which NATO and the summit have become), this mobilization depends in part on the reduction of potential veto points through the compression of participation to the lowest possible number of participants.

Here NATO with four and the UN with five have a narrow advantage over the summit's seven members. Such an advantage would assume significance should the additional capability represented by Japan, Italy, and Canada be more than offset by the net effect that these participants have in delaying or preventing summit action and consensus. It would assume further significance should the United Nations, or NATO, be more able than the summit to mobilize the reserve capability from the larger membership within the institutional system. Here the summit—with only one additional participant to mobilize to secure the capability of the full European Community—has a decisive advantage over NATO, which requires eleven additional participants to secure a broadly equal capability increment. It has a similar advantage over the UN where, among both the non-permanent Security Council members and the full membership, the number of additional participants outweighs the aggregate capability they bring.

The compression of participants (particularly through the 'major powers only' principle, which generates effective equality among them) increases institutional effectiveness in several ways. By reducing potential veto points and transaction costs, it enhances the prospect of arriving at agreements. Moreover, by reducing the obstacles to transparency, it increases the prospect that these agreements will be followed by agreed-to and appropriate action. Finally, the effective equality and collective predominance of the group's members increase the probability that each major member (including the most powerful, the US), as well as outside countries and international organizations, will adjust in ways that the agreements specify.

The third fundamental feature of the summit as concert is the common purpose of its members. At a minimum, the common characteristic of participants as major powers gives the concert a shared interest in preserving the existing order (which has enabled them to become or remain major powers) from new shocks. More ambitiously, the shared character of summit members as developed, capitalist, industrial, and open economies generates a common set of concerns, experiences, and interdependencies with the other members. Most ambitiously, their shared character as democracies, each with an open, multiparty electoral system that causes heads of state and government, and at some time governing parties, to change, generates a shared set of political values that extends this commonality into the security realm.

The transformation of the mobilizable capability that flows from concentrated power and constricted participation into actually mobilized capability depends on the likelihood that the participants, even with minimal veto points and transaction costs, will find common cause in setting an agenda, arriving at agreements, taking action, and adjusting to the consensus. Here the summit has two decisive advantages over its UN and NATO counterparts in going beyond the conservatively oriented minimum order represented by the maintenance of the status quo. These additional advantages are of particular importance at times when a rapid change in relative capability across, and alignment processes among, the major powers generates a need to revise or even transform the existing order.

In the economic domain, the uniformly high level of development and particularly the industrialized (rather than resource-based) character of all summit participants stands in sharp contrast to the ranges represented in both NATO (with Turkey) and the United Nations Security Council (with China). In the political domain, the uniformly democratic character of the summit's participants (all of whom have multiparty systems and open elections) stands in even starker contrast to the historic full NATO (with Portugal and Turkey), and the United Nations Security Council (with a still unrepentently communist and authoritarian China). Only in very specialized traditional security fields do common national attributes give the advantage to the UN Security Council (all of whose members, for example, have autonomous nuclear weapons, and are the world's major arms exporters). Moreover, because the summit's dominant members have often been of a similar political colouration (the liberal majorities of the 1970s and conservative majorities of the 1980s, with France as the counter-cyclical power throughout), they have found it even easier to agree on a common programme than have the summit's competitors (where the Anglo-American versus French party-in-power polarization lacks the common swing coalition of Germany and Canada to provide a clear majoritarian philosophy).

The effects of such multilayered commonality are clear. They make it much more likely that the summit will be able to agree on a common agenda, reach substantive agreement, and implement appropriate action. Such tendencies should be most pronounced on issues related to the core commonalities of large capitalist, industrialized, open economies, and democratic polities.

The fourth feature of the summit as concert is its political control by heads of state and government. To transform mobilized preponderant capability into flexibly focused capability well tailored to meet the new challenges of the international system requires that international institutions be directed at the highest political level. It is here that the summit has its most decisive advantage. As formal international organizations, both the United Nations and the Atlantic system are confined by the functions and geographic domains specified in their founding charters, articles of agreement, or treaties. They are managed by officials and only occasionally by portfolio ministers. And they are largely dependent upon the resources available in their organizational budgets, staffs, headquarter organizations, and standard operating procedures. In contrast, the summit, as an informal international institution, is free to take up any subject its members can collectively agree upon. Because it is managed on an ongoing basis by heads of state and government, either directly or through personal representatives, rather than by subordinate ministers with functionally confined portfolios, its deliberations and decisions are not limited by the need to seek higher political approval (vertically) or the need to harmonize with other individuals responsible for related issue areas (horizontally). And precisely because the summit is directly controlled at the highest political level, with no international organizational capacity of its own, it can and must draw upon the full resources of its constituent national bureaucracies for preparation and implementation.

Over the years there has been some movement on the part of the United Nations and Atlantic systems to adopt the features and thus acquire the advantages of an institution controlled at the highest political level. However, these efforts have been for the most part recent, and they remain limited. The United Nations Security Council is not a body that meets at the level of head of state and government. Nor do the results of its first-ever summit, in January 1992, suggest it will do so regularly in the future. Moreover, despite some recent seven-power-summit-inspired shifts (such as the autumn 1990 World Summit on Children and, perhaps, the June 1992 United Nations Conference on the Environment and Development), the full United Nations shares this tradition. Within NATO, only in the 1990s (beginning with the London summit of July 1990) has the recent tradition of summits every five years been replaced by an annual cycle (with the Rome summit of November 1991). In contrast, the seven-power summit system has since its inception centred on and been driven by the annual gathering of heads of state and government.

At the ministerial level, the United Nations system has featured annual meetings of foreign ministers, and twice-yearly meetings of finance ministers (IMF/IBRD [World Bank]), as well as regular gatherings of other ministers in the specialized portfolio relevant to the functional agencies. The Atlantic system has twice-yearly gatherings of foreign and defence (NATO), and finance (OECD) ministers. While the seven-power summit system is less extensive (including only foreign, finance, and trade ministers meeting once or more a year), it is the only integrated forum where foreign and finance ministers (the only two great internationally oriented ministries of state) annually meet together and do so in the presence of heads.

At the subministerial level there have been persistent suggestions that the summit should acquire its own supporting organization, beginning with a permanent secretariat. However, such pressures have been firmly resisted. Despite a proliferation of summit-created subordinate official-level bodies — some ongoing, some transitory; some confined to summit members, some expanding to include non-members — no intergovernmental organizational support mechanism of any kind has been established.

This unique combination of direct highest-level political control and freedom from formal organization endows the summit with four powerful advantages that render it particularly adept at dealing with new challenges to international order in a rapidly changing international system. First, it enables the summit to take the lead in international agenda-setting by immediately taking up and giving prominence to new issues, and by establishing new issue areas through the definition and legitimation of core logical linkages and ranges of acceptable considerations (e.g., debt and democracy, trade and environment). This flexibility in agenda-setting extends to the geographic domain of institutional coverage, as reflected in the summit's movement into regional security issues on a global scale, in contrast to NATO's limited ability to deal with out-of-area issues. Second, the presence of heads increases the likelihood that agreements will be made, as there are no colleagues with cognate portfolios or superior authority in national governments with whose policies prospective agreements must be harmonized, or to whom such agreements must be referred. Third, the presence of heads increases the probability that the agreements reached will be implemented, since they are made personally by heads (who understand their spirit and letter) to fellow heads (with the equality of power to sanction defection), whom one knows one will meet face-to-face in a year's time—electoral fortune permitting. Finally, the presence of heads facilitates the appropriate adjustments on national and international policy, as heads have the power to alter both the domestic and the foreign policies of their country, and ultimately to mobilize the resources required for these adjustments to be made.

The Summit as an International Institution

Although the summit has remained a heads-directed institution devoid of a supporting international organization, it has over the years developed a considerable institutional capacity through downwardly and outwardly linked systems of subordinate institutions and networks. This development has been propelled by the increase in relative power as well as the demand of the outer tier of major powers (Japan, Germany, Italy, and Canada) who have been most disenfranchised by the old international institutional security systems centred in the UN Security Council and (Germany apart) NATO's 'Berlin Dinner'.[18] The same countries were responsible for the triumph of a concert-based conception of the summit's role, centred on the recognition of a decline in American primacy and a consequent diffusion of power.

From its inception, the seven-power summit was inspired by two competing conceptions of what type of institution it should become. The Franco-German, or 'librarian' conception—put forward by Valéry Giscard D'Estaing and Helmut Schmidt on the basis of their experience as finance ministers in the 'Library Group'—conceived of the summit as a one-time or occasional event, with very limited participation and little publicity, focused on the expert-driven economic issues of exchange rates and macro-economic policy co-ordination. By contrast, the American or trilateralist conception—pioneered by Henry Kissinger on the basis of his concept of pentarchy, and his frustrated Year of Europe and new Atlantic Charter initiative—envisioned an ongoing institution, with somewhat broader participation and publicity, dealing with the major political issues of the day. From the start, the American conception prevailed, for even before the Rambouillet summit of 15-17 November 1975, Canada received a promise from the US that it would host a second summit, to which Canada would be invited.

Thus the two-day summit held in Puerto Rico on 27-28 June 1976 saw the United States, Britain, France, Germany, Japan, and Italy joined by Canada. The two-day summit held in London 7-8 May 1977 saw the European Community added in the person of the president of the Commission. The Bonn summit of 16-17 July 1978, the Tokyo summit of 28-29 June 1979, the Venice summit of 22-23 June 1980, and the Ottawa summit of 20-21 July 1981 confirmed the pattern of an institution with eight participant heads, meeting annually for two days, in May, June, or July, with a rotating host and location (the pattern generally reflecting the relative power and historic position and participation of members in the international system). The first round also saw the emergence, as part of the preparatory process, of a series of bilateral summits by the host with all summit participants, in the months immediately preceding the event itself.

The second round of summitry brought further institutional development as the summit expanded into a three-day affair, in May or June, with an occasional additional head from the European Community. Thus in addition to the president of the Commission, the president of the European Council attended when he came from a country that was not a regular summit participant. He thus attended the Versailles summit of 4-6 June 1982, was absent from the Williamsburg summit of 28-30 May 1983, the London summit of 7-9 June 1984, and the Bonn summit of 2-4 May 1985, but returned for the Tokyo summit of 4-6 May 1986, and the Venice summit of 8-10 June 1987, and was absent for the Toronto summit of 19-21 June 1988. The second round of summitry also heralded the start of additional *ad hoc* meetings of the summit heads, as six (the seven minus France) met in New York, at Ronald Reagan's invitation, to provide the US president with advice prior to his 1985 visit to Mikhail Gorbachev — the visit that marked the start of intense institutionalized superpower summitry in the modern period.

The third round of summitry maintained the three-day, eight- or nine-participant pattern, but fixed the summit date far more precisely in mid-July. More important, it was with the third round that other non-member heads began attending, or participating in, the summit, stimulating a further institutionalization of the status of the summit as a collective entity, and the role of the host as chair. Thus the Paris summit was graced by several Third World heads who were invited by summit host François Mitterrand for a separate meeting immediately before the opening of the seven-power event. These Third World heads issued an appeal for assistance to the summit leaders on 13 July, and shared a dinner with them that evening. When a second appeal for assistance to the Paris summit seven came, midway through their meeting, from Gorbachev, it was decided that a collective response would be delivered by Mitterrand, as summit host. At Houston the following year it was agreed that the host would communicate the results of the summit personally to Gorbachev in a follow-up visit. And at London in 1991 the summit principals agreed to meet collectively with the Soviet leader in London on the afternoon following the conclusion of the summit itself.

(This formula was repeated the following year at Munich with Russian President Boris Yeltsin). Arrangements for follow-up meetings with Gorbachev on behalf of the summit codified an arrangement in which the current summit's host held that position until the end of the calendar year, at which time the next summer's host took over. The London meeting also introduced the possibility of a second (and this time full and formal) *ad hoc* summit, as host Prime Minister John Major noted in his concluding press conference that he would be prepared to call the heads together should a successful conclusion to the Uruguay Round of trade negotiations not be reached.

From the beginning the heads were accompanied at their annual summit by their foreign and finance ministers. At the Bonn summit of 1978 the Germans added their minister of economics, who returned for all subsequent summits. At the inception of the second round in 1982 the Japanese brought their minister of international trade and industry, who returned for the 1983, 1986, and all subsequent summits. At the start of the third round in Paris in 1989 the Americans brought the administrator of their Environmental Protection Agency, and had their secretary of agriculture and trade representative in attendance at Houston the following year.

During the second round of the summit, first the trade, then the foreign, and finally the finance ministers of the seven began meeting apart from the annual gathering of the heads. Since a January 1982 meeting held under an American chair, the trade ministers have met two or three times a year in the 'Quadrilateral' (so called because it includes the United States, Canada, Japan, and the European Community representing all the European participants). Starting in September 1984 the G-7 foreign ministers have met annually on the margins of the autumn opening of the United Nations General Assembly in New York. The Tokyo summit of 1986 created a Group of Seven finance ministers (the seven without the European Community, which had no competence in this field), a body that met in parallel with the pre-existing Group of Five but soon came to supersede it.[19] Following the London summit of 1991, the summit's finance ministers and ministers responsible for small business were also despatched, in their summit capacity, on missions to the Soviet Union. And the summit seven environment ministers met as a group both before and at the UN Conference on Environment and Development in June 1992.

By the third round, there were signs that this separate ministerial structure too was giving rise to separate meetings among subordinate officials. During the Gulf War, the political directors (usually the senior officials responsible for international security in the foreign ministry) met in Rome on 4 November 1990, without the French (who were, by prior arrangement, briefed immediately after). And on 6 November 1991 the G-7 deputy ministers (of finance and treasuries), who had been gathering separately for several years on their core macro-economic agenda, met in Paris to discuss assistance to the expiring Soviet Union.

Over time, and with a growing frequency in recent years, the annual summit has also bred a plethora of official-level groups, both ongoing and temporary, some including summit members only, some expanding to include outsiders as well. Similarly, the task of preparing the summit—entrusted from the start not to the regular national bureaucracy but to a leader's personal representative, or 'sherpa'—has expanded to a multi-layered team of 'sous-sherpas' (one each from the foreign and finance ministries), 'sous-sous sherpas', and political directors, who since the preparations for the 1990 Houston summit have acquired an enlarged and separate role.[20]

The Summit's International Security Agenda

With increasing institutional depth has come expanding policy breadth. From its very start the seven-power summit, while publicly cast as an economic institution, also dealt importantly with political issues. For example, two issues discussed at Puerto Rico in 1976 were the mechanism for preventing the Communist party from joining the coalition government in Italy (a re-run of the concern that had bred the North Atlantic Treaty concluded in 1949), and unco-ordinated and hence excessive lending by Western banks to the Soviet Union (a precursor of the recent issue of aid to the Soviet Union, and now Russia). However, from the start France—neo-Gaullist in instinct and anxious to dilute neither its inflated five-power status as a permanent Security Council veto power nor its four-power status as part of the Berlin Dinner group—felt strongly that the summit should deal only with economic, as opposed to political or security, issues. As a formal summit co-founder and first host, France held considerable sway, to the point where in 1978 it successfully called a four-power summit in Guadeloupe focusing on political and security issues, which the United States, Britain, and Germany attended.

But despite continuing strong French resistance (even after the Socialist Mitterrand became president in 1981), the structural characteristics of the international system favouring the seven-power summit gave this institution a growing role in the political and security domain. While this growth was particularly pronounced in regard to the new and emerging security agenda, where the organizational prerogatives, capacity, and 'imperialism' of the established institutional systems were less pronounced, it also flourished from an early stage in the more traditional security areas of East-West relations, broadly defined, and regional conflict (in Europe and the Third World). Thus the most rapid and far-reaching expansion took place in new and emerging security issue areas; economically intensive (balance-of-payments support, financial lending, economic sanctions) and new areas (horizontal non-proliferation in nuclear fuels and ballistic-missile technology) of the old security agenda; and emerging, new, and old security issues involving the Third World and directly affecting the rising great powers of the international system as a whole (Japan, Germany, Italy, and Canada).

A complete understanding of the summit's expansion into the domain of international security would require a full-scale review of the subjects actually discussed by the heads at their annual summit, by the heads and sherpa teams in the preparatory process, and by the groupings created by the heads collectively to implement summit agreements. A broad overview, however, can be provided by focusing on the subjects of the authoritative, subject-specific statements the heads collectively issue at their annual summit. Despite a tendency to dismiss these as mere paper products, they do generally, if imperfectly, map the actual discussions at the summit table and in the preparatory process, and reveal what the leaders have been able to agree on and wish it to be publicly known that they are concerned about.

Whereas Rambouillet in 1975 produced only an Economic Declaration, the following summit declarations included reactions and directives in other areas, specifically air-hijacking, refugees, hostage-taking, East-West relations, and European and regional security.

Thus by the end of the first cycle of summitry, and the start of the 1980s, the summit had become a full-blown security institution. This process had begun with the new security issue of terrorism, through the concern with air-hijacking starting in 1978, and diplomatic hostage-taking added in 1980. It continued with the emerging, potentially new, security issue of refugees, beginning with the Indochinese refugees in 1979. It then moved to the economically and Third World-related area of East-West relations in 1980, with the Afghanistan issue. And by 1981 it had added the regional security issues of Europe, the Middle East, Lebanon, and Cambodia. By 1981 it had thus reached the point of issuing a general political-security statement covering East-West relations and Third World issues in two selected regions (the Middle East and the Vietnamese War remnant of Cambodia). In emerging as a security organization, then, the seven-power summit seemed to be driven first and most powerfully by the unprecedented shocks of new challenges.

The 1982 Versailles gathering added a lengthy statement on Technology, Employment and Growth, which took the summit in a major way into the micro-economic domain. By the end of the second cycle, however, the summit's full-scale development as a security institution was virtually complete. It had taken up the new security agenda with separate documents on terrorism (1978), the environment (1986), drugs (1987), and AIDS (1987). It had addressed the emerging security agenda with separate statements on refugees (1979) and democratic values (1984). In the sphere of the old security agenda it had taken up East-West relations with documents on Afghanistan (1980), and East-West relations and arms control (1984); regional security with Lebanon (1982), and Iran-Iraq (1984); and finally the global post-World War Two security order with the Political Declaration on the 40th Anniversary of the End of the Second World War (1985).

To the emerging security agenda the third cycle added human rights with a 1989 Declaration. It was at its most prolific, however, on the old security agenda. In the area of regional security it added China (1989), the Arab-Israeli conflict (1989), Southern Africa (1989), Central America (1989), Panama (1989), and Cambodia (1989). In 1990 it added a new class of transnational issues including non-proliferation, and in 1991 it issued a separate Declaration on Conventional Arms Transfers and NBC non-proliferation. From 1990 onward East-West relations disappeared as a separate item, in favour of a focus on the more comprehensive and integrated transformation of international order discussed in Securing Democracy (1990) and Strengthening the International Order (1991).

The Summit's Authoritative Reach

Even as the summit's security agenda has become vastly more comprehensive, its attempts to influence the shape of world order have become progressively more ambitious. Throughout the summit's history, there has been an ongoing debate as to whether the summits are, or should be, deliberative (the French, 'librarian', preference), or decisional (the American, 'trilateralist', preference). This debate has somewhat obscured the secular evolution of the summit from a body with decisive impact on the politics of agenda-setting to one with an important role in producing agreements, taking implementative action, and securing specified adjustments in the policies and practices of member states, other countries in the world, and other international organizations.

The authoritative reach of the seven-power summit can be assessed along a fourfold continuum of functions. The first of these is agenda-setting, which includes the assignment of prominence to particular issues in world politics, the establishment and legitimation of new areas or appropriate intergovernmental concern, the creation of new issue areas (including those created by new linkages such as debt – democracy, or trade – environment), and the specification of allowable considerations in their treatment. This agenda-setting function is the one emphasized by the 'librarians' favouring deliberative summits, who see the institution's primary value in educating the heads themselves, the watching media corps, and the public about otherwise neglected and difficult issues of international relations. Thus the agenda-setting function is conducted (and can be measured) through the summit's preparatory process, the discussions at the summit itself, its publicly issued documentation, and the media coverage of the event. Here evidence from both Canada and the United States (the weakest and strongest members of the summit respectively) demonstrate the ability of the summit to attract the attention of television news organizations and viewers to it and its participating members.

The summit's second function, focused on by the proponents of decisional summits, is that of reaching agreements. Agreements may take the limited form of giving retroactive approval to actions by the summit itself or other bodies, or the progressively more ambitious forms of committing members to action or calling upon others to act. Agreements may concern issues of process or substance, and may be confined to limited subjects or extend to broad package deals across an entire policy field.

The summit's third function, less well explored in the existing literature, is the creation of implementing action to give effect to its agreements. Such action may consist of the initiation of a summit process (e.g., the call for a report back by next summit), or the establishment of a summit group. It may also consist of instructions (with varying levels of specificity) to individual member countries and other international organizations to perform particular tasks. Such extension into the realm of implementing action is at its most ambitious when the summit issues instructions to other international institutions that are juridically separate, often much larger in membership, not formally controlled by the summit members, and busy with their autonomously identified work programmes.

The final summit function is that of ensuring that implementative activities have the desired impact by securing the specified adjustments from member and non-member countries as well as international organizations. This ultimate test of the summit's effectiveness is the subject of much pronouncement but little systematic exploration or evidence in the literature.[21] It includes the stages of outside actors' resisting (as opposed to simply ignoring) the summit's implementing actions, mobilizing to protect their policy turf or develop competitive regimes, and ultimately acceding to the summit-specified action.

In broad terms, an indication of the summit's increasing authoritative reach can be obtained by a simple comparison of the documentary records of the first summit (Rambouillet, 1975) and a more recent one (London 3, 1991) with a focus on the number and subjects of specific instructions issued to component and outside bodies ('adjustment setting'). In assessing the findings of this review, it should be recalled that Rambouillet in 1975 received some of the highest marks ever awarded by those who judge summit success by the welfare-maximizing standard of agreements reached and reliably implemented.[22] It should also be recalled that at London 3 the British hosts made an exceptional effort to restrict the length of the Declaration, in particular by eliminating references of endorsement to each participant's favourite international body, conference, or project; in addition, London 3 produced a rich array of references in its supporting security-oriented documentation, apart from the core Economic Declaration on which this review focuses.

The evidence shows a veritable explosion of such adjustment-setting instructions over the seventeen summits in question: the 6 such references at Rambouillet expanded to 88 at London 3. References to international institutions appeared in all 11 of the London Economic Declaration's subject areas — most frequently in the section on the long-standing new security issue of environment (23 references), followed by the more recent new security area of drugs (14). Then followed the most recent old security area of Central and Eastern Europe (13), the developing countries and debt (11), trade (9), the Soviet Union (6), the Middle East (4), energy (4), migration (2), economics (1) and the introduction of the Declaration. (1). Finally, whereas Rambouillet referred to only 4 international institutions (GATT, IMF, OECD, CIEC), London 3 referred to 33.

Conclusion

This analysis indeed suggests that as the summit has increasingly acquired the four central characteristics of a concert (concerted power, constricted participation, common purpose, and political control) it has developed greater institutional depth, policy breadth, and authoritative reach. These developments have been particularly pronounced during the third summit cycle, from 1989 onward, when rapid shifts in relative capability in the international system (notably the demise of the Soviet Union and diminution in capability of Russia, and the expansion of Germany with unification) have greatly enhanced the summit's structural character as a concert (concerted power), while eroding that of the United Nations Security Council and the seminal common purpose of NATO (directed at the powerful Soviet-led threat of communist expansion). Long before this decisive shift in relative capability in the international system, however, the institutional characteristic of the summit as a body personally managed by heads of state and government (political control) had given it a role in major global political and security issues, with the flexibility to respond in a timely way to new and emerging security challenges.

Indications of increasing institutional depth, policy breadth, and frequency of instructions to international institutions do not, in themselves, constitute conclusive evidence of implementative effectiveness. While it is unlikely that summit leaders would continue to give so many instructions, so publicly, to international institutions if these had proven to be ineffective (and hence embarrassing), specific case studies are required to confirm directly that summit agreements have led national governments and international organizations to adjust in the ways specified and to implement summit-designed agreements in ways that have a discernable and durable impact.

The existing case-study literature provides a firm foundation for this work. From the security-related but ultimately economic issue area of oil to the new security area of the environment, there is substantial evidence that the summit's members adjust their behaviour on important issues, against previously held preferences, in response to the dynamics of the summit process and in accordance with summit agreements.[23] Moreover, this process of adjustment takes place on the part of the summit's most powerful member, the United States, as well as its weakest, Canada (if less frequently). Indeed, Canadian leaders have implemented their summit agreements even at the cost of electoral defeat, as in 1978 and 1979 over fiscal deficit reduction and increased gasoline taxes, and have responded to summit discussions by abandoning major initiatives in diplomacy and energy, and by beginning new ones in trade policy.[24]

What remains for further research is a disciplined set of case studies, including the new security areas of terrorism, the environment, narcotics, and AIDS, that demonstrates how, across issue areas, the summit system's characteristics as a concert have increased its institutional depth, policy breadth, and authoritative reach, to the point where it has replaced the United Nations and Atlantic systems as the predominant institution for international security governance.

Notes

[1] US President Nixon's unilateral decision (15 Aug. 1971) to devalue the US dollar, and to let other currencies 'float' to find an appropriate level against it, destroyed the regime, established with the creation of the International Monetary Fund in 1945 at Bretton Woods, under which countries would when necessary renegotiate changes in the fixed value of their national currencies against each other, and agree on new fixed values that reflected underlying fundamental economic forces. The Tokyo Round of Multilateral Trade Negotiations (MTN), formally launched by members of the General Agreement on Tariffs and Trade, remained moribund as the distractions of Watergate, and then the depressing 'stagflation' caused by the rapid rise in world oil prices in October 1973, made the United States unable and unwilling to offer the initial proposals and concessions that had traditionally led MTN rounds rapidly to achieve significant reductions in tariff and non-tariff barriers. Finally, the October 1973 oil embargo by OAPEC, and consequent fourfold increase in world oil prices, overwhelmed the defensive mechanisms available to the OECD's Oil Committee, and led less developed countries to demand a 'new international economic order' well beyond the regimes then prevailing within the UN family of institutions.

[2] Although the North Atlantic Treaty of 1949 had been importantly inspired, at the outset of the cold war, by the prospect that Italy and other Western European countries would fall prey to coalition governments including communists, and then communist-dominated governments (as had Czechoslovakia), the successor North Atlantic Treaty Organization proved incapable of stemming the rise of Eurocommunism in the 1970s. Similarly, the 1974 explosion by India of a so-called 'peaceful' nuclear device exposed the limitations and ineffectiveness of the regimes established by the UN's International Atomic Energy Agency in 1957 and Non-Proliferation Treaty of 1968. The politically self-imposed military defeat of the United States with the conquest of South Vietnam by communist North Vietnam in April 1975 demonstrated the impotence of the global array of regional alliances the United States had constructed in previous decades, and the end of America's ability and willingness to act as a 'global policeman'.

[3] In addition to the post-World War II UN system, and the cold-war-inspired 'Atlantic' system, the past half century has seen the emergence of a system of geographically adjacent land-based regional economic blocs, beginning with the European Community in 1957.

[4] Michael Artis and Sylvia Ostry, *International Economic Policy Coordination* (London: Routledge and Kegan Paul, 1986); Donald Watt, *Next Steps for Summitry: Report of the Twentieth Century Fund International Conference on Economic Summitry* (New York:

Priority Press, 1984); and Robert Putnam and Nicholas Bayne, *Hanging Together: Co-operation and Conflict in the Seven-Power Summits*, rev. and enl. ed. (Cambridge, MA: Harvard Univ. Press, 1987).

[5]Wilfried Guth, ed., *Economic Policy Coordination* (Washington: International Monetary Fund, 1988); Yoichi Funabashi, *Managing the Dollar: From the Plaza to the Louvre*, 2nd ed. (Washington: Institute for International Economics, 1989); and Georges de Menil, *Les Sommets économiques: les politiques nationales à l'heure de l'interdépendance* (Paris: Economica, 1983).

[6]Cesare Merlini, ed., *Economic Summits and Western Decision-Making* (New York: St. Martin's, 1984), 197.

[7]R.G. Lipsey, 'Agendas for the 1988 and Future Summits', *Canadian Public Policy* 15 (Feb. 1989), S86-S91; and L. Waverman and T.A. Wilson, 'Macroeconomic Co-ordination and the Summit', ibid.

[8]World Institute for Development Economics Research, *World Economic Summits: The Role of Representative Groups in the Governance of the World Economy*, Study Group Series 4 (Helsinki: WIDER, 1989).

[9]Flora Lewis, 'The "G-7-1/2" Directorate', *Foreign Policy* 85 (1991-2), 25-40.

[10]Putnam and Bayne, *Hanging Together*; Waverman and Wilson, 'Macroeconomic Co-ordination', *World Economic Summits*; and Merlini, *Economic Summits*.

[11]De Menil, *Les Sommets économiques*; Artis and Ostry, *International Economic Policy Coordination*; and Funabashi, *Managing the Dollar*.

[12]Guth, *Economic Policy Coordination*; and Watt, *Next Steps for Summitry*.

[13]Artis and Ostry, *International Economic Policy Coordination*.

[14]John Kirton, 'Introduction: The Significance of the Houston Summit', in *Supplement: Documents from the 1990 Summit*, ed. Peter Hajnal (Millwood, NY: Kraus International, 1991), ix-xvii; *idem*, 'Sustainable Development at the Houston Seven-Power Summit', paper prepared for the Foreign Policy Committee of the Canadian National Roundtable on the Environment and the Economy, 6 September 1990; *idem*, 'Introduction: The Significance of the Seven-Power Summit', in *The Seven-Power Summit: Documents from the Summits of Industrialized Countries, 1975-1989*, ed. Peter Hajnal (Millwood, NY: Kraus International, 1989), xxi-xli; *idem*, 'Contemporary Concert Diplomacy: The Seven-Power Summit and the Management of International Order', a paper prepared for the annual meeting of the International Studies Association, London, 1989; and John Holmes and John Kirton, eds, *Canada and the New Internationalism* (Toronto: Canadian Institute of International Affairs, 1989).

[15]Charles Kupchan and Clifford Kupchan, 'Concerts, Collective Security and the Future of Europe', *International Security* 16 (Summer 1991), 114-61.

[16]Kirton, 'Contemporary Concert Diplomacy'.

[17]For figures on military spending, see the annual reports by the International Institute for Strategic Studies.

[18]However, it must be recalled that Germany and Italy have the attractive alternative

of the European Community as a post-war institution in which they can have a powerful first-tier, if regionally confined, place.

[19]Wendy Dobson, *Economic Policy Coordination: Requiem or Prologue?* (Washington: Institute for International Economics, 1991).

[20]From the start the individual preparing the summit on behalf of his or her leader was in name, and often in fact, a 'personal representative', to underscore the fact that this was a leader-driven forum, rather than an institution influenced by bureaucrats with any independent authority. Personal representatives thus found it appropriate to take the nickname of 'sherpa' after the Tibetans who merely bear the bags of their mountaineering masters as they ascend the real summits.

[21]For the start of systematic empirical work in this area see George M. Von Lurstenberg and Joseph P. Daniels, 'Policy Undertakings by the Seven "Summit" Countries: Ascertaining the Degree of Compliance', pp. 267-308 in Allan Meltzer and Charles Plosser, eds, *Carnegie-Rochester Conference Series on Public Policy* 35 (1991); and George M. Von Lurstenberg and Joseph P. Daniels, 'Economic Summit Declarations, 1975-1989: Examining the Written Record of International Cooperation', *Princeton Studies in International Finance* 72 (Feb. 1992).

[22]Putnam and Bayne, *Hanging Together.*

[23]John Ikenberry, 'Market Solutions for State Problems: The International and Domestic Politics of American Oil Decontrol', *International Organization* 42 (Winter 1988), 151-79; Jim MacNeill, Pieter Winsemius, and Taizo Yakushiji, *Beyond Interdependence: The Meshing of the World's Economy and the Earth's Ecology* (New York: Oxford Univ. Press, 1991); and Kirton, 'Sustainable Development at the Houston Seven-Power Summit'.

[24]George Takach, 'Moving the Embassy to Jerusalem, 1979', in Don Munton and John Kirton, eds, *Canadian Foreign Policy: Selected Cases* (Scarborough: Prentice-Hall, 1992), 273-85; David Leyton-Brown, 'Canadianizing Oil and Gas: The National Energy Program, 1980-8', in ibid., 299-310; J.L. Granatstein and Robert Bothwell, *Pirouette: Pierre Trudeau and Canadian Foreign Policy* (Toronto: Univ. of Toronto Press, 1990).

chapter fifteen

The Missile Technology Control Regime

Albert Legault

Introduction

There has been a veritable proliferation of works on non-proliferation over the past several years. This chapter offers a synthesis that seeks to demonstrate two things. First, it shows that the Missile Technology Control Regime (MTCR) did not simply drop from the sky one day in April 1987: it evolved squarely in the midst of a myriad of developing controls associated with technology transfers. Second, and related to the above, this chapter seeks to determine whether the MTCR, as one regime or several, is effective in terms both of the role played by the industrialized countries, and of the broader phenomenon of the diffusion of technology.

The Iran-Iraq War and the Gulf War are the two key events that triggered the current anxiety about the dangers of proliferation in chemical, bacteriological, and nuclear weaponry, as well as the means to deliver such weapons. To be sure, the earlier conflict neither challenged global political equilibrium nor caused much anxiety, apart from the effect of some soaring insurance premiums for oil companies. Nevertheless, as Gerard C. Smith has indicated, the Iran-Iraq War could have had a much graver impact: 'Instead of the use of chemical weapons in the . . . war, if one nuclear weapon had been exploded, that would have been an event of historical proportion.'[1] It is also difficult to contemplate what form the 1990-91 war in the Gulf might have taken had Iraq been able to unleash nuclear warheads, or even chemical or bacteriological ones.

How Far Does the Proliferation Horizon Extend?

The menace of the spread of nuclear arms is real. Table 15.1, prepared by the office of Senator Dante B. Fascell (D-Fla.), demonstrates that four countries have the ability to deploy nuclear weapons within a relatively short time span (South Africa, India, Israel, and Pakistan); that two states (Iraq and Syria) possess biological weapons; and that five other Third World countries are well along on the path to getting them. As far as chemical weapons are concerned, some twenty countries either have or are developing them. These statistics correspond to the data produced by the Washington-based specialist on chemical arms, Elisa D. Harris.[2] According to a report prepared by intelligence experts of the US Navy, six Middle Eastern countries—Egypt, Iran, Iraq, Israel, Libya, and Syria—already possess offensive capabilities in chemical weapons, and Saudi Arabia is thought likely to be in the same category.[3] Moreover, some thirty countries are either already developing ballistic-missile capabilities or likely to be doing so soon.

As for the means necessary both to build and to deliver nuclear weapons, Table 15.2 reveals that five states currently either possess or are at the stage of possessing fuel-processing facilities. Four states—Argentina, Brazil, Pakistan, and India—have constructed enrichment facilities, and Israel is a possible candidate for inclusion on this list. Three countries, and probably three others, are already well embarked on the development of nuclear-tipped missiles, while all six have aircraft capable of delivering nuclear arms for use against their adversaries' homelands.[4] In terms of research, development, and deployment of ballistic missiles, Iran, Iraq, Israel, and North Korea are at the head of the Third World class, while South Africa, India, and Pakistan have been striving to attain the same status. Four other countries are pursuing ambitious research programmes in this area. According to official American sources, at least 14 countries now have ballistic-missile capabilities, 20 countries are developing offensive capabilities in chemical weaponry, 10 have biological weapons, and several non-signatories of the Non-Proliferation Treaty (NPT) have the means to deploy nuclear weapons quickly in times of crisis.[5]

Leonard Spector, who publishes an annual update on developments relating to nuclear proliferation, is justifiably worried about what he labels the silent proliferation of nuclear warheads and missiles.[6] In large measure, this problem stems from the black market in arms transfers, as well as from clandestine flows of sensitive materials, such as the re-routing to Romania of heavy water purchased in Norway by a German company, but subsequently transferred via Dubai to Bombay. Also problematic are the absence of administrative controls in supplier countries, which are often unable or unwilling to police companies engaged in illegal commerce; the decision of some countries to lease nuclear-propelled submarines to third parties; and the absence of controls on small quantities of sensitive materials, or on larger quantities of uranium ore that can be diverted to military applications. In

Table 15.1. Weapons Proliferation

	BALLISTIC MISSILE	NUCLEAR	BIOLOGICAL	CHEMICAL
Afghanistan	C			
Argentina	S	S		
Belgium	C			
Brazil	S	S		
Bulgaria	C			
Burma				S
China	C	C	S**	S
Czechoslovakia	C			
East Germany	C			
Egypt	C		S	C
Ethiopia				S
France	C	C		C
Great Britain	C	C*		
Hungary	C			
India	S	C(1)		S
Indonesia	S			
Iran	C	S*		C
Iraq	C	S*	C	C
Israel	C	C(1)	S	S
Italy	C			
Laos				S
Libya	C	S*		C
Netherlands	C			
North Korea	C	S*	S**	S
North Yemen	C			
Pakistan	S	C(1)		S
Poland	C			
Romania	C			S
Saudi Arabia	C			
South Africa	S	C(1)	S	S
South Korea	C	S*		
South Yemen	C			
Soviet Union	C	C*	C**	C
Syria	C		C	S
Taiwan	S	S*	S**	S
United States	C	C*		C
Vietnam				S
West Germany	C			

KEY: C – confirmed or strongly suspected of having
S – suspected of seeking to acquire or develop

*Party to the 1968 Nuclear Nonproliferation Treaty (NPT)
**Party to the 1972 Convention on Biological Weapons

(1)believed to be able to deploy in a short period of time.

SOURCE: Hearings before the Committee on Foreign Affairs, May 17 and July 11, 1990 (Subcommittee on Arms Control, International Security and Science) (Washington, U.S.G.P.O., 1991), 202

Table 15.2. Nuclear Weapons Capabilities of the Threshold States

COUNTRY	Materials for nuclear weapons			Nuclear weapons production		Delivery systems	
	NPT SIGNATORY	REPROCESSING FACILITY	ENRICHMENT FACILITY	WEAPONS DESIGN PROGRAMME	NUCLEAR TEST	AIRCRAFT	MISSILES
Argentina	no	under construction	yes	no	no	yes	research
Brazil	no	no	yes	no	no	yes	research
India	no	yes	no	yes, fission and fusion	yes	yes	developing
Iran	yes	no	no	possibly	no	yes	deployed
Iraq	yes	no	no	probably	no	yes	deployed
Israel	no	yes	?	yes, fission and fusion	?	yes	deployed
North Korea	yes	may be under const.	no	unknown	no	yes	deployed
Pakistan	no	under construction	yes	yes, fission	no	yes	developing
South Africa	no	no	yes	probably, fission	?	yes	developing
South Korea	yes	no	no	no	no	yes	research
Taiwan	yes	no	no	no	no	yes	research

SOURCE: David Albright and Tom Zamora, *Journal of the FAS*, 43: 7 (September 1990)

short, there is no shortage of means of circumventing whatever non-proliferation constraints have been erected. Moreover, as discussed below, some technologies are so out of date that no one dreams of controlling their transfer; such was the case with the calutrons employed by Iraq to supply itself with fissile fuels.

Many items that were uncontrolled in the past can today have military applications.[7] Moreover, the increasing tendency of civilian industry to adopt ever more sophisticated technologies makes it all the more difficult to control goods and know-how deemed to be 'dual-use' — that is, to have both military and civilian applications.[8] To control such items would require much tighter regulations, with related administrative and bureaucratic complications — to say nothing of the negative effect upon economic interests in the affected states. Such a tightening of controls would also likely privilege certain enterprises — namely, the most well-established ones — at the expense of weaker companies, and thus could lead to a lessening of competition.

The proliferation problem is located at the intersection of three obvious realities. The first is the need to avoid economic warfare between supplier countries, many of whom have not appeared to be excessively scrupulous, in the past, regarding the promotion of their nuclear trade. The second is the need, given the link between technological and economic development, to share with others the fruits of technological progress. And the third can be found in the very notion of the security dilemma of states, many of whom fail to see the logical or ethical merit in a double standard that holds that while certain technologies may be indispensable for the security of some, they automatically become a source of instability once in the possession of others.

One need not overstate the point. There seems to exist, at the level of the international community, a consensus on the need to stop the proliferation of weapons of mass destruction, and this notwithstanding the existence of certain theoretical arguments to the effect that greater (nuclear) proliferation might prove to be a factor for stability.[9]

It should also be stressed that things are not quite as bad as they might appear. Substantial progress has been made in the realm of non-proliferation in the past several years. Following the fourth review conference of the NPT in 1990, Saudia Arabia, Kuwait, and Qatar all announced they would be ratifying the NPT. Subsequently, South Africa also made it known it would adhere to the NPT, and much the same might be said of Brazil and Argentina, each of which has decided to adhere to the (non-proliferation) Treaty of Tlatelolco. Especially significant were the announcements made by France and China, respectively on 3 June and 10 August 1991, that they too would join the NPT — announcements, it was felt, that could only have a catalyzing effect on other members of the international community.

The MTCR: Origins and Mechanisms

Martin Navias, who has written the best account of the MTCR, dates its origins to the 1976 Geneva disarmament conference, where the United States proposed—in the context of a broader set of propositions aimed at limiting the transfer of arms capable of causing massive destruction to urban centres —that supplying countries accept some self-imposed restraints on weapons transfers, and that recipient countries renounce in particular the acquisition of long-range surface-to-surface missiles and of aircraft whose combat radius extended far beyond that needed for purely defensive purposes.[10] Navias also accords great significance to the bilateral Soviet-American talks on Conventional Arms Transfers (CAT), held between 1977 and 1979 and involving the means of controlling conventional weapons flows. These talks, it will be recalled, were singularly unsuccessful.[11]

Despite that lack of success, students of the issue would be well-advised to re-examine proposals made at the time by Andrew J. Pierre regarding the mechanisms for imposing multilateral controls on conventional-weapons sales. In brief, Pierre's project for the regulation of conventional arms transfers would have required the implementation of both informal and formal rules.[12]

The four important elements of the regime stipulated at the time were (1) notification of refusal to export; (2) definition of strict criteria to determine the exportability of equipment; (3) existence of an informal grouping that would subsequently be enlarged to embrace other supplying countries; and (4) existence of a forum that could be assembled periodically, more or less along the lines of the London Suppliers' Group (which governs the export of nuclear technology).

The first element—notification of refusal—raised two difficulties.[13] Would a notification of refusal or denial entail a corresponding obligation on the part of the other potential suppliers? Further, would not the simple dynamic of size work in favour of the largest suppliers, to whom most of the requests for technology transfer would be directed? Indeed, in the first 29 months of the MTCR's existence, the United States refused 29 export licences, and the other members of the MTCR only 13.[14]

The other elements of the MTCR's control mechanism are well-known. After four years of arduous negotiations, the members of the G-7 published on 16 April 1987 a series of directives on the MTCR's 'governance'.[15] Kathleen C. Bailey has summarized the principal elements of the regime:

(1) All transfers would be considered on a case-by-case basis.
(2) Governments would implement the guidelines through national legislation.
(3) The exporting government would assume responsibility for taking all steps necessary to ensure that the item was put only to its stated end-use.
(4) The decision to export would remain the sole and sovereign judgement of the individual government.[16]

The procedure described by Bailey suggests that the MTCR constitutes a forum for exchanges and consultations in which each transfer can be discussed, although ultimate authority over decisions resides with governments. The MTCR's directives, then, constitute unilateral juridical commitments. Nevertheless, it is far from certain that such commitments would be any more binding were they to take the form of international accords.[17] Moreover, the consultative process seems clear enough with respect to goods and technology listed in the most critical Category One (the overall system operating the missile) of the technical annex of the MTCR, for which there will be a 'strong presumption of denial'.[18] But it is much less clear regarding those goods and technologies in the less critical Category Two (subsystems or elements aiding missile design). In other words, no government can proceed to transfer items listed in Category One without informing other governments in advance; but there is no obligation to give advance notice for those articles listed in Category Two, even if in practice the procedure followed in both cases is governed by the general rule of close consultations.[19]

The negotiations that led to the MTCR agreement were particularly arduous on three matters. The first concerned the question of the extraterritorial application of American laws (discussed in the following section). The second turned on the question of which interpretation to give to goods in Category One, depending upon whether they were destined for military or civilian usage. And the third involved the date at which the MTCR agreement would enter into force.

On this last point, Navias argues that the MTCR was already in place by the end of 1985, even if the official announcement of its creation had to be delayed because the French government apparently made its adherence to the MTCR conditional on Britain's and the United States' not signing the Treaty of Rarotonga, which they had still not done as of 1991.[20]

The second matter was particularly delicate, because France had consistently opposed implicit or otherwise disguised prohibitions on the export of equipment intended for the peaceful exploration of space. This position came into conflict with a presidential directive issued by Ronald Reagan in November 1982 barring the transfer of such equipment to a third country such as India or Brazil, on the grounds that it was impossible in practice to distinguish a space launcher from a ballistic missile.[21] As well, one of those countries had not adhered to the NPT, which implied that any transfer to it would justifiably be seen as attacking the legitimacy of the MTCR, given that the latter sought expressly to prevent technology transfers that might facilitate nuclear proliferation. For its part, France maintained that no state could legitimately interfere with the right of any other state to engage in the peaceful exploration of space; that in any case the technology it was seeking to transfer involved liquid-fuelled launch vehicles, hardly likely to be diverted to military purposes, given the length of time needed to prepare them for launching; and that the best means of controlling one's allies was to engage them in co-operative programmes. This last argument had some merit, and seems to have been the approach adopted by President Bush in his dealings with China and that country's most-favoured-nation status. The net effect of the debate was that the various parties, in utilizing similar political arguments, continued to maintain decidedly different aims.

France never intended to deprive itself of important and lucrative markets, while the United States continues to maintain that only unremitting pressure against recalcitrant countries can head off nuclear proliferation. In this instance the matter is far from resolved, for as Kathleen Bailey observes, Pakistan has for years preferred to continue its nuclear-weapons programmes even at the risk of having the United States suspend assistance to it.[22]

The question remains, then, in suspended animation. It is difficult to determine whether France has decided to give the green light to full co-operation with India and Brazil. Be that as it may, France can certainly appeal to wording on the announcement of the MTCR's own directives, which stipulates that their aim is not to hinder national space programmes or the international co-operation necessary to bring them to fruition. The US position on this seems firm. In her September 1990 testimony before the Subcommittee on Technology and National Security, the State Department's assistant undersecretary for political and military affairs, Elizabeth Verville, declared:

> US policy doesn't categorically prohibit assistance to foreign space programs, and the MTCR guidelines are not designed to impede national space programs. Our aim, however, is to prevent transfers that carry a risk of material contribution to ballistic missiles development, and our policy decisions in this field have been marked by restraint in the export of technology, that contributes or might contribute to foreign SLV programs and missile programs. That restraint remains in force. . . . Our policy is currently under review in the government, to ensure that it is up to date and it is valid.[23]

For the moment, nothing indicates that the US is likely to budge on the issue, but things are evolving so rapidly that a future softening of the American position cannot be ruled out.

The MTCR: One Regime or Several?

Three major developments have shaken the international system from top to bottom since 1989: the collapse of the Berlin Wall in November 1989 (and the subsequent reunification of Germany the following October); the Gulf War of 1990-1; and, most dramatic of all, the collapse of the USSR, signalling the end of the cold war and the beginning of a massive reinforcement of controls upon exports of sensitive technology to countries in the South.

The cold war's end translated into a lifting of some of the controls imposed since the late 1940s by the Coordinating Committee on Multilateral Export

Controls (CoCom) on technology transfers to Eastern Europe, particularly Poland, Hungary, and Czechoslovakia. The case of Germany was settled in the middle of the summer of 1990.[24] For the others, the operative dates were 1 October 1990 (Poland), 3 October (Hungary), and 1 February 1991 (Czechoslovakia).[25] Each country has since those dates benefited from what is called the 'China green line': namely, the privilege of importing Western technology at the same level of decontrol as that in place for China, under the obvious condition that it not be re-exported to a third country.

It is possible, alternatively, that the adherence of these countries to the control procedures embedded in the MTCR could have been obtained tacitly, in exchange for intensified bilateral programmes with the United States in the domain of peaceful nuclear co-operation.[26] It is certain that from now on, those countries will all subscribe to the principle of 'full-scope safeguards'. In April 1991, President Bush sent a memorandum to the departments of State and Energy, recommending that they give their approval to proposed nuclear co-operation programmes with the Eastern Europeans. In view of the former Soviet Union's insistence that CoCom controls against it be lifted, and that it be granted most-favoured-nation status, it must be assumed that there will be a price to pay to bring the Commonwealth of Independent States (CIS) or relevant republics fully within the MTCR.[27]

There can be no doubt that in the past CoCom's existence kept the Eastern Europeans isolated in their own technological neighbourhood, deprived of many benefits of Western commerce. Now that the Soviet threat has disappeared, those countries will constitute a set of attractive markets to exploit. The West has, accordingly, decided to revise all its control policies, lifting controls on a host of goods that are either freely available abroad or else not particularly important, and concentrating instead upon a list of key products (the CoCom core list) for which a continuation of controls will be justified on the grounds of national security, non-proliferation, or simply foreign-policy preference. Beginning in June 1990 significant initial revisions were made to the CoCom list.[28] In November 1990 Washington started to revise its industrial list, and on 5 July 1991 major changes were announced relating to products controlled for reasons of national security. This list will remain subject to further revisions relating to propulsion systems, telecommunications, and security systems.[29]

The United States has nevertheless sought to assure itself that decontrolled goods will not circulate freely among allies whose reliability is in doubt, and that those goods will not simply be included in internal lists of products that are exportable without any licences.[30] Thus an attempt has been made in the MTCR to define better the list of goods figuring in the Technical Annex of 16 April 1987, by excluding certain items deemed not worth keeping under control, and by adding others.

By the same token, Washington has had to revise its nuclear referral list, under the joint control of the departments of Commerce and Energy, as well as some other governmental agencies; this was done for reasons of non-proliferation as well as to take into account evolutions in technology. As far as missiles are concerned, allied countries are henceforth to establish a list of countries of destination, which will shortly be harmonized among them.

The second major development to have a radical impact upon the MTCR was the Gulf War. Subsequent to Iraq's seizure of Kuwait, all of America's diplomatic efforts were covered under Executive Order 12735 of 16 November 1990 and the Enhanced Proliferation Control Initiative (EPCI) of 13 December 1990. In the former, the secretaries of Commerce and State were enjoined to exercise tight controls on exports that might assist a foreign state to acquire chemical or biological weapons capabilities. The latter obliged the Commerce Department to monitor transfers of dual-use goods and technical data relative to chemical and biological arms.

Neither the Technical Annex of the MTCR nor the official communiqué of 16 April 1987, published simultaneously in the G-7 capitals, made much of the question of the extraterritorial application of American laws relative to technology transfer. Nevertheless, the American legislation of 13 March 1991 concerning the non-proliferation of missiles and bacteriological and chemical weapons is specifically directed at the following four points:

1. To mandate public authorities to refuse the export of goods requiring an export licence, for reasons other than shortness of supply, if it can be determined that the goods in question are implicated in the design, development, production, or utilization of missiles, or chemical or biological weapons;

2. To prevent the export of goods destined either for specific or indeterminate destinations when the exporter knows, or is informed by the Bureau of Export Licensing that the goods, technical data, or software are intended for the design, development, production, or utilization of missiles, or chemical or biological weapons, or are destined for installations implicated in such activities;

3. To prevent any 'US person' from participating in the activities detailed above, when the existence of such activities is known or made known to that person;

4. To restrict the participation of all 'US persons' in the construction of plants intended to produce subcomponents for chemical weapons in certain countries.

Together, these provisions embrace a variety of factors, some of which stem from the goal of better integrating objectives, and others of which really represent a reinsertion of the doctrine of extraterritoriality, since for the purposes of the regulation a 'US person' is defined as any individual who is a citizen or permanent resident of the United States, or a foreign subsidiary of companies domiciled in the United States — or even any person who finds himself on American territory.[31] What is new about the regulation is the inclusion under the same heading of everything from launch vehicles for nuclear warheads to anything that might in one way or another be useful for the manufacture of chemical and biological weapons.

Thus the US has achieved some modifications in its Export Administration Regulations (EAR) relating to the proliferation of chemical, biological, and nuclear weapons and missiles, all of which are grouped together under the new article 778 of the Export Administration Act (EAA), now entitled Proliferation Controls.[32] It also specifies a long list of countries that from now on can no longer benefit from technology transfers relating to chemical or biological weapons. This list embraces some 29 countries.[33] The same procedure is currently under study with a view to creating a list of target countries that are to be denied transfers of technology relating to missiles.

Thus what began as a matter only of controlling technology transfer involving missiles will henceforth be part of a policy of broader control, the objectives of which are to stem the proliferation of nuclear and similar weaponry. The regime has come some distance from the situation as it existed in the 1985–87 period. It is likely that in 1987 the MTCR agreement represented all that it was possible to achieve by negotiation: that is, through informal government-to-government consultations, with each state being responsible for controlling the declared use of transferred technologies or goods, and with no possible extraterritorial application of American law.

The overlapping of different control regimes for the transfer of technology has not been problem-free, precisely because in the matter of chemical or biological weapons, for instance, the United States intends to avail itself of the extraterritorial application of American legislation.[34] Where the MTCR is concerned, the US cannot pursue an American company abroad, unless that company has also violated the MTCR regulations of the host country.[35] On the other hand, the new American regulation of 13 March 1991, which bears on the imposition of controls for foreign-policy reasons, applies not only to chemical or biological weapons, but to missiles as well. Even though that category was not covered in the annex to the MTCR, it is included in Supplement 6 (Missile Technology Projects) of article 778 of the EAR. Once the new directives take effect, Washington will be in position to determine who violates American law, because the subject of the expression 'once a US person knows' will be implicitly linked to the blacklist of delinquent countries identified in regard to missiles. Furthermore, the Commerce Department, prior to the 13 March 1991 regulation, lacked the power to revoke export licences already granted for products that fell outside the reach of the MTCR's Technical Annex. The new regulations correct this situation, since from now on the Commerce Department can inform companies that a country for which a licence has been granted is now held to constitute a risk.

Where Is the MTCR Heading?

Conceived originally within the G-7, the MTCR today comprises 16 states.[36] Two other countries have adopted legal arrangements similar to MTCR directives (Sweden and Switzerland).[37] Turkey and Greece will probably be among the next batch of candidates, for given that American export regulations — at least those controls motivated by foreign-policy reasons — do not apply to goods intended for other NATO countries, it is likely that attempts will be made to bring in the two countries before the single European market comes into existence.

Whatever their formal status, the Eastern Europeans will not be far behind the Greeks and Turks. For all practical purposes, they can already be considered indirect participants in the MTCR, and the fact that there has been within CoCom a liberalization of controls on Western exports to Eastern Europe serves as a hint of what one might expect should Russia or some other republic of the former Soviet Union decide to seek MTCR membership. Following the *quid pro quo* arranged for Afghanistan — i.e., the withdrawal of Soviet troops from Cuba in exchange for the halting of American aid, via Pakistan, for the *mujahideen*, as well as the cessation of US economic assistance to the latter at the start of the 1991 fiscal year — the question had arisen as to what price the West was prepared to pay to get the Soviet Union to be a full member of the MTCR. The ante seemed broadly known in advance: the granting of most-favoured-nation (MFN) status to the USSR; the lifting of CoCom controls aimed at the latter (at least to the same extent as for China); and probably increased economic assistance from the West to the Soviets. None of these elements, in the last days of the Soviet Union, seemed to be insurmountable obstacles. It is probably safe to say that Russia, and no doubt some other republics, would be prepared to live up to obligations Moscow had hinted at accepting regarding the MTCR.[38]

The real problems will stem from the need for Russia and the other republics to develop the administrative apparatus capable both of controlling their own exports and of ensuring that imported goods and technology are not transferred to third parties. The current circumstances of the CIS suggest that the process will be a long but nevertheless possible one, given enough time. The most nettlesome issue will be the level of information exchange that the West is willing to undertake with the CIS. Can anyone truly say whether things have changed so dramatically as to allow West and East to exchange information freely in such sensitive areas as 'black-market' technology, or the import sources and technical capabilities of suspected proliferators, or the capability of such new producers as India, Brazil, or North Korea to provide certain countries with items that are being withheld from them? Large question marks remain. Nevertheless, sufficient harmony has been achieved in recent years to suggest that further progress can be characteristic of the relations between the West and the former Soviet Union. Nor can the possibility be excluded that some kind of market sharing, perhaps along the lines (with various suppliers allocated particular export markets on product lines) suggested for some time by Andrew J. Pierre for conventional weaponry, might emerge within the confines of the MTCR.[39]

This last point seems especially important given the experience of countries, such as China, that depend upon arms exports to earn the foreign exchange needed for economic modernization and technological development. Beijing's decision to join the NPT, in large measure the result of American pressure and the visit of Japanese Prime Minister Toshiki Kaifu to China, followed the recommendation of President Bush to renew for a year commercial accords with China.

If for the former Soviet republics the fundamental issue associated with their accepting the rules of the game is the need to foster economic and technological links with the West, the issue for China has for some years been the assumed impossibility of the country's associating itself with the technological hegemony of the West. China's foreign minister, Qian Qichen, declared not so long ago that the MTCR constituted a Western means of exerting pressure, and that only those countries participating in the MTCR were obligated to subscribe to its directives.[40]

The difficulties associated with trying to negotiate export controls with China have been abundantly revealed by the fact that, despite an apparent US-Chinese accord on the non-exportation of Chinese missiles to the Middle East, Beijing has continued to sell M-9 and M-11 missiles to Pakistan and Syria. In 1989, following a visit to China by National Security Adviser Brent Scowcroft, the US evidently obtained assurances that such missiles would not be sold to Syria.[41] China has since claimed that the range of its exported missiles falls below that of the missiles controlled under the MTCR. Moreover, M-11 launch pads were detected in Pakistan, which led to a visit to Beijing by Undersecretary of State Reginald Bartholomew. Little information about the nature of the talks has become available, but according to a *New York Times* report, Bartholomew declared that China was considering joining the MTCR.[42] In this regard, it should be noted that several Democratic senators have indicated they wished to link the extension of MFN status to China with the latter's promise to respect, within six months, the directives of the MTCR.

All students of the issue agree that for controls to be effective in the domain of missile-technology transfer, the MTCR must be able to count upon the effective collaboration of the major supplier countries. Enormous progress has, in fact, been made in this regard. It could well be that in future the MTCR may simply have to accept the informal participation of major producing states such as China—though it is worth recalling that Beijing has probably not yet spoken its last word on the matter.

The participation of the major producers, however, does not settle the question of emerging producers, whether they be acknowledged, clandestine, or merely potential. Given that the MTCR is directed mainly at these emerging producers, it would hardly seem likely that they would consent to join it—unless of course the West were prepared to make some important technological concessions. Those analysts who, like Admiral Brooks or Kathleen Bailey, decry either the ineffectiveness of the MTCR or its existence as a pure and simple non-proliferation institution (unlike, say, the NPT, which at least enshrines the right of all to the peaceful fruits of nuclear energy) forget that the MTCR constitutes the only viable instrument the technologically advanced states have to retard, if not bring to a halt, the phenomenon of uncontrolled nuclear proliferation.[43] As Aaron Karp notes, the MTCR remains the most important barrier to proliferation.[44] For Janne E. Nolan, for example, even if she accepts that nuclear proliferation is part of a global process of technological diffusion, the fact remains that the MTCR can hold in check some of the 'most troublesome aspects' of proliferation.[45] On the other hand, at least one former Pentagon consultant, Gary Milhollin, has a different view of the MTCR's merits, holding it to be 'too little, too late'.[46]

Conclusion

The MTCR today stands at more than one crossroads. From the US point of view, the regime is increasingly seen as one of the several instruments at the disposal of the West for responding to the otherwise untrammelled dissemination of technology, at least in its most dangerous forms. From a wider viewpoint, the MTCR stands squarely in the midst of both a rationalization and an integration of a variety of control measures, to say nothing of the vast administrative reorganization that proceeds apace with the establishment of new control criteria, now that the cold war is dead and buried and the monster of nuclear war is knocking, as the Gulf War demonstrated, at the very gates of the West's technological empire.

On the level of decision-making processes, the US had already started to rationalize its policy in 1989, by creating a position in the Defense Department for an assistant to the deputy undersecretary who would be responsible for non-proliferation policy, embracing nuclear, biological, and chemical weapons as well as missiles. The trend continued in March 1991 with the administrative decision to bring all these controls under the same regulatory device: namely, section 778 of the EAR, henceforth entitled Proliferation Controls. At the State Department also there have been administrative developments: an interdepartmental Missile Technology Control Export Group (MTEC) has been formed; a Missile Trade Analysis Group (MTAG) has been created; and the Office of Munitions Control has been strengthened.[47] At the Commerce Department, the Bureau of Export Administration (BXA) is assisted in its revision of the Commodity Control List (CCL) by several consultative groups.[48]

On the purely administrative level, the CCL is in the process of being fundamentally reviewed. The same seems true for the US munitions list, administered by the State Department. As a result of the executive order of 16 November 1990, concerning the proliferation of chemical and biological weapons, the US must remove from the munitions list all dual-use goods included in the CoCom list, except for those articles adjudged to affect national security.[49]

At the international level, states are strengthening their controls over

Table 15.3 List of Countries Participating in Various Control Regimes for Transfers of Technology, and Nuclear and Related Arms, as of 1 January 1991

	MTCR	AUSTRALIA GROUP	COCOM	NSG[1]	FSS[2]	ZANGGER COMMITTEE
Australia	X	X	X	X	X	X
Austria	X	X				X
Belgium	X	X	X	X		X
Bulgaria					X	X★
Canada	X	X	X	X	X	X
Czechoslovakia				X	X	X
Denmark	X	X	X	X		X
Finland				X		X
France	X	X	X	X		
Germany	X	X	X	X	X★	X
Great Britain	X	X	X	X		X
Greece		X	X	X		X
Hungary				X	X★	X
Ireland		X	X	X		X
Italy	X	X	X	X		X
Japan	X	X	X	X	X	X
Luxembourg	X	X	X	X		X
Netherlands	X	X	X	X	X★	X
New Zealand	X	X				
Norway	X	X	X	X	X	X
Poland				X	X	X
Portugal		X	X	X		X
Romania				X		
Spain	X	X	X	X		
Sweden				X		X
Switzerland		X		X	X	X
United States	X	X	X	X	X	X
USSR				X		X
TOTAL	16	20	17	26	12	23

★: Announced in 1990 that they would require full-scope safeguards on nuclear transfers.
[1](London) Nuclear Suppliers Group
[2]Full-Scope Safeguards
The EEC is also represented in the NSG, Australia, and MTCR Groups.

SOURCE: Report to Congress pursuant to Section 601 of the Nuclear Non-Proliferation Act of 1978 for the Year Ending December 31, 1990 (January 1991).

exports, by means of amendments to their own national legislation; at the same time, the number of adherents to the MTCR continues to grow. Their goal is simple: non-proliferation. What they offer up to attain this end is also straightforward: the creation of a vast zone of free trade in technology for those countries that know how to behave themselves.

Additionally, the MTCR faces a sweeping reorganization of all the control regimes directed toward non-proliferation. Table 15.3 lists the adherents to, or implicit participants in, a range of agreements relating—some closely, some loosely—to nuclear, chemical, biological, and missile proliferation. If the MTCR was originally an instrument of the G-7, it no longer is today; instead, it represents the multifarious and synergetic product of all those measures that have been taken in the other domains of non-proliferation.

This trend perhaps explains the Canadian desire for a global summit dedicated to the removal of weapons of mass destruction. It also explains certain other reactions elsewhere, such as that of James LeMunyon, assistant undersecretary for export administration in the US, who in 1990 urged a rationalization of non-proliferation measures within the same institutional embrace. To a congressional subcommittee in September 1990, he remarked:

> I think the issue of combining activities like the Australia Group, the Missile Tech Group, maybe other countries that participate in nuclear areas, is something that is certainly not imminent, but in my own view is probably coming some day, if for no other reason than that those of us in this business, in the international community, keep showing up at different meetings around the world, talking, in one case, on missiles, and in another case in Australia on chemicals, and in another case at CoCom on East-West trade.[50]

The overlap of activities is considerable, but still each regime corresponds to particular needs. Despite the American desire to institutionalize the MTCR, the latter continues to have no official permanent secretariat. In reality, what is needed is that participating states work within some co-ordinating structure, which even if informal could nevertheless be effective.

Faced with the task of having to plug the breaches in the non-proliferation dike(s), it would seem that anything capable of modifying the various control regimes' original mandates is worthwhile. Thus the group studying chemical weapons, at Geneva, openly lists, in table 1 of its convention relating to highly toxic chemicals, a biological toxin, saxitoxin. This was done deliberately, with a view to creating a precedent that might some day enable the convention's verification agency to police as well the 1972 Convention on the interdiction of bacteriological or toxic weapons.[51] Following the MTCR's Tokyo meeting, in March 1991, the mandate was similarly enlarged to include biological weapons, perhaps as a means of bringing into the MTCR's purview missiles with a range of less than 300 km.[52]

The above demonstrates that the MTCR has been developing, more and more, into an institution where the Western countries can harmonize their policies in a broad range of issue areas, all of which touch upon the general challenge of ensuring non-proliferation. In this sense, it does constitute a more adequate forum for international governance than the myriad of multilateral (often simply technical) forums addressing the same general objective. This high society of non-proliferation that is the MTCR comprises a fortuitous mix of political and technical competencies. The MTCR functions, because there is simply no alternative to co-operation among the Western countries most concerned about proliferation.

Notes

[1] *Hearings before the Committee on Foreign Affairs and Its Subcommittee on Arms Control, International Security and Science*, House of Representatives, 101st Congress, Second Session, 17 May and 11 July 1990 (Washington: US Government Printing Office), 3 (hereafter *Hearings*).

[2] Elisa D. Harris, 'Chemical Weapons Proliferation: Current Capabilities and Prospect for Control', in *New Threats: Responding to the Proliferation of Nuclear, Chemical, and Delivery Capabilities in the Third World*. Aspen Strategy Group Report (1990).

[3] Statement of Rear Admiral Thomas A. Brooks, USN, Director of Naval Intelligence before the Seapower, Strategic and Critical Materials Subcommittee of the House Armed Services Committee on Intelligence Issues, 7 March 1991.

[4] See Geoffrey Kemp, *Hearings*; and Uzi Rubin, 'How Much Does Missile Proliferation Matter?' *Orbis* 35 (Winter 1991), 28.

[5] See the testimony of Richard A. Clarke, US Assistant Undersecretary of State, *Hearings*, 145-6.

[6] See Leonard Spector, *Nuclear Ambitions* (Boulder, CO: Westview, 1990).

[7] Keith Krause, 'The Political Economy of the International Arms Transfer System: The Diffusion of Military Technique via Arms Transfers', *International Journal* 45 (Summer 1990), 687-722.

[8] The extreme example being the Mercedes–Benz trucks that served as launching vehicles for Iraq's Scud missiles. See *Le Monde* (26 March 1991), 5.

[9] See, for this view, Kenneth Waltz, 'The Spread of Nuclear Weapons: More May Be Better', *Adelphi Papers* 171 (London: International Institute for Strategic Studies, 1981).

[10] Martin Navias, 'Ballistic Missile Proliferation in the Third World', *Adelphi Papers* 252 (London: International Institute for Strategic Studies, 1990), 49. Also see Kathleen C. Bailey, 'Can Missile Proliferation Be Reversed?' *Orbis* 35 (Winter 1991), 5-14; Aaron Karp, 'Ballistic Missile Proliferation', *SIPRI Yearbook, 1990*, 369-93, and *SIPRI Yearbook, 1991*, 317-37; Thomas G. Mahnken and Timothy D. Hoydt, 'The Spread of Missile Technology to the Third World', *Comparative Strategy* 9 (1990), 245-63; Janne E. Nolan, 'Ballistic Missiles in the Third World: The Limits of Nonproliferation', *Arms Control Today* 19 (Nov. 1989), 9-14; and *Congressional Research Service Report* 88-742F (9 Feb. 1989).

[11] See on this subject Jo L. Husbands and Anne Hessing, 'The Conventional Arms Transfers Talks: An Experiment in Mutual Arms Trade Restraint', in Thomas Ohlson ed., *Arms Transfer Limitations and Third World Security* (New York: Oxford Univ. Press, 1988), 110-25; and especially Andrew J. Pierre, *The Global Politics of Arms Sales* (Princeton: Princeton Univ. Press 1982).

[12] Pierre, *Global Politics*, 292-3.

[13] See *Report to Congress Pursuant to Section 601 of the Nuclear Non-Proliferation Act of 1978 for the Year Ending December 31, 1990* (Jan. 1991), 17.

[14]See 'U.S. Efforts to Control the Transfer of Nuclear-Capable Missile Technology', *Report to the Honorable Dennis DeConcini*, US Senate (Washington: US General Accounting Office, June 1990), 1-2.

[15]See the written reply of the US government in *Hearings*, 285.

[16]Bailey, 'Can Missile Proliferation Be Reversed?' 19.

[17]See Edouard Sauvignon, 'Les directives de 1987 pour les tranferts sensibles de matériels concernant les missiles', *Annuaire français de droit international* 34 (1988), 699.

[18]Navias, 'Ballistic Missile Proliferation', 51.

[19]See the testimony of Richard A. Clarke, in *Hearings*, 220; and Christopher Barton, 'Controlling Missile Exports: A Catch 22?' *Christian Science Monitor* (19 March 1991).

[20]Navias, 'Ballistic Missile Proliferation', 51.

[21]Ibid., 50.

[22]See Bailey, in *Hearings*, 51. President Bush's report to Congress of January 1991 notes: 'At the beginning of the 1991 Fiscal Year in October, economic and security assistance to Pakistan was suspended because, under the Pressler Amendment to the Foreign Assistance Act, the President was unable to certify that Pakistan does not possess a nuclear explosive device and that U.S. assistance would reduce significantly the risk that Pakistan will possess such a device.' See *Report to Congress Pursuant to Section 601*, 7.

[23]*Hearing of the Subcommittee on Technology and National Security of the Joint Economic Committee*, Federal Information Systems Corporation, Federal News Service (21 Sept. 1990).

[24]See 'German Democratic Republic: Change in Country Group Status and Elimination of General License', *Federal Register* (55 FR 40825), 55 (5 Oct. 1990).

[25]'Exports to Poland, Hungary, Czechoslovakia: Exports and Re-exports of National Security Controlled Commodities and Related Technical Data', *Federal Register* (56 FR 19015), 56 (25 April 1991).

[26]In his statement of July 1990, Richard A. Clarke declared: 'To help them further into the mainstream of nuclear non-proliferation activities, as well as to create a necessary legal framework for significant peaceful nuclear commerce with the U.S., we have offered to negotiate individual agreements for peaceful nuclear cooperation with them consistent with the Atomic Energy Act.' See *Hearings*, 166.

[27]In his testimony cited in *Hearings*, 220, Undersecretary Clarke declared 'we are very opposed to the Soviets continuing to sell missiles to Afghanistan. We have said that to them. We have said to them that if they are going to be a member of the MTCR, in our view they are going to have to address that issue.' In the same *Hearings*, 92, Geoffrey Kemp recalled that more Scud missiles were fired in Afghanistan than during the 'War of the Cities' between Iraq and Iran.

[28]See 'Fact Sheet on U.S. Core List Proposal to CoCom with Contact List Released

by Department of Commerce, 1 October 1990,' Washington, Bureau of National Affairs, *Daily Report for Executives* 191 (2 Oct. 1990).

[29]'Notice of Upcoming Changes in U.S. National Security Controls', *Federal Register* (56 FR 30798) 56 (5 July 1991); and 'Revision of Commodity Control List', *Federal Register* (56 FR 42824) 56 (29 Aug. 1991).

[30]In the above-cited testimony, Clarke declared that 'MTCR Annex items controlled by Commerce have been incorporated into Commerce regulations, and Annex items licensed by State are covered by existing provisions. Because the Commerce regulations are currently tied to CoCom, Commerce may need to take some steps to retain controls on MTCR items when the CoCom lists are revised. We have also begun discussing the MTCR/CoCom relationship with our MTCR partners since, as CoCom controls are reduced, they may also need to revise their laws or regulations to ensure continued controls on missile technologies' (150).

[31]The text reads: 'The term "U.S. person" is defined for the purpose of these provisions to include foreign branches of companies organized in the United States'.

[32]According to section 778.1, 'This part defines the types of transactions that are governed by the U.S. policy concerning the non-proliferation of chemical and biological weapons, nuclear weapons or explosive devices, missile systems and the U.S. maritime nuclear propulsion policy.'

[33]See *Federal Register* (56 FR 10756) 56 (13 March 1991).

[34]See section 4 of the presidential directive of 20 Nov. 1990, 'Sanctions Against Foreign Persons', and section 5, 'Sanctions Against Foreign Countries', in 'The President Executive Order: Chemical and Biological Weapons Proliferation', *Federal Register* (55 FR 48587) 55 (20 Nov. 1990).

[35]According to testimony of Henry D. Sokolski, 'the answer is clear. They have to violate, and be found to have violated their own country's export control.' See *Hearings*, 207.

[36]Namely, Australia, Austria, Belgium, Canada, Denmark, Spain, the US, France, Italy, Japan, Luxembourg, the Netherlands, New Zealand, Norway, Germany, and the UK.

[37]Karp, 'Ballistic Missile Proliferation', 334.

[38]See *Arms Control Reporter 1991*, 706; and *San Francisco Chronicle* (7 March 1990).

[39]See Pierre, *Global Politics*, 293.

[40]Jeffrey R. Smith, 'U.S. Press China to Halt Missile Sales Deals with Syria and Pakistan Opposed', *Washington Post* (11 June 1991), A14.

[41]Clarke testimony, *Hearings*, 133.

[42]See *New York Times* (19 June 1991); and *Arms Control Reporter 1991*, 706.

[43]See Bailey, 'Can Missile Proliferation Be Reversed?' 10; and Thomas Brooks, *Jane's Defence Weekly* (International ed.) (31 March 1990), 583.

[44]Karp, 'Ballistic Missile Proliferation', 333.

[45]Nolan, 'Ballistic Missiles in the Third World', 9.

[46]Barbara Starr, 'Controlling the Spread of Ballistic Missiles', *Jane's Defence Weekly* (International ed.) (22 April 1989), 696.

[47]This position is currently filled by Henry D. Sokolski.

[48]Clarke testimony, *Hearings*, 149: 'In rough terms, for State/DTC cases we approve 92 percent; another 4 percent are approved after we receive government-to-government assurances that the item will not be used in a nuclear capable delivery system; finally about 4 percent are denied. For Commerce, the committees recommend approval of only about 22 percent immediately; for 61 percent they recommend assurances; for 17 percent, they recommend denials. Since the first of the year, they recommended denial for 29 State/DTC cases and 9 Commerce cases.'

[49]These are the Automated Manufacturing Equipment Technical Advisory Committee; Computer Peripherals, Components, and Related Test Equipment Technical Advisory Committee; Computer Systems Technical Advisory Committee; Electronic Instrumentation Technical Advisory Committee; Materials Technical Advisory Committee; Semiconductor Technical Advisory Committee; Telecommunications Equipment Technical Advisory Committee; Transportation and Related Equipment Technical Advisory Committee.

[50]See his testimony before the Subcommittee on Technology and National Security of the Joint Economic Committee, in *Federal News Service* (21 Sept. 1990).

[51]See Wolf J. Aroesty and E.C. River, 'Domestic Implementation of a Chemical Weapons Treaty', prepared for the Under Secretary of Defense for Acquisition, *Rand Corporation Report R-3745-ACQ* (Oct. 1989), 19.

[52]*The Arms Control Reporter 1991*, 706; and *Japan Economic Newswire Plus* (20 March 1991).

chapter sixteen

A New World Order?
Western Public Perceptions in the Post-Cold-War Era

Don Munton

The 'new world order' so ringingly proclaimed not long ago seems to have gone the way of the celebratory champagne bubbles. In the corridors of power politics and at the conference tables of the global élite, the realities of the old order are triumphing over the rhetoric of the new.

And whither the thoughts of the masses? By conventional assumptions, which hold that where the leaders do not go, the people will not follow, the thoughts of the masses are of little import or interest. Thus the last place many would look for, let alone expect to find, inklings of a new world order is the public mind.

Oddly enough, perhaps, that is precisely where one may not only look for but also find such evidence. Five decades after World War II, in the final decade of the twentieth century and the first of the post–cold-war era, Western publics are redefining their perceptions of global threats and security, reassessing the major world powers, and rethinking the global agenda. Indeed, these shifts have been under way in many respects for a number of years, and perhaps even for decades.

The extent of the shifts in public attitudes is now clear and unarguable, though not their significance. The central question of this chapter is whether this new public thinking about international affairs represents a 'new world order', at least at the level of public perceptions.

This analysis is based upon the concept of order outlined by Hedley Bull, in *The Anarchical Society*, and his mentor Martin Wight.[1] Bull argues that international order is maintained in large part by the collaboration of states through what he terms the five major 'institutions' of world order: war, the great powers, balance-of-power, diplomacy, and international law. The focus here is on public perceptions of and attitudes toward the first four of these. Since Bull's focus is the international system of the post-war period, he does not deal explicitly or at any length with the question of what changes might constitute a new order—a question of central importance here.[2] For the purposes of this analysis it is assumed that fundamental changes in public perceptions of these key 'institutions', taken together, constitute evidence of a perceived 'new world order'.[3]

The evidence for these assumptions and the argument that there are some prevalent conceptions of world order among Western publics can be found in part in a two-year series of co-ordinated public-opinion surveys carried out in the Federal Republic of Germany, the United Kingdom, the United States, and Canada in the late 1980s.[4] This multinational project represented the first time such co-ordinated polling on the topic of international security attitudes had ever been done in these four countries. In addition, this chapter brings together a wide variety of other poll results from the four countries, also for the first time.[5] Some of these involve comparison of results from the 1980s and 1990s with identical questions asked on surveys in the 1960s and 1970s, and some comprise lengthy time series. All of these surveys are based on national samples.

Perceptions of War

War, says Bull, is a manifestation of disorder and of the possibility of break-down of international society: 'The society of states, accordingly, is concerned to limit and contain war, to keep it within bounds of rules laid down by international society itself' (187-8). Yet his emphasis often seems to be on the 'positive role' that war plays in the maintenance of this order. Seeing war as a means of enforcing international law, preserving the balance of power, and bringing about 'just' change, Bull clearly focuses on war at the level of the interstate system rather than the individual state or person. In *Power Politics*, Martin Wight focuses more directly on war as viewed from the perspective of the state and its inhabitants. He begins with the standard realist premises that 'all powers at all times are concerned primarily with their security', and that 'most powers at most times find their security threatened' (139). In this view, the fear of war is the prime motive of international politics, and as such it must necessarily rank as a key element of any global order. Even if it were merely one of the major motives, however, it would surely rate attention here.[6]

Arguably the dominant image of the post-war period has been that of the atomic or nuclear mushroom cloud. There is certainly no lack of evidence that leaders as well as publics have given primacy to concerns about nuclear war. Superpower relations, especially during and in the decades after the Cuban missile crisis, for example, more than bear this out. Concerns about nuclear war therefore are an appropriate focus with which to begin this examination of the data. To accept a distinction between conventional and nuclear war, though, is not to assume that the former is unimportant in the nuclear age. Nor is it to deny that the former might lead to the latter. The matter of public concerns about conventional war will thus also be examined.

When asked in 1988 about the prospects of confrontation involving nuclear weapons in the next twenty-five years, Germans, Britons, Americans, and Canadians generally discounted the possibility (Table 16.1). Only minorities in each country suggested it was likely to any degree. For the relatively relaxed Germans the proportion (14 per cent) was about half what it was among the more angst-ridden Canadians (30 per cent) and Americans (33 per cent). These differences aside, a solid majority in all three countries indicated that such a war was unlikely or very unlikely. Fears about a more imminent nuclear war are even less. When the time frame proposed in survey questions is the next ten years, the perceived likelihood declines substantially. The proportions who regard such a confrontation as unlikely or very unlikely rise to more than eight out of every ten persons, except among Americans.

When public-opinion data over recent years from individual countries are examined they provide strong evidence of a common trend, not only over the course of the 1980s but also through the late 1970s. (See Figure 16.1.) In the United States, for example, the proportion who thought nuclear war likely dropped from nearly 50 per cent in the early 1980s to less than 20 per cent in 1990.[7] This pattern is entirely consistent with that found in Britain, where a downward trend over the early 1980s of about an equal magnitude seems clear.[8] The same declining concerns through the 1980s about the likelihood of nuclear war 'in your lifetime' are evident in Canada. Those who thought war likely to some degree dropped by half, from 40 per cent to about 20 per cent, over the 1984-90 period.[9]

Taking a longer time perspective, the numbers of Canadians who thought the chances of war were greater than ten years earlier had increased steadily over the course of the 1970s, as the *détente* process stalled and then collapsed with the December 1979 Soviet intervention in Afghanistan. By the late 1980s concerns were once again back down to the levels of the early 1970s.[10] A similar pattern of rise and fall is evident in both British and German concerns about a 'world war' during the late 1970s and early-mid 1980s.[11] From a low point in the late 1970s, both British and German estimates of the chances of war increased to a peak in 1980-81. They then declined more or less steadily for the rest of the decade.

These declining concerns regarding war, especially nuclear war, seem largely related to the prospect of the classic cold-war superpower confronta-

Table 16.1. Perceived Likelihood of Nuclear War in 25 Years, 1988

	UK	FRG	CANADA	US
Likely or very likely	26	14	30	33
Unlikely or very unlikely	74	86	70	66
Total	100%	100%	100%	99%

Question wording (except US): 'Within the next twenty-five years, how likely do you think it is that there would be a nuclear war?'

US wording: 'If you had to guess, how likely is it that we in the United States will get into a nuclear war within the next 25 years — very likely, fairly likely, fairly unlikely, or very unlikely?' The totals in this, and in subsequent tables below, do not always add up to 100 per cent because of rounding. Non-responses and 'don't knows' are generally omitted.

SOURCE: International Security Project (ISP), 1988: Americans Talk Security Project (ATS), #4.

Figure 16.1. Likelihood of War

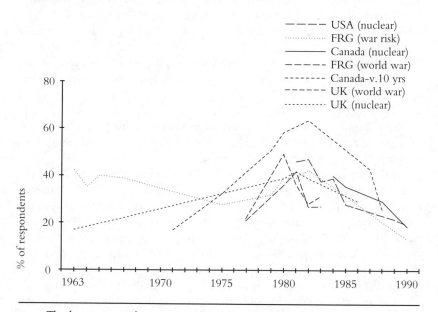

```
          ─ ─ ─ ─  USA (nuclear)
          ············  FRG (war risk)
          ─────────  Canada (nuclear)
          ─ ─ ─ ─ ─  FRG (world war)
          ---------  Canada-v.10 yrs
          ─ ─ ─ ─ ─  UK (world war)
          ··········  UK (nuclear)
```

NOTE: The data sources and survey questions are described in the text and notes.

tion.[12] As seen below, the likelihood of other types of conflict and war is not discounted to the same degree.

Perceptions of the Great Powers

A second institution of the international order identified by Wight and Bull is the special relationship among the great powers.[13] Bull argues that the great powers can, and sometimes do, promote international order: first, in managing their own bilateral relations so as to control crises, limit wars, and preserve the balance of power; and, second, in providing leadership and direction to the interstate system as a whole, by unilaterally exploiting their preponderance *vis-à-vis* lesser powers and mutually acting in concert or at least respecting each other's spheres of influence.

So prominent a feature of the interstate system as the relations between or among the great powers is obviously not lost on domestic publics. The question here is how publics perceive the great powers and what relevance these perceptions have for international order.

There are no arguments among analysts as to the identity of the two dominant great powers of the post-war period, and no doubts among domestic publics either. The capabilities of the United States, and its perceived willingness to defend not only North America but also its allies in Europe, made it indisputably the leader of the Western nations. Its policies, starting with the Marshall Plan and the establishment of NATO, went beyond self-interest. It was afforded substantial legitimacy in return.[14] The military might of the Soviet Union, and its apparently hostile intentions, on the other hand, made it clearly the major perceived threat of the post-war period. Its legitimacy in Western eyes therefore approached nil for most of the early cold-war period.

But perceptions of the Soviet Union began to change during *détente* in the late 1960s and early 1970s; the change may even have begun as early as the Cuban missile crisis of 1962. Despite the decades of the cold war, or, perhaps because after so long it had never become more than a cold war, by the mid- to late 1980s few people in Western countries believed that the Soviet Union presented a serious military threat to the West. This is abundantly evident in the responses to a variety of survey questions.

By the late 1980s, the vast majority in the UK, Germany, Canada, and the US did not regard a Soviet attack on Europe or North America as very likely (see Table 16.2.) Over 70 per cent in each country perceived little or no such danger, and thought such an attack unlikely or very unlikely.[15] Comparing across the four countries, the Germans — the allies geographically closest to Moscow — had the most benign view of the USSR as a military threat. The Americans, followed closely by the Canadians, had the least benign view. (While the latter two are indeed those farthest from the old East-West dividing line in Europe, they are not, as is often supposed by Europeans, the farthest from the USSR). The commonalities across the three countries seem

Table 16.2. Likelihood of Soviet Attack on Western Europe, 1988

	UK	FRG	CANADA	US
Likely or very likely	10	5	22	29
Unlikely or very unlikely	90	95	78	71
Total	100%	100%	100%	100%

SOURCES: US: ATS, 1988; other: International Security Project, 1988.

more striking than the differences, however. The same is true of a question in which Germans, Britons, and Canadians were asked about the greatest threat to world peace. In all three countries, few selected 'Soviet actions on the world scene' (from among a number of alternatives); in none was the proportion greater than 5 per cent. In other words, 95 per cent or more 'put the finger' on threats other than the (now former) USSR.

The fundamental changes in perceptions of the Soviet Union suggested by these data are borne out by the results of numerous questions on a variety of polls in which publics were asked to evaluate either the threat from the USSR or its degree of friendliness (see Figure 16.2.) Americans' estimation of the seriousness of the Soviet threat clearly underwent a striking shift during the second half of the 1980s. While fully three out of every four (76 per cent) regarded the Soviet Union as a serious or very serious threat in 1985, the figures dropped to 55–60 per cent by 1988 and then to around 33 per cent in

Figure 16.2 Threat from the Soviet Union

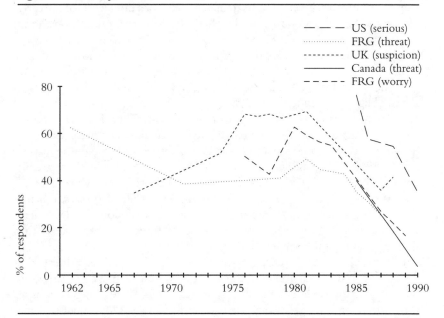

1990.[16] In Canada a similar pattern seems to emerge. Over the latter half of the 1980s there was a significant drop in the proportion of Canadians who agreed with the view of the USSR as 'an expansionist power that threatens western security'. While 40 per cent had strongly agreed with this view in 1985, only 5 per cent did so in 1990.[17]

The pattern of declining perceptions of threat is also clearly evident in Germany. In early 1980, in the aftermath of the Afghanistan invasion, two out of every three Germans (65 per cent) were worried about 'being threatened by the East' — a phrase that was understood to refer to Russia.[18] By mid-1986, and before the signing of the INF Treaty at the Washington summit in December of the following year, the proportion had declined by more than half, to 26 per cent. By mid-1989, prior to the opening of the Berlin Wall, it had again shrunk by half, to 14 per cent. In comparison with those of Americans, the threat perceptions of Germans seem to have begun to decline somewhat earlier.

An even broader perspective on changing German perceptions of the Soviet Union is provided by a unique Allensbach time series stretching back three decades. From the late 1950s through the early 1970s Germans increasingly tended to perceive 'the Russians' as 'basically committed to seeking a reconciliation with the West'. The proportion who thought so doubled, from only 17 per cent in 1959, at the height of the cold war, to 35 per cent in 1971. It then declined steadily over the course of the troubled 1970s, back down to 16 per cent the month after the Soviet invasion of Afghanistan. Elevated concerns over what that meant for East-West relations, however, did not persist long. Perceptions of the Russians as committed to reconciliation rose within eighteen months to match the record high levels of the early 1970s, and then went on to exceed them. Fully half the German population shared this view by late 1985, only months after Gorbachev had succeeded Chernenko. A related series of questions asked in Britain shows a similar trend.[19]

In short, Western public perceptions of a Soviet threat or unfriendliness in general began to decline about 1980-1 — perhaps curiously to some observers — in the aftermath of the invasion of Afghanistan. There is some evidence to suggest that this was a somewhat delayed continuation of an earlier trend. These concerns declined steadily — and substantially — through the decade of the 1980s. Considering the two unambiguous and consistent trends apparent in Western public attitudes discovered above — the reduced expectations of a nuclear war and the declining perception of threat from the Soviet Union — common sense suggests that they may not be independent of one another: a declining perception of a Soviet threat seems to have led to a declining sense of the danger of war.

It seems likely that the changing perceptions of the old Soviet threat may have influenced as well public perceptions of Soviet foreign-policy actions in general. Whether or not that is the case, it is clear that Western perceptions of the underlying interests being pursued by the Soviet Union had become

Table 16.3. Perceived Interests of the Soviet Union and United States, 1988

SOVIET INTEREST IS:	UK	FRG	CANADA	US
World domination	18	33	39	39
Protecting its own national security	83	67	61	61
Total	101%	100%	100%	100%
AMERICAN INTEREST IS:				
World domination	33	29	33	
Protecting its own national security	67	71	67	
Total	100%	100%	100%	

Question wording: 'Do you believe that the Soviet Union (United States) is mainly interested in world domination or mainly interested in protecting its own national security?'

SOURCES: UK, Germany, and Canada: the International Security Project (ISP), 1988; US data: the Americans Talk Security (ATS) series. The US percentages shown are the mean value of three surveys conducted in January, June, and December 1988.

strikingly mellow by the late 1980s. Majorities, often strong majorities, perceived it to be more concerned with protecting its own national security than with the pursuit of world domination. This judgement was most prevalent in the UK and least prevalent in the US. Those who believed that the goal was world domination, however, were at most about one in every three (see Table 16.3.)

A Soviet-American comparative perspective underscores the relatively benign nature of these judgements. Parallel public perceptions of the underlying interests pursued by the United States are available for the three ally countries (but not the US itself) for 1988. They render more or less equivalent judgements regarding basic American goals: the strong majority in all three countries regard the US too as mainly concerned with its own security. At the same time, about a third of Germans and Canadians believe the United States is more concerned with world domination than with protecting its own national security—roughly the same proportion as believe that about the Soviet Union. Among the British public there are actually more who regard world domination as the stronger American goal than regard it as the stronger Soviet one. It would seem reasonable to assume that Americans, on grounds of simple patriotism if not a firm belief in the moral rightness of their country's foreign policy, would strongly tend not to perceive an interest in world domination in that policy. Their views would thus differ from those of their allies more with respect to their own country's basic goals than those of the Soviet Union.

These judgements about the Soviet Union, and especially the similarity in public perceptions of the Soviet and American interests, suggest that it might

Table 16.4. *Confidence in the Soviet Union and United States, 1988*

CONFIDENCE IN USSR:	UK	CANADA	FRG
Very great/ considerable	42	42	33
Little/none	58	59	67
Total	100%	101%	100%
CONFIDENCE IN US:			
Very great/considerable	24	47	39
Little/none	76	52	61
Total	100%	99%	100%

Question wording: 'How much confidence do you have in the ability of the Soviet Union [United States] to deal wisely with present world problems?'

SOURCE: International Security Project, 1988.

be desirable to take a closer look at the evidence in public attitudes of what might be called parallelism, or what has been referred to, usually pejoratively, by some commentators as perceptions of 'superpower equivalence'. Perhaps the key question here, then, is the extent to which both the great powers were succeeding in the 1980s in, as Bull phrased it, 'securing and preserving the consent of other states to the special role they play in the system'. The most direct measure of this success is the general confidence held in the actions of each of the powers.

The comparative data, in short, show considerable parallelism and strong commonalities across the German, British, and Canadian publics (see Table 16.4.) Take, for example, evaluations in late 1988. In all three countries about the same proportions, or more, express confidence in the ability of the Soviet Union to deal wisely with present world problems as express such confidence in United States' ability, with one exception. In Germany the proportions with considerable or very great confidence in the USSR and US were 33 per cent and 39 per cent, respectively; in Canada, 42 per cent and 47 per cent, respectively; in Britain, 42 per cent and 24 per cent. The last figure, strikingly low, reflects a characteristically rather negative British public evaluation of American policies, an evaluation that was, of course, not evident in then Prime Minister Margaret Thatcher's official statements.

The longer-term trends in changing perceptions of the great powers are perhaps even more revealing. United States Information Agency surveys regularly carried out in the major European countries tracked changing levels of confidence in the former USSR over the 1980s. In Britain and Germany those who expressed a 'great deal' or 'fair amount' of confidence in Soviet abilities to deal with world problems rose from around 10-20 per cent in 1983-84, before Mr Gorbachev came to power, to around 60 per cent in

1988, in the aftermath of the signing of the INF treaty abolishing intermediate-range nuclear forces in Europe. This level of confidence declined only somewhat following the attempted coup of 1991 and the disintegration of the old USSR.

For most Western allies generally there was a period of long-term declining confidence in the United States through the 1960s and 1970s.[20] Confidence levels rose slightly in the early 1980s, but then fell steadily again, in reaction to the confrontational style of the Reagan administration. They recovered somewhat only in the latter Reagan years. In Britain, those with some confidence climbed from a low of 40 per cent in 1985 to over 60 per cent in 1991, in the aftermath of the Gulf War. In Germany confidence in the United States similarly rose from less than 40 per cent in 1985 to almost 70 per cent in 1991.

Surveys in Canada also have tracked the changing perceptions of the Soviet Union and the United States over these years. (The basic question was the same as that on the USIA Surveys, but a different set of responses was used.) While confidence in both was at a low ebb in the mid-1980s, the trend was for a very consistent improvement over the 1980s in both cases, as it was in Europe. With respect to the Soviet Union, the proportion of those with considerable or great confidence rose steadily from only 28 per cent in 1987 to 42 per cent in 1988 to 52 per cent in 1989 to 62 per cent in 1990.[21] The 1990 figure was almost certainly a record high level of confidence in Soviet policies.

The positiveness of Canadians' image of the USSR may have surpassed that held in the early 1970s, around the time of the first US–USSR Strategic Arms Limitation Treaty, only by the end of the 1980s. The equivalent question on the 1972 USIA poll found 54 per cent expressing great or considerable confidence in the policies of Leonid Brezhnev and company. It therefore appears that the degree of confidence held in 1990 was not unprecedented.

Confidence in the ability of the US to deal wisely with world problems rose during the 1970s, after the Vietnam and Watergate periods, but then generally fell during the Reagan years.[22] The turn-around came in 1987. From 37 per cent of Canadians in 1987, those expressing confidence rose to 75 per cent in 1990. When the current results are compared to a survey conducted in Canada in 1972 by the USIA, it appears that Canadians' confidence in their southern neighbour now exceeds the levels of the early 1970s, probably for the first time in the ensuing two decades.

The decline during the 1970s and early-mid 1980s in the perceived legitimacy of the United States as the leader of the Western alliance apparent here has, of course, not gone unnoticed. The degree of parallelism in more recent perceptions of the former USSR and the US may, however, be one of the least recognized aspects of contemporary public opinion about international affairs. While commentators began to pontificate about the end of the cold war only with the opening of the Berlin Wall in the fall of 1989, Western publics had by that time already abandoned the 'black-white' pattern of images that maintained the cold war. This development is revealed most clearly when individuals' perceptions of the US and USSR are analysed together.

During the cold-war period most, though not all, individuals in Western countries had essentially positive images of the US and essentially negative ones of the USSR. By the early 1980s, however, perceptions were no longer so. Certainly by the mid-late 1980s, most individuals had, on any given issue, either positive perceptions of both superpowers or negative perceptions of both.[23] This 'plague on both your policies' sentiment was evident among Canadians in 1987 on other parallel questions. Almost a majority of those surveyed (46 per cent) believed neither superpower's leadership was genuinely interested in disarmament. Nearly six in ten (56 per cent) expressed little or no confidence in either the American or the Soviet ability to handle world problems. And almost seven in ten (68 per cent) believed both the US and USSR were trying to increase their areas of influence.

What is particularly notable, and not widely appreciated, about these perceptions is that Western publics' images of the former Soviet Union had substantially mellowed well before the disintegration of the USSR, the collapse of communist regimes in Eastern Europe, or the fall of the Berlin Wall, and even before the conclusion of the INF treaty in December 1987, the first US–USSR arms control agreement in almost a decade. In other words, at the time of its disintegration in late 1991, the Soviet Union had, ironically, achieved substantial legitimacy as a responsible great power. It had gained legitimacy internationally in the eyes of Western publics at precisely the same time it was losing its legitimacy domestically. Arguably, it could not have both.

Perceptions of the Balance of Power

Among the concepts of international politics, perhaps none has been as controversial, none as often criticized, as that of the balance of power. It has been branded as so vague a notion, with so many differing and competing meanings, as to be without value. While it has its champions, Hedley Bull prominent among them, they seem to be outnumbered by the critics. If the scholars and theologians of the field find the notion rather too abstract, and it certainly is that, it would not be surprising if the lay public were confused about the international balance of power. The fact is, however, that Western publics have fairly often been surveyed on their perception of and attitudes toward the contemporary balance of power, and they clearly do not find it an incomprehensible notion. Their conceptions are probably as sophisticated as those of many leaders.

The general conclusion to be drawn from various opinion polls over recent decades is that there existed a rough parity between the United States and the former Soviet Union.[24] While Western publics generally perceived the USSR to be ahead, in some sense, in the period between sputnik and the Cuban missile crisis, the US was perceived to have pulled in front after October 1962, again at least in some respects. In the zero-sum context of the cold war, the post-Cuba situation was definitely to be preferred. By the 1970s, though, some change had occurred. The emergence of *détente*, regular summits, and the SALT agreements of that decade seem to have generally suggested to publics what they in fact represented: an acceptance of parity by the two major powers.

A more interesting question is what sort of balance of power Western publics think would be most desirable. The answer, which may surprise many observers, is that the public in Western countries, at least since the early 1970s, has *preferred* a situation of military parity between the Soviet Union and the United States.[25] This judgement is by no means one of a bare majority; in Germany, Britain, and Canada alike, by the late 1980s, it was the solid consensus of more than four out of five people.

Western publics are not entirely preoccupied with the great powers or the balance of power defined in military terms. They also clearly perceive changes to be under way with respect to power in the international system. Although evidence for this can be found in all countries, the most complete data are available for Canada, and these will be the focus here.

In the early 1970s, a solid majority of Canadians (60 per cent) regarded the US as the strongest country economically. Only one in six (15 per cent) pointed then to Japan. In 1990, by contrast, less than one-third chose the US as the strongest country in economic terms. The largest single number, indeed a majority (50 per cent), now pointed to Japan. The European Community came in a distant third, at 11 per cent. Most Canadians in 1972, and most in 1990, thought the US was the strongest militarily.[26]

It is clear that Canadians have sensed a relative decline in US capabilities and both an absolute and a relative rise in those of Japan and Europe.[27] This shift in perception is reinforced by qualitative judgements. Most believe that economic capabilities are now more important internationally than military strength. When presented with the statement 'Economic capabilities are now more important than military capabilities in determining a country's influence in the world today', the vast majority agreed. Indeed, a bare 16 per cent argued that military strength was still a more effective instrument of power in the international system than economic might. Together, the assessments of capabilities and of the changing sources of power suggest that what many have in mind is an emerging multipolar system, one perhaps more akin to the classical European balance-of-power system than the simple two-power balance of the cold-war era.[28]

Perceptions of the New Diplomatic Agenda

There is a widespread recognition among experts that fundamental forces have been re-shaping contemporary international politics in the past few years. East-West relations are improving rapidly, perhaps for the long term.

The reforms initiated by Gorbachev and still under way in Russia and the other republics of the former Soviet Union have changed those nations in irreversible fashion. The political map of Eastern Europe has been re-drawn. Arms control is progressing in both the nuclear and conventional spheres. Many local and regional conflicts—in Central America, in southern Africa, in Southeast Asia—are ending or at least winding down. The agenda of international politics, we are told, is shifting from long-standing concerns about armed aggression and military security to greater attention to more prosaic problems—trade protectionism, Third World debt, refugees, the international drug traffic, and the deteriorating ozone layer, for example.

Such shifts in attention have been assessed and advocated in various international reports by expert panels from the Brandt Commission report on international development prospects in the early 1980s to the Palme Report on common security to the World Commission on Environment and Development (the Brundtland report). They have been reflected not only in the front pages but also the business pages of the world's press, discussed in meetings as disparate as those of United Nations, the G-7 Economic Summit, and the Commonwealth. And they have become the staple fare of speeches by statespersons, present and past. In his historic address at Fulton, Missouri, almost half a century after Winston Churchill's warning about the 'iron curtain' and the expansion of power by Stalin's Russia, former Soviet president Mikhail Gorbachev warned about new and common dangers. He pointed to 'intensified international competition, leading to de facto trade wars and a threatened rebirth of protectionism, . . . global climatic shifts, the greenhouse effect, the "ozone hole", acid rain, contamination of the atmosphere, soil and water by industrial and household waste, the destruction of the forests, . . . and the effects of our poisoning of the spiritual sphere—drug addiction, alcoholism, terrorism, crime. . .'.[29]

Bull's fourth institution of the international order is diplomacy. In *The Anarchical Society*, however, he explicitly eschews any consideration of what he terms 'the substantive issues of world politics at the present time' (xiii). Given his concern with 'enduring structures' or institutions, he focuses on the conduct and functions of contemporary diplomacy rather than its content. It would seem only logical, however, that the emergence of a new international order would involve a change in the diplomatic agenda. The new orders ushered in by the wars of the twentieth century, for example, clearly had this effect. The question here, then, is to what extent, and how, the perceptions of Western publics are also changing with respect to the key problems and issues of the day.[30]

If East-West wars, conventionally defined and initiated, are now highly unlikely and have as a result declined in importance, are there other threats to international peace and security that have taken their place in the public mind?

The waning of the cold war, well before its passing, led Western publics by the late 1980s to discount the old standby of the Soviet threat as a serious

Table 16.5. Perceptions of Greatest Threats to World Peace, 1988

	UK	CANADA	FRG
Soviet actions on the international scene	2	5	4
US actions on the international scene	16	11	4
The superpower arms race	9	23	33
The spread of nuclear arms to smaller countries	24	32	26
The Middle East situation	46	24	25
Conflicts elsewhere in the world	3	4	8
Total	100%	99%	100%

Question wording: 'Which one of the following situations do you think poses the greatest threat to world peace?'

SOURCE: International Security Project, 1988.

military-security problem. The vast majority in some if not all Western countries came to regard factors or situations other than the Soviet Union as the greatest threat to peace (see Table 16.5). Indeed, a majority pointed either to the spread of nuclear weapons or to the Middle East situation as the greater threat.[31]

Americans and Canadians were also asked in 1989 how they thought nuclear weapons might be used, if they ever were to be.[32] The scenario judged least likely was a Soviet attack. Most likely for these two publics was the use of nuclear weapons by a terrorist or 'madman' or by a third country other than the superpowers. The accidental detonation of these weapons was judged next most likely.

When the list of possible threats is broadened to encompass a wide range of non-military-security problems, the responses change, revealing a much longer agenda. The consequences of asking such broader questions are evident in a variety of poll questions across the countries of focus here. In short, a new international agenda clearly has emerged in the public mind. Traditional security problems tend to lose pride of place. In addition to non-traditional threats from abroad, there appears to be an increasing recognition of international economic interdependence—in the Federal Republic, with the problem of integrating an economically devastated East Germany; in Britain, where the boom of the Thatcher free-market 1980s has ended; in the United States, which is struggling to meet the Japanese challenge; and in Canada, as it copes with the combined impact of recession and deindustrialization spurred by the Canada-US free trade arrangement.

In Britain and Germany, for example, more of the publics appear concerned with nuclear proliferation, terrorism, drug trafficking, and immigration than with the Middle East situation and Third World regional conflicts in general; least of all are they concerned about an attack from the former USSR (see Table 16.6).

Table 16.6. Perceived Security Threats in the United Kingdom and Federal Republic of Germany, 1991

	UK	FRG
Nuclear proliferation	23	25
International terrorism	16	10
Narcotics trafficking	14	8
Mass immigration from outside Western Europe	11	27
Instability in Eastern Europe and former USSR	9	10
Military adventurism in the Middle East	9	9
Economic competition	5	1
Regional conflicts in Third World	3	3
Military attack by USSR	2	1
Other mentions	4	6
Don't know/no answer	4	0
Total	100%	100%

NOTE: The figures are the percentage of respondents who selected each issue. Question wording: 'On this card is a list of potential threats to our national security. Please tell me which one of these, in your opinion, posed the greatest threat to our country's security.'

SOURCE: USIA survey, May 1991.

In the United States, in response to a similar question with a somewhat different set of provided choices, a very similar pattern emerges (see Table 16.7). Near the top of the list as the most frequently selected international problems, as for the Germans and the British, are nuclear proliferation, drug trafficking, and terrorism. Near the bottom of the list, once again, are conflicts in the Middle East and Central America, Soviet nuclear weapons, and Soviet aggression. Americans give somewhat more prominence to economic problems than do the Germans and British. The US list included environmental problems, which received a middle ranking, and a number of relatively highly ranked 'domestic' problems, including violent crime, the federal budget deficit, and even health-care costs.[33] Comparing this list to that from Gorbachev's Fulton speech, one is tempted to think his speechwriters had been reading the American polls.

Among Canadians as well a very similar pattern prevails, with a few differences in emphasis (see Table 16.8). As for the other countries, drug trafficking and terrorism are concerns of many. Like Americans, Canadians place economic problems relatively high on the list; unlike Americans, at least in 1990, they gave the highest ranking to environmental issues.[34] At the bottom of the Canadian list, below major war, are human-rights abuses and poverty and hunger in the Third World. This low priority suggests that Canadians simply do not see socio-economic conditions in distant lands as matters of much import for their security. Although these latter concerns were not included in the possible responses on the other countries' surveys,

Table 16.7. Perceived Threats to American National Security, 1990

	EXTREMELY SERIOUS	VERY SERIOUS	TOTAL SERIOUS
Drug trafficking	38	46	84
Proliferation of nuclear weapons	37	37	74
Environmental problems	35	39	74
Violent crime	34	38	72
Health-care costs	31	38	69
Federal budget deficit	26	38	64
Economic competition abroad	26	35	61
Terrorist activities	25	36	61
Greenhouse effect	22	30	52
Nuclear waste	21	31	52
Middle East conflicts	14	37	51
Central American conflicts	14	30	44
Soviet nuclear weapons	16	27	43
Soviet aggression	5	19	24

Question wording: 'How serious are each of the following problems to America's security?'

SOURCE: ATS, #13, February–March 1990, Report no. 3.

and hence comparison is not possible, there would seem to be little reason to think they would have received a higher ranking from other Western publics.[35]

While a new agenda has clearly emerged, the policy prescriptions to deal

Table 16.8. Perceived Problems Affecting Canada's Security, 1989

	EXTREMELY SERIOUS	VERY SERIOUS	TOTAL SERIOUS
Global pollution	54	36	90
International crime (such as drug trafficking)	51	35	86
International financial and monetary instability	26	48	74
Spread of diseases	33	39	72
World trade conflicts and protectionism	22	47	69
Terrorism	32	34	66
Major war	34	25	59
Abuses of human rights	20	36	56
Poverty and hunger in developing countries	14	30	44

Question wording: 'Listed (here) are a number of international problems that may affect Canada's security. Please rank the importance of each problem: extremely important, very important, somewhat important, or not important.'

SOURCE: Munton–CIIPS, September–October 1989.

with these problems apparently have not. In one area, though, public attitudes are unambiguous. Consistent with the consensus that the Soviet threat has disappeared, and that the danger of war directly involving the Western countries has declined, is a now widely and strongly held belief in the desirability of arms reductions. Over 75 per cent of Germans, Canadians, and Britons agree or strongly agree that 'the security of Western countries could best be increased by substantial reductions in both American and Soviet nuclear weapons'.[36] Americans display a similar attitude when posed a similarly oriented (but somewhat different) question. They were asked in 1988 whether making the 'substantial reductions' in nuclear weapons then envisaged in the strategic arms (START) negotiations would reduce security and be too risky or would improve national security and 'make the world a safer place'. By a three-to one margin, most said it would enhance national security.[37]

While much in Western publics' perceptions of the changing international diplomatic agenda is new and unprecedented, some—perhaps many—of their evident goals and values are not so new at all. Indeed, some distinctly traditional attitudes not only linger on but appear relatively robust. Despite the changing perceptions and attitudes discussed above, and despite the revolutions in Eastern Europe and the disintegration of the old USSR, attitudes about matters such as the NATO alliance have changed remarkably little.[38] In most Western countries there is also a public commitment, in principle, to the maintenance of defence forces and to continued defence spending, albeit not necessarily at 1980s levels.[39] Although this level of support for NATO and defence spending may well decline if good relations with the parts of the old USSR, especially the Russian Federation, are maintained into the future, it is nevertheless impressive testimony to the attractiveness of some old ideas.

Conclusion

While Western public opinion still finds comfortable some of the structures of the cold war (such as NATO) and some ideas (such as ensuring an adequate defence) there can be no question that thinking has shifted substantially on many key aspects of the post-war international system. Indeed, perceptions of and attitudes on what Bull and Wight term the 'institutions of international order' have been undergoing a fundamental transformation—in some respects since the 1970s, and certainly through the 1980s. In the minds of people in the West there is indeed a new world order. And this perceived new order has not come about suddenly: it has been emerging for years, if not decades.

What is most clear is that after more than forty years without direct armed superpower conflict and with the emergence of a zone of peace in Western Europe, there is a declining sense of military threat and of the likelihood of war. Amidst a transformation of East-West relations in the late 1980s, 'international security' has come to mean something quite different for the present generations — a set of concerns at once broader and more fundamental than physical security from military attack. And, prior to the disintegration of the Soviet Union, publics were expressing a new confidence in the leadership of both the superpowers and according an unprecedented degree of legitimacy to the old USSR.

Although it is much harder after the 1989 revolutions in Eastern Europe to assume that public opinion always follows and never leads, there may still be a temptation to interpret the data analysed here as providing evidence that Western publics are merely swimming with the recently changing times. That would be a mistake. The fact that so many of the trends identified here were clearly evident in the early 1980s and the 1970s suggests a keener observation of and response to events internationally by mass publics than is often assumed possible. It may be going too far to say that changing public thinking was a primary cause of the new order, but it is clearly the case that public thinking was not lagging behind that of governments. At the very least, Western publics were well prepared for the declarations of the emergence of a new world order. More than their leaders, they seem to be ready to meet the challenges such an order poses.

Notes

[1] Hedley Bull, *The Anarchical Society* (New York: Columbia University Press, 1977); Martin Wight, *Power Politics* (New York: Holmes and Meier, 1978).

[2] Although Wight also does not deal explicitly with the question of what changes are required before it is possible to say a new order has emerged, his focus ranges across the changing European inter-state system since the 15th century. He outlines, for example, the emergence of the two major inter-state systems of Europe during the seventeenth century — those of Western Europe (Spain, Holland, France and England) and of the Baltic (Sweden, Denmark, Poland and Russia) — and their eventual merger by the late eighteenth century. Thus, while Wight also does not answer explicitly the question of when a system has changed, he does deal with it implicitly in the context of surveying the various inter-state systems and great powers that have held sway at various points in time.

[3] It is further assumed that the thinking of publics in general may well reflect some of the basic ideas about international politics bandied about by scholars. See Don Munton, 'NATO up against the Wall: Changing Security Attitudes in Germany, Britain and Canada, 1960s to the 1980s', in Hans Rattinger and Don Munton, eds, *Rethinking National Security: The Public Dimension* (Frankfurt: Campus Verlag, 1991) and 'Up (or Down) on Arms: American and Canadian Public Attitudes in the Mid-1980s', in David Dewitt and Hans Rattinger, eds, *Arms Control into the 1990s* (London: Macmillan, 1991).

[4] The 'International Security Project' (ISP), a two-year multinational project, comprised common surveys in the UK, Germany and Canada in 1988 and in the USA, UK, Germany, and Canada in 1989. The two British polls were carried out by

Social Surveys (Gallup Poll) Ltd., London and directed by Robert Wybrow. Personal interviews were conducted during the periods 7-12 July 1988 and 22-27 November 1989 with, respectively, 819 and 1022 adults, aged 18 years and over.

The two German polls were carried out by the Institut für Angewandte Sozialwissenschaft (INFAS), Bonn, and directed by Hans Jurgen Hoffmann. They comprised samples of 1473 and 1465 adults, interviewed in person 11-23 July 1988 and 21-28 November 1989.

The corresponding polls in Canada were designed by Don Munton, carried out by The Longwoods Research Group, Toronto, directed by Anita Pollack, and funded by the Canadian Institute for International Peace and Security (CIIPS). The 1988 version involved 1005 adults surveyed between mid-June and early August, while the 1989 one involved 890 respondents surveyed between mid-September and late October. The Canadian surveys were carried out by mail in both English and French with a national sample selected randomly to be representative of Canadian households and chosen from a panel of 30,000 households maintained by Market Facts Ltd. Although once suspect methodologically, mail surveys are now increasingly common; this technique was used, for example, as part of the 1988 Canadian national election survey. These two polls were part of a series of annual polls carried out since 1987, all with the same organizations, format, and funding. The results of these polls have been summarized in a series of reports from the Canadian Institute for International Peace and Security: Don Munton, 'Peace and Security in the 1980s: The Views of Canadians' Working Paper, January 1988; Michael Driedger and Don Munton, 'Security, Arms Control and Defence: Public Attitudes in Canada' Working Paper No. 14, December 1988; Michael Driedger and Don Munton, 'Security, Arms Control and Defence: Public Attitudes in Canada' Working Paper, December 1989; Don Munton, 'Changing Conceptions of Security: Public Attitudes in Canada', Working Paper, December 1990. Particular themes have been the focus of a series of articles in the Institute's journal, *Peace and Security*, including Don Munton, 'Superpowers and National Security' 2, 4 (Winter 1987-88), 2-3; 'Canadians and their Defence' 3, 4 (Winter 1988-89), 2-5; 'Uncommon Threats and Common Security' 4, 4 (Winter 1989-90), 2-5.

The US survey carried out in 1989 in conjunction with the other ISP polls was done by the CBS News–New York Times Poll, New York, and directed by Kathleen Frankovic. A national sample of 1297 adults were interviewed by telephone during the period 26-28 November 1989. Percentage results for all of these surveys are accurate to within +/- 3 per cent, 95 times out of 100, with the exception of the Canadian ones (based on slightly smaller samples), which are accurate to within +/- 4 per cent, 95 times out of 100.

[5]In particular, German data were provided by the Institut für Demoskopie, Allensbach, with the kind permission of its founder and director, Professor Elisabeth Noelle-Neumann. Comparative European data have been gained from the surveys sponsored by the United States Information Agency (USIA). The data for these surveys have been obtained from the United States National Archives, Machine readable Division. American data were obtained from the Americans Talk Security series, sponsored by Alan Kay, the various reports of which are cited here by number (e.g., ATS #4). Gallup Canada, formerly the Canadian Institute of Public Opinion (CIPO), was the source of additional Canadian data. Additional sources for specific questions and years are cited individually below.

[6]Notably, Wight defines this fear as 'a rational apprehension of future evil' and not as 'an unreasoning emotion'. Unlike some contemporary analysts, then, he sees apprehensions about war as fundamental to statecraft, and not just as undermining rational calculations about war. While it is not clear Wight would accept the proposition that fears of war among domestic publics were rational in the same way as those of governmental leaders, this assumption is made here.

[7]The sources for these data are as follows: 1981-83 (AIPO); 1984 (Yankelovich for the Public Agenda Foundation); 1985-1990 (CBS-New York Times). (A much larger set of results for similar questions may be found in Thomas Graham, unpublished catalogue, Yale University.) Basic question wording: 'How likely do you think we are to get into a nuclear war within the next ten years — very likely, fairly likely, fairly unlikely, or very unlikely?' (1984 wording only: 'Within the next ten years, all out nuclear war is very likely, fairly likely, fairly unlikely, or very unlikely?') The responses have been combined into the two categories shown.

[8]Sources: Social Surveys, Gallup Political Index, September 1980, #267-November 1982, #255-November 1981, #312-August 1986. Basic question wording: 'Do you think it is likely or not that there is ever going to be a nuclear war?'

[9]Sources: 1984, 1985, 1990: CIPO, Press Release, 16 April 1990; 1988: Munton-CIIPS Survey. Question wording: '. . . within the next twenty-five years, how likely do you think it is that there would be a nuclear war?'

[10]Sources: 1971-1982: Gallup Canada/CIPO, 1987 and 1988: national surveys by the author. Basic question wording: 'Would you say that the chance of nuclear war breaking out is greater, is less, or is the same now as it was ten years ago?' The 1971 and 1975 questions referred to 'atomic war'. The surveys from 1987-89 were mail questionnaires and had fewer non-responses.

[11]Source: Eurobarometer surveys, cited in Eurobarometer no. 22, December 1984, and Eurobarometer Trends, 1974-90, March 1991. Question wording: 'Here is a sort of a scale . . . Would you . . . tell me how you assess the chances of a world war breaking out in the next ten years?' Percentages shown are those saying the chances were 50 per cent or more. Although not shown in this figure, the estimated chances rose in the late 1990 poll, especially in Britain, as the Western coalition responded to the Iraqi invasion of Kuwait. Estimates of the chances of nuclear war are unlikely to have been similarly affected by the Gulf conflict, but the data are not available to determine this with certainty. It may or may not be valid to assume that the same or similar fears are evoked by public-opinion poll questions that do not explicitly use the term 'nuclear war', but it is useful nevertheless to look at the pattern over time of responses to such questions.

[12]The reaction of Western publics to the opening of the Berlin Wall, as seen in the results of the ISP project, can perhaps best be described as cautious. When asked in September-October 1989, the month before the Berlin Wall was opened, whether the cold war was over, only a few Canadians (7 per cent) thought it was. Surveyed in the weeks after the opening of the Wall, more Germans and Britons agreed that the cold war was over (40 per cent and 20 per cent, respectively) but equal numbers or more would only say it was lessening (37 per cent and 33 per cent, respectively). After the dramatic 1989-90 year of events in Eastern Europe, the numbers of

Canadians who thought the cold war was, in fact, over had risen significantly but modestly from 7 per cent to 21 per cent.

[13]Wight's preoccupation in the fragments of writing to be found in *Power Politics* is defining the term and identifying the great powers of the European state system of various eras, but he also touches on their contribution to international order. Bull, on the other hand, deals quickly with the definitional issue and then discusses at length the roles the great powers play in maintaining that order. Early on he dismissively sets aside the term 'superpower', asserting that, while it accurately denotes a power of superior capability, it 'adds nothing' to the old concept of a great power (203). If the latter is taken to include the former, then this usage can be adopted here.

[14]Great powers, as Bull notes, are judged on the extent to which they pursue common purposes rather than self-interests.

[15]The proportions who thought unlikely or very unlikely a Soviet attack elsewhere, such as on Japan or China, were about the same.

[16]Source: Americans Talk Security project survey #13 (April 1990). Indeed, there was so much change that Americans in 1988 found it as likely that the United States and the Soviet Union might enter into a long-term military alliance as that they might fight each other in some world conflict (ATS #4, p. 65).

[17]The 1985 data are from a survey carried out for the Canadian Broadcasting Corporation (CBC); the 1990 data are from an identical question on one of the author's polls. Most Canadians and Americans in the late 1980s, when asked, said they themselves perceived the threat to be declining. In both countries, almost six in ten (57 per cent in Canada; 56 per cent in the US) said the Soviet Union was less of a threat than it had been previously. About three in ten believed that this threat had not changed (Munton–CIIPS survey, 1989; ATS #12, p. 58). At the same time, Canadians were not yet convinced that the USSR was an ordinary and peaceable power. More than two in three respondents (68 per cent) disagreed or disagreed strongly with the statement (in 1989) that 'the Soviet Union is a peace-loving nation, willing to fight only if it thinks it has to defend itself'. There is, of course, a significant difference in connotation between being an 'immediate and direct threat' and being 'peace-loving', and that distinction is clearly not lost on the Canadian public.

[18]These data are taken from Allensbach surveys; see Elisabeth Noelle-Neumann, 'The Possibilities and Limits of Opinion Polls as a Scientific Means of Determining the True State of Public Opinion', paper delivered to a NATO seminar, November 1987.

[19]Source: Social Surveys Ltd, various press releases.

[20]Source: USIA data; various surveys.

[21]Source: 1987–90: Munton–CIIPS surveys.

[22]Sources: 1987–90: Munton–CIIPS surveys; other years: Gallup Canada–CIPO.

[23]This pattern of 'black-black' and 'white-white' images, shown both in the data from the Munton–CIIPS surveys and in the European data from the USIA surveys, is

discussed in Don Munton, 'Threat Perceptions and Shifts of Public Attitudes, 1960s–1980s', in Klaus Gottstein, ed., *Western Perceptions of Soviet Policy*, (Munich: Max Planck Gesellschaft, 1989); 'NATO up against the Wall' in Rattinger and Munton, eds, *Rethinking National Security*, and 'Up (or Down) on Arms' in Dewitt and Rattinger, eds, *Arms Control into the 1990s*.

[24]Sources: USIA surveys, various years.

[25]Sources: 1988: International Security Project; other years: USIA data. Question wording: 'What would be best in your opinion. . . . for the United States to be ahead in total military strength, for the Soviet Union to be ahead in total military strength, or for the two superpowers to be about equal in total military strength?'

[26]USIA survey, 1972; Munton–CIIPS, 1990.

[27]For US data that show very similar patterns but an even greater degree of alarm about the economic threat from Japan, see ATS #5.

[28]A question mark in this new structure of power internationally is the role of united Germany. Most of the public in most countries favoured unification, with the Americans and Canadians being the most positive (MORI survey, *Economist* and *Los Angeles Times*, January 1990; Canadian data from the 1990 Munton–CIIPS survey). Of the Europeans surveyed, the Poles were the least supportive of unification, presumably for obvious historical reasons. While Europeans (more than North Americans) worry about Germany's becoming the dominant power in Europe, they generally discount the possibility of its becoming a military threat; rather, they see it as a possible economic threat.

[29]Mikhail Gorbachev, 'The River of Time', *Bulletin of the Atomic Scientists* (July–Aug. 1992), 22–7.

[30]The focus on content here is in part a practical one. While publics can be reasonably expected to have ideas about the important issues of international politics, it is unlikely they have much knowledge of, or many attitudes about, the functioning of the little-known and distant world of the diplomat.

[31]The results for Canada shown in Table 16.5, from a 1988 survey, differ only slightly from those to the same question when it was asked in 1987 and in 1989. In this case, as in others, the focus of, and the choices provided by, the survey question greatly influence the nature of the responses. (This is, it might be noted, not a frailty of public opinion as is so often supposed; it is, in fact, evidence that people respond precisely to the specific questions pollsters pose.) When the question changes, and the focus is broadened to include non-traditional security threats, the extent to which public concerns have shifted becomes more clear.

[32]The sources here were, for Canada, the 1989 Munton–CIIPS survey, and for the US, ATS #12.

[33]The concern expressed about violent crime, the federal budget deficit, and even health-care costs as 'national security problems' probably says at least as much about the designers of the survey question as it does about Americans' way of defining national security.

[34]When presented in 1989 with a choice of three categories of potential threat—

economic, environmental, and military — Canadians tended to point to environmental more than economic challenges, and more to both of these than to military ones. Indeed, fully eight in ten (83 per cent) rank military threats as the least serious of the three; fewer than one in ten, as the most serious. Canadians, however, have not always ranked environmental issues so highly. By way of comparison, a 1984 poll carried out by the Goldfarb organization for the Department of External Affairs placed environmental protection a distant third in importance for Canada's foreign policy, behind world peace and economic growth.

[35]Developed-world perceptions of Third World problems, in this respect, are thus at variance with the argument, for example, of Ivan Head (*The Hinge of History*, [Toronto: University of Toronto Press, 1991]) as to what they should be. That fact, however, is presumably one of the reasons why Head wrote his book.

[36]International Security Project, 1988; see also Munton, 'Up (or Down) on Arms' in Dewitt and Rattinger eds, *Arms Control into the 1990s*.

[37]ATS #4, p. 62. At the same time, a majority believed that nuclear-arms cuts ought to await Soviet conventional-weapons reductions in Europe (ATS #2, 42) or further evidence on Soviet compliance with existing arms-control agreements (ATS #2, question 79) and that deep cuts in nuclear weapons ought to be compensated for by a conventional buildup (ATS #7, p. 72). These reductions also did not receive highest ranking as national-security goals. When compared with a range of other objectives, achieving mutual 50 per cent cuts came out behind dealing with drug trafficking and America's trade imbalance and just ahead of keeping communist governments out of the Americas and containing Soviet aggression around the world.

[38]Tracking polls by the USIA show consistent levels of agreement that NATO is 'still essential to our country's security' across the countries of Western Europe. In Germany, in particular, most believe maintaining NATO is important despite a lack of threat. In late 1991, the Institut für Demoskopie, Allensbach, posed one of its well-known 'debate' questions in which one view argued that 'in a situation when there is little threat from Eastern Europe, NATO as a military alliance is not important any more', and the opposing view argued that 'NATO must remain a strong alliance in order to be ready for emergencies. No one knows what will happen with the Soviet Union.' In western Germany the latter view was supported by 62 per cent; even in eastern Germany, it received 39 per cent (Institut für Demoskopie, Allensbach, *Allensbacher Reports*, 1991/23 September 1991).

[39]See USIA, May 1991 Security Survey.

chapter seventeen

Conclusion: Towards the Twenty-First Century

Albert Legault

Three Major Paradigms

In the current literature on international relations there are three overarching paradigms that provide a conceptual framework through which to assess the emerging trends in international security. *Nolens volens*, two of them have dominated the history of international relations over the last three hundred years. These are the 'peace through strength' and 'peace through law' paradigms.[1] A third one is now appearing, though it is difficult to put a name on it. It might be called the 'trans-systemic'[2] or 'ecological' paradigm.

The main differences between the first and second paradigms are obvious and manifold. (See Table 17.1.) 'Peace through strength' tends to emphasize the interests of the state; 'peace through law', the interests of the international community. The two models incorporate different value and belief systems, in the sense that the primary responsibility of those working within the parameters of the first is to maintain, to conserve, or to increase the power of the unit, whereas those working within the parameters of the second paradigm are naturally inclined to favour the betterment of the community, even if some local or regional interest groups may lose some influence in the process.

Within the first paradigm there have been vast oscillations, ranging from the well-conceived balancing of the powers of one against another, as exemplified by the limited goals pursued by Bismarck, to total war as exemplified

Table 17.1. Characteristics of the Three Major Paradigms

MAJOR PARADIGM	ORIGIN	METHOD OF ANALYSIS	RESULTS	ULTIMATE GOAL
Peace through strength	scientific positivism			
		operational research and other decision making aids	strategic studies	maximize benefits for country or unit in question
	industrial revolution			
Peace through law	social justice			
		functionalism, neo-functionalism, and integration theories	studies on law and inter-national institutions	maximize benefits for the group
	peaceful settlement of disputes			
Trans-systemic (or ecological) paradigm	new ethics or values			
		marriage of hard and soft sciences	environmental studies	maximize the chances of survival for the planet
	redefining or questioning scientific progress			

SOURCE: This table is based on my *The End of a Military Century?* (Ottawa: International Development Research Centre, 1992).

by Hitler's urge for world power. Within the 'peace through law' paradigm, the visions of the world have varied from the Utopian approach of Kant's 'perpetual peace' project, or of those who favour the establishment of a world government, to the more pragmatic vision of a world policed and governed by international organizations, passing through the various steps of functionalism and neo-functionalism as approaches to integration.

The origins of these two paradigms are even more revealing. The 'peace through strength' concept draws heavily on the positivist school of science and the technological-edge concept, as if nations and nations' behaviour were a linear phenomenon destined to be repeated each time the same, or similar, conditions prevailed. History at least should warn against such preconceived ideas. In the same manner, one intuitively knows that law and reality are different, that no amount of constitutional legalism can protect against gross aggression, and that the 'peace through law' concept cannot stand on its own, unless the world is policed by a series of institutional arrangements that will make social justice more prevalent in society and the resolution of conflict more peaceful.

The historical origins of the 'peace through law' concept go back to the Greek notion of the *polis*, and draw heavily on the Judaeo-Christian notion of social justice. With the development of state systems, international law became the standard to which states had to conform. As John Temple Swing aptly points out:

> the perceived need to 'find some better way' was a principal motivation behind American idealism that led to U.S. attempts to introduce arbitration as the preferred method of settling international disputes early in this century, in President Wilson's Fourteen Points, and in American leadership in the creation of the concept of collective security embodied first in the League of Nations and then, at the end of the most disastrous war in history in 1945, in the Charter of the United Nations.[3]

Though some may see the concept of peaceful settlement of disputes as no more than a policy prescription, it is one of the strongest pillars of the 'peace through law' paradigm. 'Peace-through-strength' traditionalists who hold that power capability is the ultimate way to measure the influence of the state tend to forget that international law would not have been born without the state, and that the peaceful settlement of conflict cannot be achieved without the institutional support necessary to regulate the realm of law. For example, there could not be a Europe without institutions, and institutions make sense only if they lead to political authority.[4]

The realists and neo-realists of the peace-through-strength approach may describe the world as an anarchic system, and by the same token declare the death of the United Nations system, but in the absence of world order some kind of system is needed to regulate international conflict. The Charter of the United Nations from that point of view is a marriage of the first two paradigms of international relations. Chapter VI of the Charter postulates that all efforts to find a peaceful settlement to a conflict must be exhausted before the use of force can even be contemplated. But chapter VII authorizes the organization to contemplate the use of force in the event of a breach of the peace, or of a military threat against international peace, providing there is a consensus among the system's ruling powers to counteract that breach or threat.

In the Gulf War, those who favoured a peaceful settlement of the dispute asked for more time for the sanctions to operate. Rightly or wrongly, an ultimatum was voted upon, and the deadline of 15 January 1991 was established. It is clear that from that date onwards the 'peace through strength' paradigm prevailed, though this did not by any means mark the end of diplomacy. In other words, force was interjected into the settlement of the dispute. The cutting edge between war and peace in times of crisis will always remain at this particular juncture of the first two schools of thought.

The debate between the traditionalists and the neo-realists became particularly acute in the 1980s. David J. Scheffer succinctly summarizes the argument of the neo-realists:

> First, the neorealists urge unilateral military intervention (direct or indirect) by the United States in response to Soviet bloc intervention in other countries. They rarely suggest that the United States be inhibited in responding with force by the procedural requirements of the UN Charter or other multilateral charters. [. . .] Second, the neorealists see the use of force as an effective instrument to further other principles that they believe are integral to the UN Charter; self-determination, human rights, and, above all, democracy. The neorealists' point of view poses an intriguing paradox. On the one hand, they challenge the legitimacy of long-held views about international law, such as the prohibitions on aiding insurgencies fighting established governments and intervening on behalf of either side in a civil war. On the other hand, they want to unleash the United States to enforce international law unilaterally.[5]

Beyond the debates over the sempiternal question of whether law is to be obeyed by the state, or whether the state should bind the law to serve its interests — hence the debate on the double standards of policy on the Gulf War and the Palestinian question — there is a deeper debate that divides the two schools. This is the debate over the definition of realism.

In the United States, the prevailing idealist conception of international relations after World War II was soon to be replaced in the early fifties by Morgenthau's power paradigm: that is, the 'peace through strength' concept. In short, peace fell apart because it rested on an idealist conception of international relations, and because power alone could command enough respect to maintain what was to become a balance of terror between the main protagonists. Some European scholars would take exception to this definition. They tend to believe that they never miscalculated the difficulty of distinguishing between what Stanley Hoffmann calls the 'is', the iron rule of power politics, and the 'ought', that which should be: in other words, a world regulated by law and diplomacy. For many European scholars, it is the United States that developed the Wilsonian concept of peace and tried to make the world safer for democracy, firmly believing, at the time, in the strength and virtues of international organizations.

The difference here is an exercise in semantics. The realist in Europe is the one who measures the distance that remains between the 'is' and the 'ought', or between chapter VI and chapter VII of the UN Charter, whereas on the other side of the Atlantic the realist is the one who sees the UN as a defunct organization that has proven impotent in most of the crises of the cold war. The debate on the new world order — or disorder — is symptomatic of the inability of the specialist to foresee the future and, most particularly, to assess the stability of the international system: that is, whether the system will be more prone to war or to peace if its structure is bipolar, multilateral, multipolar, or rearranged in a complex diffusion of power.[6] But this inability to foresee the future does not affect the basic cleavages between the first two paradigms. Neither does it render less imperative the necessity of developing institutional procedures that will help to resolve international conflict on a peaceful basis.

In sum, many see those strategic analysts concerned with power as myopic, and those concerned with the betterment of the international community through international co-operation and integration as the real internationalists. There is nothing farther from the truth. As long as the need for security exists, the sword will exist, and the law will continue to be perceived as a legitimate shield if, and only if, it is universally accepted and equitably implemented.

The third paradigm partly bridges the gap between the first two, but it is not a synthesis of them. There is no doubt that the arms race between the East and the West has diverted enormous quantities of resources to nonproductive ends; that economic progress has produced a serious deterioration of our biosphere; that deforestation, desertification, and the depletion of the ozone layer are interrelated factors linked to the ill-considered exploitation of our planet — more often by the rich countries at the expense of the poorer ones. The most deleterious effects produced by humankind on the environment under the banner of progress, coupled with the most nefarious effects of the power paradigm on international relations, have led many to a new consciousness: the need to protect the environment and to maximize the chances of survival of the planet. The resolution of these long-term problems will necessitate a marriage between the hard (physical) and the soft (social) sciences.

This paradigm has its origins in the increased dissatisfaction with the notion of linear progress in the realms of science and economic development, and in the search for new fundamental values, at a time when genetic manipulation constitutes the new frontier of science and medicine. What is new in the third paradigm is that it expands human consciousness in all fields. One now talks about global and common security, sustainable development, pollution control, and a common future. Obviously, those problems will be very difficult to tackle unless one is willing to talk about the ethical implications and legitimacy of the rules of the game.[7]

The German philosopher Hegel said it before our time. Death is the only equalizer between the rich and the poor. Humans are mortal, and our planet too is mortal, because the sun will implode in the distant future. Caught between those two absurdities, the first one very close and the second very remote, the only hope is to improve the consciousness of humankind, and to make sure that new values will eventually contribute to the development of initiatives that will bridge the gap between the major powers of the system and the rest of the world. Stanley Hoffmann has properly distinguished the existential rules from the deliberative rules, 'the former being the rules of nuclear deterrence and of competition and the latter being the operative rules to carry out the existential ones'.[8] This said, if nuclear weapons have rendered war obsolete, both as an instrument of foreign policy and as a way to conduct military operations between the major nuclear powers of the system, it remains to be seen how much more 'deliberation' will be needed to forge new realities that will work in this supposedly increasingly interdependent world. It may well be that the world is on the brink of a new Renaissance.

There are three dialectical areas where the power paradigm is flawed. First, are all models built on the assumption that states and nations behave in a rational way, and that power is the ultimate foundation on which security is to be based? Many authors who have written on the cold war, notably Richard Rosecrance and Raymond Aron, point out that it was when the United States enjoyed the monopoly of the atom bomb, or when the East and the West were in a period of *détente*, that the Soviet Union engaged in its most expansionist moves: that is, in the aftermath of the cold war in Central Europe and in the Third World, particularly in Africa. Second, deterrence in itself no longer has the aura it had for many decades in the West. Its credibility was seriously weakened by Chernobyl and the prospect of nuclear winter long before the collapse of the Soviet Union. This revision process had gone so far in the Soviet Union that Moscow proclaimed the irrationality of even a conventional war in Europe, because of the fragility of the European industrial infrastructure. It is an irony of history that the developing states are now beginning to cling desperately to deterrence at a time when the industrial states are having second thoughts about it. Third, if there is any lesson to be drawn from the failures of deterrence, the Gulf War is a case in point. Diplomacy failed, deterrence failed, and the coalition fell into the situation it wanted to avoid in the first place: war.

But now that war has been waged, it is a moot point to ask, as some Arab states now do, if Saddam is, or was, preferable to war. The issue has now been transformed into a refugee problem, Iraq for all practical purposes is under the trusteeship of the Security Council, and the Kurdish issue may in the future become analogous to the Palestinian question. The peace process in the Middle East is bogged down over the intransigence of the Israeli government, which makes it more difficult to trade territory in exchange for peace. This in turn almost kills the possibility of ensuring a transitional phase from the power to the peace paradigm.

Change and Integration in Europe and the Three Paradigms

Forty-eight years after World War II, Europe is still talking about European integration, monetary union, and a common defence and foreign policy. Some argue that it was Robert Schuman, Konrad Adenauer, and Alcide De Gasperi who put the train of European integration in motion;

others, that European unity began and progressed because of Stalin. If the first argument is correct, there is no reason to believe that Europe will not one day be an important political entity, capable of achieving some common European goals and objectives. This hypothesis would be in line both with the early integration theories and with current functionalist and neo-functionalist approaches.

If the second argument also contains an element of truth—coalitions coalesce only to counterbalance the presence of an enemy[9]—it would also mean that Europe will in the future try to distance itself from the United States (if only to mark its European identity), and quite surely from the former USSR, if this erstwhile enemy goes into terrible turmoil. If both hypotheses are true, and there is no reason to believe otherwise, Europe may have a future of its own. But the irony of the situation is that as the threat disappears, there is also more than a marked tendency towards a reaffirmation of national identities throughout Europe.

Will the Europe of tomorrow be composed of the Twelve, of the Twelve plus Central Europe, and/or of the Twelve plus all of Europe: that is, including Russia? The path towards European unity is well understood in the West: a second floor cannot be added to the European house unless the first floor is firmly established.[10] In other words, the European Community must be deepened before it can be widened. Events indicate that the EC will try to strengthen the web of its political co-operation and institutions before it accepts any new members.

This also raises the question of where Germany stands in this whole process. In the course of its history, Berlin has constantly oscillated between the Stresemann model, which has consisted in anchoring Germany to the West—and which Adenauer practised so well in the 1950s—and the Schumacher model—a political vision clear of any military alliance—which the socialists Egon Bahr and Willy Brandt have partially espoused in the course of their Ostpolitik.[11] The actual division of philosophy between Chancellor Helmut Kohl and the former foreign affairs minister Hans-Dietrich Genscher reflects this basic dilemma of German foreign policy. Many believe today that a fundamental debate in Bonn on Germany's future course of action is yet to come. But if history can be of any help here, there is no reason to believe that Bonn will cease to be faithful to the West, any more than it will be irresistibly attracted to the East, even though Russian soil contains a wealth of natural resources that, according to Genscher, could be exploited to the benefit of all. After its reunification, Germany is again the power *in* the middle as well as *of* the middle. Economically, Bonn will do its utmost to stabilize the Eastern European countries through financial aid and monetary assistance, investment, and joint ventures. Bonn also takes no satisfaction in the crumbling of the Soviet empire, if only for reasons of long-term stability. Bonn is therefore properly insisting on reinserting the former USSR into the economic structures of the West, on the basis of a non-zero-sum game scenario. Whatever the future holds, it seems unlikely that Germany would engage in any rash political action that could compromise its future relations with the West.

If the path towards European unity seems to be on course, many problems still remain to be settled. The intergovernmental discussions in Rome in September and December 1990, as well as the negotiations at the beginning of 1991 on political union, are indicative of the European mood concerning further integration. Political union means nothing unless there are proper political institutions to regulate this process. The ability of the 'peace through law' paradigm to reign over this process will depend as much on the potential for evolution of the current European institutions as on the willingness of the European states to divest themselves of certain powers that eventually could be transferred to the Community. There is still a long way to go, all the more so since the traditional instruments of foreign policy, notably defence and foreign affairs, are still very much vested in national governments.

Other indicators point to a marked deceleration in the process of European integration. In addition to the effects of the power paradigm on alliance formation, the unexpected costs of German reunification may very well slow the process of economic and monetary union, which in turn will delay political union. The necessity for Germany to stabilize its eastern flank at a time when the reforms are slow and when Western aid comes up short, despite the promises of the BERD (Bank for European Reconstruction and Development), may also have a centrifugal impact on the whole process of European integration.

However, Europe has a wealth of regulatory institutions, which are beginning to be effective to the point that national legislation now has to conform to the jurisprudence of Brussels. This is true with regard to refugees and border movements, and the issue of pollution control has recently been dealt with by the European Council as well as by other multilateral bodies. These are encouraging signs. They have the virtue of demonstrating the close links that exist between the second and third paradigms. There can be no peaceful settlement of disputes without adequate institutions, and there can be no substantial progress in the third paradigm unless it is backed by the full power of the institutions.

Cultural Values and the Trans-systemic Paradigm

A large aspect of culture is mass communication. Though the mass media may be too strong or too weak, they necessarily form an important part of the democratic process. If they are too strong, interested pressure groups may experience difficulties in gaining access to the media, or the mass media may become absolutely contemptuous of the incumbents in power: either way, the legitimacy of the system would be undermined. If, on the other hand, they are too weak, governments will so thoroughly filter the truth that 'all the news that's fit to print' will not be published, or else pressure groups or interest groups alone will gain access to the incumbents in power, and as a result the influence of public opinion on the government will be diminished.[12]

There is an element of truth, but not more, in C. Wright Mills's thesis to the effect that modern media would lead to public apathy and the destruction of democracy. Those who insist on freedom of information cannot be seen as the same who insist on the naked truth. When there are strong dissonances between beliefs and reality, between the values that respect life and the dire reality of war, cultural differences may emerge in full, and the ground become fertile for psychological propaganda exercises.

In the Gulf War, for instance, information was heavily filtered if not created by the governments. If, day after day, one had actually seen on television the destruction wreaked on the Iraqi soldiers and civilians, it is far from sure that the air war could have continued for more than thirty days. Those images would quickly have connected with the dominant feeling that war is wrong, with the overwhelming feeling that disputes should be settled on a peaceful basis—at least if one espouses the views of the second paradigm—and with the values inherent in the third paradigm, such as respect for human life and the environment.

The dominant image transmitted by the governments of the coalition, however, was in line with the first paradigm: if war becomes a necessity, it should be waged according to the rules: respect for civilians, destruction of military targets with minimum collateral damage, and use of force only to the extent necessary to accomplish clear and limited objectives. That was the message. The reality was perhaps different.

World War I was waged in the name of democracy, or in the hope of making the world safer for democracy. World War II was fought to protect democracy from the dangers of fascism and Nazism. The Gulf War was declared simply because many felt the Gordian knot had to be cut. If there was no war, the future held chaos. If there was a war, chaos would reign too. If the West curbed its instinct to wage war with the USSR for forty-five years, before the Berlin Wall fell and democracy supposedly triumphed, it was because everyone knew at any time and for all time that there was no solution to the dilemma of democracy versus totalitarianism but mutual suicide. For better or for worse, the West decided it could not wait after 15 January 1991.

In the meantime, it is true that media communication is creating a transformation of consciousness. But has the realist approach to security been challenged because of the media, or have the media become purely instrumental in disseminating the new concepts of the Palme and Brundtland commissions through their reports (A World at Peace and Our Common Future)? This question touches upon the various relationships between the three major paradigms defined above. The relationship between the first and second paradigms is fairly obvious: they are two sides of the same coin. The links between the first two paradigms and the third are also easy to establish, as long as one's analysis is limited to the philosophical origins of those approaches. The trans-systemic or ecological paradigm has been present in various literatures published over the last two decades or so.

However, the effects of implementing these three paradigms are so different that they may in fact correspond to deep cultural differences. In the first paradigm, science and technology serve the state and the objective is to maximize its benefits. In the third paradigm, political élites ask the state to make science and technology serve humanity at large. The debate obviously overlaps the question of political ends and hence bears on different value orders. It deals not with politics, but with ethics. The relative strength of each paradigm will always be a question of the proper allocation of resources at the political level. But the progress within each and across each of those levels will depend to a great extent on the political understanding of history, and on the proper assessment of what political responsibility means. The best hope one can entertain about the first two paradigms is that every effort will be made to minimize the most nefarious effects of the use of force and to maximize the 'peace through law' approach.

The twenty-first century will be a time of crisis and values will change accordingly. Will states and persons be prepared to face this new ontological barrage of questions, ranging from genetic manipulation to the superordinate goal of wanting to share a common planet and its resources? Is it too late to intervene now? Have we now reached the point of no return as environmental damage progresses and the world's population grows? This is perhaps a pessimistic question, but it has the merit of being the right one at the right time.

A Three-Tiered Security System

Questions of peace and security have always been on the mind of every social scientist. With the end of the cold war, the world has now reached a stage that both historians and political analysts feel is an important historical juncture. To look at the world of tomorrow is not an easy task, but at least one author has had the courage to try. Michael Vlahos, director of the Centre for the Study of Foreign Policy, has produced a study called 'Seeking a New World: The Year 2010'.[13] Four or five predictions emerge from this study: a drifting apart of the major economic blocs, further collapse of the states of the former Soviet empire, an increase of regional conflicts, the emergence of a new European bloc, and, perhaps, a renewed American isolationism coupled ironically with a greater willingness to intervene—but only if US interests are threatened.

What are the lessons to be drawn from the end of the cold war and the outburst of war in the Gulf? If Vlahos is right in his assessment of world trends, three points deserve to be emphasized. The cold war is over, but the former Soviet republics have not succeeded in joining the club of industrial nations, and they are very unlikely to do so in the near future. The future of these states has tremendous consequences for whether the new world order will be a mere remnant of the order established at Yalta, or a reflection of a world transformed.

From the perspective of the first and second paradigms, a three-tiered security system seems to be in the offing, consisting of a reinforced collective-security system, a hard-core security system still composed of European NATO powers, and a soft security system, to emerge perhaps from the CSCE and such institutions as the G-7 summit.

A Reinforced Collective Security System

In the summer of 1990, the Gulf crisis proved the possibility of establishing a new world order through the United Nations. It is now doubtful that the Gulf experience could be repeated elsewhere, simply because the first authentic attempt to use chapter VII of the UN Charter turned into a need to use force. Had the Gulf crisis been resolved peacefully—that is, had chapter VI of the Charter proved effective—it may be that Germany and Japan would be more than happy to amend their respective constitutions to permit their military participation in the collective effort. This would at least facilitate the process of earmarking national contingents to the Charter-prescribed Military Staff Committee of the United Nations. This possibility cannot be totally excluded in the future, but it will have to wait until the ashes of war have fallen back into the Gulf. This may take years.

Depending on how one wants to look at the question, the UN Security Council is either a legacy of the cold war—perhaps even of Yalta—or an international body whose functions must be protected and enhanced in the future. If Germany and Japan were to become permanent members of the Security Council, the system would become skewed in favour of the industrial democracies. The South is already under-represented, and there is no reason to let India and Brazil, to name but two, wait at the door of this international forum. Sooner or later, the legitimacy of the Security Council will have to rest on a more legitimate representation of the organization's important member states.

Moreover, if the states of the former USSR are abandoned to the economic havoc that may result from internal turmoil, their foreign policy will hibernate for a long time, as in the period that followed the Crimean War of 1856 or the Russo-Japanese war of 1905. This unhappy situation may allow the Western world greater manoeuvrability within the Security Council, though admittedly Russia and China will retain their ultimate rights of veto.

It is also doubtful that the system could be made effective if it had to intervene in special zones of influence, such as between Tibet and China, or between Bhutan and India, or between Azerbaijan and Armenia. The war against Iraq was unique from a strategic point of view: most of the Iraqi heartland is vulnerable to both air and sea power, and oil revenues represent almost ninety per cent of Baghdad's income from foreign trade.

The distinctive characteristics of the Gulf situation suggest the dangers of a renewed intensity of regional conflicts in the future. There is no alternative but to reinforce the universal and regional institutions that were specifically established to promote the peaceful settlement of conflict. The Gulf crisis was *sui generis*, and the fact that it resulted in the legally decided, common use of force does not mean that in different contexts and situations, chapter VI could not be put to use with considerable success.

A Hard-Core Security System

In the future NATO is likely to continue to exercise its hard-core security functions as it expands its political consultative process. Since the London Declaration of July 1990, NATO looks more and more like an insurance policy against unforeseen circumstances, as opposed to a full-scale military alliance. The core function of the alliance nonetheless is to prevent a resurgence of the circumstances that divided the world into two camps in the late 1940s.

The 'existential' rules of nuclear deterrence are now relegated to the background. On the intra-alliance agenda, the main question is the distribution of responsibilities among the allies. The WEU is likely to play a more important role in the future, but the outcome of this particular structural revision will probably be decided mainly by the Europe of the Twelve. If the European Community forges a realistic common policy on security and defence, a better distribution of power and responsibilities may be achieved between the United States and Europe.

If the hopes are high on this particular issue, they are much less so with regard to out-of-area responsibilities. The Gulf operations have shown that the West is still as dependent on its air and sea-lift capabilities as it was in World War II. They also have reinforced the traditional maritime and air links between the United States and Great Britain. If the air and sea operations are still important for the West, it means that the Washington-London-Oslo axis will have to be given priority in future, whereas the continental powers, essentially France and Germany, will continue to play a vital role for the defence of the continent.

Any attempt at designing a common European defence and foreign policy will have to face some difficult realities. In fact, out-of-area operations could be a source of division rather than strength within the Atlantic Alliance if the continental powers were to insist on developing a common policy that did not take into account the operational requirements of the strongest partner within the Alliance, the US. A common defence and foreign policy is possible in regard to Europe, but it is doubtful the main European countries could achieve the same degree of cohesion with respect to conflicts in peripheral areas.

This would point to the necessity of giving the UN the teeth to deal with the political aspects of out-of-area operations, and of using NATO as an operational arm if a show of force is needed to support the peaceful-resolution process (pending a revision of the UN and the potential actualization of its military committee). Such arrangements would facilitate the transition from the first to the second paradigm, at least as far as the peaceful resolution of regional conflicts is concerned.

A Soft Security System

Since the beginning of the 1970s, two major conferences have profoundly marked the evolution of East-West relations: the Mutual and Balanced Force Reductions (MBFR) Conference and the Conference on Security and Co-operation in Europe (CSCE). The MBFR Conference has become moribund but the CSCE forum has now become a full-scale process, and the Conventional Forces in Europe (CFE) treaty, though its implementation still causes some trouble, was signed in November 1991. Within the context of the reduced presence of military forces and with the dissolution of the Warsaw Pact, the scepticism that once surrounded the CSCE has been replaced by a degree of optimism. Former US Undersecretary of Defense for Policy Paul Wolfowitz has concluded that NATO and the CSCE do 'provide a structure for political reconciliation and a regime of openness and transparency in the military sphere'.[14]

The CSCE is the only pan-European body that provides the European countries with an overall architecture for policy discussions. It now has a small secretariat and a small centre for conflict prevention. But the organization has no teeth. Moreover, all its decisions are taken under the rule of consensus, which is a serious handicap if multilateral diplomacy is to work. Nonetheless, considerable success has been achieved within the CSCE, and it is still the only organization that can accommodate the evolution of change in Eastern and Central Europe without excluding the former Soviet Union.[15]

Within this particular structure, new security arrangements could emerge in the future. The CSCE may even be empowered with some limited peace-making capabilities, and ultimately with peace-keeping functions, though the latter seems unlikely in the absence of a political directorate within the pan-European body. Such a directorate is resisted by the small powers, which do not want to be kept out of the principal deliberations of what would amount to another Security Council.

In the long run, the CSCE could become as ineffective as the United Nations once was. In the short run, it has two merits. The organization is institutionalizing itself. This is not a guarantee of success,[16] but it is a necessary condition if conflicts are to be settled peacefully. In the second place, NATO has some peace-making functions, at least in the field of arms control and in the achievement of greater military transparency in Europe, but the CSCE could progressively take over these roles in the future, with the possible consequence that greater security could be achieved through negotiations based on common security, instead of through the mechanism of the past, which has consisted in negotiating on the basis of strength.

Conclusion

The time ahead is fraught with promises and dangers. In the North one was led to believe, not so long ago, that co-operation between the industrial democracies could very well stretch from San Francisco to Vladivostok — as if history had stopped in 1917, and with the end of the cold war it could finally resume. Unfortunately, the clock of history cannot be turned back. This optimistic scenario is now being increasingly repudiated, partly because of ethnic violence in Eastern Europe and the fracturing of the Soviet empire, and partly because it is difficult to know whether the North should include China, which may also become a difficult partner in the future.

The rapid disintegration of the Soviet Union has created a cauldron of renewed nationalism and religious fervour that will have devastating consequences for stability. The same phenomenon is now appearing in the South. Whereas in the past the threat of a major confrontation between the superpowers has at times helped to restrain regional conflicts, the nationalist and religious fervour of the past is now resurfacing with a new vigour. And in Asia, the potential reunification of Korea may revive the old antagonism between Japan and Seoul.

Hope remains. In the best of circumstances, institutional arrangements of a regional kind may help assuage the tensions between the first and the second paradigms. From the viewpoint of the North, the tentative new order will have to be based on a greater regulative process for questions pertaining to peace and war issues; from the viewpoint of the South, however, it will succeed only if the structural imbalances between the poor and the rich countries are progressively eliminated. A transformation in consciousness is needed to assess what the purposes of development should be. The value systems of both the North and the South must be reviewed, notably the ethics and legitimacy of the rules of the game.

The third paradigm sounds good on paper, but it ultimately depends on the successful functioning of the second paradigm. The third paradigm is also directly linked to the first, in the sense that no amount of rhetoric will solve the world's ecological problems, unless vast resources are urgently allocated to make the environment safer and the world more equitable. Clearly, unless all agree on the need to share the same planet, it will be difficult to do away with the first paradigm. And unless states are willing to give up some of their prerogatives and abandon the principle of enforcing an illusory security based on territory, it is to be feared that the resources that are desperately needed to prevent the further deterioration of the environment will continue to be pumped into arms. If arms-race technology could be put to use to solve ecological problems, the world might still stand a chance of being a better place in the long run.

Notes

[1] For a fascinating discussion of these two paradigms, see *Right versus Might: International Law and the Use of Force* (New York: Council on Foreign Relations Press, 1989), 123 (hereafter cited as *Right vs Might*).

[2] The prefix *trans* here means 'throughout', as in *transparent*, not 'beyond', as in *Transcaucasian*.

[3] Cited in *Right vs Might*, vii.

[4] A fundamental point that has long been argued by Jean Monnet, a founding father of Europe. See Jean-Louis Quermonne, 'Existe-t-il un modèle politique européen?', *Revue française de science politique* 40, 2 (avril 1990), 192.

[5] Cited in *Right vs Might*, 10-11.

[6] All current works on this particular empirical question are contradictory. See, for instance, Jonathan Wilkenfeld, Michael Brecher, and Sheila Moser, *Crises in the Twentieth Century II, Handbook of Foreign Policy Crises* (New York: Pergamon, 1988). See also James Patrick, 'Structure et conflit en politique internationale: une analyse séquentielle des crises internationales de 1929 à 1979', *Études internationales* 20, 4 (décembre 1989), 791-809; Michael Brecher and Jonathan Wilkenfeld, *Crisis, Conflict and Instability* (New York: Pergamon, 1989), 29-42.

[7] Two points on which Stanley Hoffmann properly insists in his paper 'Ethics and Rules of the Game between the Superpowers', in *Right vs Might*, 71-94.

[8] See David J. Scheffer in *Right vs Might*, 15.

[9] This reflects the power paradigm, which has been considerably corrected by Karl Deutsch with his notion of a security community based on common values.

[10] See Quermonne, 'Existe-t-il un modèle politique européen?', 192-211.

[11] See Walter F. Hahn, 'NATO and Germany', *Global Affairs* (Winter 1990), 1-19.

[12] These may look like sweeping statements, but they have been carefully developed in my article 'La démocratie et les sciences chinoises, 2000 ans avant Jésus-Christ', *Cahiers internationaux de sociologie* LXXXVI (1989), 337-51.

[13] *Los Angeles Times* (11 Dec. 1990), 4.

[14] 'New Security Architecture in Europe Discussed', United States Embassy, Press Offices, Text 31 (26 April 1991).

[15] The only other organization would be the EC, but nobody seriously expects that Russia will join this body.

[16] It could even become another bureaucratized organization with no power of decision.

Index

Adenauer, Konrad, 71, 330, 406, 407
Afghanistan, 32, 46, 49, 90, 239, 242, 244, 245, 250, 302, 304, 369; weapons, 360
Agriculture, 194-7, 200, 201, 202, 206-7
Albania, 71, 81
Algeciras conference (1906), 285
Algeria, 239, 242, 244, 245, 250
Angola, 90, 239, 242, 245, 250, 302
Antarctic Treaty (1959), 298
Anti-Ballistic Missile (ABM) Treaty, 299
Arab League, 278
Argentina, 239, 250, 306, 362; weapons, 98, 126, 278, 359, 360, 361
Armenia, 61
Arms, see Weapons
Arms control/disarmament, 4, 53, 54, 59, 124, 126, 318, 328, 331-2, 363; and UN, 276, 277, 287, 295-9; see also Conventional Forces in Europe; Missile Technology Control Regime; Nuclear Non-Proliferation Treaty
Arms Control and Disarmament Agency (ACDA), 124, 126
Arms transfers, 271, 298, 358; 'black market', 127, 359; conventional arms, 123-7; and G-7, 352; and Third World, 95-8, 124-7
Asia Pacific Economic Community (APEC), 7
Assam, 199-200, 211
Association of South East Asian Nations (ASEAN), 7, 54
Atlantic Alliance, 76, 336, 337, 342, 412; see also North Atlantic Treaty Organization
Australia, 240, 241, 242, 245, 251, 372
Austria, 74, 245, 372; Austria-Hungary, 27, 235, 236
Azerbaijan, 61, 72

Bahr, Egon, 407
Baker, James, 150
Balkan states, 2; see also Yugoslavia
Baltic states, 55, 61, 72
Bangladesh, 199-200, 211, 239, 244, 245, 250, 253
Bank for European Reconstruction and Development (BERD), 408
Bargaining, 233; collective, 143; 'offensive' and 'defensive', 231
Belarus, 56, 61
Belgium, 73, 236, 240, 241, 242, 244, 247, 251, 372; and NATO, 319, 322; weapons, 360
Benelux states, 66-7
Bentham, Jeremy, 261, 284
Berlin congresses: (1878), 284; (1884-5), 285
Biological weapons, 358, 359, 360, 373; Biological Weapons Convention (1972), 128, 298-9
Bipolarity, 3, 4, 23, 63, 64, 65, 258, 313
Bismarck, Otto von, 27, 145, 401
Bolivia, 239, 250
Bosnia-Herzegovina, 72; see also Yugoslavia
Botswana, 248
Boutros Ghali, Boutros, 275, 302
Brandt, Willy, 268, 407
Brazil, 43, 54, 239, 250, 252, 302, 306; and UN, 273, 309; weapons, 98, 126, 127, 278, 359, 360, 361
Bretton Woods system, 151, 152, 335
Brezhnev, Leonid, 41, 42, 43, 47, 48, 49, 387; 'doctrine', 53, 62
British Army of the Rhine (BAOR), 320, 321
Brundtland, Gro Harlem, 170; commission, 268, 409
Bulgaria, 53, 71, 72, 360, 372
Bull, Hedley, 379, 382, 388, 390, 394

Burma, 240, 245, 250, 360
Burundi, 240, 244, 245, 251
Bush, George, 68, 176, 294, 328

Cambodia, 90, 302; and UN, 266, 270, 277, 294, 306, 307
Cameroon, 239, 242, 244, 250
Canada, 5, 162, 240, 241, 242, 245, 251, 252, 372; and CSCE, 81; and G-7, 343, 344, 345, 347, 348, 352, 354; and NATO, 319-20, 324, 327; and UN, 273, 276, 293; see also Public-opinion data
Carbon dioxide (CO_2) emissions, 249-53
Caucasus, 61, 69, 72
Chad, 74, 239, 245, 248, 250, 278
Chemical weapons, 128-9, 267, 358, 359, 360; Chemical Weapons Convention, 277
China, 35, 49, 239, 241, 244, 245, 250, 414; CO_2 emissions, 253; and global economy, 143; imperial, 235, 236; missile sales, 370; and MTCR, 362, 370; population, 206, 248-9; power, 17, 33; resources, 196, 248; technology transfers, 366; and UN, 279, 292, 303-4, 411; and USSR, 50; weapons, 98, 128, 297, 360
Chlorofluorocarbons (CFCs), 186
Class: ideology, 41, 49-50; struggle, 148
Climate change, 185, 186, 188, 196-7; see also Environmental change
Colombia, 126, 239, 244, 250, 294, 306
Colonialism, post-, 8; see also Decolonization
Commonwealth, 7
Commonwealth of Independent States (CIS), 18, 33, 69; and MTCR, 366, 369; see also Russia; USSR, successor states
Communications: and conflict, 172; and democracy, 165, 166; and empowerment, 159, 172; global, 162-6; and mass publics, 172-4; media, 160-1, 167; and nationalism/ internationalism, 161, 162; and political élites, 174; and security, 168-

9; and statehood, 175; and state system, 174-5; and Third World, 172; and UN, 265-6; and values, 174-6, 408-10
Computer technology, 168-9
Concert of Europe, 261, 285, 342
Conference on Disarmament (CD), 296-7
Conference on International Economic Co-operation (CIEC), 354
Conference on Security and Co-operation in Europe (CSCE), 7, 61, 62, 63, 64, 71, 73, 75, 79, 80, 278, 331, 411, 413; and EC, 79; and European security, 81-2; institutions, 79-80; and interstate/ethnic conflict, 80; membership, 81; and US, 81; and USSR, 68-9
Conflict: ethnic, 65-6, 72-3, 88, 246; and globalization, 149, 155; regional, 8, 90, 412; social (types), 207-15; subnational, 8, 266; Third World, 86-99; see also Environmental change; Wars
Congo, 239, 244, 250
Contadora Group, 306
Conventional Forces in Europe (CFE), 62, 69, 80, 328, 413
Coordinating Committee on Multilateral Export (CoCom), 365-6, 369
'Cornucopian' view, 202-5
Costa Rica, 306
Council for Mutual Economic Assistance (CMEA), 61, 62, 63
Council of Europe, 64
Crimea, 70
Croatia, 270; see also Yugoslavia
Crucé, Emeric, 284
Cuba, 42, 294
Culture, globalization of, 161, 162-3
Cyprus, 80, 267, 300, 302
Czechoslovakia, 42, 71, 72, 360, 366, 372

Dante, 284
Davignon Report (1970), 77
Decision-making (individual, group, state), 23-4
Decolonization, 240-3, 302-3
de Gaulle, Charles, 151

Demographic pressures, *see* Population
Deng Xiaoping, 33
Denmark, 245, 372
Deterrence, 33, 41, 96, 259, 406, 412
Deutsch, Karl, 161
Developing countries, *see* Third World
Disarmament, *see* Arms control
Dominican Republic, 240, 251
Drug trade, 5, 271, 341
DuBois, Pierre, 260, 284

'Ecological capital', 202-3
'Ecological paradigm', *see* Trans-
systemic paradigm
Economic Community of West African States, 278
Economy, global, *see* Globalization
Egypt, 126, 239, 244, 250, 265, 273;
weapons, 299, 359, 360
El Salvador, 245, 302, 306
Empires, 235, 236, 241-2
Environmental change/degradation, 5,
7, 185, 186-7; and agriculture, 194-7;
and conflict, 149, 187-93, 200, 207-
13, 215-17; and economic decline,
197-9; major kinds and interrelations,
192-3; and post-Fordism, 149; social
effects, 187-92, 193-200, 207-13; and
security, 187-8, 230-1, 232, 249-53,
268, 269, 341, 405; and Third World,
187, 192, 200-13
Eritrea, 270
Ethiopia, 244, 245, 360
Europe: and German unification, 62-3,
330-1; and global economy, 94, 143,
154-5; and Gulf War, 66, 74; and
NATO, 75, 331; and out-of-area
conflicts, 67, 68, 74-5; political identity, 60-1; and Russia, 63-4; security
institutions, 74-81; security agenda,
59-60, 65-73, 313-15; and Third
World, 74; and UN, 75, 80; and US,
63, 64; and USSR successor states, 61,
62, 68-70
Europe, Eastern, 26, 54, 66, 73, 75,
163; and EC, 63, 79, 80; conflict, 53,
65-6, 314
European Community (EC), 60-1, 63,
64, 331, 342, 389, 407, 408; and

CSCE, 79; defence policy, 412; and
Eastern Europe, 79, 80; and European
security, 78, 81-2; and G-7, 335, 348;
and Germany, 71; and Maastricht
agreement, 77; and NATO, 79, 326;
and Third World, 74-5; and UN, 273;
and WEU, 76, 79; and Yugoslavia, 72,
73, 78
European Council, 76, 78, 408
European Defence Community, 77,
320
European Free Trade Association
(EFTA), 61, 79
European Political Co-operation
(EPC), 77-8
Expansionism, 406; economic, 154;
and 'lateral pressure', 234, 235-6

Falklands War, 74
Finland, 74, 372
Forces françaises en Allemagne (FFA), 321
Fordism, 141-2, 143; and military
power, 144-7; post-Fordism, 142-4,
147-50
France, 73, 74, 77, 236, 240, 242, 245,
247, 251, 372; and G-7, 345, 350,
352; military technology, 124; and
MTCR, 364, 365; and NATO, 75,
321, 322, 324, 331; and NPT, 362;
power cycle, 27; and UN, 273, 276,
279, 292; and Vietnam, 151; weapons,
128, 360; and WEU, 76
Francophonie, la, 7

G-7 summits, 3, 7, 336-9, 341-7, 411;
authority, 352-4; 'concert' characteristics, 338-9, 343-7; and EC, 348; and
human rights, 351; institutional
capacity, 347-50; 'librarian' conception, 347, 352; locations, 348; membership, 342-3; and MTCR, 373;
official-level meetings, 350; statements, 351-2; origins, 335-6; 'Quadrilateral', 349; and refugees, 351; and
Russia, 337; security issues, 350-2,
353-4; separate ministerial structure,
349; and Third World, 350, 351;
'trilateralist' conception, 347, 352
Gasperi, Alcide De, 406

General Agreement on Tariffs and
Trade (GATT), 66, 354
Geneva Protocol (1925), 128
Genscher, Hans Dietrich, 317, 407
Georgia, 61
Germany, 23, 31, 74, 245, 372, 407;
and Eastern Europe, 66, 407; East
Germany (GDR), 62, 314, 316, 321,
324, 360; and EC, 30, 72; and G-7,
337, 345, 347; and NATO, 314-31;
power, 27-30, 62-3, 64; 'singularization', 318, 325; and UN, 265, 273,
308; and unification, 28, 53, 66, 70-1,
321, 330, 408; and WEU, 76; West
Germany (FRG), 124, 126, 152, 324,
329-30, 360; and Yugoslavia, 31, 72;
weapons, 330; see also Public-opinion
data
Ghana, 240, 250
Giscard D'Estaing, Valéry, 347
Globalization, economic, 2, 5; and
conflict, 155; and post-Fordism, 142-
4, 148-50; and Third World, 155; vs
territorial principle, 143, 150-1, 154
Gorbachev, Mikhail, 25-6, 32, 47, 55,
62, 90, 259, 390; and Europe, 69; and
G-7, 348, 349
Goulding, Marrack, 307
Great Britain, 22-3, 27, 74, 154, 236,
372; and NATO, 320-1, 322; and UN,
273; weapons, 124, 360; and WEU,
77; see also United Kingdom
Greece, 71, 80, 240, 242, 251, 269, 372
Greenhouse warming, 185, 196, 249;
see also Climate change
Gromyko, Andrei, 25
Grotius, 261
Guatemala, 239, 244, 245, 250, 306
Guinea-Bissau, 242
Gulf War, 2, 4, 6, 8, 14, 54, 259, 266,
271, 358, 406; and Europe, 66, 74;
and MTCR, 367; as regional conflict,
87; TV coverage, 173-4; and
territorialism/globalization, 150-1;
and UN, 274, 275, 285, 294; and US,
92, 329; and USSR, 55, 90

Hague conferences (1899, 1907), 288
Haiti, 267, 276, 302, 306

Hammarskjöld, Dag, 300-1
Hegel, G.W.F., 160, 405
Hegemonic-stability theory, 14
Helsinki process, 59, 63, 79; see also
CSCE
Hitler, Adolph, 28, 402
Hobbes, Thomas, 172
Honduras, 197, 306
Human rights, 4, 5, 8-9, 268, 277, 351
Hungary, 65, 71, 242, 360, 366, 372;
Austria-Hungary, 27, 235, 236
Hussein, Saddam, 93, 94, 275

Independent Commission on Disar-
mament and Security Issues, 170
India, 90, 239, 244, 250, 300; popula-
tion, 206, 249; and UN, 265, 273,
309; weapons, 96, 97, 98, 126, 128,
335, 359, 360, 361
Indochina, 2, 242
Indonesia, 197, 198, 239, 242, 244,
250, 252, 300, 360
Industrial Revolution, 111, 112
Innis, Harold Adams, 160-1, 165
Intelsat, 336
Intergovernmental Conference on
Political Union, 78
Intermediate Nuclear Force (INF), 49;
treaty, 299, 387, 388
Intermediate Range Ballistic Missile
(IRBM), 98
International Atomic Energy Agency
(IAEA), 96, 97, 128, 295-6, 306
International Bank for Reconstruction
and Development (World Bank), 7,
202, 275, 346
International Court of Justice, 272, 288
International Energy Agency, 336
International Labour Organization
(ILO), 296
International Monetary Fund (IMF),
152, 202, 278, 337, 346
Iran, 239, 244, 245, 250, 253; weap-
ons, 128, 129, 299, 359, 360, 361
Iran-Iraq War, 90, 95, 129, 150, 302,
304
Iraq, 9, 239, 244, 245, 247, 250, 263,
306, 362, 411; and Kurds, 295, 406;
and Kuwait, 87, 93 (see also Gulf War);

weapons,7–8, 128, 129, 288, 299, 359, 360, 361
Ireland, 71, 74, 372
Israel, 90, 240, 244, 251, 406; weapons, 96, 126, 127, 299, 359, 360, 361
Italy, 124, 126, 253, 262, 273, 360, 372; and G-7, 343, 344

Japan, 5, 24, 249, 372, 389; aerospace industry, 146; economy, 17, 22, 94, 154; and G-7, 337, 342, 343, 344, 347; and global economy, 143; and globalization, 154–5; in international system, 35; power, 17, 18, 33; and USSR, 31, 49; and UN, 265, 273, 308; and US, 146–7, 153–4
Johnson, Lyndon B., 151
Jordan, 239, 250

Kampuchea, 49, 245
Kant, Immanuel, 171, 261, 284, 402
Kennedy, Paul, 13, 15, 16, 17, 145
Kenya, 239, 242
Khrushchev, Nikita, 41, 48
Kissinger, Henry, 24, 347
Kohl, Helmut, 70, 407
Korea, 263, 414; Korean War, 241, 242, 291, 293; North Korea, 128, 240, 251, 359, 360, 361; South Korea, 42, 126, 127, 240, 244, 251, 360
Kurds, 9, 261, 267, 268
Kuwait, 87, 150–1, 240, 245, 247, 251, 306, 362; see also Gulf War

Labour, organized, 142, 145, 148, 149
Laos, 239, 245, 248, 250, 360
League of Nations, 81, 264, 261–2, 274, 285, 286, 287
Lebanon, 242, 244, 267, 278
Lenin, Vladimir, 42, 47, 145; Marxism-Leninism, 2, 4, 238
Leveraging, 233; offensive/defensive, 231
Liberia, 278
Library Group, 347
Libya, 240, 247, 251, 288, 299, 360
Lithuania, 46; see also Baltic states
Lomé Conventions, 74
London conferences (1871, 1912, 1913), 284

London Suppliers' Group, 96, 363, 372 (table)
Luxembourg, 372

Maastricht agreement, 76, 77, 78, 81
Macedonia, 72
Major, John, 349
Malaysia, 294
Malthusians: anti-, 188 (see also Cornucopians); neo-, 202–7
Market, self-regulating, 143; and resource scarcity, 201–7
Marx, Karl, 160
Marxism-Leninism, 2, 4, 238
Mauretania, 245
McLuhan, Marshall, 160, 161, 167
McNamara, Robert, 278
Mearsheimer thesis, 65, 71, 313, 314
Media, see Communications
Mexico, 22, 306
Mill, J.S., 261
Mills, C. Wright, 166, 409
Missile Technology Control Regime (MTCR), 98, 126, 358–73; categories, 364; and G-7, 373; governance, 363–4; and Gulf War, 367; membership, 368–9; origins, 363–4; and space programmes, 364–5
Mitterand, François, 70, 321, 350
Moldova, 61, 72
Monnet, Jean, 71
Morgenthau, Hans, 404
Morocco, 239, 242, 250
Mozambique, 239, 242, 244, 250
Mujahideen, 369
Multilateral Trade Negotiations, Tokyo Round, 335
Multipolarity, 24, 64
Mutual and Balanced Force Reduction (MBFR) Conference, 413

Nagorno-Karabakh, 46
Namibia, 90, 267, 302, 305
Napoleonic Wars, 111
Nationalism, 2, 4; and communications, 161, 162; economic, 142; sub-state, 270
Netherlands, 236, 240, 241, 242, 245, 251, 360; and NATO, 319, 322–3

New Guinea, 252
New International Economic Order, 144
'New World Information Order', 164, 176
'New world order', 2, 4, 68, 75, 264; public perceptions, 378-95
New Zealand, 245, 372
Nicaragua, 90, 239, 245, 250, 267, 302, 306
Nigeria, 239, 244, 250, 265, 273, 309
Nixon, Richard, 24
Non-aligned Movement, 92, 273
Nordic countries, 276, 293
North Atlantic Co-operation Council, 75
North Atlantic Treaty, 350
North Atlantic Treaty Organization (NATO), 7, 14, 59, 60, 63, 64, 75, 76, 263, 336, 354, 394, 413; 'Berlin Dinner', 347, 350; and EC, 76, 79, 326; and European security, 75-6, 80, 81-2; Franco-German 'Euro-Corps', 321, 331 and Germany, 71, 313-32; London Declaration (1990), 412; membership, 342-5; Main Defence and Augmentation Forces, 318; mutual co-operation, 326; Rapid Reaction Corps (RRC), 318, 321; stationing agreements, 316; strategy review, 317; summits, 346; and USSR successor states, 61-2, 75; and Warsaw Pact, 75; and WEU, 76, 78
Norway, 245, 372
Nuclear Non-Proliferation Treaty (NPT), 96, 128, 277-8, 297, 298, 330, 359, 362, 370-1
Nuclear weapons, 4, 115, 117, 240, 277-8, 345, 358, 359, 360; Partial Test-Ban Treaty (1963), 298; Short Range Nuclear Forces (SNF), 328; states with nuclear capacity, 127-8, 360; and Third World, 96-8; and UN, 288; and USSR collapse, 299
Nyrere, Julius, 268

Oman, 240, 247, 251
Organization for Economic Cooperation and Development (OECD), 336, 337

Organization of African Unity (OAU), 278
Organization of American States (OAS), 278, 306
Organization of Arab Petroleum Exporting Countries (OAPEC), 335
Organization of Petroleum Exporting Countries (OPEC), 151
Ottoman empire, 235, 236
Ozone depletion, 186, 188, 197

Pakistan, 46, 239, 244, 250, 300, 304; weapons, 96, 97, 98, 359, 360, 361, 365, 370
Palestine, 300
Palme, Olof, 170; Palme commission, 268, 409
Panama, 242, 278, 306
Paris, Congress of (1856), 284
Paris Treaty (1990), 278
Peace enforcement, 259, 263; see also Collective security; United Nations
'Peace-through-law' and 'peace-through-strength' (power) paradigms, 401-5, 406, 409-10, 414
Pearson, Lester B., 163, 299-300
Penn, William, 284
Pérez de Cuellar, Javier, 258, 268, 301-2, 305-6
Peru, 239, 250, 306
Philippines, 194, 197, 239, 250, 252; environmental change and conflict, 213-14, 215
Pickering, Thomas, 304
Poland, 42, 70, 360, 366, 372
Population: control, 248-9; and environment, 189-92; pressures, 9, 191; and security, 230; interaction with technology and resources, 206, 231, 232-3, 234, 237-40, 247; movement, 5, 21, 66, 194, 199-200, 244-7, 341; stabilization level, 206
Portugal, 236, 240, 241, 242, 251, 345, 372
Power-cycle theory, 12, 13, 15-18, 19-23, 145; absolute and relative power, 13
Power, military, and production, 141-55

Production, mass, 141-2, 144-5, 147; *see also* Fordism
Public-opinion data (Canada, FRG, UK, US): on arms reduction, 394; on balance of power, 388-9; on NATO, 394; on US, 382, 385-9; on USSR, 382-9; on threats to security, 389-94, 395; on war, 380-1

Qatar, 362

Rarotonga, Treaty of, 298, 364
Reagan, Ronald, 149, 259, 348, 387; and US military build-up, 18, 22, 145
Refugees, 244-6, 247, 351, 306
Regional organizations, 7, 8, 9, 278, 285, 307
Resources: interactions with population and technology, 231, 232-3, 234, 237-40, 247-9; scarcity, 201-7; and security, 150-1, 231, 269
Rhodesia, 242
Romania, 65, 71, 72, 360, 372
Rousseau, J.-J., 261, 284
Russia, 31-2, 33, 56, 235, 236; and Europe, 62, 63-4, 69, 407; and G-7, 337; and MTCR, 369; power, 12; and regional conflict, 69-70; and Third World, 90-1; and UN, 69, 273, 279, 411; and US, 65, 318
Rwanda, 245

Saint-Pierre, Abbé de, 284
Saudi Arabia, 92, 93, 150-1, 247; and NPT, 362; weapons, 359, 360
Schmidt, Helmut, 347
Schumacher, Kurt, 407
Schuman, Robert, 71, 406
Security: collective, *see below*; 'comprehensive', 269; 'co-operative', 5, 6; and computer technology, 168-9; cultural, 65, 66-7; definitions, 8, 173, 229, 230-2, 268-9, 271, 308, 340-1; demographic, 65, 66, 68; economic, 65, 66-7, 268, 269; environmental, 187-8, 230-1, 232, 249-54, 268, 269; new agenda, 2, 5, 8, 63-73, 169-76, 339-41, 350-2, 389-94; regionalization of, 8

Security, collective, 5, 7, 75, 258-80, 411-12; defined, 259; historical development, 260-4; 'objective and subjective conditions', 263-4; and sovereignty, 268, 269, 270; and UN, 259, 287, 293, 342
Shevardnadze, Eduard, 25, 259
Somalia, 9, 239, 245, 248, 250, 305, 306; and UN, 166, 275
South Africa, 244, 245, 278; weapons, 96, 126, 359, 360, 361; and NPT, 96, 362
Sovereignty, 268, 270, 293
Space programmes, 364-5
Spain, 73, 236, 240, 241, 245, 251, 372
Sri Lanka, 240, 245, 250
Stalin, Joseph, 42, 43, 44, 47, 48, 50, 407
States: population/resources/technology ratios, 237-40; uneven growth and development, 232, 233, 234, 239-40 (tables), 252-3
Status of Forces Agreement, Supplementary Agreement to, 324
Stockholm Initiative, 269
Stockholm International Peace Research Institute (SIPRI), 124, 126, 296
Strategic Arms Limitation Treaty (SALT) agreements, 299, 387, 389
Strategic Communications Initiative (SCI), 176
Strategic Defense Initiative (SDI), 107, 145, 147
Stresemann, Gustav, 407
Sudan, 239, 244, 245, 250
Sully, Duc de, 284
Summits, G-7, *see* G-7
'Sustainability', 232, 253-4
Sweden, 74, 245, 369, 372
Switzerland, 245, 369, 372
Syria, 128, 209-11, 239, 244, 250, 299, 359, 360, 370

Taiwan, 43, 126, 263, 360
Tajikistan, 46
Tanzania, 239, 250
Taylorism, 142
Technology: and environmental

security, 206, 230-1, 252-3; interactions with population and resources,
201-2, 205, 207, 231, 232-3, 234,
237-40, 247-9; and UN operations,
265-6; military, *see below*; *see also*
Communications

Technology, military, 3, 122, 170;
black-market, 127, 369; change,
nature of, 111-15; and civil technology, 117-20, 130, 146; definitional
distinctions, 107-11; diffusion of,
123-30, 366, 367-8; 'dual-use', 116-
17, 129, 362, 371; emerging, 120-2;
history, 111-13; NBC, 127-30; and
Third World, 95-8, 124-7; offensive/
defensive, 115-17; *see also* Biological,
Chemical, and Nuclear weapons

Television, 165-6, 167, 175-6

Territoriality, 5, 143, 150-1, 154, 175

Terrorism, 271, 276

Thailand, 239, 250

Thatcher, Margaret, 259, 294, 386

Third World: agricultural production,
194-5; arms and technology transfers,
95-8, 124-7, 359-62, 369-70; and
communications, 161, 162, 172; and
conflict, 86-90, 172, 258; and 'cultural imperialism', 164; and *détente*,
92-3; and deterrence, 96; and environmental change, 187-8, 192, 200-7,
207-13; and globalization, 155; and
great powers, 87-9; population
growth, 206; refugees, 246-7; security issues, 86-99; state-making, 88;
and UN, 273, 278, 290-1; and US,
86, 91-5; wars, 241-3, 243-4

Thirty Years War, 111

Tlatelolco, Treaty of, 298, 362

'Trans-systemic paradigm', 401, 405,
410, 414

Transylvania, 53

Tunisia, 239, 242, 250

Turkey, 61, 71, 80, 239, 250, 345;
Euphrates dam, 209-11; and MTCR,
369

Turkmenistan, 46

Uganda, 240, 244, 251

Ukraine, 56-7, 61, 72, 332

Union of Soviet Socialist Republics,
240, 251, 372; and Afghanistan, 244,
304; arms control/disarmament, 52,
53, 328, 363; and China, 49, 50; class
ideology, 41, 49-50, 51; collapse, 2, 4,
6, 86, 90, 95, 162, 236, 243, 244, 299,
313; and colonial wars, 241; Communist party (CPSU), 42, 44, 47, 50;
decline, 42-8; democratization, 45-6,
47; and *détente*, 25, 41; and Eastern
Europe, 26, 40, 49, 50, 51, 53, 54;
economy, 18, 25-6, 30-1, 40, 42-4,
45, 51-2, 53, 316; and Europe, 49, 60;
ethnic and nationalist conflict, 46, 53,
69-70; expansionism, 236, 406; foreign policy, 25, 41-2, 48-55, 90; and
GDR, 314, 315-16; and German
unification, 30; *glasnost*, 25-6, 47; and
Gulf War, 34, 55; instability, 270; and
international socialism, 41-2; and
Japan, 49; military, 18, 113, 124, 145;
and MTCR, 98, 369; 'new thinking',
48-9, 259, 268; *perestroika*, 13, 25-6,
69; political system, 42, 46-7; power
cycle, 12, 18, 25-7, 30-2; reform, 45-
8; social malaise, 44; successor states,
61, 65, 68-70, 71, 75, 369 (*see also*
Russia); and Third World, 40, 41-2,
49, 50, 54, 90-1; and UN, 292; weapons, 297, 360; and Yugoslavia, 50; *see
also* Public-opinion data

United Kingdom, 73, 240, 244, 245,
251; and CSCE, 79; colonial wars,
241; and Korean War, 242; and UN,
279, 292; *see also* Great Britain;
Public-opinion data

United Nations, 3, 4, 7-8; and arms
control, 276, 277, 287, 295- 9; Charter, 6-7, 262-3, 269, 285-91, 403; and
collective security, 259, 287, 293,
342; decision-making, 272-4; and
decolonization, 302-3; economic
development programme, 74; economic sanctions, 267, 275; finances,
285, 307; General Assembly, 265,
289, 290, 292; great-power veto, 263,
264, 272, 273, 280, 285, 292-3, 304;
and Gulf War, 285, 294; humanitarian
aid, 167, 176-7; and human rights,

268, 302, 305-6; information-gathering, 271-2, 275; and Iran-Iraq War, 302, 304; military capacity, 263, 269-70, 272, 275-6, 279, 294, 308; obstacles to change, 270-1; oversight role, 267; 'pacific settlement of disputes', 280, 286, 288-9; 'peace enforcement', 280, 286, 289-91, 293-4; peace-keeping, 263, 267, 275, 276, 280, 291, 299-302, 305-7; 'preventive diplomacy', 68, 300-1; recent changes, 303-4; and refugees, 306; and regional organizations, 278, 285, 307; representation of states/groups, 265, 266, 273, 308-9, 411; Secretary-General, 6-7, 266, 273, 274-5, 289, 291, 301, 306; Security Council, 6-7, 263, 266, 267, 272-4, 271, 279, 285, 286, 287, 288, 289, 290, 303, 308-9, 342, 343, 345, 347; Security Council Commission, 274-5; Security Council summit (1992), 259, 276, 307-8, 346; and self-help, 8, 288; and sovereignty, 293; and subnational conflict, 266; and Third World, 278, 290-1; and US, 293-4; voting, 274; 'ward' system, 276; and Yugoslavia, 80

UN commissions, offices, etc.: Assembly Declaration on the Granting of Independence to Colonial Countries and Peoples (1960), 303; Atomic Energy Commission, 295; Committee on the Indian Ocean, 296; Conference on Disarmament, 129; Conference on Environment and Development, 232, 349; Consular Commission, 300; Disarmament Commission, 295, 298; Department of Peacekeeping Operations, 307; Economic Commission for Europe, 63; Educational, Scientific, and Cultural Organization (UNESCO), 296; Emergency Force in the Middle East (UNEF), 300; Environmental Program (UNEP), 296; First Committee, 295; Food and Agricultural Organization (FAO), 296; Humanitarian Assistance Teams (UNHAT), 267; Military Observer Group in India and Pakistan

(UNMOGIP), 300; Military Staff Committee (MSC), 75, 263, 276, 289, 293, 294, 411, 413; Observer Group in Central America (ONUCA), 306; Office of Research and Collection of Information (ORCI), 266, 302; Office of Special Political Affairs, 307; Scientific Committee on the Effects of Atomic Radiation (UNSCEAR), 296; Special Committee on the Balkans (1947), 300; Special Committee on Colonialism (Committee of 24), 303; Special Committee on Peacekeeping Operations, 277; Special General Assembly on Disarmament, 297; Transitional Assistance Group (UNTAG), 305; Truce Supervision Organization (UNTSO), 300; Trusteeship Council, 303; Uniting for Peace Resolution (1950), 291; World Disarmament Conference, 296

United States, 240, 244, 245, 247, 251, 372; carbon emissions, 252; Civil War, 144; and colonial wars, 241; and CSCE, 79, 81; Conventional Arms Transfers (CAT) talks, 363; culture, 163; 'decline', 12-36, 54, 279; defence planning, 107; economy, 13, 14, 15, 18, 22, 95, 151, 152-3, 243, 318, 328 (see also military spending, below); and Europe, 63, 64, 66, 75, 327; Export Administration Regulations (EAR), 368, 371; expansionism, 236, 241; foreign policy, 33, 34-5; and G-7, 337, 347, 352, 354; and global economy, 94, 143, 154; and Gulf War, 92; and Japan, 146, 147, 154; and Korean War, 242; and League of Nations, 262; military build-up, 18, 22, 145; military spending and debt, 22, 145, 151, 152-3, 243, 328; military technology, 113-14, 124; and MTCR, 371; and NATO, 14, 317, 318-19, 322, 325, 327-9, 331-2; power cycle, 12-36; and Russia, 65, 318; and Third World, 86, 91-5; and UN, 74, 279, 292, 293-4, 295, 304; 'unipolar moment', 63-4, 258, 279; and Vietnam, 242; weapons, 318,

360; and WEU, 77; and Yugoslavia, 328; *see also* Public-opinion data
Urquhart, Brian, 265
Uruguay, 306

Vance, Cyrus, 170
Vattel, Emmerich de, 261
Venezuela, 306
Vienna, Congress of (1815), 261, 284
Vietnam, 239, 245, 250; War, 151, 241, 242, 244, 335, 360

Waltz, Kenneth, 65, 171
Wars: causes of, 171-2, 236; civil, 230, 243-4, 294; of collision, 235-6; colonial, 235, 240-3; and 'lateral pressure', 234, 235-6; and uneven growth and development, 238
Warsaw Treaty Organization (Warsaw Pact), 40, 53, 62, 63, 263, 313, 315
Weapons: proliferation, 341, 359-62 (table, 360); 'mass destruction', 3, 7, 8; *see also* Arms control; Biological, Chemical, and Nuclear weapons
Weber, Max, 160
Welfare state, 142, 143, 149
Western European Union (WEU), 62, 63, 64, 68, 74, 321, 330, 331, 412; and

EC, 76; and European security, 76-7; membership, 76
Westphalia, Treaty of, 8
Wight, Martin, 379, 382, 394
Wilson, Woodrow, 262, 300
Wolff, Christian, 261
World Bank, *see* International Bank for Reconstruction and Development
World Commission on Environment and Development, 170, 232
World Health Organization (WHO), 296
World Meteorological Organization (WMO), 296
World Resources Institute, 196

Xenophobia, 66, 211

Yeltsin, Boris, 55, 69, 349
Yemen, 247, 294; North, 360; South, 360
Yugoslavia (former), 9, 53, 65, 71; and EC, 78, 81; and UN, 80, 266, 270, 275, 277, 294; and US, 328; and USSR, 50

Zaire, 244, 245
Zimbabwe, 239, 242, 244, 250